Lectures

TO MY STUDENTS

COMPLETE AND UNABRIDGED

Cover image of Charles Haddon Spurgeon (1834–92), engraved by D. J. Pound from a photograph, from *The Drawing-Room of Eminent Personages, Volume 2*, published in London, 1860 (engraving) by John Jabez Edwin Paisley Mayall (1810–1901).

Lectures
TO MY STUDENTS

COMPLETE AND UNABRIDGED

CHARLES SPURGEON

ZONDERVAN®

ZONDERVAN.com/
AUTHORTRACKER
follow your favorite authors

Lectures to My Students
New edition containing Selected Lectures from Series 1, 2, and 3
1954

Requests for information should be addressed to:
Zondervan, *Grand Rapids, Michigan 49530*

ISBN-10: 0-310-32911-6
ISBN-13: 978-0-310-32911-4

Printed in the United States of America

07 08 09 10 11 12 • 55 54 53 52 51 50 49 48 47 46 45

CONTENTS

CONTENTS

Lectures

TO MY STUDENTS

COMPLETE AND UNABRIDGED

I

The Minister's Self-watch

"Take heed unto thyself, and unto the doctrine."—1 Timothy iv. 16.

EVERY workman knows the necessity of keeping his tools in a good state of repair, for "if the iron be blunt, and he do not whet the edge, then must he put to more strength." If the workman lose the edge from his adze, he knows that there will be a greater draught upon his energies, or his work will be badly done. Michael Angelo, the elect of the fine arts, understood so well the importance of his tools, that he always made his own brushes with his own hands, and in this he gives us an illustration of the God of grace, who with special care fashions for himself all true ministers. It is true that the Lord, like Quintin Matsys in the story of the Antwerp well-cover, can work with the faultiest kind of instrumentality, as he does when he occasionally makes very foolish preaching to be useful in conversion; and he can even work without agents, as he does when he saves men without a preacher at all, applying the word directly by his Holy Spirit; but we cannot regard God's absolutely sovereign acts as a rule for our action. He may, in His own absoluteness, do as pleases Him best, but we must act as His plainer dispensations instruct us; and one of the facts which is clear enough is this, that the Lord usually adapts means to ends, from which the plain lesson is, that we shall be likely to accomplish most when we are in the best spiritual condition; or in other words, we shall usually do our Lord's work best when our gifts and graces are in good order, and we shall do worst when they are most out of trim. This is a practical truth for our guidance. When the Lord makes exceptions, they do but prove the rule.

We are, in a certain sense, our own tools, and therefore must keep ourselves in order. If I want to preach the gospel, I can only use my own voice; therefore I must train my vocal powers. I can only think with my own brains, and feel with my own heart, and therefore I must educate my intellectual and emotional faculties. I can only weep and agonise for souls in my own renewed nature, therefore must I watch-fully maintain the tenderness which was in Christ Jesus. It will be in vain for me to stock my library, or organise societies, or project schemes, if I neglect the culture of myself; for books, and agencies, and systems, are only remotely the instruments of my holy calling; my

7

own spirit, soul, and body, are my nearest machinery for sacred service; my spiritual faculties, and my inner life, are my battle axe and weapons of war. M'Cheyne, writing to a ministerial friend, who was travelling with a view to perfecting himself in the German tongue, used language identical with our own:—"I know you will apply hard to German, but do not forget the culture of the inner man—I mean of the heart. How diligently the cavalry officer keeps his sabre clean and sharp; every stain he rubs off with the greatest care. Remember you are God's sword, His instrument—I trust, a chosen vessel unto Him to bear His name. In great measure, according to the purity and perfection of the instrument, will be the success. It is not great talents God blesses so much as likeness to Jesus. A holy minister is an awful weapon in the hand of God."

For the herald of the gospel to be spiritually out of order in his own proper person is, both to himself and to his work, a most serious calamity; and yet, my brethren, how easily is such an evil produced, and with what watchfulness must it be guarded against! Travelling one day by express from Perth to Edinburgh, on a sudden we came to a dead stop, because a very small screw in one of the engines—every railway locomotive consisting virtually of two engines—had been broken, and when we started again we were obliged to crawl along with one piston-rod at work instead of two. Only a small screw was gone. If that had been right the train would have rushed along its iron road, but the absence of that insignificant piece of iron disarranged the whole. A train is said to have been stopped on one of the United States' railways by flies in the grease-boxes of the carriage wheels. The analogy is perfect; a man in all other respects fitted to be useful, may by some small defect be exceedingly hindered, or even rendered utterly useless. Such a result is all the more grievous, because it is associated with the gospel, which in the highest sense is adapted to effect the grandest results. It is a terrible thing when the healing balm loses its efficacy through the blunderer who administers it. You all know the injurious effects frequently produced upon water through flowing along leaden pipes; even so the gospel itself, in flowing through men who are spiritually unhealthy, may be debased until it grows injurious to their hearers. It is to be feared that Calvinistic doctrine becomes most evil teaching when it is set forth by men of ungodly lives, and exhibited as if it were a cloak for licentiousness; and Arminianism, on the other hand, with its wide sweep of the offer of mercy, may do most serious damage to the souls of men, if the careless tone of the preacher leads his hearers to believe that they *can* repent whenever they please; and that, therefore, no urgency surrounds the gospel message. Moreover, when a preacher is poor in grace, any lasting good which may be the result of his ministry, will usually be feeble and utterly out of proportion with what might have been expected. Much sowing will be followed by little reaping; the interest upon the talents will be inappreciably small. In two or three of the battles which were lost in the late American war, the result is said to have been due to the bad gunpowder which was served out by certain "shoddy" contractors to the army, so that the due effect of a cannonade was not produced. So it may be with us. We may miss our mark, lose our end and aim, and waste our time, through not possessing true vital force within ourselves, or not possessing it in such a degree that God could consistently bless us. Beware of being "shoddy" preachers.

IT SHOULD BE ONE OF OUR FIRST CARES THAT WE OURSELVES BE SAVED MEN.

That a teacher of the gospel should first be a partaker of it is a simple truth, but at the same time a rule of the most weighty importance. We are not among those who accept the apostolical succession of young men simply because they assume it; if their college experience has been rather vivacious than spiritual, if their honours have been connected rather with athletic exercises than with labours for Christ, we demand evidence of another kind than they are able to present to us. No amount of fees paid to learned doctors, and no amount of classics received in return, appear to us to be evidences of a call from above. True and genuine piety is necessary as the first indispensable requisite; whatever "call" a man may pretend to have, if he has not been called to holiness, he certainly has not been called to the ministry.

"First be trimmed thyself, and then adorn thy brother," say the rabbins. "The hand," saith Gregory, "that means to make another clean, must not itself be dirty." If your salt be unsavoury how can you season others? Conversion is a *sine qua non* in a minister. Ye aspirants to our pulpits, "ye must be born again." Nor is the possession of this first qualification a thing to be taken for granted by any man, for there is very great possibility of our being mistaken as to whether we are converted or not. Believe me, it is no child's play to "make your calling and election sure." The world is full of counterfeits, and swarms with panderers to carnal self-conceit, who gather around a minister as vultures around a carcass. Our own hearts are deceitful, so that truth lies not on the surface, but must be drawn up from the deepest well. We must search ourselves very anxiously and very thoroughly, lest by any means after having preached to others we ourselves should be castaways.

How horrible to be a preacher of the gospel and yet to be unconverted! Let each man here whisper to his own inmost soul, "What a dreadful thing it will be *for me* if I should be ignorant of the power of the truth which I am preparing to proclaim!" Unconverted ministry involves the most unnatural relationships. A graceless pastor is a blind man elected to a professorship of optics, philosophising upon light and vision, discoursing upon and distinguishing to others the nice shades and delicate blendings of the prismatic colours, while he himself is absolutely in the dark! He is a dumb man elevated to the chair of music; a deaf man fluent upon symphonies and harmonies! He is a mole professing to educate eaglets; a limpet elected to preside over angels. To such a relationship one might apply the most absurd and grotesque metaphors, except that the subject is too solemn. It is a dreadful position for a man to stand in, for he has undertaken a work for which he is totally, wholly, and altogether unqualified, but from the responsibilities of which this unfitness will not screen him, because he wilfully incurred them. Whatever his natural gifts, whatever his mental powers may be, he is utterly out of court for spiritual work if he has no spiritual life; and it is his duty to cease the ministerial office till he has received this first and simplest of qualifications for it.

Unconverted ministry must be equally dreadful in another respect. If the man has no commission, what a very *unhappy* position for him to occupy! What can he see in the experience of his people to give him comfort? How must he feel when he hears the cries of penitents; or listens to their anxious doubts and solemn fears? He must be astonished to think that his words should be owned to that end! The word of an unconverted man may be blessed to the conversion of souls, since the Lord, while He disowns the man, will still honour His own truth. How perplexed such a man must be when he is consulted concerning the difficulties of mature Christians! In the pathway of experience, in which his own regenerate hearers are led, he must feel himself quite at a loss. How can he listen to their deathbed joys, or join in their rapturous fellowships around the table of their Lord?

In many instances of young men put to a trade which they cannot endure, they run away to sea sooner than follow an irksome business; but where shall that man flee who is apprenticed for life to this holy calling, and yet is a total stranger to the power of godliness? How can he daily bid men come to Christ, while he himself is a stranger to His dying love? O sirs, surely this must be perpetual slavery. Such a man must hate the sight of a pulpit as much as a galley-slave hates the oar.

And *how unserviceable* such a man must be. He has to guide travellers along a road which he has never trodden, to navigate a vessel along a coast of which he knows none of the landmarks! He is called to instruct others, being himself a fool. What can he be but a cloud without rain, a tree with leaves only. As when the caravan in the wilderness, all athirst and ready to die beneath the broiling sun, comes to the long desired well, and, horror of horrors! finds it without a drop of water; so when souls thirsting after God come to a graceless ministry, they are ready to perish because the water of life is not to be found. Better abolish pulpits than fill them with men who have no experimental knowledge of what they teach.

Alas! *the unregenerate pastor becomes terribly mischievous* too, for of all the causes which create infidelity, ungodly ministers must be ranked among the first. I read the other day, that no phase of evil presented so marvellous a power for destruction, as the unconverted minister of a parish, with a £1200 organ, a choir of ungodly singers, and an aristocratic congregation. It was the opinion of the writer, that there could be no greater instrument for damnation out of hell than that. People go to their place of worship and sit down comfortably, and think they must be Christians, when all the time all that their religion consists in, is listening to an orator, having their ears tickled with music, and perhaps their eyes amused with graceful action and fashionable manners; the whole being no better than what they hear and see at the opera—not so good, perhaps, in point of æsthetic beauty, and not an atom more spiritual. Thousands are congratulating themselves, and even blessing God that they are devout worshippers, when at the same time they are living in an unregenerate Christless state, having the form of godliness, but denying the power thereof. He who presides over a system which aims at nothing higher than formalism, is far more a servant of the devil than a minister of God.

A formal preacher is mischievous while he preserves his outward equilibrium, but as he is without the preserving balance of godliness, sooner or later he is almost sure to make a trip in his moral character, and what a position is he in then! How is God blasphemed, and the gospel abused!

Terrible is it to consider *what a death must await such a man! and what must be his after-condition!* The prophet pictures the king of Babylon going down to hell, and all the kings and princes whom he had destroyed, and whose capitals he had laid waste, rising up from their places in Pandemonium, and saluting the fallen tyrant with the cutting sarcasm, "Art thou become like unto us?". And cannot you suppose a man who has been a minister, but who has lived without Christ in his heart, going down to hell, and all the imprisoned spirits who used to hear him, and all the ungodly of his parish rising up and saying to him in bitter tones, "Art thou also become as we are? Physician, didst thou not heal thyself? Art thou who claimed to be a shining light cast down into the darkness for ever?" Oh! if one must be lost, let it not be in this fashion! To be lost under the shadow of a pulpit is dreadful, but how much more so to perish from the pulpit itself!

There is an awful passage in John Bunyan's treatise, entitled "Sighs from Hell," which full often rings in my ears: "How many souls have blind priests been the means of destroying by their ignorance? Preaching that was no better for their souls than rats-bane to the body. Many

of them, it is to be feared, have whole towns to answer for. Ah! friend,
I tell thee, thou that hast taken in hand to preach to the people, it
may be thou hast taken in hand thou canst not tell what. Will it not
grieve thee to see thy whole parish come bellowing after thee into
hell? crying out, 'This we have to thank thee for, thou wast afraid to tell
us of our sins, lest we should not put meat fast enough into thy mouth.
O cursed wretch, who wast not content, blind guide as thou wast, to
fall into the ditch thyself, but hast also led us thither with thee.'"

Richard Baxter, in his "Reformed Pastor," amid much other solemn
matter, writes as follows: "Take heed to yourselves lest you should
be void of that saving grace of God which you offer to others, and
be strangers to the effectual working of that gospel which you preach;
and lest, while you proclaim the necessity of a Saviour to the world,
your hearts should neglect him, and you should miss of an interest in
him and his saving benefits. Take heed to yourselves, lest you perish
while you call upon others to take heed of perishing, and lest you
famish yourselves while you prepare their food. Though there be a
promise of shining as stars to those that turn many to righteousness
(Dan. xii. 3), this is but on supposition that they be first turned to it
themselves: such promises are made *cæteris paribus, et suppositis
supponendis.* Their own sincerity in the faith is the condition of their
glory simply considered, though their great ministerial labours may
be a condition of the promise of their greater glory. Many men have
warned others that they come not to that place of torment, which yet
they hasted to themselves; many a preacher is now in hell, that hath
an hundred times called upon his hearers to use the utmost care and
diligence to escape it. Can any reasonable man imagine that God
should save men for offering salvation to others, while they refused
it themselves, and for telling others those truths which they themselves
neglected and abused? Many a tailor goes in rags that maketh costly
clothes for others; and many a cook scarce licks his fingers, when he
hath dressed for others the most costly dishes. Believe it, brethren,
God never saved any man for being a preacher, nor because he was
an able preacher; but because he was a justified, sanctified man, and
consequently faithful in his Master's work. Take heed, therefore, to
yourselves first, that you be that which you persuade others to be,
and believe that which you persuade them daily to believe, and have
heartily entertained that Christ and Spirit which you offer unto others.
He that bade you love your neighbours as yourselves, did imply that
you should love yourselves and not hate and destroy both yourselves
and them."

My brethren, let these weighty sentences have due effect upon you.
Surely there can be no need to add more; but let me pray you to
examine yourselves, and so make good use of what has been addressed
to you.

This first matter of true religion being settled, IT IS OF THE NEXT IMPORTANCE TO THE MINISTER THAT HIS PIETY BE VIGOROUS.

He is not to be content with being equal to the rank and file of Christians, he must be a mature and advanced believer; for the ministry of Christ has been truly called "the choicest of his choice, the elect of his election, a church picked out of the church." If he were called to an ordinary position, and to common work, common grace might perhaps satisfy him, though even then it would be an indolent satisfaction; but being elect to extraordinary labours, and called to a place of unusual peril, he should be anxious to possess that superior strength which alone is adequate to his station. His pulse of vital godliness must beat strongly and regularly; his eye of faith must be bright; his foot of resolution must be firm; his hand of activity must be quick; his whole inner man must be in the highest degree of sanity. It is said of the Egyptians that they chose their priests from the most learned of their philosophers, and then they esteemed their priests so highly, that they chose their kings from them. We require to have for God's ministers the pick of all the Christian host; such men indeed, that if the nation wanted kings they could not do better than elevate them to the throne. Our weakest-minded, most timid, most carnal, and most ill-balanced men are not suitable candidates for the pulpit. There are some works which we should never allot to the invalid or deformed. A man may not be qualified for climbing lofty buildings, his brain may be too weak, and elevated work might place him in great danger; by all means let him keep on the ground and find useful occupation where a steady brain is less important: there are brethren who have analogous spiritual deficiencies, they cannot be called to service which is conspicuous and elevated, because their heads are too weak. If they were permitted a little success they would be intoxicated with vanity—a vice all too common among ministers, and of all things the least becoming in them, and the most certain to secure them a fall. Should we as a nation be called to defend our hearths and homes, we should not send out our boys and girls with swords and guns to meet the foe, neither may the church send out every fluent novice or inexperienced zealot to plead for the faith. The fear of the Lord must teach the young man wisdom, or he is barred from the pastorate; the grace of God must mature his spirit, or he had better tarry till power be given him from on high.

The highest moral character must be sedulously maintained. Many are disqualified for office in the church who are well enough as simple members. I hold very stern opinions with regard to Christian men who have fallen into gross sin; I rejoice that they may be truly converted, and may be with mingled hope and caution received into the church; but I question, gravely question whether a man who has grossly sinned should be very readily restored to the pulpit. As John Angell James remarks, "When a preacher of righteousness has stood in the way of sinners, he should never again open his lips in the great congregation until his repentance is as notorious as his sin." Let those who have been shorn by the sons of Ammon tarry at Jericho till their beards be grown; this has often been used as a taunt to beardless boys to whom it is evidently inapplicable, it is an accurate enough metaphor for dishonoured and characterless men, let their age be what it may. Alas! the beard of reputation once shorn is hard to grow again. Open immorality, in most cases, however deep the repentance, is a fatal sign that ministerial graces were never in the man's character. Cæsar's wife must be beyond suspicion, and there must be no ugly rumours as to ministerial inconsistency in the past, or the hope of usefulness will be slender. Into the church such fallen ones are to be received as penitents, and into the ministry they may be received if God puts them there; my doubt is not about that, but as to whether God ever did place them there; and my belief is that we should be very slow to help back to the pulpit men, who having been once tried, have proved themselves to have too little grace to stand the crucial test of ministerial life.

For some work we choose none but the strong; and when God calls us to ministerial labour we should endeavour to get grace that we may be strengthened into fitness for our position, and not be mere novices carried away by the temptations of Satan, to the injury of the church and our own ruin. We are to stand equipped with the whole armour of God, ready for feats of valour not expected of others: to us self-denial, self-forgetfulness, patience, perseverance, longsuffering, must be every-day virtues, and who is sufficient for these things? We had need live very near to God, if we would approve ourselves in our vocation.

Recollect, as ministers, that your whole life, your whole pastoral life especially, will be affected by the vigour of your piety. If your zeal grows dull, you will not pray well in the pulpit; you will pray worse in the family, and worst in the study alone. When your soul becomes lean, your hearers, without knowing how or why, will find that your prayers in public have little savour for them; they will feel your barrenness, perhaps, before you perceive it yourself. Your discourses will next betray your declension. You may utter as well-chosen words, and as fitly-ordered sentences, as aforetime; but there will be a perceptible loss of spiritual force. You will shake yourselves as at other times, even as Samson did, but you will find that your great strength has departed. In your daily communion with your people, they will not be slow to mark the all-pervading decline of your graces. Sharp eyes will see the grey hairs here and there long before you do. Let a man be afflicted with a disease of the heart, and all evils are wrapped up in that one—stomach, lungs, viscera, muscles, and nerves will all suffer; and so, let a man have his heart weakened in spiritual things, and very soon his entire life will feel the withering influence. Moreover, as the result of your own decline, everyone of your hearers will suffer more or less; the vigorous amongst them will overcome the depressing tendency, but the weaker sort will be seriously damaged. It is with us and our hearers as it is with watches and the public clock; if our watch be wrong, very few will be misled by it but ourselves; but if the Horse Guards or Greenwich Observatory should go amiss, half London would lose its reckoning. So is it with the minister; he is the parish-clock, many take their time from him, and if he be incorrect, then they all go wrongly, more or less, and he is in a great measure accountable for all the sin which he occasions. This we cannot endure to think of, my brethren. It will not bear a moment's comfortable consideration, and yet it must be looked at that we may guard against it.

You must remember, too, that we have need of very vigorous piety, *because our danger is so much greater than that of others.* Upon the whole, no place is so assailed with temptation as the ministry. Despite the popular idea that ours is a snug retreat from temptation, it is *no less* true that our dangers are more numerous and more insidious than those of ordinary Christians. Ours may be a vantage-ground for height, but that height is perilous, and to many the ministry has proved a Tarpeian rock. If you ask what these temptations are, time might fail us to particularise them; but among them are both the coarser and the more refined; the coarser are such temptations as self-indulgence at the table, enticements to which are superabundant among a hospitable people, the temptations of the flesh, which are incessant with young unmarried men set on high among an admiring throng of young women : but enough of this, your own observation will soon reveal to you a thousand snares, unless indeed your eyes are blinded. There are more secret snares than these, from which we can less easily escape; and of these the worst is the temptation to ministerialism— the tendency to read our Bibles as ministers, to pray as ministers, to get into doing the whole of our religion as not ourselves personally, but only relatively, concerned in it. To lose the personality of repentance and faith is a loss indeed. "No man," says John Owen, "preaches his sermon well to others if he doth not first preach it to his own heart." Brethren, it is eminently hard to keep to this. Our office, instead of helping our piety, as some assert, is through the evil of our natures turned into one of its most serious hindrances; at least, I find it so. How one kicks and struggles against officialism, and yet how easily doth it beset us, like a long garment which twists around the racer's feet and impedes his running! Beware, dear brethren, of this and all the other seductions of your calling; and if you have done so until now, continue still to watch till life's latest hour.

We have noted but one of the perils, but indeed they are legion. The great enemy of souls takes care to leave no stone unturned for the preacher's ruin. "Take heed to yourselves," says Baxter, "because the tempter will make his first and sharpest onset upon you. If you will be the leaders against him, he will spare you no further than God restraineth him. He beareth you the greatest malice that are engaged to do him the greatest mischief. As he hateth Christ more than any of us, because he is the General of the field, and the 'Captain of our salvation,' and doth more than all the world besides against the kingdom of darkness; so doth he note the leaders under him more than the common soldiers, on the like account, in their proportion. He knows what a rout he may make among the rest, if the leaders fall before their eyes. He hath long tried that way of fighting, 'neither with small nor great,' comparatively, but these; and of 'smiting the shepherds, that he may scatter the flock.' And so great has been his success this way, that he will follow it on as far as he is able. Take heed, therefore, brethren, for the enemy hath a special eye upon you. You shall have his most subtle insinuations, and incessant solicitations, and violent assaults. As wise and learned as you are, take heed to yourselves lest he overwit you. The devil is a greater scholar than you, and a nimbler disputant; he can 'transform himself into an angel of light' to deceive. He will get within you and trip up your heels before you are aware; he will play the juggler with you undiscerned, and cheat you of your faith or innocency, and you shall not know that you have lost it; nay, he will make you believe it is multiplied or increased when it is lost. You shall see neither hook nor line, much less the subtle angler himself, while he is offering you his bait. And his baits shall be so fitted to your temper and disposition, that he will be sure to find advantages within you, and make your own principles and inclinations to betray you; and whenever he ruineth you, he will make you the instrument of your own ruin. Oh, what a conquest will he think he hath got, if he can make a minister lazy and unfaithful; if he can tempt a minister into covetousness or scandal! He will glory against the church, and say, 'These are your holy preachers: you see what their preciseness is, and whither it will bring them.' He will glory against Jesus Christ Himself, and say, 'These are thy champions! I can make thy chiefest servants to abuse thee; I can make the stewards of thy house unfaithful.' If he did so insult against God upon a false surmise, and tell Him he could make Job to curse Him to His face (Job i. 2), what would he do if he should indeed prevail against us? And at last he will insult as much over you that ever he could draw you to be false to your great trust, and to blemish your holy profession, and to do him so much service that was your enemy. O do not so far gratify Satan; do not make him so much sport: suffer him not to use you as the Philistines did Samson—first to deprive you of your strength, and then to put out your eyes, and so to make you the matter of his triumph and derision."

Once more. We must cultivate the highest degree of godliness *because our work imperatively requires it.* The labour of the Christian ministry is well performed in exact proportion to the vigour of our renewed nature. Our work is only well done when it is well with ourselves. As is the workman, such will the work be. To face the enemies of truth, to defend the bulwarks of the faith, to rule well in the house of God, to comfort all that mourn, to edify the saints, to guide the perplexed, to bear with the froward, to win and nurse souls—all these and a thousand other works beside are not for a Feeble-mind or a Ready-to-halt, but are reserved for Great-heart whom the Lord has made strong for Himself. Seek then strength from the Strong One, wisdom from the Wise One, in fact, all from the God of all.

Thirdly, let the minister take care THAT HIS PERSONAL CHARACTER AGREES IN ALL RESPECTS WITH HIS MINISTRY.

We have all heard the story of the man who preached so well and lived so badly, that when he was in the pulpit everybody said he ought never to come out again, and when he was out of it they all declared he never ought to enter it again. From the imitation of such a Janus may the Lord deliver us. May we never be priests of God at the altar, and sons of Belial outside the tabernacle door; but on the contrary, may we, as Nazianzen says of Basil, "thunder in our doctrine, and lighten in our conversation." We do not trust those persons who have two faces, nor will men believe in those whose verbal and practical testimonies are contradictory. As actions, according to the proverb, speak louder than words, so an ill life will effectually drown the voice of the most eloquent ministry. After all, our truest building must be performed with our hands; our characters must be more persuasive than our speech. Here I would not alone warn you of sins of commission, but of sins of omission. Too many preachers forget to serve God when they are out of the pulpit, their lives are negatively inconsistent. Abhor, dear brethren, the thought of being clockwork ministers who are not alive by abiding grace within, but are wound up by temporary influences; men who are only ministers for the time being, under the stress of the hour of ministering, but cease to be ministers when they descend the pulpit stairs. True ministers are always ministers. Too many preachers are like those sand-toys we buy for our children; you turn the box upside down, and the little acrobat revolves and revolves till the sand is all run down, and then he hangs motionless; so there are some who persevere in the ministrations of truth as long as there is an official necessity for their work, but after that, no pay, no paternoster; no salary, no sermon.

It is a horrible thing to be an inconsistent minister. Our Lord is said to have been like Moses, for this reason, that He was "a prophet mighty in word and in deed." The man of God should imitate his Master in this; he should be mighty both in the word of his doctrine and in the deed of his example, and mightiest, if possible, in the second. It is remarkable that the only church history we have is, "*The Acts* of the apostles." The Holy Spirit has not preserved their sermons. They were very good ones, better than we shall ever preach, but still the Holy Spirit has only taken care of their "acts." We have no books of the resolutions of the apostles; when we hold our church-meetings we record our minutes and resolutions, but the Holy Spirit only puts down the "acts." Our acts should be such as to bear recording, for recorded they will be. We must live as under the more immediate eye of God, and as in the blaze of the great all-revealing day.

Holiness in a minister is at once his chief necessity and his goodliest ornament. Mere moral excellence is not enough, there must be the higher virtue; a consistent character there must be, but this must be anointed with the sacred consecrating oil, or that which makes us most fragrant to God and man will be wanting. Old John Stoughton, in his treatise entitled "The Preacher's Dignity and Duty," insists upon the minister's holiness in sentences full of weight. "If Uzzah must die but for *touching the ark of God,* and that to stay it when it was like to fall; if the men of Beth-shemesh for *looking into it*; if the very beasts that do but come near the holy mount be threatened; then what manner of persons ought they to be who shall be admitted to talk with God familiarly, to 'stand before him,' as the angels do, and 'behold his face continually;' 'to bear the ark upon their shoulders,' 'to bear his name before the Gentiles;' in a word, to be his ambassadors? 'Holiness becometh thy house, O Lord;' and were it not a ridiculous thing to imagine, that the vessels must be holy, the vestures must be holy, all must be holy, but only he upon whose very garments must be written 'holiness to the Lord,' might be unholy; that the bells of the horses should have an inscription of holiness upon them, in Zechariah, and the saints' bells, the bells of Aaron, should be un-hallowed? No, they must be 'burning and shining lights,' or else their influence will dart some malignant quality; they must 'chew the cud and divide the hoof,' or else they are unclean; they must 'divide the word aright,' and walk uprightly in their life, and so join life to learning. If holiness be wanting, the ambassadors dishonour the country from whence they come, and the prince from whom they come; and this dead Amasa, this dead doctrine not quickened with a good life, lying in the way, stops the people of the Lord, that they cannot go on cheerfully in their spiritual warfare."

The life of the preacher should be a magnet to draw men to Christ, and it is sad indeed when it keeps them from him. Sanctity in ministers is a loud call to sinners to repent, and when allied with holy cheerfulness it becomes wondrously attractive. Jeremy Taylor in his own rich language tells, "Herod's doves could never have invited so many strangers to their dove-cotes, if they had not been besmeared with opobalsamum : but, ἐὰν μύρῳ χρίσῃς τάς περιστερὰς, καί ἔξωθεν ἄλλας ἄξουσιν, said Didymus, 'make your pigeons smell sweet, and they will allure whole flocks;' and if your life be excellent, if your virtues be like a precious ointment, you will soon invite your charges to run 'in odorem unguentorum,' 'after your precious odours :' but you must be excellent, not 'tanquam unus de populo,' but 'tanquam homo Dei;' you must be a man of God, not after the common manner of men, but 'after God's own heart;' and men will strive to be like you, if you be like to God : but when you only stand at the door of virtue, for nothing but to keep sin out, you will draw into the folds of Christ none but such as fear drives in. 'Ad majorem Dei gloriam,' 'To do what will most glorify God,' that is the line you must walk by : for to do no more than all men needs must is servility, not so much as the affection of sons; much less can you be fathers to the people, when you go not so far as the sons of God : for a dark lantern, though there be a weak brightness on one side, will scarce enlighten one, much less will it conduct a multitude, or allure many followers by the brightness of its flame."

Another equally admirable episcopal divine has well and pithily said, "The star which led the wise men unto Christ, the pillar of fire which led the children unto Canaan, did not only shine, but go before them. Matt. ii. 9; Exod. xiii. 21. The voice of Jacob will do little good if the hands be the hands of Esau. In the law, no person who had any blemish was to offer the oblations of the Lord (Lev. xxi. 17–20); the Lord thereby teaching us what graces ought to be in his ministers. The priest was to have in his robes bells and pomegranates; the one a figure of sound doctrine, and the other of a fruitful life. Exod. xxviii. 33, 34. The Lord will be sanctified in all those that draw near unto him (Isa. lii. 11); for the sins of the priests make the people abhor the offering of the Lord (1 Sam. ii. 17); their wicked lives do shame their doctrine; Passionem Christi annunciant profitendo, male agendo exhonorant, as St. Austin speaks : with their doctrine they build, and with their lives they destroy. I conclude this point with that wholesome passage of Hierom ad Nepotianum. Let not, saith he, thy works shame thy doctrine, lest they who hear thee in the church tacitly answer, Why doest thou not thyself what thou teachest to others? He is too delicate a teacher who persuadeth others to fast with a full belly. A robber may accuse covetousness. Sacerdotis Christi os, mens, manusque concordent; a minister of Christ should have his tongue, and his heart, and his hand agree."

Very quaint also is the language of Thomas Playfere in his "Say Well, Do Well." "There was a ridiculous actor in the city of Smyrna, who, pronouncing *O cælum!* O heaven! pointed with his finger towards the ground; which when Polemo, the chiefest man in the place, saw, he could abide to stay no longer, but went from the company in a great chafe, saying 'This fool hath made a solecism with his hand, he has spoken false Latin with his finger.' And such are they who *teach* well and *do* ill; that however they have *heaven* at their tongue's end, yet the *earth* is at their finger's end; such as do not only speak false Latin with their tongue, but false divinity with their hands; such as live not according to their preaching. But He that sits in the heaven will laugh them to scorn, and hiss them off the stage, if they do not mend their action."

Even in little things the minister should take care that his life is consistent with his ministry. He should be especially careful never to fall short of his word. This should be pushed even to scrupulosity; we cannot be too careful; truth must not only be in us, but shine from us. A celebrated doctor of divinity in London, who is now in heaven I have no doubt—a very excellent and godly man—gave notice one Sunday that he intended to visit all his people, and said, that in order to be able to get round and visit them and their families once in the year, he should take all the seatholders in order. A person well known to me, who was then a poor man, was delighted with the idea that the minister was coming to his house to see him, and about a week or two before he conceived it would be his turn, his wife was very careful to sweep the hearth and keep the house tidy, and the man ran home early from work, hoping each night to find the doctor there. This went on for a considerable time. He either forgot his promise, or grew weary in performing it, or for some other reason never went to this poor man's house, and the result was this, the man lost confidence in all preachers, and said, "They care for the rich, but they do not care for us who are poor." That man never settled down to any one place of worship for many years, till at last he dropped into Exeter Hall and remained my hearer for years till providence removed him. It was no small task to make him believe that any minister could be an honest man, and could impartially love both rich and poor. Let us avoid doing such mischief, by being very particular as to our word.

We must remember that we are very much looked at. Men hardly have the impudence to break the law in the open sight of their fellows, yet in such publicity we live and move. We are watched by a thousand eagle eyes; let us so act that we shall never need to care if all heaven, and earth, and hell, swelled the list of spectators. Our public position is a great gain if we are enabled to exhibit the fruits of the Spirit in our lives; take heed, brethren, that you throw not away the advantage.

When we say to you, my dear brethren, take care of your life, we mean be careful of even the minutiæ of your character. Avoid little debts, unpunctuality, gossiping, nicknaming, petty quarrels, and all other of those little vices which fill the ointment with flies. The self-indulgences which have lowered the repute of many must not be tolerated by us. The familiarities which have laid others under suspicion, we must chastely avoid. The roughnesses which have rendered some obnoxious, and the fopperies which have made others contemptible, we must put away. We cannot afford to run great risks through little things. Our care must be to act on the rule, "giving no offence in anything, that the ministry be not blamed."

By this is not intended that we are to hold ourselves bound by every whim or fashion of the society in which we move. As a general rule, I hate the fashions of society, and detest conventionalities, and if I conceived it best to put my foot through a law of etiquette, I should feel gratified in having it to do. No, we are men, not slaves; and are not to relinquish our manly freedom, to be the lackeys of those who affect gentility or boast refinement. Yet, brethren, anything that verges upon the coarseness which is akin to sin, we must shun as we would a viper. The rules of Chesterfield are ridiculous to us, but not the example of Christ; and He was never coarse, low, discourteous, or indelicate.

Even in your recreations, remember that you are ministers. When you are off the parade you are still officers in the army of Christ, and as such demean yourselves. But if the lesser things must be looked after, how careful should you be in the great matters of morality, honesty, and integrity! Here the minister must not fail. His private life must ever keep good tune with his ministry, or his day will soon set with him, and the sooner he retires the better, for his continuance in his office will only dishonour the cause of God and ruin himself.

II

The Call to the Ministry

ANY Christian has a right to disseminate the gospel who has the ability to do so; and more, he not only has the right, but it is his duty so to do as long as he lives. Rev. xxii. 17. The propagation of the gospel is left, not to a few, but to all the disciples of the Lord Jesus Christ: according to the measure of grace entrusted to him by the Holy Spirit, each man is bound to minister in his day and generation, both to the church and among unbelievers. Indeed, this question goes beyond men, and even includes the whole of the other sex; whether believers are male or female, they are all bound, when enabled by divine grace, to exert themselves to the utmost to extend the knowledge of the Lord Jesus Christ. Our service, however, need not take the particular form of preaching—certainly, in some cases it must not, as for instance in the case of females, whose public teaching is expressly prohibited: 1 Tim. ii. 12; 1 Cor. xiv. 34. But yet if we have the ability to preach, we are bound to exercise it. I do not, however, in this lecture allude to occasional preaching, or any other form of ministry common to all the saints, but to the work and office of the bishopric, in which is included both teaching and bearing rule in the church, which requires the dedication of a man's entire life to spiritual work, and separation from every secular calling, 2 Tim. ii. 4; and entitles the man to cast himself for temporal supplies upon the church of God, since he gives up all his time, energies, and endeavours, for the good of those over whom he presides. 1 Cor. ix. 11; 1 Tim. v. 18. Such a man is addressed by Peter in the words, "Feed the flock of God which is among you, taking the oversight thereof." 1 Pet. v. 2. Now, all in a church cannot oversee, or rule—there must be some to be overseen and ruled; and we believe that the Holy Ghost appoints in the church of God some to act as overseers, while others are made willing to be watched over for their good. All are not called to labour in word and doctrine, or to be elders, or to exercise the office of a bishop; nor should all aspire to such works, since the gifts necessary are nowhere promised to all; but those should addict themselves to such important engagements who feel, like the apostle, that they have "received this ministry." 2 Cor. iv. 1. No man may intrude into the sheepfold as an under-shepherd; he must have an eye to the chief Shepherd, and wait His beck and command. Or ever a man stands

22

forth as God's ambassador, he must wait for the call from above; and if he does not so, but rushes into the sacred office, the Lord will say of him and others like him, "I sent them not, neither commanded them; therefore they shall not profit this people at all, saith the Lord." Jer. xxiii. 32.

By reference to the Old Testament, you will find the messengers of God in the old dispensation claiming to hold commissions from Jehovah. Isaiah tells us that one of the seraphim touched his lips with a live coal from off the altar, and the voice of the Lord said, "Whom shall I send, and who will go for us?" Isa. vi. 8. Then said the prophet, "Here am I, send me." He ran not before he had been thus especially visited of the Lord and qualified for his mission. "How shall they preach, except they be sent?" were words as yet unuttered, but their solemn meaning was well understood. Jeremiah details his call in his first chapter: "Then the word of the Lord came unto me, saying, Before I formed thee in the belly I knew thee; and before thou camest forth out of the womb, I sanctified thee, and I ordained thee a prophet unto the nations. Then said I, Ah, Lord God! behold, I cannot speak: for I am a child. But the Lord said unto me, Say not, I am a child: for thou shalt go to all that I shall send thee, and whatsoever I command thee thou shalt speak. Be not afraid of their faces: for I am with thee to deliver thee, saith the Lord. Then the Lord put forth his hand, and touched my mouth; and the Lord said unto me, Behold, I have put my words in thy mouth. See, I have this day set thee over the nations and over the kingdoms, to root out, and to pull down, and to destroy, and to throw down, and to build, and to plant." Jer. i. 4–10. Varying in its outward form, but to the same purport, was the commission of Ezekiel; it runs thus in his own words: "And he said unto me, Son of man, stand upon thy feet, and I will speak unto thee. And the Spirit entered into me when he spake unto me, and set me upon my feet, that I heard him that spake unto me. And he said unto me, Son of man, I send thee to the children of Israel, to a rebellious nation that hath rebelled against me: they and their fathers have transgressed against me, even unto this very day." Ezek. ii. 1–3. "Moreover he said unto me, Son of man, eat that thou findest; eat this roll, and go speak unto the house of Israel. So I opened my mouth, and he caused me to eat that roll. And he said unto me, Son of man, cause thy belly to eat, and fill thy bowels with this roll that I give thee. Then did I eat it; and it was in my mouth as honey for sweetness. And he said unto me, Son of man, go, get thee unto the house of Israel, and speak with my words unto them." Ezek. iii. 1–4. Daniel's call to prophesy, although not recorded, is abundantly attested by the visions granted to him, and the exceeding favour which he had with the Lord, both in his solitary meditations and public acts. It is not needful to pass all the other prophets in review, for they all claimed to speak with "thus saith the Lord." In the present dispensation, the priesthood is common to all the saints; but to prophesy, or what is analogous thereto, namely, to be moved by the Holy Ghost to give oneself up wholly to the proclamation of the gospel, is, as a matter of fact, the gift and calling of only a comparatively small number; and surely these need to be as sure of the rightfulness of their position as were the prophets; and yet how can they justify their office, except by a similar call?

Nor need any imagine that such calls are a mere delusion, and that none are in this age separated for the peculiar work of teaching and overseeing the church, for the very names given to ministers in the New Testament imply a previous call to their work. The apostle says, "Now then we are *ambassadors* for God;" but does not the very soul of the ambassadorial office lie in the appointment which is made by the monarch represented? An ambassador unsent would be a laughing-stock. Men who dare to avow themselves ambassadors for Christ, must feel most solemnly that the Lord has "committed" to them the word of reconciliation. 2 Cor. v. 18, 19. If it be said that this is restricted to the apostles, I answer that the epistle is written not in the name of Paul only, but of Timothy also, and hence includes other ministry besides apostleship. In the first epistle to the Corinthians we read, "Let a man so account of us (the *us* here meaning Paul and Sosthenes, 1 Cor. i. 1), as of the ministers of Christ, and *stewards* of the mysteries of God." 1 Cor. iv. 1. Surely a steward must hold his office from the Master. He cannot be a steward merely because he chooses to be so, or is so regarded by others. If any of us should elect ourselves stewards to the Marquis of Westminster, and proceed to deal with his property, we should have our mistake very speedily pointed out to us in the most convincing manner. There must evidently be authority ere a man can legally become a bishop, "the steward of God." Titus i. 7.

The Apocalyptic title of *Angel* (Rev. ii. 1) means a messenger; and how shall men be Christ's heralds, unless by his election and ordination? If the reference of the word *Angel* to the minister be questioned, we should be glad to have it shown that it can relate to any one else. To whom would the Spirit write in the church as its representative, but to some one in a position analogous to that of the presiding elder?

Titus was bidden to make full proof of his ministry—there was surely something to prove. Some are "vessels unto honour, sanctified and meet for the Master's use, and prepared unto every good work." 2 Tim. ii. 21. The Master is not to be denied the choice of the vessels which he uses; he will still say of certain men as he did of Saul of Tarsus, "He is a chosen vessel unto me, to bear my name before the

Gentiles." Acts ix. 15. When our Lord ascended on high he gave gifts unto men, and it is noteworthy that these gifts were men set apart for various works: "He gave some, apostles; and some, prophets; and some, evangelists; and some, pastors and teachers" (Eph. iv. 11); from which it is evident that certain individuals are, as the result of our Lord's ascension, bestowed upon the churches as pastors; they are given of God, and consequently not self-elevated to their position. Brethren, I trust you may be able one day to speak of the flock over whom "the Holy Ghost has made you overseers" (Acts xx. 28), and I pray that every one of you may be able to say with the apostle of the Gentiles, that your ministry is not of man, neither by man, but that you have received it of the Lord. Gal. i. 1. In you may that ancient promise be fulfilled, "I will give them pastors according to mine heart." Jer. iii. 15. "I will set up shepherds over them, which shall feed them." Jer. xxiii. 4. May the Lord himself fulfil in your several persons his own declaration: "I have set watchmen upon thy walls, O Jerusalem, which shall never hold their peace day nor night." May you take forth the precious from the vile, and so be as God's mouth. Jer. xv. 19. May the Lord make manifest by you the savour of the knowledge of Jesus in every place, and make you "unto God a sweet savour of Christ, in them that are saved, and in them that perish." 2 Cor. ii. 15. Having a priceless treasure in earthen vessels, may the excellency of the divine power rest upon you, and so may you both glorify God and clear yourselves from the blood of all men. As the Lord Jesus went up to the Mount and called to him whom he would, and then sent them forth to preach (Mark iii. 13), even so may he select you, call you upward to commune with himself, and send you forth as his elect servants to bless both the church and the world.

How may a young man know whether he is called or not? That is a weighty enquiry, and I desire to treat it most solemnly. O for divine guidance in so doing! That hundreds have missed their way, and stumbled against a pulpit is sorrowfully evident from the fruitless ministries and decaying churches which surround us. It is a fearful calamity to a man to miss his calling, and to the church upon whom he imposes himself, his mistake involves an affliction of the most grievous kind. It would be a curious and painful subject for reflection—the frequency with which men in the possession of reason mistake the end of their existence, and aim at objects which they were never intended to pursue. The writer who penned the following lines must surely have had his eyes upon many ill-occupied pulpits:

> "Declare, ye sages, if ye find
> 'Mongst animals of every kind,

Of each condition, sort, and size,
From whales and elephants to flies,
A creature that mistakes his plan,
And errs so constantly as man!

Each kind pursues its proper good,
And seeks enjoyment, rest and food,
As nature points, and never errs
In what it chooses or prefers;
Man only blunders, though possessed
Of reason far above the rest.

Descend to instances and try:
An ox will not attempt to fly,
Or leave his pasture in the wood
With fishes to explore the flood.
Man only acts of every creature
In opposition to his nature."

When I think upon the all but infinite mischief which may result from a mistake as to our vocation for the Christian pastorate, I feel overwhelmed with fear lest any of us should be slack in examining our credentials; and I had rather that we stood too much in doubt, and examined too frequently, than that we should become cumberers of the ground. There are not lacking many exact methods by which a man may test his call to the ministry if he earnestly desires to do so. It is imperative upon him not to enter the ministry until he has made solemn quest and trial of himself as to this point. His own personal salvation being secure, he must investigate as to the further matter of his call to office; the first is vital to himself as a Christian, the second equally vital to him as a pastor. As well be a professor without conversion, as a pastor without calling. In both cases there is a name and nothing more.

1. The first sign of the heavenly calling is *an intense, all-absorbing desire for the work.* In order to a true call to the ministry there must be an irresistible, overwhelming craving and raging thirst for telling to others what God has done to our own souls; what if I call it a kind of στοργή, such as birds have for rearing their young when the season is come; when the mother-bird would sooner die than leave her nest. It was said of Alleine by one who knew him intimately, that "he was infinitely and insatiably greedy of the conversion of souls." When he might have had a fellowship at his university, he preferred a chaplaincy, because he was "inspired with an impatience to be occupied in direct ministerial work." "Do not enter the ministry *if you can help it,*" was the deeply sage advice of a divine to one who sought his judgment. If any student in this room could be content to be a newspaper editor, or a grocer, or a farmer, or a doctor, or a

. . .

lawyer, or a senator, or a king, in the name of heaven and earth let him go his way; he is not the man in whom dwells the Spirit of God in its fulness, for a man so filled with God would utterly weary of any pursuit but that for which his inmost soul pants. If on the other hand, you can say that for all the wealth of both the Indies you could not and dare not espouse any other calling so as to be put aside from preaching the gospel of Jesus Christ, then, depend upon it, if other things be equally satisfactory, you have the signs of this apostleship We must feel that woe is unto us if we preach not the gospel; the word of God must be unto us as fire in our bones, otherwise, if we undertake the ministry, we shall be unhappy in it, shall be unable to bear the self-denials incident to it, and shall be of little service to those among whom we minister. I speak of self-denials, and well I may; for the true pastor's work is full of them, and without a love to his calling he will soon succumb, and either leave the drudgery, or move on in discontent, burdened with a monotony as tiresome as that of a blind horse in a mill.

> "There is a comfort in the strength of love;
> 'Twill make a thing endurable which else
> Would break the heart."

Girt with that love, you will be undaunted; divested of that more than magic-belt of irresistible vocation, you will pine away in wretchedness.

This desire must be a *thoughtful* one. It should not be a sudden impulse unattended by anxious consideration. It should be the outgrowth of our heart in its best moments, the object of our reverent aspirations, the subject of our most fervent prayers. It must continue with us when tempting offers of wealth and comfort come into conflict with it, and remain as a calm, clear-headed resolve after everything has been estimated at its right figure, and the cost thoroughly counted. When living as a child at my grandfather's in the country, I saw a company of huntsmen in their red coats riding through his fields after a fox. I was delighted! My little heart was excited; I was ready to follow the hounds over hedge and ditch. I have always felt a natural taste for that sort of business, and, as a child, when asked what I would be, I usually said I was going to be a huntsman. A fine profession, truly! Many young men have the same idea of being parsons as I had of being a huntsman—a mere childish notion that they would like the coat and the horn-blowing; the honour, the respect, the ease; and they are probably even fools enough to think, the riches of the ministry. (Ignorant beings they must be if they look for wealth in connection with the Baptist ministry.) The fascination of the preacher's office is very great to weak minds, and hence I earnestly caution all young men not to mistake whim for inspiration, and a childish preference for a call of the Holy Spirit.

Mark well, that the desire I have spoken of must be *thoroughly disinterested.* If a man can detect, after the most earnest self-examination, any other motive than the glory of God and the good of souls in his seeking the bishopric, he had better turn aside from it at once; for the Lord will abhor the bringing of buyers and sellers into His temple: the introduction of anything mercenary, even in the smallest degree, will be like the fly in the pot of ointment, and will spoil it all.

This desire should be one which *continues with us,* a passion which bears the test of trial, a longing from which it is quite impossible for us to escape, though we may have tried to do so; a desire, in fact, which grows more intense by the lapse of years, until it becomes a yearning, a pining, a famishing to proclaim the Word. This intense desire is so noble and beautiful a thing, that whenever I perceive it glowing in any young man's bosom, I am always slow to discourage him, even though I may have my doubts as to his abilities. It may be needful, for reasons to be given you further on, to repress the flame, but it should always be reluctantly and wisely done. I have such a profound respect for this "fire in the bones," that if I did not feel it myself, I must leave the ministry at once. If you do not feel the consecrated glow, I beseech you return to your homes and serve God in your proper spheres; but if assuredly the coals of juniper blaze within, do not stifle them, unless, indeed, other considerations of great moment should prove to you that the desire is not a fire of heavenly origin.

2. In the second place, combined with the earnest desire to become a pastor, there must be *aptness to teach and some measure of the other qualities needful for the office of a public instructor.* A man to prove his call must make a successful trial of these. I do not claim that the first time a man rises to speak he must preach as well as Robert Hall did in his later days. If he preaches no worse than that great man did at the first, he must not be condemned. You are aware that Robert Hall broke down altogether three times, and cried, "If this does not humble me, nothing will." Some of the noblest speakers were not in their early days the most fluent. Even Cicero at first suffered from a weak voice and a difficulty of utterance. Still, a man must not consider that he is called to preach until he has proved that he can speak. God certainly has not created behemoth to fly; and should leviathan have a strong desire to ascend with the lark, it would evidently be an unwise aspiration, since he is not furnished with wings. If a man be called to preach, he will be endowed with a degree of speaking ability, which he will cultivate and increase. If the gift of utterance be not

there in a measure at the first, it is not likely that it will ever be developed.

I have heard of a gentleman who had a most intense desire to preach, and pressed his suit upon his minister, until after a multitude of rebuffs he obtained leave to preach a trial sermon. That opportunity was the end of his importunity, for upon announcing his text he found himself bereft of every idea but one, which he delivered feelingly, and then descended the rostrum. "My brethren," said he, "if any of you think it an easy thing to preach, I advise you to come up here and have all the conceit taken out of you." The trial of your powers will go far to reveal to you your deficiency, if you have not the needed ability. I know of nothing better. We must give ourselves a fair trial in this matter, or we cannot assuredly know whether God has called us or not; and during the probation we must often ask ourselves whether, upon the whole, we can hope to edify others with such discourses.

We must, however, do much more than put it to our own conscience and judgment, for we are poor judges. A certain class of brethren have a great facility for discovering that they have been very wonderfully and divinely helped in their declamations; I should envy them their glorious liberty and self-complacency if there were any ground for it; for alas! I very frequently have to bemoan and mourn over my non-success and shortcomings as a speaker. There is not much dependence to be placed upon our own opinion, but much may be learned from judicious, spiritual-minded persons. It is by no means a law which ought to bind all persons, but still it is a good old custom in many of our country churches for the young man who aspires to the ministry to preach before the church. It can hardly ever be a very pleasant ordeal for the youthful aspirant, and, in many cases, it will scarcely be a very edifying exercise for the people; but still it may prove a most salutary piece of discipline, and save the public exposure of rampant ignorance. The church book at Arnsby contains the following entry:

A short account of the Call of Robert Hall, Junior, to the work of the Ministry, by the Church at Arnsby, August 13th, 1780.

"The said Robert Hall was born at Arnsby, May 2nd, 1764; and was, even from his childhood, not only serious, and *given to secret prayer before he could speak plain,* but was always wholly inclined to the work of the ministry. He began to compose hymns before he was quite seven years old, and therein discovered marks of piety, deep thought, and genius. Between eight and nine years he made several hymns, which were much admired by many, one of which was printed in the Gospel Magazine about that time. He wrote his thoughts on various religious subjects, and select portions of Scripture. He was likewise possessed of an intense inclination for learning, and made such progress that the country master under whom he was could not instruct him any further. He was then sent to North-ampton boarding school, under the care of the Rev. John Ryland, where he continued about a year and a half, and made great progress in Latin and Greek. In October, 1778, he went to the Academy at Bristol, under the care of the Rev. Mr. Evans; and on August 13th, 1780, was sent out to the ministry by this church, being sixteen years and three months old. The manner in which the church obtained satisfaction with his abilities for the great work, was his speaking in his turn at conference meetings from various portions of Scripture; in which, and in prayer, he had borne a part for upwards of four years before; and having when at home, at their request, frequently preached on Lord's-day mornings, to their great satisfaction. They therefore earnestly and unanimously requested his being in a solemn manner set apart to public employ. Accordingly, on the day aforesaid, he was examined by his father before the church, respecting his inclination, motives, and end, in reference to the ministry, and was likewise desired to make a declaration of his religious sentiments. All which being done, to the entire satisfaction of the church, they therefore set him apart by lifting up their right hands, and by solemn prayer. His father then delivered a discourse to him from 2 Tim. ii. 1, 'Thou therefore, my son, be strong in the grace that is in Christ Jesus.' Being thus sent forth, he preached in the afternoon from 2 Thess. i. 7, 8. 'May the Lord bless him, and grant him great success!'"

Considerable weight is to be given to the judgment of men and women who live near to God, and in most instances their verdict will not be a mistaken one. Yet this appeal is not final nor infallible, and is only to be estimated in proportion to the intelligence and piety of those consulted. I remember well how earnestly I was dissuaded from preaching by as godly a Christian matron as ever breathed; the value of her opinion I endeavoured to estimate with candour and patience —but it was outweighed by the judgment of persons of wider ex-perience. Young men in doubt will do well to take with them their wisest friends when next they go out to the country chapel or village meeting-room and essay to deliver the Word. I have noted—and our venerable friend, Mr. Rogers, has observed the same—that you, gentlemen, students, as a body, in your judgment of one another, are seldom if ever wrong. There has hardly ever been an instance, take the whole house through, where the general opinion of the entire college concerning a brother has been erroneous. Men are not quite so unable to form an opinion of each other as they are sometimes supposed to be. Meeting as you do in class, in prayer-meeting, in conversation, and in various religious engagements, you gauge each other; and a wise man will be slow to set aside the verdict of the house.

I should not complete this point if I did not add that mere ability to edify, and aptness to teach, is not enough; there must be other talents to complete the pastoral character. Sound judgment and solid experience must instruct you; gentle manners and loving affections must sway you; firmness and courage must be manifest; and tenderness and sympathy must not be lacking. Gifts administrative in ruling well will be as requisite as gifts instructive in teaching well. You must be fitted to lead, prepared to endure, and able to persevere. In grace, you should be head and shoulders above the rest of the people, able to be their father and counsellor. Read carefully the qualifications of a bishop, given in 1 Tim. iii. 2–7, and in Titus i. 6–9. If such gifts and graces be not in you and abound, it may be possible for you to succeed as an evangelist, but as a pastor you will be of no account.

3. In order further to prove a man's call, after a little exercise of his gifts, such as I have already spoken of, *he must see a measure of conversion-work going on under his efforts,* or he may conclude that he has made a mistake, and, therefore, may go back by the best way he can. It is not to be expected that upon the first or even twentieth effort in public we shall be apprized of success; and a man may even give himself a life trial of preaching if he feels called to do so, but it seems to me, that as a man to be set apart to the ministry, his commission is without seals until souls are won by his instrumentality to the knowledge of Jesus. As a worker, he is to work on whether he succeeds or no, but as a minister he cannot be sure of his vocation till results are apparent. How my heart leaped for joy when I heard tidings of my first convert! I could never be satisfied with a full congregation, and the kind expressions of friends; I longed to hear that hearts had been broken, that tears had been seen streaming from the eyes of penitents. How did I rejoice, as one that findeth great spoil, over one poor labourer's wife who confessed that she felt the guilt of sin, and had found the Saviour under my discourse on Sunday afternoon: I have the cottage in which she lived in my eye now; believe me, it always appears picturesque. I remember well her being received into the church, and her dying, and her going home to heaven. She was the first seal to my ministry, and, I can assure you, a very precious one indeed. No mother was ever more full of happiness at the sight of her first-born son. Then could I have sung the song of the Virgin Mary, for my soul did magnify the Lord for remembering my low estate, and giving me the great honour to do a work for which all generations should call me blessed, for so I counted the conversion of one soul. There must be some measure of conversion-work in your irregular labours before you can believe that preaching is to be your life-work. Remember the Lord's words by the prophet Jeremiah; they are very much to the point, and should alarm all fruitless preachers. "I have not sent these prophets, yet they ran; I have not spoken to them, yet they prophesied. But if they had stood in my counsel, and had caused my people to hear my words, then they

should have turned them from their evil way, and from the evil of
their doings." Jer. xxiii. 21, 22. It is a marvel to me how men continue
at ease in preaching year after year without conversions. Have they
no bowels of compassion for others? no sense of responsibility upon
themselves? Dare they, by a vain misrepresentation of divine
sovereignty, cast the blame on their Master? Or is it their belief that
Paul plants and Apollos waters, and that God gives no increase?
Vain are their talents, their philosophy, their rhetoric, and even their
orthodoxy, without the signs following. How are they sent of God
who bring no men to God? Prophets whose words are powerless,
sowers whose seed all withers, fishers who take no fish, soldiers who
give no wounds—are these God's men? Surely it were better to be a
mud-raker, or a chimney-sweep, than to stand in the ministry as an
utterly barren tree. The meanest occupation confers some benefit upon
mankind, but the wretched man who occupies a pulpit and never
glorifies his God by conversions is a blank, a blot, an eyesore, a
mischief. He is not worth the salt he eats, much less his bread; and if
he writes to newspapers to complain of the smallness of his salary,
his conscience, if he has any, might well reply, "And what you have
is undeserved." Times of drought there may be; ay, and years of lean-
ness may consume the former years of usefulness, but still there will
be fruit in the main, and fruit to the glory of God; and meanwhile
the transient barrenness will fill the soul with unutterable anguish.
Brethren, if the Lord gives you no zeal for souls, keep to the lapstone
or the trowel, but avoid the pulpit as you value your heart's peace
and your future salvation.

4. A step beyond all this is, however, needful in our enquiry. The
will of the Lord concerning pastors is made known through the
prayerful judgment of His church. It is needful as a proof of your
vocation that *your preaching should be acceptable to the people of
God.* God usually opens doors of utterance for those whom He calls
to speak His name. Impatience would push open or break down
the door, but faith waits upon the Lord, and in due season her
opportunity is awarded her. When the opportunity comes then comes
our trial. Standing up to preach, our spirit will be judged of the
assembly, and if it be condemned, or if, as a general rule, the church
is not edified, the conclusion may not be disputed, that we are not
sent of God. The signs and marks of a true bishop are laid down in
the Word for the guidance of the church; and if in following such
guidance the brethren see not in us the qualifications, and do not elect
us to office, it is plain enough that however well we may evangelise,
the office of the pastor is not for us. Churches are not all wise, neither
do they all judge in the power of the Holy Ghost, but many of them
judge after the flesh; yet I had sooner accept the opinion of a company
of the Lord's people than my own upon so personal a subject as my

own gifts and graces. At any rate, whether you value the verdict of the church or no, one thing is certain, that none of you can be pastors without the loving consent of the flock; and therefore this will be to you a practical indicator if not a correct one. If your call from the Lord be a real one you will not long be silent. As surely as the man wants his hour, so surely the hour wants its man. The church of God is always urgently in need of living ministers; to her a man is always more precious than the gold of Ophir. Formal officials do lack and suffer hunger, but the anointed of the Lord need never be without a charge, for there are quick ears which will know them by their speech, and ready hearts to welcome them to their appointed place. Be fit for your work, and you will never be out of it. Do not run about inviting yourselves to preach here and there; be more concerned about your ability than your opportunity, and more earnest about your walk with God than about either. The sheep will know the God-sent shepherd; the porter of the fold will open to you, and the flock will know your voice.

At the time of my first delivery of this lecture, I had not read John Newton's admirable letter to a friend on this subject; it so nearly tallies with my own thoughts, that at the risk of being thought to be a copyist, which I certainly am not in this instance, I will read you the letter:

"Your case reminds me of my own; my first desires towards the ministry were attended with great uncertainties and difficulties, and the perplexity of my own mind was heightened by the various and opposite judgments of my friends. The advice I have to offer is the result of painful experience and exercise, and for this reason, perhaps, may not be unacceptable to you. I pray our gracious Lord to make it useful.

"I was long distressed, as you are, about what was or was not a proper call to the ministry. It now seems to me an easy point to solve; but, perhaps, it will not be so to you, till the Lord shall make it clear to yourself in your own case. I have not room to say so much as I could. In brief, I think it principally includes three things:

"1. A warm and earnest desire to be employed in this service. I apprehend the man who is once moved by the Spirit of God to this work, will prefer it, if attainable, to thousands of gold and silver; so that, though he is at times intimidated by a sense of its importance and difficulty, compared with his own great insufficiency (for it is to be presumed a call of this sort, if indeed from God, will be accompanied with humility and self-abasement), yet he cannot give it up. I hold it a good rule to enquire in this point, whether the desire to preach is most fervent in our most lively and spiritual frames, and when we are most laid in the dust before the Lord? If so, it is a good sign. But if, as is sometimes the case, a person is very earnest to be a preacher to others, when he finds but little hungerings and thirstings after grace in his own soul, it is then to be feared his zeal springs rather from a selfish principle than from the Spirit of God.

"2. Besides this affectionate desire and readiness to preach, there must in due season appear some competent sufficiency as to gifts, knowledge, and utterance. Surely, if the Lord sends a man to teach others, He will furnish him with the means. I believe many have intended well in setting up for preachers, who yet went beyond or before their call in so doing. The main difference between a minister and a private Christian, seems to consist in those ministerial gifts, which are imparted to him, not for his own sake, but for the edification of others. But then I say these are to appear in due season; they are not to be expected instantaneously, but gradually, in the use of proper means. They are necessary for the discharge of the ministry, but not necessary as pre-requisites to warrant our desires after it. In your case, you are young, and have time before you; therefore, I think you need not as yet perplex yourself with enquiring if you have these gifts already. It is sufficient if your desire is fixed, and you are willing, in the way of prayer and diligence, to wait upon the Lord for them; as yet you need them not.[1]

"3. That which finally evidences a proper call, is a correspondent opening in providence, by a gradual train of circumstances pointing out the means, the time, the place, of actually entering upon the work. And until this coincidence arrives, you must not expect to be always clear from hesitation in your own mind. The principal caution on this head is, not to be too hasty in catching at first appearances. If it be the Lord's will to bring you into His ministry, He has already appointed your place and service, and though you know it not at present, you shall at a proper time. If you had the talents of an angel, you could do no good with them till His hour is come, and till He leads you to the people whom He has determined to bless by your means. It is very difficult to restrain ourselves within the bounds of prudence here, when our zeal is warm: a sense of the love of Christ upon our hearts, and a tender compassion for poor sinners, is ready to prompt us to break out too soon; but he that believeth shall not make haste. I was about five years under this constraint; sometimes I thought I must preach, though it was in the streets. I listened to everything that seemed plausible, and to many things which were not so. But the Lord graciously, and as it were insensibly, hedged up my way with thorns; otherwise, if I had been left to my own spirit, I

---

[1] We should hesitate to speak precisely in this manner. The gifts must be somewhat apparent before the desire should be encouraged. Still, in the main we agree with Mr. Newton.

should have put it quite out of my power to have been brought into such a sphere of usefulness, as He in His good time has been pleased to lead me to. And I can now see clearly, that at the time I would first have gone out, though my intention was, I hope, good in the main, yet I overrated myself, and had not that spiritual judgment and experience which are requisite for so great a service."

Thus much may suffice, but the same subject will be before you if I detail a little of my experience in dealing with aspirants for the ministry. I have constantly to fulfil the duty which fell to the lot of Cromwell's Triers. I have to form an opinion as to the advisability of aiding certain men in their attempts to become pastors. This is a most responsible duty, and one which requires no ordinary care. Of course, I do not set myself up to judge whether a man shall enter the ministry or not, but my examination merely aims at answering the question whether this institution shall help him, or leave him to his own resources. Certain of our charitable neighbours accuse us of having "a parson manufactory" here, but the charge is not true at all. We never tried to make a minister, and should fail if we did; we receive none into the College but those who profess to be ministers already. It would be nearer the truth if they called me a parson killer, for a goodly number of beginners have received their quietus from me; and I have the fullest ease of conscience in reflecting upon what I have so done. It has always been a hard task for me to discourage a hopeful young brother who has applied for admission to the College. My heart has always leaned to the kindest side, but duty to the churches has compelled me to judge with severe discrimination. After hearing what the candidate has had to say, having read his testimonials and seen his replies to questions, when I have felt convinced that the Lord had not called him, I have been obliged to tell him so. Certain of the cases are types of all. Young brethren apply who earnestly desire to enter the ministry, but it is painfully apparent that their main motive is an ambitious desire to shine among men. These men are from a common point of view to be commended for aspiring, but then the pulpit is never to be the ladder by which ambition is to climb. Had such men entered the army they would never have been satisfied till they had reached the front rank, for they are determined to push their way up—all very laudable and very proper so far; but they have embraced the idea that if they entered the ministry they would be greatly distinguished; they have felt the buddings of genius, and have regarded themselves as greater than ordinary persons, and, therefore, they have looked upon the ministry as a platform upon which to display their supposed abilities. Whenever this has been visible I have felt bound to leave the man "to gang his ain gate," as the Scotch say; believing that such spirits always come to nought if they enter the Lord's service. We find that we have nothing whereof to glory, and if we had, the very worst place in which to hang it out would be a pulpit; for there we are brought daily to feel our own insignificance and nothingness.

Men who since conversion have betrayed great feebleness of mind and are readily led to embrace strange doctrines, or to fall into evil company and gross sin, I never can find it in my heart to encourage to enter the ministry, let their professions be what they may. Let them, if truly penitent, keep in the rear ranks. Unstable as water they will not excel.

So, too, those who cannot endure hardness, but are of the kid-gloved order, I refer elsewhere. We want soldiers, not fops, earnest labourers, not genteel loiterers. Men who have done nothing up to their time of application to the college, are told to earn their spurs before they are publicly dubbed as knights. Fervent lovers of souls do not wait till they are trained, they serve their Lord at once.

Certain good men appeal to me who are distinguished by enormous vehemence and zeal, and a conspicuous absence of brains; brethren who would talk for ever and ever upon nothing—who would stamp and thump the Bible, and get nothing out of it all; earnest, awfully earnest, mountains in labour of the most painful kind; but nothing comes of it all, not even the *ridiculus mus*. There are zealots abroad who are not capable of conceiving or uttering five consecutive thoughts, whose capacity is most narrow and their conceit most broad, and these can hammer, and bawl, and rave, and tear, and rage, but the noise all arises from the hollowness of the drum. I conceive that these brethren will do quite as well without education as with it, and there-fore I have usually declined their applications.

Another exceedingly large class of men seek the pulpit they know not why. They cannot teach and will not learn, and yet must fain be ministers. Like the man who slept on Parnassus, and ever after imagined himself a poet, they have had impudence enough once to thrust a sermon upon an audience, and now nothing will do but preaching. They are so hasty to leave off sewing garments, that they will make a rent in the church of which they are members to accomplish their design. The encounter is distasteful, and a pulpit cushion is coveted; the scales and weights they are weary of, and must needs try their hands at the balances of the sanctuary. Such men, like raging waves of the sea usually foam forth their own shame, and we are happy when we bid them adieu.

Physical infirmities raise a question about the call of some excellent men. I would not, like Eusthenes, judge men by their features, but their general physique is no small criterion. That narrow chest does not indicate a man formed for public speech. You may think it odd, but still I feel very well assured, that when a man has a contracted chest, with no distance between his shoulders, the all-wise Creator did not intend him habitually to preach. If he had meant him to speak he would have given him·in some measure breadth of chest, sufficient to yield a reasonable amount of lung force. When the Lord means a creature to run, He gives it nimble legs, and if He means another creature to preach, He will give it suitable lungs. A brother who has to pause in the middle of a sentence and work his air-pump, should ask himself whether there is not some other occupation for which he is better adapted. A man who can scarcely get through a sentence without pain, can hardly be called to "Cry aloud and spare not." There may be exceptions, but is there not weight in the general rule? Brethren with defective mouths and imperfect articulation are not usually called to preach the gospel. The same applies to brethren with no palate, or an imperfect one.

Application was received some short time ago from a young man who had a sort of rotary action of his jaw of the most painful sort to the beholder. His pastor commended him as a very holy young man, who had been the means of bringing some to Christ, and he expressed the hope that I would receive him, but I could not see the propriety of it. I could not have looked at him while preaching without laughter if all the gold of Tarshish had been my reward, and in all probability nine out of ten of his hearers would have been more sensitive than myself. A man with a big tongue which filled up his mouth and caused indistinctness, another without teeth, another who stammered, another who could not pronounce all the alphabet, I have had the pain of declining on the ground that God had not given them those physical appliances, which are as the prayer-book would put it, "generally necessary."

One brother I have encountered—one did I say? I have met ten, twenty, a hundred brethren, who have pleaded that they were sure, quite sure that they were called to the ministry—they were quite certain of it, because they had failed in everything else. This is a sort of model story: "Sir, I was put into a lawyer's office, but I never could bear the confinement, and I could not feel at home in studying law; Providence clearly stopped up my road, for I lost my situation." "And what did you do then?" "Why sir, I was induced to open a grocer's shop." "And did you prosper?" "Well, I do not think, Sir, I was ever meant for trade, and the Lord seemed quite to shut my way up there, for I failed and was in great difficulties. Since then I have done a little in life-assurance agency, and tried to get up a school, besides selling tea; but my path is hedged up, and something within me makes me feel that I ought to be a minister." My answer generally is, "Yes, I see; you have failed in everything else, and therefore you think the Lord has especially endowed you for His service; but I fear you have forgotten that the ministry needs the very best of men, and not those who cannot do anything else." A man who would succeed as a preacher would probably do right well either as a grocer, or a lawyer, or anything else. A really valuable minister would have excelled at anything. There is scarcely anything impossible to a man who can keep a congregation together for years, and be the means of edifying them for hundreds of consecutive Sabbaths; he must be possessed of some abilities, and be by no means a fool or ne'er-do-well. Jesus Christ deserves the best men to preach His cross, and not the empty-headed and the shiftless.

One young gentleman with whose presence I was once honoured, has left on my mind the photograph of his exquisite self. That same face of his looked like the title-page to a whole volume of *conceit* and *deceit*. He sent word into my vestry one Sabbath morning that he must see me at once. His audacity admitted him; and when he was before me he said, "Sir, I want to enter your College, and should like to enter it at once." "Well, Sir," said I, "I fear we have no room for you at present, but your case shall be considered." "But mine is a very remarkable case, Sir; you have probably never received such an application as mine before." "Very good, we'll see about it; the secretary will give you one of the application papers, and you can see me on Monday." He came on the Monday bringing with him the questions, answered in a most extraordinary manner. As to books, he claimed to have read all ancient and modern literature, and after giving an immense list he added, "this is but a selection; I have read most extensively in all departments." As to his preaching, he could produce the highest testimonials, but hardly thought they would be needed, as a personal interview would convince me of his ability at once. His surprise was great when I said, "Sir, I am obliged to tell you that I cannot receive you." "Why not, Sir?" "I will tell you plainly. You are so dreadfully clever that I could not insult you by receiving you into our College, where we have none but rather ordinary men; the president, tutors, and students, are all men of moderate attainments, and you would have to condescend too much in coming among us." He looked at me very severely, and said with dignity, "Do you mean to say, that because I have an unusual genius, and have produced in myself a gigantic mind such as is rarely seen, I am refused admittance into your College?" "Yes," I replied, as calmly as I could, considering the overpowering awe which his genius inspired, "for that very reason." "Then, Sir, you ought to allow me a trial of my preaching abilities; select me any text you like, or suggest any subject you please, and here in this very room I will speak upon it, or preach upon it without deliberation, and you will be surprised." "No, thank you, I would rather not have the trouble of listening to you." "Trouble, Sir! I assure you it would be the greatest possible

pleasure you could have." I said it might be, but I felt myself unworthy of the privilege, and so bade him a long farewell. The gentleman was unknown to me at the time, but he has since figured in the
police court as too clever by half.

We have occasionally had applications at which, perhaps, you
would be amazed, from men who are evidently fluent enough, and
who answer all our questions very well, except those upon their
doctrinal views, to which repeatedly we have had this answer: "Mr.
So-and-so is prepared to receive the doctrines of the College whatever
they may be!" In all such cases we never deliberate a moment; the
instantaneous negative is given. I mention it, because it illustrates our
conviction that men are not called to the ministry who have no
knowledge and no definite belief. When young fellows say that they
have not made up their minds upon theology, they ought to go back
to the Sunday-school until they have. For a man to come shuffling
into a College, pretending that he holds his mind open to any form
of truth, and that he is eminently receptive, but has not settled in his
mind such things as whether God has an election of grace, or whether
he loves his people to the end, seems to me to be a perfect monstrosity.
"Not a novice," says the apostle; yet a man who has not made up his
mind on such points as these, is confessedly and egregiously "a
novice," and ought to be relegated to the catechism-class till he has
learned the first truths of the gospel.

After all, gentlemen, we shall have to prove our call by the practical
proof of our ministry in after life, and it will be a lamentable thing
for us to start in our course without due examination, for if so, we
may have to leave it in disgrace. On the whole, experience is our
surest test, and if God upholds us from year to year, and gives us his
blessing, we need make no other trial of our vocation. Our moral and
spiritual fitnesses will be tried by the labour of our ministry, and this
is the most trustworthy of all tests. From some one or other I heard
in conversation of a plan adopted by Matthew Wilks, for examining
a young man who wanted to be a missionary; the drift, if not the
detail of the test, commends itself to my judgment though not to my
taste. The young man desired to go to India as a missionary in
connection with the London Missionary Society. Mr. Wilks was
appointed to consider his fitness for such a post. He wrote to the
young man, and told him to call upon him at six o'clock the next
morning. The brother lived many miles off, but he was at the house
at six o'clock punctually. Mr. Wilks did not, however, enter the room
till hours after. The brother waited wonderingly, but patiently. At
last, Mr. Wilks arrived, and addressed the candidate thus, in his usual
nasal tones, "Well, young man, so you want to be a missionary?"
"Yes, Sir." "Do you love the Lord Jesus Christ?" "Yes, Sir, I hope
I do." "And have you had any education?" "Yes, Sir, a little."

"Well, now, we'll try you; can you spell 'cat'?" The young man looked confused, and hardly knew how to answer so preposterous a question. His mind evidently halted between indignation and submission, but in a moment he replied steadily, "C, a, t, cat." "Very good," said Mr. Wilks; "now can you spell 'dog'?" Our young martyr hesitated, but Mr. Wilks said in his coolest manner, "Oh, never mind; don't be bashful; you spelt the other word so well that I should think you will be able to spell this: high as the attainment is, it is not so elevated but what you might do it without blushing." The youthful Job replied, "D, o, g, dog." "Well, that is right; I see you will do in your spelling, and now for your arithmetic; how many are twice two?" It is a wonder that Mr. Wilks did not receive "twice two" after the fashion of muscular Christianity, but the patient youth gave the right reply and was dismissed. Matthew Wilks at the committee meeting said, "I cordially recommend that young man; his testimonials and character I have duly examined, and besides that, I have given him a rare personal trial such as few could bear. I tried his self-denial, he was up in the morning early; I tried his temper, and I tried his humility; he can spell 'cat' and 'dog,' and can tell that 'twice two make four,' and he will do for a missionary exceedingly well." Now, what the old gentleman is thus said to have done with exceedingly bad taste, we may with much propriety do with ourselves. We must try whether we can endure brow-beating, weariness, slander, jeering, and hardship; and whether we can be made the off-scouring of all things, and be treated as nothing for Christ's sake. If we can endure all these, we have some of those points which indicate the possession of the rare qualities which should meet in a true servant of the Lord Jesus Christ. I gravely question whether some of us will find our vessels, when far out at sea, to be quite so seaworthy as we think them. O my brethren, make sure work of it while you are yet in this retreat; and diligently labour to fit yourselves for your high calling. You will have trials enough, and woe to you if you do not go forth armed from head to foot with armour of proof. You will have to run with horsemen, let not the footmen weary you while in your preliminary studies. The devil is abroad, and with him are many. Prove your own selves, and may the Lord prepare you for the crucible and the furnace which assuredly await you. Your tribulation may not in all respects be so severe as that of Paul and his companions, but you must be ready for a like ordeal. Let me read you his memorable words, and let me entreat you to pray, while you hear them, that the Holy Ghost may strengthen you for all that lies before you. "Giving no offence in anything, that the ministry be not blamed: but in all things approving ourselves as the ministers of God, in much patience, in affliction, in necessities, in distresses, in stripes, in imprisonments, in tumults, in labours, in watchings, in fastings; by pureness, by knowledge, by long-suffering, by kindness, by the Holy Ghost, by love unfeigned, by the word of truth, by the power of God, by the armour of righteousness on the right hand and on the left, by honour and dishonour, by evil report and good report: as deceivers, and yet true; as unknown, and yet well known; as dying, and, behold, we live; as chastened, and not killed; as sorrowful, yet always rejoicing; as poor, yet making many rich; as having nothing, and yet possessing all things."

III

The Preacher's Private Prayer

OF COURSE the preacher is above all others distinguished as a man of prayer. He prays as an ordinary Christian, else he were a hypocrite. He prays more than ordinary Christians, else he were disqualified for the office which he has undertaken. "It would be wholly monstrous," says Bernard, "for a man to be highest in office and lowest in soul; first in station and last in life." Over all his other relationships the pre-eminence of the pastor's responsibility casts a halo, and if true to his Master, he becomes distinguished for his prayerfulness in them all. As a citizen, his country has the advantage of his intercession; as a neighbour those under his shadow are remembered in supplication. He prays as a husband and as a father; he strives to make his family devotions a model for his flock; and if the fire on the altar of God should burn low anywhere else, it is well tended in the house of the Lord's chosen servant—for he takes care that the morning and evening sacrifice shall sanctify his dwelling. But there are some of his prayers which concern his office, and of those our plan in these lectures leads us to speak most. He offers peculiar supplications *as a minister,* and he draws near to God in this respect, over and above all his approaches in his other relationships.

I take it that as a minister *he is always praying.* Whenever his mind turns to his work, whether he is in it or out of it, he ejaculates a petition, sending up his holy desires as well-directed arrows to the skies. He is not always in the act of prayer, but he lives in the spirit of it. If his heart be in his work, he cannot eat or drink, or take recreation, or go to his bed, or rise in the morning, without evermore feeling a fervency of desire, a weight of anxiety, and a simplicity of dependence upon God; thus, in one form or other he continues in prayer. If there be any man under heaven, who is compelled to carry out the precept—"Pray without ceasing," surely it is the Christian minister. He has peculiar temptations, special trials, singular difficulties, and remarkable duties; he has to deal with God in awful relationships, and with men in mysterious interests; he therefore needs much more grace than common men, and as he knows this, he is led constantly to cry to the strong for strength, and say, "I will lift up mine eyes unto the hills, from whence cometh my help." Alleine once wrote to a dear friend, "Though I am apt to be unsettled and quickly set off the hinges, yet, methinks, I am like a bird out of the nest, I am never quiet till I am in my old way of communion with God; like the needle in the compass, that is restless till it be turned towards the pole. I can say, through grace, with the church, 'With my soul have I desired thee in the night, and with my spirit within me have I sought thee early.' My heart is early and late with God; 'tis the business and delight of my life to seek him." Such must be the even tenor of your way, O men of God. If you as ministers are not very prayerful, you are much to be pitied. If, in the future, you shall be called to sustain pastorates, large or small, if you become lax in secret devotion, not only will *you* need to be pitied, but your people also; and, in addition to that, you shall be blamed, and the day cometh in which you shall be ashamed and confounded.

It may scarcely be needful to commend to you the sweet uses of private devotion, and yet I cannot forbear. To you, as the ambassadors of God, the mercy-seat has a virtue beyond all estimate; the more familiar you are with the court of heaven the better shall you discharge your heavenly trust. Among all the formative influences which go to make up a man honoured of God in the ministry, I know of none more mighty than his own familiarity with the mercy-seat. All that a college course can do for a student is coarse and external compared with the spiritual and delicate refinement obtained by communion with God. While the unformed minister is revolving upon the wheel of preparation, prayer is the tool of the great potter by which he moulds the vessel. All our libraries and studies are mere emptiness compared with our closets. We grow, we wax mighty, we prevail in private prayer.

Your prayers will be your ablest assistants *while your discourses are yet upon the anvil.* While other men, like Esau, are hunting for their portion, you, by the aid of prayer, will find the savoury meat near at home, and may say in truth what Jacob said so falsely, "The Lord brought it to me." If you can dip your pens into your hearts, appealing in earnestness to the Lord, you will write well; and if you can gather your matter on your knees at the gate of heaven, you will not fail to speak well. Prayer, as a mental exercise, will bring many subjects before the mind, and so help in the selection of a topic, while as a high spiritual engagement it will cleanse your inner eye that you may see truth in the light of God. Texts will often refuse to reveal their treasures till you open them with the key of prayer. How wonderfully were the books opened to Daniel when he was in supplication! How much Peter learned upon the housetop! The closet is the best study. The commentators are good instructors, but the Author Himself is far better, and prayer makes a direct appeal to Him and enlists Him in our cause. It is a great thing to pray one's self into the spirit and marrow of a text; working into it by sacred feeding thereon, even as the worm bores its way into the kernel of the nut.

Prayer supplies a leverage for the uplifting of ponderous truths. One marvels how the stones of Stonehenge could have been set in their places; it is even more to be enquired after whence some men obtained such admirable knowledge of mysterious doctrines: was not prayer the potent machinery which wrought the wonder? Waiting upon God often turns darkness into light. Persevering enquiry at the sacred oracle uplifts the veil and gives grace to look into the deep things of God. A certain Puritan divine at a debate was observed frequently to write upon the paper before him; upon others curiously seeking to read his notes, they found nothing upon the page but the words, "More light, Lord," "More light, Lord," repeated scores of times: a most suitable prayer for the student of the Word when preparing his discourse.

You will frequently find fresh streams of thought leaping up from the passage before you, as if the rock had been struck by Moses' rod; new veins of precious ore will be revealed to your astonished gaze as you quarry God's Word and use diligently the hammer of prayer. You will sometimes feel as if you were entirely shut up, and then suddenly a new road will open before you. He who hath the key of David openeth, and no man shutteth. If you have ever sailed down the Rhine, the water scenery of that majestic river will have struck you as being very like in effect to a series of lakes. Before and behind the vessel appears to be enclosed in massive walls of rock, or circles of vine-clad terraces, till on a sudden you turn a corner, and before you the rejoicing and abounding river flows onward in its strength. So the laborious student often finds it with a text; it appears to be fast closed against you, but prayer propels your vessel, and turns its prow into fresh waters, and you behold the broad and deep stream of sacred truth flowing in its fulness, and bearing you with it. Is not this a convincing reason for abiding in supplication? Use prayer as a boring rod, and wells of living water will leap up from the bowels of the Word. Who will be content to thirst when living waters are so readily to be obtained!

The best and holiest men have ever made prayer the most important part of pulpit preparation. It is said of M'Cheyne, "Anxious to give his people on the Sabbath what had cost him somewhat, he never, without an urgent reason, went before them without much previous meditation and prayer. His principle on this subject was embodied in a remark he made to some of us who were conversing on the matter. Being asked his view of diligent preparation for the pulpit, he reminded us of Exodus xxvii. 20. '*Beaten oil—beaten oil for the lamps of the sanctuary.*' And yet his prayerfulness was greater still. Indeed, he could not neglect fellowship with God before entering the congregation. He needed to be bathed in the love of God. His ministry was so much a bringing out of views that had first sanctified his own soul, that the healthiness of his soul was absolutely needful to the vigour and power of his ministrations." "With him the commencement of all labour invariably consisted in the preparation of his own soul. The walls of his chamber were witnesses of his prayerfulness and of his tears, as well as of his cries."

Prayer will singularly assist you in the delivery of your sermon; in fact, nothing can so gloriously fit you to preach as descending fresh from the mount of communion with God to speak with men. None are so able to plead with men as those who have been wrestling with God on their behalf. It is said of Alleine, "He poured out his very heart in prayer and preaching. His supplications and his exhortations were so affectionate, so full of holy zeal, life and vigour, that they quite overcame his hearers; he melted over them, so that he thawed and mollified, and sometimes dissolved the hardest hearts." There could have been none of this sacred dissolving of heart if his mind had not been previously exposed to the tropical rays of the Sun of Righteousness by private fellowship with the risen Lord. A truly pathetic delivery, in which there is no affectation, but much affection, can only be the offspring of prayer. There is no rhetoric like that of the heart, and no school for learning it but the foot of the cross. It were better that you never learned a rule of human oratory, but were full of the power of heavenborn love, than that you should master Quintilian, Cicero, and Aristotle, and remain without the apostolic anointing.

Prayer may not make you eloquent after the human mode, but it will make you truly so, for you will speak out of the heart; and is not that the meaning of the word eloquence? It will bring fire from heaven upon your sacrifice, and thus prove it to be accepted of the Lord.

As fresh springs of thought will frequently break up during preparation in answer to prayer, so will it be in the delivery of the sermon. Most preachers who depend upon God's Spirit will tell you that their freshest and best thoughts are not those which were premeditated, but ideas which come to them, flying as on the wings of angels; unexpected treasures brought on a sudden by celestial hands, seeds of the flowers of paradise, wafted from the mountains of myrrh. Often and often when I have felt hampered, both in thought and expression, my secret groaning of heart has brought me relief, and I have enjoyed more than usual liberty. But how dare we pray in the battle if we have never cried to the Lord while buckling on the harness! The remembrance of his wrestlings at home comforts the fettered preacher when in the pulpit: God will not desert us unless we have deserted him. You, brethren, will find that prayer will ensure you strength equal to your day.

As the tongues of fire came upon the apostles, when they sat watching and praying, even so will they come upon you. You will find yourselves, when you might perhaps have flagged, suddenly upborne, as by a seraph's power. Wheels of fire will be fastened to your chariot, which had begun to drag right heavily, and steeds angelic will be in a moment harnessed to your fiery car, till you climb the heavens like Elijah, in a rapture of flaming inspiration.

After the sermon, how would a conscientious preacher give vent to his feelings and find solace for his soul if access to the mercy seat were denied him? Elevated to the highest pitch of excitement, how can we relieve our souls but in importunate pleadings. Or depressed by a fear of failure, how shall we be comforted but in moaning out our complaint before our God. How often have some of us tossed to and fro upon our couch half the night because of conscious short-comings in our testimony! How frequently have we longed to rush back to the pulpit again to say over again more vehemently, what we have uttered in so cold a manner! Where could we find rest for our spirits but in confession of sin, and passionate entreaty that our infirmity or folly might in no way hinder the Spirit of God! It is not possible in a public assembly to pour out all our heart's love to our flock. Like Joseph, the affectionate minister will seek where to weep; his emotions, however freely he may express himself, will be pent up in the pulpit, and only in private prayer can he draw up the sluices and bid them flow forth. If we cannot prevail with men for God, we will, at least, endeavour to prevail with God for men. We cannot save them, or even persuade them to be saved, but we can at least bewail their madness and entreat the interference of the Lord. Like Jeremiah, we can make it our resolve, "If ye will not hear it, my soul shall weep in secret places for your pride, and mine eye shall weep sore and run down with tears." To such pathetic appeals the Lord's heart can never be indifferent; in due time the weeping intercessor will become the rejoicing winner of souls. There is a distinct connection between importunate agonising and true success, even as between the travail and the birth, the sowing in tears and the reaping in joy. "How is it that your seed comes up so soon?" said one gardener to another. "Because I steep it," was the reply. We must steep all our teachings in tears, "when none but God is nigh," and their growth will surprise and delight us. Could any one wonder at Brainerd's success, when his diary contains such notes as this: "Lord's Day, April 25th—This morning spent about two hours in sacred duties, and was enabled, more than ordinarily, to agonize for immortal souls; though it was early in the morning, and the sun scarcely shone at all, yet my body was quite wet with sweat." The secret of Luther's power lay in the same direction. Theodorus said of him: "I overheard him in prayer, but, good God, with what life and spirit did he pray! It was with so much reverence, as if he were speaking to God, yet with so much confidence as if he were speaking to his friend." My brethren, let me beseech you to be men of prayer. Great talents you may never have, but you will do well enough without them if you abound in intercession. If you do not pray over what you have sown, God's sovereignty may possibly determine to give a blessing, but you have no right to expect it, and if it comes it will bring no comfort to your own heart. I was reading yesterday a book by Father Faber, late of the Oratory, at Brompton, a marvellous compound of truth and error. In it he relates a legend to this effect. A certain preacher, whose sermons converted men by scores, received a revelation from heaven that not one of the conversions was owing to his talents or eloquence, but all to the prayers of an illiterate lay-brother, who sat on the pulpit steps, pleading all the time for the success of the sermon. It may in the all-revealing day be so with us. We may discover, after having laboured long and wearily in preaching, that all the honour belongs to another builder, whose prayers were gold, silver, and precious stones, while our sermonisings being apart from prayer, were but hay and stubble.

When we have done with preaching, we shall not, if we are true ministers of God, have done with praying, because the whole church, with many tongues, will be crying, in the language of the Macedonian, "Come over and help us" in prayer. If you are enabled to prevail in prayer you will have many requests to offer for others who will flock to you, and beg a share in your intercessions, and so you will find yourselves commissioned with errands to the mercy-seat for friends and hearers. Such is always my lot, and I feel it a pleasure to have such requests to present before my Lord. Never can you be short of themes for prayer, even if no one should suggest them to you. Look at your congregation. There are always sick folk among them, and many more who are soul-sick. Some are unsaved, others are seeking and cannot find. Many are desponding, and not a few believers are backsliding or mourning. There are widows' tears and orphans' sighs to be put into our bottle, and poured out before the Lord. If you are a genuine minister of God you will stand as a priest before the Lord, spiritually wearing the ephod and the breast-plate whereon you bear the names of the children of Israel, pleading for them within the veil. I have known brethren who have kept a list of persons for whom they felt bound especially to pray, and I doubt not such a record often reminded them of what might otherwise have slipped their memory. Nor will your people wholly engross you; the nation and the world will claim their share. The man who is mighty in prayer may be a wall of fire around his country, her guardian angel and her shield. We have all heard how the enemies of the Protestant cause dreaded the prayers of Knox more than they feared armies of ten thousand men. The famous Welch was also a great intercessor for his country; he used to say, "he wondered how a Christian could lie in his bed all night and not rise to pray." When his wife, fearing that he would take cold, followed him into the room to which he had withdrawn, she heard him pleading in broken sentences, "Lord, wilt thou not grant me Scotland?" O that we were thus wrestling at midnight, crying, "Lord, wilt thou not grant us our hearers' souls?"

The minister who does not earnestly pray over his work must surely be a vain and conceited man. He acts as if he thought himself sufficient of himself, and therefore needed not to appeal to God. Yet what a baseless pride to conceive that our preaching can ever be in itself so powerful that it can turn men from their sins, and bring them to God without the working of the Holy Ghost. If we are truly humble-minded we shall not venture down to the fight until the Lord of Hosts has clothed us with all power, and said to us, "Go in this thy might." The preacher who neglects to pray much must be very careless about his ministry. He cannot have comprehended his calling. He cannot have computed the value of a soul, or estimated the meaning of eternity. He must be a mere official, tempted into a pulpit because the piece of bread which belongs to the priest's office is very necessary to him, or a detestable hypocrite who loves the praise of men, and cares not for the praise of God. He will surely become a mere superficial talker, best approved where grace is least valued and a vain show most admired. He cannot be one of those who plough deep and reap abundant harvests. He is a mere loiterer, not a labourer. As a preacher he has a name to live and is dead. He limps in his life like the lame man in the Proverbs, whose legs were not equal, for his praying is shorter than his preaching.

I am afraid that, more or less, most of us need self-examination as to this matter. If any man here should venture to say that he prays as much as he ought, as a student, I should gravely question his statement; and if there be a minister, deacon, or elder present who can say that he believes he is occupied with God in prayer to the full extent to which he might be, I should be pleased to know him. I can only say, that if he can claim this excellence, he leaves me far behind, for I can make no such claim: I wish I could; and I make the confession with no small degree of shame-facedness and confusion, but I am obliged to make it. If we are not more negligent than others, this is no consolation to us; the shortcomings of others are no excuses for us. How few of us could compare ourselves with Mr. Joseph Alleine, whose character I have mentioned before? "At the time of his health," writes his wife, "he did rise constantly at or before four of the clock, and would be much troubled if he heard smiths or other craftsmen at their trades before he was at communion with God; saying to me often, 'How this noise shames me. Does not my Master deserve more than theirs?' From four till eight he spent in prayer, holy contemplation, and singing psalms, in which he much delighted and did daily practise alone, as well as in the family. Sometimes he would suspend the routine of parochial engagements, and devote whole days to these secret exercises, in order to which, he would contrive to be alone in some void house, or else in some sequestered spot in the open valley. Here there would be much prayer and meditation on God and heaven." Could we read Jonathan Edwards' description of David Brainerd and not blush? "His life," says Edwards, "shows the right way to success in the works of the ministry. He sought it as a resolute soldier seeks victory in a siege or battle; or as a man that runs a race for a great prize. Animated with love to Christ and souls, how did he labour always fervently, not only in word and doctrine, in public and private, but in *prayers* day and night, 'wrestling with God' in secret, and 'travailing in birth,' with unutterable groans and agonies! 'until Christ were formed' in the hearts of the people to whom he was sent! How did he thirst for a blessing upon his ministry, 'and watch for souls as one that must give account!' How did he 'go forth in the strength of the Lord God, seeking and depending on the special influence of the Spirit to assist and succeed him! And what was the happy fruit at last, after long waiting and many dark and discouraging appearances: like a true son of Jacob, he persevered in wrestling through all the darkness of the night, until the breaking of the day."

Might not Henry Martyn's journal shame us, where we find such entries as these; "Sept. 24th—The determination with which I went to bed last night, of devoting this day to prayer and fasting, I was enabled to put into execution. In my first prayer for deliverance from worldly thoughts, depending on the power and promises of God, for fixing my soul while I prayed, I was helped to enjoy much abstinence from the world for nearly an hour. Then read the history of Abraham, to see how familiarly God had revealed himself to mortal men of old. Afterwards, in prayer for my own sanctification, my soul breathed freely and ardently after the holiness of God, and this was the best season of the day." We might perhaps more truly join with him in his lament after the first year of his ministry that "he judged he had dedicated too much time to public ministrations, and too little to private communion with God."

How much of blessing we may have missed through remissness in supplication we can scarcely guess, and none of us can know how poor we are in comparison with what we might have been if we had lived habitually nearer to God in prayer. Vain regrets and surmises are useless, but an earnest determination to amend will be far more useful. We not only ought to pray more, but we *must*. The fact is, the secret of all ministerial success lies in prevalence at the mercy-seat.

One bright benison which private prayer brings down upon the ministry is an indescribable and inimitable something, better understood than named; it is a dew from the Lord, a divine presence which you will recognise at once when I say it is "an unction from the holy One." What is it? I wonder how long we might beat our brains before we could plainly put into words what is meant by *preaching with unction;* yet he who preaches knows its presence, and he who hears soon detects its absence; Samaria, in famine, typifies a discourse without it; Jerusalem, with her feasts of fat things full of marrow, may represent a sermon enriched with it. Every one knows what the freshness of the morning is when orient pearls abound on every blade of grass, but who can describe it, much less produce it of itself? Such is the mystery of spiritual anointing; we know, but we cannot tell to others what it is. It is as easy as it is foolish to counterfeit it, as some do who use expressions which are meant to betoken fervent love, but oftener indicate sickly sentimentalism or mere cant. "Dear Lord!" "Sweet Jesus!" "Precious Christ!" are by them poured out wholesale, till one is nauseated. These familiarities may have been not only tolerable, but even beautiful when they first fell from a saint of God, speaking, as it were, out of the excellent glory, but when repeated flippantly they are not only intolerable, but indecent, if not profane. Some have tried to imitate unction by unnatural tones and whines; by turning up the whites of their eyes, and lifting their hands in a most ridiculous manner. M'Cheyne's tone and rhythm one hears from Scotchmen continually: we much prefer his spirit to his mannerism; and all mere mannerism without power is as foul carrion of all life bereft, obnoxious, mischievous. Certain brethren aim at inspiration through exertion and loud shouting; but it does not come: some we have known to stop the discourse, and exclaim, "God bless you," and others gesticulate wildly, and drive their finger nails into the palms of their hands as if they were in convulsions of celestial ardour. Bah! The whole thing smells of the green-room and the stage. The getting up of fervour in hearers by the simulation of it in the preacher is a loathsome deceit to be scorned by honest men. "To affect feeling," says Richard Cecil, "is nauseous and soon detected, but to feel is the readiest way to the hearts of others." Unction is a thing which you cannot manufacture, and its counterfeits are worse than worthless; yet it is in itself priceless, and beyond measure needful if you would edify believers and bring sinners to Jesus. To the secret pleader with God this secret is committed; upon him rests the dew of the Lord, about him is the perfume which makes glad the heart. If the anointing which we bear come not from the Lord of hosts we are deceivers, and since only in prayer can we obtain it, let us continue instant, constant, fervent in supplication. Let your fleece lie on the threshing-floor of supplication till it is wet with the dew of heaven. Go not to minister in the temple till you have washed in the laver. Think not to be a messenger of grace to others till you have seen the God of grace for yourselves, and had the word from his mouth.

Time spent in quiet prostration of soul before the Lord is most invigorating. David "sat before the Lord;" it is a great thing to hold these sacred sittings; the mind being receptive, like an open flower drinking in the sunbeams, or the sensitive photographic plate accepting the image before it. Quietude, which some men cannot abide, because it reveals their inward poverty, is as a palace of cedar to the wise, for along its hallowed courts the King in his beauty deigns to walk.

> "Sacred silence! thou that art
> Floodgate of the deeper heart,
> Offspring of a heavenly kind;
> Frost o' the mouth, and thaw o' the mind."
>   FLECKNOE.

Priceless as the gift of utterance may be, the practice of silence in some aspects far excels it. Do you think me a Quaker? Well, be it so. Herein I follow George Fox most lovingly; for I am persuaded that we most of us think too much of speech, which after all is but the shell of thought. Quiet contemplation, still worship, unuttered rapture, these are mine when my best jewels are before me. Brethren, rob not your heart of the deep sea joys; miss not the far-down life, by for ever babbling among the broken shells and foaming surges of the shore.

I would seriously recommend to you, when settled in the ministry, the celebration of extraordinary seasons of devotion. If your ordinary prayers do not keep up the freshness and vigour of your souls, and you feel that you are flagging, get alone for a week, or even a month if possible. We have occasional holidays, why not frequent holy days? We hear of our richer brethren finding time for a journey to Jerusalem; could we not spare time for the less difficult and far more profitable journey to the heavenly city? Isaac Ambrose, once pastor at Preston, who wrote that famous book, *Looking unto Jesus,* always set apart one month in the year for seclusion in a hut in a wood at Garstang. No wonder that he was so mighty a divine, when he could regularly spend so long a time in the mount with God. I notice that the Romanists are accustomed to secure what they call "Retreats," where a number of priests will retire for a time into perfect quietude, to spend the whole of the time in fasting and prayer, so as to inflame their souls with ardour. We may learn from our adversaries. It would be a great thing every now and then for a band of truly spiritual brethren to spend a day or two with each other in real burning agony of prayer. Pastors alone could use much more freedom than in a mixed company. Times of humiliation and supplication for the whole church will also benefit us if we enter into them heartily. Our seasons of fasting and prayer at the Tabernacle have been high days indeed; never has heaven-gate stood wider; never have our hearts been nearer the central glory. I look forward to our month of special devotion, as mariners reckon upon reaching land. Even if our public work were laid aside to give us space for special prayer, it might be a great gain to our churches. A voyage to the golden rivers of fellowship and meditation would be well repaid by a freight of sanctified feeling and elevated thought. Our silence might be better than our voices if our solitude were spent with God. That was a grand action of old Jerome, when he laid all his pressing engagements aside to achieve a purpose to which he felt a call from heaven. He had a large congregation, as large a one as any of us need want; but he said to his people, "Now it is of necessity that the New Testament should be translated, you must find another preacher: the translation must be made; I am bound for the wilderness, and shall not return till my task is finished." Away he went with his manuscripts, and prayed and laboured, and produced a work—the Latin Vulgate—which will last as long as the world stands; on the whole a most wonderful translation of Holy Scripture. As learning and prayerful retirement together could thus produce an immortal work, if we were sometimes to say to our people when we felt moved to do so, "Dear friends, we really must be gone for a little while to refresh our souls in solitude," our profiting would soon be apparent, and if we did not write Latin Vulgates, yet we should do immortal work, such as would abide the fire.

IV

Our Public Prayer

IT HAS sometimes been the boast of Episcopalians that Churchmen go to their churches to pray and worship God, but that Dissenters merely assemble to hear sermons. Our reply to this is, that albeit there may be some professors who are guilty of this evil, it is not true of the people of God among us, and these are the only persons who ever will in any church really enjoy devotion. Our congregations gather together to worship God, and we assert, and feel no hesitation in so asserting, that there is as much true and acceptable prayer offered in our ordinary Nonconformist services as in the best and most pompous performances of the Church of England.

Moreover, if the observation be meant to imply that the hearing of sermons is not worshipping God, it is founded on a gross mistake, for rightly to listen to the gospel is one of the noblest parts of the adoration of the Most High. It is a mental exercise, when rightly performed, in which all the faculties of the spiritual man are called into devotional action. Reverently hearing the word exercises our humility, instructs our faith, irradiates us with joy, inflames us with love, inspires us with zeal, and lifts us up towards heaven. Many a time a sermon has been a kind of Jacob's ladder upon which we have seen the angels of God ascending and descending, and the covenant God himself at the top thereof. We have often felt when God has spoken through His servants into our souls, "This is none other than the house of God, and the very gate of heaven." We have magnified the name of the Lord and praised Him with all our heart while He has spoken to us by His Spirit which He has given unto men. Hence there is not the wide distinction to be drawn between preaching and prayer that some would have us admit; for the one part of the service softly blends into the other, and the sermon frequently inspires the prayer and the hymn. True preaching is an acceptable adoration of God by the manifestation of His gracious attributes: the testimony of His gospel, which pre-eminently glorifies Him, and the obedient hearing of revealed truth, are an acceptable form of worship to the Most High, and perhaps one of the most spiritual in which the human mind can be engaged. Nevertheless, as the old Roman poet tells us, it is right to learn from our enemies, and therefore it may be possible that our liturgical opponents have pointed out to us what is in some instances a weak place in our public services. It is to be feared that our exercises are not in every case moulded into the best form, or presented in the most commendable fashion. There are meeting-houses in which the supplications are neither so devout nor so earnest as we desire; in other places the earnestness is so allied with ignorance, and the devotion so marred with rant, that no intelligent believer can enter into the service with pleasure. Praying in the Holy Ghost is not universal among us, neither do all pray with the understanding as well as with the heart. There is room for improvement, and in some quarters there is an imperative demand for it. Let me, therefore, very earnestly caution you, beloved brethren, against spoiling your services by your prayers: make it your solemn resolve that all the engagements of the sanctuary shall be of the best kind.

Be assured that free prayer is the most scriptural, and should be the most excellent form of public supplication. If you lose faith in what you are doing you will never do it well; settle it in your minds therefore, that before the Lord you are worshipping in a manner which is warranted by the word of God, and accepted of the Lord. The expression, "reading prayers," to which we are now so accustomed, is not to be found in Holy Scripture, rich as it is in words for conveying religious thought; and the phrase is not there because the thing itself had no existence. Where in the writings of the apostles meet we with the bare idea of a liturgy? Prayer in the assemblies of the early Christians was unrestricted to any form of words. Tertullian writes, "we pray *without a prompter* because from the heart."[1] Justin Martyr describes the presiding minister as praying "according to his ability."[2] It would be difficult to discover when and where liturgies began; their introduction was gradual, and as we believe, co-extensive with the decline of purity in the church; the introduction of them among Nonconformists would mark the era of our decline and fall. The subject tempts me to linger, but it is not the point in hand, and therefore I pass on, only remarking that you will find the matter of liturgies ably handled by Dr. John Owen, whom you will do well to consult.[3]

Be it ours to prove the superiority of extempore prayer by making it more spiritual and earnest than liturgical devotion. It is a great pity when the observation is forced from the hearer, our minister preaches far better than he prays: this is not after the model of our Lord; He spake as never man spake—and as for His prayers, they so impressed His disciples that they said, "Lord, teach us to pray." All our faculties should concentrate their energy, and the whole man should be elevated

---

[1] "Denique sine monitore, quia de pectore oramus." Tertulliani Apologet. c. 30.
[2] "Ὅση δύναμις αὐτῷ." Justin Martyr, Apol. I, c. 68, p. 270. Ed Otto.
[3] A Discourse concerning Liturgies and their Imposition. Vol. XV. Owen's Works, Goold's Edition.

to his highest point of vigour while in public prayer, the Holy Ghost meanwhile baptizing soul and spirit with His sacred influence; but slovenly, careless, lifeless talk in the guise of prayer, made to fill up a certain space in the service, is a weariness to man, and an abomination to God. Had free prayer been universally of a higher order a liturgy would never have been thought of, and to-day forms of prayer have no better apology than the feebleness of extemporaneous devotions. The secret is that we are not so really devout at heart as we should be. Habitual communion with God must be maintained, or our public prayers will be vapid or formal. If there be no melting of the glacier high up in the ravines of the mountain, there will be no descending rivulets to cheer the plain. Private prayer is the drill ground for our more public exercises, neither can we long neglect it without being out of order when before the people.

Our prayers must never grovel, they must soar and mount. We need a heavenly frame of mind. Our addresses to the throne of grace must be solemn and humble, not flippant and loud, or formal and careless. The colloquial form of speech is out of place before the Lord; we must bow reverently and with deepest awe. We may speak boldly with God, but still He is in heaven and we are upon earth, and we are to avoid presumption. In supplication we are peculiarly before the throne of the Infinite, and as the courtier in the king's palace puts on another mien and another manner than that which he exhibits to his fellow courtiers, so should it be with us. We have noticed in the churches of Holland, that as soon as the minister begins to preach every man puts his hat on, but the instant he turns to pray everybody takes his hat off: this was the custom in the older Puritanic congregations of England, and it lingered long among the Baptists; they wore their caps during those parts of the service which they conceived were not direct worship, but put them off as soon as there was a direct approach to God, either in song or in prayer. I think the practice unseemly, and the reason for it erroneous. I have urged that the distinction between prayer and hearing is not great, and I feel sure no one would propose to return to the old custom or the opinion of which it was the index; but still there is a difference, and inasmuch as in prayer we are more directly talking with God rather than seeking the edification of our fellow men, we must put our shoes from off our feet, for the place whereon we stand is holy ground.

Let the Lord alone be the object of your prayers. Beware of having an eye to the auditors; beware of becoming rhetorical to please the listeners. Prayer must not be transformed into "an oblique sermon." It is little short of blasphemy to make devotion an occasion for display. Fine prayers are generally very wicked prayers. In the presence of the Lord of hosts it ill becomes a sinner to parade the feathers and finery of tawdry speech with the view of winning applause from his fellow mortals. Hypocrites who dare to do this have their reward, but it is one to be dreaded. A heavy sentence of condemnation was passed upon a minister when it was flatteringly said that his prayer was the most eloquent ever offered to a Boston congregation. We may aim at exciting the yearnings and aspirations of those who hear us in prayer; but every word and thought must be Godward, and only so far touching upon the people as may be needful to bring them and their wants before the Lord. Remember the people in your prayers, but do not mould your supplications to win their esteem : look up, look up with both eyes.

Avoid all vulgarities in prayer. I must acknowledge to having heard some, but it would be unprofitable to recount them; the more especially as they become less frequent every day. We seldom now meet with the vulgarities of prayer which were once so common in Methodist prayer-meetings, much commoner probably by report than in reality. Uneducated people must, when in earnest, pray in their own way, and their language will frequently shock the fastidious if not the devout; but for this allowance must be made, and if the spirit is evidently sincere we may forgive uncomely expressions. I once, at a prayer-meeting, heard a poor man pray thus : "Lord, watch over these young people during the feast time, for thou knowest, Lord, how their enemies watch for them as a cat watches for mice." Some ridiculed the expression, but it appeared to me to be natural and expressive, considering the person using it. A little gentle instruction and a hint or two will usually prevent a repetition of anything objectionable in such cases, but we, who occupy the pulpit, must be careful to be quite clear ourselves. The biographer of that remarkable American Methodist preacher, Jacob Gruber, mentions as an instance of his ready wit, that after having heard a young Calvinistic minister violently attack his creed, he was asked to conclude with prayer, and among other petitions, prayed that the Lord would bless the young man who had been preaching, and grant him much grace, "that his heart might become as soft as his head." To say nothing of the bad taste of such public animadversion upon a fellow minister, every right-minded man will see that the throne of the Most High is not the place for uttering such vulgar witticisms. Most probably the young orator deserved a castigation for his offence against charity, but the older one sinned ten times more in his want of reverence. Choice words are for the King of kings, not such as ribald tongues have defiled.

Another fault equally to be avoided in prayer is an unhallowed and sickening superabundance of endearing words. When "Dear Lord," and "Blessed Lord," and "Sweet Lord," come over and over again as vain repetitions, they are among the worst of blots. I must confess I should feel no revulsion in my mind to the words, "Dear Jesus," if they fell from the lips of a Rutherford, or a Hawker, or a Herbert; but when I hear fond and familiar expressions hackneyed by persons not at all remarkable for spirituality, I am inclined to wish that they could, in some way or other, come to a better understanding of the true relation existing between man and God. The word "dear" has come from daily use to be so common, and so small, and in some cases so silly and affected a monosyllable, that interlarding one's prayers with it is not to edification.

The strongest objection exists to the constant repetition of the word "Lord," which occurs in the early prayers of young converts, and even among students. The words, "O Lord! O Lord! O Lord!" grieve us when we hear them so perpetually repeated. "Thou shalt not take the name of the Lord thy God in vain," is a great commandment, and although the law may be broken unwittingly, yet its breach is still a sin and a very solemn one. God's name is not to be a stop-gap to make up for our want of words. Take care to use most reverently the name of the infinite Jehovah. The Jews in their sacred writings either leave a space for the word "Jehovah," or else write the word, "Adonai," because they conceive that holy name to be too sacred for common use: we need not be so superstitious, but it were well to be scrupulously reverent. A profusion of "ohs!" and other interjections may be well dispensed with; young speakers are often at fault here.

Avoid that kind of prayer which may be called—though the subject is one on which language has not given us many terms—*a sort of peremptory demanding of God.* It is delightful to hear a man wrestle with God, and say, "I will not let thee go except thou bless me," but that must be said softly, and not in a hectoring spirit, as though we could command and exact blessings from the Lord of all. Remember, it is still a man wrestling, even though permitted to wrestle with the eternal I AM. Jacob halted on his thigh after that night's holy conflict, to let him see that God is terrible, and that his prevailing power did not lie in himself. We are taught to say, "Our Father," but still it is, "Our Father *who art in heaven.*" Familiarity there may be, but holy familiarity; boldness, but the boldness which springs from grace and is the work of the Spirit; not the boldness of the rebel who carries a brazen front in the presence of his offended king, but the boldness of the child who fears because he loves, and loves because he fears. Never fall into a vainglorious style of impertinent address to God; he is not to be assailed as an antagonist, but entreated with as our Lord and God. Humble and lowly let us be in spirit, and so let us pray.

Pray when you profess to pray, and don't talk about it. Business men say, "A place for everything and everything in its place;" preach in the sermon and pray in the prayer. Disquisitions upon our need of help in prayer are not prayer. Why do not men go at once to prayer

—why stand beating about the bush; instead of saying what they ought to do and want to do, why not set to work in God's name and do it? In downright earnestness, address yourself to intercession, and set your face towards the Lord. Plead for the supply of the great and constant needs of the church, and do not fail to urge, with devout fervour, the special requirements of the present time and audience. Let the sick, the poor, the dying, the heathen, the Jew, and all forgotten classes of people, be mentioned as they press upon your heart. Pray for your people as saints and sinners—not as if they were all saints. Mention the young and the aged; the impressed and the careless; the devout and the backsliding. Never turn to the right hand or to the left, but plough on in the furrow of real prayer. Let your confessions of sin and your thanksgivings be truthful and to the point; and let your petitions be presented as if you believed in God and had no doubt as to the efficacy of prayer: I say this, because so many pray in such a formal manner as to lead observers to conclude that they thought it a very decent thing to pray, but, after all, a very poor and doubtful business as to any practical result. Pray as one who has tried and proved his God, and therefore comes with undoubting confidence to renew his pleadings: and do remember to pray to God right through the prayer, and never fall to talking or preaching—much less, as some do, to scolding and grumbling.

As a rule, if called upon to preach, conduct the prayer yourself; and if you should be highly esteemed in the ministry, as I trust you may be, make a point, with great courtesy, but equal firmness, to resist the practice of choosing men to pray with the idea of honouring them by giving them something to do. Our public devotions ought never to be degraded into opportunities for compliment. I have heard prayer and singing now and then called "the preliminary services," as if they were but a preface to the sermon; this is rare I hope among us—if it were common it would be to our deep disgrace. I endeavour invariably to take all the service myself for my own sake, and I think also for the people's. I do not believe that "anybody will do for the praying." No, sirs, it is my solemn conviction that the prayer is one of the most weighty, useful, and honourable parts of the service, and that it ought to be even more considered than the sermon. There must be no putting up of anybodies and nobodies to pray, and then the selection of the abler man to preach. It may happen through weakness, or upon a special occasion, that it may be a relief to the minister to have some one to offer prayer for him; but if the Lord has made you love your work you will not often or readily fulfil this part of it by proxy. If you delegate the service at all, let it be to one in whose spirituality and present preparedness you have the fullest confidence; but to pitch on a giftless brother unawares, and put him forward to get through the devotions, is shameful.

"Shall we serve *heaven* with less respect
Than we do minister to our gross selves?"

Appoint the ablest man to pray, and let the sermon be slurred sooner than the approach to heaven. Let the Infinite Jehovah be served with our best; let prayer addressed to the Divine Majesty be carefully weighed, and presented with all the powers of an awakened heart and a spiritual understanding. He who has been by communion with God prepared to minister to the people, is usually of all men present the most fit to engage in prayer; to lay out a programme which puts up another brother in his place, is to mar the harmony of the service, to rob the preacher of an exercise which would brace him for his sermon, and in many instances to suggest comparisons between one part of the service and the other which ought never to be tolerated. If unprepared brethren are to be sent into the pulpit to do my praying for me when I am engaged to preach, I do not see why I might not be allowed to pray, and then retire to let these brethren do the sermonizing. I am not able to see any reason for depriving me of the holiest. sweetest, and most profitable exercise which my Lord has allotted me; if I may have my choice, I will sooner yield up the sermon than the prayer. Thus much I have said in order to impress upon you that you must highly esteem public prayer, and seek of the Lord for the gifts and graces necessary to its right discharge.

Those who despise all extempore prayer will probably catch at these remarks and use them against it, but I can assure them that the faults adverted to are not common among us, and are indeed almost extinct; while the scandal caused by them never was, at the worst, so great as that caused by the way in which the liturgical service is often performed. Far too often is the church service hurried through in a manner as indevout as if it were a ballad-singer's ditty. The words are parroted without the slightest appreciation of their meaning; not sometimes, but very frequently, in the places set apart for Episcopal worship, you may see the eyes of the people, and the eyes of the choristers, and the eyes of the parson himself, wandering about in all directions, while evidently from the very tone of the reading there is no feeling of sympathy with what is being read.[1] I have been at funerals when the burial service of the church of England has been galloped through so indecorously that it has taken all the grace I had to prevent my throwing a hassock at the creature's head. I have felt so indignant that I have not known what to do, to hear, in the presence of mourners whose hearts were bleeding, a man rattling through the service as if he were paid by the piece, and had more work to follow, and therefore desired to get it through as quickly as possible. What

[1] It is but fair to admit, and we do so with pleasure, that of late years this fault has grown more and more rare.

effect he could think he was producing, or what good result could come from words jerked forth and hurled out with vengeance and vehemence, I cannot imagine. It is really shocking to think of how that very wonderful burial service is murdered, and made into an abomination by the mode in which it is frequently read. I merely mention this because, if they criticise our prayers too severely, we can bring a formidable countercharge to silence them. Better far, however, for us to amend our own blunders than find fault with others.

In order to make our public prayer what it should be, the first necessary is, that *it must be a matter of the heart*. A man must be really in earnest in supplication. It must be true prayer, and if it be such, it will, like love, cover a multitude of sins. You can pardon a man's familiarities and his vulgarities too, when you clearly see that his inmost heart is speaking to his Maker, and that it is only the man's defects of education which create his faults, and not any moral or spiritual vices of his heart. The pleader in public must be in earnest; for a sleepy prayer—what can be a worse preparation for a sermon? A sleepy prayer—what can make people more dislike going up to the house of God at all? Cast your whole soul into the exercise. If ever your whole manhood was engaged in anything, let it be in drawing near unto God in public. So pray, that by a divine attraction, you draw the whole congregation with you up to the throne of God. So pray, that by the power of the Holy Spirit resting on you, you express the desires and thoughts of every one present, and stand as the one voice for the hundreds of beating hearts which are glowing with fervour before the throne of God.

Next to this, our prayers must be *appropriate*. I do not say go into every minute detail of the circumstances of the congregation. As I have said before, there is no need to make the public prayer a gazette of the week's events, or a register of the births, deaths, and marriages of your people, but the general movements that have taken place in the congregation should be noted by the minister's careful heart. He should bring the joys and sorrows of his people alike before the throne of grace, and ask that the divine benediction may rest upon his flock in all their movements, their exercises, engagements, and holy enterprises, and that the forgiveness of God may be extended to their shortcomings and innumerable sins.

Then, by way of negative canon, I should say, *do not let your prayer be long*. I think it was John Macdonald who used to say, "If you are in the spirit of prayer, do not be long, because other people will not be able to keep pace with you in such unusual spirituality; and if you are not in the spirit of prayer, do not be long, because you will then be sure to weary the listeners." Livingstone says of Robert Bruce, of Edinburgh, the famous co-temporary of Andrew Melville,

"No man in his time spoke with such evidence and power of the Spirit. No man had so many seals of conversion; yea, many of his hearers thought no man, since the apostles, spake with such power. . . . He was very short in prayer when others were present, but every sentence was like a strong bolt shot up to heaven. I have heard him say that he wearied when others were long in prayer; but, being alone, he spent much time in wrestling and prayer." A man may, on special occasions, if he be unusually moved and carried out of himself, pray for twenty minutes in the long morning prayer, but this should not often happen. My friend, Dr. Charles Brown, of Edinburgh, lays it down, as a result of his deliberate judgment, that ten minutes is the limit to which public prayer ought to be prolonged. Our Puritanic forefathers used to pray for three-quarters of an hour, or more, but then you must recollect that they did not know that they would ever have the opportunity of praying again before an assembly, and there-fore, took their fill of it; and besides, people were not inclined in those days to quarrel with the length of prayers or of sermons so much as they do nowadays. You cannot pray too long in private. We do not limit you to ten minutes there, or ten hours, or ten weeks if you like. The more you are on your knees alone the better. We are now speak-ing of those public prayers which come before or after the sermon, and for these ten minutes is a better limit than fifteen. Only one in a thousand would complain of you for being too short, while scores will murmur at your being wearisome in length. "He prayed me into a good frame of mind," George Whitfield once said of a certain preacher, "and if he had stopped there, it would have been very well; but he prayed me out of it again by keeping on." The abundant long-suffering of God has been exemplified in his sparing some preachers, who have been great sinners in this direction; they have done much injury to the piety of God's people by their long-winded orations, and yet God, in his mercy, has permitted them still to officiate in the sanctuary. Alas! for those who have to listen to pastors who pray in public for five-and-twenty minutes, and then ask God to for-give their "shortcomings"! Do not be too long, for several reasons. First, because you weary yourselves and the people; and secondly, because being too long in prayer puts your people out of heart for hearing the sermon. All those dry, dull, prolix talkifications in prayer do but blunt the attention, and the ear gets, as it were, choked up. Nobody would think of blocking up Ear-gate with mud or stones when he meant to storm the gate. No, let the portal be cleared that the battering-ram of the gospel may tell upon it when the time comes to use it. Long prayers either consist of repetitions, or else of un-necessary explanations which God does not require; or else they degenerate into downright preachings, so that there is no difference between the praying and the preaching, except that in the one the minister has his eyes shut, and in the other he keeps them open. It is not necessary in prayer to rehearse the Westminster Assembly's Catechism. It is not necessary in prayer to relate the experience of all the people who are present, or even your own. It is not necessary in prayer to string a selection of texts of Scripture together, and quote David, and Daniel, and Job, and Paul, and Peter, and every other body, under the title of "thy servant of old." It *is* necessary in prayer to draw near unto God, but it is not required of you to prolong your speech till everyone is longing to hear the word "*Amen.*"

One little hint I cannot withhold—never appear to be closing, and then start off again for another five minutes. When friends make up their minds that you are about to conclude, they cannot with a jerk proceed again in a devout spirit. I have known men tantalize us with the hope that they were drawing to a close, and then take a fresh lease two or three times; this is most unwise and unpleasant.

Another canon is—*do not use cant phrases.* My brethren, have done with those vile things altogether; they have had their day, and let them die. These pieces of spiritual fustian cannot be too much reprobated. Some of them are pure inventions; others are passages taken from the Apocrypha; others are texts fathered upon Scripture, but which have been fearfully mangled since they came from the Author of the Bible. In the Baptist Magazine for 1861 I made the following remarks upon the common vulgarities of prayer-meetings. "Cant phrases are a great evil. Who can justify such expressions as the following? '*We would not rush into thy presence as the unthinking* (!!) *horse into the battle.*' As if horses ever did think, and as if it were not better to exhibit the spirit and energy of the horse than the sluggishness and stupidity of the ass! As the verse from which we imagine this fine sentence to be derived has more to do with sinning than with praying, we are glad that the phrase is on its last legs. '*Go from heart to heart, as oil from vessel to vessel,*' is probably a quotation from the nursery romance of *Ali Baba, and the Forty Thieves,* but as destitute of sense, Scripture, and poetry, as ever sentence could be conceived to be. We are not aware that oil runs from one vessel to another in any very mysterious or wonderful manner; it is true it is rather slow in coming out, and is therefore an apt symbol of some people's earnestness; but surely it would be better to have the grace direct from heaven than to have it out of another vessel—a Popish idea which the metaphor seems to insinuate, if indeed it has any meaning at all. '*Thy poor unworthy dust,*' an epithet generally applied to themselves by the proudest men in the congregation, and not seldom by the most moneyed and grovelling, in which case the last two words are not so very inappropriate. We have heard of a good man who, in pleading for his children and grandchildren, was so completely beclouded in the blinding influence of this expression, that he exclaimed, 'O Lord, save thy dust, and thy dust's dust, and thy dust's dust's dust.' When Abraham said, 'I have taken upon me to speak unto the Lord, which am but dust and ashes,' the utterance was forcible and expressive; but in its misquoted, perverted, and abused form, the sooner it is consigned to its own element the better. A miserable conglomeration of perversions of Scripture, uncouth similes, and ridiculous metaphors, constitute a sort of spiritual slang, the offspring of unholy ignorance, unmanly imitation, or graceless hypocrisy; they are at once a dishonour to those who constantly repeat them, and an intolerable nuisance to those whose ears are jaded with them."

Dr. Charles Brown, of Edinburgh, in an admirable address at a meeting of the New College Missionary Association, gives instances of current misquotations indigenous to Scotland, which sometimes, however, find their way across the Tweed. By his permission, I shall quote at length. "There is what might be called an unhappy, sometimes, quite grotesque, mingling of Scripture texts. Who is not familiar with the following words addressed to God in prayer, 'Thou art the high and lofty One that inhabiteth eternity, *and the praises thereof*'! which is but a jumble of two glorious texts, each glorious taken by itself—both marred, and one altogether lost indeed, when thus combined and mingled. The one is Isaiah lvii. 15, 'Thus saith the high and lofty One, *that inhabiteth eternity*, whose name is Holy.' The other is, Psalm xxii. 3, 'Thou art holy, O thou that *inhabitest the praises of Israel*.' The inhabiting of the praises *of eternity*, to say the least, is meagre; there were no praises in the *past* eternity to inhabit. But what a glory is there in God's condescending to inhabit, take up his very abode, in the praises of Israel, of the ransomed church. Then there is an example nothing less than grotesque under this head, and yet one in such frequent use that I suspect it is very generally regarded as having the sanction of Scripture. Here it is, 'We would put our hand on our mouth, and our mouth in the dust, and cry out, Unclean, unclean; God be merciful to us sinners.' This is no fewer than *four* texts joined, each beautiful by itself. First, Job xl. 4, 'Behold, I am vile; what shall I answer thee? I will lay my hand upon my mouth.' Second, Lamentations iii. 29, 'He putteth his mouth in the dust; if so be there may be hope.' Third, Leviticus xiii. 45, where the leper is directed to put a covering upon his upper lip, and to cry, Unclean, unclean. And fourth, the publican's prayer. But how incongruous a man's first putting his hand on his mouth, then putting his mouth in the dust, and, last of all, crying out, etc.! The only other example I give is an expression nearly universal among us, and, I suspect, almost universally thought to be in Scripture, 'In thy favour is life, and thy lovingkindness is better than life.' The fact is, that this also is just an unhappy combination of two passages, in which the term *life* is used in altogether different, and even incompatible senses, namely,

Psalm lxiii. 3, 'Thy lovingkindness is better than life,' where, evidently, life means the present temporal life.

"A second class may be described as unhappy alterations of Scripture language. Need I say that the 130th Psalm, 'Out of the depths,' etc., is one of the most precious in the whole book of the Psalms? Why must we have the words of David and of the Holy Ghost thus given in public prayer, and so constantly that our pious people come all to adopt it into their social and family prayers, 'There is forgiveness with thee, that thou mayest be feared, and plenteous redemption *that thou mayest be sought after*,' or 'unto'? How precious the simple words as they stand in the Psalm (verse 4), 'There is forgiveness with thee, that thou mayest be feared' (verses 7, 8); 'With the Lord there is mercy, and with him is plenteous redemption; and he shall redeem Israel from all his iniquities!' Again, in this blessed Psalm, the words of the third verse, 'If thou, Lord, shouldest mark iniquities, O Lord, who shall stand?' too seldom are left us in their naked simplicity, but must undergo the following change, 'If thou wert *strict* to mark iniquity,' etc. I remember in my old college days, we used to have it in a much more offensive shape, 'If thou wert strict to mark and *rigorous to punish!*' Another favourite change is the following, 'Thou art in heaven, and we upon earth; therefore let our words be few *and well ordered.*' Solomon's simple and sublime utterance (full of instruction, surely, on the whole theme I am dealing with) is, 'God is in heaven, and thou upon earth; therefore let thy words *be few.*' Eccles. v. 2. For another example under this class see how Habakkuk's sublime words are tortured, 'Thou art of purer eyes than to behold evil, and canst not look on sin *without abhorrence.*' The words of the Holy Ghost are (Heb. i. 13), 'Thou art of purer eyes than to behold evil, and canst not look on iniquity.' Need I say that the power of the figure, 'canst not look on iniquity' is nearly lost when you add that God *can* look on it, only not without abhorrence?

"A third class is made up of meaningless pleonasms, vulgar, common-place redundancies of expression, in quoting from the Scriptures. One of these has become so universal, that I venture to say you seldom miss it, when the passage referred to comes up at all. 'Be in the midst of us' (or, as some prefer to express it, somewhat unfortunately, as I think, 'in our midst'), 'to bless us, *and to do us good.*' What additional idea is there in the last expression, 'and to do us good'? The passage referred to is Exodus xx. 24, 'In all places where I record my name, I will come unto you, and I will bless you.' Such is the simplicity of Scripture. Our addition is, 'Bless us, and do us good.' In Daniel iv. 35, we read the noble words, 'None can stay his hand, or say unto him, What doest thou?' The favourite change is, 'None can stay thy hand *from working.*' 'Eye hath not seen, nor ear heard, neither have entered into the heart of man the things which

God hath prepared for them that love him!' This is changed, 'Neither hath it entered into the heart of man *to conceive* the things.' Constantly we hear God addressed as 'the hearer *and answerer* of prayer,' a mere vulgar and useless pleonasm, for the Scripture idea of God's hearing prayer is just his answering it—'O thou that hearest prayer, unto thee shall all flesh come;' 'Hear my prayer O Lord;' 'I love the Lord because he hath heard my voice and my supplications.' Whence, again, that commonplace of public prayer, 'Thy consolations are neither few nor small'? The reference, I suppose, is to those words of Job, 'Are the consolations of God small with thee?' So one scarce ever hears that prayer of the seventy-fourth Psalm, 'Have respect to the covenant, for the dark places of the earth are full of the habitations of cruelty,' without the addition, '*horrid* cruelty;' nor the call to prayer in Isaiah, 'Keep not silence, and give him no rest, till he establish, and till he make Jerusalem a praise in the earth,' without the addition, 'the *whole earth*;' nor that appeal of the Psalmist, 'Whom have I in heaven but thee, and there is none upon earth that I desire beside thee,' without the addition, 'none in *all* the earth.' These last may seem small matters indeed. And so they are; nor were worth finding fault with, did they occur but occasionally. But viewed as stereotyped commonplaces, weak enough in themselves, and occurring so often as to give an impression of their having Scripture authority, I humbly think they ought to be discountenanced and discarded— banished wholly from our Presbyterian worship. It will, perhaps, surprise you to learn that the only Scripture authority for that favourite, and somewhat peculiar expression, about the 'wicked rolling sin as a sweet morsel under their tongue,' is the following words in the book of Job (xx. 12), 'Though wickedness be sweet in his mouth, though he *hide* it under his tongue.'"

But enough of this. I am only sorry to have felt bound in conscience to be so long upon so unhappy a subject. I cannot, however, leave the point without urging upon you literal accuracy in all quotations from the word of God.

It ought to be a point of honour among ministers always to quote Scripture correctly. It is difficult to be always correct, and because it is difficult, it should be all the more the object of our care. In the halls of Oxford or Cambridge it would be considered almost treason or felony for a fellow to misquote Tacitus, or Virgil, or Homer; but for a preacher to misquote Paul, or Moses, or David, is a far more serious matter, and quite as worthy of the severest censure. Mark, I said a "fellow," not a freshman, and from a pastor we expect, at least, equal accuracy in his own department as from the holder of a fellowship. You who so unwaveringly believe in the verbal-inspiration theory (to my intense satisfaction), ought never to quote at all until you can give the precise words, because, according to your own showing, by the alteration of a single word you may miss altogether God's sense of the passage. If you cannot make extracts from Scripture correctly, why quote it at all in your petitions? Make use of an expression fresh from your own mind, and it will be quite as acceptable to God as a scriptural phrase defaced or clipped. Vehemently strive against garblings and perversions of Scripture, and renounce for ever all cant phrases, for they are the disfigurement of free prayer.

I have noticed a habit among some—I hope you have not fallen into it—of praying with their eyes open. It is unnatural, unbecoming, and disgusting. Occasionally the opened eye uplifted to heaven may be suitable and impressive, but to be gazing about while professing to address the unseen God is detestable. In the earliest ages of the church the fathers denounced this unseemly practice. Action in prayer should be very little used, if at all. It is scarcely comely to lift and move the arm, as if in preaching; the outstretched arms however, or the clasped hands, are natural and suggestive when under strong holy excitement. The voice should accord with the matter, and should never be boisterous, or self-asserting: humble and reverent let those tones be in which man talketh with his God. Doth not even nature itself teach you this? If grace does not I despair.

With special regard to your prayers in the Sabbath services, a few sentences may be useful. In order to prevent custom and routine from being enthroned among us, it will be well to *vary the order of service as much as possible.* Whatever the free Spirit moves us to do, that let us do at once. I was not till lately aware of the extent to which the control of deacons has been allowed to intrude itself upon ministers in certain benighted churches. I have always been accustomed to conduct religious services in the way I have thought most suitable and edifying, and I never have heard so much as a word of objection, although I trust I can say I live on the dearest intimacy with my officers; but a brother minister told me this morning that on one occasion he prayed in the morning service at the commencement instead of giving out a hymn, and when he retired into the vestry after service the deacons informed him that they would have no innovations. We hitherto understood that Baptist churches are not under bondage to traditions and fixed rules as to modes of worship, and yet these poor creatures, these would-be lords, who cry out loudly enough against a liturgy, would bind their minister with rubrics made by custom. It is time that such nonsense were for ever silenced. We claim to conduct service as the Holy Spirit moves us, and as we judge best. We will not be bound to sing here and pray there, but will vary the order of service to prevent monotony. Mr. Hinton, I have heard, once preached the sermon at the commencement of the service, so that those who came late might at any rate have an opportunity to pray. And why not? Irregularities would do good, monotony works weariness. It will frequently be a most profitable thing to let the people sit quite still in profound silence for two or five minutes. Solemn silence makes noble worship.

> True prayer is not the noisy sound
> That clamorous lips repeat,
> But the deep silence of a soul
> That clasps Jehovah's feet.

Vary the order of your prayers, then, for the sake of maintaining attention, and preventing people going through the whole thing as a clock runs on till the weights are down.

Vary the length of your public prayers. Do you not think it would be much better if sometimes instead of giving three minutes to the first prayer and fifteen minutes to the second, you gave nine minutes to each? Would it not be better sometimes to be longer in the first, and not so long in the second prayer? Would not two prayers of tolerable length be better than one extremely long and one extremely short? Would it not be as well to have a hymn after reading the chapter, or a verse or two before the prayer? Why not sing four times, occasionally? Why not be content with two hymns, or only one, occasionally? Why sing after sermon? Why, on the other hand, do some never sing at the close of the service? Is a prayer after sermon always, or even often, advisable? Is it not sometimes most impressive? Would not the Holy Spirit's guidance secure us a variety at present unknown? Let us have anything so that our people do not come to regard any form of service as being appointed, and so relapse into the superstition from which they have escaped.

Vary the current of your prayers in intercession. There are many topics which require your attention; the church in its weakness, its backslidings, its sorrows, and its comforts; the outside world, the neighbourhood, unconverted hearers, the young people, the nation. Do not pray for all these every time, or otherwise your prayers will be long and probably uninteresting. Whatever topic shall come uppermost to your heart, let that be uppermost in your supplications. There is a way of taking a line of prayer, if the Holy Spirit shall guide you therein, which will make the service all of a piece, and harmonize with the hymns and discourse. It is very useful to maintain unity in the service where you can; not slavishly, but wisely, so that the effect is one. Certain brethren do not even manage to keep unity in the sermon, but wander from Britain to Japan, and bring in all imaginable subjects; but you who have attained to the preservation of unity in the sermon might go a little farther, and exhibit a degree of unity in the service, being careful in both the hymn, and the prayer, and the chapter, to keep the same subject prominent. Hardly commendable is the practice, common with some preachers, of rehearsing the sermon in the last prayer. It may be instructive to the audience, but that is an object altogether foreign to prayer. It is stilted, scholastic, and unsuitable; do not imitate the practice.

As you would avoid a viper, *keep from all attempts to work up spurious fervour in public devotion.* Do not labour to seem earnest. Pray as your heart dictates, under the leading of the Spirit of God, and if you are dull and heavy tell the Lord so. It will be no ill thing to confess your deadness, and bewail it, and cry for quickening; it will be real and acceptable prayer; but simulated ardour is a shameful form of lying. Never imitate those who are earnest. You know a good man who groans, and another whose voice grows shrill when he is carried away with zeal, but do not therefore moan or squeak in order to appear as zealous as they are. Just be natural the whole way through, and ask of God to be guided in it all.

Lastly—this is a word I utter in confidence to yourselves—*prepare your prayer.* You say with astonishment, "Whatever can you mean by that?" Well, I mean what some do not mean. The question was once discussed in a society of ministers, "Was it right for the minister to prepare his prayer beforehand?" It was earnestly asserted by some that it was wrong; and very properly so. It was with equal earnestness maintained by others that it was right; and they were not to be gainsayed. I believe both parties to have been right. The first brethren understood by preparing the prayer, the studying of expressions, and the putting together of a train of thought, which they all said was altogether opposed to spiritual worship, in which we ought to leave ourselves in the hand of God's Spirit to be taught of him both as to matter and words. In these remarks we altogether agree; for if a man writes his prayers and studies his petitions, let him use a liturgy at once. But the brethren in opposition meant by preparation quite another thing, not the preparation of the head, but of the heart, which consists in the solemn consideration beforehand of the importance of prayer, meditation upon the needs of men's souls, and a remembrance of the promises which we are to plead; and thus coming before the Lord with a petition written upon the fleshy tables of the heart. This is surely better than coming to God at random, rushing before the throne at haphazard, without a definite errand or desire. "I never am tired of praying," said one man, "because I always have a definite errand when I pray." Brethren, are your prayers of this sort? Do you strive to be in a fit frame to lead the supplications of your people? Do you order your cause in coming before the Lord? I feel, my brethren, that we ought to prepare ourselves by private prayer for public praying. By living near to God we ought to maintain prayerfulness of spirit, and then we shall not fail in our vocal pleadings. If anything beyond this is to be tolerated, it would be the commitment to memory of the Psalms and parts of Scripture containing promises, supplications, praises, and confessions, such as may be helpful in the act of prayer. It is said of Chrysostom, that he had learned his Bible by heart, so as to be able to repeat it at his pleasure: no wonder that he was called golden-mouthed. Now, in our converse with God, no speech can be more appropriate than the words of the Holy Ghost—"Do as thou hast said," will always prevail with the Most High. We counsel, therefore, the committing to memory of the inspired devotional exercises of the word of truth, and then your continued reading of the Scriptures will keep you always furnished with fresh supplications, which will be as ointment poured forth, filling the whole house of God with its fragrance, when you present your petitions in public before the Lord. Seeds of prayer thus sown in the memory will yield a constant golden harvest, as the Spirit shall warm your soul with hallowed fire in the hour of congregational prayer. As David used the sword of Goliath for after victories, so may we at times employ a petition already answered, and find ourselves able to say with the son of Jesse, "There is none like unto it," as God shall yet again fulfil it in our experience.

Let your prayers be earnest, full of fire, vehemence, prevalence. I pray the Holy Ghost to instruct every student of this College so to offer public prayer, that God shall always be served of his best. Let your petitions be plain and heart-felt; and while your people may sometimes feel that the sermon was below the mark, may they also feel that the prayer compensated for all.

V

Sermons—their Matter

SERMONS *should have real teaching in them,* and their doctrine should be solid, substantial, and abundant. We do not enter the pulpit to talk for talk's sake; we have instructions to convey important to the last degree, and we cannot afford to utter pretty nothings. Our range of subjects is all but boundless, and we cannot, therefore, be excused if our discourses are threadbare and devoid of substance. If we speak as ambassadors for God, we need never complain of want of matter, for our message is full to overflowing. The entire gospel must be presented from the pulpit; the whole faith once delivered to the saints must be proclaimed by us. The truth as it is in Jesus must be instructively declared, so that the people may not merely hear, but *know,* the joyful sound. We serve not at the altar of "the unknown God," but we speak to the worshippers of Him of whom it is written, "they that know Thy name will put their trust in Thee." To divide a sermon well may be a very useful art, but how if there is nothing to divide? A mere division maker is like an excellent carver with an empty dish before him. To be able to deliver an exordium which shall be appropriate and attractive, to be at ease in speaking with propriety during the time allotted for the discourse, and to wind up with a respectable peroration, may appear to mere religious performers to be all that is requisite; but the true minister of Christ knows that the true value of a sermon must lie, not in its fashion and manner, but in the truth which it contains. Nothing can compensate for the absence of teaching; all the rhetoric in the world is but as chaff to the wheat in contrast to the gospel of our salvation. However beautiful the sower's basket it is a miserable mockery if it be without seed. The grandest discourse ever delivered is an ostentatious failure if the doctrine of the grace of God be absent from it; it sweeps over men's heads like a cloud, but it distributes no rain upon the thirsty earth; and therefore the remembrance of it to souls taught wisdom by an experience of pressing need is one of disappointment, or worse. A man's style may be as fascinating as that of the authoress of whom one said that she should write with a crystal pen dipped in dew upon silver paper, and use for pounce the dust of a butterfly's wing; but to an audience whose souls are in instant jeopardy, what will mere elegance be but "altogether lighter than vanity"?

Horses are not to be judged by their bells or their trappings, but by limb and bone and blood; and sermons, when criticised by judicious hearers, are largely measured by the amount of gospel truth and force of gospel spirit which they contain. Brethren, weigh your sermons. Do not retail them by the yard, but deal them out by the pound. Set no store by the quantity of words which you utter, but strive to be esteemed for the quality of your matter. It is foolish to be lavish in words and niggardly in truth. He must be very destitute of wit who would be pleased to hear himself described after the manner of the world's great poet, who says, "Gratiano speaks an infinite deal of nothing, more than any man in all Venice: his reasons are as two grains of wheat hidden in two bushels of chaff; you shall seek all day ere you find them; and when you have them they are not worth the search."

Rousing appeals to the affections are excellent, but if they are not backed up by instruction they are a mere flash in the pan, powder consumed and no shot sent home. Rest assured that the most fervid revivalism will wear itself out in mere smoke, if it be not maintained by the fuel of teaching. The divine method is to put the law in the mind, and then write it on the heart; the judgment is enlightened, and then the passions subdued. Read Hebrews viii. 10, and follow the model of the covenant of grace. Gouge's note on that place may with fitness be quoted here: "Ministers are herein to imitate God, and, to their best endeavour, to instruct people in the mysteries of godliness, and to teach them what to believe and practise, and then to stir them up in act and deed, to do what they are instructed to do. Their labour otherwise is like to be in vain. Neglect of this course is a main cause that men fall into many errors as they do in these days." I may add that this last remark has gained more force in our times; it is among uninstructed flocks that the wolves of popery make havoc; sound teaching is the best protection from the heresies which ravage right and left among us.

Sound information upon scriptural subjects your hearers crave for, and must have. Accurate explanations of Holy Scripture they are entitled to, and if you are "an interpreter, one of a thousand," a real messenger of heaven, you will yield them plenteously. Whatever else may be present, the absence of edifying, instructive truth, like the absence of flour from bread, will be fatal. Estimated by their solid contents rather than their superficial area, many sermons are very poor specimens of godly discourse. I believe the remark is too well grounded that if you attend to a lecturer on astronomy or geology, during a short course you will obtain a tolerably clear view of his system; but if you listen, not only for twelve months, but for twelve years, to the common run of preachers, you will not arrive at anything like an idea of their system of theology. If it be so, it is a grievous fault, which cannot be too much deplored. Alas! the indistinct utterances of many concerning the grandest of eternal realities, and the dimness of thought in others with regard to fundamental truths, have given too much occasion for the criticism! Brethren, if you are not theologians you are in your pastorates just nothing at all. You may be fine rhetoricians, and be rich in polished sentences; but without knowledge of the gospel, and aptness to teach it, you are but a sounding brass and a tinkling cymbal. Verbiage is too often the fig-leaf which does duty as a covering for theological ignorance. Sounding periods are offered instead of sound doctrine, and rhetorical flourishes in the place of robust thought. Such things ought not to be. The abounding of empty declamation, and the absence of food for the soul, will turn a pulpit into a box of bombast, and inspire contempt instead of reverence. Unless we are instructive preachers, and really feed the people, we may be great quoters of elegant poetry, and mighty retailers of second-hand windbags, but we shall be like Nero of old, fiddling while Rome was burning, and sending vessels to Alexandria to fetch sand for the arena while the populace starved for want of corn.

We insist upon it, that there must be abundance of matter in sermons, and next, that *this matter must be congruous to the text*. The discourse should spring out of the text as a rule, and the more evidently it does so the better; but at all times, to say the least, it should have a very close relationship thereto. In the matter of spiritualising and accommodation very large latitude is to be allowed; but liberty must not degenerate into license, and there must always be a connection, and something more than a remote connection—a real relationship between the sermon and its text. I heard the other day of a remarkable text, which was appropriate or inappropriate, as you may think. A squire of a parish had given away a number of flaming scarlet cloaks to the oldest matrons of the parish. These resplendent beings were required to attend the parish church on the following Sunday, and to sit in front of the pulpit, from which one of the avowed successors of the apostles edified the saints from the words, "Solomon in all his glory was not arrayed like one of these." It is reported that on a subsequent occasion, when the same benefactor of the parish had given a bushel of potatoes to every man who had a family, the topic on the following Sunday was, "And they said, It is manna." I cannot tell whether the matter in that case was congruous to the selection of the text; I suppose it may have been, for the probabilities are that the whole performance was foolish throughout. Some brethren have done with their text as soon as they have read it. Having paid all due honour to that particular passage by announcing it, they feel no necessity further to refer to it. They touch their hats, as it were, to that part of Scripture, and pass on to fresh fields and pastures new. Why do such men take a text at all? Why limit their own glorious liberty? Why make Scripture a horsing-block by which to mount upon their unbridled Pegasus? Surely the words of inspiration were never meant to be boothooks to help a Talkative to draw on his seven-leagued boots in which to leap from pole to pole.

The surest way to maintain variety is to keep to the mind of the Holy Spirit in the particular passage under consideration. No two texts are exactly similar; something in the connection or drift of the passage gives to each apparently identical text a shade of difference. Keep to the Spirit's track and you will never repeat yourself or be short of matter: his paths drop fatness. A sermon, moreover, comes with far greater power to the consciences of the hearers when it is plainly the very word of God—not a lecture about the Scripture, but Scripture itself opened up and enforced. It is due to the majesty of inspiration that when you profess to be preaching from a verse you do not thrust it out of sight to make room for your own thinkings.

Brethren, if you are in the habit of keeping to the precise sense of the Scripture before you, I will further recommend you to hold to the *ipsissima verba*, the very words of the Holy Ghost; for, although in many cases topical sermons are not only allowable, but very proper, those sermons which expound the exact words of the Holy Spirit are the most useful and the most agreeable to the major part of our congregations. They love to have the words themselves explained and expounded. The many are not always sufficiently capable of grasping the sense apart from the language—of gazing, so to speak, upon the truth disembodied; but when they hear the precise words reiterated again and again, and each expression dwelt upon after the manner of such preachers as Mr. Jay, of Bath, they are more edified, and the truth fixes itself more firmly upon their memories. Let your matter, then, be copious, and let it grow out of the inspired word, as violets and primroses spring up naturally from the sod, or as the virgin honey drops from the comb.

Take care that your deliverances are always weighty, and full of really important teaching. Build not with wood, hay, and stubble, but with gold, silver, and precious stones. It is scarcely needful to warn you against the grosser degradations of pulpit eloquence, or the example of the notorious orator Henley might be instanced. That loquacious adventurer, whom Pope has immortalized in his "Dunciad," was wont to make the passing events of the week the themes of his buffoonery on week days, and theological topics suffered the same fate on Sundays. His forte lay in his low wit and in tuning his voice and balancing his hands. The satirist says of him, "How fluent nonsense trickles from his tongue." Gentlemen, it were better never to have been born, than to have the like truthfully said of us; we are on peril of our souls bound to deal with the solemnities of eternity and with no earth-born topics. There are, however, other and more inviting methods of wood and hay-building, and it behoves you not to be duped by them. This remark is necessary, especially to those gentlemen who mistake highflying sentences for eloquence, and latinized utterances for great depth of thought. Certain homiletical instructors, by their example, if not by their precepts, encourage rhodomontade and great swelling words, and, therefore, are most perilous to young preachers. Think of a discourse commencing with such an amazing and stupendous assertion as the following, which by its native grandeur will strike you at once with a sense of the sublime and beautiful: "MAN IS MORAL." This genius might have added, "A cat has four feet." There would have been as much novelty in the one information as the other. I remember a sermon by a would-be profound writer which quite stunned the reader with grenadier words of six-feet length, but which, when properly boiled down, came to as much essence of meat as this—Man has a soul, his soul will live in another world, and therefore he should take care that it occupies a happy place. No one can object to the teaching, but it is not so novel as to need a blast of trumpets and a procession of bedizened phrases to introduce it to public attention. The art of saying commonplace things elegantly, pompously, grandiloquently, bombastically, is not lost among us, although its utter extinction were "a consummation devoutly to be wished." Sermons of this sort have been held up as models, and yet they are mere bits of bladder which would lie on your finger-nail, blown out until they remind you of those coloured balloons which itinerant dealers carry about the streets to sell at a halfpenny a-piece for the delectation of the extremely juvenile; the parallel, I am sorry to say, holding good a little further, for in some cases these discourses contain just a tinge of poison by way of colouring, which some of the weaker sort have found out to their cost. It is infamous to ascend your pulpit and pour over your people rivers of language, cataracts of words, in which mere platitudes are held in solution like infinitesimal grains of homœopathic medicine in an Atlantic of utterance. Better far give the people masses of unprepared truth in the rough, like pieces of meat from a butcher's block, chopped off anyhow, bone and all, and even dropped down in the sawdust, than ostentatiously and delicately hand them out upon a china dish a delicious slice of nothing at all, decorated with the parsley of poetry, and flavoured with the sauce of affectation.

It will be a happy circumstance if you are so guided by the Holy Spirit as to *give a clear testimony to all the doctrines which constitute or lie around the gospel.* No truth is to be kept back. The doctrine of reserve, so detestable in the mouths of Jesuits, is not one whit the less villainous when accepted by Protestants. It is not true that some doctrines are only for the initiated; there is nothing in the Bible which is ashamed of the light. The sublimest views of divine sovereignty have a practical bearing, and are not, as some think, mere metaphysical subtleties; the distinctive utterances of Calvinism have their bearing upon every-day life and ordinary experience, and if you hold such views, or the opposite, you have no dispensation permitting you to conceal your beliefs. Cautious reticence is, in nine cases out of ten, cowardly betrayal. The best policy is never to be politic, but to proclaim every atom of the truth so far as God has taught it to you. Harmony requires that the voice of one doctrine shall not drown the rest, and it also demands that the gentler notes shall not be omitted because of the greater volume of other sounds. Every note appointed by the great minstrel must be sounded, each note having its own proportionate power and emphasis; the passage marked with *forte* must not be softened, and those with *piano* must not be rolled out like thunder, but each must have its due hearing. All revealed truth in harmonious proportion must be your theme.

Brethren, if you resolve in your pulpit utterances to deal with important verities, *you must not for ever hover around the mere angles of truth.* Those doctrines which are not vital to the soul's salvation, nor even essential to practical Christianity, are not to be considered upon every occasion of worship. Bring in all the features of truth in due proportion, for every part of Scripture is profitable, and you are not only to preach the truth, but the whole truth. Do not insist perpetually upon one truth alone. A nose is an important feature in the human countenance, but to paint a man's nose alone is not a satisfactory method of taking his likeness: a doctrine may be very important, but an exaggerated estimate of it may be fatal to an harmonious and complete ministry. Do not make minor doctrines main points. Do not paint the details of the background of the gospel picture with the same heavy brush as the great objects in the foreground of it. For instance, the great problems of sublapsarianism and supralapsarianism, the trenchant debates concerning eternal filiation, the earnest dispute concerning the double procession, and the pre or post millenarian schemes, however important some may deem them, are practically of very little concern to that godly widow woman, with seven children to support by her needle, who wants far more to hear of the loving-kindness of the God of providence than of these mysteries profound; if you preach to her on the faithfulness of God to his people, she will be cheered and helped in the battle of life; but difficult questions will perplex her or send her to sleep. She is, however, the type of hundreds of those who most require your care. Our great master theme is the good news from heaven; the tidings of mercy through the atoning death of Jesus, mercy to the chief of sinners upon their believing in Jesus.

We must throw all our strength of judgment, memory, imagination, and eloquence into the delivery of the gospel; and not give to the preaching of the cross our random thoughts while wayside topics engross our deeper meditations. Depend upon it, if we brought the intellect of a Locke or a Newton, and the eloquence of a Cicero, to bear upon the simple doctrine of "believe and live," we should find no surplus strength. Brethren, first and above all things, keep to plain evangelical doctrines; whatever else you do or do not preach, be sure incessantly to bring forth the soul-saving truth of Christ and him crucified. I know a minister whose shoe latchet I am unworthy to unloose, whose preaching is often little better than sacred miniature painting— I might almost say holy trifling. He is great upon the ten toes of the beast, the four faces of the cherubim, the mystical meaning of badgers' skins, and the typical bearings of the staves of the ark, and the windows of Solomon's temple: but the sins of business men, the temptations of the times, and the needs of the age, he scarcely ever touches upon. Such preaching reminds me of a lion engaged in mouse-hunting, or a man-of-war cruising after a lost water-butt. Topics scarcely in importance equal to what Peter calls "old wives' fables" are made great matters of by those microscopic divines to whom the nicety of a point is more attractive than the saving of souls. You will have read in Todd's "Student's Manual" that Harcatius, king of Persia, was a notable mole-catcher; and Briantes, king of Lydia, was equally *au fait* at filing needles; but these trivialities by no means prove them to have been great kings: it is much the same in the ministry; there is such a thing as meanness of mental occupation unbecoming the rank of an ambassador of heaven.

Among a certain order of minds at this time the Athenian desire of telling or hearing some new thing appears to be predominant. They boast of new light, and claim a species of inspiration which warrants them in condemning all who are out of their brotherhood, and yet their grand revelation relates to a mere circumstantial of worship, or to an obscure interpretation of prophecy; so that, at sight of their great fuss and loud cry concerning so little, we are reminded of

"Ocean into tempest toss'd
To waft a feather or to drown a fly."

Worse still are those who waste time in insinuating doubts concerning the authenticity of texts, or the correctness of Biblical statements concerning natural phenomena. Painfully do I call to mind hearing one Sabbath evening a deliverance called a sermon, of which the theme was a clever inquiry as to whether an angel did actually descend, and stir the pool at Bethesda, or whether it was an intermitting spring, concerning which Jewish superstition had invented a legend. Dying men and women were assembled to hear the way of salvation, and they were put off with such vanity as this! They came for bread, and received a stone; the sheep looked up to the shepherd, and were not fed. Seldom do I hear a sermon, and when I do I am grievously unfortunate, for one of the last I was entertained with was intended to be a justification of Joshua for destroying the Canaanites, and another went to prove that it was not good for man to be alone. How many souls were converted in answer to the prayers before these sermons I have never been able to ascertain, but I shrewdly suspect that no unusual rejoicing disturbed the serenity of the golden streets.

Believing my next remark to be almost universally unneeded, I bring it forward with diffidence—*do not overload a sermon with too much matter.* All truth is not to be comprised in one discourse. Sermons are not to be bodies of divinity. There is such a thing as having too much to say, and saying it till hearers are sent home loathing rather than longing. An old minister walking with a young preacher, pointed to a cornfield, and observed, "Your last sermon had too much in it, and it was not clear enough, or sufficiently well-arranged; it was like that field of wheat, it contained much crude food, but none fit for use. You should make your sermons like a loaf of bread, fit for eating, and in convenient form." It is to be feared that human heads (speaking phrenologically) are not so capacious for theology as they once were, for our forefathers rejoiced in sixteen ounces of divinity, undiluted and unadorned, and could continue receiving it for three or four hours at a stretch, but our more degenerate, or perhaps more busy, generation requires about an ounce of doctrine at a time, and that must be the concentrated extract or essential oil, rather than the entire substance of divinity. We must in these times say a great deal in a few words, but not too much, nor with too much amplification. One thought fixed on the mind will be better than fifty thoughts made to flit across the ear. One tenpenny nail driven home and clenched will be more useful than a score of tin-tacks loosely fixed, to be pulled out again in an hour.

Our matter should be well arranged according to the true rules of mental architecture. Not practical inferences at the basis and doctrines as the topstones; not metaphors in the foundations, and propositions at the summit; not the more important truths first and the minor teachings last, after the manner of an anticlimax; but the thought must climb and ascend; one stair of teaching leading to another; one door of reasoning conducting to another, and the whole elevating the hearer to a chamber from whose windows truth is seen gleaming in the light of God. In preaching, have a place for everything, and everything in its place. Never suffer truths to fall from you pell-mell. Do not let your thoughts rush as a mob, but make them march as a troop of soldiery. Order, which is heaven's first law, must not be neglected by heaven's ambassadors.

Your doctrinal teaching should be clear and unmistakable. To be so it must first of all be clear to yourself. Some men think in smoke

and preach in a cloud. Your people do not want a luminous haze, but
the solid terra firma of truth. Philosophical speculations put certain
minds into a semi-intoxicated condition, in which they either see
everything double, or see nothing at all. The head of a certain college
in Oxford was years ago asked by a stranger what was the motto of
the arms of that university. He told him that it was "*Dominus
illuminatio mea.*" But he also candidly informed the stranger that, in
his private opinion, a motto more appropriate might be, "*Aristoteles
meæ tenebræ.*" Sensational writers have half crazed many honest men
who have conscientiously read their lucubrations out of a notion that
they ought to be abreast of the age, as if such a necessity might not
also require us to attend the theatres in order to be able to judge the
new plays, or frequent the turf that we might not be too bigoted in
our opinions upon racing and gambling. For my part, I believe that
the chief readers of heterodox books are ministers, and that if they
would not notice them they would fall still-born from the press. Let
a minister keep clear of mystifying himself, and then he is on the
road to becoming intelligible to his people. No man can hope to be
felt who cannot make himself understood. If we give our people
refined truth, pure Scriptural doctrine, and all so worded as to have
no needless obscurity about it, we shall be true shepherds of the sheep,
and the profiting of our people will soon be apparent.

*Endeavour to keep the matter of your sermonising as fresh as you
can.* Do not rehearse five or six doctrines with unvarying monotony
of repetition. Buy a theological barrel-organ, brethren, with five tunes
accurately adjusted, and you will be qualified to practise as an ultra-
Calvinistic preacher at Zoar and Jireh, if you also purchase at some
vinegar factory a good supply of bitter, acrid abuse of Arminians, and
duty-faith men. Brains and grace are optional, but the organ and the
wormwood are indispensable. It is ours to perceive and rejoice in a
wider range of truth. All that these good men hold of grace and
sovereignty we maintain as firmly and boldly as they; but we dare
not shut our eyes to other teachings of the word, and we feel bound
to make full proof of our ministry, by declaring the whole counsel
of God. With abundant themes diligently illustrated by fresh metaphors and experiences, we shall not weary, but, under God's hand,
shall win our hearers' ears and hearts.

Let your teachings grow and advance; let them deepen with your
experience, and rise with your soul-progress. I do not mean preach
new truths; for, on the contrary, I hold that man happy who is so
well taught from the first that, after fifty years of ministry, he has
never had to recant a doctrine or to mourn an important omission;
but I mean, let our depth and insight continually increase, and where
there is spiritual advance it will be so. Timothy could not preach
like Paul. Our earlier productions must be surpassed by those of our

riper years; we must never make these our models; they will be best burned, or only preserved to be mourned over because of their superficial character. It were ill, indeed, if we knew no more after being many years in Christ's school; our progress may be slow, but progress there must be, or there will be cause to suspect that the inner life is lacking or sadly unhealthy. Set it before you as most certain that you have not yet attained, and may grace be given you to press forward towards that which is yet beyond. May you all become able ministers of the New Testament, and not a whit behind the very chief of preachers, though in yourselves you will still be nothing.

The word "sermon" is said to signify *a thrust*, and, therefore, in sermonising it must be our aim to *use the subject in hand with energy and effect, and the subject must be capable of such employment*. To choose mere moral themes will be to use a wooden dagger; but the great truths of revelation are as sharp swords. Keep to doctrines which stir the conscience and the heart. Remain unwaveringly the champions of a soul-winning gospel. God's truth is adapted to man, and God's grace adapts man to it. There is a key which, under God, can wind up the musical box of man's nature; get it, and use it daily. Hence I urge you to keep to the old-fashioned gospel, and to that only, for assuredly it is the power of God unto salvation.

Of all I would wish to say this is the sum; my brethren, preach CHRIST, always and evermore. He is the whole gospel. His person, offices, and work must be our one great, all-comprehending theme. The world needs still to be told of its Saviour, and of the way to reach him. Justification by faith should be far more than it is the daily testimony of Protestant pulpits; and if with this master-truth there should be more generally associated the other great doctrines of grace, the better for our churches and our age. If with the zeal of Methodists we can preach the doctrine of Puritans a great future is before us. The fire of Wesley, and the fuel of Whitfield, will cause a burning which shall set the forests of error on fire, and warm the very soul of this cold earth. We are not called to proclaim philosophy and metaphysics, but the simple gospel. Man's fall, his need of a new birth, forgiveness through an atonement, and salvation as the result of faith, these are our battle-axe and weapons of war. We have enough to do to learn and teach these great truths, and accursed be that learning which shall divert us from our mission, or that wilful ignorance which shall cripple us in its pursuit. More and more am I jealous lest any views upon prophecy, church government, politics, or even systematic theology, should withdraw one of us from glorying in the cross of Christ. Salvation is a theme for which I would fain enlist every holy tongue. I am greedy after witnesses for the glorious gospel of the blessed God. O that Christ crucified were the universal burden of men of God. Your guess at the number of the beast, your

Napoleonic speculations, your conjectures concerning a personal Anti-christ—forgive me, I count them but mere bones for dogs; while men are dying, and hell is filling, it seems to me the veriest drivel to be muttering about an Armageddon at Sebastopol or Sadowa or Sedan, and peeping between the folded leaves of destiny to discover the fate of Germany. Blessed are they who read and hear the words of the prophecy of the Revelation, but the like blessing has evidently not fallen on those who pretend to expound it, for generation after generation of them have been proved to be in error by the mere lapse of time, and the present race will follow to the same inglorious sepulchre. I would sooner pluck one single brand from the burning than explain all mysteries. To win a soul from going down into the pit is a more glorious achievement than to be crowned in the arena of theological controversy as *Doctor Sufficientissimus;* to have faithfully unveiled the glory of God in the face of Jesus Christ will be in the final judgment accounted worthier service than to have solved the problems of the religious Sphinx, or to have cut the Gordian knot of Apocalyptic difficulty. Blessed is that ministry of which CHRIST IS ALL.

VI

On the Choice of a Text

I TRUST, my brethren, that we all feel very deeply the importance of conducting every part of divine worship with the utmost possible efficiency. When we remember that the salvation of a soul may hang, instrumentally, upon the choice of a hymn, we should not consider so small a matter as the selection of the psalms and hymns to be a trifle. An ungodly stranger, stepping into one of our services at Exeter Hall, was brought to the cross by the words of Wesley's verse—"Jesu, lover of my soul." "Does Jesus love me?" said he: "then why should I live in enmity to him?" When we reflect, too, that God may very especially bless an expression in our prayer to the conversion of a wanderer; and that prayer in the unction of the Holy Spirit, may minister greatly to the edification of God's people, and bring unnumbered blessings down upon them, we shall endeavour to pray with the best gift and the highest grace within our reach. Since, also, in the reading of the Scriptures comfort and instruction may be plenteously distributed, we shall pause over our opened Bibles, and devoutly seek to be guided to that portion of Holy Writ which shall be most likely to be made useful.

With regard to the sermon, we shall be most anxious, first of all, respecting the selection of the text. No one amongst us looks upon the sermon in so careless a light as to conceive that a text picked up at random will be suitable for every, or indeed, for any occasion. We are not all of Sydney Smith's mind, when he recommended a brother at a loss for a text, to preach from "Parthians, and Medes, and Elamites, and the dwellers in Mesopotamia;" as though anything would do for a sermon. I hope we all make it a matter of very earnest and serious consideration, every week, what shall be the subjects upon which we shall address our people on the Sabbath morning and evening; for, although all Scripture is good and profitable, yet it is not all equally appropriate for every occasion.[1] To everything there

---

[1] "A moment's reflection upon the eternal consequences that may issue from the preaching of a single sermon in the name of the great Author and Finisher of faith, should be sufficient to effectually rebuke the haphazard carelessness and the reckless self-conceit with which texts are sometimes taken and treated, and to impress every true minister of the gospel with the duty of choosing his texts in such a frame of mind as may harmonise with the divine guidance as often as he may perform that important task."—DANIEL P. KIDDER.

is a season; and everything is the better for being seasonable. A wise householder labours to give to each one of the family his portion of meat in due season; he does not serve out rations indiscriminately, but suits the viands to the needs of the guests. Only a mere official, the slave of routine, the lifeless automaton of formalism, will be content to snatch at the first subject which comes to hand. The man who plucks topics as children in the meadows gather buttercups and daisies, just as they offer themselves, may act in accordance with his position in a church into which a patron may have thrust him, and out of which the people cannot eject him; but those who profess to be called of God, and selected to their positions by the free choice of believers, will need to make fuller proof of their ministry than can be found in such carelessness. Among many gems we have to select the jewel most appropriate for the setting of the occasion. We dare not rush into the King's banquet hall with a confusion of provisions as though the entertainment were to be a vulgar scramble, but as well-mannered servitors we pause and ask the great Master of the feast, "Lord, what wouldst thou have us set upon thy table this day?"

Some texts have struck us as most unhappily chosen. We wonder what Mr. Disraeli's rector did with the words, "In my flesh shall I see God," when lately preaching at a village harvest home! Exceedingly unfortunate was the funeral text for a murdered clergyman (Mr. Plow), from, "So he giveth his beloved sleep." Most manifestly idiotic was he who selected "Judge not, that ye be not judged," for a sermon before the judges at an assize.

Do not be misled by the sound and seeming fitness of scriptural words. M. Athanase Coquerel confesses to having preached on a third visit to Amsterdam, from the words, "This is the third time I am coming to you," 2 Corinthians xiii. 1—well may he add, that he "found great difficulty in afterwards putting into this discourse what was fitting to the occasion." A parallel case was that of one of the sermons on the death of the Princess Charlotte from, "She was sick and died." It is still worse to select words out of a miserable facetiousness, as in the case of a recent sermon on the death of Abraham Lincoln, from the sentence, "Abraham is dead." It is said that a student, who it is to be hoped never emerged from the shell, preached a sermon in public, before his tutor, Dr. Philip Doddridge. Now the good man was accustomed to place himself immediately in front of the student, and look him full in the face. Judge therefore of his surprise, if not indignation, when the text announced ran in these words, "Have I been so long time with you, and yet hast thou not known me, Philip?" Gentlemen, fools sometimes become students: let us hope none of that order may dishonour our *Alma Mater.* I pardon the man who preached before that drunken Solomon, James I of England and VI of Scotland, from James i. 6; the temptation was too great to be resisted. But let the wretch be for ever execrated, if such a man ever lived, who celebrated the decease of a deacon by a tirade from, "It came to pass that the beggar died." I forgive the liar who attributed such an outrage to me, but I hope he will not try his infamous arts upon any one else.

As we would avoid a careless accidental pitching upon topics, so would we equally *avoid a monotonous regularity.* I have heard of a divine who had fifty-two Sunday sermons, and a few extra ones for holy days, from which he was wont to preach in regular order, year after year. In his case, there would be no need that the people should entreat that the same things should be spoken to them on the next Sabbath-day, nor would there be much wonder if imitators of Eutychus should be found in other places beside the third loft. It is not very long ago since a clergyman said to a farmer friend of mine, "Do you know, Mr. D——, I was turning over my sermons the other day, and really the parsonage is so damp, especially in my study, that my sermons have become quite musty." My friend, who although he was churchwarden, attended a Dissenting place of worship, was not so rude as to say that *he thought it very likely*; but as the village venerables had frequently heard the aforesaid discourses, it is possible they were musty in more senses than one. There are persons in the ministry who, having accumulated a little stock of sermons, repeat them *ad nauseam,* with horrible regularity. Itinerating brethren must be far more subject to this temptation than those who are stationed for several years in one place. If they fall victims to the habit, it must surely be the end of their usefulness, and send an intolerable death-chill into their hearts, of which their people must soon be conscious while they hear them parroting forth their time-worn productions. The very best invention for promoting spiritual idleness must be the plan of acquiring a two or three years' stock of sermons, and repeating them in order again and again. As we, my brethren, hope to live for many years, if not for life, in one place, rooted to the spot by the mutual affection which will grow up between ourselves and our people, we have need of a far different method from that which may suit a sluggard or an itinerant evangelist.

It must be burdensome to some, and very easy to others, I should imagine, to find their subject, as they do whose lot is cast in the Episcopal establishment, where the preacher usually refers to the gospel or the epistle, or the lesson for the day, and feels himself bound —not by any law, but by a sort of precedent—to preach from a verse in either the one or the other. When Advent and Epiphany, and Lent and Whitsuntide, bring their stereotyped round, no man needs to agonise at heart over the question, "What shall I say unto this people?" The voice of the church is clear and distinct, "Master, say on; there is your work, give yourself wholly to it." There may be some advantages connected with this pre-arrangement, but the Episcopalian public do not appear to have been made partakers of them, for their public writers are always groaning over the dreariness of sermons, and bemoaning the sad condition of a longsuffering laity who are compelled to listen to them. The slavish habit of following the course of the sun and the revolution of the months, instead of waiting upon the Holy Spirit is, to my mind, quite enough to account for the fact that in many churches, their own writers being judges, the sermons are nothing better than specimens of "that decent debility which alike guards their authors from ludicrous errors, and precludes them from striking beauties."

Be it then taken for granted, that we all feel it to be most important, not only to preach the truth, but to preach the right truth for each particular occasion; our effort will be to descant upon such subjects as shall be best adapted to our people's wants, and most likely to prove a channel of grace to their hearts.

Is there any difficulty in obtaining texts? I remember, in my earlier days, reading somewhere in a volume of lectures upon Homiletics, a statement which considerably alarmed me at the time; it was something to this effect: "If any man shall find a difficulty in selecting a text, he had better at once go back to the grocer's shop, or to the plough, for he evidently has not the capacity required for a minister." Now, as such had been very frequently my cross and burden, I enquired within myself whether I should resort to some form of secular labour, and leave the ministry; but I have not done so, for I still have the conviction that, although condemned by the sweeping judgment of the lecturer, I follow a call to which God has manifestly set his seal. I was so much in trouble of conscience through the aforesaid severe remark, that I asked my grandfather, who had been in the ministry some fifty years, whether he was ever perplexed in choosing his theme. He told me frankly that this had always been his greatest trouble, compared with which, preaching in itself was no anxiety at all. I remember the venerable man's remark, "The difficulty is not because there are not enough texts, but because there are so many, that I am in a strait betwixt them." Brethren, we are sometimes like the lover of choice flowers, who finds himself surrounded by all the beauties of the garden, with permission to select but one. How long he lingers between the rose and the lily, and how great the difficulty to prefer one among ten thousand blooming lovelinesses! To me still, I must confess, my text selection is a very great embarrassment— *embarras de richesses,* as the French say—an embarrassment of riches, very different from the bewilderment of poverty—the anxiety of attending to the most pressing of so many truths, all clamouring for a hearing, so many duties all needing enforcing, and so many spiritual needs of the people all demanding supply. I confess that I frequently sit hour after hour praying and waiting for a subject, and that this is the main part of my study; much hard labour have I spent in manipulating topics, ruminating upon points of doctrine, making skeletons out of verses and then burying every bone of them in the catacombs of oblivion, sailing on and on over leagues of broken water, till I see the red lights and make sail direct to the desired haven. I believe that almost any Saturday in my life I make enough outlines of sermons, if I felt at liberty to preach them, to last me for a month, but I no more dare to use them than an honest mariner would run to shore a cargo of contraband goods. Themes flit before the mind one after another, like images passing across the photographer's lens, but until the mind is like the sensitive plate, which retains the picture, the subjects are valueless to us.

What is the right text? How do you know it? We know it by the signs of a friend. When a verse gives your mind a hearty grip, from which you cannot release yourself, you will need no further direction as to your proper theme. Like the fish, you nibble at many baits, but when the hook has fairly pierced you, you will wander no more. When the text gets a hold of us, we may be sure that we have a hold of it, and may safely deliver our souls upon it. To use another simile: you get a number of texts in your hand, and try to break them up; you hammer at them with might and main, but your labour is lost; at last you find one which crumbles at the first blow, and sparkles as it falls in pieces, and you perceive jewels of the rarest radiance flashing from within. It grows before your eye like the fabled seed which developed into a tree while the observer watched it. It charms and fascinates you, or it weights you to your knees and loads you with the burden of the Lord. Know then that this is the message which the Lord would have you deliver; and, feeling this, you will become so bound by that scripture that you will never feel at rest until you have yielded your whole mind to its power, and have spoken upon it as the Lord shall give you utterance. Wait for that elect word, even if you wait till within an hour of the service. This may not be understood by cool, calculating men, who are not moved by impulses as we are, but to some of us these things are a law in our hearts against which we dare not offend. We tarry at Jerusalem till power is given.

"I believe in the Holy Ghost." This is one of the articles of the creed, but it is scarcely believed among professors so as to be acted on. Many ministers appear to think that *they* are to choose the text; *they* are to discover its teaching; *they* are to find a discourse in it. We do not think so. We are to use our own volitions, of course, as well as our understandings and affections, for we do not pretend that the Holy Ghost will compel us to preach from a text against our wills. He does not deal with us as though we were musical boxes, to be wound up and set to a certain tune; but that glorious inspirer of all truth deals with us as with rational intelligences, who are swayed by spiritual forces congruous to our natures: still, devout minds ever-more desire that the choice of the text should rest with the all-wise Spirit of God, and not with their own fallible understandings, and therefore they humbly put themselves into his hand, asking him to condescend to direct them to the portion of meat in due season which he has ordained for his people. Gurnal says, "Ministers have no ability of their own for their work. Oh! how long may they sit tumbling their books over, and puzzling their brains, until God comes to their help, and then—as Jacob's venison—it is brought to their hand. If God drop not down his assistance, we write with a pen that hath no ink: if any one need walk dependently upon God more than another, the minister is he."

If any one enquire of me, *"How shall I obtain the most proper text?"* I should answer, *"Cry to God for it."* Harrington Evans, in his "Rules for Sermons," lays down as the first, "Seek God in prayer for choice of a passage. Enquire why such a passage is decided upon. Let the question be fairly answered. Sometimes the answer may be such as ought to decide the mind against the choice." If prayer alone should not guide you to the desired treasure, it will in any case be a profitable exercise to you to have prayed. The difficulty of settling upon a topic, if it makes you pray more than usual, will be a very great blessing to you. Praying is the best studying. Luther said so of old—*"Bene orasse est bene studuisse,"* and the well-worn proverb will bear repeating. Pray over the Scripture; it is as the treading of grapes in the wine-vat, the threshing of corn on the barn floor, the melting of gold from the ore. Prayer is twice blest; it blesseth the pleading preacher, and the people to whom he ministers. When your text comes in answer to prayer, it will be all the dearer to you; it will come with a divine savour and unction altogether unknown to the formal orator to whom one theme is as another.

After prayer, *we are bound with much earnestness to use fitting means for concentrating our thoughts, and directing them in the best channel.* Consider the condition of your hearers. Reflect upon their spiritual state as a whole and as individuals, and prescribe the medicine adapted to the current disease, or prepare the food suitable for the prevailing necessity. Let me caution you, however, against considering the whims of your hearers, or the peculiarities of the wealthy and influential. Do not give too much weight to the gentleman and lady who sit in the green pew, if you are so unfortunate as to possess such an abominable place of distinction in a house where all are on a level. Let the large contributor be considered by all means as much as others, and let not his spiritual infirmities be neglected; but he is not everybody, and you will grieve the Holy Spirit if you think him to be so. Look at the poor in the aisles with equal interest, and select topics which are within their range of thought, and which may cheer them in their many sorrows. Do not suffer your heads to be turned by respect to those one-sided members of the congregation, who have a sweet tooth for one portion of the gospel, and turn a deaf ear to other parts of truth; never go out of your way either to give them a feast or a scolding. It may be satisfactory to think that they are pleased, if they are good people, and one respects their predilections, but faithfulness demands that we should not become mere pipers to our hearers, playing such tunes as they may demand of us, but should remain as the Lord's mouth to declare all his counsels. I return to the remark, think over what your people really want for their edification, and let that be your theme. That famous apostle of the north of Scotland, Dr. Macdonald, gives an instance to the point in his *Diary of Work in St. Kilda:*—"Friday, May 27. At our morning exercise this day, I read and gave some illustrations of Romans xii., which afforded me an opportunity of stating the connection between faith and practice, and that the doctrines of grace are according to godliness, and lead to holiness in heart and life. This I deemed necessary, as from the high ground I had occupied for some days past, I was afraid the people might veer towards Antinomianism, an extreme as dangerous as Arminianism, if not more so."

Consider what sins appear to be most rife in the church and congregation—worldliness, covetousness, prayerlessness, wrath, pride, want of brotherly love, slander, and such like evils. Take into account, affectionately, the trials of your people, and seek for a balm for their wounds. It is not necessary to go into minute details, either in the prayer or in the sermon, as to all these trials of your congregation, although this was the custom of a venerable minister who was once a great bishop in this neighbourhood, and has now gone to heaven. He was wont, in his abundant love to his people, to give such hints as to births, deaths, and marriages, in his flock, that one of the Sunday afternoon's enjoyments of his constant hearers must have consisted in finding out to whom the minister referred in the various parts of his prayer and sermon. This was tolerated, and even admired *from him*—from us it would be ridiculous: a patriarch may do with propriety what a young man must scrupulously avoid. The venerable divine whom I have just mentioned, had learned this particularising from the example of his father, for he was one of a family in which the children, having observed that something particular had occurred during the day, would say to each other, "We must wait till family prayer, when we shall know all about it." But I digress; this instance shows how an excellent habit may degenerate into a fault, but the rule which I have laid down is not affected by it. Certain trials will occur, at particular junctures, to many in the congregation, and as these afflictions will invite your mind into new fields of thought, you will do ill to be deaf to their call. Again, we must watch the spiritual state of our people, and if we notice that they are falling into a backsliding condition; if we fear that they are likely to be inoculated by any mischievous heresy or perverse imagining; if anything, in fact, in the whole physiological character of the church should strike our mind, we must hasten to prepare a sermon which, by God's grace, may stay the plague. These are the indications among his hearers which the Spirit of God gives to the careful, observant pastor as to his line of action. The careful shepherd often examines his flock, and governs his mode of treatment by the state in which he finds it. He will be likely to supply one sort of food but sparingly, and another in greater abundance, and medicine in its due quantity, according as his practised judgment finds the one or the other necessary. We shall be rightly directed if we do but associate ourselves with "that great Shepherd of the sheep."

Do not, however, let us allow our preaching right home to our people to degenerate into scolding them. They call the pulpit "Cowards' Castle," and it is a very proper name for it in some respects, especially when fools mount the platform and impudently insult their hearers by holding up their faults or infirmities to public derision. There is a personality—an offensive, wanton, unjustifiable personality—which is to be studiously avoided; it is of the earth, earthy, and is to be condemned in unmeasured terms; while there is another personality, wise, spiritual, heavenly, which is to be aimed at unceasingly. The word of God is sharper than any two-edged sword, and therefore you can leave the word of God to wound and kill, and need not be yourselves cutting in phrase and manner. God's truth is searching: leave it to search the hearts of men without offensive additions from yourself. He is a mere bungler in portrait painting who needs to write the name under the picture when it is hung up in the family parlour where the person himself is sitting. Compel your hearers to perceive that you speak of them, though you have not even in the remotest degree named them, or pointed them out. Occasions may possibly occur when you may be bound to go as far as Hugh Latimer, when speaking upon bribery—he said, "He that took the silver basin and ewer for a bribe, thinketh that it will never come out. But he may not know that I know it, and I know it not alone; there be more beside me that know it. Oh, briber and bribery! He was never a good man that will so take bribes; nor can I believe that he that is a briber will be a good justice." Here was as much prudent reticence as bold disclosure; and if you go no further than this, no man dare, for shame sake, accuse you of too great personality.

In the next place, the minister in looking after his text, should *consider what his previous topics have been.* It would be unwise to insist perpetually upon one doctrine to the neglect of others. Some of our profounder brethren may be able to deal with the same subject in a series of discourses, and may be able, by a turn of the kaleido-scope, to present new forms of beauty with no change of subject, but the most of us, who are of less fertile abilities, will find it best to study variety, and deliver ourselves upon a wide range of truth. I think it well frequently to look over the list of my sermons, and see whether any doctrine has escaped my attention, or any Christian grace has been neglected in my ministrations. It is well to enquire whether we have been too doctrinal lately, or too barely practical, or too exclusively experimental. We do not desire to degenerate into Antinomians, nor, on the other hand, to descend to be mere teachers of a cold morality, but our ambition is to make full proof of our ministry. We would give every portion of Scripture its fair share in our heart and head. Doc-trine, precept, history, type, psalm, proverb, experience, warning, promise, invitation, threatening, or rebuke—we would include the whole of inspired truth within the circle of our teachings. Let us abhor all one-sidedness, all exaggeration of one truth and disparage-ment of another, and let us endeavour to paint the portrait of truth with balanced features and blended colours, lest we dishonour her by presenting distortion instead of symmetry, and a caricature for a faithful copy.

Supposing, however, that you have prayed in that little room of yours, have wrestled hard and supplicated long, and have thought over your people and their wants, and still you cannot meet with *the* text—well, do not fret about it, nor give way to despair. If you were about to go a warfare at your own charges, it would be a very miser-able thing to be short of powder, and the battle so near; but as your Captain has to provide, there is no doubt that all in good time he will serve out the ammunition. *If you trust in God, he will not, he cannot, fail you.* Continue pleading and watching, for to the industrious student heavenly help is certain. If you had gone up and down idly all the week, and given no heed to proper preparation, you could not expect divine aid; but if you have done your best, and are now waiting to know your Lord's message, your face shall never be ashamed.

Two or three incidents have occurred to me which may seem rather odd to you, but then I am an odd man. When I lived at Cambridge, I had, as usual, to preach in the evening at a neighbouring village, to which I had to walk. After reading and meditating all day, I could not meet with the right text. Do what I would, no response came from the sacred oracle, no light flashed from the Urim and Thummim; I prayed, I meditated, I turned from one verse to another, but the mind would not take hold, or I was, as Bunyan would say, "much tumbled up and down in my thoughts." Just then I walked to the window and looked out. On the other side of the narrow street in which I lived, I saw a poor solitary canary bird upon the slates, surrounded by a crowd of sparrows, who were all pecking at it as if they would tear it to pieces. At that moment the verse came to my mind— "Mine heritage is unto me as a speckled bird, the birds round about are against her." I walked off with the greatest possible composure, considered the passage during my long and lonely walk, and preached upon the peculiar people, and the persecutions of their enemies, with freedom and ease to myself, and I believe with comfort to my rustic audience. The text was sent to me, and if the ravens did not bring it, certainly the sparrows did. At another time, while labouring at Water-beach, I had preached on the Sunday morning, and gone home to dinner, as was my wont, with one of the congregation. Unfortunately, there were three services, and the afternoon sermon came so close upon the back of the morning, that it was difficult to prepare the soul, especially as the dinner is a necessary but serious inconvenience where a clear brain is required. Alas! for those afternoon services in our English villages, they are usually a doleful waste of effort. Roast beef and pudding lie heavy on the hearers' souls, and the preacher himself is deadened in his mental processes while digestion claims the mastery of the hour. By a careful measuring of diet, I remained, on that occasion, in an earnest, lively condition, but to my dismay, I found that the pre-arranged line of thought was gone from me. I could not find the trail of my prepared sermon, and press my forehead as I might, the missing topic would not come. Time was brief, the hour was striking, and in some alarm I told the honest farmer that I could not for the life of me recollect what I had intended to preach about. "Oh!" he said, "never mind; you will be sure to have a good word for us." Just at that moment a blazing block of wood fell out of the fire upon the hearth at my feet, smoking into one's eyes and nose at a great rate. "There," said the farmer, "there's a text for you, sir—'Is not this a brand plucked out of the fire?'" No, I thought, it was not plucked out, for it fell out of itself. Here was a text, an illustration, and a leading thought as a nest egg for more. Further light came, and the sermon was certainly not worse than my more prepared effusions; it was better in the best sense, for one or two came forward declaring themselves to have been aroused and converted through that after-noon's sermon. I have always considered that it was a happy circum-stance that I had forgotten the text from which I had intended to preach. At New Park Street I once passed through a very singular experience, of which witnesses are present in this room. I had passed happily through all the early parts of divine service in the evening of the Sabbath, and was giving out the hymn before sermon. I opened the Bible to find the text, which I had carefully studied as the topic of discourse, when on the opposite page another passage of Scrip-ture sprang upon me like a lion from a thicket, with vastly more power than I had felt when considering the text which I had chosen.

The people were singing and I was sighing. I was in a strait betwixt two, and my mind hung as in the balances. I was naturally desirous to run in the track which I had carefully planned, but the other text would take no refusal, and seemed to tug at my skirts, crying, "No, no, you must preach from me. God would have you follow me." I deliberated within myself as to my duty, for I would neither be fanatical nor unbelieving, and at last I thought within myself, "Well, I should like to preach the sermon which I have prepared, and it is a great risk to run to strike out a new line of thought, but still as this text constrains me, it may be of the Lord, and therefore I will venture upon it, come what may." I almost always announce my divisions very soon after the exordium, but on this occasion, contrary to my usual custom, I did not do so, for a reason which some of you may probably guess. I passed through the first head with considerable liberty, speaking perfectly extemporaneously both as to thought and word. The second point was dwelt upon with a consciousness of unusual quiet efficient power, but I had no idea what the third would or could be, for the text yielded no more matter just then, nor can I tell even now what I could have done had not an event occurred upon which I had never calculated. I had brought myself into great difficulty by obeying what I thought to be a divine impulse, and I felt comparatively easy about it, believing that God would help me, and knowing that I could at least close the service should there be nothing more to be said. I had no need to deliberate, for in one moment we were in total darkness—the gas had gone out, and as the aisles were choked with people, and the place everywhere crowded, it was a great peril, but a great blessing. What was I to do then? The people were a little frightened, but I quieted them instantly by telling them not to be at all alarmed, though the gas was out, for it would soon be re-lighted; and as for myself, having no manuscript, I could speak just as well in the dark as in the light, if they would be so good as to sit and listen. Had my discourse been ever so elaborate, it would have been absurd to have continued it, and so as my plight was, I was all the less embarrassed. I turned at once mentally to the well-known text which speaks of the child of light walking in darkness, and the child of darkness walking in the light, and found appropriate remarks and illustrations pouring in upon me, and when the lamps were again lit, I saw before me an audience as rapt and subdued as ever a man beheld in his life. The odd thing of all was, that some few church-meetings afterwards, two persons came forward to make confession of their faith, who professed to have been converted that evening; but the first owed her conversion to the former part of the discourse, which was on the new text that came to me, and the other traced his awakening to the latter part, which was occasioned by the sudden darkness. Thus, you see, Providence befriended me. I cast myself upon God, and his arrangements quenched the light at the proper time for me. Some may ridicule, but I adore; others may even censure, but I rejoice. Anything is better than mechanical sermonising, in which the direction of the Spirit is practically ignored. Every Holy Ghost preacher, I have no doubt, will have such recollections clustering around his ministry. I say, therefore, watch the course of Providence; cast yourselves upon the Lord's guidance and help. If you have solemnly done your best to get a text, and the subject does not start up before you, go up into the pulpit firmly convinced that you will receive a message when the time comes, even though you have not a word at that moment.

In the life of Samuel Drew, a famous Methodist preacher, we read, "Whilst stopping at a friend's house, in Cornwall, after preaching, a person who had attended the service, observing to him, that he had, on that occasion, surpassed his usual ability; and other individuals concurring in the opinion, Mr. Drew said, 'If it be true, it is the more singular, because my sermon was entirely unpremeditated. I went into the pulpit designing to address you from another text, but looking upon the Bible, which lay open, that passage from which you heard me speak just now, 'Prepare to meet thy God, O Israel,' arrested my attention so forcibly as to put to flight my former ideas; and though I had never considered the passage before, I resolved instantly to make it the subject of my discourse." Mr. Drew did well to be obedient to the heavenly direction.

Under certain circumstances you will be absolutely compelled to cast away the well-studied discourse, and rely upon the present help of the Holy Spirit, using purely extempore speech. You may find yourself in the position of the late Kingman Nott, when preaching in the National Theatre, New York. In one of his letters, he says, "The building was filled full, and mostly with young men and boys of the roughest type. I went with a sermon in my mind, but as soon as I came upon the stage, greeted with a 'Hi! hi!' and saw the motley and uproarious crowd I had to do with, I let all thoughts of the sermon go, and catching up the parable of the Prodigal Son, tried to interest them in that, and succeeded in keeping most of them inside the house, and tolerably attentive." What a simpleton would he have been had he persevered in his unsuitable prelection! Brethren, I beseech you, believe in the Holy Ghost, and practically carry out your faith.

As a further assistance to a poor stranded preacher, who cannot launch his mind for want of a wave or two of thought, I recommend him in such a case, to *turn again and again to the Word of God itself*, and read a chapter, and ponder over its verses one by one; or let him select a single verse, and get his mind fully exercised upon it. It may be that he will not find his text in the verse or chapter which he reads, but the right word will come to him through his mind being actively engaged upon holy subjects. According to the relation of thoughts to each other, one thought will suggest another, and another, until a long procession will have passed before the mind, out of which one or other will be the predestinated theme.

Read also good suggestive books, and get your mind aroused by them. If men wish to get water out of a pump which has not been lately used, they first pour water down, and then the pump works. Reach down one of the Puritans, and thoroughly study the work, and speedily you will find yourself like a bird on the wing, mentally active and full of motion.

By way of precaution, however, let me remark, that *we ought to be always in training for text-getting and sermon-making.* We should constantly preserve the holy activity of our minds. Woe unto the minister who dares to waste an hour. Read John Foster's "Essay on the Improvement of Time," and resolve never to lose a second of it. A man who goes up and down from Monday morning till Saturday night, and indolently dreams that he is to have his text sent down by an angelic messenger in the last hour or two of the week, tempts God, and deserves to stand speechless on the Sabbath. We have no leisure as ministers; we are never off duty, but are on our watchtowers day and night. Students, I tell you solemnly, nothing will excuse you from the most rigid economy of time; it is at your peril that you trifle with it. The leaf of your ministry will soon wither unless, like the blessed màn in the first Psalm, you meditate in the law of the Lord both day and night. I am most anxious that you should not throw away time in religious dissipation, or in gossiping and frivolous talk. Beware of running about from this meeting to that, listening to mere twaddle, and contributing your share to the general blowing up of windbags. A man great at tea-drinkings, evening parties, and Sunday-school excursions, is generally little everywhere else. Your pulpit preparations are your first business, and if you neglect these, you will bring no credit upon yourself or your office. Bees are making honey from morning till night, and we should be always gathering stores for our people. I have no belief in that ministry which ignores laborious preparation. When travelling in Northern Italy, our driver at night slept in the carriage, and when I called him up in the morning, he leaped out, cracked his whip three times, and said he was quite ready. Such a rapid toilet I hardly appreciated, and wished that he had slept elsewhere, or that I had to occupy another seat. You who are ready to preach in a hop, skip, and jump, will pardon me if I take a pew somewhere else. Habitual mental exercise in the direction of our work is advisable. Ministers should always be making their hay, but especially while the sun shines. Do you not find yourself sometimes wonderfully ready at sermonising? Mr. Jay said that when he felt in such a condition, he would take out his paper and jot down texts and divisions of sermons, and keep them in store, that they might serve him at times when his mind was not so ready. The lamented Thomas Spencer wrote, "I keep a little book, in which I enter every text of Scripture which comes into my mind with power and sweetness. Were I to dream of a passage of Scripture I should enter it, and when I sit down to compose I look over the book, and have never found myself at a loss for a subject." Watch for subjects as you go about the city or the country.[1] Always keep your eyes and ears open, and you will hear and see angels. The world is full of sermons—catch them on the wing. A sculptor believes, whenever he sees a rough block of marble, that there is a noble statue concealed within it, and that he has only to chip away the superfluities and reveal it. So do you believe that there is within the husk of everything the kernel of a sermon for the wise man. Be wise, and see the heavenly in its earthly pattern. Hear the voices from the skies, and translate them into the language of men. Always a preacher be thou, O man of God, foraging for the pulpit, in all provinces of nature and art, storing and preparing at all hours and seasons.

I am asked whether it is a good thing to announce arrangements, and publish *lists of projected sermons.* I answer, Every man in his own order. I am not a judge for others; but I dare not attempt such a thing, and should signally fail if I were to venture upon it. Precedents are much against my opinion, and at the head of them the sets of discourses by Matthew Henry, John Newton, and a host of others. Still I can only speak my own personal impressions, and leave each man to be a law unto himself. Many eminent divines have delivered valuable courses of sermons upon pre-arranged topics, but we are not eminent, and must counsel others like ourselves to be cautious how they act. I dare not announce what I shall preach from to-morrow, much less what I shall preach from in six weeks' or six months' time, the reason being partly this, that I am conscious of not possessing those peculiar gifts which are necessary to interest an assembly in one subject or set of subjects, for any length of time. Brethren of extraordinary research and profound learning can do it, and brethren with none of these, and no common sense, may pretend to do it, but I cannot. I am obliged to owe a great deal of my strength to variety rather than profundity. It is questionable whether the great majority of list preachers had not far better burn their programmes if they would succeed. I have a very lively, or rather a deadly, recollection of a certain series of discourses on the Hebrews, which made a deep impression on my mind of the most undesirable kind. I wished frequently that the Hebrews had kept the epistle to themselves, for it

[1] "I was led into a profitable strain of meditation, on our good Shepherd's care of his flock, by seeing some lambs exposed to the cold, and a poor sheep perishing for want of care."—ANDREW FULLER'S DIARY.

sadly bored one poor Gentile lad. By the time the seventh or eighth
discourse had been delivered, only the very good people could stand
it: these, of course, declared that they never heard more valuable
expositions, but to those of a more carnal judgment it appeared that
each sermon increased in dulness. Paul, in that epistle, exhorts us
to *suffer* the word of exhortation, and we did so. Are all courses of
sermons like this? Perhaps not, and yet I fear the exceptions are few,
for it is even said of that wonderful expositor, Joseph Caryl, that he
commenced his famous lectures upon Job with eight hundred hearers,
and closed the book with only eight! A prophetical preacher enlarged
so much upon "the little horn" of Daniel, that one Sabbath morning
he had but seven hearers remaining. They doubtless thought it

> "Strange that a harp of thousand strings,
> Should play one tune so long."

Ordinarily, and for ordinary men, it seems to me that pre-arranged
discourses are a mistake, are never more than an apparent benefit,
and generally a real mischief. Surely to go through a long epistle
must require a great deal of genius in the preacher, and demand a
world of patience on the part of the hearers. I am moved by a yet
deeper consideration in what I have now said: it strikes me that
many a truly living, earnest preacher, would feel a programme to be
a fetter. Should the preacher announce for next Lord's day a topic
full of joy, requiring liveliness and exaltation of spirit, it is very
possible that he may, from various causes, find himself in a sad and
burdened state of mind; nevertheless, he must put the new wine into
his old bottle, and go up to the wedding feast wearing his sackcloth
and ashes, and worst of all, this he may be bound to repeat for a
whole month. Is this quite as it should be? It is important that the
speaker should be in tune with his theme, but how is this to be secured
unless the election of the topic is left to influences which shall work
at the time? A man is not a steam engine, to run on metals, and it is
unwise to fix him in one groove. Very much of the preacher's power
will lie in his whole soul being in accord with the subject, and I should
be afraid to appoint a subject for a certain date lest, when the time
come, I should not be in the key for it. Besides, it is not easy to see
how a man can exhibit dependence upon the guidance of the Spirit
of God, when he has already prescribed his own route. Perhaps you
will say, "That is a singular objection, for why not rely upon him for
twenty weeks as well as for one?" True, but we have never had a
promise to warrant such faith. God promises to give us grace according to our days, but he says nothing of endowing us with a reserve
fund for the future.

> "Day by day the manna fell;
> Oh, to learn this lesson well!"

Even so will our sermons come to us, fresh from heaven, when required. I am jealous of anything which should hinder your daily dependence upon the Holy Spirit, and therefore I register the opinion already given. To you, my younger brethren, I feel safe in saying with authority, leave ambitious attempts at elaborate series of discourses to older and abler men. We have but a small share of mental gold and silver; let us invest our little capital in useful goods which will obtain a ready market, and leave the wealthier merchants to deal in more expensive and cumbrous articles. We know not what a day may bring forth—let us wait for daily teaching, and do nothing which might preclude us from using those materials which providence may to-day or to-morrow cast in our way.

Perhaps you will ask whether you should preach from *texts which persons select for you, and request you to preach upon!* My answer would be, as a rule, *never*; and if there must be exceptions let them be few. Let me remind you that you do not keep a shop to which customers may come and give their orders. When a friend suggests a topic, think it over, and consider whether it be appropriate, and see whether it comes to you with power. Receive the request courteously, as you are in duty bound to do as a gentleman and a Christian; but if the Lord whom you serve does not cast his light upon the text, do not preach from it, let who may persuade you.

I am quite certain that if we will wait upon God for our subjects, and make it a matter of prayer that we may be rightly directed, we shall be led forth by a right way; but if we are puffed up with the idea that we can very easily choose for ourselves, we shall find that even in the selection of a subject, without Christ we can do nothing. Wait upon the Lord, hear what he would speak, receive the word direct from God's mouth, and then go forth as an ambassador fresh from the court of heaven. "Wait, I say, on the Lord."

VII

On Spiritualizing

MANY writers upon Homiletics condemn in unmeasured terms even the occasional spiritualizing of a text.[1] "Select texts," say they, "which give a plain, literal sense; never travel beyond the obvious meaning of the passage; never allow yourself to accommodate or adapt; it is an artifice of men of artificial culture, a trick of mountebanks, a miserable display of bad taste and impudence." Honour to whom honour is due, but I humbly beg leave to dissent from this learned opinion, believing it to be more fastidious than correct, more plausible than true. A great deal of real good may be done by occasionally taking forgotten, quaint, remarkable, out-of-the-way texts; and I feel persuaded that if we appeal to a jury of practical, successful preachers, who are not theorizers, but men actually in the field, we shall have a majority in our favour. It may be that the learned rabbis of this generation are too sublime and celestial to condescend to men of low estate; but we who have no high culture, or profound learning, or enchanting eloquence to boast of, have deemed it wise to use the very method which the grandees have proscribed; for we find it one of the best ways of keeping out of the rut of dull formality, and it yields us a sort of salt with which to give flavour to unpalatable truth. Many great soul-winners have felt it meet to give a fillip to their ministry, and to arrest their people's attention by now and then striking out a path which had not been trodden heretofore. Experience has not taught them that they were in error, but the reverse. Within limit, my brethren, be not afraid to spiritualize, or to take singular texts. Continue to look out passages of Scripture, and not only give their plain meaning, as you are bound to do, but also draw from them meanings which may not lie upon their surface. Take the advice for what it is worth, but I seriously recommend you to show the superfine critics that everybody does not worship the golden image which they have set up. I counsel you to employ spiritualizing within certain limits and boundaries, but I pray you do not, under cover of this advice, rush headlong into incessant and injudicious "imaginings," as George Fox would call them. Do not drown yourselves because

---

[1] "Allegorical preaching debases the taste, and fetters the understanding both of preacher and hearers."—ADAM CLARKE.

Wesley's rule is better: "Be sparing in allegorizing or spiritualizing."

you are recommended to bathe, or hang yourselves on an oak because *tannin* is described as a valuable astringent. An allowable thing carried to excess is a vice, even as fire is a good servant in the grate, but a bad master when raging in a burning house. Too much even of a good thing surfeits and disgusts, and in no case is this fact more sure than in the one before us.

The first canon to be observed is this—*do not violently strain a text by illegitimate spiritualizing*. This is a sin against common sense. How dreadfully the word of God has been mauled and mangled by a certain band of preachers who have laid texts on the rack to make them reveal what they never would have otherwise spoken. Mr. Slopdash, of whom Rowland Hill tells us in his Village Dialogues, is but a type of a numerous generation. That worthy is described as delivering himself of a discourse upon, "I had three white baskets on my head," from the dream of Pharaoh's baker. Upon this the "thrice-anointed ninny-hammer," as a friend of mine would call him, discoursed upon the doctrine of the Trinity! A dear minister of Christ, a venerable and excellent brother, one of the most instructive ministers in his county, told me that he missed one day a labouring man and his wife from his chapel. He missed them again and again, Sunday after Sunday, and one Monday, meeting the husband in the street, he said to him, "Well, John, I have not seen you lately." "No sir," was the reply, "We did not seem to profit under your ministry as we used to do." "Indeed, John, I am very sorry to hear it." "Well, me and my missis likes the doctrines of grace, and therefore we've gone to hear Mr. Bawler lately." "Oh! you mean the good man at the High Calvanist Meeting?" "Yes, sir, and we are *so* happy; we get right good food there, sixteen ounces to the pound. We were getting half starved under your ministry—though I always shall respect you as a man, sir." "All right, my friend; of course you ought to go where you get good for your soul, I only hope it *is* good; but what did you get last Sunday?" "Oh! we had a most refreshing time, sir. In the morning we had—I don't seem to like to tell you—however, we had really a most precious time." "Yes, but what was it, John?" "Well, sir, Mr. Bawler led us blessedly into that passage, 'Art thou a man given to appetite? Put a knife to thy throat when thou sittest before a ruler.' "Whatever did he make out of that?" "Well, sir, I can tell you what he made out of it, but I should like to know first what you would have said upon it." "I don't know, John; I don't think I should have taken it at all, but if I must have spoken about it, I should have said that a person given to eating and drinking should take care what he was about when he was in the presence of great men, or he would ruin himself. Gluttony even in this life is ruinous." "Ah!" said the man, "that is your dead-letter way of rendering it. As I told my missis the other day, ever since we have been to hear

Mr. Bawler, the Bible has been opened up to us so that we can see a great deal more in it than we used to do." "Yes, but what did Mr. Bawler tell you about his text?" "Well, he said a man given to appetite was a young convert, who is sure to have a tremendous appetite for preaching, and always wants food; but he ain't always nice about what sort of food it is." "What next, John?" "He said that if the young convert went to sit before a ruler—that is to say, a legal preacher, or a duty-faith man, it would be the worse for him." "But how about the knife, John?" "Well, sir, Mr. Bawler said it was a very dangerous thing to hear legal preachers, it would be sure to ruin the man; and he might just as well cut his throat at once, sir!" The subject was, I suppose, the mischievous effects of young Christians listening to any preachers but those of the hyper school; and the moral drawn from it was, that sooner than this brother should go to hear his former minister, he had better cut his throat! That was accommodating considerably! Ye critics, we give over such dead horses as these to your doggish teeth. Rend and devour as ye will, we will not upbraid. We have heard of another performer who delivered his mind upon Proverbs xxi. 17. "He that loveth pleasure shall be a poor man: he that loveth wine and oil shall not be rich." The Proverbs are a favourite field for spiritualizers to disport themselves withal. Our worthy disposed of the proverb in this fashion: "'He that loveth pleasure,' that is, the Christian who enjoys the means of grace, 'shall be a poor man,' that is, he shall be poor in spirit; 'and he that loveth wine and oil;' that is to say, rejoices in covenant provisions, and enjoys the oil and wine of the gospel, 'shall not be rich,' that is, he shall not be rich in his own esteem;" showing the excellence of those who are poor in spirit, and how they shall enjoy the pleasures of the gospel—a very proper sentiment, but my carnal eyes fail to see it in the text. You have all heard of William Huntingdon's famous rendering of the passage in Isaiah xi. 8: "The sucking child shall play on the hole of the asp, and the weaned child shall put his hand on the cockatrice' den." "'The sucking child,' that is, the babe in grace, 'shall play on the hole of the asp,' 'the asp,' that is, the Arminian: 'the hole of the asp,' that is, the Arminian's mouth." Then follows an account of the games in which simple minds are more than a match for Arminian wisdom. Professors of the other school of divinity have usually had the good sense not to return the compliment, or the Antinomians might have found themselves ranked with cockatrices, and their opponents boastfully defying them at the mouths of their dens. Such abuse only injures those who use it. Theological differences are better expounded and enforced than by such buffoonery.

Ludicrous results sometimes arise from sheer stupidity inflated with conceit. One instance may suffice. A worthy minister told me the other day that he had been preaching lately to his people upon the nine and twenty knives of Ezra. I am sure he would handle these edged tools discreetly, but I could not refrain from saying that I hoped he had not imitated the very sage interpreter who saw in that odd number of knives a reference to the four-and-twenty elders of the Apocalypse.

A passage in the Proverbs reads as follows: "For three things the earth is disquieted, and for four which it cannot bear: for a servant when he reigneth; and a fool when he is filled with meat: for an odious woman when she is married; and an handmaid that is heir to her mistress." A raving spiritualizer declares that this is a sweet picture of the work of grace in the soul, and shows what it is that disquiets Arminians, and sets them by the ears. "'A servant when he reigneth,' that is, poor servants like ourselves, when we are made to reign with Christ; 'a fool when he is filled with meat,' that is, poor foolish men like us, when we are fed with the finest of the wheat of gospel truth; 'an odious woman when she is married,' that is, a sinner when he is united to Christ; 'A handmaid that is heir to her mistress,' that is, when we poor handmaids that were under the law, bondslaves, come into the privileges of Sarah, and become heirs to our own mistress."

These are a few specimens of ecclesiastical curiosities which are as numerous and valuable as the relics which are every day gathered so plentifully on the battle-field of Waterloo, and accepted by the more verdant as priceless treasures. But we have surfeited you, and have no wish to waste more of your time. From all such rank absurdity need you be admonished to turn away! Such maunderings dishonour the Bible, are an insult to the common-sense of the hearers, and a deplorable lowering of the minister. This, however, is no more the spiritualizing which we recommend to you than the thistle in Lebanon is the cedar of Lebanon. Avoid that childish trifling and outrageous twisting of texts which will make you a wise man among fools, but a fool among wise men.

Our second is, *never spiritualize upon indelicate subjects*. It is needful to say this, for the Slopdash family are never more at home than when they speak in a way to crimson the cheek of modesty. There is a kind of beetle which breeds in filth, and this creature has its prototype among men. Do I not at this moment call to mind a savoury divine who enlarged with wonderful gusto and sensuous unction upon the concubine cut into ten pieces: Greenacre himself could not have done it better. What abominable things have been said upon some of the sterner and more horrifying similes of Jeremiah and Ezekiel! Where the Holy Spirit is veiled and chaste, these men have torn away the veil, and spoken as none but naughty tongues would venture to do. I am not squeamish, indeed, far from it, but explanations of the new birth by analogies suggested by a monthly nurse, expositions of the rite of circumcision, and minute descriptions of married life, would arouse my temper and make me feel inclined to command with Jehu that the shameless one should be thrown down from the exalted position disgraced by such brazen-faced impudence. I know it is said, *"Honi soit qui mal y pense,"* but I aver that no pure mind ought to be subjected to the slightest breath of indelicacy from the pulpit. Cæsar's wife must be without suspicion, and Christ's ministers must be without speck in their lives or stain in their speech. Gentlemen, the kissing and hugging which some preachers delight in is disgusting: Solomon's Song had better be let alone than dragged in the mire as it often is. Young men especially must be scrupulously, jealously modest and pure in word: an old man is pardoned, I scarce know why, but a young man is utterly without excuse should he overstep the strict line of delicacy.

Next, and thirdly, *never spiritualize for the sake of showing what an uncommonly clever fellow you are.* Such an intention will be wicked, and the method used will be foolish. Only an egregious simpleton will seek to be noted for doing what nine out of ten could do quite as well. A certain probationer once preached a sermon upon the word "but," thus hoping to ingratiate himself with the congregation, who would, he thought, be enraptured with the powers of a brother who could enlarge so marvellously upon a mere conjunction. His subject appears to have been, the fact that whatever there may be of good in a man's character, or admirable in a man's position, there is sure to be some difficulty, some trial in connection with us all: "Naaman was a great man with his master, but——." When the orator descended from the pulpit the deacons said, "Well, sir, you have given us a singular sermon, *but*—you are not the man for the place; that we can see very clearly." Alas! for wit when it becomes so common, and withal puts a weapon into the hand of its own adversaries! Remember that spiritualizing is not such a wonderful display of ingenuity, even if you are able to do it well, and that without discretion it is the most ready method of revealing your egregious folly. Gentlemen, if you aspire to emulate Origen in wild, daring, interpretations, it may be as well to read his life and note attentively the follies into which even his marvellous mind was drawn by allowing a wild fancy to usurp absolute authority over his judgment; and if you set yourselves to rival the vulgar declaimers of a past generation, let me remind you that the cap and bells do not now command the same patronage as fell to their share a few years ago.

Our fourth caution is, *never pervert Scripture* to give it a novel and so-called spiritual meaning, lest you be found guilty of that solemn curse with which the roll of inspiration is guarded and closed. Mr. Cook, of Maidenhead, felt himself obliged to separate from William

Huntingdon because of his making the seventh commandment to mean the Lord speaking to his Son and saying, "Thou shalt not covet the devil's wife, *i.e.*, the non-elect." One can only say, horrible! Perhaps it would be an insult to your reason and your religion to say, loathe the thought of such profanity. You instinctively shrink from it.

Once more, *in no case allow your audience to forget that the narratives which you spiritualize are facts,* and not mere myths or parables. The first sense of the passage must never be drowned in the outflow of your imagination; it must be distinctly declared and allowed to hold the first rank; your accommodation of it must never thrust out the original and native meaning, or even push it into the background. The Bible is not a compilation of clever allegories or instructive poetical traditions; it teaches literal facts and reveals tremendous realities : let your full persuasion of this truth be manifest to all who attend your ministry. It will be an ill day for the church if the pulpit should even appear to endorse the sceptical hypothesis that Holy Scripture is but the record of a refined mythology, in which globules of truth are dissolved in seas of poetic and imaginary detail.

However, there is a legitimate range for spiritualizing, or rather for the particular gift which leads men to spiritualize. For instance, you have frequently been shown that *the types* yield ample scope for the exercise of a sanctified ingenuity. Why need you go about to find "odious women" to preach upon, when you have before you the tabernacle in the wilderness, with all its sacred furniture, the burnt-offering, the peace-offering, and all the various sacrifices which were offered before God? Why struggle for novelties when the temple and all its glories are before you? The largest capacity for typical interpretation will find abundant employment in the undoubted symbols of the Word of God, and it will be safe to enter upon such an exercise, because the symbols are of divine appointment.

When you have exhausted all the Old Testament types, you have left to you an heirloom of a thousand *metaphors*. Benjamin Keach, in his laborious treatise, proves most practically what mines of truth lie concealed in the metaphors of Scripture. His work, by the way, is open to much criticism on the score of making metaphors run not only on all-fours, but on as many legs as a centipede; but it does not deserve the condemnation of Dr. Adam Clarke, when he says it has done more to debase the taste both of preachers and people than any other work of the kind. A discreet explanation of the poetical allusions of Holy Scripture will be most acceptable to your people, and, with God's blessing, not a little profitable.

But supposing you have expounded all the usually accepted types, and have cast light upon the emblems and figurative expressions, must your fancy and delight in similitudes go to sleep? By no means. When the apostle Paul finds a mystery in Melchisedek, and speaking of Hagar and Sarah, says, "Which things are an allegory," he gives us a precedent for discovering scriptural *allegories* in other places besides the two mentioned. Indeed, the historical books not only yield us here and there an allegory, but seem as a whole to be arranged with a view to symbolical teaching. A passage from Mr. Andrew Jukes' preface to his work on the types of Genesis, will show how, without violence, a most elaborate theory may be constructed by a devout mind: "As a base or ground for what is to follow, we first are shown what springs from man, and all the different forms of life, which either by nature or grace can grow out of the root of old Adam. This is the book of Genesis. Then we see, that be it bad or good which has come out of Adam, there must be redemption; so an elect people by the blood of the Lamb are saved from Egypt. This is Exodus. After redemption is known, we come to the experience of the elect as needing access, and learning the way of it, to God the Redeemer in the sanctuary. This we get in Leviticus. Then in the wilderness of this world, as pilgrims from Egypt, the house of bondage, to the promised land beyond Jordan, the trials of the journey are learnt, from that land of wonders and man's wisdom to the land flowing with milk and honey. This is the book of Numbers. Then comes the desire to exchange the wilderness for the better land, from entering which for a season after redemption is known the elect yet shrink; answering to the desire of the elect at a certain stage to know the power of the resurrection, to live even now as in heavenly places. The rules and precepts which must be obeyed, if this is to be done, come next. Deuteronomy, a second giving of the law, a second cleansing, tells the way of progress. After which Canaan is indeed reached. We go over Jordan: we know practically the death of the flesh, and what it is to be circumcised, and to roll away the reproach of Egypt. We know now what it is to be risen with Christ, and to wrestle, not with flesh and blood, but with principalities and powers in heavenly places. This is Joshua. Then comes the failure of the elect in heavenly places, failure arising from making leagues with Canaanites instead of overcoming them. This is Judges. After which the different forms of rule, which the church may know, pass in review in the books of Kings, from the first setting up of rule in Israel down to its extinction, when for their sin the rule of Babylon supersedes that of the elect. When this is known with all its shame, we see the remnants of the elect, each according to its measure, doing what may be done, if possible, to restore Israel; some, like Ezra, returning to build the temple, that is, to restore the forms of true worship; and some coming up, like Nehemiah, to build the wall, that is, to re-establish, by Gentile permission, a feeble imitation of the ancient polity; while a third remnant in Esther is seen in bonds, but faithful, providentially saved, though God's name (and this is characteristic of their state) never appears throughout the whole record." I should be far from recommending you to become as fanciful as the ingenious author I have just quoted sometimes becomes, through the large indulgence of his tendency to mysticism, but nevertheless, you will read the Word with greatly increased interest if you are a sufficiently careful reader to have noticed the general run of the books of the Bible, and their consecutiveness as a system of types.

Then, too, the faculty which turns to spiritualizing will be well employed *in generalizing the great universal principles evolved by minute and separate facts.* This is an ingenious, instructive, and legitimate pursuit. Perhaps you might not elect to preach upon, "Take it by the tail," but the remark arising from it is natural enough —"there is a way of taking everything." Moses took the serpent by the tail, so there is a mode of grasping our afflictions and finding them stiffen in our hands into a wonder-working rod; there is a way of holding the doctrines of grace, a way of encountering ungodly men, and so on. In hundreds of scriptural incidents you may find great general principles which may nowhere be expressed in so many words. Take the following instances from Mr. Jay. From Psalm lxxiv. 14, "Thou brakest the heads of leviathan in pieces, and gavest him to be meat to the people inhabiting the wilderness," he teaches the doctrine that the greatest foes of God's pilgrim people shall be slain, and the remembrance of the mercy shall refresh the saints. From Genesis xxxv. 8, "But Deborah, Rebekah's nurse died, and she was buried beneath Beth-el, under an oak: and the name of it was called Allon-bachuth," he discourses upon good servants, and the certainty of death. Upon 2 Samuel xv. 15, "And the king's servants said unto the king, Behold, thy servants are ready to do whatsoever my lord the king shall apoint," he shows that such language may with propriety be adopted by Christians, and addressed to Christ. Should anyone take exception to the form of spiritualizing which Mr. Jay so efficiently and judiciously indulged in, he must be a person whose opinion need not sway you in the least. After my own ability I have taken the liberty to do the same, and the outlines of many sermons of the kind may be found in my little work entitled *Evening by Evening,* and a less liberal sprinkling in its companion, *Morning by Morning.*

A notable instance of a good sermon fixed upon a strained and unjustifiable basis, is that of Everard, in his *Gospel Treasury.* In the discourse upon Joshua xv. 16, 17, where the words are, "And Caleb said, He that smiteth Kirjath-sepher, and taketh it, to him will I give Achsah my daughter to wife. And Othniel the son of Kenaz, the brother of Caleb, took it: and he gave him Achsah his daughter to wife;" here the run of the preacher's utterance is based upon the translation of the Hebrew proper names, so that he makes it read, "A good heart said, Whosoever smiteth and taketh the city of the letter, to him will I give the rending of the veil; and Othniel took it as being God's fit time or opportunity, and he married Achsah, that is, enjoyed the rending of the veil, and thereby had the blessing both of the upper and nether springs." Was there no other method of showing that we are to search after the inner sense of Scripture, and not rest in the mere words or letter of the Book?

The parables of our Lord in their expounding and enforcement afford the amplest scope for a matured and disciplined fancy, and if these have all passed before you, *the miracles* still remain, rich in symbolical teaching. There can be no doubt that the miracles are the acted sermons of our Lord Jesus Christ. You have his "word sermons" in his matchless teaching, and his "deed sermons" in his peerless acts. Despite many doctrinal failures, you will find Trench, on the miracles, most helpful in this direction. All our Lord's mighty works are full of teaching. Take the story of the healing of the deaf and dumb man. The poor creature's maladies are eminently suggestive of man's lost estate, and our Lord's mode of procedure most instructively illustrates the plan of salvation. "Jesus took him aside from the multitude"—the soul must be made to feel its own personality and individuality, and must be led into loneliness. He "put his fingers into his ears," the source of the mischief indicated; sinners are convinced of their state. "And spat"—the gospel is a simple and a despised means, and the sinner, in order to salvation, must humble himself to receive it. He "touched his tongue," further pointing out where the mischief lay—our sense of need grows on us. He "looked up to heaven"—Jesus reminded his patient that all strength must come from above—a lesson which every seeker must learn. "He sighed," showing that the sorrows of the Healer are the means of our healing. And then he said, "Ephphatha, Be opened"—here was the effectual word of grace which wrought an immediate, perfect, and lasting cure. From this one exposition learn all, and ever believe that the miracles of Christ are a great picture gallery, illustrating His work among the sons of men.

Let it be an instruction, however, to all who handle either the parables or the metaphors, to be discreet. Dr. Gill is one whose name must ever be mentioned with honour and respect in this house in which his pulpit still stands, but his exposition of the parable of the Prodigal Son strikes me as being sadly absurd in some points. The learned commentator tells us, "the fatted calf" was the Lord Jesus Christ! Really, one shudders to see spiritualizing come to this. Then also there is his exposition of the Good Samaritan. The beast on which the wounded man was placed is again our Lord Jesus, and the two pence which the Good Samaritan gave to the host, are the Old and New Testament, or the ordinances of Baptism and the Lord's Supper.

Despite this caution, you may allow much latitude in spiritualizing to men of rare poetical temperament, such as John Bunyan. Gentlemen, did you ever read John Bunyan's spiritualizing of Solomon's Temple? It is a most remarkable performance, and even when a little strained it is full of a consecrated ingenuity. Take, for a specimen, one of his most far-fetched explanations, and see if it can be improved. It is on "the leaves of the Gate of the Temple." "The *leaves* of this gate or door, as I told you before, were *folding*, and so, as was hinted, have something of signification in them. For by this means a man, especially *a young disciple*, may easily be mistaken; thinking that the whole passage, when yet but a part, was open, whereas three parts might be yet kept undiscovered to him. For these doors, as I said before, were never yet set wide open, I mean in the *antitype*; never man yet saw all the riches and fulness which is in Christ. So that I say, *a new comer*, if he judged by present sight, especially if he saw but little, might easily be mistaken, wherefore such for the most part are most horribly afraid that they shall never get in thereat. How sayest thou, young comer, is not this the case with thy soul? So it seems to thee that thou art too big, being so great, so *tun-bellied* a sinner! But, O thou sinner, fear not, the doors are *folding-doors*, and may be opened wider, and wider again after that; wherefore when thou comest to this gate, and imaginest that there is not space enough for thee to enter, *knock, and it shall be wider opened unto thee,* and thou shalt be received. Luke xi. 9; John vi. 37. So then, whoever thou art, thou art come to the door of which the temple was a type, trust not to thy first conceptions of things, but believe there is grace abundant. Thou knowest not yet what Christ can do, the doors *are folding-doors. He can 'do exceeding abundantly above all that we can ask or think.'* Eph. iii. 20. The *hinges* on which these doors do hang, were, as I told you, gold; to signify that they both turned upon motives and motions of *love*, and also that the openings thereof were *rich.* Golden hinges the gate to God doth turn upon. The posts on which these doors did hang *were of the olive tree*, that *fat* and *oily* tree, to show that they do never open with *lothness*, or sluggishness as doors do whose hinges want oil. They are always *oily,* and so open easily and quickly to those who knock at them. Hence you read that he that dwells in this house gives freely, loves freely, and doth us good with all his heart. 'Yea,' saith he, 'I will rejoice over them to do them good, and I will plant them in this land assuredly, with my whole heart, and with my whole soul.' Jer. iii. 12, 14, 22; xxxii. 41; Rev. xxi. 6; xxii. 17. Wherefore, the oil of grace, signified by this oily tree, or these *olive-posts*, on which these doors do hang, do cause that they open glibly or frankly to the soul."

When Bunyan opens up the meaning of the doors being made of fir wood, who but he would have said, "The *fir tree* is also the house of the *stork,* that unclean bird, even as Christ is a harbour and shelter for sinners. As for the stork, saith the text, the fir tree is her house; and Christ saith to the sinners that see their want of shelter, 'Come unto me, and I will give you rest.' He is a refuge for the oppressed, a refuge in time of trouble. Deut. xiv. 18; Lev. xi. 19; Ps. civ. 17; lxxiv. 2, 3; Matt. xi. 27, 28; Heb. vi. 17–20." In his "House of the Forest of Lebanon" he is still more puzzled, but works his way out as no other man could have done. He finds the three rows of pillars of fifteen each to be an enigma rather too deep for him, and gives it up, but not until he has made some brave attempts upon it. Mr. Bunyan is the chief, and head, and lord of all allegorists, and is not to be followed by us into the deep places of typical and symbolical utterance. He was a swimmer, we are but mere waders, and must not go beyond our depth.

I am tempted before I close this address to give a sketch or two of spiritualizings which were familiar to me in my earliest days. I shall never forget a sermon preached by an uneducated but remarkable man, who was my near neighbour in the country. I had the notes of the discourse from his own lips, and I trust they will remain as notes, and never be preached from again in this world. The text was, "The night-hawk, the owl, and the cuckoo." That might not strike you as being exceedingly rich in matter; it did not so strike me, and there-fore I innocently enquired, "And what were the heads?" He replied most archly, "Heads? why, wring the bird's necks, and there are three directly, 'the night-hawk, the owl, and the cuckoo.'" He showed that these birds were all unclean under the law, and were plain types of unclean sinners. Night-hawks were persons who pilfered on the sly, also people who adulterated their goods, and cheated their neigh-bours in an underhand way without being suspected to be rogues. As for the owls, they typified drunkards, who are always liveliest at night, while by day they will almost knock their heads against a post because they are so sleepy. There were owls also among professors. The owl is a very small bird when he is plucked; he only looks big because he wears so many feathers; so, many professors are all feathers, and if you could take away their boastful professions there would be very little left of them. Then the cuckoos were the church clergy, who always utter the same note whenever they open their mouths in the church, and live on other birds' eggs with their church-rates and tithes. The cuckoos were also, I think, the free-willers, who were always saying, "Do-do-do-do." Was not this rather too much of a good thing? Yet from the man who delivered it the sermon would not seem at all remarkable or odd. The same venerable brother delivered a sermon equally singular but far more original and useful; those who heard it will remember it to their dying day. It was from this text: "The slothful man roasteth not that which he took in hunting." The good old man leaned upon the top of the pulpit, and said, "Then, my brethren, he *was* a lazy fellow!" That was the exordium; and then he went on to say, "He went out a hunting, and after much trouble he caught his hare, and then was too idle to roast it. He was a lazy fellow indeed!" The good man made us all feel how ridiculous such idleness was, and then he said, "But then you are very likely quite as much to blame as this man, for you do just the same. You hear of a popular minister coming down from London, and you put the horse in the cart, and drive ten or twenty miles to hear him; and then when you have heard the sermon you forget to profit by it. You catch the hare and do not roast it; you go hunting after the truth, and then you do not receive it." Then he went on to show, that just as meat needs cooking to prepare it for assimilation in the bodily system—I do not think he used that word though—so the truth needs to go through a process before it can be received into the mind so that we may feed thereon and grow. He said he should show how to cook a sermon, and he did so most instructively. He began as the cookery books do— "First catch your hare." "So," he said, "first get a gospel sermon." Then he declared that a great many sermons were not worth hunting for, and that good sermons were mournfully scarce, and it was worth while to go any distance to hear a solid, old-fashioned, Calvinistic discourse. Then after the sermon had been caught, there was much about it which might be necessary because of the preacher's infirmity, which was not profitable, and must be put away. Here he enlarged upon discerning and judging what we heard, and not believing every word of any man. Then followed directions as to roasting a sermon; run the spit of memory through it from end to end, turn it round upon the roasting-jack of meditation, before the fire of a really warm and earnest heart, and in that way the sermon would be cooked and ready to yield real spiritual nourishment. I do but give you the outline, and though it may look somewhat laughable, it was not so esteemed by the hearers. It was full of allegory, and kept up the attention of the people from the beginning to the end. "Well, my dear sir, how are you?" was my salutation to him one morning, "I'm pleased to see you so well at your age." "Yes, I am in fine order for an old man, and hardly feel myself failing at all." "I hope your good health will continue for years to come, and that like Moses you will go down to your grave with your eye un-dimmed and your natural force unabated." "All very fine," said the old gentleman, "but in the first place, Moses never went down to his grave at all, he went up to it; and in the next place, what is the meaning of all you have been talking about? Why did not the eye of Moses wax dim?" "I suppose, sir," said I, very meekly, "that his natural mode of life and quiet spirit had helped to preserve his faculties and make him a vigorous old man." "Very likely," said he, "but that's not what I am driving at: what's the meaning, the spiritual teaching of the whole matter? Is it not just this: Moses is the law, and what a glorious end of the law the Lord gave it on the mount of His finished work; how sweetly its terrors are all laid to sleep with a kiss from God's mouth! and, mark you, the reason why the law no more condemns us is not because its eye is dim, so that it cannot see our sins, or because its force is abated with which to curse and punish; but Christ has taken it up to the mount, and gloriously made an end of it." Such was his usual talk and such was his ministry. Peace to his ashes. He fed sheep the first years of his life, and was a shepherd of men the next, and, as he used to tell me, "found men by far the more sheepish of the two." The converts who found the road to heaven under him were so many that, when we remember them, we are like those who saw the lame man leaping through the word of Peter and John; they were disposed to criticise, but "beholding the man that was healed standing with Peter and John, they could say nothing against it."

With this I close, re-asserting the opinion, that guided by discretion and judgment, we may occasionally employ spiritualizing with good effect to our people; certainly we shall interest them and keep them awake.

VIII

On the Voice

OUR FIRST rule with regard to the voice would be—*do not think too much about it,* for recollect the sweetest voice is nothing without something to say, and however well it may be managed, it will be like a well-driven cart with nothing in it, unless you convey by it important and seasonable truths to your people. Demosthenes was doubtless right in giving a first, second, and third place to a good delivery; but of what value will that be if a man has nothing to deliver? A man with a surpassingly excellent voice who is destitute of a well-informed head, and an earnest heart, will be "a voice crying in the wilderness;" or, to use Plutarch's expression, "*Vox et praeterea nihil.*" Such a man may shine in the choir, but he is useless in the pulpit. Whitfield's voice, without his heart-power, would have left no more lasting effects upon his hearers than Paganini's fiddle. You are not singers but preachers: your voice is but a secondary matter; do not be fops with it, or puling invalids over it, as so many are. A trumpet need not be made of silver, a ram's-horn will suffice; but it must be able to endure rough usage, for trumpets are for war's conflicts, not for the drawing-rooms of fashion.

On the other hand, *do not think too little of your voice,* for its excellence may greatly conduce to the result which you hope to produce. Plato, in confessing the power of eloquence, mentions the *tone* of the speaker. "So strongly," says he, "does the speech and the tone of the orator ring in my ears, that scarcely in the third or fourth day do I recollect myself, and perceive where on the earth I am; and for a while I am willing to believe myself living in the isles of the blessed." Exceedingly precious truths may be greatly marred by being delivered in monotonous tones. I once heard a most esteemed minister, who mumbled sadly, compared to "a humble bee in a pitcher," a vulgar metaphor no doubt, but so exactly descriptive, that it brings to my mind the droning sound at this instant most distinctly, and reminds me of the parody upon Gray's Elegy:

> "Now fades the glimmering subject from the sight,
> And all the air a sleepy stillness holds,
> Save where the parson hums his droning flight,
> And drowsy tinklings lull the slumb'ring folds."

What a pity that a man who from his heart delivered doctrines of undoubted value, in language the most appropriate, should commit ministerial suicide by harping on one string, when the Lord had given him an instrument of many strings to play upon! Alas! alas! for that dreary voice, it hummed and hummed like a mill-wheel to the same unmusical tune, whether its owner spake of heaven or hell, eternal life or everlasting wrath. It might be, by accident, a little louder or softer, according to the length of the sentence, but its tone was still the same, a dreary waste of sound, a howling wilderness of speech in which there was no possible relief, no variety, no music, nothing but horrible sameness.

When the wind blows through the Æolian harp, it swells through all the chords, but the heavenly wind, passing through some men, spends itself upon one string, and that, for the most part, the most out of tune of the whole. Grace alone could enable hearers to edify under the drum—drum—drum of some divines. I think an impartial jury would bring in a verdict of justifiable slumbering in many cases where the sound emanating from the preacher lulls to sleep by its reiterated note. Dr. Guthrie charitably traces the slumbers of a certain Scotch congregation to bad ventilation in the meeting-house; this has something to do with it, but a bad condition of the valves of the preacher's throat might be a still more potent cause. Brethren, in the name of everything that is sacred, ring the whole chime in your steeple, and do not dun your people with the ding-dong of one poor cracked bell.

When you do pay attention to the voice, *take care not to fall into the habitual and common affectations of the present day.* Scarcely one man in a dozen in the pulpit talks like a man. This affectation is not confined to Protestants, for the Abbé Mullois remarks, "Everywhere else, men speak: they speak at the bar and the tribune; but they no longer speak in the pulpit, for there we only meet with a factitious and artificial language, and a false tone. This style of speaking is only tolerated in the church, because, unfortunately, it is so general there; elsewhere it would not be endured. What would be thought of a man who should converse in a similar way in a drawing-room? He would certainly provoke many a smile. Some time ago there was a warder at the Pantheon—a good sort of fellow in his way —who, in enumerating the beauties of the monument, adopted precisely the tone of many of our preachers, and never failed thereby to excite the hilarity of the visitors, who were as much amused with his style of address as with the objects of interest which he pointed out to them. A man who has not a natural and true delivery, should not be allowed to occupy the pulpit; from thence, at least, everything that is false should be summarily banished. . . . In these days of mistrust everything that is false should be set aside; and the best way of correcting one's self in that respect, as regards preaching, is frequently to listen to certain monotonous and vehement preachers. We shall come away in such disgust, and with such a horror of their delivery, that we shall prefer condemning ourselves to silence rather than imitate them. The instant you abandon the natural and the true, you forego the right to be believed, as well as the right of being listened to." You may go all round, to church and chapel alike, and you will find that by far the larger majority of our preachers have a holy tone for Sundays. They have one voice for the parlour and the bedroom, and quite another tone for the pulpit; so that, if not double-tongued sinfully, they certainly are so literally. The moment some men shut the pulpit door, they leave their own personal manhood behind them, and become as official as the parish beadle. There they might almost boast with the Pharisee, that they are not as other men are, although it would be blasphemy to thank God for it. No longer are they carnal and speak as men, but a whine, a broken hum-haw, an *ore rotundo*, or some other graceless mode of noise-making, is adopted, to prevent all suspicion of being natural and speaking out of the abundance of the heart. When that gown is once on, how often does it prove to be the shroud of the man's true self, and the effeminate emblem of officialism!

There are two or three modes of speech which I dare say you will recognise as having frequently heard. That dignified, doctorial, inflated, bombastic style, which I just now called the *ore rotundo*, is not quite so common now as it used to be, but it is still admired by some. [Unfortunately, the Lecturer could not here be reported by any known form of letter-press, as he proceeded to read a hymn with a round, rolling swelling voice.] When a reverend gentleman was once blowing off steam in this way, a man in the aisle said he thought the preacher "had swallowed a dumpling," but another whispered, "No, Jack, he ain't swaller'd un; he's got un in his mouth a-wobblin." I can imagine Dr. Johnson talking in that fashion at Bolt Court; and from men to whom it is natural it rolls with Olympian grandeur, but in the pulpit away for ever with all imitation of it; if it comes naturally, well and good, but to mimic it is treason to common decency: indeed, all mimicry is in the pulpit near akin to an unpardonable sin.

There is another style, at which I beseech you not to laugh. [Giving another illustration], a method of enunciation said to be very lady-like, mincing, delicate, servant-girlified, dawdling, Dundrearyish, I know not how else to describe it. We have, most of us, had the felicity of hearing these, or some others, of the extensive genus of falsettos, high-stilts, and affectations. I have heard many different varieties, from the fulness of the Johnsonian to the thinness of the little genteel whisper; from the roaring of the Bulls of Bashan up to the chip, chip, chip of a chaffinch. I have been able to trace some of

our brethren to their forefathers—I mean their ministerial forefathers, from whom they first of all gathered these heavenly, melodious, sanctified, in every way beautiful, but I must honestly add
detestable modes of speech. The undoubted order of their oratorical
pedigree is as follows: Chip, which was the son of Lisp, which was
the son of Simper, which was the son of Dandy, which was the son
of Affectation; or Wobbler, which was the son of Grandiose, which
was the son of Pomposity, the same was the father of many sons.
Understand, that where even these horrors of sound are natural, I
do not condemn them—let every creature speak in its own tongue;
but the fact is, that in nine cases out of ten, these sacred brogues,
which I hope will soon be dead languages, are unnatural and strained.
I am persuaded that these tones and semitones and monotones are
Babylonian, that they are not at all the Jerusalem dialect; for the
Jerusalem dialect has this one distinguishing mark, that it is a man's
own mode of speech, and is the same out of the pulpit as it is in it.
Our friend of the affected *ore rotundo* school was never known to talk
out of the pulpit as he does in, or to say in the parlour in the same
tone which he uses in the pulpit: "Will you be so good as to give me
another cup of tea; I take sugar, if you please." He would make himself ludicrous if he did so, but the pulpit is to be favoured with the
scum of his voice, which the parlour would not tolerate. I maintain
that the best notes a man's voice is capable of should be given to
the proclamation of the gospel, and these are such as nature teaches
him to use in earnest conversation. Ezekiel served his Master with
his most musical and melodious powers, so that the Lord said, "Thou
art unto them as a very lovely song of one that hath a pleasant voice,
and can play well on an instrument." Although this, alas! was of
no use to Israel's hard heart, as nothing will be but the Spirit of God,
yet it well became the prophet to deliver the word of the Lord in the
best style of voice and manner.

In the next place, *if you have any idiosyncrasies of speech, which are
disagreeable to the ear, correct them, if possible.*[1] It is admitted that
this is much more easy for the teacher to inculcate than for you to
practise. Yet to young men in the morning of their ministry, the
difficulty is not insuperable. Brethren from the country have a flavour
of their rustic diet in their mouths, reminding us irresistibly of the
calves of Essex, the swine of Berkshire, or the runts of Suffolk. Who
can mistake the Yorkshire or Somersetshire dialects, which are not
merely provincial pronunciations, but tones also? It would be difficult to discover the cause, but the fact is clear enough, that in some
counties of England men's threats seem to be furred up, like long-
used teakettles, and in others, they ring like brass music, with a vicious

[1] "Take care of anything awkward or affected either in your gesture, phrase, or pronunciation."—JOHN WESLEY.

metallic sound. Beautiful these variations of nature may be in their season and place, but my taste has never been able to appreciate them. A sharp discordant squeak, like a rusty pair of scissors, is to be got rid of at all hazards; so also is a thick, inarticulate utterance in which no word is complete, but nouns, adjectives, and verbs are made into a kind of hash. Equally objectionable is that ghostly speech in which a man talks without using his lips, ventriloquising most horribly: sepulchral tones may fit a man to be an undertaker, but Lazarus is not called out of his grave by hollow moans. One of the surest ways to kill yourself is to speak from the throat instead of the mouth. This misuse of nature will be terribly avenged by her; escape the penalty by avoiding the offence. It may be well in this place to urge you as soon as you detect yourself interposing hum-haw pretty plentifully in your discourse, to purge yourself of the insinuating but ruinous habit at once. There is no need whatever for it, and although those who are now its victims may never be able to break the chain, you, who are beginners in oratory, must scorn to wear the galling yoke. It is even needful to say, open your mouths when you speak, for much of inarticulate mumbling is the result of keeping the mouth half closed. It is not in vain that the evangelists have written of our Lord, "*He opened His mouth* and taught them." Open wide the doors from which such goodly truth is to march forth. Moreover, brethren, avoid the use of the nose as an organ of speech, for the best authorities are agreed that it is intended to smell with. Time was, when the nasal twang was the correct thing, but in this degenerate age you had better obey the evident suggestion of nature, and let the mouth keep to its work without the interference of the olfactory instrument. Should an American student be present he must excuse my pressing this remark upon his attention. Abhor the practice of some men, who will not bring out the letter "r;" such a habit is "vewy wuinous and wediculous, vewy wetched and wepwehensible." Now and then a brother has the felicity to possess a most winning and delicious lisp. This is perhaps among the least of evils, *where the brother himself is little and winning,* but it would ruin any being who aimed at manliness and force. I can scarcely conceive of Elijah lisping to Ahab, or Paul prettily chipping his words on Mars' Hill. There may be a peculiar pathos about a weak and watery eye, and a faltering style; we will go further, and admit that where these are the result of intense passion, they are sublime; but some possess them by birth, and use them rather too freely: it is, to say the least, unnecessary for you to imitate them. Speak as educated nature suggests to you, and you will do well; but let it be educated, and not raw, rude, uncultivated nature. Demosthenes took, as you know, unbounded pains with his voice, and Cicero, who was naturally weak, made a long journey into Greece to correct his manner of speaking. With far nobler themes, let us not be less ambitious to excel. "Deprive me of everything else," says Gregory, of Nazianzen, "but leave me eloquence, and I shall never regret the voyages which I have made in order to study it."

Always speak so as to be heard. I know a man who weighs sixteen stone, and ought to be able to be heard half-a-mile, who is so gracelessly indolent, that in his small place of worship you can scarcely hear him in the front of the gallery. What is the use of a preacher whom men cannot hear? Modesty should lead a voiceless man to give place to others who are more fitted for the work of proclaiming the messages of the King. Some men are loud enough, but they are not distinct; their words overlap each other, play at leap-frog, or trip each other up. Distinct utterance is far more important than windpower. Do give a word a fair chance, do not break its back in your vehemence, or run it off its legs in your haste. It is hateful to hear a big fellow mutter and whisper when his lungs are quite strong enough for the loudest speech; but at the same time, let a man shout ever so lustily, he will not be well heard unless he learns to push his words forward with due space between. To speak too slowly is miserable work, and subjects active-minded hearers to the disease called the "horrors." It is impossible to hear a man who crawls along at a mile an hour. One word to-day and one to-morrow is a kind of slow-fire which martyrs only could enjoy. Excessively rapid speaking, tearing and raving into utter rant, is quite as inexcusable; it is not, and never can be powerful, except with idiots, for it turns what should be an army of words into a mob, and most effectually drowns the sense in floods of sound. Occasionally, one hears an infuriated orator of indistinct utterance, whose impetuosity hurries him on to such a confusion of sounds, that at a little distance one is reminded of Lucan's lines :

> "Her gabbling tongue a muttering tone confounds,
> Discordant and unlike to human sounds;
> It seem'd of dogs the bark, of wolves the howl,
> The doleful screeching of the midnight owl;
> The hiss of snakes, the hungry lion's roar,
> The bound of billows beating on the shore;
> The groan of winds among the leafy wood,
> And burst of thunder from the rending cloud!
> 'Twas these, all these in one."

It is an infliction not to be endured twice, to hear a brother who mistakes perspiration for inspiration, tear along like a wild horse with a hornet in its ear till he has no more wind, and must needs pause to pump his lungs full again; a repetition of this indecency several times in a sermon is not uncommon, but is most painful. Pause soon enough to prevent that "hough, hough," which rather creates pity for the breathless orator than sympathy with the subject in hand.

Your audience ought not to know that you breathe at all—the process of respiration should be as unobserved as the circulation of the blood. It is indecent to let the mere animal function of breathing cause any hiatus in your discourse.

Do not as a rule exert your voice to the utmost in ordinary preaching. Two or three earnest men, now present, are tearing themselves to pieces by needless bawling; their poor lungs are irritated, and their larynx inflamed by boisterous shouting, from which they seem unable to refrain. Now it is all very well to "Cry aloud and spare not," but "Do thyself no harm" is apostolical advice. When persons can hear you with half the amount of voice, it is as well to save the superfluous force for times when it may be wanted. "Waste not, want not" may apply here as well as elsewhere. Be a little economical with that enormous volume of sound. Do not give your hearers head-aches when you mean to give them heart-aches: you aim to keep them from sleeping in their pews, but remember that it is not needful to burst the drums of their ears. "The Lord is not in the wind." Thunder is not lightning. Men do not hear in proportion to the noise created; in fact, too much noise stuns the ear, creates reverberations and echoes, and effectually injures the power of your sermons. Adapt your voice to your audience; when twenty thousand are before you, draw out the stops and give the full peal, but not in a room which will only hold a score or two. Whenever I enter a place to preach, I unconsciously calculate how much sound is needed to fill it, and after a few sentences my key is pitched. If you can make the man at the end of the chapel hear, if you can see that he is catching your thought, you may be sure that those nearer can hear you, and no more force is needed, perhaps a little less will do—watch and see. Why speak so as to be heard in the street when there is nobody there who is listening to you? Whether indoors or out, see that the most remote hearers can follow you, and that will be sufficient. By the way, I may observe, that brethren should, out of mercy to the weak, always attend carefully to the force of their voices in sick rooms, and in congregations where some are known to be very infirm. It is a cruel thing to sit down by a sick man's bedside, and shout out "THE LORD IS MY SHEPHERD." If you act so thoughtlessly, the poor man will say as soon as you are down stairs, "Dear me! how my head aches. I am glad the good man is gone, Mary; that is a very precious Psalm and so quiet like, but he read it out like thunder and lightning, and almost stunned me!" Recollect, you younger and unmarried men, that soft whispers will suit the invalid better than roll of drum and culverin.

Observe carefully the rule to *vary the force of your voice.* The old rule was, to begin very softly, gradually rise higher, and bring out your loudest notes at the end. Let all such regulations be blown to pieces at the cannon's mouth; they are impertinent and misleading.

Speak softly or loudly, as the emotion of the moment may suggest, and observe no artificial and fanciful rules. Artificial rules are an utter abomination, As M. de Cormorin satirically puts it, "Be impassioned, thunder, rage, weep, up to the fifth word, of the third sentence, of the tenth paragraph, of the tenth leaf. How easy that would be! Above all, how very natural!" In imitation of a popular preacher, to whom it was unavoidable, a certain minister was accustomed in the commencement of his sermon to speak in so low a key, that no one could possibly hear him. Everybody leaned forward, fearing that something good was being lost in the air, but their straining was in vain; a holy mutter was all they could discern. If the brother *could not* have spoken out none should have blamed him, but it was a most absurd thing to do this when in a short time he proved the power of his lungs by filling the whole structure by sonorous sentences. If the first half of his discourse was of no importance, why not omit it? and if of any value at all, why not deliver it distinctly? *Effect*, gentlemen, that was the point aimed at; he knew that one who spake in that fashion had produced great effects, and he hoped to rival him. If any of you dare commit such a folly for such a detestable object, I heartily wish you had never entered this Institution. I tell you most seriously, that the thing called "*effect*," is hateful, because it is untrue, artificial, tricky, and therefore despicable. Never do anything for effect, but scorn the stratagems of little minds, hunting after the approval of connoisseurs in preaching, who are a race as obnoxious to a true minister as locusts to the Eastern husbandman. But I digress: be clear and distinct at the very first. Your exordia are too good to be whispered to space. Speak them out boldly, and command attention at the very outset by your manly tones. Do not start at the highest pitch as a rule, for then you will not be able to rise when you warm with the work; but still be outspoken from the first. Lower the voice when suitable even to a whisper; for soft, deliberate, solemn utterances are not only a relief to the ear, but have a great aptitude to reach the heart. Do not be afraid of the low keys, for if you throw force into them they are as well heard as the shouts. You need not speak in a loud voice in order to be heard well. Macaulay says of William Pitt, "His voice, even when it sank to a whisper, was heard to the remotest benches of the House of Commons." It has been well said that the most noisy gun is not the one which carries a ball the furthest: the crack of a rifle is anything but noisy. It is not the loudness of your voice, it is the force which you put into it that is effective. I am certain that I could whisper so as to be heard throughout every corner of our great Tabernacle, and I am equally certain that I could holloa and shout so that nobody could understand me. The thing could be done here, but perhaps the example is needless, as I fear some of you perform the business with remarkable success. Waves of air may dash upon the ear in such rapid succession that they create no translatable impression on the auditory nerve. Ink is necessary to write with, but if you upset the ink bottle over the sheet of paper you convey no meaning thereby; so is it with sound. Sound is the ink, but management is needed, not quantity, to produce an intelligible writing upon the ear. If your sole ambition be to compete with—

> "Stentor the strong, endued with brazen lungs,
> Whose throat surpass'd the force of fifty tongues,"

then bawl yourselves into Elysium as rapidly as possible, but if you wish to be understood, and so to be of service, shun the reproach of being "impotent and loud." You are aware that shrill sounds travel the farthest: the singular cry which is used by travellers in the wilds of Australia, owes its remarkable power to its shrillness. A bell will be heard much farther off than a drum; and, very singularly, the more musical a sound is the farther it travels. It is not the thumping of the piano which is needed, but the judicious sounding of the best keys. You will therefore feel at liberty to ease the strain very frequently in the direction of loudness, and you will be greatly relieving both the ears of the audience and your own lungs. Try all methods, from the sledge-hammer to the puff-ball. Be as gentle as a zephyr and as furious as a tornado. Be, indeed, just what every common-sense person is in his speech when he talks naturally, pleads vehemently, whispers confidentially, appeals plaintively, or publishes distinctly.

Next to the moderation of lung-force, I should place the rule, *modulate your tones*. Alter the key frequently and vary the strain constantly. Let the bass, the treble, and the tenor, take their turn. I beseech you to do this out of pity to yourself and to those who hear you. God has mercy upon us and arranges all things to meet our cravings for variety; let us have mercy upon our fellow creatures, and not persecute them with the tedium of sameness. It is a most barbarous thing to inflict upon the tympanum of a poor fellow-creature's ear the anguish of being bored and gimbleted with the same sound for half an hour. What swifter mode of rendering the mind idiotic or lunatic could be conceived than the perpetual droning of a beetle, or buzzing of a blue-bottle, in the organ of hearing? What dispensation have you by which you are to be tolerated in such cruelty to the helpless victims who sit under your drum-drum ministrations? Kind nature frequently spares the drone's unhappy victims the full effect of his tortures by steeping them in sweet repose. This, however, you do not desire; then speak with varied voice. How few ministers remember that monotony causes sleep. I fear the charge brought by a writer in the *Imperial Review* is true to the letter of numbers of my brethren. "We all know how the noise of running water, or the murmur of the sea, or the sighing of the south wind among the pines, or the moaning of wood-doves, induces a delicious dreamy languor. Far be it from us to say that the voice of a modern divine resembles, in the slightest degree, any of these sweet sounds, yet the effect is the same, and few can resist the drowsy influences of a lengthy dissertation, delivered without the slightest variation of tone or alteration of expression. Indeed, the very exceptional use of the phrase 'an awakening discourse,' even by those most familiar with such matters, conveys the implication that the great majority of pulpit harangues are of a decidedly soporific tendency. It is an ill case when the preacher

> "Leaves his hearers perplex'd—
> Twixt the two to determine:
> 'Watch and pray,' says the text,
> 'Go to sleep,' says the sermon."

However musical your voice may be in itself, if you continue to sound the same chord perpetually, your hearers will perceive that its notes are by distance made more sweet. Do in the name of humanity cease intoning and take to rational speaking. Should this argument fail to move you, I am so earnest about this point, that if you will not follow my advice out of mercy to your hearers, yet do it out of mercy to yourselves; for as God in His infinite wisdom has been pleased always to append a penalty to every sin against His natural as well as moral laws, so the evil of monotony is frequently avenged by that dangerous disease called *dysphonia clericorum*, or, "Clergyman's sore throat." When certain of our brethren are so beloved by their hearers that they do not object to pay a handsome sum to get rid of them for a few months, when a journey to Jerusalem is recommended and provided for, bronchitis of a modified order is so remarkably overruled for good, that my present argument will not disturb their equanimity. But such is not *our* lot; to us bronchitis means real misery, and therefore, to avoid it, we would follow any sensible suggestion. If you wish to ruin your throats you can speedily do so, but if you wish to preserve them, note what is now laid before you. I have often in this room compared the voice to a drum. If the drummer should always strike in one place on the head of his drum, the skin would soon wear into a hole; but how much longer it would have lasted him if he had varied his thumping and had used the entire surface of the drum-head! So it is with a man's voice. If he uses always the same tone, he will wear a hole in that part of the throat which is most exercised in producing that monotony, and very soon he will suffer from bronchitis. I have heard surgeons affirm, that Dissenting bronchitis differs from the Church of England article. There is an ecclesiastical twang which is much admired in the Establishment, a sort of steeple-

in-the-throat grandeur, an aristocratic, theologic, parsonic, supernatural, infra-human mouthing of language and rolling over of words.
It may be illustrated by the following specimen: "He that hath yaws
to yaw let him yaw," which is a remarkable, if not impressive, rendering of a Scripture text. Who does not know the hallowed way of
pronouncing—"Dearly beloved brethren, the Scripture moveth us in
divers places"? It rolls in my ears now like Big Ben—coupled with
boyish memories of monotonous peals of "The Prince Albert, Albert
Prince of Wales, and all the Royal Family. . . . Amen." Now, if a
man who talks so unnaturally does *not* get bronchitis, or some other
disease, I can only say that throat diseases must be very sovereignly
dispensed. At the Nonconformist hobbies of utterance I have already
struck a blow, and I believe it is by them that larynx and lungs become
delicate, and good men succumb to silence and the grave. Should
you desire my authority for the threat which I have held out to you,
I shall give you the opinion of Mr. Macready, the eminent tragedian,
who, since he looks at the matter from an impartial but experimental
standpoint, is worthy of a respectful hearing. "Relaxed throat is
usually caused, not so much by exercising the organ, as by the kind
of exercise; that is, not so much by long or loud speaking, as by
speaking in a feigned voice. I am not sure that I shall be understood
in this statement, but there is not one person in, I may say, ten
thousand, who in addressing a body of people, does so in his natural
voice; and this habit is more especially observable in the pulpit. I
believe that relaxation of the throat results from violent efforts in
these affected tones, and that severe irritation, and often ulceration,
is the consequence. The labour of a whole day's duty in a church is
nothing, in point of labour, compared with the performance of one
of Shakespeare's leading characters, nor I should suppose, with any of
the very great displays made by our leading statesmen in the Houses
of Parliament; and I feel very certain that the disorder, which you
designate as 'Clergyman's sore throat,' is attributable generally to the
mode of speaking, and not to the length of time or violence of effort
that may be employed. I have known several of my former contemporaries on the stage suffer from sore throat, but I do not think,
among those eminent in their art, that it could be regarded as a
prevalent disease." Actors and barristers have much occasion to strain
their vocal powers, and yet there is no such thing as a counsel's sore
throat, or a tragedian's bronchitis; simply because these men dare
not serve the public in so slovenly a manner as some preachers serve
their God. Samuel Fenwick, Esq., M.D., in a popular treatise upon
"Diseases of the Throat and Lungs," has most wisely said, "From
what was stated respecting the physiology of the vocal chords, it will
be evident that continued speaking in one tone is much more fatiguing
than frequent alterations in the pitch of the voice; because by the

former, one muscle or set of muscles alone is strained, whilst by the latter, different muscles are brought into action, and thus relieve one another. In the same way, a man raising his arm at right angles to his body, becomes fatigued in five or ten minutes, because only one set of muscles has to bear the weight; but these same muscles can work the whole day if their action is alternated with that of others. Whenever, therefore, we hear a clergyman droning through the church service, and in the same manner and tone of voice reading, praying, and exhorting, we may be perfectly sure that he is giving ten times more labour to his vocal chords than is absolutely necessary."

This may be the place to reiterate an opinion which I have often expressed in this place, of which I am reminded by the author whom I have quoted. If ministers would speak oftener, their throats and lungs would be less liable to disease. Of this I am quite sure; it is matter of personal experience and wide observation, and I am confident that I am not mistaken. Gentlemen, twice a week preaching is very dangerous, but I have found five or six times healthy, and even twelve or fourteen not excessive. A costermonger set to cry cauliflowers and potatoes one day in the week would find the effort most laborious, but when he for six successive days fills streets and lanes and alleys with his sonorous din, he finds no *dysphonia pomariorum,* or "Costermonger's sore throat," laying him aside from his humble toils. I was pleased to find my opinion, that infrequent preaching is the root of many diseases, thus plainly declared by Dr. Fenwick: "All the directions which have been here laid down will, I believe, be ineffectual without regular daily practice of the voice. Nothing seems to have such a tendency to produce this disease as the occasional prolonged speaking, alternating with long intervals of rest, to which clergymen are more particularly subject. Anyone giving the subject a moment's consideration will readily understand this. If a man, or any other animal, be intended for any unusual muscular exertion, he is regularly exercised in it, day by day, and labour is thus rendered easy which otherwise it would be almost impossible to execute. But the generality of the clerical profession undergo a great amount of muscular exertion in the way of speaking only on one day of the week, whilst in the remaining six days they scarcely ever raise their voice above the usual pitch. Were a smith or a carpenter thus occasionally to undergo the fatigue connected with the exercise of his trade, he would not only be quite unfitted for it, but he would lose the skill he had acquired. The example of the most celebrated orators the world has seen proves the advantages of regular and constant practice of speaking; and I would on this account most strongly recommend all persons subject to this complaint to read aloud once or twice a day, using the same pitch of voice as in the pulpit, and paying especial attention to the position of the chest and throat, and to clear and proper articulation of the words." Mr. Beecher is of the same opinion, for he remarks, "Newsboys show what out-of-door practice will do for a man's lungs. What would the pale and feeble-speaking minister do who can scarcely make his voice reach two hundred auditors if he were set to cry newspapers? Those New York newsboys stand at the head of a street, and send down their voices through it, as an athlete would roll a ball down an alley. We advise men training for speaking professions to peddle wares in the streets for a little time. Young ministers might go into partnership with newsboys awhile, till they got their mouths open and their larynx nerved and toughened."

Gentlemen, a needful rule is—*always suit your voice to your matter.* Do not be jubilant over a doleful subject, and on the other hand, do not drag heavily where the tones ought to trip along merrily, as though they were dancing to the tune of the angels in heaven. This rule I shall not enlarge upon, but rest assured it is of the utmost importance, and if obediently followed, will always secure attention, provided your matter is worth it. Suit your voice to your matter always, and, above all, *in everything be natural.* Away for ever with slavish attention to rules and models. Do not imitate other people's voices, or, if from an unconquerable propensity you must follow them, emulate every orator's excellencies, and the evil will be lessened. I am myself, by a kind of irresistible influence, drawn to be an imitator, so that a journey to Scotland or Wales will for a week or two materially affect my pronunciation and tone. Strive against it I do, but there it is, and the only cure I know of is to let the mischief die a natural death. Gentlemen, I return to my rule—use your own natural voices. Do not be monkeys, but men; not parrots, but men of originality in all things. It is said that the most becoming way for a man to wear his beard is that in which it grows, for both in colour and form it will suit his face. Your own modes of speech will be most in harmony with your methods of thought and your own personality. The mimic is for the playhouse, the cultured man in his sanctified personality is for the sanctuary. I would repeat this rule till I wearied you if I thought you would forget it; be natural, be natural, be natural evermore. An affectation of voice, or an imitation of the manner of Dr. Silvertongue, the eminent divine, or even of a well-beloved tutor or president will inevitably ruin you. I charge you throw away the servility of imitation and rise to the manliness of originality.

We are bound to add—*endeavour to educate your voice.* Grudge no pains or labour in achieving this, for as it has been well observed, "However prodigious may be the gifts of nature to her elect, they can only be developed and brought to their extreme perfection by labour and study." Think of Michael Angelo working for a week without taking off his clothes, and Handel hollowing out every key of his harpsichord, like a spoon, by incessant practice. Gentlemen, after this, never talk of difficulty or weariness. It is almost impossible to see the utility of Demosthenes' method of speaking with stones in his mouth, but any one can perceive the usefulness of his pleading with the boisterous billows, that he might know how to command a hearing amidst the uproarious assemblies of his countrymen; and in his speaking as he ran up hill that his lungs might gather force from laborious use the reason is as obvious as the self-denial is commendable. We are bound to use every possible means to perfect the voice by which we are to tell forth the glorious gospel of the blessed God. Take great care of the consonants, enunciate every one of them clearly; they are the features and expression of the words. Practise indefatigably till you give every one of the consonants its due; the vowels have a voice of their own, and therefore they can speak for themselves. In all other matters exercise a rigid discipline until you have mastered your voice, and have it in hand like a well-trained steed. Gentlemen with narrow chests are advised to use the dumb-bells every morning, or better still, those clubs which the College has provided for you. You need broad chests, and must do your best to get them. Do not speak with your hands in your waistcoat pockets so as to contract your lungs, but throw the shoulders back, as public singers do. Do not lean over a desk while speaking, and never hold the head down on the breast while preaching. Upward rather than downward let the body bend. Off with all tight cravats and button-up waistcoats; leave room for the full play of the bellows and the pipes. Observe the statues of the Roman or Greek orators, look at Raphael's picture of Paul, and, without affectation, fall naturally into the graceful and appropriate attitudes there depicted, for these are best for the voice. Get a friend to tell you your faults, or better still, welcome an enemy who will watch you keenly and sting you savagely. What a blessing such an irritating critic will be to a wise man, what an intolerable nuisance to a fool! Correct yourself diligently and frequently, or you will fall into errors unawares, false tones will grow, and slovenly habits will form insensibly; therefore criticise yourself with unceasing care. Think nothing little by which you may be even a little more useful. But, gentlemen, never degenerate in this business into pulpit fops, who think gesture and voice to be everything. I am sick at heart when I hear of men taking a whole week to get up a sermon, much of the getting up consisting in repeating their precious productions before a glass! Alas! for this age, if graceless hearts are to be forgiven for the sake of graceful manners. Give us all the vulgarities of the wildest back-woods' itinerant rather than the perfumed prettinesses of effeminate gentility. I would no more advise you to be fastidious with your voices than I would recommend you to imitate Rowland Hill's Mr. Taplash with his diamond ring, his richly-scented pocket handkerchief, and his eyeglass. Exquisites are out of place in the pulpit, they should be set up in a tailor's window, with a ticket, *"This style complete, including MSS., £10 10s."*

Perhaps here may be the place to observe that it were well if all parents were more attentive to the teeth of their children, since faulty teeth may cause serious damage to a speaker. There are men, whose articulation is faulty, who should at once consult the dentist (I mean, of course, a thoroughly scientific and experienced one); for a few false teeth or some other simple arrangement would be a permanent blessing to them. My own dentist very sensibly remarks in his circular, "When a portion or the whole of the teeth are lost, a contraction of the muscles of the face and throat follows, the other organs of the voice which have been accustomed to the teeth are impaired, and put out of their common play, producing a break, languor, or depression, as in a musical instrument which is deficient in a note. It is vain to expect perfect symphony, and proportional and consistent accent on the key, tone, and pitch of the voice, with deficiencies in its organs, and of course the articulation becomes defective; such defect adds much to the *labour* of speaking, to say the least, and in most cases lisping, a too hasty or sudden drop, or a faint delivery, is the result; from more serious deficiencies a mumbling and clattering is almost sure to follow." Where this is the mischief, and the cure is within reach, we are bound for our works' sake to avail ourselves of it. Teeth may seem unimportant, but be it remembered, that nothing is little in so great a calling as ours. I shall in succeeding remarks mention even smaller matters, but it is with the deep impression that hints upon insignificant things may be of unknown value in saving you from serious neglects or gross errors.

Lastly, I would say with regard to your throats—*take care of them.* Take care always to clear them well when you are about to speak, but do not be constantly clearing them while you are preaching. A very esteemed brother of my acquaintance always talks in this way—"My dear friends—hem—hem—this is a most—hem—important subject which I have now—hem—hem—to bring before you, and—hem—hem—I have to call upon you to give me—hem—hem—your most serious—hem—attention." Avoid this most zealously. Others, from want of clearing the throat, talk as if they were choked up, and were just about to expectorate; it were far better to do so at once than to sicken the hearer by repeated unpleasant sounds. Snuffling and sniffing are excusable enough when a man has a cold, but they are extremely unpleasant, and when they become habitual, they ought to be indicted under the "Nuisances Act." Pray excuse me, it may appear vulgar to mention such things, but your attention to the plain and free observations made in this lecture room may save many remarks at your expense hereafter.

When you have done preaching take care of your throat by *never wrapping it up tightly.* From personal experience I venture with some diffidence to give this piece of advice. If any of you possess delightfully warm woollen comforters, with which there may be associated the most tender remembrances of mother or sister, treasure them—treasure them in the bottom of your trunk, but do not expose them to any vulgar use by wrapping them round your necks. If any brother wants to die of influenza let him wear a warm scarf round his neck, and then one of these nights he will forget it, and catch such a cold as will last him the rest of his natural life. You seldom see a sailor wrap his neck up. No, he always keeps it bare and exposed, and has a turn-down collar, and if he has a tie at all, it is but a small one loosely tied,.so that the wind can blow all round his neck. In this philosophy I am a firm believer, having never deviated from it for these fourteen years, and having before that time been frequently troubled with colds, but very seldom since. If you feel that you want something else, why, then grow your beards! A habit most natural, scriptural, manly, and beneficial. One of our brethren, now present, has for years found this of great service. He was compelled to leave England on account of the loss of his voice, but he has become as strong as Samson now that his locks are unshorn. If your throats become affected consult a good physician, or if you cannot do this, give what attention you please to the following hint. Never purchase "Marsh-mallow Rock," "Cough-no-more Lozenges," "Pulmonic Wafers," Horehound, Ipecacuanha, or any of the ten thousand emollient compounds. They may serve your turn for a time by removing present uneasiness, but they ruin the throat by their laxative qualities. If you wish to improve your throat take a good share of pepper—good Cayenne pepper, and other astringent substances, as much as your stomach can bear. Do not go beyond that, because you must recollect that you have to take care of your stomach as well as your throat, and if the digesting apparatus be out of order, nothing can be right. Common sense teaches you that astringents must be useful. Did you ever hear of a tanner making a piece of hide into leather by laying it to soak in sugar? Neither would tolu, ipecacuanha, or treacle serve his purpose, but the very reverse; if he wants to harden and strengthen the skin, he places it in a solution of oak-bark, or some astringent substance which draws the material together and strengthens it. When I began to preach at Exeter Hall my voice was weak for such a place—as weak as the usual run of voices, and it had frequently failed me altogether in street preaching, but in Exeter Hall (which is an unusually difficult place to preach in, from its excessive width in proportion to its length), I always had a little glass of Chili vinegar and water just in front of me, a draught of which appeared to give a fresh force to the throat whenever it grew weary and the voice appeared likely to break down. When my throat becomes a little relaxed I usually ask the cook to prepare me a basin of beef-tea, as strong with pepper as can be borne, and hitherto this has been a sovereign remedy. However, as I am not qualified to practise in medicine, you will probably pay no more attention to me in medical matters than to any other quack. My belief is that half the difficulties connected with the voice in our early days will vanish as we advance in years, and find in use a second nature. I would encourage the truly earnest to persevere; if they feel the Word of the Lord like fire in their bones, even stammering may be overcome, and fear, with all its paralysing results, may be banished. Take heart, young brother, persevere, and God, and nature, and practice, will help you.

IX

Attention !

OUR subject is one which I find scarcely ever noticed in any books upon homiletics—a very curious fact, for it is a most important matter, and worthy of more than one chapter. I suppose the homiletical *savans* consider that their entire volumes are seasoned with this subject, and that they need not give it to us in lumps, because, like sugar in tea, it flavours the whole. That overlooked topic is, How TO OBTAIN AND RETAIN THE ATTENTION OF OUR HEARERS. Their attention must be gained, or nothing can be done with them: and it must be retained, or we may go on word-spinning, but no good will come of it.

Over the head of military announcements our English officers always place the word "ATTENTION!" in large capitals, and we need some such word over all our sermons. We need the earnest, candid, wakeful, continued attention of all those who are in the congregation. If men's minds are wandering far away they cannot receive the truth, and it is much the same if they are inactive. Sin cannot be taken out of men, as Eve was taken out of the side of Adam, while they are fast asleep. They must be awake, understanding what we are saying, and feeling its force, or else we may as well go to sleep too. There are preachers who care very little whether they are attended to or not; so long as they can hold on through the allotted time it is of very small importance to them whether their people hear for eternity, or hear in vain: the sooner such ministers sleep in the churchyard and preach by the verse on their gravestones the better. Some brethren speak up the ventilator, as if they sought the attention of the angels; and others look down upon their book as if they were absorbed in thought, or had themselves for an audience, and felt much honoured thereby. Why do not such brethren preach on the prairie and edify the stars? If their preaching has no reference to their hearers they might do so with evident propriety; if a sermon be a soliloquy, the more lonely the performer the better. To a rational preacher (and all are not rational) it must seem essential to interest all his audience, from the eldest to the youngest. We ought not to make even children inattentive. "Make them inattentive," say you, "who does that?" I say that most preachers do; and when children are not quiet in a meeting it is often as much our fault as theirs. Can you not put in a little story or parable on purpose for the little ones? Can you not catch the eye of the boy in the gallery, and the little girl downstairs, who have begun to fidget, and smile them into order? I often talk with my eyes to the orphan boys at the foot of my pulpit. We want all eyes fixed upon us and all ears open to us. To me it is an annoyance if even a blind man does not look at me with his face. If I see anybody turning round, whispering, nodding, or looking at his watch, I judge that I am not up to the mark, and must by some means win these minds. Very seldom have I to complain, and when I do, my general plan is to complain of myself, and own that I have no right to attention unless I know how to command it.

Now, there are some congregations whose attention you do not readily gain; they do not care to be interested. It is useless to scold them; that will be like throwing a bush at a bird to catch it. The fact is, that in most cases there is another person whom you should scold, and that is yourself. It may be their duty to attend, but it is far more your duty to make them do so. You must attract the fish to your hook, and if they do not come you should blame the fisherman and not the fish. Compel them to stand still a while and hear what God the Lord would speak to their souls. The minister who recommended the old lady to take snuff in order to keep from dozing was very properly rebuked by her reply,—that if he would put more snuff into the sermon she would be awake enough. We must plentifully cast snuff into the sermon, or something yet more awakening. Recollect that to some of our people it is not so easy to be attentive; many of them are not interested in the matter, and they have not felt enough of any gracious operation on their hearts to make them confess that the gospel is of any special value to them. Concerning the Saviour whom you preach you may say to them,

> "Is it nothing to you, all ye that pass by,
> Is it nothing to you that Jesus should die?"

Many of them have through the week been borne down by the press of business cares. They ought to roll their burden on the Lord; but do *you* always do so? Do *you* always find it easy to escape from anxieties? Are *you* able to forget the sick wife and the ailing children at home? There is no doubt whatever that many come into the house of God loaded heavily with the thoughts of their daily avocations. The farmer recollects the fields that are to be ploughed or to be sown; it is a wet Sunday, and he is reflecting upon the yellow look of the young wheats. The merchant sees that dishonoured bill fluttering before his eyes, and the tradesman counts over his bad debts. I should not wonder if the colours of the ladies' ribbons and the creak of the gentlemen's boots disturb many. There are troublesome flies about, you know: Beelzebub, the god of flies, takes care that wherever there is a gospel feast the guests should be worried with petty annoyances. Often mental mosquitoes sting the man while you are preaching to him, and he is thinking more of trifling distractions than of your discourse; is it so very wonderful that he does? You must drive the mosquitoes away, and secure your people's undistracted thoughts, turning them out of the channel in which they have been running six days into one suitable for the Sabbath. You must have sufficient leverage in your discourse and its subject to lift them right up from the earth to which they cleave, and to elevate them a little nearer heaven.

Frequently it is very difficult for congregations to attend, because of the place and the atmosphere. For instance, if the place is like this room at present, sealed against the pure air, with every window closed, they have enough to do to breathe, and cannot think of anything else: when people have inhaled over and over again the air which has been in other people's lungs, the whole machinery of life gets out of gear, and they are more likely to feel an aching head than a broken heart. The next best thing to the grace of God for a preacher is oxygen. Pray that the windows of heaven may be opened, but begin by opening the windows of your meeting-house. Look at many of our country places, and I am afraid our city chapels too, and you will find that the windows are not made to open. The modern barbarous style of building gives us no more ceiling than a barn, and no more openings for ventilation than would be found in an oriental dungeon, where the tyrant expected his prisoner to die by inches. What would we think of *a house* where the windows could not be opened? Would any of you hire such a dwelling? Yet Gothic architecture and silly pride make many persons renounce the wholesome sash window for little holes in the ceiling, or bird traps in the windows, and so places are made far less comfortable than Nebuchadnezzar's furnace was to Shadrach, Meshach, and Abednego. Provided all such chapels were properly insured, I could not pray for their preservation from fire. Even where the windows will open they are often kept closed by the month together, and from Sunday to Sunday the impure atmosphere is unchanged. This ought not to be endured. I know some people do not notice such things, and I have heard it remarked that foxes are not killed by the stench of their own holes; but I am not a fox, and bad air makes me dull, and my hearers dull too. A gust of fresh air through the building might be to the people the next best thing to the gospel itself; at least it would put them into a fit frame of mind to receive the truth. Take trouble on week days to remove the hindrance arising from foul air. In my former chapel in Park Street I mentioned to my deacons several times my opinion that the upper panes of the iron-framed windows had better be taken out, as the windows were not made to open. I mentioned this several times, and nothing came of it; but it providentially happened one Monday that somebody removed most of those panes in a masterly manner, almost as well as if they had been taken out by a glazier. There was considerable consternation, and much conjecture as to who had committed the crime, and I proposed that a reward of five pounds should be offered for the discovery of the offender, who when found should receive the amount as a present. The reward was not forthcoming, and therefore I have not felt it to be my duty to inform against the individual. I trust none of you will suspect *me*, for if you do I shall have to confess that I have walked with the stick which let the oxygen into that stifling structure.

Sometimes the manners of our people are inimical to attention; they are not in the habit of attending; they attend the chapel but do not attend to the preacher. They are accustomed to look round at every one who enters the place, and they come in at all times, sometimes with much stamping, squeaking of boots, and banging of doors. I was preaching once to a people who continually looked round, and I adopted the expedient of saying, "Now, friends, as it is so very interesting to you to know who comes in, and it disturbs me so very much for you to look round, I will, if you like, describe each one as he comes in, so that you may sit and look at me, and keep up at least a show of decency." I described one gentleman who came in, who happened to be a friend whom I could depict without offence, as "a very respectable gentleman who had just taken his hat off," and so on; and after that one attempt I found it was not necessary to describe any more, because they felt shocked at what I was doing, and I assured them that I was much more shocked that they should render it necessary for me to reduce their conduct to such an absurdity. It cured them for the time being, and I hope for ever, much to their pastor's joy.

We will now suppose that this is set right. You have let the foul air out of the place, and reformed the manners of the people. What next? *In order to get attention, the first golden rule is, always say something worth hearing.* Most persons possess an instinct which leads them to desire to hear a good thing. They have a similar instinct, also, which you had better take note of, namely, that which prevents their seeing the good of attentively listening to mere words. It is not a severe criticism to say that there are ministers whose words stand in a very large proportion to their thoughts. In fact, their words hide their thoughts, if they have any. They pour out heaps of chaff, and, perhaps, there may be somewhere or other an oat or two, but it would be hard to say where. Congregations will not long attend to words, words, words, words, and nothing else. Amongst the commandments I am not aware of one which runs thus: "Thou shalt not be verbose," but it may be comprehended under the command, "Thou shalt not steal;" for it is a fraud upon your hearers to give them words instead of spiritual food. "In the multitude of words there wanteth not sin," even in the best preacher. Give your hearers something which they can treasure up and remember; something likely to be useful to them, the best matter from the best of places, solid doctrine from the divine Word. Give them manna fresh from the skies; not the same thing over and over again, in the same form *ad nauseam*, like workhouse bread cut into the same shape all the year round. Give them something striking, something that a man might get up in the middle of the night to hear, and which is worth his walking fifty miles to listen to. You are quite capable of doing that. *Do it,* brethren. Do it continually, and you will have all the attention you can desire.

Let the good matter which you give them be very clearly arranged. There is a great deal in that. It is possible to heap up a vast mass of good things all in a muddle. Ever since the day I was sent to shop with a basket, and purchased a pound of tea, a quarter-of-a-pound of mustard, and three pounds of rice, and on my way home saw a pack of hounds and felt it necessary to follow them over hedge and ditch (as I always did when I was a boy), and found when I reached home that all the goods were amalgamated—tea, mustard, and rice— into one awful mess, I have understood the necessity of packing up my subjects in good stout parcels, bound round with the thread of my discourse; and this makes me keep to firstly, secondly, and thirdly, however unfashionable that method may now be. People will not drink your mustardy tea, nor will they enjoy muddled-up sermons, in which you cannot tell head from tail, because they have neither, but are like Mr. Bright's Skye terrier, whose head and tail were both alike. Put the truth before men in a logical, orderly manner, so that they can easily remember it, and they will the more readily receive it.

Be sure, moreover, to speak plainly; because, however excellent your matter, if a man does not comprehend it, it can be of no use to him; you might as well have spoken to him in the language of Kamskatka as in your own tongue, if you use phrases that are quite out of his line, and modes of expression which are not suitable to his mind. Go up to his level if he is a poor man; go down to his understanding if he is an educated person. You smile at my contorting the terms in that manner, but I think there is more going up in being plain to the illiterate, than there is in being refined for the polite; at any rate, it is the more difficult of the two, and most like the Saviour's mode of speech. It is wise to walk in a path where your auditors can accompany you, and not to mount the high horse and ride over their heads. Our Lord and Master was the King of preachers, and yet He never was above anybody's comprehension, except so far as the grandeur and glory of His matter were concerned; His words and utterances were such that He spake like "the holy child Jesus." Let your hearts indite a good matter, clearly arranged and plainly put, and you are pretty sure to gain the ear, and so the heart.

Attend also to your manner of address; aim in that at the promotion of attention. And here I should say, as a rule do not read your sermons. There have been a few readers who have exercised great power, as, for instance, Dr. Chalmers, who could not have had a more attentive audience had he been extemporising; but then I do not suppose that we are equal to Dr. Chalmers: men of such eminence may read if they prefer it, but for us there is "a more excellent way." The best reading I have ever heard has tasted of paper, and has stuck in my throat. I have not relished it, for my digestion is not good enough to dissolve foolscap. It is better to do without the manuscript, even if you are driven to recite. It is best of all if you need neither to recite nor to read. If you must read, mind that you do it to perfection. Be the very best of readers, and you had need to be if you would secure attention.

Here let me say, *if you would be listened to, do not extemporise in the emphatic sense,* for that is as bad as reading, or perhaps worse, unless the manuscript was written extemporaneously; I mean without previous study. Do not go into the pulpit and say the first thing that comes to hand, for the uppermost thing with most men is mere froth. Your people need discourses which have been prayed over and laboriously prepared. People do not want raw food; it must be cooked and made ready for them. We must give out of our very souls, in the words which naturally suggest themselves, the matter which has been as thoroughly prepared by us as it possibly could have been by a sermon-writer; indeed, it should be even better prepared, if we would speak well. The best method is, in my judgment, that in which the man does not extemporise the matter, but extemporises the words; the language comes to him at the moment, but the theme has been well thought out, and like a master in Israel he speaks of that which he knows, and testifies of what he has seen.

In order to get attention, make your manner as pleasing as it can possibly be. Do not, for instance, indulge in monotones. Vary your voice continually. Vary your speed as well—dash as rapidly as a lightning flash, and anon, travel forward in quiet majesty. Shift your accent, move your emphasis, and avoid sing-song. Vary the tone; use the bass sometimes, and let the thunders roll within; at other times speak as you ought to do generally—from the lips, and let your speech be conversational. Anything for a change. Human nature craves for variety, and God grants it in nature, providence and grace; let us have it in sermons also. I shall not, however, dwell much upon this, because preachers have been known to arouse and sustain attention by their matter alone, when their mode of speech has been very imperfect. If Richard Sibbes, the Puritan, were here this afternoon,

I would guarantee him fixed attention to anything that he used to say, and yet he stammered dreadfully. One of his contemporaries says he *Sib*-ilated, he lisped and hissed so much. We need not look far for instances in modern pulpits, for there are too many of them; but we may remember that Moses was slow of speech, and yet every ear was attent to his words; probably Paul also laboured under a similar infirmity, for his speech was said to be contemptible; of this, however, we are not sure, for it was only the criticism of his enemies. Paul's power in the churches was very great, and yet he was not always able to maintain attention when his sermon was long, for at least one hearer went to sleep under him with serious result. Manner is not everything. Still, if you have gathered good matter, it is a pity to convey it meanly; a king should not ride in a dust-cart; the glorious doctrines of grace should not be slovenly delivered. Right royal truths should ride in a chariot of gold. Bring forth the noblest of your milk-white steeds, and let the music sound forth melodiously from the silver trumpets, as truth rides through the streets. If people do not attend, do not let them find excuses in our faulty utterance. If, however, we cannot mend in this respect let us be the more diligent to make up for it by the richness of our matter, and on all occasions let us do our very best.

As a rule, *do not make the introduction too long.* It is always a pity to build a great porch to a little house. An excellent Christian woman once heard John Howe, and, as he took up an hour in his preface, her observation was, that the dear good man was so long a time in laying the cloth, that she lost her appetite : she did not think there would be any dinner after all. Spread your table quickly, and have done with the clatter of the knives and the plates. You may have seen a certain edition of Doddridge's *Rise and Progress of Religion in the Soul,* with an introductory essay by John Foster. The essay is both bigger and better than the book and deprives Doddridge of the chance of being read. Is not this preposterous? Avoid this error in your own productions. I prefer to make the introduction of my sermon very like that of the town-crier, who rings his bell and cries, "Oh, yes! Oh, yes! This is to give notice," merely to let people know that he has news for them, and wants them to listen. To do that, the introduction should have something striking in it. It is well to fire a startling shot as the signal gun to clear the decks for action. Do not start at the full pitch and tension of your mind, but yet in such way that all will be led to expect a good time. Do not make your exordium a pompous introduction into nothing, but a step to something better still. Be alive at the very commencement.

In preaching, *do not repeat yourselves.* I used to hear a divine who had a habit, after he had uttered about a dozen sentences, of saying, "As I have already observed," or, "I repeat what I before remarked."

Well, good soul, as there was nothing particular in what he had said, the repetition only revealed the more clearly the nakedness of the land. If it was very good, and you said it forcibly, why go over it again? And if it was a feeble affair, why exhibit it a second time? Occasionally, of course, the repetition of a few sentences may be very telling; anything may be good occasionally, and yet be very vicious as a habit. Who wonders that people do not listen the first time when they know it is all to come over again?

Yet further, do not repeat the same idea over and over again in other words. Let there be something fresh in each sentence. Be not for ever hammering away at the same nail: yours is a large Bible; permit the people to enjoy its length and breadth. And, brethren, do not think it necessary or important every time you preach to give a complete summary of theology, or a formal digest of doctrines, after the manner of Dr. Gill—not that I would discredit or speak a word against Dr. Gill—his method is admirable for a body of divinity, or a commentary, but not suitable for preaching. I know a divine whose sermons whenever they are printed read like theological summaries, more fitted for a classroom than for a pulpit—they fall flat on the public ear. Our hearers do not want the bare bones of technical definition, but meat and flavour. Definitions and differences are all very well; but when they are the staple of a sermon they remind us of the young man whose discourse was made up of various important distinctions. Upon this performance an old deacon observed that there was one distinction which he had omitted, namely, the distinction between meat and bones. If preachers do not make that distinction, all their other distinctions will not bring them much distinction.

In order to maintain attention, *avoid being too long.* An old preacher used to say to a young man who preached an hour,—"My dear friend, I do not care what else you preach about, but I wish you would always preach *about* forty minutes." We ought seldom to go much beyond that—forty minutes, or, say, three-quarters of an hour. If a fellow cannot say all he has to say in that time, when will he say it? But somebody said he liked "to do justice to his subject." Well, but ought he not to do justice to his people, or, at least, have a little mercy upon them, and not keep them too long? The subject will not complain of you, but the people will. In some country places, in the afternoon especially, the farmers have to milk their cows, and one farmer bitterly complained to me about a young man—I think from this College—"Sir, he ought to have given over at four o'clock, but he kept on till half-past, and there were all my cows waiting to be milked! *How would he have liked it if he had been a cow?*" There was a great deal of sense in that question. The Society for the Prevention of Cruelty to Animals ought to have prosecuted that young sinner. How can farmers hear to profit when they have cows-on-the-brain? The mother feels morally certain during that extra ten minutes of your sermon that the baby is crying, or the fire is out, and she cannot and will not give her heart to your ministrations. You are keeping her ten minutes longer than she bargained for, and she looks upon it as a piece of injustice on your part. There is a kind of moral compact between you and your congregation that you will not weary them more than an hour-and-a-half, and if you keep them longer, it amounts to an infraction of a treaty and a piece of practical dishonesty of which you ought not to be guilty. Brevity is a virtue within the reach of all of us; do not let us lose the opportunity of gaining the credit which it brings. If you ask me how you may shorten your sermons, I should say, *study them better*. Spend more time in the study that you may need less in the pulpit. We are generally longest when we have least to say. A man with a great deal of well-prepared matter will probably not exceed forty minutes; when he has less to say he will go on for fifty minutes, and when he has absolutely nothing he will need an hour to say it in. Attend to these minor things and they will help to retain attention.

If you want to have the attention of your people—to have it thoroughly and always, *it can only be accomplished by their being led by the Spirit of God into an elevated and devout state of mind.* If your people are teachable, prayerful, active, earnest, devout, they will come up to the house of God on purpose to get a blessing. They will take their seats prayerfully, asking God to speak to them through you; they will remain on the watch for every word, and will not weary. They will have an appetite for the gospel, for they know the sweetness of the heavenly manna, and they will be eager to gather their appointed portions. No man will ever have a congregation to preach to which surpasses my own in this respect. Indeed, those with whom the preacher is most at home are usually the best hearers for him. It is comparatively easy to me to preach at the Tabernacle; my people come on purpose to hear something, and their expectation helps to fulfil itself. If they would hear another preacher with the same expectancy, I believe they would generally be satisfied; though there are exceptions.

When the preacher first settles, he cannot expect that his congregation will give him that solemn earnest attention which those obtain who stand up like fathers among their own children, endeared to their people by a thousand memories, and esteemed for age and experience. Our whole life must be such as to add weight to our words, so that in after years we shall be able to wield the invincible eloquence of a long-sustained character, and obtain, not merely the attention, but the affectionate veneration of our flock. If by our prayers and tears and labours our people become spiritually healthy, we need not fear that we shall lose their attention. A people hungering after righteousness, and a minister anxious to feed their souls, will act in sweetest harmony with each other when their common theme is the Word of the Lord.

If you need another direction for winning attention, I should say, *be interested yourself,* and you will interest others. There is more in those words than there seems to be, and so I will follow a custom which I just now condemned, and repeat the sentence,—be interested yourself, and you will interest other people. Your subject must weigh so much upon your own mind that you dedicate all your faculties at their best to the deliverance of your soul concerning it; and then when your hearers see that the topic has engrossed you, it will by degrees engross them.

Do you wonder that people do not attend to a man who does not feel that he has anything important to say? Do you wonder that they do not listen with all their ears when a man does not speak with all his heart? Do you marvel that their thoughts ramble to subjects which are real to them when they find that the preacher is wasting time over matters which he treats as if they were fiction? Romaine used to say it was well to understand the *art* of preaching, but infinitely better to know the *heart* of preaching; and in that saying there is no little weight. The *heart* of preaching, the throwing of the soul into it, the earnestness which pleads as for life itself, is half the battle as to gaining attention. At the same time, you cannot hold men's minds in rapt attention by mere earnestness if you have nothing to say. People will not stand at their doors for ever to hear a fellow beat a drum; they will come out to see what he is at, but when they find that it is much ado about nothing, they will slam the door and go in again, as much as to say, "You have taken us in and we do not like it." Have something to say, and say it earnestly, and the congregation will be at your feet.

It may be superfluous to remark that for the mass of our people it is well that *there should be a goodly number of illustrations in our discourses.* We have the example of our Lord for that: and most of the greatest preachers have abounded in similes, metaphors, allegories, and anecdotes. But beware of overdoing this business. I read the other day the diary of a German lady who has been converted from Lutheranism to our faith, and she speaks of a certain village where she lives: "There is a mission-station here, and young men come down to preach to us. I do not wish to find fault with these young gentlemen, but they tell us a great many very pretty little stories, and I do not think there is much else in what they say. Also I have heard some of their little stories before, therefore they do not so much interest me, as they would do if they would tell us some good doctrine out of the Scriptures." The same thing has no doubt crossed many other minds. "Pretty stories" are all very well, but it will never do to rely upon them as the great attraction of a sermon. Moreover, take warning concerning certain of these "pretty little stories," for their day is over and gone; the poor things are worn threadbare and ought to go into the rag-bag. I have heard some of them so many times, that I could tell them myself, but there is no need. From stock anecdotes may both ourselves and our hearers be mercifully delivered. Ancient jests sicken us when witlings retail them as their own ideas, and anecdotes to which our great-grandfathers listened have much the same effect upon the mind. Beware of those extremely popular compilations of illustrations which are in every Sunday-school teacher's hand, for nobody will thank you for repeating what everybody already knows by heart: if you tell anecdotes let them have some degree of freshness and originality; keep your eyes open, and gather flowers from the garden and the field with your hands; they will be far more acceptable than withered specimens borrowed from other men's bouquets, however beautiful those may once have been. Illustrate richly and aptly, but not so much with parables imported from foreign sources as with apt similes growing out of the subject itself. Do not, however, think the illustration everything; it is the window, but of what use is the light which it admits if you have nothing for the light to reveal? Garnish your dishes, but remember that the joint is the main point to consider, not the garnishing. Real instruction must be given and solid doctrine taught, or you will find your imagery pall upon your hearers, and they will pine for spiritual meat.

In your sermons *cultivate what Father Taylor calls "the surprise power."* There is a great deal of force in that for winning attention. Do not say what everybody expected you would say. Keep your sentences out of ruts. If you have already said, "Salvation is all of grace" do not always add, "and not by human merit," but vary it and say, "Salvation is all of grace; self-righteousness has not a corner to hide its head in." I fear I cannot recall one of Mr. Taylor's sentences so as to do it justice, but it was something like this: "Some of you make no advance in the divine life, because you go forward a little way and then you float back again: just like a vessel on a tidal river which goes down with the stream just far enough to be carried back again on the return tide. So you make good progress for a while, and then all of a sudden"—what did he say?—"you hitch up in some muddy creek." Did he not also repeat us a speech to this effect,— "He felt sure that if they were converted they would walk uprightly and keep their bullocks out of their neighbour's corn."? Occasional resorts to this system of surprise will keep an audience in a state of proper expectancy. I sat last year about this time on the beach at Mentone by the Mediterranean Sea. The waves were very gently rising and falling, for there is little or no tide, and the wind was still.

The waves crept up languidly one after another, and I took little heed of them, though they were just at my feet. Suddenly, as if seized with a new passion, the sea sent up one far-reaching billow, which drenched me thoroughly. Quiet as I had been before, you can readily conceive how quickly I was on my feet, and how speedily my day-dreaming ended. I observed to a ministering brother at my side, "This shows us how to preach, to wake people up we must astonish them with something they were not looking for." Brethren, take them at unawares. Let your thunderbolt drop out of a clear sky. When all is calm and bright let the tempest rush up, and by contrast make its terrors all the greater. Remember, however, that nothing will avail if you go to sleep yourself while you are preaching. Is that possible? Oh, possible! It is done every Sunday. Many ministers are more than half-asleep all through the sermon; indeed, they never were awake at any time, and probably never will be unless a cannon should be fired off near their ear: tame phrases, hackneyed expressions, and dreary monotones make the staple of their discourses, and they wonder that the people are so drowsy: I confess I do not.

A very useful help in securing attention is a *pause*. Pull up short every now and then, and the passengers on your coach will wake up. The miller goes to sleep while the mill wheels revolve; but if by some means or other the grinding ceases, the good man starts and cries, "What now?" On a sultry summer's day, if nothing will keep off the drowsy feeling, be very short, sing more than usual, or call on a brother or two to pray. A minister who saw that the people would sleep, sat down and observed, "I saw you were all resting, and I thought I would rest too." Andrew Fuller had barely commenced a sermon when he saw the people going to sleep. He said, "Friends, friends, friends, this won't do. I have thought sometimes when you were asleep that it was my fault, but now you are asleep before I begin, and it must be your fault. Pray wake up and give me an opportunity of doing you some good." Just so. Know how to pause. Make a point of interjecting arousing parentheses of quietude. Speech is silver, but silence is golden when hearers are inattentive. Keep on, on, on, on, on, with commonplace matter and monotonous tone, and you are rocking the cradle, and deeper slumbers will result; give the cradle a jerk, and sleep will flee.

I suggest again that in order to secure attention all through a discourse we must *make the people feel that they have an interest in what we are saying to them.* This is, in fact, a most essential point, because nobody sleeps while he expects to hear something to his advantage. I have heard of some very strange things, but I never did hear of a person going to sleep while a will was being read in which he expected a legacy, neither have I heard of a prisoner going to sleep while the judge was summing up, and his life was hanging in jeopardy.

Self-interest quickens attention. Preach upon practical themes, pressing, present, personal matters, and you will secure an earnest hearing.

It will be well to *prevent attendants traversing the aisles* to meddle with gas or candles, or to distribute plates for collections, or to open windows. Deacons and sextons trotting over the place are a torture never to be patiently endured, and should be kindly, but decidedly, requested to suspend their perambulations.

Late attendance, also, needs remedying, and our gentlest reasonings and expostulations must be brought to bear upon it. I feel sure that the devil has a hand in many disturbances in the congregation, which jar upon our nerves, and distract our thoughts: the banging of a pew door, the sharp fall of a stick on the floor, or the cry of a child, are all convenient means in the hands of the evil one for hindering us in our work; we may, therefore, very justifiably beg our people to preserve our usefulness from this class of assaults.

I gave you a golden rule for securing attention at the commencement, namely, always say something worth hearing; I will now give you a diamond rule, and conclude. *Be yourself clothed with the Spirit of God,* and then no question about attention or non-attention will arise. Come fresh from the closet and from communion with God, to speak to men for God with all your heart and soul, and you must have power over them. You have golden chains in your mouth which will hold them fast. When God speaks men must listen; and though He may speak through a poor feeble man like themselves, the majesty of the truth will compel them to regard His voice. Supernatural power must be your reliance. We say to you, perfect yourselves in oratory, cultivate all the fields of knowledge, make your sermon mentally and rhetorically all it ought to be (you ought to do no less in such a service), but at the same time remember, "it is not by might, nor by power," that men are regenerated or sanctified, but "by my Spirit, saith the Lord." Are you not conscious sometimes of being clad with zeal as with a cloak, and filled to the full with the Spirit of God? At such times you have had a hearing people, and, ere long, a believing people; but if you are not thus endowed with power from on high, you are to them no more than a musician who plays upon a goodly instrument, or sings a sweet song with a clear voice, reaching the ear but not the heart. If you do not touch the heart you will soon weary the ear. Clothe yourself, then, with the power of the Spirit of God, and preach to men as those who must soon give an account, and who desire that their account may not be painful to their people and grievous to themselves, but that it may be to the glory of God.

Brethren, may the Lord be with you, while you go forth in His name and cry, "He that hath ears to hear, let him hear."

X

The Faculty of Impromptu Speech

WE ARE not about to discuss the question as to whether sermons should be written and read, or written, committed to memory and repeated, or whether copious notes should be employed, or no notes at all. Neither of these is the subject now under consideration, although we may incidentally allude to each of them, but we are now to speak of extemporaneous speech in its truest and most thorough form—speech impromptu, without special preparation, without notes or immediate forethought.

Our first observation shall be that *we would not recommend any man to attempt preaching in this style as a general rule.* If he did so, he would succeed, we think, most certainly, in producing a vacuum in his meeting-house; his gifts of dispersion would be clearly manifested. Unstudied thoughts coming from the mind without previous research, without the subjects in hand having been investigated at all, must be of a very inferior quality, even from the most superior men; and as none of us would have the effrontery to glorify ourselves as men of genius or wonders of erudition, I fear that our unpremeditated thoughts upon most subjects would not be remarkably worthy of attention. Churches are not to be held together except by an instructive ministry; a mere filling up of time with oratory will not suffice. Everywhere men ask to be fed, really fed. Those new-fangled religionists, whose public worship consists of the prelections of any brother who chooses to jump up and talk, notwithstanding their flattering inducements to the ignorant and garrulous, usually dwindle away, and die out; because even men with the most violently crotchety views, who conceive it to be the mind of the Spirit that every member of the body should be a mouth, soon grow impatient of hearing other people's nonsense, though delighted to dispense their own; while the mass of the good people grow weary of prosy ignorance, and return to the churches from which they were led aside, or would return if their pulpits were well supplied with solid teaching. Even Quakerism, with all its excellences, has scarcely been able to survive the poverty of thought and doctrine displayed in many of its assemblies by impromptu orators. The method of unprepared ministrations is practically a failure, and theoretically unsound. The Holy Spirit has made no promise to supply spiritual food to the saints by an impromptu ministry. He will never do for us what we can do for ourselves. If we can study and do not, if we can have a studious ministry and will not, we have no right to call in a divine agent to make up the deficits of our idleness or eccentricity. The god of providence has promised to feed his people with temporal food; but if we came together to a banquet, and no one had prepared a single dish, because all had faith in the Lord that food would be given in the selfsame hour, the festival would not be eminently satisfactory, but folly would be rebuked by hunger; as, indeed, it is in the case of spiritual banquets of the impromptu kind, only men's spiritual receptacles are hardly such powerful orators as their stomachs. Gentlemen, do not attempt, as a rule, to follow a system of things which is so generally unprofitable that the few exceptions only prove the rule. All sermons ought to be well considered and prepared by the preacher; and, as much as possible, every minister should, with much prayer for heavenly guidance, enter fully into his subject, exert all his mental faculties in original thinking, and gather together all the information within his reach. Viewing the whole matter from all quarters, the preacher should think it out, get it well masticated and digested; and having first fed upon the word himself should then prepare the like nutriment for others. Our sermons should be our mental life-blood —the out-flow of our intellectual and spiritual vigour; or, to change the figure, they should be diamonds well cut and well set—precious, intrinsically, and bearing the marks of labour. God forbid that we should offer to the Lord that which costs us nothing.

Very strongly do I warn all of you against reading your sermons, but I recommend, as a most healthful exercise, and as a great aid towards attaining extemporising power, the frequent writing of them. Those of us who write a great deal in other forms, for the press, etc., may not so much require that exercise; but if you do not use the pen in other ways, you will be wise to write at least some of your sermons, and revise them with great care. Leave them at home afterwards, but still write them out, that you may be preserved from a slipshod style. M. Bautain in his admirable work on extempore speaking, remarks, "You will never be capable of speaking properly in public unless you acquire such mastery of your own thought as to be able to decompose it into its parts, to analyse it into its elements, and then, at need, to re-compose, re-gather, and concentrate it again by a synthetical process. Now this analysis of the idea, which displays it, as it were, before the eyes of the mind, is well executed only by writing. The pen is the scalpel which dissects the thoughts, and never, except when you write down what you behold internally, can you succeed in clearly discerning all that is contained in a conception, or in obtaining its well-marked scope. You then understand yourself, and make others understand you."

We do not recommend the plan of learning sermons by heart, and repeating them from memory; that is both a wearisome exercise of an inferior power of the mind and an indolent neglect of other and superior faculties. The most arduous and commendable plan is to store your mind with matter upon the subject of discourse, and then to deliver yourself with appropriate words which suggest themselves at the time. This is not extemporaneous preaching; the words are extemporal, as I think they always should be, but the thoughts are the result of research and study. Only thoughtless persons think this to be easy; it is at once the most laborious and the most efficient mode of preaching, and it has virtues of its own of which I cannot now speak particularly, since it would lead us away from the point in hand.

Our subject is the faculty of pure, unmixed, genuinely extemporaneous speaking, and to this let us return. This power is extremely useful, and in most cases is, with a little diligence, to be acquired. It is possessed by many, yet not by so many that I shall be incorrect if I say that the gift is rare. The *improvisatori* of Italy possessed the power of impromptu speech to such an extent, that their extemporaneous verses upon subjects suggested on the spot by the spectators, frequently amounted to hundreds and even thousands of lines. They would produce whole tragedies as spontaneously as springs bubble up with water, and rhyme away by the half-hour and the hour together, on the spur of the moment, and perhaps also on the spur of a little Italian wine. Their printed works seldom rise above mediocrity, and yet one of them, Perfetti, gained the laurel crown which had been awarded only to Petrarch and Tasso. Many of them at this hour produce off-hand verses which are equal to the capacities of their hearers, and secure their breathless attention. Why cannot we acquire just such a power in prose? We shall not be able, I suppose, to produce verses, nor need we desire the faculty. Many of you have no doubt versified a little (as which of us in some weak moment has not?) but we have put away childish things now that the sober prose of life and death, and heaven and hell, and perishing sinners, demands all our thought.[1]

Many *lawyers* possess the gift of extemporaneous speech in a high degree. They should have some virtues! Some weeks ago a wretched being was indicted for the horrible crime of libelling a lawyer; it is well for him that I was not his judge, for had such a difficult and atrocious crime been fairly brought home to him, I would have delivered him over to be cross-examined during the term of his natural life, hoping for mercy's sake that it might be a brief one.

---

[1] Mr. Wesley thought it needful to say, "Sing no hymns of your own composing." The habit of giving out rhymes of their own concoction was rife among the divines of his day: it is to be hoped it is now utterly extinct.

But the gentlemen of the bar are many of them most ready speakers, and as you will clearly see, they must to a considerable degree be extemporaneous speakers too, because it would be impossible for them always to foresee the line of argument which the evidence, or the temper of the judge, or the pleadings on the other side would require. However well a case may be prepared, points must and will arise requiring an active mind and a fluent tongue to deal with them. Indeed, I have been astonished to observe the witty, sharp, and in every way appropriate replies which counsel will throw off without forethought in our courts of law. What a barrister can do in advocating the cause of his client, you and I should surely be able to do in the cause of God. The bar must not be allowed to excel the pulpit. We will be as expert in intellectual arms as any men, be they who they may, God helping us.

Certain Members of the House of Commons have exercised the faculty of extemporaneous speaking with great results. Usually, of all tasks of hearing, the most miserable is that of listening to one of the common ruck of speakers from the House of Lords and Commons. Let it be proposed that when capital punishment is abolished, those who are found guilty of murder shall be compelled to listen to a selection of the dreariest parliamentary orators. The members of the Royal Humane Society forbid. Yet in the House some of the Members are able to speak extemporaneously, and to speak well. I should imagine that some of the finest things which have been said by John Bright, and Gladstone, and Disraeli, were altogether what Southey would call jets from the great Geyser when the spring is in full play. Of course, their long orations upon the Budget, the Reform Bill, and so on, were elaborated to the highest degree by previous manipulation; but many of their briefer speeches have, no doubt, been the offspring of the hour, and yet have an amazing amount of power about them. Shall the representatives of the nation attain an expertness of speech beyond the representatives of the court of heaven? Brethren, covet earnestly this good gift, and go about to win it.

You are all convinced that the ability which we are considering must be a priceless possession for a minister. Did we hear a single heart whisper, "I wish I had it, for then I should have no need to study so arduously"? Ah! then you must not have it, you are unworthy of the boon, and unfit to be trusted with it. If you seek this gift as a pillow for an idle head, you will be much mistaken; for the possession of this noble power will involve you in a vast amount of labour in order to increase and even to retain it. It is like the magic lamp in the fable, which would not shine except it was well rubbed, and became a mere dim globe as soon as the rubbing ceased. What the sluggard desires for the sake of ease, we may, however, covet for the best of reasons.

Occasionally one has heard or read of men agreeing, by way of bravado, to preach upon texts given them at the time in the pulpit, or in the vestry: such vainglorious displays are disgusting, and border on profanity. As well might we have exhibitions of juggling on the Sabbath as such mountebankism of oratory. Our talents are given us for far other ends. Such a prostitution of gift I trust you will never be allowed to perpetrate. Feats of speech are well enough in a debating club, but in the ministry they are abominable even when a Bossuet lends himself to them.

The power of impromptu speech is invaluable, because it enables a man on the spur of the moment, in an emergency, to deliver himself with propriety. These emergencies will arise. Accidents will occur in the best regulated assemblies. Singular events may turn the premeditated current of your thoughts quite aside. You will see clearly that the subject selected would be inopportune, and you will as a wise man drift into something else without demur. When the old road is closed, and there is no help for it but to make a new way for the chariot, unless you are qualified to drive the horses over a ploughed field as well as along the macadamised road on which you hoped to travel, you will find yourself off the coach-box, and mischief will befall the company. It is a great acquisition to be able at a public meeting, when you have heard the speeches of your brethren, and believe that they have been too frivolous, or it may be, on the other hand, too dull, without any allusions to them, quietly to counteract the mischief, and lead the assembly into a more profitable line of thought. This gift may be of the utmost importance in the church-meeting, where business may arise which it would be difficult to foresee. All the troublers of Israel are not yet dead. Achan was stoned, and his wife, and his children, but others of his family must have escaped, for the race has certainly been perpetuated, and needs to be dealt with discreetly and vigorously. In some churches certain noisy men will rise and speak, and when they have done so, it is of great importance that the pastor should readily and convincingly reply, lest bad impressions should remain. A pastor who goes to the church-meeting in the spirit of his Master, feeling sure that in reliance upon the Holy Spirit he is quite able to answer any untoward spirit, sits at ease, keeps his temper, rises in esteem on each occasion, and secures a quiet church; but the unready brother is flurried, probably gets into a passion, commits himself, and inherits a world of sorrow. Besides this, a man may be called upon to preach at a moment's notice, through the non-arrival of the expected minister, or his sudden sickness; at a public meeting one may feel stirred to speak where silence had been resolved upon; and at any form of religious exercise emergencies may arise which will render impromptu speech as precious as the gold of Ophir.

The gift is valuable—how is it to be obtained? The question leads us to remark that *some men will never obtain it.* There must be a natural adaptedness for extemporaneous speech; even as for the poetic art: a poet is born, not made. "Art may develop and perfect the talent of a speaker, but cannot produce it." All the rules of rhetoric, and all the artifices of oratory cannot make a man eloquent; it is a gift from heaven, and where it is withheld it cannot be obtained. This "gift of utterance," as we call it, is born with some people, inherited probably from the mother's side.[1] To others the gift is denied; their confirmation of jaw, and yet more their confirmation of brain, never will allow of their becoming fluent and ready speakers. They may, perhaps, make moderate stutterers and slow deliverers of sober truth, but they can never be impromptu orators; unless they should rival Methuselah in age, and then perhaps on the Darwinian theory, which educes an Archbishop of Canterbury from an oyster, they might develop into speakers. If there be not a natural gift of oratory a brother may attain to a respectable post in other departments, but he is not likely to shine as a bright particular star in extemporary speech.

If a man would speak without any present study, he must usually study much. This is a paradox perhaps, but its explanation lies upon the surface. If I am a miller, and I have a sack brought to my door, and am asked to fill that sack with good fine flour within the next five minutes, the only way in which I can do it, is by keeping the flour-bin of my mill always full, so that I can at once open the mouth of the sack, fill it, and deliver it. I do not happen to be grinding at that time, and so far the delivery is extempory; but I have been grinding before, and so have the flour to serve out to the customer. So, brethren, you must have been grinding, or you will not have the flour. You will not be able to extemporise good thinking unless you have been in the habit of thinking and feeding your mind with abundant and nourishing food. Work hard at every available moment. Store your minds very richly, and then, like merchants with crowded warehouses, you will have goods ready for your customers, and having arranged your good things upon the shelves of your mind, you will be able to hand them down at any time without the laborious process of going to market, sorting, folding, and preparing. I do not believe that any man can be successful in continuously maintaining the gift of extemporaneous speech, except by ordinarily using far more labour than is usual with those who write and commit their discourses to memory. Take it as a rule without exception, that to be able to over-flow spontaneously you must be full.

The collection of a fund of ideas and expressions is exceedingly

---

[1] "There are men organised to speak well, as there are birds organised to sing well, bees to make honey, and beavers to build."—M. Bautain.

helpful. There is a wealth and a poverty in each of these respects. He who has much information, well arranged, and thoroughly understood, with which he is intimately familiar, will be able like some prince of fabulous wealth to scatter gold right and left among the crowd. To you, gentlemen, an intimate acquaintance with the Word of God, with the inward spiritual life, with the great problems of time and eternity will be indispensable. Out of the abundance of the heart the mouth speaketh. Accustom yourselves to heavenly meditations, search the Scriptures, delight yourselves in the law of the Lord, and you need not fear to speak of things which you have tasted and handled of the good word of God. Men may well be slow of speech in discussing themes beyond the range of their experience; but you, warmed with love towards the King, and enjoying fellowship with him, will find your hearts inditing a good matter, and your tongues will be as the pens of ready writers. Get at the roots of spiritual truths by an experimental acquaintance with them, so shall you with readiness expound them to others. Ignorance of theology is no rare thing. in our pulpits, and the wonder is not that so few men are extempore speakers, but that so many are, when theologians are so scarce. We shall never have great preachers till we have great divines. You cannot build a man-of-war out of a currant bush, nor can great soul-moving preachers be formed out of superficial students. If you would be fluent, that is to say flowing, be filled with all knowledge, and especially with the knowledge of Christ Jesus your Lord. But we remarked that a fund of expressions would be also of much help to the extempore speaker; and, truly, second only to a store of ideas is a rich vocabulary. Beauties of language, elegancies of speech, and above all forcible sentences are to be selected, remembered, and imitated. You are not to carry that gold pencil-case with you, and jot down every polysyllabic word which you meet with in your reading, so as to put it in your next sermon, but you are to know what words mean, to be able to estimate the power of a synonym, to judge the rhythm of a sentence, and to weigh the force of an expletive. You must be masters of words; they must be your genii, your angels, your thunderbolts, or your drops of honey. Mere word-gatherers are hoarders of oyster shells, bean husks, and apple-parings; but to a man who has wide information and deep thought, words are baskets of silver in which to serve up his apples of gold. See to it that you have a good team of words to draw the wagon of your thoughts.

I think, too, that a man who would speak well, extemporaneously, *must be careful to select a topic which he understands.* This is the main point. Ever since I have been in London, in order to get into the habit of speaking extemporaneously, I have never studied or prepared anything for the Monday evening prayer-meeting. I have all along selected that occasion as the opportunity for off-hand exhortation; but you will observe that I do not on such occasions select difficult expository topics or abstruse themes, but restrict myself to simple homely talk about the elements of our faith. When standing up on such occasions, one's mind makes a review, and enquires, "What subject has already taken up my thought during the day? What have I met with in my reading during the past week? What is most laid upon my heart at this hour? What is suggested by the hymns or the prayers?" It is of no use to rise before an assembly, and hope to be inspired upon subjects of which you know nothing; if you are so unwise, the result will be that as you know nothing you will probably say it, and the people will not be edified. But I do not see why a man cannot speak extemporaneously upon a subject which he fully understands. Any tradesman, well versed in his line of business, could explain it to you without needing to retire for meditation; and surely we ought to be equally as familiar with the first principles of our holy faith; we ought not to feel at a loss when called upon to speak upon topics which constitute the daily bread of our souls. I do not see what benefit is gained in such a case, by the mere manual labour of writing before speaking; because in so doing, a man would write extemporaneously, and extemporaneous writing is likely to be even feebler than extemporaneous speech. The gain of the writing lies in the opportunity of careful revision; but as able writers are able to express their thoughts correctly at the first, so also may able speakers. The thought of a man who finds himself upon his legs, dilating upon a theme with which he is familiar, may be very far from being his first thought; it may be the cream of his meditations warmed by the glow of his heart. He, having studied the subject well before, though not at that moment, may deliver himself most powerfully; whereas another man, sitting down to write, may only be penning his first ideas, which may be vague and vapid. Do not attempt to be impromptu then, unless you have well studied the theme—this paradox is a counsel of prudence. I remember to have been tried rather sharply upon one occasion, and had I not been versed in impromptu address, I know not how it would have sped with me. I was expected to preach in a certain chapel, and there was a crowded congregation, but I was not in time, being delayed by some blockade upon the railroad; so another minister went on with the service, and when I reached the place, all breathless with running, he was already preaching a sermon. Seeing me appear at the front door and pass up the aisle, he stopped and said, "There he is," and looking at me, he added, "I'll make way for you; come up and finish the sermon." I asked him what was the text and how far he had gone with it. He told me what the text was, and said he had just passed through the first head; without hesitation I took up the discourse at that point and finished the sermon, and I should be ashamed of any man here who could not have done the same, the circumstances being such as to make the task a remarkably easy one. In the first place the minister was my grandfather, and, in the second place, the text was—"By grace are ye saved, through faith, and that not of yourselves, it is the gift of God." He must have been a more foolish animal than that which Balaam rode, if, at such a juncture, he had not found a tongue. "By grace are ye saved," had been spoken of as indicating *the source* of salvation; who could not follow by describing the next clause— "through faith," as *the channel*? One did not need to study much to show that salvation is received by us through faith. Yet, on that occasion, I had a further trial; for when I had proceeded a little, and was warming to my work, a hand patted my back approvingly, and a voice said, "That's right—that's right; tell them that again, for fear they should forget it." Thereupon I repeated the truth, and a little further on, when I was becoming rather deeply experimental I was gently pulled by my coat-tail, and the old gentleman stood up in front and said, "Now, my grandson can tell you this as a theory, but I am here to bear witness to it as a matter of practical experience: I am older than he is, and I must give you my testimony as an old man." Then after having given us his personal experience, he said, "There, now, my grandson can preach the gospel a great deal better than I can, but he cannot preach a better gospel, can he?" Well, gentlemen, I can easily imagine that if I had not possessed some little power of extemporaneous speech upon that occasion, I might have been somewhat ruffled; but as it was, it came as naturally as if it had been pre-arranged.

The acquisition of another language affords a fine drilling for the practice of extempore speech. Brought into connection with the roots of words, and the rules of speech, and being compelled to note the differentia of the two languages, a man grows by degrees to be much at home with parts of speech, moods, tenses, and inflections; like a workman he becomes familiar with his tools, and handles them as everyday companions. I know of no better exercise than to translate with as much rapidity as possible a portion of Virgil or Tacitus, and then with deliberation to amend one's mistakes. Persons who know no better think all time thrown away which is spent upon the classics, but if it were only for the usefulness of such studies to the sacred orator, they ought to be retained in all our collegiate institutions. Who does not see that the perpetual comparison of the terms and idioms of two languages must aid facility of expression? Who does not see, moreover, that by this exercise the mind becomes able to appreciate refinements and subtleties of meaning, and so acquires the power of distinguishing between things that differ—a power essential to an expositor of the Word of God, and an extempore declarer of His truth. Learn, gentlemen, to put together, and unscrew all the machinery of language, mark every cog, and wheel, and bolt, and rod, and you will feel the more free to drive the engine, even at an express speed should emergencies demand it.

Every man who wishes to acquire this art must practise it. It was by slow degrees, as Burke says, that Charles Fox became the most brilliant and powerful debater that ever lived. He attributed his success to the resolution which he formed when very young, of speaking well or ill, at least once every night. "During five whole sessions," he used to say, "I spoke every night but one, and I regret only that I did not speak on that night too." At first he may do so with no other auditory than the chairs and books of his study, imitating the example of a gentleman who, upon applying for admission to this college, assured me that he had for two years practised himself in extempore preaching in his own room. Students living together might be of great mutual assistance by alternately acting the part of audience and speaker, with a little friendly criticism at the close of each attempt. Conversation, too, may be of essential service, if it be a matter of principle to make it solid and edifying. Thought is to be linked with speech; that is the problem; and it may assist a man in its solution, if he endeavours in his private musings to think aloud. So has this become habitual to me that I find it very helpful to be able, in private devotion, to pray with my voice; reading aloud is more beneficial to me than the silent process; and when I am mentally working out a sermon, it is a relief to me to speak to myself as the thoughts flow forth. Of course this only masters half the difficulty, and you must practise in public, in order to overcome the trepidation occasioned by the sight of an audience; but half way is a great part of a journey. Good impromptu speech is just the utterance of a practised thinker—a man of information, meditating on his legs, and allowing his thoughts to march through his mouth into the open air. Think aloud as much as you can when you are alone, and you will soon be on the high road to success in this matter. The discussion and debates in the class-room are of vital importance as a further step, and I would urge the more retiring brethren to take a part in them. The practice of calling upon you to speak upon a topic drawn at random from a bowl out of a wide selection has been introduced among you, and we must more frequently resort to it. What I condemned as a part of religious worship, we may freely use as a scholastic exercise among ourselves. It is calculated to try a man's readiness and self-command, and those who fail in it are probably as much benefited as those who succeed, for self-knowledge may be as useful to one as practice to another. If the discovery that you are as yet a bungler in oratory should drive you to severer study and more resolute endeavours, it may be the true path to ultimate eminence.

In addition to the practice commended, I must urge upon you the necessity of being *cool and confident*. As Sydney Smith says, "A great deal of talent is lost to the world for want of a little courage." This is not to be easily acquired by the young speaker. Cannot you young speakers sympathise with Blondin, the rope walker? Do you not sometimes feel when you are preaching as though you were walking on a rope high in the air, and do you not tremble and wonder whether you will reach the other end in safety? Sometimes when you have been flourishing that beautiful balancing pole, and watching the metaphorical spangles which flash poetry upon your audience, have you not been half regretful that you ever exposed yourself to such risks of sudden descent, or, to drop the figure, have you not wondered whether you would be able to conclude the sentence, or find a verb for the nominative, or an accusative for the verb? Everything depends upon your being cool and unflurried. Forebodings of failure, and fear of man, will ruin you. Go on, trusting in God, and all will be well. If you have made a blunder in grammar, and you are half inclined to go back to correct it, you will soon make another, and your hesitation will involve you as in a net. Let me whisper—for it is meant for your ear alone—it is always a bad thing to go back. If you make a verbal blunder, go on, and do not notice it. My father gave me a very good rule when I was learning to write, which I think of equal utility in learning to speak. He used to say: "When you are writing, if you make a mistake by misspelling a word, or by writing a wrong word, do not cross it out and make a mess of it, but see how you can in the readiest way alter what you were going to say so as to bring in what you have written, and leave no trace of mistake." So in speaking, if the sentence will not finish in the best way, conclude it in another. It is of very little use to go back to amend, for you thus call attention to the flaw which perhaps few had noticed, and you draw off the mind from your subject to your language, which is the last thing which the preacher should do. If, however, your *lapsus linguae* should be noticed, all persons of sense will forgive a young beginner, and they will rather admire you than otherwise for attaching small importance to such slips, and pressing on with your whole heart towards your main design. A novice at public speaking is like a rider unused to horseback; if his horse stumbles he fears he will be down and throw him over his head, or if it be a little fresh, he feels assured that it will run away; and the eye of a friend, or the remark of a little boy, will make him as wretched as if he were lashed to the back of the great red dragon. But when a man is well used to mount he knows no dangers, and he meets with none, because his courage prevents them. When a speaker feels, "I am master of the situation," he usually is so. His confidence averts the disasters which trembling would be certain to create. My brethren, if the Lord has indeed ordained you to the ministry, you have the best reasons for being bold and calm, for whom have you to fear? You have to deliver your Lord's errand as he enables you, and if this be done, you are responsible to no one but your heavenly Master, who is no harsh judge. You do not enter the pulpit to shine as an orator, or to gratify the predilections of your audience; you are the messenger of heaven and not the servant of men.[1] Remember the words of the Lord to Jeremiah, and be afraid to be afraid. "Thou therefore gird up thy loins, and arise, and speak unto them all that I command thee: be not dismayed at their faces, lest I confound thee before them." Jer. i. 17. Trust in the Holy Spirit's present help, and the fear of man which bringeth a snare will depart from you. When you are able to feel at home in the pulpit, and can look round and speak to the people as a brother talking to brethren, then you will be able to extemporise, but not till then. Bashfulness and timidity which are so beautiful in our younger brethren, will be succeeded by that true modesty which forgets self, and is not careful as to its own reputation so long as Christ is preached in the most forcible manner at command.

To attain the holy and useful exercise of extemporal speech the Christian minister must cultivate a childlike *reliance upon the immediate assistance of the Holy Spirit.* "I believe in the Holy Ghost," says the Creed. It is to be feared that many do not make this a real article of belief. To go up and down all the week wasting time, and then to cast ourselves upon the Spirit's aid, is wicked presumption, an attempt to make the Lord minister to our sloth and self-indulgence; but in an emergency the case is widely different. When a man finds himself unavoidably called upon to speak without any preparation, then he may with fullest confidence cast himself upon the Spirit of God. The Divine mind beyond a doubt comes into contact with the human intellect, lifts it out of its weakness and distraction, makes it soaring and strong, and enables it both to understand and to express divine truth in a manner far beyond its unaided powers. Such interpositions, like miracles, are not meant to supersede our efforts or slacken our diligence, but are the Lord's assistance which we may count upon at an emergency. His Spirit will be ever with us, but especially under severe stress of service. Earnestly as I advise you not to try purely impromptu speaking more than you are obliged to do, till you have become somewhat matured in your ministry, I yet exhort you to speak in that manner whenever compelled to do so,

---

[1] "At first my chief solicitude used to be what I should find to say; I hope it is now rather that I may not speak in vain. For the Lord hath not sent me here to acquire the character of a ready speaker, but to win souls to Christ and to edify His people. Often when I begin I am at a loss how I shall proceed, but one thing insensibly offers after another, and in general the best and most useful parts of my sermon occur *de novo,* while I am preaching."—JOHN NEWTON. *Letters to a Student in Divinity.*

believing that in the selfsame hour it shall be given you what you shall speak.

If you are happy enough to acquire the power of extemporary speech, pray recollect that *you may very readily lose it.* I have been struck with this in my own experience, and I refer to that because it is the best evidence that I can give you. If for two successive Sundays I make my notes a little longer and fuller than usual, I find on the third occasion that I require them longer still; and I also observe that if on occasions I lean a little more to my recollection of my thoughts, and am not so extemporaneous as I have been accustomed to be, there is a direct craving and even an increased necessity for pre-composition. If a man begins to walk with a stick merely for a whim, he will soon come to *require* a stick; if you indulge your eyes with spectacles they will speedily demand them as a permanent appendage; and if you were to walk with crutches for a month, at the end of the time they would be almost necessary to your movements, although naturally your limbs might be as sound and healthy as any man's. Ill uses create an ill nature. You must continually practise extemporising, and if to gain suitable opportunities you should frequently speak the word in cottages, in the school-rooms of our hamlets, or to two or three by the wayside, your profiting shall be known unto all men.

It may save you much surprise and grief if you are forewarned that there will be great variations in your power of utterance. To-day your tongue may be the pen of a ready writer, to-morrow your thoughts and words may be alike frost-bound. Living things are sensitive, and are affected by a variety of forces; only the merely mechanical can be reckoned upon with absolute certainty. Think it not strange if you should frequently feel yourself to have failed, nor wonder if it should turn out that at such times you have best succeeded. You must not expect to become sufficient as of yourself; no habit or exercise can render you independent of divine assistance; and if you have preached well forty-nine times when called upon without notice, this is no excuse for self-confidence on the fiftieth occasion, for if the Lord should leave you you will be at a dead stand. Your variable moods of fluency and difficulty will by God's grace tend to keep you humbly looking up to the strong for strength.

Above all things beware of letting your tongue outrun your brains. Guard against a feeble fluency, a garrulous prosiness, a facility of saying nothing. What a pleasure it is to hear of a brother breaking down who presumed upon his powers to keep on when he really had nothing to say! May such a consummation come to all who err in that direction. My brethren, it is a hideous gift to possess, to be able to say nothing at extreme length. Elongated nonsense, paraphrastic platitude, wire-drawn common-place, or sacred rhodomontade, are common enough, and are the scandal and shame of extemporising. Even when sentiments of no value are beautifully expressed, and neatly worded, what is the use of them? Out of nothing comes nothing. Extemporary speech without study is a cloud without rain, a well without water, a fatal gift, injurious equally to its possessor and his flock. Men have applied to me whom I have denied admission to this College, because being utterly destitute both of education and of a sense of their own ignorance, their boundless conceit and enormous volubility made them dangerous subjects for training. Some have even reminded me of the serpent in the Apocalypse, which cast out of his mouth water as a flood so plenteously that the woman was likely to have been carried away with it. Wound up like clocks, they keep on, and on, and on, till they run down, and blessed is he who has least acquaintance with them. The sermons of such preachers are like Snug the joiner's part when he acted the lion. "You may do it extempore, for it is nothing but roaring." Better to lose, or rather never to possess, the gift of ready utterance, than to degrade ourselves into mere noise makers, the living representations of Paul's sounding brass and tinkling cymbal.

I might have said much more if I had extended the subject to what is *usually called* extempore preaching, that is to say, the preparation of the sermon so far as thoughts go, and leaving the words to be found during delivery; but this is quite another matter, and although looked upon as a great attainment by some, it is, as I believe, an indispensable requisite for the pulpit, and by no means a mere luxury of talent; but of this we will speak on another occasion.

XI

The Minister's Fainting Fits

As IT is recorded that David, in the heat of battle, waxed faint, so may it be written of all the servants of the Lord. Fits of depression come over the most of us. Usually cheerful as we may be, we must at intervals be cast down. The strong are not always vigorous, the wise not always ready, the brave not always courageous, and the joyous not always happy. There may be here and there men of iron, to whom wear and tear work no perceptible detriment, but surely the rust frets even these; and as for ordinary men, the Lord knows, and makes them to know, that they are but dust. Knowing by most painful experience what deep depression of spirit means, being visited therewith at seasons by no means few or far between, I thought it might be consolatory to some of my brethren if I gave my thoughts thereon, that younger men might not fancy that some strange thing had happened to them when they became for a season possessed by melancholy; and that sadder men might know that one upon whom the sun has shone right joyously did not always walk in the light.

It is not necessary by quotations from the biographies of eminent ministers to prove that seasons of fearful prostration have fallen to the lot of most, if not all of them. The life of Luther might suffice to give a thousand instances, and he was by no means of the weaker sort. His great spirit was often in the seventh heaven of exultation, and as frequently on the borders of despair. His very death-bed was not free from tempests, and he sobbed himself into his last sleep like a great wearied child. Instead of multiplying cases, let us dwell upon the reasons why these things are permitted; why it is that the children of light sometimes walk in the thick darkness; why the heralds of the daybreak find themselves at times in tenfold night.

Is it not first that *they are men*? Being men, they are compassed with infirmity, and heirs of sorrow. Well said the wise man in the Apocrypha, Ecclus xl. 1, 2, 3, 4, 5–8, "Great travail is created for all men, and a heavy yoke on the sons of Adam, from the day that they go out of their mother's womb unto that day that they return to the mother of all things—namely, their thoughts and fear of their hearts, and their imagination of things that they wail for, and the day of death. From him that sitteth in the glorious throne, to him that sitteth beneath in the earth and ashes; from him that is clothed in blue silk, and weareth a crown, to him that is clothed in simple linen —wrath, envy, trouble, and unquietness, and fear of death and rigour, and such things come to both man and beast, but sevenfold to the ungodly." Grace guards us from much of this, but because we have not more of grace we still suffer even from ills preventible. Even under the economy of redemption it is most clear that we are to endure infirmities, otherwise there were no need of the promised Spirit to help us in them. It is of need be that we are sometimes in heaviness. Good men are promised tribulation in this world, and ministers may expect a larger share than others, that they may learn sympathy with the Lord's suffering people, and so may be fitting shepherds of an ailing flock. Disembodied spirits might have been sent to proclaim the word, but they could not have entered into the feelings of those who, being in this body, do groan, being burdened; angels might have been ordained evangelists, but their celestial attributes would have disqualified them from having compassion on the ignorant; men of marble might have been fashioned, but their impassive natures would have been a sarcasm upon our feebleness, and a mockery of our wants. Men, and men subject to human passions, the all-wise God has chosen to be his vessels of grace; hence these tears, hence these perplexities and castings down.

Moreover, *most of us are in some way or other unsound physically.* Here and there we meet with an old man who could not remember that ever he was laid aside for a day; but the great mass of us labour under some form or other of infirmity, either in body or mind. Certain bodily maladies, especially those connected with the digestive organs, the liver, and the spleen, are the fruitful fountains of despondency; and, let a man strive as he may against their influence, there will be hours and circumstances in which they will for awhile overcome him. As to mental maladies, is any man altogether sane? Are we not all a little off the balance? Some minds appear to have a gloomy tinge essential to their very individuality; of them it may be said, "Melancholy marked them for her own;" fine minds withal, and ruled by noblest principles, but yet most prone to forget the silver lining, and to remember only the cloud. Such men may sing with the old poet:

> "Our hearts are broke, our harps unstringèd be,
>   Our only music's sighs and groans,
>   Our songs are to the tune of *lachrymae*,
>   We're fretted all to skin and bones."
>   THOMAS WASHBOURNE.

These infirmities may be no detriment to a man's career of special usefulness; they may even have been imposed upon him by divine wisdom as necessary qualifications for his peculiar course of service. Some plants owe their medicinal qualities to the marsh in which they

grow; others to the shades in which alone they flourish. There are
precious fruits put forth by the moon as well as by the sun. Boats
need ballast as well as sail; a drag on the carriage-wheel is no
hindrance when the road runs downhill. Pain has probably in some
cases developed genius; hunting out the soul which otherwise might
have slept like a lion in its den. Had it not been for the broken wing,
some might have lost themselves in the clouds, some even of those
choice doves who now bear the olive-branch in their mouths and show
the way to the ark. But where in body and mind there are predisposing
causes to lowness of spirit, it is no marvel if in dark moments the
heart succumbs to them; the wonder in many cases is—and if inner
lives could be written, men would see it so—how some ministers keep
at their work at all, and still wear a smile upon their countenances.
Grace has its triumphs still, and patience has its martyrs; martyrs
none the less to be honoured because the flames kindle about their
spirits rather than their bodies, and their burning is unseen of human
eyes. The ministries of Jeremiahs are as acceptable as those of
Isaiahs, and even the sullen Jonah is a true prophet of the Lord, as
Nineveh felt full well. Despise not the lame, for it is written that they
take the prey; but honour those who, being faint, are yet pursuing.
The tender-eyed Leah was more fruitful than the beautiful Rachel,
and the griefs of Hannah were more divine than the boastings of
Peninnah. "Blessed are they that mourn," said the Man of Sorrows,
and let none account them otherwise when their tears are salted with
grace. We have the treasure of the gospel in earthen vessels, and if
there be a flaw in the vessel here and there, let none wonder.

*Our work, when earnestly undertaken, lays us open to attacks in the
direction of depression.* Who can bear the weight of souls without
sometimes sinking to the dust? Passionate longings after men's
conversion, if not fully satisfied (and when are they?), consume the
soul with anxiety and disappointment. To see the hopeful turn aside,
the godly grow cold, professors abusing their privileges, and sinners
waxing more bold in sin—are not these sights enough to crush us to
the earth? The kingdom comes not as we would, the reverend name
is not hallowed as we desire, and for this we must weep. How can
we be otherwise than sorrowful, while men believe not our report,
and the divine arm is not revealed? All mental work tends to weary
and to depress, for much study is a weariness of the flesh; but ours is
more than mental work—it is heart work, the labour of our inmost
soul. How often, on Lord's-day evenings, do we feel as if life were
completely washed out of us! After pouring out our souls over our
congregations, we feel like empty earthen pitchers which a child might
break. Probably, if we were more like Paul, and watched for souls
at a nobler rate, we should know more of what it is to be eaten up
by the zeal of the Lord's house. It is our duty and our privilege to

exhaust our lives for Jesus. We are not to be living specimens of men in fine preservation, but living *sacrifices,* whose lot is to be consumed; we are to spend and to be spent, not to lay ourselves up in lavender, and nurse our flesh. Such soul-travail as that of a faithful minister will bring on occasional seasons of exhaustion, when heart and flesh will fail. Moses' hands grew heavy in intercession, and Paul cried out, "Who is sufficient for these things?" Even John the Baptist is thought to have had his fainting fits, and the apostles were once amazed, and were sore afraid.

Our position in the church will also conduce to this. A minister fully equipped for his work will usually be a spirit by himself, above, beyond, and apart from others. The most loving of his people cannot enter into his peculiar thoughts, cares, and temptations. In the ranks, men walk shoulder to shoulder, with many comrades, but as the officer rises in rank, men of his standing are fewer in number. There are many soldiers, few captains, fewer colonels, but only one commander-in-chief. So, in our churches, the man whom the Lord raises as a leader becomes, in the same degree in which he is a superior man, a solitary man. The mountain-tops stand solemnly apart, and talk only with God as He visits their terrible solitudes. Men of God who rise above their fellows into nearer communion with heavenly things, in their weaker moments feel the lack of human sympathy. Like their Lord in Gethsemane, they look in vain for comfort to the disciples sleeping around them; they are shocked at the apathy of their little band of brethren, and return to their secret agony with all the heavier burden pressing upon them, because they have found their dearest companions slumbering. No one knows, but he who has endured it, the solitude of a soul which has outstripped its fellows in zeal for the Lord of hosts: it dares not reveal itself, lest men count it mad; it cannot conceal itself, for a fire burns within its bones: only before the Lord does it find rest. Our Lord's sending out his disciples by two and two manifested that he knew what was in men; but for such a man as Paul, it seems to me that no helpmeet was found; Barnabas, or Silas, or Luke, were hills too low to hold high converse with such a Himalayan summit as the apostle of the Gentiles. This loneliness, which if I mistake not is felt by many of my brethren, is a fertile source of depression; and our ministers' fraternal meetings, and the cultivation of holy intercourse with kindred minds will, with God's blessing, help us greatly to escape the snare.

There can be little doubt that *sedentary habits* have a tendency to create despondency in some constitutions. Burton, in his *Anatomy of Melancholy,* has a chapter upon this cause of sadness; and, quoting from one of the myriad authors whom he lays under contribution, he says—"Students are negligent of their bodies. Other men look to their tools; a painter will wash his pencils; a smith will look to his hammer, anvil, forge; a husbandman will mend his plough-irons, and grind his hatchet if it be dull; a falconer or huntsman will have an especial care of his hawks, hounds, horses, dogs, etc.; a musician will string and unstring his lute; only scholars neglect that instrument (their brain and spirits I mean) which they daily use. Well saith Lucan, 'See thou twist not the rope so hard that it break.'" To sit long in one posture, poring over a book, or driving a quill, is in itself a taxing of nature; but add to this a badly ventilated chamber, a body which has long been without muscular exercise, and a heart burdened with many cares, and we have all the elements for preparing a seething cauldron of despair, especially in the dim months of fog:

> "When a blanket wraps the day,
> When the rotten woodland drips,
> And the leaf is stamped in clay."

Let a man be naturally as blithe as a bird, he will hardly be able to bear up year after year against such a suicidal process; he will make his study a prison and his books the warders of a gaol, while nature lies outside his window calling him to health and beckoning him to joy. He who forgets the humming of the bees among the heather, the cooing of the wood-pigeons in the forest, the song of birds in the woods, the rippling of rills among the rushes, and the sighing of the wind among the pines, needs not wonder if his heart forgets to sing and his soul grows heavy. A day's breathing of fresh air upon the hills, or a few hours' ramble in the beech woods' umbrageous calm, would sweep the cobwebs out of the brain of scores of our toiling ministers who are now but half alive. A mouthful of sea air, or a stiff walk in the wind's face, would not give grace to the soul, but it would yield oxygen to the body, which is next best.

> "Heaviest the heart is in a heavy air,
> Ev'ry wind that rises blows away despair."

The ferns and the rabbits, the streams and the trouts, the fir trees and the squirrels, the primroses and the violets, the farm-yard, the new-mown hay, and the fragrant hops—these are the best medicine for hypochondriacs, the surest tonics for the declining, the best refreshments for the weary. For lack of opportunity, or inclination, these great remedies are neglected, and the student becomes a self-immolated victim.

The times most favourable to fits of depression, so far as I have experienced, may be summed up in a brief catalogue. First among them I must mention *the hour of great success*. When at last a long-cherished desire is fulfilled, when God has been glorified greatly by our means, and a great triumph achieved, then we are apt to faint.

It might be imagined that amid special favours our soul would soar to heights of ecstacy, and rejoice with joy unspeakable, but it is generally the reverse. The Lord seldom exposes His warriors to the perils of exultation over victory; he knows that few of them can endure such a test, and therefore dashes their cup with bitterness. See Elias after the fire has fallen from heaven, after Baal's priests have been slaughtered and the rain has deluged the barren land! For him no notes of self-complacent music, no strutting like a conqueror in robes of triumph; he flees from Jezebel, and feeling the revulsion of his intense excitement, he prays that he may die. He who must never see death, yearns after the rest of the grave, even as Cæsar, the world's monarch, in his moments of pain cried like a sick girl. Poor human nature cannot bear such strains as heavenly triumphs bring to it; there must come a reaction. Excess of joy or excitement must be paid for by subsequent depressions. While the trial lasts, the strength is equal to the emergency; but when it is over, natural weakness claims the right to show itself. Secretly sustained, Jacob can wrestle all night, but he must limp in the morning when the contest is over, lest he boast himself beyond measure. Paul may be caught up to the third heaven, and hear unspeakable things, but a thorn in the flesh, a messenger of Satan to buffet him, must be the inevitable sequel. Men cannot bear unalloyed happiness; even good men are not yet fit to have "their brows with laurel and with myrtle bound," without enduring secret humiliation to keep them in their proper place. Whirled from off our feet by a revival, carried aloft by popularity, exalted by success in soul-winning, we should be as the chaff which the wind driveth away, were it not that the gracious discipline of mercy breaks the ships of our vain glory with a strong east wind, and casts us shipwrecked, naked and forlorn, upon the Rock of Ages.

Before any great achievement, some measure of the same depression is very usual. Surveying the difficulties before us, our hearts sink within us. The sons of Anak stalk before us, and we are as grasshoppers in our own sight in their presence. The cities of Canaan are walled up to heaven, and who are we that we should hope to capture them? We are ready to cast down our weapons and take to our heels. Nineveh is a great city, and we would flee unto Tarshish sooner than encounter its noisy crowds. Already we look for a ship which may bear us quietly away from the terrible scene, and only a dread of tempest restrains our recreant footsteps. Such was my experience when I first became a pastor in London. My success appalled me; and the thought of the career which it seemed to open up, so far from elating me, cast me into the lowest depth, out of which I uttered my *miserere* and found no room for a *gloria in excelsis*. Who was I that I should continue to lead so great a multitude? I would betake me to my village obscurity, or emigrate to America, and find a solitary nest in the backwoods, where I might be sufficient for the things which would be demanded of me. It was just then that the curtain was rising upon my life-work, and I dreaded what it might reveal. I hope I was not faithless, but I was timorous and filled with a sense of my own unfitness. I dreaded the work which a gracious providence had prepared for me. I felt myself a mere child, and trembled as I heard the voice which said, "Arise, and thresh the mountains, and make them as chaff." This depression comes over me whenever the Lord is preparing a larger blessing for my ministry; the cloud is black before it breaks, and overshadows before it yields its deluge of mercy. Depression has now become to me as a prophet in rough clothing, a John the Baptist, heralding the nearer coming of my Lord's richer benison. So have far better men found it. The scouring of the vessel has fitted it for the Master's use. Immersion in suffering has preceded the baptism of the Holy Ghost. Fasting gives an appetite for the banquet. The Lord is revealed in the backside of the desert, while His servant keepeth the sheep and waits in solitary awe. The wilderness is the way to Canaan. The low valley leads to the towering mountain. Defeat prepares for victory. The raven is sent forth before the dove. The darkest hour of the night precedes the day-dawn. The mariners go down to the depths, but the next wave makes them mount to the heaven; their soul is melted because of trouble before he bringeth them to their desired haven.

In the midst of a long stretch of unbroken labour, the same affliction may be looked for. The bow cannot be always bent without fear of breaking. Repose is as needful to the mind as sleep to the body. Our Sabbaths are our days of toil, and if we do not rest upon some other day we shall break down. Even the earth must lie fallow and have her Sabbaths, and so must we. Hence the wisdom and compassion of our Lord, when He said to His disciples, "Let us go into the desert and rest awhile." What! when the people are fainting? When the multitudes are like sheep upon the mountains without a shepherd? Does Jesus talk of rest? When Scribes and Pharisees, like grievous wolves, are rending the flock, does He take His followers on an excursion into a quiet resting place? Does some red-hot zealot denounce such atrocious forgetfulness of present and pressing demands? Let him rave in his folly. The Master knows better than to exhaust His servants and quench the light of Israel. Rest time is not waste time. It is economy to gather fresh strength. Look at the mower in the summer's day, with so much to cut down ere the sun sets. He pauses in his labour—is he a sluggard? He looks for his stone, and begins to draw it up and down his scythe, with "rink-a-tink—rink-a-tink—rink-a-tink." Is that idle music—is he wasting precious moments? How much he might have mown while he has been ringing out those notes on his scythe! But he is sharpening his tool, and he will do far more when once again he gives his strength to those long sweeps which lay the grass prostrate in rows before him. Even thus a little pause prepares the mind for greater service in the good cause. Fishermen must mend their nets, and we must every now and then repair our mental waste and set our machinery in order for future service. To tug the oar from day to day, like a galley-slave who knows no holidays, suits not mortal men. Mill-streams go on and on for ever, but we must have our pauses and our intervals. Who can help being out of breath when the race is continued without intermission? Even beasts of burden must be turned out to grass occasionally; the very sea pauses at ebb and flood; earth keeps the Sabbath of the wintry months; and man, even when exalted to be God's ambassador, must rest or faint; must trim his lamp or let it burn low; must recruit his vigour or grow prematurely old. It is wisdom to take occasional furlough. In the long run, we shall do more by sometimes doing less. On, on, on for ever, without recreation, may suit spirits emancipated from this "heavy clay," but while we are in this tabernacle, we must every now and then cry halt, and serve the Lord by holy inaction and consecrated leisure. Let no tender conscience doubt the lawfulness of going out of harness for a while, but learn from the experience of others the necessity and duty of taking timely rest.

One crushing stroke has sometimes laid the minister very low. The brother most relied upon becomes a traitor. Judas lifts up his heel against the man who trusted him, and the preacher's heart for the moment fails him. We are all too apt to look to an arm of flesh, and from that propensity many of our sorrows arise. Equally overwhelming is the blow when an honoured and beloved member yields to temptation, and disgraces the holy name with which he was named. Anything is better than this. This makes the preacher long for a lodge in some vast wilderness, where he may hide his head for ever, and hear no more the blasphemous jeers of the ungodly. Ten years of toil do not take so much life out of us as we lose in a few hours by Ahithophel the traitor, or Demas the apostate. Strife, also, and division, and slander, and foolish censures, have often laid holy men prostrate, and made them go "as with a sword in their bones." Hard words wound some delicate minds very keenly. Many of the best of ministers, from the very spirituality of their character, are exceedingly sensitive—too sensitive for such a world as this. "A kick that scarce would move a horse would kill a sound divine." By experience the soul is hardened to the rough blows which are inevitable in our warfare; but at first these things utterly stagger us, and send us to our homes wrapped in a horror of great darkness. The trials of a true minister are not few, and such as are caused by ungrateful professors are harder to bear than the coarsest attacks of avowed enemies. Let no man who looks for ease of mind and seeks the quietude of life enter the ministry; if he does so he will flee from it in disgust.

To the lot of the few does it fall to pass through such a horror of great darkness as that which fell upon me after the deplorable accident at the Surrey Music Hall. I was pressed beyond measure and out of bounds with an enormous weight of misery. The tumult, the panic, the deaths, were day and night before me, and made life a burden. Then I sang in my sorrow:

> "The tumult of my thoughts
> Doth but increase my woe,
> My spirit languisheth, my heart
> Is desolate and low."

From that dream of horror I was awakened in a moment by the gracious application to my soul of the text, "Him hath God the Father exalted." The fact that Jesus is still great, let His servants suffer as they may, piloted me back to calm reason and peace. Should so terrible a calamity overtake any of my brethren, let them both patiently hope and quietly wait for the salvation of God.

When troubles multiply, and discouragements follow each other in long succession, like Job's messengers, then, too, amid the perturbation of soul occasioned by evil tidings, despondency despoils the heart of all its peace. Constant dropping wears away stones, and the bravest minds feel the fret of repeated afflictions. If a scanty cupboard is rendered a severer trial by the sickness of a wife or the loss of a child, and if ungenerous remarks of hearers are followed by the opposition of deacons and the coolness of members, then, like Jacob, we are apt to cry, "All these things are against me." When David returned to Ziklag and found the city burned, goods stolen, wives carried off, and his troops ready to stone him, we read, "he encouraged himself in his God"; and well was it for him that he could do so, for he would then have fainted if he had not believed to see the goodness of the Lord in the land of the living. Accumulated distresses increase each other's weight; they play into each other's hands, and, like bands of robbers, ruthlessly destroy our comfort. Wave upon wave is severe work for the strongest swimmer. The place where two seas meet strains the most seaworthy keel. If there were a regulated pause between the buffetings of adversity, the spirit would stand prepared; but when they come suddenly and heavily, like the battering of great hailstones, the pilgrim may well be amazed. The last ounce breaks the camel's back, and when that last ounce is laid upon us, what wonder if we for awhile are ready to give up the ghost!

This evil will also come upon us, we know not why, and then it is all the more difficult to drive it away. Causeless depression is not to be reasoned with, nor can David's harp charm it away by sweet discoursings. As well fight with the mist as with this shapeless, undefinable, yet all-beclouding hopelessness. One affords himself no pity when in this case, because it seems so unreasonable, and even sinful, to be troubled without manifest cause; and yet troubled the man is, even in the very depths of his spirit. If those who laugh at such melancholy did but feel the grief of it for one hour, their laughter would be sobered into compassion. Resolution might, perhaps, shake it off, but where are we to find the resolution when the whole man is unstrung? The physician and the divine may unite their skill in such cases, and both find their hands full, and more than full. The iron bolt which so mysteriously fastens the door of hope and holds our spirits in gloomy prison, needs a heavenly hand to push it back; and when that hand is seen we cry with the apostle, "Blessed be God, even the Father of our Lord Jesus Christ, the Father of mercies, and the God of all comfort; who comforteth us in all our tribulation, that we may be able to comfort them which are in any trouble, by the comfort wherewith we ourselves are comforted of God" 2 Cor. i. 3, 4. It is the God of all consolation who can:

> "With sweet oblivious antidote
> Cleanse our poor bosoms of that perilous stuff
> Which weighs upon the heart."

Simon sinks till Jesus takes him by the hand. The devil within rends and tears the poor child till the word of authority commands him to come out of him. When we are ridden with horrible fears, and weighed down with an intolerable incubus, we need but the Sun of Righteousness to rise, and the evils generated of our darkness are driven away; but nothing short of this will chase away the nightmare of the soul. Timothy Rogers, the author of a treatise on Melancholy, and Simon Browne, the writer of some remarkably sweet hymns, proved in their own cases how unavailing is the help of man if the Lord withdraw the light from the soul.

If it be enquired why the Valley of the Shadow of Death must so often be traversed by the servants of King Jesus, the answer is not far to find. All this is promotive of the Lord's mode of working, which is summed up in these words: "Not by might nor by power, but by my Spirit, saith the Lord." Instruments shall be used, but their intrinsic weakness shall be clearly manifested; there shall be no division of the glory, no diminishing the honour due to the Great Worker. The man shall be emptied of self, and then filled with the Holy Ghost. In his own apprehension he shall be like a sere leaf driven of the tempest, and then shall be strengthened into a brazen wall against the enemies of truth. To hide pride from the worker is the great difficulty. Uninterrupted success and unfading joy in it would be more than our weak heads could bear. Our wine must needs be mixed with water, lest it turn our brains. My witness is, that those who are honoured of their Lord in public have usually to endure a secret chastening, or to carry a peculiar cross, lest by any means they exalt themselves, and fall into the snare of the devil. How constantly the Lord calls Ezekiel "Son of man"! Amid his soarings into the superlative splendours, just when with eye undimmed he is strengthened to gaze into the excellent glory, the word "Son of man" falls on his ears, sobering the heart which else might have been intoxicated with the honour conferred upon it. Such humbling but salutary messages our depressions whisper in our ears; they tell us in a manner not to be mistaken that we are but men, frail, feeble, apt to faint.

By all the castings down of His servants God is glorified, for they are led to magnify Him when He sets them on their feet, and even while prostrate in the dust their faith yields Him praise. They speak all the more sweetly of His faithfulness, and are the more firmly established in His love. Such mature men as some elderly preachers are, could scarcely have been produced if they had not been emptied from vessel to vessel, and made to see their own emptiness and the vanity of all things round about them. Glory be to God for the furnace, the hammer, and the file. Heaven shall be all the fuller of bliss because we have been filled with anguish here below, and earth shall be better tilled because of our training in the school of adversity.

The lesson of wisdom is, *be not dismayed by soul-trouble.* Count it no strange thing, but a part of ordinary ministerial experience. Should the power of depression be more than ordinary, think not that all is over with your usefulness. Cast not away your confidence, for it hath great recompense of reward. Even if the enemy's foot be on your neck, expect to rise and overthrow him. Cast the burden of the present, along with the sin of the past and the fear of the future, upon the Lord, who forsaketh not His saints. Live by the day—ay, by the hour. Put no trust in frames and feelings. Care more for a grain of faith than a ton of excitement. Trust in God alone, and lean not on the needs of human help. Be not surprised when friends fail you: it is a failing world. Never count upon immutability in man: inconstancy you may reckon upon without fear of disappointment. The disciples of Jesus forsook Him; be not amazed if your adherents wander away to other teachers: as they were not your all when with you, all is not gone from you with their departure. Serve God with all your might while the candle is burning, and then when it goes out for a season, you will have the less to regret. Be content to be nothing, for that is what you are. When your own emptiness is painfully forced upon your consciousness, chide yourself that you ever dreamed of being full, except in the Lord. Set small store by present rewards; be grateful for earnests by the way, but look for the recompensing joy hereafter. Continue with double earnestness to serve your Lord when no visible result is before you. Any simpleton can follow the narrow path in the light: faith's rare wisdom enables us to march on in the dark with infallible accuracy, since she places her hand in that of her Great Guide. Between this and heaven there may be rougher weather yet, but it is all provided for by our covenant Head. In nothing let us be turned aside from the path which the divine call has urged us to pursue. Come fair or come foul, the pulpit is our watch-tower, and the ministry our warfare; be it ours, when we cannot see the face of our God, to trust under THE SHADOW OF HIS WINGS.

XII

The Minister's Ordinary Conversation

OUR subject is to be the minister's common conversation when he mingles with men in general, and is supposed to be quite at his ease. How shall he order his speech among his fellow-men? First and foremost, let me say, *let him give himself no ministerial airs,* but avoid everything which is stilted, official, fussy, and pretentious. "The Son of Man" is a noble title; it was given to Ezekiel, and to a greater than he: let not the ambassador of heaven be other than a son of man. In fact, let him remember that the more simple and unaffected he is, the more closely will he resemble that child-man, the holy child Jesus. There is such a thing as trying to be too much a minister, and becoming too little a man; though the more of a true man you are, the more truly will you be what a servant of the Lord should be. Schoolmasters and ministers have generally an appearance peculiarly their own; in the wrong sense, they "are not as other men are." They are too often speckled birds, looking as if they were not at home among the other inhabitants of the country, but awkward and peculiar. When I have seen a flamingo gravely stalking along, an owl blinking in the shade, or a stork demurely lost in thought, I have been irresistibly led to remember some of my dignified brethren of the teaching and preaching fraternity, who are so marvellously proper at all times that they are just a shade amusing. Their very respectable, stilted, dignified, important, self-restrained manner is easily acquired; but is it worth acquiring?

Theodore Hook once stepped up to a gentleman who was parading the street with great pomposity, and said to him, "Sir, are you not a person of great importance?" and one has felt half inclined to do the same with certain brethren of the cloth. I know brethren who, from head to foot, in garb, tone, manner, necktie, and boots, are so utterly *parsonic* that no particle of manhood is visible. One young sprig of divinity must needs go through the streets in a gown, and another of the High Church order has recorded it in the newspapers with much complacency that he traversed Switzerland and Italy, wearing in all places his biretta; few boys would have been so proud of a fool's cap. None of us are likely to go as far as that in our apparel; but we may do the like by our mannerism. Some men appear to have a white cravat twisted round their souls, their manhood is throttled with that starched rag. Certain brethren maintain an air of superiority which they think impressive, but which is simply offensive, and eminently opposed to their pretensions as followers of the lowly Jesus. The proud Duke of Somerset intimated his commands to his servants by signs, not condescending to speak to such base beings; his children never sat down in his presence, and when he slept in the afternoon one of his daughters stood on each side of him during his august slumbers. When proud Somersets get into the ministry, they affect dignity in other ways almost equally absurd. "Stand by, I am holier than thou," is written across their foreheads.

A well-known minister was once rebuked by a sublime brother for his indulgence in a certain luxury, and the expense was made a great argument. "Well, well," he replied, "there may be something in that; but remember, I do not spend half so much upon my weakness as you do in starch." That is the article I am deprecating, that dreadful ministerial starch. If you have indulged in it, I would earnestly advise you to "go and wash in Jordan seven times," and get it out of you, every particle of it. I am persuaded that one reason why our working-men so universally keep clear of ministers is because they abhor their artificial and unmanly ways. If they saw us, in the pulpit and out of it, acting like real men, and speaking naturally, like honest men, they would come around us. Baxter's remark still holds good: "The want of a familiar tone and expression is a great fault in most of our deliveries, and that which we should be very careful to amend." The vice of the ministry is that ministers will *parsonificate* the gospel. We must have humanity along with our divinity if we would win the masses. Everybody can see through affectations, and people are not likely to be taken in by them. Fling away your stilts, brethren, and walk on your feet; doff your ecclesiasticism, and array yourselves in truth.

Still, a minister, wherever he is, is a minister, and should recollect that he is on duty. A policeman or a soldier may be off duty, but a minister never is. Even in our recreations we should still pursue the great object of our lives; for we are called to be diligent "in season and out of season." There is no position in which we may be placed but the Lord may come with the question, "What doest thou here, Elijah?" and we ought to be able at once to answer, "I have something to do for thee even here, and I am trying to do it." The bow, of course, must be at times unstrung, or else it will lose its elasticity; but there is no need to cut the string. I am speaking at this time of the minister in times of relaxation; and I say that even then he should conduct himself as the ambassador of God, and seize opportunities of doing good: this will not mar his rest, but sanctify it. A minister should be like a certain chamber which I saw at Beaulieu, in the New Forest, in which a cobweb is never seen. It is a large lumber-room, and is never swept; yet no spider ever defiles it with the emblems of neglect. It is roofed with chestnut, and for some reason, I know not what, spiders will not come near that wood by the year together. The same thing was mentioned to me in the corridors of Winchester School: I was told, "No spiders ever come here." Our minds should be equally clear of idle habits.

On our public rests for porters in the City of London you may read the words, "Rest, but do not loiter"; and they contain advice worthy of our attention. I do not call the *dolce far niente* laziness; there is a sweet doing of nothing which is just the finest medicine in the world for a jaded mind. When the mind gets fatigued and out of order, to rest it is no more idleness than sleep is idleness; and no man is called lazy for sleeping the proper time. It is far better to be industriously asleep than lazily awake. Be ready to do good even in your resting times and in your leisure hours; and so be really a minister, and there will be no need for you to proclaim that you are so.

The Christian minister out of the pulpit should be a sociable man. He is not sent into the world to be a hermit, or a monk of La Trappe. It is not his vocation to stand on a pillar all day, above his fellow-men, like that hare-brained Simon Stylites of olden time. You are not to warble from the top of a tree, like an invisible nightingale; but to be a man among men, saying to them, "I also am as you are in all that relates to man." Salt is of no use in the box; it must be rubbed into the meat; and our personal influence must penetrate and season society. Keep aloof from others, and how can you benefit them? Our Master went to a wedding, and ate bread with publicans and sinners, and yet was far more pure than those sanctimonious Pharisees, whose glory was that they were separate from their fellow-men. Some ministers need to be told that they are of the same species as their hearers. It is a remarkable fact, but we may as well state it, that bishops, canons, archdeacons, prebendaries, rural deans, rectors, vicars and even archbishops, are only men after all; and God has not railed off a holy corner of the earth to serve as a chancel for them, to abide therein by themselves.

It would not be amiss if there could be a revival of holy talk in the churchyard and the meeting-yard. I like to see the big yew-trees outside our ancient churches with seats all round them. They seem to say: "Sit down here, neighbour, and talk upon the sermon; here comes the pastor; he will join us, and we shall have a pleasant, holy chat." It is not every preacher we would care to talk with; but there are some whom one would give a fortune to converse with for an hour. I love a minister whose face invites me to make him my friend—a man upon whose doorstep you read, "Salve," "*Welcome*"; and feel that there is no need of that Pompeian warning, "Cave Canem,"

"Beware of the dog." Give me the man around whom the children come, like flies around a honey-pot: they are first-class judges of a good man. When Solomon was tried by the Queen of Sheba, as to his wisdom, the rabbis tell us that she brought some artificial flowers with her, beautifully made and delicately scented, so as to be fac-similes of real flowers. She asked Solomon to discover which were artificial and which were real. The wise man bade his servants open the window, and when the bees came in they flew at once to the natural flowers, and cared nothing for the artificial. So you will find that children have their instincts, and discover very speedily who is their friend, and depend upon it the children's friend is one who will be worth knowing. Have a good word to say to each and every member of the family—the big boys, and the young ladies, and the little girls, and everybody. No one knows what a smile and a hearty sentence may do. A man who is to do much with men must love them, and feel at home with them. An individual who has no geniality about him had better be an undertaker, and bury the dead, for he will never succeed in influencing the living. I have met somewhere with the observation that to be a popular preacher one must have bowels. I fear that the observation was meant as a mild criticism upon the bulk to which certain brethren have attained: but there is truth in it. A man must have a great heart if he would have a great congregation. His heart should be as capacious as those noble harbours along our coast, which contain sea-room for a fleet. When a man has a large, loving heart, men go to him as ships to a haven, and feel at peace when they have anchored under the lee of his friendship. Such a man is hearty in private as well as in public; his blood is not cold and fishy, but he is warm as your own fireside. No pride and selfishness chill you when you approach him; he has his doors all open to receive you, and you are at home with him at once. Such men I would persuade you to be, every one of you.

The Christian minister should also be very cheerful. I don't believe in going about like certain monks whom I saw in Rome, who salute each other in sepulchral tones, and convey the pleasant information, "Brother, we must die:" to which lively salutation each lively brother of the order replies, "Yes, brother, we must die." I was glad to be assured upon such good authority that all these lazy fellows are about to die; upon the whole, it is about the best thing they can do; but till that event occurs, they might use some more comfortable form of salutation.

No doubt there are some people who will be impressed by the very solemn appearance of ministers. I have heard of one who felt con-vinced that there must be something in the Roman Catholic religion, from the extremely starved and pinched appearance of a certain ecclesiastic. "Look," said he, "how the man is worn to a skeleton by his daily fastings and nightly vigils! How he must mortify his flesh!" Now, the probabilities are that the emaciated priest was labouring under some internal disease, which he would have been heartily glad to be rid of, and it was not conquest of appetite, but failure in digestion, which had so reduced him; or possibly a troubled conscience, which made him fret himself down to the light weights. Certainly, I have never met with a text which mentions prominence of bone as an evidence of grace. If so, "The Living Skeleton" should have been exhibited, not merely as a natural curiosity, but as the standard of virtue. Some of the biggest rogues in the world have been as mortified in appearance as if they had lived on locusts and wild honey. It is a very vulgar error to suppose that a melancholy countenance is the index of a gracious heart. I commend cheerfulness to all who would win souls; not levity and frothiness, but a genial happy spirit. There are more flies caught with honey than with vinegar, and there will be more souls led to heaven by a man who wears heaven in his face than by one who bears Tartarus in his looks.

Young ministers, and, indeed, all others, when they are in company, *should take care not to engross all the conversation.* They are quite qualified to do so, no doubt; I mean from their capacity to instruct, and readiness of utterance; but they must remember that people do not care to be perpetually instructed; they like to take a turn in the conversation themselves. Nothing pleases some people so much as to let them talk, and it may be for their good to let them be pleased. I spent an hour one evening with a person who did me the honour to say that he found me a very charming companion, and most instructive in conversation, yet I do not hesitate to confess that I said scarcely anything at all, but allowed him to have the talk to himself. By exercising patience I gained his good opinion, and an opportunity to address him on other occasions. A man has no more right at table to talk all than to eat all. We are not to think ourselves Sir Oracle, before whom no dog must open his mouth. No; let all the company contribute of their stores, and they will think all the better of the godly words with which you try to season the discourse.

There are some companies into which you will go, especially when you are first settled, where everybody will be awed by the majesty of your presence, and people will be invited because the new minister is to be there. Such a position reminds me of the choicest statuary in the Vatican. A little room is screened off, a curtain is drawn, and lo! before you stands the great Apollo! If it be your trying lot to be the Apollo of the little party, put an end to the nonsense. If I were the Apollo, I should like to step right off the pedestal and shake hands all round, and you had better do the same; for sooner or later the fuss they make about you will come to an end, and the wisest course is to end it yourself. Hero-worship is a kind of idolatry, and must not be encouraged. Heroes do well when they, like the apostles at Lystra, are horrified at the honours done to them, and run in among the people crying, "Sirs, why do ye these things? We also are men of like passions with you." Ministers will not have to do it long; for their foolish admirers are very apt to turn round upon them, and if they do not stone them nearly to death, they will go as far as they dare in unkindness and contempt.

While I say, "Do not talk all, and assume an importance which is mere imosture;" still, *do not be a dummy*. People will form their estimate of you and your ministry by what they see of you in private as well as by your public deliverances. Many young men have ruined themselves in the pulpit by being indiscreet in the parlour, and have lost all hope of doing good by their stupidity or frivolity in company. Don't be an inanimate log. At Antwerp Fair, among many curiosities advertised by huge paintings and big drums, I observed a booth containing "a great wonder," to be seen for a penny a head; it was *a petrified man*. I did not expend the amount required for admission, for I had seen so many petrified men for nothing, both in and out of the pulpit—lifeless, careless, destitute of common sense, and altogether inert, though occupied with the weightiest business which man could undertake.

Try to turn the conversation to profitable use. Be sociable and cheerful and all that, but labour to accomplish something. Why should you sow the wind, or plough a rock? Consider yourself, after all, as being very much responsible for the conversation which goes on where you are; for such is the esteem in which you will usually be held, that you will be the helmsman of the conversation. Therefore, steer it into a good channel. Do this without roughness or force. Keep the points of the line in good order, and the train will run on to your rails without a jerk. Be ready to seize opportunities adroitly, and lead on imperceptibly in the desired track. If your heart is in it and your wits are awake, this will be easy enough, especially if you breathe a prayer for guidance.

I shall never forget the manner in which a thirsty individual once begged of me upon Clapham Common. I saw him with a very large truck, in which he was carrying an extremely small parcel, and I wondered why he had not put the parcel into his pocket, and left the machine at home. I said, "It looks odd to see so large a truck for such a small load." He stopped, and looking me seriously in the face, he said, "Yes, sir, it is a very odd thing; but, do you know, I have met with an odder thing than that this very day. I've been about, working and sweating all this 'ere blessed day, and till now I haven't met a single gentleman that looked as if he'd give me a pint of beer, till I saw you." I considered that turn of the conversation very neatly managed, and we, with a far better subject upon our minds, ought to be equally able to introduce the topic upon which our heart is set. There was an ease in the man's manner which I envied, for I did not find it quite so simple a matter to introduce my own topic to his notice; yet if I had been thinking as much about how I could do him good as he had upon how to obtain a drink, I feel sure I should have succeeded in reaching my point. If by any means we may save some, we must, like our Lord, talk at table to good purpose—yes, and on the margin of the well, and by the road, and on the sea-shore, and in the house, and in the field. To be a holy talker for Jesus might be almost as fruitful an office as to be a faithful preacher. Aim at excellence in both exercises, and if the Holy Spirit's aid be called in, you will attain your desire.

Here, perhaps, I may insert a canon, which nevertheless I believe to be quite needless, in reference to each one of the honourable brethren whom I am now addressing. *Do not frequent rich men's tables to gain their countenance, and never make yourself a sort of general hanger-on at tea-parties and entertainments.* Who are you that you should be dancing attendance upon this wealthy man and the other, when the Lord's poor, his sick people, and his wandering sheep require you? To sacrifice the study to the parlour is criminal. To be a tout for your church, and waylay people at their homes to draw them to fill your pews, is a degradation to which no man should submit. To see ministers of different sects fluttering round a wealthy man, like vultures round a dead camel, is sickening. Deliciously sarcastic was that famous letter "from an old and beloved minister to his dear son" upon his entrance into the ministry, the following extract from which hits our present point. It is said to have been copied from the *Smellfungus Gazette,* but I suspect our friend Paxton Hood knows all about its authorship: "Keep also a watchful eye on all likely persons, especially wealthy or influential, who may come to your town; call upon them, and attempt to win them over by the devotions of the drawing-room to your cause. Thus you may most efficiently serve the Master's interests. People need looking after, and the result of a long experience goes to confirm my conviction, long cherished, that the power of the pulpit is trifling compared with the power of the parlour. We must imitate and sanctify, by the word of God and prayer, the exercises of the Jesuits. They succeeded not by the pulpit so much as by the parlour. In the parlour you can whisper —you can meet people on all their little personal private ideas. The pulpit is a very unpleasant place; of course it is the great power of God, and so on, but it is the parlour that tells, and a minister has not the same chance of success if he be a good preacher as if he is a perfect gentleman; nor in cultivated society has any man a legitimate prospect of success if he is not, whatever he may be, a gentleman. I have always admired Lord Shaftesbury's character of St. Paul in his

'Characteristics'—that he was a fine gentleman. And I would say to you, be a gentleman. Not that I need to say so, but am persuaded that only in this way can we hope for the conversion of our growing wealthy middle classes. We must show that our religion is the religion of good sense and good taste; that we disapprove of strong excitements and strong stimulants; and oh, my dear boy, if you would be useful, often in your closet make it a matter of earnest prayer that you may be proper. If I were asked what is your first duty, *be proper*; and your second, *be proper*; and your third, *be proper*." Those who remember a class of preachers who flourished fifty years ago will see the keenness of the satire in this extract. The evil is greatly mitigated now; in fact, I fear we may be drifting into another extreme.

In all probability, sensible conversation will sometimes drift into controversy, and here many a good man runs upon a snag. *The sensible minister will be particularly gentle in argument.* He, above all men, should not make the mistake of fancying that there is force in temper, and power in speaking angrily. A heathen who stood in a crowd in Calcutta, listening to a missionary disputing with a Brahmin, said he knew which was right though he did not understand the language—he knew that he was in the wrong who lost his temper first. For the most part, that is a very accurate way of judging. Try to avoid debating with people. State your opinion and let them state theirs. If you see that a stick is crooked, and you want people to see how crooked it is, lay a straight rod down beside it; that will be quite enough. But if you are drawn into controversy, use very hard arguments and very soft words. Frequently you cannot convince a man by tugging at his reason, but you can persuade him by winning his affections. The other day I had the misery to need a pair of new boots, and though I bade the fellow make them as large as canoes, I had to labour fearfully to get them on. With a pair of boot-hooks I toiled like the men on board the vessel with Jonah, but all in vain. Just then my friend put in my way a little French chalk, and the work was done in a moment. Wonderfully coaxing was that French chalk. Gentlemen, always carry a little French chalk with you into society, a neat packet of Christian persuasiveness, and you will soon discover the virtues of it.

And lastly, with all his amiability, *the minister should be firm for his principles, and bold to avow and defend them in all companies.* When a fair opportunity occurs, or he has managed to create one, let him not be slow to make use of it. Strong in his principles, earnest in his tone, and affectionate in heart, let him speak out like a man and thank God for the privilege. There need be no reticence—there should be none. The maddest romances of Spiritualists, the wildest dreams of Utopian reformers, the silliest chit-chat of the town, and the vainest nonsense of the frivolous world, demand a hearing and get it. And shall not Christ be heard? Shall His message of love remain untold, for fear we should be charged with intrusion or accused of cant? Is religion to be tabooed—the best and noblest of all themes forbidden? If this be the rule of any society, we will not comply with it. If we cannot break it down, we will leave the society to itself, as men desert a house smitten with leprosy. We cannot consent to be gagged. There is no reason why we should be. We will go to no place where we cannot take our Master with us. While others take liberty to sin, we shall not renounce our liberty to rebuke and warn them.

Wisely used, our common conversation may be a potent means for good. Trains of thought may be started by a single sentence which may lead to the conversion of persons whom our sermons have never reached. The method of button-holing people, or bringing the truth before them individually, has been greatly successful: this is another subject, and can hardly come under the head of Common Conversation; but we will close by saying that it is to be hoped that we shall never, in our ordinary talk, any more than in the pulpit, be looked upon as nice sort of persons, whose business it is to make things agreeable all round, and who never by any possibility cause uneasiness to any one, however ungodly their lives may be. Such persons go in and out among the families of their hearers, and make merry with them, when they ought to be mourning over them. They sit down at their tables and feast at their ease, when they ought to be warning them to flee from the wrath to come. They are like that American alarum I have heard of, which was warranted not to wake you if you did not wish it to do so.

Be it ours to sow, not only on the honest and good soil, but on the rock and on the highway, and at the last great day to reap a glad harvest. May the bread which we cast upon the waters in odd times and strange occasions be found again after many days.

XIII

To Workers with Slender Apparatus

WHAT are those ministers to do who have a slender apparatus? By a slender apparatus I mean that they have few books, and little or no means wherewith to purchase more. This is a state of things which ought not to exist in any case; the churches ought to take care that it should be rendered impossible. Up to the highest measure of their ability they should furnish their minister, not only with the food which is needful to sustain the life of his body, but with mental nutriment, so that his soul may not be starved. A good library should be looked upon as an indispensable part of church furniture; and the deacons, whose business it is "to serve tables," will be wise if, without neglecting the table of the Lord, or of the poor, and without diminishing the supplies of the minister's dinner-table, they give an eye to his study-table, and keep it supplied with new works and standard books in fair abundance. It would be money well laid out, and would be productive far beyond expectation. Instead of waxing eloquent upon the declining power of the pulpit, leading men in the church should use the legitimate means for improving its power, by supplying the preacher with food for thought. Put the whip into the manger is my advice to all grumblers.

Some years ago I tried to induce our churches to have ministers' libraries as a matter of course, and some few thoughtful people saw the value of the suggestion, and commenced carrying it out. With much pleasure I have seen here and there the shelves provided and a few volumes placed upon them. I earnestly wish that such a beginning had been made everywhere; but, alas! I fear that a long succession of starveling ministers will alone arouse the miserly to the conviction that parsimony with a minister is false economy. Those churches which cannot afford a liberal stipend should make some amends by founding a library as a permanent part of their establishment; and, by making additions to it from year to year, it would soon become very valuable. My venerable grandfather's manse had in it a collection of very valuable ancient Puritanic volumes, which had descended from minister to minister: well do I remember certain ponderous tomes, whose chief interest to me lay in their curious initial letters, adorned with pelicans, griffins, little boys at play, or patriarchs at work. It may be objected that the books would be lost

175

through change of users, but I would run the risk of that; and trustees, with a little care over the catalogue, could keep the libraries as securely as they keep the pews and pulpit.

If this scheme be not adopted, let another and simpler one be tried; let all the subscribers towards the preacher's support add ten per cent or more to their subscriptions, expressly to provide food for the minister's brain. They would get back what they gave in the improved sermons they would hear. If some little annual income could be secured to poor ministers, to be sacredly spent in books, it would be a God-send to them, and an incalculable blessing to the community. Sensible persons do not expect a garden to yield them herbs from year to year unless they enrich the soil; they do not expect a locomotive to work without fuel, or even an ox or an ass to labour without food; let them, therefore, give over expecting to receive instructive sermons from men who are shut out of the storehouse of knowledge by their inability to purchase books.

But the subject is, what are men to do who have no stores, who have no church library, and no allowance made them to provide books? Let us remark at once that, if these men succeed, greater honour is due to them than to those who have large appliances.

Quintin Matsys is said to have had all his tools except his hammer and file taken from him by his fellow workmen, and to have produced his famous well-cover without them; so much the more honour to him! Great credit is due to those workers for God who have done great things without helpful tools. Their labour would have been greatly lightened if they had possessed them; but what they have done is the more wonderful. At the present International Exhibition at Kensington, Mr. Buckmaster's School of Cookery is mainly admired because he produces such savoury dishes from unpromising material; from a handful of bones and a little macaroni he serves up royal dainties. If he had all the materials employed in French cookery, and used them all, every person would say, "Well, anybody could do that;" but when he shows you scraps of meat and bones, and tells you that he bought them at the butcher's for a few pence, and that he can make out of them a dinner for a family of five or six, all the good wives open their eyes, and wonder how on earth it can be done; and when he passes round his dish, and they taste how delicious it is, they are full of admiration. Work away, then, poor brother, for you may yet succeed in doing great things in your ministry, and your welcome of "Well done, good and faithful servant," will be all the more emphatic because you laboured under serious difficulties.

If a man can purchase but very few books, my first advice to him would be, *let him purchase the very best*. If he cannot spend much, let him spend well. The best will always be the cheapest. Leave mere dilutions and attenuations to those who can afford such luxuries. Do not buy milk and water, but get condensed milk, and put what water you like to it yourself. This age is full of word-spinners— professional book-makers, who hammer a grain of matter so thin that it will cover a five-acre sheet of paper; these men have their uses, as gold-beaters have, but they are of no use to you. Farmers on our coast used to cart wagon-loads of seaweed and put them upon their land; the heaviest part was the water: now they dry the weeds, and save a world of labour and expense. Don't buy thin soup; purchase the essence of meat. Get much in little. Prefer books which abound in what James Hamilton used to call "Bibline," or the essence of books. You require accurate, condensed, reliable, standard books, and should make sure that you get them. In preparing his *Horae Biblicae Quotidianae*, which is an admirable comment upon the Bible, Dr. Chalmers used only the *Concordance*, the *Pictorial Bible*, *Poole's Synopsis*, *Matthew Henry's Commentary*, and *Robinson's Researches in Palestine*. "These are the books I use," said he to a friend; "all that is Biblical is there; I have to do with nothing besides in my Biblical study." This shows that those who have unlimited stores at their command, yet find a few standard books sufficient. If Dr. Chalmers were now alive, he would probably take Thomson's *Land and the Book* instead of *Robinson's Researches*, and give up the *Pictorial Bible* for Kitto's *Daily Bible Illustrations*; at least I should recommend the alteration to most men. This is clear evidence that some most eminent preachers have found that they could do better with few books than with many when studying the Scriptures, and this, I take it, is our main business.

Forgo, then, without regret, the many books which, like poor Hodge's razors, of famous memory, "are made to sell," and do sell those who buy them, as well as themselves. Matthew Henry's Commentary having been mentioned, I venture to say that no better investment can be made, by any minister, than that peerless· exposition. Get it, if you sell your coat to buy it.

The next rule I shall lay down is, *master those books you have*. Read them thoroughly. Bathe in them until they saturate you. Read and re-read them, masticate them, and digest them. Let them go into your very self. Peruse a good book several times, and make notes and analyses of it. A student will find that his mental constitution is more affected by one book thoroughly mastered than by twenty books which he has merely skimmed, lapping at them, as the classic proverb puts it "As the dogs drink of Nilus." Little learning and much pride come of hasty reading. Books may be piled on the brain till it cannot work. Some men are disabled from thinking by their putting meditation away for the sake of much reading. They gorge themselves with book-matter, and become mentally dyspeptic.

Books *on* the brain cause disease. Get the book *into* the brain, and you will grow. In D'Israeli's *Curiosities of Literature* there is an invective of Lucian upon those men who boast of possessing large libraries, which they either never read or never profit by. He begins by comparing such a person to a pilot who never learned the art of navigation, or a cripple who wears embroidered slippers but cannot stand upright in them. Then he exclaims, "Why do you buy so many books? You have no hair, and you purchase a comb; you are blind, and you must need buy a fine mirror; you are deaf, and you will have the best musical instrument!"—a very well-deserved rebuke to those who think that the possession of books will secure them learning. A measure of that temptation happens to us all; for do we not feel wiser after we have spent an hour or two in a bookseller's shop? A man might as well think himself richer for having inspected the vaults of the Bank of England. In reading books let your motto be, "Much, not many." Think as well as read, and keep the thinking always proportionate to the reading, and your small library will not be a great misfortune.

There is very much sound sense in the remark of a writer in the *Quarterly Review* many years back. "Give us the *one* dear book, cheaply picked from the stall by the price of the dinner, thumbed and dog-eared, cracked in the back and broken in the corner, noted on the fly-leaf and scrawled on the margin, sullied and scorched, torn and worn, smoothed in the pocket and grimed on the hearth, damped by the grass and dusted among the cinders, over which you have dreamed in the grove and dozed before the embers, but read again, again, and again, from cover to cover. It is by this one book, and its three or four single successors, that more real cultivation has been imparted than by all the myriads which bear down the mile-long, bulging, bending shelves of the Bodleian."

But if you feel you must have more books, *I recommend to you a little judicious borrowing.* You will most likely have some friends who have books, and who will be kind enough to let you use them for a time; and I specially advise you, in order to borrow again, to return whatsoever is lent, promptly, and in good condition. I hope there is not so much need that I should say much about returning books, as there would have been a few months ago, for I have lately met with a statement by a clergyman, which has very much raised my opinion of human nature; for he declares that he has a personal acquaintance with three gentlemen who have actually returned borrowed umbrellas! I am sorry to say that he moves in a more favoured circle than I do, for I have personal acquaintance with several young men who have borrowed books and never returned them. The other day, a certain minister, who had lent me *five* books, which I have used for two years or more, wrote to me a note to request the return of *three* of them. To his surprise, he had them back by the next "Parcels' Delivery," and two others which he had forgotten. I had carefully kept a list of books borrowed, and, therefore, could make a complete return to the owner. I am sure he did not expect their prompt arrival, for he wrote me a letter of mingled astonishment and gratitude, and when I visit his study again, I feel sure I shall be welcome to another loan. You know the rhyme which has been written in many a man's book—

> "If thou art borrowed by a friend,
> Right welcome shall he be
> To read, to study, not to lend,
> But to return to me.
> Not that imparted knowledge doth
> Diminish learning's store,
> But books I find when once they're lent,
> Return to me no more."

Sir Walter Scott used to say that his friends might be very indifferent accountants, but he was sure they were good "book-keepers." Some have even had to go the length of the scholar who, when asked to lend a book, sent word by the servant that he would not let the book go out of his chamber, but that the gentleman who sought the loan might come and sit there and read as long as he liked. The rejoinder was unexpected but complete, when, his fire being slow to burn, he sent to the same person to borrow a pair of bellows, and received for answer that the owner would not lend the bellows out of his own chamber, but the gentleman might come and blow there as long as he liked. Judicious borrowing may furnish you with much reading, but remember the man's axe-head in the Scriptures, and be careful of what you borrow. "The wicked borroweth and payeth not again."

In case the famine of books should be sore in the land, *there is one book which you all have, and that is your Bible*; and a minister with his Bible is like David with his sling and stone, fully equipped for the fray. No man may say that he has no well to draw from while the Scriptures are within reach. In the Bible we have a perfect library, and he who studies it thoroughly will be a better scholar than if he had devoured the Alexandrian Library entire. To understand the Bible should be our ambition; we should be familiar with it, as familiar as the housewife with her needle, the merchant with his ledger, the mariner with his ship. We ought to know its general run, the contents of each book, the details of its histories, its doctrines, its precepts, and everything about it. Erasmus, speaking of Jerome, asks, "Who but he ever learned by heart the whole Scripture? or imbibed, or meditated on it as he did?" It is said of Witsius, a learned Dutchman, author of the famous work on "The Covenants," that he also was able, not merely to repeat every word of Scripture in the original tongues, but to give the context, and the criticisms of the best authors; and I have heard of an old minister in Lancashire, that he was "a walking Concordance," and could either give you chapter and verse for any passage quoted, or, *vice versa,* could correctly give the words when the place was mentioned. That may have been a feat of memory, but the study needful to it must have been highly profitable. I do not say that you must aspire to that; but if you could, it would be well worth the gaining. It was one of the fortes of that singular genius, William Huntington (whom I will not now either condemn or commend), that in preaching he incessantly quoted Holy Scripture, and was accustomed, whenever he did so, to give the chapter and the verse; and in order to show his independence of the printed book, it was his uncomely habit to remove the Bible from the front of the pulpit.

A man who has learned not merely the letter of the Bible, but its inner spirit, will be no mean man, whatever deficiencies he may labour under. You know the old proverb, *"Cave ab homine unius libri"—Beware of the man of one book.* He is a terrible antagonist. A man who has his Bible at his fingers' ends and in his heart's core is a champion in our Israel; you cannot compete with him: you may have an armoury of weapons, but his Scriptural knowledge will overcome you; for it is a sword like that of Goliath, of which David said, "There is none like it." The gracious William Romaine, I believe, in the latter part of his life, put away all his books and read nothing at all but his Bible. He was a scholarly man, yet he was monopolised by the one Book, and was made mighty by it. If we are driven to do the same by necessity, let us recollect that some have done it by choice, and let us not bemoan our lot, for the Scriptures will be sweeter than honey to our taste, and will make us "wiser than the ancients." We shall never be short of holy matter if we are continually studying the inspired volume; nay, it is not only matter that we shall find there, but illustration too; for the Bible is its own best illustrator. If you want anecdote, simile, allegory, or parable, turn to the sacred page. Scriptural truth never looks more lovely than when she is adorned with jewels from her own treasury. I have lately been reading the Books of the Kings and the Chronicles, and I have become enamoured of them; they are as full of divine instruction as the Psalms or Prophets, if read with opened eyes. I think it was Ambrose who used to say, "I adore the infinity of Scripture." I hear that same voice which sounded in the ears of Augustine, concerning the Book of God, *"Tolle, lege"—Take, read.* It may be you will dwell in retirement in some village, where you will find no one to converse with who is above your own level, and where you will meet with very few books worth your reading; then read and meditate in the law of the Lord both day and night, and you shall be "as a tree planted by the rivers of water." Make the Bible the man of your right hand, the companion of every hour, and you will have little reason to lament your slender equipment in inferior things.

I would earnestly impress upon you the truth, that a man who is short of apparatus can *make up for it by much thought.* Thinking is better than possessing books. Thinking is an exercise of the soul which both develops its powers and educates them. A little girl was once asked whether she knew what her soul was, and, to the surprise of all, she said, "Sir, my soul is my think." If this be correct, some persons have very little soul. Without thinking, reading cannot benefit the mind, but it may delude the man into the idea that he is growing wise. Books are a sort of idol to some men. As the image with the Roman Catholic is intended to make him think of Christ, and in effect keeps him from Christ, so books are intended to make men think, but are often a hindrance to thought. When George Fox took a sharp knife and cut out for himself a pair of leather breeches, and, having done with the fashions of society, hid himself in a hollow tree, to think by the month together, he was growing into a man of thought before whom men of books speedily beat a retreat. What a flutter he made, not only among the Poperies, and Prelacies, and Presbyteries of his day, but also among the well-read proprieties of Dissent. He swept no end of cobwebs out of the sky, and gave the bookworms a hard time of it. Thought is the backbone of study, and if more ministers would think, what a blessing it would be! Only, we want men who will think about the revealed truth of God, and not dreamers who evolve religions out of their own consciousness. Nowadays we are pestered with a set of fellows who must needs stand on their heads and think with their feet. Romancing is their notion of meditation. Instead of considering revealed truth, they excogitate a mess of their own, in which error, and nonsense, and conceit appear in about equal parts; and they call this broth "modern thought." We want men who will try to think straight, and yet think deep, because they think God's thoughts. Far be it from me to urge you to imitate the boastful thinkers of this age, who empty their meeting-houses, and then glory that they preach to the cultivated and intellectual. It is miserable cant. Earnest thought upon the things which are assuredly believed among us is quite another matter, and to that I urge you. Personally I owe much to many hours, and even days, spent alone, under an old oak-tree, by the river Medway. Happening to be somewhat indisposed at the time when I was leaving school, I was allowed considerable leisure, and, armed with an excellent fishing-rod, I caught a few small fishes, and enjoyed many day-dreams, intermingled with searchings of heart, and much ruminating of knowledge acquired. If boys would think, it would be well to give them less class work and more opportunity for thought. All cram and no digestion makes flesh destitute of muscle, and this is even more deplorable mentally than physically. If your people are not numerous enough to supply you with a library, they will make fewer demands on your time, and, in having time for meditation, you will be even better off than your brethren with many books and little space for quiet contemplation.

Without books *a man may learn much by keeping his eyes open.* Current history, incidents which transpire under his own nose, events recorded in the newspaper, matters of common talk—he may learn from them all. The difference between eyes and no eyes is wonderful. If you have no books to try your eyes, keep them open wherever you go, and you will find something worth looking at. Can you not learn from nature? Every flower is waiting to teach you. "Consider the lilies," and learn from the roses. Not only may you go to the ant, but every living thing offers itself for your instruction. There is a voice in every gale, and a lesson in every grain of dust it bears. Sermons glisten in the morning on every blade of grass, and homilies fly by you as the sere leaves fall from the trees. A forest is a library, a cornfield is a volume of philosophy, the rock is a history, and the river at its base a poem. Go, thou who hast thine eyes opened, and find lessons of wisdom everywhere, in heaven above, in the earth beneath, and in the waters under the earth. Books are poor things compared with these.

Moreover, however scant your libraries, *you can study yourself.* This is a mysterious volume, the major part of which you have not read. If any man think that he knows himself thoroughly, he deceives himself; for the most difficult book you will ever read is your own heart. I said to a doubter the other day, who seemed to be wandering in a maze, "Well, really I cannot understand you; but I am not vexed, for I never could understand myself;" and I certainly meant what I said. Watch the twists and turns and singularities of your own mind, and the strangeness of your own experience; the depravity of your heart, and the work of divine grace; your tendency to sin, and your capacity for holiness; how akin you are to a devil, and yet how allied to God Himself! Note how wisely you can act when taught of God, and how foolishly you behave when left to yourself. You will find the study of your heart to be of immense importance to you as a watcher over the souls of others. A man's own experience should be to him the laboratory in which he tests the medicines which he prescribes for others. Even your own faults and failures will instruct you if you bring them to the Lord. Absolutely sinless men would be unable to sympathise with imperfect men and women. Study the Lord's dealings with your own souls, and you will know more of His ways with others.

Read other men; they are as instructive as books. Suppose there should come up to one of our great hospitals a young student so poor that he could not purchase surgical books; it would certainly be a great detriment to him; but if he had the run of the hospital, if he saw operations performed, and watched cases from day to day, I should not wonder but what he might turn out as skilful a surgeon as his more favoured companions. His observation would show him what books alone could not; and as he stood by to see the removal of a limb, the binding up of a wound, or the tying up of an artery, he might, at any rate, pick up enough practical surgery to be of immense service to him. Now, much that a minister needs to know he must learn by actual observation. All wise pastors have walked the hospitals spiritually, and dealt with inquirers, hypocrites, backsliders, the despairing, and the presumptuous. A man who has had a sound practical experience in the things of God Himself, and watched the hearts of his fellows, other things being equal, will be a far more useful man than he who knows only what he has read. It is a great pity for a man to be a college Jack-a-dandy, who comes out of the class-room as out of a band-box, into a world he has never seen before, to deal with men he has never observed, and handle facts with which he has never come into personal contact. "Not a novice," says the apostle; and it is possible to be a novice and yet a very accomplished scholar, a classic, a mathematician, and a theoretical theologian. We should have practical familiarity with men's souls; and if we have much of it, the fewness of our books will be a light affliction. "But," says an inquiring brother, "how can you read a man?" I have heard of a gentleman of whom it was said that you could never stop five minutes under an archway with him but what he would teach you something. That was a wise man; but he would be a wiser man still who would never stop five minutes under an archway without learning somewhat from other people. Wise men can learn as much from a fool as from a philosopher. A fool is a splendid book to read from, because every leaf is open before you; there is a dash of the comic in the style, which entices you to read on, and if you gather nothing else, you are warned not to publish your own folly.

Learn from experienced saints. What deep things some of them can teach to us younger men! What instances God's poor people can narrate of the Lord's providential appearances for them; how they glory in His upholding grace and His faithfulness to His covenant! What fresh light they often shed upon the promises, revealing meanings hidden from the carnally wise, but made clear to simple hearts! Know you not that many of the promises are written with invisible ink, and must be held to the fire of affliction before the letters will show themselves? Tried spirits are grand instructors for ministers.

As for the inquirer, how much is to be gathered from him! I have seen very much of my own stupidity while in conversation with seeking souls. I have been baffled by a poor lad while trying to bring him to the Saviour; I thought I had him fast, but he has eluded me again and again with perverse ingenuity of unbelief. Sometimes inquirers who are really anxious surprise me with their singular skill in battling against hope; their arguments are endless and their difficulties countless. They put us to a *non plus* again and again. The grace of God at last enables us to bring them to the light, but not until we have seen our own inefficiency. In the strange perversities of unbelief, the singular constructions and misconstructions which the desponding put upon their feelings and upon scriptural statements, you will often find a world of instruction. I would sooner give a young man an hour with inquirers and the mentally depressed than a week in the best of our classes, so far as practical training for the pastorate is concerned.

Once more, *be much at death-beds*; they are illuminated books. There shall you read the very poetry of our religion, and learn the secrets thereof. What splendid gems are washed up by the waves of Jordan! What fair flowers grow on its banks! The everlasting fountains in the glory-land throw their spray aloft, and the dew-drops fall on this side the narrow stream! I have heard humble men and women, in their departing hours, talk as though they were inspired, uttering strange words, aglow with supernal glory. These they learned from no lips beneath the moon; they must have heard them while sitting in the suburbs of the New Jerusalem. God whispers them in their ears amid their pain and weakness; and then they tell us a little of what the Spirit has revealed. I will part with all my books, if I may see the Lord's Elijahs mount their chariots of fire.

XIV

The Holy Spirit in Connection with our Ministry

I HAVE selected a topic upon which it would be difficult to say anything which has not been often said before; but as the theme is of the highest importance it is good to dwell upon it frequently, and even if we bring forth only old things and nothing more, it may be wise to put you in remembrance of them. Our subject is "THE HOLY SPIRIT IN CONNECTION WITH OUR MINISTRY," or—the work of the Holy Ghost in relation to ourselves as ministers of the gospel of Jesus Christ.

"I BELIEVE IN THE HOLY GHOST." Having pronounced that sentence as a matter of creed, I hope we can also repeat it as a devout soliloquy forced to our lips by personal experience. To us the presence and work of the Holy Spirit are the ground of our confidence as to the wisdom and hopefulness of our life work. If we had *not* believed in the Holy Ghost we should have laid down our ministry long ere this, for "who is sufficient for these things?" Our hope of success, and our strength for continuing the service, lie in our belief that the Spirit of the Lord resteth upon us.

I will for the time being take it for granted that we are all of us conscious of the existence of the Holy Spirit. We have said we *believe* in Him; but in very deed we have advanced beyond faith in this matter, and have come into the region of consciousness. Time was when most of us believed in the existence of our present friends, for we had heard of them by the hearing of the ear, but we have now seen each other, and returned the fraternal grip, and felt the influence of happy companionship, and therefore we do not now so much believe as know. Even so we have *felt* the Spirit of God operating upon our hearts, we have known and perceived the power which He wields over human spirits, and we know Him by frequent, conscious, personal contact. By the sensitiveness of our spirit we are as much made conscious of the presence of the Spirit of God as we are made cognizant of the existence of the souls of our fellow-men by their action upon our souls, or as we are certified of the existence of matter by its action upon our senses. We have been raised from the dull sphere of mere mind and matter into the heavenly radiance of the spirit-world; and

185

now, as spiritual men, we discern spiritual things, we feel the forces which are paramount in the spirit-realm, and we know that there is a Holy Ghost, for we feel Him operating upon our spirits. If it were not so, we should certainly have no right to be in the ministry of Christ's church. Should we even dare to remain in her membership? But, my brethren, we have been spiritually quickened. We are distinctly conscious of a new life, with all that comes out of it: we are new creatures in Christ Jesus, and dwell in a new world. We have been illuminated, and made to behold the things which eye hath not seen; we have been guided into truth such as flesh and blood could never have revealed. We have been comforted of the Spirit: full often have we been lifted up from the deeps of sorrow to the heights of joy by the sacred Paraclete. We have also, in a measure, been sanctified by Him; and we are conscious that the operation of sanctification is going on in us in different forms and ways. Therefore, because of all these personal experiences, we know that there is a Holy Ghost, as surely as we know that we ourselves exist.

I am tempted to linger here, for the point is worthy of longer notice. Unbelievers ask for phenomena. The old business doctrine of Gradgrind has entered into religion, and the sceptic cries, "What I want is facts." *These are our facts:* let us not forget to use them. A sceptic challenges me with the remark, "I cannot pin my faith to a book or a history; I want to see present facts." My reply is, "*You* cannot see them, because your eyes are blinded; but the facts are there none the less. Those of us who have eyes see marvellous things, though you do not." If he ridicules my assertion, I am not at all astonished. I expected him to do so, and should have been very much surprised if he had not done so; but I demand respect to my own position as a witness to facts, and I turn upon the objector with the enquiry— "What right have you to deny my evidence? If I were a blind man, and were told by you that you possessed a faculty called sight, I should be unreasonable if I railed at you as a conceited enthusiast. All you have a right to say is—that you know nothing about it, but you are not authorized to call us all liars or dupes. You may join with revilers of old and declare that the spiritual man is mad, but that does not disprove his statements." Brethren, to me the phenomena which are produced by the Spirit of God demonstrate the truth of the Christian religion as clearly as ever the destruction of Pharaoh at the Red Sea, or the fall of manna in the wilderness, or the water leaping from the smitten rock, could have proved to Israel the presence of God in the midst of her tribes.

We will now come to the core of our subject. To us, as ministers, the Holy Spirit is absolutely essential. Without Him our office is a mere name. We claim no priesthood over and above that which belongs to every child of God; but we are the successors of those who, in olden times, were moved of God to declare His word, to testify against transgression, and to lead His cause. Unless we have the spirit of the prophets resting upon us, the mantle which we wear is nothing but a rough garment to deceive. We ought to be driven forth with abhorrence from the society of honest men for daring to speak in the name of the Lord if the Spirit of God rests not upon us. We believe ourselves to be spokesmen for Jesus Christ, appointed to continue His witness upon earth; but upon Him and His testimony the Spirit of God always rested, and if it does not rest upon us, we are evidently not sent forth into the world as He was. At Pentecost the commencement of the great work of converting the world was with flaming tongues and a rushing mighty wind, symbols of the presence of the spirit; if, therefore, we think to succeed without the Spirit, we are not after the Pentecostal order. If we have not the Spirit which Jesus promised, we cannot perform the commission which Jesus gave.

I need scarcely warn any brother here against falling into the delusion that we may have the Spirit so as to become inspired. Yet the members of a certain litigious modern sect need to be warned against this folly. They hold that their meetings are under "the presidency of the Holy Spirit": concerning which notion I can only say that I have been unable to discover in holy Scripture either the term or the idea. I do find in the New Testament a body of Corinthians eminently gifted, fond of speaking, and given to party strifes—true representatives of those to whom I allude, but as Paul said of them, "I thank God I baptized *none of you*," so also do I thank the Lord that few of that school have ever been found in our midst. It would seem that their assemblies possess a peculiar gift of inspiration, not quite perhaps amounting to infallibility, but nearly approximating thereto. If you have mingled in their gatherings, I greatly question whether you have been more edified by the prelections produced under celestial presidency, than you have been by those of ordinary preachers of the Word, who only consider themselves to be under the influence of the Holy Spirit, as one spirit is under the influence of another spirit, or one mind under the influence of another mind. We are not the passive communicators of infallibility, but the honest teachers of such things as we have learned, so far as we have been able to grasp them. As our minds are active, and have a personal existence while the mind of the Spirit is acting upon them, *our* infirmities are apparent as well as *His* wisdom; and while we reveal what He has made us to know, we are greatly abased by the fear that our own ignorance and error are in a measure manifested at the same time, because we have not been more perfectly subject to the divine power. I do not suspect that you will go astray in the direction I have hinted at: certainly the results of previous experiments are not likely to tempt wise men to that folly.

This is our first question. *Wherein may we look for the aid of the Holy Spirit?* When we have spoken on this point, we will, very solemnly, consider a second—*How may we lose that assistance?* Let us pray that, by God's blessing, this consideration may help us to retain it.

Wherein may we look for the aid of the Holy Spirit? I should reply,—in seven or eight ways.

1. First, *He is the Spirit of knowledge,*—"He shall guide you into all truth." In this character we need His teaching.

We have urgent need to study, for the teacher of others must himself be instructed. Habitually to come into the pulpit unprepared is unpardonable presumption: nothing can more effectually lower ourselves and our office. After a visitation discourse by the Bishop of Lichfield upon the necessity of earnestly studying the Word, a certain vicar told his lordship that he could not believe his doctrine, "for," said he, "often when I am in the vestry I do not know what I am going to talk about; but I go into the pulpit and preach, and think nothing of it." His lordship replied, "And you are quite right in thinking nothing of it, for your churchwardens have told me that they share your opinion." If we are not instructed, how can we instruct? If we have not thought, how shall we lead others to think? It is in our study-work, in that blessed labour when we are alone with the Book before us, that we need the help of the Holy Spirit. He holds the key of the heavenly treasury, and can enrich us beyond conception; He has the clue of the most labyrinthine doctrine, and can lead us in the way of truth. He can break in pieces the gates of brass, and cut in sunder the bars of iron, and give to us the treasures of darkness, and hidden riches of secret places. If you study the original, consult the commentaries, and meditate deeply, yet if you neglect to cry mightily unto the Spirit of God your study will not profit you; but even if you are debarred the use of helps (which I trust you will not be), if you wait upon the Holy Ghost in simple dependence upon His teaching, you will lay hold of very much of the divine meaning.

The Spirit of God is peculiarly precious to us, because He especially instructs us as to the person and work of our Lord Jesus Christ; and that is the main point of our preaching. He takes of the things *of Christ*, and shows them unto us. If He had taken of the things of doctrine or precept, we should have been glad of such gracious assistance; but since He especially delights in the things of Christ, and focusses His sacred light upon the cross, we rejoice to see the centre of our testimony so divinely illuminated, and we are sure that the light will be diffused over all the rest of our ministry. Let us wait upon the Spirit of God with this cry—"O Holy Spirit, reveal to us the Son of God, and thus show us the Father."

As the Spirit of knowledge, He not only instructs us as to the gospel, but He leads us to see the Lord in all other matters. We are not to shut our eyes to God in nature, or to God in general history, or to God in the daily occurrences of providence, or to God in our own experience; and the blessed Spirit is the interpreter to us of the mind of God in all these. If we cry, "Teach me what thou wouldst have me to do; or, show me wherefore thou contendest with me; or, tell me what is thy mind in this precious providence of mercy, or in that other dispensation of mingled judgment and grace,"—we shall in each case be well instructed; for the Spirit is the seven-branched candlestick of the sanctuary, and by His light all things are rightly seen. As Goodwin well observes, "There must be light to accompany the truth if we are to know it. The experience of all gracious men proves this. What is the reason that you shall see some things in a chapter at one time, and not at another; some grace in your hearts at one time, and not at another; have a sight of spiritual things at one time, and not at another? The eye is the same, but it is the Holy Ghost that openeth and shutteth this dark lantern, as I may so call it; as He openeth it wider, or contracts it, or shutteth it narrower, so do we see more or less: and sometimes He shutteth it wholly, and then the soul is in darkness, though it have never so good an eye."

Beloved brethren, wait upon Him for this light, or you will abide in darkness and become blind leaders of the blind.

2. In the second place, the Spirit is called *the Spirit of wisdom*, and we greatly need Him in that capacity; for knowledge may be dangerous if unaccompanied with wisdom, which is the art of rightly using what we know. Rightly to divide the Word of God is as important as fully to understand it, for some who have evidently understood a part of the gospel have given undue prominence to that one portion of it, and have therefore exhibited a distorted Christianity, to the injury of those who have received it, since they in their turn have exhibited a distorted character in consequence thereof. A man's nose is a prominent feature in his face, but it is possible to make it so large that eyes and mouth and everything else are thrown into insignificance, and the drawing is a caricature and not a portrait: so certain important doctrines of the gospel can be so proclaimed in excess as to throw the rest of truth into the shade, and the preaching is no longer the gospel in its natural beauty, but a caricature of the truth, of which caricature, however, let me say, some people seem to be mightily fond. The Spirit of God will teach you the use of the sacrificial knife to divide the offerings; and He will show you how to use the balances of the sanctuary so as to weigh out and mix the

precious spices in their proper quantities. Every experienced preacher feels this to be of the utmost moment, and it is well if he is able to resist all temptation to neglect it. Alas, some of our hearers do not desire to hear the whole counsel of God. They have their favourite doctrines, and would have us silent on all besides. Many are like the Scotchwoman, who, after hearing a sermon, said, "It was very well if it hadna been for the trash of duties at the *hinner* end." There are brethren of that kind; they enjoy the comforting part—the promises and the doctrines, but practical holiness must scarcely be touched upon. Faithfulness requires us to give them a four-square gospel, from which nothing is omitted, and in which nothing is exaggerated, and for this much wisdom is requisite. I gravely question whether any of us have so much of this wisdom as we need. We are probably afflicted by some inexcusable partialities and unjustifiable leanings; let us search them out and have done with them. We may be conscious of having passed by certain texts, not because we do not understand them (which might be justifiable), but because we do understand them, and hardly like to say what they have taught us, or because there may be some imperfection in ourselves, or some prejudice among our hearers which those texts would reveal too clearly for our comfort. Such sinful silence must be ended forthwith. To be wise stewards and bring forth the right portions of meat for our Master's household we need Thy teaching, O Spirit of the Lord!

Nor is this all, for even if we know how rightly to divide the Word of God, we want wisdom in the selection of the particular part of truth which is most applicable to the season and to the people assembled; and equal discretion in the tone and manner in which the doctrine shall be presented. I believe that many brethren who preach human responsibility deliver themselves in so legal a manner as to disgust all those who love the doctrines of grace. On the other hand, I fear that many have preached the sovereignty of God in such a way as to drive all persons who believe in man's free agency entirely away from the Calvinistic side. We should not hide truth for a moment, but we should have wisdom so to preach it that there shall be no needless jarring or offending, but a gradual enlightenment of those who cannot see it at all, and a leading of weaker brethren into the full circle of gospel doctrine.

Brethren, we also need wisdom in the way of putting things to different people. You can cast a man down with the very truth which was intended to build him up. You can sicken a man with the honey with which you meant to sweeten his mouth. The great mercy of God has been preached unguardedly, and has led hundreds into licentiousness; and, on the other hand, the terrors of the Lord have been occasionally fulminated with such violence that they have driven men into despair, and so into a settled defiance of the Most High.

Wisdom is profitable to direct, and He who hath it brings forth each truth in its season, dressed in its most appropriate garments. Who can give us this wisdom but the blessed Spirit? O, my brethren, see to it, that in lowliest reverence you wait for His direction.

3. Thirdly, we need the Spirit in another manner, namely, as the live coal from off the altar, touching our lips, so that when we have knowledge and wisdom to select the fitting portion of truth, we may enjoy *freedom of utterance* when we come to deliver it. "Lo, this hath touched thy lips." Oh, how gloriously a man speaks when his lips are blistered with the live coal from the altar—feeling the burning power of the truth, not only in his inmost soul, but on the very lip with which he is speaking! Mark at such times how his very utterance quivers. Did you not notice in the prayer-meeting just now, in two of the suppliant brethren, how their tones were tremulous, and their bodily frames were quivering, because not only were their hearts touched, as I hope all our hearts were, but their lips were touched, and their speech was thereby affected. Brethren, we need the Spirit of God to open our mouths that we may show forth the praises of the Lord, or else we shall not speak with power.

We need the divine influence to keep us back from saying many things which, if they actually left our tongue, would mar our message. Those of us who are endowed with the dangerous gift of humour have need, sometimes, to stop and take the word out of our mouth and look at it, and see whether it is quite to edification; and those whose previous lives have borne them among the coarse and the rough had need watch with lynx eyes against indelicacy. Brethren, far be it from us to utter a syllable which would suggest an impure thought, or raise a questionable memory. We need the Spirit of God to put bit and bridle upon us to keep us from saying that which would take the minds of our hearers away from Christ and eternal realities, and set them thinking upon the grovelling things of earth.

Brethren, we require the Holy Spirit also to incite us in our utterance. I doubt not you are all conscious of different states of mind in preaching. Some of those states arise from your body being in different conditions. A bad cold will not only spoil the clearness of the voice, but freeze the flow of the thoughts. For my own part if I cannot speak clearly I am unable to think clearly, and the matter becomes hoarse as well as the voice. The stomach, also, and all the other organs of the body, affect the mind; but it is not to these things that I allude. Are you not conscious of changes altogether independent of the body? When you are in robust health do you not find yourselves one day as heavy as Pharaoh's chariots with the wheels taken off, and at another time as much at liberty as "a hind let loose"? To-day your branch glitters with the dew, yesterday it was parched with drought. Who knoweth not that the Spirit of God is in all this? The divine Spirit will sometimes work upon us so as to bear us completely out of ourselves. From the beginning of the sermon to the end we might at such times say, "Whether in the body or out of the body I cannot tell: God knoweth." Everything has been forgotten but the one all-engrossing subject in hand. If I were forbidden to enter heaven, but were permitted to select my state for all eternity, I should choose to be as I sometimes feel in preaching the gospel. Heaven is foreshadowed in such a state: the mind shut out from all disturbing influences, adoring the majestic and consciously present God, every faculty aroused and joyously excited to its utmost capability, all the thoughts and powers of the soul joyously occupied in contemplating the glory of the Lord, and extolling to listening crowds the Beloved of our soul; and all the while the purest conceivable benevolence towards one's fellow creatures urging the heart to plead with them on God's behalf—what state of mind can rival this? Alas, we have reached this ideal, but we cannot always maintain it, for we know also what it is to preach in chains, or beat the air. We may not attribute holy and happy changes in our ministry to anything less than the action of the Holy Spirit upon our souls. I am sure the Spirit does so work. Often and often, when I have had doubts suggested by the infidel, I have been able to fling them to the winds with utter scorn, because I am distinctly conscious of a power working upon me when I am speaking in the name of the Lord, infinitely transcending any personal power of fluency, and far surpassing any energy derived from excitement such as I have felt when delivering a secular lecture or making a speech—so utterly distinct from such power that I am quite certain it is not of the same order or class as the enthusiasm of the politician or the glow of the orator. May we full often feel the divine energy, and speak with power.

4. But then, fourthly, the Spirit of God acts also as *an anointing oil,* and this relates to *the entire delivery*—not to the utterance merely from the mouth, but to the whole delivery of the discourse. He can make you feel your subject till it thrills you, and you become depressed by it so as to be crushed into the earth, or elevated by it so as to be borne upon its eagle wings; making you feel, besides your subject, your object, till you yearn for the conversion of men, and for the uplifting of Christians to something nobler than they have known as yet. At the same time, another feeling is with you, namely, an intense desire that God may be glorified through the truth which you are delivering. You are conscious of a deep sympathy with the people to whom you are speaking, making you mourn over some of them because they know so little, and over others because they have known much, but have rejected it. You look into some faces, and your heart silently says, "The dew is dropping there;" and, turning to

others, you sorrowfully perceive that they are as Gilboa's dewless mountain. All this will be going on during the discourse. We cannot tell how many thoughts can traverse the mind at once. I once counted eight sets of thoughts which were going on in my brain simultaneously, or at least within the space of the same second. I was preaching the gospel with all my might, but could not help feeling for a lady who was evidently about to faint, and also looking out for our brother who opens the windows that he might give us more air. I was thinking of that illustration which I had omitted under the first head, casting the form of the second division, wondering if A felt my rebuke, and praying that B might get comfort from the consoling observation, and at the same time praising God for my own personal enjoyment of the truth I was proclaiming. Some interpreters consider the cherubim with their four faces to be emblems of ministers, and assuredly I see no difficulty in the quadruple form, for the sacred Spirit can multiply our mental states, and make us many times the men we are by nature. How much He can make of us, and how grandly He can elevate us, I will not dare to surmise: certainly, He can do exceeding abundantly above what we ask or even think.

Especially is it the Holy Spirit's work to maintain in us a devotional frame of mind whilst we are discoursing. This is a condition to be greatly coveted—to continue praying while you are occupied with preaching; to do the Lord's commandments, hearkening unto the voice of His word; to keep the eye on the throne, and the wing in perpetual motion. I hope we know what this means; I am sure we know, or may soon experience, its opposite, namely, the evil of preaching in an undevotional spirit. What can be worse than to speak under the influence of a proud or angry spirit? What more weakening than to preach in an unbelieving spirit? But, oh, to burn in our secret heart while we blaze before the eyes of others! This is the work of the Spirit of God. Work it in us, O adorable Comforter!

In our pulpits we need the spirit of dependence to be mixed with that of devotion, so that all along, from the first word to the last syllable, we may be looking up to the strong for strength. It is well to feel that though you have continued up to the present point, yet if the Holy Spirit were to leave you, you would play the fool ere the sermon closed. Looking to the hills whence cometh your help all the sermon through, with absolute dependence upon God, you will preach in a brave confident spirit all the while. Perhaps I was wrong to say "brave," for it is not a brave thing to trust God: to true believers it is a simple matter of sweet necessity—how can they help trusting Him? Wherefore should they doubt their ever faithful Friend? I told my people the other morning, when preaching from the text, "My grace is sufficient for thee," that for the first time in my life I experienced what Abraham felt when he fell upon his face and laughed. I was riding home, very weary with a long week's work, when there came to my mind this text: "My grace is sufficient for thee"; but it came with the emphasis laid upon two words. "*My* grace is sufficient for *thee*." My soul said, "Doubtless it is. Surely the grace of the infinite God is more than sufficient for such a mere insect as I am," and I laughed, and laughed again, to think how far the supply exceeded all my needs. It seemed to me as though I were a little fish in the sea, and in my thirst I said, "Alas, I shall drink up the ocean." Then the Father of the waters lifted up His head sublime, and smilingly replied, "Little fish, the boundless main is sufficient for thee." The thought made unbelief appear supremely ridiculous, as indeed it is. Oh, brethren, we ought to preach feeling that God means to bless the word, for we have His promise for it; and when we have done preaching we should look out for the people who have received a blessing. Do you ever say, "I am overwhelmed with astonishment to find that the Lord has converted souls through my poor ministry"? Mock humility! Your ministry is poor enough. Everybody knows that, and you ought to know it most of all: but, at the same time, is it any wonder that God, who said "My word shall not return unto me void," has kept His promise? Is the meat to lose its nourishment because the dish is a poor platter? Is divine grace to be overcome by our infirmity? No, but we have this treasure in earthen vessels, that the excellency of the power may be of God and not of us.

We need the Spirit of God, then, all through the sermon to keep our hearts and minds in a proper condition, for if we have not the right spirit we shall lose the tone which persuades and prevails, and our people will discover that Samson's strength has departed from him. Some speak scoldingly, and so betray their bad temper; others preach themselves, and so reveal their pride. Some discourse as though it were a condescension on their part to occupy the pulpit, while others preach as though they apologised for their existence. To avoid errors of manners and tone, we must be led of the Holy Spirit, who alone teacheth us to profit.

5. Fifthly, we depend entirely upon the Spirit of God *to produce actual effect from the gospel,* and at this effect we must always aim. We do not stand up in our pulpits to display our skill in spiritual sword play, but we come to actual fighting: our object is to drive the sword of the Spirit through men's hearts. If preaching can ever in any sense be viewed as a public exhibition, it should be like the exhibition of a ploughing match, which consists in actual ploughing. The competition does not lie in the appearance of the ploughs, but in the work done; so let ministers be judged by the way in which they drive the gospel plough, and cut the furrow from end to end of the field.

Always aim at effect. "Oh," says one, "I thought you would have said, 'Never do that.'" I do also say, never aim at effect, in the unhappy sense of that expression. Never aim at effect after the manner of the climax makers, poetry quoters, handkerchief manipulators, and bombast blowers. Far better for a man that he had never been born than that he should degrade a pulpit into a show box to exhibit himself in. Aim at the right sort of effect; the inspiring of saints to nobler things, the leading of Christians closer to their Master, the comforting of doubters till they rise out of their terrors, the repentance of sinners, and their exercise of immediate faith in Christ. Without these signs following, what is the use of our sermons? It would be a miserable thing to have to say with a certain archbishop, "I have passed through many places of honour and trust, both in Church and State, more than any of my order in England, for seventy years before; but were I assured that by my preaching I had but converted one soul to God, I should herein take more comfort than in all the honoured offices that have been bestowed upon me." Miracles of grace must be the seals of our ministry; who can bestow them but the Spirit of God? Convert a soul without the Spirit of God! Why, you cannot even make a fly, much less create a new heart and a right spirit. Lead the children of God to a higher life without the Holy Ghost! You are inexpressibly more likely to conduct them into carnal security, if you attempt their elevation by any method of your own. Our ends can never be gained if we miss the co-operation of the Spirit of the Lord. Therefore, with strong crying and tears, wait upon Him from day to day.

The lack of distinctly recognizing the power of the Holy Ghost lies at the root of many useless ministries. The forcible words of Robert Hall are as true now as when he poured them forth like molten lava upon a semi-socinian generation. "On the one hand it deserves attention, that the most eminent and successful preachers of the gospel in different communities, a Brainerd, a Baxter, and a Schwartz, have been the most conspicuous for simple dependence on spiritual aid; and on the other that no success whatever has attended the ministrations of those by whom this doctrine has been either neglected or denied. They have met with such a rebuke of their presumption, in the total failure of their efforts, that none will contend for the reality of Divine interposition, as far as they are concerned; for when has the arm of the Lord been revealed to those pretended teachers of Christianity, who believe there is no such arm? We must leave them to labour in a field respecting which God has commanded the clouds not to rain upon it. As if conscious of this, of late they have turned their efforts into a new channel, and despairing of the conversion of sinners, have confined themselves to the seduction of the faithful; in which, it must be confessed, they have acted in a manner perfectly consistent with their principles; the propagation of heresy requiring, at least, no divine assistance."

6. Next we need the Spirit of God as *the Spirit of supplications,* who maketh intercession for the saints according to the will of God. A very important part of our lives consists in praying in the Holy Ghost, and that minister who does not think so had better escape from his ministry. Abundant prayer must go with earnest preaching. We cannot be always on the knees of the body, but the soul should never leave the posture of devotion. The habit of prayer is good, but the spirit of prayer is better. Regular retirement is to be maintained, but continued communion with God is to be our aim. As a rule, we ministers ought never to be many minutes without actually lifting up our hearts in prayer. Some of us could honestly say that we are seldom a quarter of an hour without speaking to God, and that not as a duty but as an instinct, a habit of the new nature for which we claim no more credit than a babe does for crying after its mother. How could we do otherwise? Now, if we are to be much in the spirit of prayer, we need secret oil to be poured upon the sacred fire of our heart's devotion; we want to be again and again visited by the Spirit of grace and of supplications.

As to our prayers in public, let it never be truthfully said that they are official, formal, and cold; yet they will be so if the supply of the Spirit be scant. Those who use a liturgy I judge not; but to those who are accustomed to free prayer I say,—you cannot pray acceptably in public year after year without the Spirit of God; dead praying will become offensive to the people long before that time. What then? Whence shall our help come? Certain weaklings have said, "Let us have a liturgy!" Rather than seek divine aid they will go down to Egypt for help. Rather than be dependent upon the Spirit of God, they will pray by a book! For my part, if I cannot pray, I would rather know it, and groan over my soul's barrenness till the Lord shall again visit me with fruitfulness of devotion. If you are filled with the Spirit, you will be glad to throw off all formal fetters, that you may commit yourself to the sacred current, to be borne along till you find waters to swim in. Sometimes you will enjoy closer fellowship with God in prayer in the pulpit than you have known anywhere else. To me my greatest secrecy in prayer has often been in public; my truest loneliness with God has occurred to me while pleading in the midst of thousands. I have opened my eyes at the close of a prayer and come back to the assembly with a sort of a shock at finding myself upon earth and among men. Such seasons are not at our command, neither can we raise ourselves into such conditions by any preparations or efforts. How blessed they are both to the minister and his people no tongue can tell! How full of power and blessing habitual prayerfulness must also be I cannot here pause to declare, but for it all we must look to the Holy Spirit, and blessed be God we shall not look in vain, for it is especially said of Him that He helped our infirmities in prayer.

7. Furthermore, it is important that we be under the influence of the Holy Ghost, as He is the *Spirit of Holiness;* for a very considerable and essential part of Christian ministry lies in example. Our people take much note of what we say out of the pulpit, and what we do in the social circle and elsewhere. Do you find it easy, my brethren, to be saints?—such saints that others may regard you as examples? We ought to be such husbands that every husband in the parish may safely be such as we are. Is it so? We ought to be the best of fathers. Alas! some ministers, to my knowledge, are far from this, for as to their families, they have kept the vineyards of others, but their own vineyards they have not kept. Their children are neglected, and do not grow up as a godly seed. Is it so with yours? In our converse with our fellow men are we blameless and harmless, the sons of God without rebuke? Such we ought to be. I admire Mr. Whitfield's reasons for always having his linen scrupulously clean. "No, no," he would say, "these are not trifles; a minister must be without spot, even in his garments, if he can." Purity cannot be carried too far in a minister. You have known an unhappy brother bespatter himself, and you have affectionately aided in removing the spots, but you have felt that it would have been better had the garments been always white. O to keep ourselves unspotted from the world! How can this be in such a scene of temptation, and with such besetting sins unless we are preserved by superior power? If you are to walk in all holiness and purity, as becometh ministers of the gospel, you must be daily baptized into the Spirit of God.

8. Once again, we need the Spirit as *a Spirit of discernment,* for He knows the minds of men as He knows the mind of God, and we need this very much in dealing with difficult characters. There are in this world some persons who might possibly be allowed to preach, but they should never be suffered to become pastors. They have a mental or spiritual disqualification. In the church of San Zeno, at Verona, I saw the statue of that saint in a sitting posture, and the artist has given him knees so short that he has no lap whatever, so that he could not have been a nursing father. I fear there are many others who labour under a similar disability: they cannot bring their minds to enter heartily into the pastoral care. They can dogmatize upon a doctrine, and controvert upon an ordinance, but as to sympathizing with an experience, it is far from them. Cold comfort can such render to afflicted consciences; their advice will be equally valuable with that of the highlander who is reported to have seen an Englishman sinking in a bog on Ben Nevis. "I am sinking!" cried the traveller. "Can you tell me how to get out?" The highlander calmly

replied, "I think it is likely you never will," and walked away. We have known ministers of that kind, puzzled, and almost annoyed with sinners struggling in the slough of despond. If you and I, untrained in the shepherd's art, were placed among the ewes and young lambs in the early spring, what should we do with them? In some such perplexity are those found who have never been taught of the Holy Spirit how to care for the souls of men. May His instructions save us from such wretched incompetence.

Moreover, brethren, whatever our tenderness of heart, or loving anxiety, we shall not know how to deal with the vast variety of cases unless the Spirit of God shall direct us, for no two individuals are alike; and even the same case will require different treatment at different times. At one period it may be best to console, at another to rebuke; and the person with whom you sympathized even to tears to-day may need that you confront him with a frown to-morrow, for trifling with the consolation which you presented. Those who bind up the broken-hearted, and set free the captives, must have the Spirit of the Lord upon them.

In the oversight and guidance of a church the Spirit's aid is needed. At bottom the chief reason for secession from our denomination has been the difficulty arising out of our church government. It is said to "tend to the unrest of the ministry." Doubtless, it is very trying to those who crave for the dignity of officialism, and must need be Sir Oracles, before whom not a dog must bark. Those who are no more capable of ruling than mere babes are the very persons who have the greatest thirst for authority, and, finding little of it awarded to them in these parts, they seek other regions. If you cannot rule yourself, if you are not manly and independent, if you are not superior in moral weight, if you have not more gift and more grace than your ordinary hearers, you may put on a gown and claim to be the ruling person in the church; but it will not be in a church of the Baptist or New Testament order. For my part I should loathe to be the pastor of a people who have nothing to say, or who, if they do say anything, might as well be quiet, for the pastor is Lord Paramount, and they are mere laymen and nobodies. I would sooner be the leader of six free men, whose enthusiastic love is my only power over them, than play the dictator to a score of enslaved nations. What position is nobler than that of a spiritual father who claims no authority and yet is universally esteemed, whose word is given only as tender advice, but is allowed to operate with the force of law? Consulting the wishes of others he finds that they first desire to know what he would recommend, and deferring always to the desires of others, he finds that they are glad to defer to him. Lovingly firm and graciously gentle, he is the chief of all because he is the servant of all. Does not this need wisdom from above? What can require it more? David when established on the throne said, "It is He that subdueth my people under me," and so may every happy pastor say when he sees so many brethren of differing temperaments all happily willing to be under discipline, and to accept his leadership in the work of the Lord. If the Lord were not among us how soon there would be confusion. Ministers, deacons, and elders may all be wise, but if the sacred Dove departs, and the spirit of strife enters, it is all over with us. Brethren, our system will not work without the Spirit of God, and I am glad it will not, for its stoppages and breakages call our attention to the fact of His absence. Our system was never intended to promote the glory of priests and pastors, but it is calculated to educate manly Christians, who will not take their faith at second-hand. What am I, and what are you, that we should be lords over God's heritage? Dare any of us say with the French king, "*L'état, c'est moi*" —"the state is myself,"—I am the most important person in the church? If so, the Holy Spirit is not likely to use such unsuitable instruments; but if we know our places and desire to keep them with all humility, He will help us, and the churches will flourish beneath our care.

I have given you a lengthened catalogue of matters wherein the Holy Spirit is absolutely necessary to us, and yet the list is very far from complete. I have intentionally left it imperfect, because if I attempted its completion all our time would have expired before we were able to answer the question, How MAY WE LOSE THIS NEEDFUL ASSISTANCE? Let none of us ever try the experiment, but it is certain that ministers may lose the aid of the Holy Ghost. Each man here may lose it. You shall not perish as believers, for everlasting life is in you; but you may perish as ministers, and be no more heard of as witnesses for the Lord. Should this happen it will not be without a cause. The Spirit claims a sovereignty like that of the wind which bloweth where it listeth; but let us never dream that sovereignty and capriciousness are the same thing. The blessed Spirit acts as He wills, but He always acts justly, wisely, and with motive and reason. At times He gives or withholds His blessing, for reasons connected with ourselves. Mark the course of a river like the Thames; how it winds and twists according to its own sweet will: yet there is a reason for every bend and curve: the geologist studying the soil and marking the conformation of the rock, sees a reason why the river's bed diverges to the right or to the left: and so, though the Spirit of God blesses one preacher more than another, and the reason cannot be such that any man could congratulate himself upon his own goodness, yet there are certain things about Christian ministers which God blesses, and certain other things which hinder success. The Spirit of God falls like the dew, in mystery and power, but it is in the spiritual world as in the natural: certain substances are wet with the celestial moisture while others are always dry. Is there not a cause? The wind blows where it lists; but if we desire to feel a stiff breeze we must go out to sea, or climb the hills. The Spirit of God has His favoured places for displaying His might. He is typified by a dove, and the dove has its chosen haunts: to the rivers of waters, to the peaceful and quiet places, the dove resorts; we meet it not upon the battlefield, neither does it alight on carrion. There are things congruous to the Spirit and things contrary to His mind. The Spirit of God is compared to light, and light can shine where it wills, but some bodies are opaque, while others are transparent; and so there are men through whom God the Holy Ghost can shine, and there are others through whom His brightness never appears. Thus, then, it can be shown that the Holy Ghost, though He be the "free Spirit" of God, is by no means capricious in His operations.

But, dear brethren, the Spirit of God may be grieved and vexed, and even resisted: to deny this is to oppose the constant testimony of Scripture. Worst of all, we may do despite to Him, and so insult Him that He will speak no more by us, but leave us as He left King Saul of old. Alas, that there should be men in the Christian ministry to whom this has happened; but I am afraid there are.

Brethren, what are those evils which will grieve the Spirit? I answer, anything that would have disqualified you as an ordinary Christian for communion with God also disqualifies you for feeling the extraordinary power of the Holy Spirit as a minister: but, apart from that, there are special hindrances.

Among the first we must mention a want of sensitiveness, or that unfeeling condition which arises from disobeying the Spirit's influences. We should be delicately sensitive to His faintest movement, and then we may expect His abiding presence, but if we are as the horse and as the mule, which have no understanding, we shall feel the whip, but we shall not enjoy the tender influences of the Comforter.

Another grieving fault is a want of truthfulness. When a great musician takes a guitar, or touches a harp, and finds that the notes are false, he stays his hand. Some men's souls are not honest; they are sophistical and double-minded. Christ's Spirit will not be an accomplice with men in the wretched business of shuffling and deceiving. Does it really come to this—that you preach certain doctrines, not because you believe them, but because your congregation expects you to do so? Are you biding your time till you can, without risk, renounce your present creed and tell out what your dastardly mind really holds to be true? Then are you fallen indeed, and are baser than the meanest slaves. God deliver us from treacherous men, and if they enter our ranks, may they speedily be drummed out to the tune of the Rogue's March. If we feel an abhorrence of them, how much more must the Spirit of truth detest them!

You can greatly grieve the Holy Spirit by a general scantiness of grace. The phrase is awkward, but it describes certain persons better than any other which occurs to me. The Scanty-grace family usually have one of the brothers in the ministry. I know the man. He is not dishonest, nor immoral, he is not bad tempered, nor self-indulgent, but there is a something wanting: it would not be easy to prove its absence by any overt offence, but it is wanting in the whole man, and its absence spoils everything. He wants the one thing needful. He is not spiritual, he has no savour of Christ, his heart never burns within him, his soul is not alive, he wants grace. We cannot expect the Spirit of God to bless a ministry which never ought to have been exercised, and certainly a graceless ministry is of that character.

Another evil which drives away the divine Spirit is pride. The way to be very great is to be very little. To be very noteworthy in your own esteem is to be unnoticed of God. If you must needs dwell upon the high places of the earth, you shall find the mountain summits cold and barren: the Lord dwells with the lowly, but He knows the proud afar off.

The Holy Ghost is also vexed by laziness. I cannot imagine the Spirit waiting at the door of a sluggard, and supplying the deficiencies created by indolence. Sloth in the cause of the Redeemer is a vice for which no excuse can be invented. We ourselves feel our flesh creep when we see the dilatory movements of sluggards, and we may be sure that the active Spirit is equally vexed with those who trifle in the work of the Lord.

Neglect of private prayer and many other evils will produce the same unhappy result, but there is no need to enlarge, for your own consciences will tell you, brethren, what it is that grieves the Holy One of Israel.

And now, let me entreat you, listen to this word: *Do you know what may happen if the Spirit of God be greatly grieved and depart from us? There are two suppositions.* The first is that we never were God's true servants at all, but were only temporarily used by him, as Balaam was, and even the ass on which he rode. Suppose, brethren, that you and I go on comfortably preaching a while, and are neither suspected by ourselves nor others to be destitute of the Spirit of God: our ministry may all come to an end on a sudden, and we may come to an end with it; we may be smitten down in our prime, as were Nadab and Abidu, no more to be seen ministering before the Lord, or removed in riper years, like Hophni and Phineas, no longer to serve in the tabernacle of the congregation. We have no inspired annalist to record for us the sudden cutting off of promising men, but if we had, it may be we should read with terror--of zeal sustained by strong drink, of public Phariseeism associated with secret defilement, of avowed orthodoxy concealing absolute infidelity, or of some other form of strange fire presented upon the altar till the Lord would endure it no more, and cut off the offenders with a sudden stroke. Shall this terrible doom happen to any one of us?

Alas, I have seen some deserted by the Holy Spirit, as Saul was. It is written that the Spirit of God came upon Saul, but he was faithless to the divine influence, and it departed, and an evil spirit occupied its place. See how the deserted preacher moodily plays the cynic, criticises all others, and hurls the javelin of detraction at a better man than himself. Saul was once among the prophets, but he was more at home among the persecutors. The disappointed preacher worries the true evangelist, resorts to the witchcraft of philosophy, and seeks help from dead heresies; but his power is gone, and the Philistines will soon find him among the slain. "Tell it not in Gath, publish it not in the streets of Askelon! ye daughters of Israel weep over Saul! How are the mighty fallen in the midst of the battle!"

Some, too, deserted by the Spirit of God, have become like the sons of one Sceva, a Jew. These pretenders tried to cast out devils in the name of Jesus, whom Paul preached, but the devils leaped upon them and overcame them; thus while certain preachers have declaimed against sin, the very vices which they denounced have overthrown them. The sons of Scevo have been among us in England: the devils of drunkenness have prevailed over the very man who denounced the bewitching cup, and the demon of unchastity has leaped upon the preacher who applauded purity. If the Holy Ghost be absent, ours is of all positions the most perilous; therefore let us beware.

Alas, some ministers become like Balaam. He was a prophet, was he not? Did he not speak in the name of the Lord? Is he not called "the man whose eyes are opened, which saw the vision of the Almighty?" Yet Balaam fought against Israel, and cunningly devised a scheme by which the chosen people might be overthrown. Ministers of the gospel have become Papists, infidels, and freethinkers, and plotted the destruction of what they once professed to prize. We may be apostles, and yet, like Judas, turn out to be sons of perdition. Woe unto us if this be the case!

Brethren, I will assume that we really are the children of God, and what then? Why, even then, if the Spirit of God depart from us, we may be taken away on a sudden as the deceived prophet was who failed to obey the command of the Lord in the days of Jeroboam. He was no doubt a man of God, and the death of his body was no evidence of the loss of his soul, but he broke away from what he knew to be the command of God given specially to himself, and his ministry ended there and then, for a lion met him by the way and slew him. May the Holy Spirit preserve us from deceivers, and keep us true to the voice of God.

Worse still, we may reproduce the life of Samson, upon whom the Spirit of God came in the camps of Dan; but in Delilah's lap he lost his strength, and in the dungeon he lost his eyes. He bravely finished his life-work, blind as he was, but who among us wishes to tempt such a fate?

Or—and this last has saddened me beyond all expression, because it is much more likely than any of the rest—we may be left by the Spirit of God, in a painful degree, to mar the close of our life-work as Moses did. Not to lose our souls, nay, not even to lose our crowns in heaven, or even our reputations on earth; but, still, to be under a cloud in our last days through once speaking unadvisedly with our lips. I have lately studied the later days of the great prophet of Horeb, and I have not yet recovered from the deep gloom of spirit which it cast over me. What was the sin of Moses? You need not enquire. It was not gross like the transgression of David, nor startling like the failure of Peter, nor weak and foolish like the grave fault of his brother Aaron; indeed, it seems an infinitesimal offence as weighed in the balances of ordinary judgment. But then, you see, it was the sin of Moses, of a man favoured of God beyond all others, of a leader of the people, of a representative of the divine King. The Lord could have overlooked it in anyone else, but not in Moses: Moses must be chastened by being forbidden to lead the people into the promised land. Truly, he had a glorious view from the top of Pisgah, and everything else which could mitigate the rigour of the sentence, but it was a great disappointment never to enter the land of Israel's inheritance, and that for once speaking unadvisedly. I would not shun my Master's service, but I tremble in His presence. Who can be faultless when even Moses erred? It is a dreadful thing to be beloved of God. "Who among us shall dwell with devouring fire? Who among us shall dwell with everlasting burnings? He that walketh righteously and speaketh uprightly"—he alone can face that sin-consuming flame of love. Brethren, I beseech you, crave Moses's place, but tremble as you take it. Fear and tremble for all the good that God shall make to pass before you. When you are fullest of the fruits of the Spirit bow lowest before the throne, and serve the Lord with fear. "The Lord our God is a jealous God." Remember that God has come unto us, not to exalt *us*, but to exalt *Himself*, and we must see to it that His glory is the one sole object of all that we do. "He must increase, and I must *decrease*." Oh, may God bring us to this, and make us walk very carefully and humbly before Him. God will search us and try us, for judgment begins at His house, and in that house it begins with His ministers. Will any of us be found wanting? Shall the pit of hell draw a portion of its wretched inhabitants from among our band of pastors? Terrible will be the doom of a fallen preacher: his condemnation will astonish common transgressors. "Hell from beneath is moved for thee to meet thee at thy coming." All they shall speak and say unto thee, "Art thou also become weak as we? Art thou become like unto us?" O for the Spirit of God to make and keep us alive unto God, faithful to our office, and useful to our generation, and clear of the blood of men's souls. Amen.

XV

The Necessity of Ministerial Progress[1]

DEAR FELLOW SOLDIERS! We are few, and we have a desperate fight before us, therefore it is needful that every man should be made the most of, and nerved to his highest point of strength. It is desirable that the Lord's ministers should be the picked men of the church, yea, of the entire universe, for such the age demands; therefore, in reference to yourselves and your personal qualifications, I give you the motto, *"Go forward."* Go *forward* in personal attainments, *forward* in gifts and in grace, *forward* in fitness for the work, and *forward* in conformity to the image of Jesus. The points I shall speak upon begin at the base, and ascend.

1. First, dear brethren, I think it necessary to say to myself and to you that *we must go forward in our mental acquirements.* It will never do for us continually to present ourselves to God at our worst. We are not worth His having at our best; but at any rate let not the offering be maimed and blemished by our idleness. "Thou shalt love the Lord thy God with all thy heart" is, perhaps, more easy to comply with, than to love Him with all our mind; yet we must give Him our mind as well as our affections, and that mind should be well furnished, that we may not offer Him an empty casket. Our ministry demands mind. I shall not insist upon "the enlightenment of the age"; still it is quite certain that there is a great educational advance among all classes, and that there will yet be much more of it. The time is passed when ungrammatical speech will suffice for a preacher. Even in a country village, where, according to tradition, "nobody knows nothing," the schoolmaster is now abroad, and want of education will hinder usefulness more than it once did; for, when the speaker wishes his audience to remember the gospel, they on the other hand will remember his ungrammatical expressions, and will repeat them as themes for jest, when we could have wished they had rehearsed the divine doctrines to one another in solemn earnest. Dear brethren, we must cultivate ourselves to the highest possible point, and we should do this, first, by gathering in knowledge that we may fill the barn, then by acquiring discrimination that we may winnow the heap, and lastly by a firm retentiveness of mind, by which we may lay up the winnowed grain in the storehouse. These three points may

[1] This lecture was delivered to ministers who had been educated at the Pastors' College as well as to students, hence certain differences of expression.

not be equally important, but they are all necessary to a complete man.

We must, I say, make great efforts to *acquire* information, especially of a Biblical kind. We must not confine ourselves to one topic of study, or we shall not exercise our whole mental manhood. God made the world for man, and He made man with a mind intended to occupy and use all the world; he is the tenant, and nature is for a while his house; why should he shut himself out of any of its rooms? Why refuse to taste any of the cleansed meats the great Father has put upon the table? Still, our main business is to study the Scriptures. The smith's main business is to shoe horses; let him see that he knows how to do it, for should he be able to belt an angel with a girdle of gold he will fail as a smith if he cannot make and fix a horse-shoe. It is a small matter that you should be able to write the most brilliant poetry, as possibly you could, unless you can preach a good and telling sermon, which will have the effect of comforting saints and convincing sinners. Study the Bible, dear brethren, through and through, with all helps that you can possibly obtain: remember that the appliances now within the reach of ordinary Christians are much more extensive than they were in our fathers' days, and therefore you must be greater Biblical scholars if you would keep in front of your hearers. Intermeddle with all knowledge, but above all things meditate day and night in the law of the Lord.

Be well instructed in theology, and do not regard the sneers of those who rail at it because they are ignorant of it. Many preachers are not theologians, and hence the mistakes which they make. It cannot do any hurt to the most lively evangelist to be also a sound theologian, and it may often be the means of saving him from gross blunders. Nowadays we hear men tear a single sentence of Scripture from its connection, and cry "Eureka! Eureka!" as if they had found a new truth; and yet they have not discovered a diamond, but a piece of broken glass. Had they been able to compare spiritual things with spiritual, had they understood the analogy of the faith, and had they been acquainted with the holy learning of the great Bible students of ages past, they would not have been quite so fast in vaunting their marvellous knowledge. Let us be thoroughly well acquainted with the great doctrines of the Word of God, and let us be mighty in expounding Scripture. I am sure that no preaching will last so long, or build up a church so well, as the expository. To renounce altogether the hortatory discourse for the expository would be running to a preposterous extreme; but I cannot too earnestly assure you that if your ministries are to be lastingly useful you must be expositors. For this you must understand the Word yourselves, and be able so to comment upon it that the people may be built up by the Word. Be masters of your Bibles, brethren: whatever other works you have not searched, be at home with the writings of the prophets and apostles. "Let the word of God dwell in you richly."

Having given precedence to the inspired writings, neglect no field of knowledge. The presence of Jesus on the earth has sanctified the realms of nature, and what He has cleansed call not you common. All that your Father has made is yours, and you should learn from it. You may read a naturalist's journal, or a traveller's voyage, and find profit in it. Yes, and even an old herbal, or a manual of alchemy may, like Samson's dead lion, yield you honey. There are pearls in oyster shells, and fruits on thorny boughs. The paths of true science, especially natural history and botany, drop fatness. Geology, so far as it is fact, and not fiction, is full of treasures. History—wonderful are the visions which it makes to pass before you—is eminently instructive; indeed, every portion of God's dominion in nature teems with precious teachings. Follow the trails of knowledge, according as you have the time, the opportunity, and the peculiar faculty; and do not hesitate to do so because of any apprehension that you will educate yourselves up to too high a point. When grace abounds, learning will not puff you up, or injure your simplicity in the gospel. Serve God with such education as you have, and thank Him for blowing through you if you are a ram's horn, but if there be a possibility of your becoming a silver trumpet, choose it rather.

I have said that we must also learn to *discriminate*, and at this particular time that point needs insisting on. Many run after novelties, charmed with every invention: learn to judge between truth and its counterfeits, and you will not be led astray. Others adhere like limpets to old teachings, and yet these may only be ancient errors: prove all things, and hold fast that which is good. The use of the sieve, and the winnowing fan, is much to be commended. Dear brethren, a man who has asked of the Lord to give him clear eyes by which he shall see the truth and discern its bearings, and who, by reason of the constant exercise of his faculties, has obtained an accurate judgment, is one fit to be a leader of the Lord's host; but all are not such. It is painful to observe how many embrace anything if it be but earnestly brought before them. They swallow the medicine of every spiritual quack who has enough of brazen assurance to appear to be sincere. Be ye not such children in understanding, but test carefully before you accept. Ask the Holy Spirit to give you the faculty of discerning, so shall you conduct your flocks far from poisonous meadows, and lead them into safe pasturage.

When in due time you have gained the power of acquiring knowledge, and the faculty of discrimination, seek next for ability to *retain* and hold firmly what you have learned. In these times certain men glory in being weathercocks; they hold fast nothing, they have, in fact, nothing worth the holding. They believed yesterday, but not that which they believe to-day, nor that which they will believe to-morrow; and he would be a greater prophet than Isaiah who should be able to tell what they will believe when next the moon doth fill her horns, for they are constantly altering, and seem to be born under that said moon, and to partake of her changing moods. These men may be as honest as they claim to be, but of what use are they? Like good trees oftentimes transplanted, they may be of a noble nature, but they bring forth nothing; their strength goes out in rooting and re-rooting, they have no sap to spare for fruit. Be sure you have the truth, and then be sure you hold it. Be ready for fresh truth, *if it be truth,* but be very chary how you subscribe to the belief that a better light has been found than that of the sun. Those who hawk new truth about the street, as the boys do a second edition of the evening paper, are usually no better than they should be. The fair maid of truth does not paint her cheeks and tire her head like Jezebel, following every new philosophic fashion; she is content with her own native beauty, and her aspect is in the main the same yesterday, to-day, and for ever. When men change often they generally need to be changed in the most emphatic sense. Our "modern thought" gentry are doing incalculable mischief to the souls of men, and resemble Nero fiddling upon the top of a tower with Rome burning at his feet. Souls are being damned, and yet these men are spinning theories. Hell gapes wide, and with her open mouth swallows up myriads, and those who should spread the tidings of salvation are "pursuing fresh lines of thought." Highly cultured soul-murderers will find their boasted "culture" to be no excuse in the day of judgment. For God's sake, let us know how men are to be saved, and get to the work: to be for ever deliberating as to the proper mode of making bread while a nation dies of famine is detestable trifling. It is time we knew what to teach, or else renounced our office. "For ever learning and never coming to the truth" is the motto of the worst rather than the best of men. I saw in Rome a statue of a boy extracting a thorn from his foot; I went my way, and returned in a year's time, and there sat the selfsame boy, extracting the intruder still. Is this to be our model? "I shape my creed every week," was the confession of one of these divines to me. Whereunto shall I liken such unsettled ones? Are they not like those birds which frequent the Golden Horn, and are to be seen from Constantinople, of which it is said that they are always on the wing, and never rest? No one ever saw them alight on the water or on the land, they are for ever poised in mid-air. The natives call them "lost souls," seeking rest and finding none. Assuredly, men who have no personal rest in the truth, if they are not saved themselves, are, at least, very unlikely to save others. He who has no assured truth to tell must not wonder if his hearers set small store by him. We must know the truth, understand it, and hold it with firm grip, or we cannot hope to lead others to believe it. Brethren, I charge you, seek to know and to discriminate; and then, having discriminated, labour to be rooted and grounded in the truth. Keep in full operation the processes of filling the barn, winnowing the grain, and storing it in granaries, so shall you mentally "Go forward."

2. We need to go forward in *oratorical qualifications*. I am beginning at the bottom, but even this is important, for it is a pity that even the feet of this image should be of clay. Nothing is trifling which can be of any service to our grand design. Only for want of a nail the horse lost his shoe, and so became unfit for the battle; that shoe was only a trifling rim of iron which smote the ground, and yet the neck clothed with thunder was of no avail when the shoe was gone. A man may be irretrievably ruined for spiritual usefulness, not because he fails either in character or spirit, but because he breaks down mentally or oratorically, and, therefore, I have begun with these points, and again remark that we must improve in. utterance. It is not every one of us who can speak as some can do, and even these men cannot speak up to their own ideal. If there be any brother here who thinks he can preach as well as he should, I would advise him to leave off altogether. If he did so he would be acting as wisely as the great painter who broke his palette, and, turning to his wife, said, "My painting days are over, for I have satisfied myself, and therefore I am sure my power is gone." Whatever other perfection may be reachable, I am certain that he who thinks he has gained perfection in oratory mistakes volubility for eloquence, and verbiage for argument. Whatever you may know, you cannot be truly efficient ministers if you are not "apt to teach." You know ministers who have mistaken their calling, and evidently have no gifts for it: make sure that none think the same of you. There are brethren in the ministry whose speech is intolerable; either they rouse you to wrath, or else they send you to sleep. No chloral can ever equal some discourses in sleep-giving properties; no human being, unless gifted with infinite patience, could long endure to listen to them, and nature does well to give the victim deliverance through sleep. I heard one say the other day that a certain preacher had no more gifts for the ministry than an oyster, and in my own judgment this was a slander on the oyster, for that worthy bivalve shows great discretion in his openings, and knows when to close. If some men were sentenced to hear their own sermons it would be a righteous judgment upon them, and they would soon cry out with Cain, "My punishment is greater than I can bear." Let us not fall under the same condemnation.

Brethren, we should cultivate a *clear style*. When a man does not make me understand what he means, it is because he does not himself know what he means. An average hearer, who is unable to follow the course of thought of the preacher, ought not to worry himself, but to blame the preacher, whose business it is to make the matter plain. If you look down into a well, if it be empty it will appear to be very deep, but if there be water in it you will see its brightness. I believe that many "deep" preachers are simply so because they are like dry wells with nothing whatever in them, except decaying leaves, a few stones, and perhaps a dead cat or two. If there be living water in your preaching it may be very deep, but the light of truth will give clearness to it. It is not enough to be so plain that you can be understood, you must speak so that you cannot be misunderstood.

We must cultivate a *cogent* as well as a clear style; our speech must be forceful. Some imagine that this consists in speaking loudly, but I can assure them they are in error. Nonsense does not improve by being bellowed. God does not require us to shout as if we were speaking to ten thousand when we are only addressing three hundred. Let us be forcible by reason of the excellence of our matter, and the energy of spirit which we throw into the delivery of it. In a word, let our speaking be *natural* and living. I hope we have foresworn the tricks of professional orators, the strain for effect, the studied climax, the pre-arranged pause, the theatric strut, the mouthing of words, and I know not what besides, which you may see in certain pompous divines who still survive upon the face of the earth. May such become extinct animals ere long, and may a living, natural, simple way of talking out the gospel be learned by us all; for I am persuaded that such a style is one which God is likely to bless.

Among many other things, we must cultivate *persuasiveness*. Some of our brethren have great influence over men, and yet others with greater gifts are devoid of it; these last do not appear to get near to the people, they cannot grip them and make them feel. There are preachers who in their sermons seem to take their hearers one by one by the button-hole, and drive the truth right into their souls, while others generalise so much, and are so cold withal, that one would think they were speaking of dwellers in some remote planet, whose affairs did not much concern them. Learn the art of pleading with men. You will do this well if you often see the Lord. If I remember rightly, the old classic story tells us that, when a soldier was about to kill Darius, his son, who had been dumb from his childhood, suddenly cried out in surprise, "Know you not that he is the king?" His silent tongue was unloosed by love to his father, and well may ours find earnest speech when the Lord is seen by us crucified for sin. If there be any speech in us, this will rouse it. The knowledge of the terrors of the Lord should also bestir us to persuade men. We cannot do other than plead with them to be reconciled to God.

Brethren, mark those who woo sinners to Jesus, find out their secret, and never rest till you obtain the same power. If you find them very simple and homely, yet if you see them really useful, say to yourself, "That is my fashion"; but if on the other hand you listen to a preacher who is much admired, and on inquiry find that no souls are savingly converted, say to yourself, "This is not the thing for me, for I am not seeking to be great, but to be really useful."

Let your oratory, therefore, constantly improve in clearness, cogency, naturalness, and persuasiveness. Try, dear brethren, to get such a style of speaking that you *suit yourselves to your audiences*. Much lies in that. The preacher who should address an educated congregation in the language which he would use in speaking to a company of costermongers would prove himself a fool: and on the other hand, he who goes down amongst miners and colliers with technical theological terms and drawing-room phrases acts like an idiot. The confusion of tongues at Babel was more thorough than we imagine. It did not merely give different lauguages to great nations, but it made the speech of each class to vary from that of others. A fellow of Billingsgate cannot understand a Fellow of Brasenose. Now as the costermonger cannot learn the language of the college, let the college learn the language of the costermonger. "We use the language of the market," said Whitfield, and this was much to his honour; yet when he stood in the drawing-room of the Countess of Huntingdon, and his speech entranced the infidel noblemen whom she brought to hear him, he adopted another style. His language was equally plain in each case, because it was equally familiar to the audience: he did not use the *ipsissima verba*, or his language would have lost its plainness in the one case or the other, and would either have been slang to the nobility, or Greek to the crowd. In our modes of speech we should aim at being "all things to all men." He is the greatest master of oratory who is able to address any class of people in a manner suitable to their condition, and likely to touch their hearts.

Brethren, let none excel us in power of speech: let none surpass us in the mastery of our mother tongue. Beloved fellow-soldiers, our tongues are the swords which God has given us to use for Him, even as it is said of our Lord, "Out of His mouth went a two-edged sword." Let these swords be sharp. Cultivate your powers of speech, and be amongst the foremost in the land for utterance. I do not exhort you to this because you are remarkably deficient; far from it, for everybody says to me, "We know the college men by their plain, bold speech." This leads me to believe that you have the gift largely in you, and I beseech you to take pains to perfect it.

3. Brethren, we must be even more earnest to go forward in *moral qualities*. Let the points I shall mention here come home to those who shall require them, but I assure you I have no special persons

among you in my mind's eye. We desire to rise to the highest style of ministry, and if so, even if we obtain the mental and oratorical qualifications, we shall fail, unless we also possess high moral qualities.

There are evils which we must shake off, as Paul shook the viper from his hand, and there are virtues which we must gain at any cost.

Self-indulgence has slain its thousands; let us tremble lest we perish by the hands of that Delilah. Let us have every passion and habit under due restraint: if we are not masters of ourselves we are not fit to be leaders in the church.

We must put away all notion of self-importance. God will not bless the man who thinks himself great. To glory even in the work of God the Holy Spirit in yourself is to tread dangerously near to self-adulation. "Let another praise thee, and not thine own lips," and be very glad when that other has sense enough to hold his tongue.

We must also have our tempers well under restraint. A vigorous temper is not altogether an evil. Men who are as easy as an old shoe are generally of as little worth. I would not say to you, "Dear brethren, have a temper," but I do say, "If you have it, control it carefully." I thank God when I see a minister have temper enough to be indignant at wrong, and to be firm for the right; still, temper is an edged tool, and often cuts the man who handles it. "Gentle, easy to be entreated," preferring to bear evil rather than inflict it, this is to be our spirit. If any brother here naturally boils over too soon, let him mind that when he does do so he scalds nobody but the devil, and then let him boil away.

We must conquer—some of us especially—our tendency to levity. A great distinction exists between holy cheerfulness, which is a virtue, and that general levity, which is a vice. There is a levity which has not enough heart to laugh, but trifles with everything; it is flippant, hollow, unreal. A hearty laugh is no more levity than a hearty cry. I speak of that religious veneering which is pretentious, but thin, superficial, and insincere about the weightiest matters. Godliness is no jest, nor is it a mere form. Beware of being actors. Never give earnest men the impression that you do not mean what you say, and are mere professionals. To be burning at the lip and freezing at the soul is a mark of reprobation. God deliver us from being superfine and superficial: may we never be the butterflies of the garden of God.

At the same time, we should avoid everything like the ferocity of bigotry. I know a class of religious people who, I have no doubt, were born of a woman, but they appear to have been suckled by a wolf. I have done them no dishonour: were not Romulus and Remus, the founders of Rome, so reared? Some warlike men of this order have had sufficient mental power to found dynasties of thought; but human kindness and brotherly love consort better with the kingdom of Christ. We are not to go about the world searching out heresies, like terrier dogs sniffing for rats; nor are we to be so confident of our own infallibility as to erect ecclesiastical stakes at which to roast all who differ from us, not, 'tis true, with fagots of wood, but with those coals of juniper, which consist of strong prejudice and cruel suspicion.

In addition to all this, there are mannerisms, and moods, and ways which I cannot now describe, against which we must struggle, for little faults may often be the source of failure, and to get rid of them may be the secret of success. Count nothing little which even in a small degree hinders your usefulness; cast out from the temple of your soul the seats of them that sell doves as well as the traffickers in sheep and oxen.

And, dear brethren, we must acquire certain moral faculties and habits, as well as put aside their opposites. He will never do much for God who has not integrity of spirit. If we be guided by policy, if there be any mode of action for us but that which is straightforward, we shall make shipwreck before long. Resolve, dear brethren, that you can be poor, that you can be despised, that you can lose life itself, but that you cannot do a crooked thing. For you, let the only policy be honesty.

May you also possess the grand moral characteristic of courage. By this we do not mean impertinence, impudence, or self-conceit; but real courage to do and say calmly the right thing, and to go straight on at all hazards, though there should be none to give you a good word. I am astonished at the number of Christians who are afraid to speak the truth to their brethren. I thank God I can say this, there is no member of my church, no officer of the church, and no man in the world to whom I am afraid to say before his face what I would say behind his back. Under God I owe my position in my own church to the absence of all policy, and the habit of saying what I mean. The plan of making things pleasant all round is a perilous as well as a wicked one. If you say one thing to one man, and another to another, they will one day compare notes and find you out, and then you will be despised. The man of two faces will sooner or later be the object of contempt, and justly so. Above all things avoid cowardice, for it makes men liars. If you have anything that you feel you ought to say about a man, let the measure of what you say be this—"How much dare I say to his face?" You must not allow yourselves a word more in censure of any man living. If that be your rule, your courage will save you from a thousand difficulties, and win you lasting respect.

Having the integrity and the courage, dear brethren, may you be gifted with an indomitable zeal. Zeal—what is it? How shall I describe it? Possess it, and you will know what it is. Be consumed with love for Christ, and let the flame burn continuously, not flaming up at public meetings and dying out in the routine work of every day. We need indomitable perseverance, dogged resolution, and a combination of sacred obstinacy, self-denial, holy gentleness, and invincible courage.

Excel also in one power, which is both mental and moral, namely, the power of concentrating all your forces upon the work to which you are called. Collect your thoughts, rally all your faculties, mass your energies, focus your capacities. Turn all the springs of your soul into one channel, causing it to flow onward in an undivided stream. Some men lack this quality. They scatter themselves and fail. Mass your battalions, and hurl them upon the enemy. Do not try to be great at this and great at that—to be "everything by turns, and nothing long"; but suffer your entire nature to be led in captivity by Jesus Christ, and lay everything at His dear feet who bled and died for you.

4. Above all these, we need *spiritual qualifications,* graces which must be wrought in us by the Lord Himself. This is the main matter, I am sure. Other things are precious, but this is priceless; we must be rich towards God.

We need to know ourselves. The preacher should be great in the science of the heart, the philosophy of inward experience. There are two schools of experience, and neither is content to learn from the other; let us be content, however, to learn from both. The one school speaks of the child of God as one who knows the deep depravity of his heart, who understands the loathsomeness of his nature, and daily feels that in his flesh there dwelleth no good thing. "That man has not the life of God in his soul," say they, "who does not know and feel this, and feel it by bitter and painful experience from day to day." It is in vain to talk to them about liberty, and joy in the Holy Ghost; they will not have it. Let us learn from these one-sided brethren. They know much that should be known, and woe to that minister who ignores their set of truths. Martin Luther used to say that temptation is the best teacher for a minister. There is truth on that side of the question. Another school of believers dwell much upon the glorious work of the Spirit of God, and rightly and blessedly so. They believe in the Spirit of God as a cleansing power, sweeping the Augean stable of the soul, and making it into a temple for God. But frequently they talk as if they had ceased to sin, or to be annoyed by temptation; they glory as if the battle were already fought, and the victory won. Let us learn from these brethren. All the truth they can teach us let us know. Let us become familiar with the hill-tops, and the glory that shines thereon, the Hermons and the Tabors, where we may be transfigured with our Lord. Do not be afraid of becoming too holy. Do not be afraid of being too full of the Holy Spirit. I would have you wise on all sides, and able to deal with man both in his conflicts and in his joys, as one familiar with both. Know where Adam left you; know where the Spirit of God has placed you. Do not know either of these so exclusively as to forget the other. I believe that if any men are likely to cry, "O wretched man that I am! Who shall deliver me from the body of this death?" it will always be the ministers, because we need to be tempted in all points, so that we may be able to comfort others. In a railway carriage last week I saw a poor man with his leg placed upon the seat. An official happening to see him in this posture, remarked, "Those cushions were not made for you to put your dirty boots on." As soon as the guard was gone the man put up his leg again, and said to me, "He has never broken his leg in two places, I am sure, or he would not be so sharp with me." When I have heard brethren who have lived at ease, enjoying good incomes, condemning others who are much tried, because they could not rejoice in their fashion, I have felt that they knew nothing of the broken bones which others have to carry throughout the whole of their pilgrimage.

Brethren, know man in Christ, and out of Christ. Study him at his best, and study him at his worst; know his anatomy, his secrets, and his passions. You cannot do this by books; you must have personal spiritual experience; God alone can give you that.

Among spiritual acquirements, it is beyond all other things needful to know him who is the sure remedy for all human diseases. Know Jesus. Sit at His feet. Consider His nature, His work, His sufferings, His glory. Rejoice in His presence: commune with Him from day to day. To know Christ is to understand the most excellent of sciences. You cannot fail to be wise if you commune with wisdom; you cannot miss of strength if you have fellowship with the mighty Son of God. I saw the other day in an Italian grotto a little fern, which grew where its leaves continually glistened and danced in the spray of a fountain. It was always green, and neither summer's drought nor winter's cold affected it. So let us for ever abide under the sweet influence of Jesus' love. Dwell in God, brethren; do not occasionally visit Him, but abide in Him. They say in Italy that where the sun does not enter the physician must. Where Jesus does not shine the soul is sick. Bask in His beams and you shall be vigorous in the service of the Lord. Last Sunday night I had a text which mastered me: "No man knoweth the Son but the Father." I told the people that poor sinners who had gone to Jesus and trusted Him thought they knew Him, but that they knew only a little of Him. Saints of sixty years' experience, who have walked with Him every day, think they know

Him; but they are only beginners yet. The perfect spirits before the throne, who have been for five thousand years perpetually adoring Him, perhaps think they know Him, but they do not to the full. "No man knoweth the Son but the Father." He is so glorious, that only the infinite God has full knowledge of Him, therefore there will be no limit to our study, or narrowness in our line of thought, if we make our Lord the great object of all our meditations.

Brethren, as the outcome of this, if we are to be strong men, we must be conformed to our Lord. Oh, to be like Him! Blessed be that cross on which we shall suffer, if we suffer for being made like unto the Lord Jesus. If we obtain conformity to Christ, we shall have a wondrous unction upon our ministry, and without that, what is a ministry worth?

In a word, we must labour for holiness of character. What is holiness? Is it not wholeness of character? a balanced condition in which there is neither lack nor redundance? It is not morality: that is a cold lifeless statue; holiness is life. You must have holiness; and, dear brethren, if you should fail in mental qualifications (as I hope you will not), and if you should have a slender measure of the oratorical faculty (as I trust you will not), yet, depend upon it, a holy life is, in itself, a wonderful power, and will make up for many deficiencies; it is, in fact, the best sermon the best man can deliver. Let us resolve that all the purity which can be had we will have, that all the sanctity which can be reached we will obtain, and that all the likeness to Christ that is possible in this world of sin shall certainly be in us through the work of the Spirit of God. The Lord lift us all as a college right up to a higher platform, and He shall have the glory!

5. Still I have not done, dear brethren. I have to say to you, go forward in *actual work,* for, after all, we shall be known by what we have done. We ought to be mighty in deed as well as word. There are good brethren in the world who are impractical. The grand doctrine of the second advent makes them stand with open mouths, peering into the skies, so that I am ready to say, "Ye men of Plymouth, why stand ye here gazing up into heaven?" The fact that Jesus Christ is to come is not a reason for star-gazing, but for working in the power of the Holy Ghost. Be not so taken up with speculations as to prefer a Bible reading over a dark passage in the Revelation to teaching in a ragged-school or discoursing to the poor concerning Jesus. We must have done with day-dreams, and get to work. I believe in eggs, but we must get chickens out of them. I do not mind how big your egg is; it may be an ostrich's egg if you like, but if there is nothing in it, pray clear away the shells. If something comes of it, God bless your speculations, and even if you should go a little further than I think it wise to venture, still, if you are more useful, God be

praised for it. We want facts—deeds done, souls saved. It is all very well to write essays, but what souls have you saved from going down to hell? Your excellent management of your school interests me, but how many children have been brought into the church by it? We are glad to hear of those special meetings, but how many have really been born to God in them? Are saints edified? Are sinners converted? To swing to and fro on a five-barred gate is not progress, yet some seem to think so. I see them in perpetual Elysium, humming over to themselves and their friends, "We are very comfortable." God save us from living in comfort while sinners are sinking into hell. In travelling along the mountain roads in Switzerland you will continually see marks of the boring-rod; and in every minister's life there should be traces of stern labour. Brethren, do something; do something; do something: While committees waste their time over resolutions, do something. While Societies and Unions are making constitutions, let us win souls. Too often we discuss, and discuss, and discuss, and Satan laughs in his sleeve. It is time we had done planning and sought something to plan. I pray you, be men of action all of you. Get to work and quit yourselves like men. Old Suvarov's idea of war is mine: "Forward and strike! No theory! Attack! Form column! Charge bayonets! Plunge into the centre of the enemy." Our one aim is to save sinners, and this we are not to talk about, but to do in the power of God.

6. Lastly, and here I am going to deliver a message which weighs upon me,—Go forward in the matter of *the choice of your sphere of action*. I plead this day for those who cannot plead for themselves, namely, the great outlying masses of the heathen world. Our existing pulpits are tolerably well supplied, but we need men who will build on new foundations. Who will do this? Are we, as a company of faithful men, clear in our consciences about the heathen? Millions have never heard the name of Jesus. Hundreds of millions have seen a missionary only once in their lives, and know nothing of our King. Shall we let them perish? Can we go to our beds and sleep while China, India, Japan, and other nations are being damned? Are we clear of their blood? Have they no claim upon us? We ought to put it on this footing—not "Can I prove that I *ought* to go?" but "Can I prove that I *ought not* to go?" When a man can prove honestly that he ought not to go then he is clear, but not else. What answer do you give, my brethren? I put it to you man by man. I am not raising a question among you which I have not honestly put to myself. I have felt that if some of our leading ministers would go forth it would have a grand effect in stimulating the churches, and I have honestly asked myself whether I ought to go. After balancing the whole thing I feel bound to keep my place, and I think the judgment of most Christians would be the same; but I hope I would cheerfully

go if it were my duty to do so. Brethren, put yourselves through the same process. We must have the heathen converted; God has myriads of His elect among them, we must go and search for them till we find them. Many difficulties are now removed, all lands are open to us, and distance is annihilated. True we have not the Pentecostal gift of tongues, but languages are now readily acquired, while the art of printing is a full equivalent for the lost gift. The dangers incident to missions ought not to keep any true man back, even if they were very great, but they are now reduced to a minimum. There are hundreds of places where the cross of Christ is unknown, to which we can go without risk. Who will go? The men who ought to go are young brethren of good abilities who have not yet taken upon themselves family cares.

Each student entering the college should consider this matter, and surrender himself to the work unless there are conclusive reasons for his not doing so. It is a fact that even for the colonies it is very difficult to find men, for I have had openings in Australia which I have been obliged to decline. It ought not to be so. Surely there is some self-sacrifice among us yet, and some among us are willing to be exiled for Jesus. The Mission languishes for want of men. If the men were forthcoming the liberality of the church would supply their needs, and, in fact, the liberality of the church had made the supply, and yet there are not the men to go. I shall never feel, brethren, that we, as a band of men, have done our duty until we see our comrades fighting for Jesus in every land in the van of conflict. I believe that if God moves you to go, you will be among the best of missionaries, because you will make the preaching of the gospel the great feature of your work, and that is God's sure way of power. I wish that our churches would imitate that of Pastor Harms, in Germany, where every member was consecrated to God indeed and of a truth. The farmers gave the produce of their lands, the working-men their labour; one gave a large house to be used as a missionary college, and Pastor Harms obtained money for a ship which he fitted out, to make voyages to Africa, and then he sent missionaries, and little companies of his people with them, to form Christian communities among the Bushmen. When will our churches be equally self-denying and energetic? Look at the Moravians! how every man and woman becomes a missionary, and how much they do in consequence. Let us catch their spirit. Is it a right spirit? Then it is right for us to have it. It is not enough for us to say, "Those Moravians are very wonderful people!" We ought to be wonderful people too. Christ did not purchase the Moravians any more than He purchased us; they are under no more obligation to make sacrifices than we are. Why then this backwardness? When we read of heroic men who gave up all for Jesus, we are not merely to admire, but to imitate them. Who will imitate them now? Come to the point. Are there not some among you willing to consecrate yourselves to the Lord? "Forward" is the watchword to-day! Are there no bold spirits to lead the van? Pray all of you that during this Pentecost the Spirit may say, "Separate me Barnabas and Saul for the work."

Forward! In God's name, FORWARD!!

XVI

The Need of Decision for the Truth

SOME things are true and some things are false: I regard that as an axiom; but there are many persons who evidently do not believe it. The current principle of the present age seems to be, "Some things are either true or false, according to the point of view from which you look at them. Black is white, and white is black according to circumstances; and it does not particularly matter which you call it. Truth of course is true, but it would be rude to say that the opposite is a lie; we must not be bigoted, but remember the motto, 'So many men, so many minds,'" Our forefathers were particular about maintaining landmarks; they had strong notions about fixed points of revealed doctrine, and were very tenacious of what they believed to be scriptural; their fields were protected by hedges and ditches, but their sons have grubbed up the hedges, filled up the ditches, laid all level, and played at leap-frog with the boundary stones. The school of modern thought laughs at the ridiculous positiveness of Reformers and Puritans; it is advancing in glorious liberality, and before long will publish a grand alliance between heaven and hell, or, rather, an amalgamation of the two establishments upon terms of mutual concession, allowing falsehood and truth to lie side by side, like the lion with the lamb. Still, for all that, my firm old-fashioned belief is that some doctrines are true, and that statements which are diametrically opposite to them are not true,—that when "No" is the fact, "Yes" is out of court, and that when "Yes" can be justified, "No" must be abandoned. I believe that the gentleman who has for so long a time perplexed our courts is either Sir Roger Tichborne or somebody else; I am not yet able to conceive of his being the true heir and an impostor at the same time. Yet in religious matters the fashionable standpoint is somewhat in that latitude.

We have a fixed faith to preach, my brethren, and we are sent forth with a definite message from God. We are not let to fabricate the message as we go along. We are not sent forth by our Master with a general commission arranged on this fashion: "As you shall think in your heart and invent in your head, so preach. Keep abreast of the times. Whatever the people want to hear, tell them that, and they shall be saved." Verily, we read not so. There is something definite in the Bible. It is not quite a lump of wax to be shaped at our will, or a roll of cloth to be cut according to the prevailing fashion. Your great thinkers evidently look upon the Scriptures as a box of letters for them to play with, and make what they like of, or a wizard's bottle, out of which they may pour anything they choose, from atheism up to spiritualism. I am too old-fashioned to fall down and worship this theory. There is something told me in the Bible—told me for certain—not put before me with a "but" and a "perhaps," and an "if," and a "may be," and fifty thousand suspicions behind it, so that really the long and the short of it is, that it may not be so at all; but revealed to me as infallible fact, which must be believed, the opposite of which is deadly error, and comes from the father of lies.

Believing, therefore, that there is such a thing as truth, and such a thing as falsehood, that there are truths in the Bible, and that the gospel consists in something definite which is to be believed by men, it becomes us to be decided as to what we teach, and to teach it in a decided manner. We have to deal with men who will be either lost or saved, and they certainly will not be saved by erroneous doctrine. We have to deal with God, whose servants we are, and He will not be honoured by our delivering falsehoods; neither will He give us a reward, and say, "Well done, good and faithful servant, thou hast mangled the gospel as judiciously as any man that ever lived before thee." We stand in a very solemn position, and ours should be the spirit of old Micaiah, who said, "As the Lord my God liveth, before whom I stand, whatsoever the Lord saith unto me that will I speak." Neither less nor more than God's word are we called to state, but that word we are bound to declare in a spirit which convinces the sons of men that, whatever they may think of it, we believe God, and are not to be shaken in our confidence in Him.

Brethren, in what ought we to be positive? Well, there are gentlemen alive who imagine that there are no fixed principles to go upon. "Perhaps a few doctrines," said one to me, "perhaps a few doctrines may be considered as established. It is, perhaps, ascertained that there is a God; but one ought not to dogmatise upon His personality: a great deal may be said for pantheism." Such men creep into the ministry, but they are generally cunning enough to conceal the breadth of their minds beneath Christian phraseology, thus acting in consistency with their principles, for their fundamental rule it that truth is of no consequence.

As for us—as for me, at any rate—I am certain that there is a God, and I mean to preach it as a man does who is absolutely sure. He is the Maker of heaven and earth, the Master of providence, and the Lord of grace: let His name be blessed for ever and ever! We will have no questions and debates as to Him.

We are equally certain that the book which is called "the Bible" is His word, and is inspired: not inspired in the sense in which Shakespeare, and Milton, and Dryden may be inspired, but in an infinitely higher sense; so that, provided we have the exact text, we regard the words themselves as infallible. We believe that everything stated in the book that comes to us from God is to be accepted by us as His sure testimony, and nothing less than that. God forbid we should be ensnared by those various interpretations of the *modus* of inspiration, which amount to little more than frittering it away. The book is a divine production; it is perfect, and is the last court of appeal —"the judge which ends the strife." I would as soon dream of blaspheming my Maker as of questioning the infallibility of His word.

We are also sure concerning the doctrine of the blessed Trinity. We cannot explain how the Father, Son, and Spirit can be each one distinct and perfect in himself, and yet that these three are one, so that there is but one God; yet we do verily believe it, and mean to preach it, notwithstanding Unitarian, Socinian, Sabellian, or any other error. We shall hold fast evermore the doctrine of the Trinity in Unity.

And, brethren, there will be no uncertain sound from us as to the atonement of our Lord Jesus Christ. We cannot leave the blood out of our ministry, or the life of it will be gone; for we may say of the gospel, "The blood is the life thereof." The proper substitution of Christ, the vicarious sacrifice of Christ, on the behalf of His people, that they might live through Him,—this we must publish till we die.

Neither can we waver in our mind for a moment concerning the great and glorious Spirit of God—the fact of His existence, His personality, the power of His working, the necessity of His influences, the certainty that no man is regenerated except by Him; that we are born again by the Spirit of God, and that the Spirit dwells in believers, and is the author of all good in them, their sanctifier and preserver, without whom they can do no good thing whatsoever: we shall not at all hesitate as to preaching these truths.

The absolute necessity of the new birth is also a certainty. We come down with demonstration when we touch that point. We shall never poison our people with the notion that a moral reformation will suffice, but we will over and over again say to them, "Ye must be born again." We have not got into the condition of the Scotch minister who, when old John Macdonald preached to his congregation a sermon to sinners, remarked, "Well, Mr. Macdonald, that was a very good sermon which you have preached, but it is very much out of place, for I do not know one single unregenerate person in my congregation." Poor soul, he was in all probability unregenerated himself. No, we dare not flatter our hearers, but we must continue to tell them that they are born sinners, and must be born saints, or they will never see the face of God with acceptance.

The tremendous evil of sin—we shall not hesitate about that. We shall speak on that matter both sorrowfully and positively; and, though some very wise men raise difficult questions about hell, we shall not fail to declare the terrors of the Lord, and the fact that the Lord has said, "These shall go away into everlasting punishment, but the righteous into life eternal."

Neither will we ever give an uncertain sound as to the glorious truth that salvation is all of grace. If ever we ourselves are saved, we know that sovereign grace alone has done it, and we feel it must be the same with others. We will publish, "Grace! grace! grace!" with all our might, living and dying.

We shall be very decided, also, as to justification by faith; for salvation is "Not of works, lest any man should boast." "Life in a look at 'the Crucified One'" will be our message. Trust in the Redeemer will be that saving grace which we will pray the Lord to implant in all our hearers' hearts.

And everything else which we believe to be true in the Scriptures we shall preach with decision. If there be questions which may be regarded as moot, or comparatively unimportant, we shall speak with such a measure of decision about them as may be comely. But points which cannot be moot, which are essential and fundamental, will be declared by us without any stammering, without any enquiring of the people, "What would you wish us to say?" Yes, and without the apology, "Those are my views, but other people's views may be correct." We ought to preach the gospel, not as *our views* at all, but as the mind of God—the testimony of Jehovah concerning His own Son, and in reference to salvation for lost men. If we had been entrusted with the making of the gospel, we might have altered it to suit the taste of this modest century, but never having been employed to originate the good news, but merely to repeat it, we dare not stir beyond the record. What we have been taught of God we teach. If we do not do this, we are not fit for our position. If I have a servant in my house, and I send a message by her to the door, and she amends it on her own authority, she may take away the very soul of the message by so doing, and she will be responsible for what she has done. She will not remain long in my employ, for I need a servant who will repeat what I say, as nearly as possible, word for word; and if she does so, I am responsible for the message, she is not. If any one should be angry with her on account of what she said, they would be very unjust; their quarrel lies with me, and not with the person whom I employ to act as mouth for me. He that hath God's Word, let him speak it faithfully, and he will have no need to answer gainsayers, except with a "Thus saith the Lord." This, then, is the matter concerning which we are decided.

How are we to show this decision? We need not be careful to answer this question; our decision will show itself in its own way. If we really believe a truth, we shall be decided about it. Certainly we are not to show our decision by that obstinate, furious, wolfish bigotry which cuts off every other body from the chance and hope of salvation and the possibility of being regenerate or even decently honest if they happen to differ from us about the colour of a scale of the great leviathan. Some individuals appear to be naturally cut on the cross; they are manufactured to be rasps, and rasp they will. Sooner than not quarrel with you they would raise a question upon the colour of invisibility, or the weight of a non-existent substance. They are up in arms with you, not because of the importance of the question under discussion, but because of the far greater importance of their being always the Pope of the party. Don't go about the world with your fist doubled up for fighting, carrying a theological revolver in the leg of your trousers. There is no sense in being a sort of doctrinal game-cock, to be carried about to show your spirit, or a terrier of orthodoxy, ready to tackle heterodox rats by the score. Practise the *suaviter in modo* as well as the *fortiter in re*. Be prepared to fight, and always have your sword buckled on your thigh, but wear a scabbard; there can be no sense in waving your weapon about before everybody's eyes to provoke conflict, after the manner of our beloved friends of the Emerald Isle, who are said to take their coats off at Donnybrook Fair, and drag them along the ground, crying out, while they flourish their shillelaghs, "Will any gentleman be so good as to tread on the tail of my coat?" These are theologians of such warm, generous blood, that they are never at peace till they are fully engaged in war.

If you really believe the gospel, you will be decided for it in more sensible ways. Your very tone will betray your sincerity; you will speak like a man who has something to say, which he knows to be true. Have you ever watched a rogue when he is about to tell a falsehood? Have you noticed the way in which he has to mouth it? It takes a long time to be able to tell a lie well, for the facial organs were not originally constituted and adapted for the complacent delivery of falsehood. When a man knows he is telling you the truth, every-thing about him corroborates his sincerity. Any accomplished cross-examining lawyer knows within a little whether a witness is genuine or a deceiver. Truth has her own air and manner, her own tone and emphasis. Yonder is a blundering, ignorant country fellow in the witness-box; the counsel tries to bamboozle and confuse him, if possible, but all the while he feels that he is an honest witness, and he says to himself, "I should like to shake this fellow's evidence, for it will greatly damage my side of the question." There ought to be always that same air of truth about the Christian minister; only as he is not only bearing witness to the truth, but wants other people to feel that truth and own the power of it, he ought to have more decision in his tone than a mere witness who is stating facts which may be believed or not without any serious consequences following either way. Luther was the man for decision. Nobody doubted that he believed what he spoke. He spoke with thunder, for there was lightning in his faith. The man preached all over, for his entire nature believed. You felt, "Well, he may be mad, or he may be altogether mistaken, but he assuredly believes what he says. He is the incarnation of faith; his heart is running over at his lips."

If we would show decision for the truth, we must not only do so by our tone and manner, but by our daily actions. A man's life is always more forcible than his speech; when men take stock of him they reckon his deeds as pounds and his words as pence. If his life and his doctrines disagree, the mass of lookers-on accept his practice and reject his preaching. A man may know a great deal about truth, and yet be a very damaging witness on its behalf, because he is no credit to it. The quack who in the classic story cried up an infallible cure for colds, coughing and sneezing between every sentence of his panegyric, may serve as the image and symbol of an unholy minister. The Satyr in Æsop's fable was indignant with the man who blew hot and cold with the same mouth, and well he might be. I can conceive no surer method of prejudicing men against the truth than by sounding her praises through the lips of men of suspicious character. When the devil turned preacher in our Lord's day, the Master bade him hold his peace; He did not care for Satanic praises. It is very ridiculous to hear good truth from a bad man; it is like flour in a coal-sack. When I was last in one of our Scottish towns I heard of an idiot at the asylum, who thought himself a great historic character. With much solemnity the poor fellow put himself into an impressive attitude and exclaimed, "I'm Sir William Wallace! Gie me a bit of bacca." The descent from Sir William Wallace to a piece of tobacco was too absurd for gravity; yet it was neither so absurd nor so sad as to see a professed ambassador of the cross covetous, worldly, passionate, or sluggish. How strange it would be to hear a man say, "I am a servant of the Most High God, and I will go wherever I can get the most salary. I am called to labour for the glory of Jesus only, and I will go nowhere unless the church is of most respectable standing. For me to live is Christ, but I cannot do it under five hundred pounds per annum."

Brother, if the truth be in thee it will flow out of thine entire being as the perfume streams from every bough of the sandal-wood tree; it will drive thee onward as the trade-wind speeds the ships, filling all their sails; it will consume thy whole nature with its energy as the forest fire burns up all the trees of the wood. Truth has not fully given thee her friendship till all thy doings are marked with her seal.

We must show our decision for the truth by the sacrifices we are ready to make. This is, indeed, the most efficient as well as the most trying method. We must be ready to give up anything and everything for the sake of the principles which we have espoused, and must be ready to offend our best supporters, to alienate our warmest friends, sooner than belie our consciences. We must be ready to be beggars in purse, and offscourings in reputation, rather than act treacherously. We can die, but we cannot deny the truth. The cost is already counted, and we are determined to buy the truth at any price, and sell it at no price. Too little of this spirit is abroad nowadays. Men have a saving faith, and save their own persons from trouble; they have great discernment, and know on which side their bread is buttered; they are large-hearted, and are all things to all men, if by any means they may save a sum. There are plenty of curs about, who would follow at the heel of any man who would keep them in meat. They are among the first to bark at decision, and call it obstinate dogmatism, and ignorant bigotry. Their condemnatory verdict causes us no distress; it is what we expected.

Above all we must show our zeal for the truth by continually, in season and out of season, endeavouring to maintain it in the tenderest and most loving manner, but still very earnestly and firmly. We must not talk to our congregations as if we were half asleep. Our preaching must not be articulate snoring. There must be power, life, energy, vigour. We must throw our whole selves into it, and show that the zeal of God's house has eaten us up.

How are we to manifest our decision? Certainly not by harping on one string and repeating over and over again the same truths with the declaration that we believe them. Such a course of action could only suggest itself to the incompetent. The barrel-organ grinder is not a pattern of decision; he may have persistency, but that is not the same thing as consistency. I could indicate certain brethren who have learned four or five doctrines, and they grind them over and over again with everlasting monotony. I am always glad when they grind their tunes in some street far removed from my abode. To weary with perpetual repetition is not the way to manifest our firmness in the faith.

My brethren, you will *strengthen your decision* by the recollection of the importance of these truths to your own souls. Are your sins forgiven? Have you a hope of heaven? How do the solemnities of eternity affect you? Certainly you are not saved apart from these things, and therefore you must hold them, for you feel you are a lost man if they be not true. You have to die, and, being conscious that these things alone can sustain you in the last article, you hold them with all your might. You cannot give them up. How can a man resign a truth which he feels to be vitally important to his own soul? He daily feels—"I have to live on it, I have to die on it, I am wretched now, and lost for ever apart from it, and therefore by the help of God I cannot relinquish it."

Your own experience from day to day will sustain you, beloved brethren. I hope you have realised already and will experience much more the power of the truth which you preach. I believe the doctrine of election, because I am quite sure that if God had not chosen me I should never have chosen Him; and I am sure He chose me before I was born, or else He never would have chosen me afterwards; and He must have elected me for reasons unknown to me, for I never could find any reason in myself why He should have looked upon me with special love. So I am forced to accept that doctrine. I am bound to the doctrine of the depravity of the human heart, because I find myself depraved in heart, and have daily proofs that there dwelleth in my flesh no good thing. I cannot help holding that there must be an atonement before there can be pardon, because my conscience demands it, and my peace depends upon it. The little court within my own heart is not satisfied unless some retribution be exacted for dishonour done to God. They tell us sometimes that such and such statements are not true; but when we are able to reply that we have tried them and proved them, what answer is there to such reasoning? A man propounds the wonderful discovery that honey is not sweet. "But I had some for breakfast, and I found it very sweet," say you, and your reply is conclusive. He tells you that salt is poisonous, but you point to your own health, and declare that you have eaten salt these twenty years. He says that to eat bread is a mistake—a vulgar error, an antiquated absurdity; but at each meal you make his protest the subject for a merry laugh. If you are daily and habitually experienced in the truth of God's Word, I am not afraid of your being shaken in mind in reference to it. Those young fellows who never felt conviction of sin, but obtained their religion as they get their bath in the morning, by jumping into it—these will as readily leap out of it as they leaped in. Those who feel neither the joys nor yet the depressions of spirit which indicate spiritual life, are torpid, and their palsied hand has no firm grip of truth. Mere skimmers of the Word, who, like swallows, touch the water with their wings, are the first to fly from one land to another as personal considerations guide them. They believe this, and then believe that, for, in truth, they believe nothing intensely. If you have ever been dragged through the mire and clay of soul-despair, if you have been turned upside down, and wiped out like a dish as to all your own strength and pride, and have then been filled with the joy and peace of God, through Jesus Christ, I will trust you among fifty thousand infidels. Whenever I hear the sceptic's stale attacks upon the Word of God, I smile within myself and think, "Why, you simpleton! how can you urge such trifling objections? I have felt, in the contentions of my own unbelief, ten times greater difficulties." We who have contended with horses are not to be wearied by footmen. Gordon Cumming and other lion-killers are not to be scared by wild cats, nor will those who have stood foot to foot with Satan resign the field to pretentious sceptics, or any other of the evil one's inferior servants.

If, my brethren, we have fellowship with the Lord Jesus Christ, we cannot be made to doubt the fundamentals of the gospel; neither can we be undecided. A glimpse at the thorn-crowned head and pierced hands and feet is the sure cure for "modern doubt" and all its vagaries. Get into the "Rock of Ages, cleft for you," and you will abhor the quicksand. That eminent American preacher, the seraphic Summerfield, when he lay a-dying, turned round to a friend in the room and said, "I have taken a look into eternity. Oh, if I could come back and preach again, how differently would I preach from what I have done before!" Take a look into eternity, brethren, if you want to be decided. Remember how Atheist met Christian and Hopeful on the road to the New Jerusalem, and said, "There is no celestial country. I have gone a long way, and could not find it." Then Christian said to Hopeful, "Did we not see it from the top of Mount Clear, when we were with the shepherds?" There was an answer! So when men have said, "There is no Christ—there is no truth in religion," we have replied to them, "Have we not sat under His shadow with great delight? Was not His fruit sweet to our taste? Go with your scepticisms to those who do not know whom they have believed. We have tasted and handled the good word of life. What we have seen and heard, that we do testify; and whether men receive our testimony or not, we cannot but speak it, for we speak what we do know, and testify what we have seen." That, my brethren, is the sure way to be decided.

And now, lastly, *why should we at this particular age be decided and bold?* We should be so because this age is a doubting age. It swarms with doubters as Egypt of old with frogs. You rub against them everywhere. Everybody is doubting everything, not merely in religion, but in politics and social economics, in everything indeed. It is the era of progress, and I suppose it must be the age, therefore, of unloosening, in order that the whole body politic may move on a little further. Well, brethren, as the age is doubting, it is wise for us to put our foot down and stand still where we are sure we have truth beneath us. Perhaps, if it were an age of bigotry, and men would not learn, we might be more inclined to listen to new teachers; but now the Conservative side must be ours, or rather the Radical side, which is the truly Conservative side. We must go back to the radix, or root of truth, and stand sternly by that which God has revealed, and so meet the wavering of the age. Our eloquent neighbour, Mr. Arthur Mursell, has well hit off the present age:

"Have we gone too far in saying that modern thought has grown impatient with the Bible, the gospel, and the cross? Let us see. What part of the Bible has it not assailed? The Pentateuch it has long ago swept from the canon as unauthentic. What we read about the creation and the flood is branded as fable. And the laws about the landmarks, from which Solomon was not ashamed to quote, are buried or laid upon the shelf.

"Different men assail different portions of the book, and various systems level their batteries of prejudice at various points; until by some the Scripture is torn all to pieces, and cast to the four winds of heaven, and by even the most forbearing of the cultured Vandals of what is called modern thought, it is condensed into a thin pamphlet of morality, instead of the tome of teaching through which we have eternal life. There is hardly a prophet but has been *reviewed* by the wiseacres of the day in precisely the same spirit as they would review a work from Mudie's library. The Temanite and the Shuhite never misconstrued the baited Job with half the prejudice of the acknowledged intellects of our time. Isaiah, instead of being sawn asunder, is quartered and hacked in pieces. The weeping prophet is drowned in his own tears. Ezekiel is ground to atoms amidst his wheels. Daniel is devoured bodily by the learned lions. And Jonah is swallowed by the deep monsters with a more inexorable voracity than the fish, for they never cast him up again. The histories and events of the great chronicle are rudely contradicted and gainsaid, because some schoolmaster with a slate and pencil cannot bring his sums right. And every miracle which the might of the Lord wrought for the favour of His people, or the frustration of their foes, is pooh-poohed as an absurdity, because the professors cannot do the like with their enchantments. A few of what are called miracles may be credible, because our leaders think they can do them themselves. A few natural phenomena, which some doctor can show to a company of martinets in a dark room, or with a table-full of apparatus, will account for the miracle of the Red Sea. An aeronaut goes up in a balloon, and then comes down again, and quite explains away the pillar of fire and of cloud, and trifles of that kind. And so our great men are satisfied when they think that their toy wand has swallowed up the wand of Aaron: but when Aaron's wand threatens to swallow up theirs, they say that part is not authentic, and that miracle never occurred.

"Nor does the New Testament fare any better than the Old at the hands of these invaders. There is no toll of deference levied on their homage as they pass across the line. They recognise no voice of warning with the cry, 'Take thy shoes from off thy feet, because the place whereon thou standest is holy ground.' The mind which halts in its career of spiritual rapine on any reverential pretext, is denounced as ignorant or slavish. To hesitate to stamp the hoof upon a lily or a spring flower is the sentimental folly of a child, and the vanguard of the thought of the age has only pity and a sneer for such a feeling, as it stalks upon its boasted march of progress. We are told that the legends of our nurseries are obsolete, and that broader views are gaining ground with thoughtful minds. We are unwilling to believe it. The truth is, that a few, a very few, thoughtful men, whose thinking consists in negation from first to last, and whose minds are tortured with a chronic twist or curve, which turns them into intellectual notes of interrogation, have laid the basis of this system; these few honest doubters have been joined by a larger band who are simply restless; and these again by men who are inimical to the spirit and the truths of Scripture, and together they have formed a coterie, and called themselves the leaders of the thought of the age. They have a following, it is true; but of whom does it consist? Of the mere satellites of fashion. Of the wealth, the pedantry, and the stupidity of our large populations. A string of carriages is seen 'setting down' and 'taking up' at the door where an advanced professor is to lecture, and because the milliner is advertised from floor to ceiling in the lecture room, these views are said to be gaining ground. But in an age of fashion like this, who ever suspects these minions of the mode of having any views at all? It becomes respectable to follow a certain name for a time, and so the vainlings go to follow the name and to display the dress. But as to views, one would no more suspect such people of having any views than they would dream of charging more than a tenth part of the crowds who go to the Royal Academy's exhibition with understanding the laws of perspective. It is the thing to do: and so every one who has a dress to show and a lounge to air, goes to show it, and all who would be in the fashion (and who would not?) are bound to advance with the times. And hence we find the times advancing over the sacred precincts of the New Testament, as though it were the floor of St. Alban's or of a professor's lecture room; and ladies drag their trains, and dandies set their dress-boots on the authenticity of this, or the authority of that, or the inspiration of the other. People who never heard of Strauss, of Bauer, or of Tübingen, are quite prepared to say that our Saviour was but a well-meaning man, who had a great many faults, and made a great many mistakes; that His miracles, as recorded in the New Testament, were in part imaginary, and in part accountable by natural theories; that the raising of Lazarus never occurred, since the Gospel of John is a forgery from first to last; that the atonement is a doctrine to be scouted as bloody and unrighteous; that Paul was a fanatic who wrote unthinkingly, and that much of what bears his name was never written by him at all. Thus is the Bible rubbed through the tribulum of criticism from Genesis to Revelation, until, in the faith of the age in which we live, as represented by its so-called leaders, there are but a few inspired fragments here and there remaining."

Moreover, after all, this is not an earnestly doubting age; we live among a careless, frivolous race. If the doubters were honest there would be more infidel places of concourse than there are; but infidelity as an organised community does not prosper. Infidelity in London, open and avowed, has come down to one old corrugated iron shed opposite St. Luke's. I believe that is the present position of it. "The Hall of Science" is it not called? Its literature was carried on for a long time in half a shop in Fleet Street; that was all it could manage to support, and I don't know whether even that half shop is used now. It is a poor, doting, drivelling thing. In Tom Paine's time it bullied like a vigorous blasphemer, but it was outspoken, and, in its own way, downright and earnest in its outspokenness. It commanded in former days some names which one might mention with a measure of respect; Hume, to wit, and Bolingbroke, and Voltaire were great in talent, if not in character. But where now will you find a Hobbes or a Gibbon? The doubters now are usually doubters because they do not care about truth at all. They are indifferent altogether. Modern scepticism is playing and toying with truth; and it takes to "modern thought" as an amusement, as ladies take to croquet or archery. This is nothing less than an age of millinery and dolls and comedy. Even good people do not believe out and out as their fathers used to do. Some even among Nonconformists are shamefully lax in their convictions; they have few masterly convictions such as would lead them to the stake, or even to imprisonment. Molluscs have taken the place of men, and men are turned to jelly-fishes. Far from us be the desire to imitate them.

Moreover it is an age which is very impressible, and therefore I should like to see you very decided, that you may impress it. The wonderful progress made in England by the High Church movement shows that earnestness is power. The Ritualists believe something, and that fact has given them influence. To me their distinctive creed is intolerable nonsense, and their proceedings are childish foolery; but they have dared to go against the mob, and have turned the mob round to their side. Bravely did they battle, let us say it to their honour; when their churches became the scenes of riot and disorder, and there was raised the terrible howl of "No Popery" by the lower orders, they boldly confronted the foe and never winced. They went against the whole current of what was thought to be the deep-seated feeling of England in favour of Protestantism, and with scarcely a bishop to patronise them, and but few loaves and fishes of patronage, they have increased from a handful to become the dominant and most vital party in the Church of England, and to our intense surprise and horror they have brought people to receive again the Popery which we thought dead and buried. If anybody had told me twenty years ago that the witch of Endor would become Queen of England, I should as soon have believed it as that we should now have such a High Church development; but the fact is, the men were earnest and decided, and held what they believed most firmly, and did not hesitate to push their cause. The age, therefore, can be impressed; it will receive what is taught by zealous men, whether it be truth or falsehood. It may be objected that falsehood will be received the more readily; that is just possible, but anything will be accepted by men if you will but preach it with tremendous energy and living earnestness. If they will not receive it into their hearts in a spiritual sense, yet at any rate there will be a mental assent and consent, very much in proportion to the energy with which you proclaim it; ay, and God will bless our decision too, so that when the mind is gained by our earnestness, and the attention is won by our zeal, the heart itself will be opened by the Spirit of God.

We must be decided. What have Dissenters been doing to a great extent lately but trying to be fine? How many of our ministers are labouring to be grand orators or intellectual thinkers? That is not the thing. Our young ministers have been dazzled by that, and have gone off to bray like wild asses under the notion that they would then be reputed to have come from Jerusalem, or to have been reared in Germany. The world has found them out. There is nothing now I believe that genuine Christians despise more than the foolish affectation of intellectualism. You will hear a good old deacon say, "Mr. So-and-so, whom we had here, was a very clever man, and preached wonderful sermons, but the cause has gone down through it. We can hardly support the minister, and we mean next time to have one of the old-fashioned ministers back again who believe in something and preach it. There will be no addition to our church else." Will you go out and tell the people that you believe you can say something, but you hardly know what; you are not quite sure that what you preach is correct, but the trust-deed requires you to say it, and therefore you say it? Why, you may cause fools and idiots to be pleased with you, and you will be sure to propagate infidelity, but you cannot do more. When a prophet comes forward he must speak as from the Lord, and if he cannot do that, let him go back to his bed. It is quite certain, dear friends, that now or never we must be decided, because the age is manifestly drifting. You cannot watch for twelve months without seeing how it is going down the tide; the anchors are pulled up, and the vessel is floating to destruction. It is drifting now, as near as I can tell you, south-east, and is nearing Cape Vatican, and if it drives much further in that direction it will be on the rocks of the Roman reef. We must get aboard her, and connect her with the glorious steam-tug of gospel truth, and drag her back. I should be glad if I could take her round by Cape Calvin, right up into the Bay of Calvary, and anchor her in the fair haven which is close over by Vera Cruz, or the cross. God grant us grace to do it. We must have a strong hand, and have our steam well up, and defy the current; and so by God's grace we shall both save this age and the generations yet to come.

XVII

Open-air Preaching—a Sketch of its History

THERE are some customs for which nothing can be pleaded, except that they are very old. In such cases antiquity is of no more value than the rust upon a counterfeit coin. It is, however, a happy circumstance when the usage of ages can be pleaded for a really good and scriptural practice, for it invests it with a halo of reverence. Now, it can be argued, with small fear of refutation, that open-air preaching is as old as preaching itself. We are at full liberty to believe that Enoch, the seventh from Adam, when he prophesied, asked for no better pulpit than the hill-side, and that Noah, as a preacher of righteousness, was willing to reason with his contemporaries in the ship-yard wherein his marvellous ark was builded. Certainly, Moses and Joshua found their most convenient place for addressing vast assemblies beneath the unpillared arch of heaven. Samuel closed a sermon in the field at Gilgal amid thunder and rain, by which the Lord rebuked the people and drove them to their knees. Elijah stood on Carmel, and challenged the vacillating nation, with "How long halt ye between two opinions?" Jonah, whose spirit was somewhat similar, lifted up his cry of warning in the streets of Nineveh, and in all her places of concourse gave forth the warning utterance, "Yet forty days and Nineveh shall be overthrown!" To hear Ezra and Nehemiah "all the people gathered themselves together as one man into the street that was before the water gate." Indeed, we find examples of open-air preaching everywhere around us in the records of the Old Testament.

It may suffice us, however, to go back as far as the origin of our own holy faith, and there we hear the forerunner of the Saviour crying in the wilderness and lifting up his voice from the river's bank. Our Lord Himself, who is yet more our pattern, delivered the larger proportion of His sermons on the mountain's side, or by the sea shore, or in the streets. Our Lord was to all intents and purposes an open-air preacher. He did not remain silent in the synagogue, but He was equally at home in the field. We have no discourse of His on record delivered in the chapel royal, but we have the sermon on the mount, and the sermon in the plain; so that the very earliest and most divine kind of preaching was practised out of doors by Him who spake as never man spake.

There were gatherings of His disciples after His decease, within walls, especially that in the upper room; but the preaching was even then most frequently in the court of the temple, or in such other open spaces as were available. The notion of holy places and consecrated meeting-houses had not occurred to them as Christians; they preached in the temple because it was the chief place of concourse, but with equal earnestness "in every house they ceased not to teach and preach Jesus Christ."

The apostles and their immediate successors delivered their message of mercy not only in their own hired houses, and in the synagogues, but also anywhere and everywhere as occasion served them. This may be gathered incidentally from the following statement of Eusebius. "The divine and admirable disciples of the apostles built up the super-structure of the churches, the foundations whereof the apostles had laid, in all places where they came; they everywhere prosecuted the preaching of the gospel, sowing the seeds of heavenly doctrine throughout the whole world. Many of the disciples then alive distributed their estates to the poor; and, leaving their own country, did the work of evangelists to those who had never yet heard the Christian faith, preaching Christ, and delivering the evangelical writings to them. No sooner had they planted the faith in any foreign countries, and ordained guides and pastors, to whom they committed the care of these new plantations, but they went to other nations, assisted by the grace and powerful working of the Holy Spirit. As soon as they began to preach the gospel the people flocked universally to them, and cheerfully worshipped the true God, the Creator of the world, piously and heartily believing in His name."

As the dark ages lowered, the best preachers of the gradually declining church were also preachers in the open air; as were also those itinerant friars and great founders of religious orders who kept alive such piety as remained. We hear of Berthold, of Ratisbon, with audiences of sixty or a hundred thousand, in a field near Glatz in Bohemia. There were also Bernards, and Bernardines, and Anthonys, and Thomases of great fame as travelling preachers, of whom we cannot find time to speak particularly. Dr. Lavington, Bishop of Exeter, being short of other arguments, stated, as a proof that the Methodists were identical with the Papists, that the early Friar Preachers were great at holding forth in the open fields. Quoting from Ribadeneira, he mentions Peter of Verona, who had "a divine talent in preaching; neither churches, nor streets, nor market-places could contain the great concourse that resorted to hear his sermons." The learned bishop might have easily multiplied his examples, as we also could do, but they would prove nothing more than that, for good or evil, field preaching is a great power.

When Antichrist had commenced its more universal sway, the Reformers before the Reformation were full often open-air preachers, as, for instance, Arnold of Brescia, who denounced Papal usurpations at the very gates of the Vatican.

It would be very easy to prove that revivals of religion have usually been accompanied, if not caused, by a considerable amount of preaching out of doors, or in unusual places. The first avowed preaching of protestant doctrine was almost necessarily in the open air, or in buildings which were not dedicated to worship, for these were in the hands of the Papacy. True, Wycliffe for a while preached the gospel in the church at Lutterworth; Huss, and Jerome, and Savonarola for a time delivered semi-gospel addresses in connection with the ecclesiastical arrangements around them; but when they began more fully to know and proclaim the gospel, they were driven to find other platforms. The Reformation when yet a babe was like the new-born Christ, and had not where to lay its head, but a company of men comparable to the heavenly host proclaimed it under the open heavens, where shepherds and common people heard them gladly. Throughout England we have several trees remaining called "gospel oaks." There is one spot on the other side of the Thames known by the name of "Gospel Oak," and I have myself preached at Addlestone, in Surrey, under the far-spreading boughs of an ancient oak, beneath which John Knox is said to have proclaimed the gospel during his sojourn in England. Full many a wild moor, and lone hillside, and secret spot in the forest have been consecrated in the same fashion, and traditions still linger over caves, and dells, and hill tops, where of old time the bands of the faithful met to hear the word of the Lord. Nor was it alone in solitary places that in days of yore the voice of the preacher was heard, for scarcely is there a market cross which has not served as a pulpit for itinerant gospellers. During the lifetime of Wycliffe his missionaries traversed the country, everywhere preaching the word. An Act of Parliament of Richard II (1382) sets it forth as a grievance of the clergy that a number of persons in frieze gowns went from town to town, without the licence of the ordinaries, and preached not only in churches, but in churchyards, and market-places, and also at fairs. To hear these heralds of the cross the country people flocked in great numbers, and the soldiers mingled with the crowd, ready to defend the preachers with their swords if any offered to molest them. After Wycliffe's decease his followers scrupled not to use the same methods. It is specially recorded of William Swinderby that "being excommunicated, and forbidden to preach in any church or churchyard, he made a pulpit of two mill-stones in the High-street of Leicester, and there preached 'in contempt of the bishop.' 'There,' says Knighton, 'you might see throngs of people from every part, as well from the town as the country, double the number there used to be when they might hear him lawfully.'"

In Germany and other continental countries the Reformation was greatly aided by the sermons delivered to the masses out of doors. We read of Lutheran preachers perambulating the country proclaiming the new doctrine to crowds in the market-places, and burial-grounds, and also on mountains and in meadows. At Goslar a Wittemberg student preached in a meadow planted with lime-trees, which procured for his hearers the designation of "the Lime-tree Brethren." D'Aubigné tells us that at Appenzel, as the crowds could not be contained in the churches, the preaching was held in the fields and public squares, and, notwithstanding keen opposition, the hills, meadows, and mountains echoed with the glad tidings of salvation. In the life of Farel we meet with incidents connected with out-of-doors ministry; for instance, when at Metz he preached his first sermon in the churchyard of the Dominicans, his enemies caused all the bells to be tolled, but his voice of thunder overpowered the sound. In Neuchâtel we are told that "the whole town became his church. He preached in the market-place, in the streets, at the gates, before the houses, and in the squares, and with such persuasion and effect that he won over many to the gospel. The people crowded to hear his sermons, and could not be kept back either by threats or persuasions."

From Dr. Wylie's *History of Protestantism* I borrow the following: "It is said that the first field-preaching in the Netherlands took place on the 14th of June, 1566, and was held in the neighbourhood of Ghent. The preacher was Herman Modet, who had formerly been a monk, but was now the reformed pastor at Oudenard. 'This man,' says a Popish chronicler, 'was the first who ventured to preach in public, and there were 7,000 persons at his first sermon.' . . . The second great field-preaching took place on the 23rd of July following, the people assembling in a large meadow in the vicinity of Ghent. The 'Word' was precious in those days, and the people, eagerly thirsting to hear it, prepared to remain two days consecutively on the ground. Their arrangements more resembled an army pitching their camp than a peaceful multitude assembled for worship. Around the worshippers was a wall of barricades in the shape of carts and waggons. Sentinels were placed at all the entrances. A rude pulpit of planks was hastily run up and placed aloft on a cart. Modet was preacher, and around him were many thousands of persons, who listened with their pikes, hatchets, and guns lying by their sides ready to be grasped on a sign from the sentinels who kept watch all around the assembly. In front of the entrances were erected stalls, whereat pedlars offered prohibited books to all who wished to buy. Along the roads running into the country were stationed certain persons, whose office it was to bid the casual passenger turn in and hear the Gospel. . . . When the services were finished, the multitude would repair to other districts, where they encamped after the same fashion, and remained for the same space of time, and so passed through the whole of West Flanders. At these conventicles the Psalms of David, which had been translated into Low Dutch from the version of Clement Marot, and Theodore Beza, were always sung. The odes of the Hebrew king, pealed forth by from five to ten thousand voices, and borne by the breeze over the woods and meadows, might be heard at great distances, arresting the ploughman as he turned the furrow, or the traveller as he pursued his way, and making him stop and wonder whence the minstrelsy proceeded." It is most interesting to observe that congregational singing is sure to revive at the same moment as gospel-preaching. In all ages a Moody has been attended by a Sankey. History repeats itself because like causes are pretty sure to produce like effects.

It would be an interesting task to prepare a volume of notable facts connected with open-air preaching, or, better still, a consecutive history of it. I have no time for even a complete outline, but would simply ask you, where would the Reformation have been if its great preachers had confined themselves to churches and cathedrals? How would the common people have become indoctrinated with the gospel had it not been for those far wandering evangelists, the colporteurs, and those daring innovators who found a pulpit on every heap of stones, and an audience chamber in every open space near the abodes of men?

Among examples within our own highly favoured island I cannot forbear mentioning the notable case of holy Wishart. This I quote from Gillie's *Historical Collections*:

"George Wishart was one of the early preachers of the doctrines of the Reformers, and suffered martyrdom in the days of Knox. His public exposition of the Epistle to the Romans especially excited the fears and hatred of the Romish ecclesiastics, who caused him to be silenced at Dundee. He went to Ayr, and began to preach the gospel with great freedom and faithfulness. But Dunbar, the then Archbishop of Glasgow, being informed of the great concourse of people who crowded to his sermons, at the instigation of Cardinal Beaton, went to Ayr, with the resolution to apprehend him; but first took possession of the church, to prevent him from preaching in it. The news of this brought Alexander, Earl of Glencairn, and some gentlemen of the neighbourhood immediately to town. They wished and offered to put Wishart into the church, but he would not consent, saying that 'the Bishop's sermon would not do much hurt, and that, if they pleased, he would go to the market cross,' which he accordingly did, and preached with such success, that several of his hearers, formerly enemies to the truth, were converted on the occasion.

"Wishart continued with the gentlemen of Kyle, after the archbishop's departure; and being desired to preach next Lord's-day at the church of Mauchline, he went thither with that design, but the sheriff of Ayr had, in the night time, put a garrison of soldiers into the church to keep him out. Hugh Campbell, of Kinzeancleugh, with others in the parish, were exceedingly offended at this impiety, and would have entered the church by force; but Wishart would not suffer it, saying, 'Brethren, it is the word of peace which I preach unto you; the blood of no man shall be shed for it this day: Jesus Christ is as mighty in the fields as in the church, and He Himself, while He lived in the flesh, preached oftener in the desert and upon the sea side than in the temple of Jerusalem.' Upon this the people were appeased, and went with him to the edge of the moor, on the south-west of Mauchline, where having placed himself upon a ditch-dike, he preached to a great multitude. He continued speaking for more than three hours, God working wondrously by him; insomuch that Laurence Ranken, the Laird of Shield, a very profane person, was converted by his means. About a month after the above circumstance, he was informed that the plague had broken out at Dundee, the fourth day after he had left it; and that it still continued to rage in such a manner that great numbers were swept off daily. This affected him so much, that he resolved to return to them, and accordingly took leave of his friends in the west, who were filled with sorrow at his departure. The next day, after his arrival at Dundee, he caused intimation to be made that he would preach; and for that purpose chose his station at the head of the east gate, the infected persons standing without, and those that were whole, within. His text on this occasion was Psalm cvii. 20: 'He sent his word and healed them, and delivered them from their destructions.' By this discourse he so comforted the people, that they thought themselves happy in having such a preacher, and entreated him to remain with them while the plague continued." What a scene must this have been? Seldom has preacher had such an audience, and, I may add, seldom has audience had such a preacher. Then, to use the words of an old author, "Old time stood at the preacher's side with his scythe, saying with hoarse voice, 'Work while it is called to-day, for at night I will mow thee down.' There, too, stood grim death hard by the pulpit, with his sharp arrows, saying, 'Do thou shoot God's arrows and I will shoot mine.'" This is, indeed, a notable instance of preaching out of doors.

I wish it were in my power to give more particulars of that famous discourse by John Livingstone in the yard of the Kirk of Shotts, when not less than five hundred of his hearers found Christ, though it rained in torrents during a considerable part of the time. It remains as one of the great out-door sermons of history, unsurpassed by any within walls. Here is the gist of what we know about it:

"It was not usual, it seems, in those times, to have any sermon on the Monday after dispensing the Lord's Supper. But God had given so much of His gracious presence, and afforded His people so much communion with Himself, on the foregoing days of that solemnity, that they knew not how to part without thanksgiving and praise. There had been a vast confluence of choice Christians, with several eminent ministers, from almost all the corners of the land. There had been many of them there together for several days before the sacrament, hearing sermons, and joining together in larger or lesser companies, in prayer, praise, and spiritual conferences. While their hearts were warm with the love of God, some expressing their desire of a sermon on the Monday, were joined by others, and in a little the desire became very general. Mr. John Livingstone, chaplain to the Countess of Wigtoun (at that time only a preacher, not an ordained minister, and about twenty-seven years of age), was with very much ado prevailed on to think of giving the sermon. He had spent the night before in prayer and conference; but when he was alone in the fields, about eight or nine in the morning, there came such a misgiving of heart upon him under a sense of unworthiness and unfitness to speak before so many aged and worthy ministers, and so many eminent and experienced Christians; that he was thinking to have stolen quite away, and was actually gone away to some distance; but when just about to lose sight of the Kirk of Shotts these words, 'Have I been a wilderness unto Israel? a land of darkness?' were brought into his heart with such an overcoming power, as constrained him to think it his duty to return and comply with the call to preach; which he accordingly did with good assistance for about an hour and a half on the points he had meditated from that text, Ezek. xxxvi. 25, 26: 'Then will I sprinkle clean water upon you, and ye shall be clean: from all your filthiness, and from all your idols, will I cleanse you. A new heart also will I give you, and a new spirit will I put within you: and I will take away the stony heart out of your flesh, and I will give you an heart of flesh.' As he was about to close, a heavy shower coming suddenly on, which made the people hastily take to their cloaks and mantles, he began to speak to the following purpose: 'If a few drops of rain from the clouds so discomposed them, how discomposed would they be, how full of horror and despair, if God should deal with them as they deserved: and thus He will deal with all the finally impenitent. That God might justly rain fire and brimstone upon them, as upon Sodom and Gomorrah, and the other cities of the plain. That the Son of God, by tabernacling in our nature, and obeying and suffering in it, is the only refuge and covert from the storm of divine wrath due to us for sin. That His merits and mediation are the only screen from that storm, and none but penitent believers shall have the benefit of that shelter.' In these or some expressions to this purpose, and many others, he was led on for about an hour's time (after he had done with what he had premeditated) in a strain of exhortation and warning, with great enlargement and melting of heart."

We must not forget the regular out-of-doors ministry at Paul's Cross, under the eaves of the old cathedral. This was a famous institution, and enabled the notable preachers of the times to be heard by the citizens in great numbers. Kings and princes did not disdain to sit in the gallery built upon the cathedral wall, and listen to the preacher for the day. Latimer tells us that the graveyard was in such an unhealthy condition that many died through attending the sermons; and yet there was never a lack of hearers. Now that the abomination of intra-mural burial is done away with, the like evil would not arise, and Paul's Cross might be set up again; perhaps a change to the open space might blow away some of the Popery which is gradually attaching itself to the services of the cathedral. The restoration of the system of public preaching of which Paul's Cross was the central station is greatly to be desired. I earnestly wish that some person possessed of sufficient wealth would purchase a central space in our great metropolis, erect a pulpit, and a certain number of benches, and then set it apart for the use of approved ministers of the gospel, who should there freely declare the gospel to all comers without favour or distinction. It would be of more real service to our ever-growing city than all its cathedrals, abbeys, and grand Gothic edifices. Before all open spaces are utterly swept away by the ever-swelling tide of mortar and brick, it would be a wise policy to secure Gospel Fields, or God's-acres-for-the-living, or whatever else you may please to call open spaces for free gospel preaching.

All through the Puritan times there were gatherings in all sorts of out-of-the-way places, for fear of persecutors. "We took," says Archbishop Laud, in a letter dated Fulham, June, 1632, "another conventicle of separatists in Newington Woods, in the very brake where the king's stag was to be lodged, for his hunting next morning." A hollow or gravel pit on Hounslow Heath sometimes served as a conventicle, and there is a dell near Hitchin where John Bunyan was wont to preach in perilous times. All over Scotland the straths, and dells, and vales, and hill-sides are full of covenanting memories to this day. You will not fail to meet with rock pulpits whence the stern fathers of the Presbyterian church thundered forth their denunciations of Erastianism, and pleaded the claims of the King of kings. Cargill and Cameron and their fellows found congenial scenes for their brave ministries mid the lone mountains' rents and ravines.

"Long ere the dawn, by devious ways,
O'er hills, through woods, o'er dreary wastes, they sought
The upland moors, where rivers, there but brooks,
Dispart to different seas: fast by such brooks,
A little glen is sometimes scoop'd, a plat
With greensward gay, and flowers that strangers seem
Amid the heathery wild, that all around
Fatigues the eye: in solitudes like these
Thy persecuted children, Scotia, foil'd
A tyrant's and a bigot's bloody law.
There, leaning on his spear . . .
The lyart veteran heard the word of God
By Cameron thunder'd, or by Renwick pour'd
In gentle stream: then rose the song, the loud
Acclaim of praise; the wheeling plover ceased
Her plaint; the solitary place was glad,
And on the distant cairns, the watcher's ear
Caught doubtfully at times the breeze-borne note.
But years more gloomy follow'd; and no more
The assembled people dared, in face of day,
To worship God, or even at the dead
Of night, save when the wintry storm raved fierce,
And thunder-peals compell'd the men of blood
To couch within their dens; then dauntlessly
The scatter'd few would meet, in some deep dell
By rocks o'er-canopied, to hear the voice,
Their faithful pastor's voice: he by the gleam
Of sheeted lightning oped the sacred book,
And words of comfort spake: over their souls
His accents soothing came, as to her young
The heathfowl's plumes, when at the close of eve
She gathers in, mournful, her brood dispersed
By murderous sport, and o'er the remnant spreads
Fondly her wings; close nestling 'neath her breast
They cherish'd cower amid the purple blooms."

At the risk of being prolix I feel I must add the following touching description of one of these scenes. The prose picture even excels the poet's painting.

"We entered on the administration of the holy ordinance, committing it and ourselves to the invisible protection of the Lord of hosts, in whose name we were met together. Our trust was in the arm of Jehovah, which was better than weapons of war, or the strength of the hills. The place where we convened was every way commodious, and seemed to have been formed on purpose. It was a green and pleasant haugh, fast by the water side (the Whittader). On either hand there was a spacious brae, in the form of a half round, covered with delightful pasture, and rising with a gentle slope to a goodly height.

Above us was the clear blue sky, for it was a sweet and calm Sabbath morning, promising indeed to be 'one of the days of the Son of man.' There was a solemnity in the place befitting the occasion, and elevating the whole soul to a pure and holy frame. The communion tables were spread on the green by the water, and around them the people had arranged themselves in decent order. But the far greater multitude sat on the brae face, which was crowded from top to bottom—full as pleasant a sight as ever was seen of that sort. Each day at the congregation's dismissing the ministers with their guards, and as many of the people as could, retired to their quarters in three several country towns, where they might be provided with necessaries. The horsemen drew up in a body till the people left the place, and then marched in goodly array behind at a little distance, until all were safely lodged in their quarters. In the morning, when the people returned to the meeting, the horsemen accompanied them: all the three parties met a mile from the spot, and marched in a full body to the consecrated ground. The congregation being all fairly settled in their places, the guardsmen took their several stations, as formerly. These accidental volunteers seemed to have been the gift of Providence, and they secured the peace and quiet of the audience; for, from Saturday morning, when the work began, until Monday afternoon, we suffered not the least affront or molestation from enemies, which appeared wonderful. At first there was some apprehension, but the people sat undisturbed, and the whole was closed in as orderly a way as it had been in the time of Scotland's brightest noon. And truly the spectacle of so many grave, composed, and devout faces must have struck the adversaries with awe, and been more formidable than any outward ability of fierce looks and warlike array. We desired not the countenance of earthly kings: there was a spiritual and divine Majesty shining on the work, and sensible evidence that the great Master of assemblies was present in the midst. It was indeed the doing of the Lord, who covered us a table in the wilderness, in presence of our foes; and reared a pillar of glory between us and the enemy, like the fiery cloud of old that separated between the camp of Israel and the Egyptians—encouraging to the one, but dark and terrible to the other. Though our vows were not offered within the courts of God's house, they wanted not sincerity of heart, which is better than the reverence of sanctuaries. Amidst the lonely mountains we remembered the words of our Lord, that true worship was not peculiar to Jerusalem or Samaria—that the beauty of holiness consisted not in consecrated buildings or material temples. We remembered the ark of the Israelites which had sojourned for years in the desert, with no dwelling place but the tabernacle of the plain. We thought of Abraham and the ancient patriarchs, who laid their victims on the rocks for an altar, and burnt sweet incense under the shade of the green tree.

"The ordinance of the Last Supper, that memorial of His dying love till His second coming, was signally countenanced and backed with power and refreshing influence from above. Blessed be God, for He hath visited and confirmed his heritage when it was weary. In that day Zion put on the beauty of Sharon and Carmel; the mountains broke forth into singing, and the desert place was made to bud and blossom as the rose. Few such days were seen in the desolate Church of Scotland; and few will ever witness the like. There was a rich effusion of the Spirit shed abroad in many hearts; their souls, filled with heavenly transports, seemed to breathe a diviner element, and to burn upwards as with the fire of a pure and holy devotion. The ministers were visibly assisted to speak home to the conscience of the hearers. It seemed as if God had touched their lips with a live coal from off His altar: for they who witnessed declared they carried themselves more like ambassadors from the court of heaven than men cast in earthly mould.

"The tables were served by some gentlemen and persons of the gravest deportment. None were admitted without tokens as usual, which were distributed on the Saturday, but only to such as were known to some of the ministers or persons of trust to be free of public scandals. All the regular forms were gone through. The communicants entered at one end and retired at the other, a way being kept clear to take their seats again on the hillside. Mr. Welsh preached the action sermon and served the two first tables, as he was ordinarily put to do so on such occasions. The other four ministers, Mr. Blackader, Mr. Dickson, Mr. Riddell, and Mr. Rae, exhorted the rest in their turn; the table service was closed by Mr. Welsh with solemn thanksgiving, and solemn it was, and sweet and edifying to see the gravity and composure of all present, as well as of all parts of the service. The communion was peaceably concluded, all the people heartily offering up their gratitude, and singing with a joyful voice to the Rock of their salvation. It was pleasant as the night fell to hear their melody swelling in full unison along the hill, the whole congregation joining with one accord, and praising God with the voice of psalms.

"There were two long tables and one short across the head, with seats on each side. About a hundred sat at every table. There were sixteen tables in all, so that about three thousand two hundred communicated that day."

Perhaps the most remarkable place ever chosen for a discourse was the centre of the river Tweed, where Mr. John Welsh often preached during hard frosts, in order that he might escape from the authorities of either Scotland or England, whichever might interfere. Prize-fighters have often selected the borders of two counties for their performances, but their prudence would seem to have been anticipated by the children of light.

It is amusing also to read of Archbishop Sharp's commanding the militia to be sent to disperse the crowd who had gathered on the hillside to hear Mr. Blackader, and of his being informed that they had all gone an hour before to attend the sermon.

What the world would have been if there had not been preaching outside of walls, and beneath a more glorious roof than these rafters of fir, I am sure I cannot guess. It was a brave day for England when Whitefield began field preaching. When Wesley stood and preached a sermon on his father's grave, at Epworth, because the parish priest would not allow him admission within the (so-called) sacred edifice, Mr. Wesley writes: "I am well assured that I did far more good to my Lincolnshire parishioners by preaching three days on my father's tomb than I did by preaching three years in his pulpit." The same might be said of all the open-air preaching which followed, as compared with the regular discourses within doors. "The thought of preaching in the open air was suggested to Whitefield by a crowd of a thousand people unable to gain admission to Bermondsey church, where he preached one Sunday afternoon. He met with no encouragement when he mentioned it to some of his friends; they thought it was a 'mad notion.' However, it would have been carried out the next Sunday at Ironmongers' Almshouses had not the preacher been disappointed in his congregation, which was small enough to hear him from the pulpit. He took two sermons with him, one for within and the other for without." The idea which had thus ripened into a resolve had not long to wait before it was carried into execution. The Chancellor of the Diocese having put impediments in the way of Whitefield's preaching in the churches of Bristol on behalf of his Orphanhouse, he went to preach to the colliers at Kingswood "for the first time on a Saturday afternoon, taking his stand on Hannan Mount. He spoke on Matt. v. 1, 2, 3, to as many as came to hear; upwards of two hundred attended. His only remark in his journal is, Blessed be God that the ice is now broke, and I have now taken the field! Some may censure me. But is there not a cause? Pulpits are denied; and the poor colliers ready to perish for lack of knowledge." Now he was the owner of a pulpit that no man could take from him, and his heart rejoiced in this great gift. On the following day the journal relates, "All the church doors being now shut, and if open not able to contain half that came to hear, at three in the afternoon I went to Kingswood among the colliers. God highly favoured us in sending us a fine day, and near two thousand people were assembled on that occasion. I preached and enlarged on John iii. 3 for near an hour, and, I hope, to the comfort and edification of those that heard me." Two days afterwards he stood upon the same spot, and preached to a congregation of four or five thousand with great freedom. The bright sun overhead, and the immense throng standing around him in awful silence formed a picture which filled him with 'holy admiration.' On a subsequent Sunday, Bassleton, a village two miles from Bristol, opened its church to him, and a numerous congregation coming together, he first read prayers in the church, and then preached in the churchyard. At four he hastened to Kingswood. Though the month was February the weather was unusually open and mild; the setting sun shone with its fullest power; the trees and hedges were crowded with hearers who wanted to see the preacher as well as to hear him. For an hour he spoke with a voice loud enough to be heard by every one, and his heart was not without joy in his own message. He writes in his journal: 'Blessed be God, The fire is kindled; may the gates of hell never be able to prevail against it!' It is important to know what were his feelings when he met those immense field congregations, whose numbers had grown from two hundred to twenty thousand, and what were the effects of his preaching upon his audience. His own words are, 'Having no righteousness of their own to renounce, the colliers were glad to hear of Jesus who was a friend to publicans, and came not to call the righteous, but sinners, to repentance. The first discovery of their being affected was, to see the white gutters made by their tears, which plentifully fell down their black cheeks, as they came out of their coal pits. Hundreds and hundreds of them were soon brought under deep convictions, which (as the event proved) happily ended in a sound and thorough conversion. The change was visible to all, though numbers chose to impute it to anything rather than the finger of God. As the scene was quite new, and I had just begun to be an extempore preacher, it often occasioned many inward conflicts. Sometimes, when twenty thousand people were before me, I had not, in my own apprehension, a word to say, either to God or them. But I was never totally deserted, and frequently knew by happy experience what our Lord meant when he said, 'Out of his belly shall flow rivers of living water.' The open firmament above me, the prospect of the adjacent fields, with the sight of thousands and thousands, some in coaches, some on horseback, and some on the trees, and, at times, all affected and drenched in tears together, to which sometimes was added the solemnity of the approaching evening, was almost too much for, and quite overcame, me."

Wesley writes in his journal, "Saturday, 31 [March, 1731]. In the evening I reached Bristol, and met Mr. Whitefield there. I could scarce reconcile myself at first to this strange way of preaching in the fields, of which he set me an example on Sunday; having been all my life (till very lately) so tenacious of every point relating to decency and order, that I should have thought the saving of souls almost a sin, if had it not been done in a church." Such were the feelings of a man who in after life became one of the greatest open-air preachers that ever lived!

I shall not tarry to describe Mr. Whitefield on our own Kennington Common among the tens of thousands, or at Moorfields early in the morning, when the lanterns twinkled like so many glow-worms on a grassy bank on a summer's night, neither will I mention the multitudes of glorious scenes with Wesley and his more renowned preachers; but a picture more like that which some of you can easily copy has taken a strong hold upon my memory; and I set it before you that you may never in times to come despise the day of small things:

"Wesley reached Newcastle on Friday, the 28th of May. On walking out, after tea, he was surprised and shocked at the abounding wickedness. Drunkenness and swearing seemed general, and even the mouths of little children were full of curses. How he spent the Saturday we are not informed; but, on Sunday morning at seven, he and John Taylor took their stand near the pump, in Sandgate, 'the poorest and most contemptible part of the town,' and began to sing the Old Hundredth Psalm and tune. Three or four people came about them, to see what was the matter; these soon increased in number, and, before Wesley finished preaching, his congregation consisted of from twelve to fifteen hundred persons. When the service was ended, the people still stood gaping, with the most profound astonishment, upon which Wesley said, 'If you desire to know who I am, my name is John Wesley. At five in the evening, with God's help, I design to preach here again.'"

Glorious were those great gatherings in fields and commons which lasted throughout the long period in which Wesley and Whitefield blessed our nation. Field-preaching was the wild note of the birds singing in the trees, in testimony that the true springtime of religion had come. Birds in cages may sing more sweetly, perhaps, but their music is not so natural, nor so sure a pledge of the coming summer. It was a blessed day when Methodists and others began to proclaim Jesus in the open air; then were the gates of hell shaken, and the captives of the devil set free by hundreds and by thousands.

Once recommenced, the fruitful agency of field-preaching was not allowed to cease. Amid jeering crowds and showers of rotten eggs and filth, the immediate followers of the two great Methodists continued to storm village after village and town after town. Very varied were their adventures, but their success was generally great. One smiles often when reading incidents in their labours. A string of packhorses is so driven as to break up a congregation, and a fire-engine is brought out and played over the throng to achieve the same purpose. Hand-bells, old kettles, marrow-bones and cleavers, trumpets, drums, and entire bands of music were engaged to drown the preachers' voices. In one case the parish bull was let loose, and in others dogs were set to fight. The preachers needed to have faces set like flints, and so indeed they had. John Furz says: "As soon as I began to preach, a man came straight forward, and presented a gun at my face; swearing that he would blow my brains out, if I spake another word. However, I continued speaking, and he continued swearing, sometimes putting the muzzle of the gun to my mouth, sometimes against my ear. While we were singing the last hymn, he got behind me, fired the gun, and burned off part of my hair." After this, my brethren, we ought never to speak of petty interruptions or annoyances. The proximity of a blunderbuss in the hands of a son of Belial is not very conducive to collected thought and clear utterance, but the experience of Furz was probably no worse than that of John Nelson, who coolly says, "But when I was in the middle of my discourse, one at the outside of the congregation threw a stone, which cut me on the head: however, that made the people give greater attention, especially when they saw the blood run down my face; so that all was quiet till I had done, and was singing a hymn."

The life of Gideon Ouseley, by Dr. Arthur, is one of the most powerful testimonies to the value of outdoor preaching. In the early part of the present century, from 1800 to 1830, he was in full vigour, riding throughout the whole of Ireland, preaching the gospel of Jesus in every town. His pulpit was generally the back of his horse, and he himself and his coadjutors were known as the men with the black caps, from their habit of wearing skull caps. This cavalry ministry was in its time the cause of a great revival in Ireland, and gave promise of really touching Erin's deep-seated curse—the power of the priesthood, and the superstition of the people. Ouseley showed at all times much shrewdness, and a touch of common-sense humour; hence he generally preached in front of the apothecary's window because the mob would be the less liberal with their stones, or next best he chose to have the residence of a respectable Catholic in his rear, for the same reason. His sermon from the stone stairs of the market house of Enniscorthy was a fair specimen of his dexterous method of meeting an excited mob of Irishmen. I will give it you at length, that you may know how to act if ever you are placed in similar circumstances: "He took his stand, put off his hat, assumed his black velvet cap, and, after a few moments spent in silent prayer, commenced to sing. People began to gather round him, and, during the singing of a few verses, were quiet, and apparently attentive, but soon began to be restless and noisy. He then commenced to pray, and quietness for a short time followed; but presently, as the crowd increased, it became uneasy, and even turbulent. He closed his prayer, and began to preach; but evidently his audience were not disposed to hear him. Before many sentences had been uttered, missiles began to fly—at first not of a very destructive character, being refuse—vegetables, potatoes, turnips, etc., but before long harder materials were thrown— brickbats and stones, some of which reached him and inflicted slight wounds. He stopped, and, after a pause, cried out, 'Boys dear, what's the matter with you to-day? Won't you let an old man talk to you a little?' 'We don't want to hear a word out of your old head,' was the prompt reply from one in the crowd. 'But I want to tell you what, I think, you would like to hear.' 'No, we'll like nothing you can tell us.' 'How do you know? I want to tell you a story about one you all say you respect and love.' 'Who's that?' 'The blessed Virgin.' 'Och, and what do *you* know about the blessed Virgin?' 'More than you think; and I'm sure you'll be pleased with what I have to tell you, if you'll only listen to me.' 'Come then,' said another voice, 'let us hear what he has to say about the Holy Mother.' And there was a lull, and the missionary began: 'There was once a young couple to be married, belonging to a little town called Cana. It's away in that country where our blessed Saviour spent a great part of his life among us; and the decent people whose children were to be married thought it right to invite the blessed Virgin to the wedding feast, and her blessed Son too, and some of His disciples; and they all thought it right to come. As they sat at table, the Virgin Mother thought she saw that the wine provided for the entertainment began to run short, and she was troubled lest the decent young people should be shamed before their neighbours; and so she whispered to her blessed Son, "They have no wine." "Don't let that trouble you, ma'am," said He. And in a minute or two after, she, knowing well what was in His good heart, said to one of the servants that was passing behind them, "Whatsoever he saith unto you, do it." Accordingly, by-and-by, our blessed Lord said to another of them—I suppose they had passed the word among themselves—"Fill those large waterpots with water." (There were six of them standing in a corner of the room, and they held nearly three gallons apiece, for the people of those countries use a great deal of water every day.) And, remembering the words of the Holy Virgin, they did His bidding, and came back, and said, "Sir, they are full to the brim." "Take some, then, to the master, at the head of the table," He said. And they did so, and the master tasted it, and lo and behold you! it was wine, and the best of wine too. And there was plenty of it for the feast, ay, and, it may be, some left to help the young couple setting up house-keeping. And all that, you see, came of the servants taking the advice of the blessed Virgin, and doing what she bid them. Now, if she was here among us this day, she would give just the same advice to every one of us, "Whatsoever *He* saith to you, do it," and with good reason too, for well she knows there is nothing but love in His heart to us, and nothing but wisdom comes from His lips. And now I'll tell you some of the things He says to us. He says, "Strive to enter in at the strait gate; for many, I say unto you, will strive to enter in, and shall not be able."'' And straightway the preacher briefly, but clearly and forcibly, expounded the nature of the gate of life, its straitness, and the dread necessity for pressing into it, winding up with the Virgin's counsel, 'Whatsoever he saith unto you, do it.' In like manner he explained, and pressed upon his hearers, some other of the weighty words of our divine Lord.—'Except a man be born of water and of the Spirit, he cannot enter into the kingdom of God'; and, 'If any man will come after me, let him deny himself, and take up his cross daily and follow me,'— enforcing His exhortation in each instance by the Virgin's counsel to the servants at Cana. 'But no,' at last he broke forth, 'no; with all the love and reverence you pretend for the blessed Virgin, you won't take her advice, but will listen willingly to any drunken schoolmaster that will wheedle you into a public-house, and put mischief and wickedness into your heads.' Here he was interrupted by a voice, which seemed to be that of an old man, exclaiming, 'True for you, true for ye. If you were tellin' lies all the days of your life, it's the truth you're tellin' now.' And so the preacher got leave to finish his discourse with not a little of good effect."

The history of *Primitive Methodism* might here be incorporated bodily as part of our sketch of Field-preaching, for that wonderful mission movement owed its rise and progress to this agency. It is, however, a singular reproduction of the events which attended the earlier Methodism of eighty or ninety years before. The Wesleyans had become respectable, and it was time that the old fire should burn up among another class of men. Had Wesley been alive he would have glorified in the poor but brave preachers who risked their lives to proclaim the message of eternal love among the depraved, and he would have headed them in their crusade. As it was, other leaders came forward, and it was not long before their zeal called forth a host of fervent witnesses who could not be daunted by mobs, or squires, or clergymen; nor even chilled by the genteel brethren whose proprieties they so dreadfully shocked. Then came forth the old weapons in abundance. Agricultural produce in all stages of decomposition rewarded the zealous apostles—turnips and potatoes were a first course, and rotten eggs followed in special abundance, these last we note were frequently *goose* eggs, selected we suppose for their size. A tub of coal-tar was often in readiness, filth from the horse-ponds was added, and all this to the music of tin whistles, horns, and watchmens' rattles. Barrels of ale were provided by the advocates of "Church and king" to refresh the orthodox assailants, while both preachers and disciples were treated with brutality such as to excite compassion even in the hearts of adversaries. All this was, happily, a violation of law, but the great unpaid winked at the transgressors, and endeavoured to bully the preacher into silence. For Christ's sake they were content to be treated as vagrants and vagabonds, and the Lord put great honour upon them. Disciples were made and the

Ranters multiplied. Even till a late period these devoted brethren have been opposed with violence, but their joyful experience has led them to persevere in their singing through the streets, camp-meetings, and other irregularities: blessed irregularities by which hundreds of wanderers have been met with and led to the fold of Jesus.

I have no time further to illustrate my subject by descriptions of the work of Christmas Evans and others in Wales, or of the Haldanes in Scotland, or even of Rowland Hill and his brethren in England. If you wish to pursue the subject these names may serve as hints for discovering abundant materials; and I may add to the list *The Life of Dr. Guthrie,* in which he records notable open-air assemblies at the time of the Disruption, when as yet the Free Church had no places of worship built with human hands.

I must linger a moment over Robert Flockhart, of Edinburgh, who, though a lesser light, was a constant one, and a fit example to the bulk of Christ's street witnesses. Every evening, in all weathers and amid many persecutions, did this brave man continue to speak in the street for *forty-three years.* Think of that, and never be discouraged. When he was tottering to the grave the old soldier was still at his post. "Compassion to the souls of men drove me," said he, "to the streets and lanes of my native city, to plead with sinners and persuade them to come to Jesus. The love of Christ constrained me." Neither the hostility of the police, nor the insults of Papists, Unitarians, and the like could move him, he rebuked error in the plainest terms, and preached salvation by grace with all his might. So lately has he passed away that Edinburgh remembers him still. There is room for such in all our cities and towns, and need for hundreds of his noble order in this huge *nation* of London—can I call it less?

In America men like Peter Cartwright, Lorenzo Dow, Jacob Gruber, and others of a past generation, carried on a glorious warfare under the open heavens in their own original fashion; and in later times Father Taylor has given us another proof of the immeasurable power of this mode of crusade in his *Seven Years of Street Preaching in San Francisco, California.* Though sorely tempted, I shall forbear at this time from making extracts from that very remarkable work.

The camp-meeting is a sort of associated field-preaching, and has become an institution in the United States, where everything must needs be done upon a great scale. This would lead me into another subject, and therefore I shall merely give you a glimpse at that means of usefulness, and then forbear.

The following description of the earlier camp meetings in America is from the pen of the author of a *Narrative of a Mission to Nova Scotia*: "The tents are generally pitched in the form of a crescent, in the centre of which is an elevated stand for the preachers, round which, in all directions, are placed rows of planks for the people to sit upon while they hear the word. Among the trees, which spread their tops over this forest church, are hung the lamps, which burn all night, and give light to the various exercises of religion which occupy the solemn midnight hours. It was nearly eleven o'clock at night when I first arrived on the border of the camp. I left my boat at the edge of the wood, one mile from the scene; and when I opened upon the camp ground, my curiosity was converted into astonishment, to behold the pendant lamps among the trees; the tents half-encircling a large space; four thousand people in the centre of this, listening with profound attention to the preacher, whose stentorian voice and animated manner carried the vibration of each word to a great distance through the deeply umbrageous wood, where, save the twinkling lamps of the camp, brooding darkness spread a tenfold gloom. All excited my astonishment, and forcibly brought before my view the Hebrews in the wilderness. The meetings generally begin on Monday morning, and on Friday morning following break up. The daily exercises are carried forward in the following manner: in the morning at five o'clock the horn sounds through the camp, either for preaching or for prayer; this, with similar exercises, or a little intermission, brings on the breakfast hour, eight o'clock; at ten, the horn sounds for public preaching, after which, until noon, the interval is filled up with little groups of praying persons, who scatter themselves up and down the camp, both in the tents and under the trees. After dinner the horn sounds at two o'clock; this is for preaching. I should have observed that a female or two is generally left in each tent, to prepare materials for dinner. A fire is kept burning in different parts of the camp, where water is boiled for tea, the use of ardent spirits being forbidden. After the afternoon preaching things take nearly the same course as in the morning, only the praying groups are upon a larger scale, and more scope is given to animated exhortations and loud prayers. Some who exercise on these occasions soon lose their voices, and, at the end of a camp meeting, many of both preachers and people can only speak in a whisper. At six o'clock in the evening the horn summons to preaching, after which, though in no regulated form, all the above means continue until evening; yea, and during whatever part of the night you awake, the wilderness is vocal with praise."

Whether or not under discreet management some such gatherings could be held in our country I cannot decide, but it does strike me as worthy of consideration whether in some spacious grounds services might not be held in summer weather, say for a week at a time, by ministers who would follow each other in proclaiming the gospel beneath the trees. Sermons and prayer-meetings, addresses and hymns, might follow each other in wise succession, and perhaps thousands might be induced to gather to worship God, among whom would be scores and hundreds who never enter our regular sanctuaries. Not only must *something* be done to evangelize the millions, but *everything* must be done, and perhaps amid variety of effort the best thing would be discovered. "If by any means I may save some" must be our motto, and this must urge us onward to go forth into the highways and hedges and compel them to come in. Brethren, I speak as unto wise men, consider what I say.

XVIII

Open-air Preaching—Remarks Thereon

I FEAR that in some of our less enlightened country churches there are conservative individuals who almost believe that to preach anywhere except in the chapel would be a shocking innovation, a sure token of heretical tendencies, and a mark of zeal without knowledge. Any young brother who studies his comfort among them must not suggest anything so irregular as a sermon outside the walls of their Zion. In the olden times we are told "Wisdom crieth without, she uttereth her voice in the streets, she crieth in the chief places of concourse, in the openings of the gates"; but the wise men of orthodoxy would have wisdom gagged except beneath the roof of a licensed building. These people believe in a New Testament which says, "Go out into the highways and hedges and compel them to come in," and yet they dislike a literal obedience to the command. Do they imagine that a special blessing results from sitting upon a particular deal board with a piece of straight-up panelling at their back—an invention of discomfort which ought long ago to have made people prefer to worship outside on the green grass? Do they suppose that grace rebounds from sounding-boards, or can be beaten out of pulpit cushions in the same fashion as the dust? Are they enamoured of the bad air, and the stifling stuffiness which in some of our meeting-houses make them almost as loathsome to the nose and to the lungs as the mass-houses of Papists with their cheap and nasty incense? To reply to these objectors is a task for which we have no heart: we prefer foemen worthy of the steel we use upon them, but these are scarcely worth a passing remark. One smiles at their prejudice, but we may yet have to weep over it, if it be allowed to stand in the way of usefulness.

No sort of defence is needed for preaching out of doors; but it would need very potent arguments to prove that a man had done his duty who has never preached beyond the walls of his meeting-house. A defence is required rather for services within buildings than for worship outside of them. Apologies are certainly wanted for architects who pile up brick and stone into the skies when there is so much need for preaching rooms among poor sinners down below. Defence is greatly needed for forests of stone pillars, which prevent the preacher's being seen and his voice from being heard; for high-pitched Gothic roofs in which all sound is lost, and men are killed by being compelled to shout till they burst their bloodvessels; and also for the wilful creation of echoes by exposing hard, sound-refracting surfaces to satisfy the demands of art, to the total overlooking of the comfort of both audience and speaker. Surely also some decent excuse is badly wanted for those childish people who must needs waste money in placing hobgoblins and monsters on the outside of their preaching houses, and must have other ridiculous pieces of Popery stuck up both inside and outside, to deface rather than to adorn their churches and chapels: but no defence whatever is wanted for using the heavenly Father's vast audience chamber, which is in every way so well fitted for the proclamation of a gospel so free, so full, so expansive, so sublime. The usual holding of religious assemblies under cover may be excused in England, because our climate is so execrably bad; but it were well to cease from such use when the weather is fine and fixed, and space and quiet can be obtained. We are not like the people of Palestine, who can foresee their weather, and are not every hour in danger of a shower; but if we meet *sub Jove,* as the Latins say, we must expect the Jove of the hour to be *Jupiter pluvius.* We can always have a deluge if we do not wish for it, but if we fix a service out of doors for next Sunday morning, we have no guarantee that we shall not all be drenched to the skin. It is true that some notable sermons have been preached in the rain, but as a general rule the ardour of our auditors is hardly so great as to endure much damping. Besides, the cold of our winters is too intense for services out of doors all the year round, though in Scotland I have heard of sermons amid the sleet, and John Nelson writes of speaking to "a crowd too large to get into the house, though it was dark and snowed." Such things may be done now and then, but exceptions only prove the rule. It is fair also to admit that when people will come within walls, if the house be so commodious that a man could not readily make more persons hear, and if it be always full, there can be no need to go out of doors to preach to fewer than there would be indoors; for, all things considered, a comfortable seat screened from the weather, and shut in from noise and intrusion, is helpful to a man's hearing the gospel with solemnity and quiet thought. A well ventilated, well managed building is an advantage if the crowds can be accommodated and can be induced to come; but these conditions are very rarely met, and therefore my voice is for the fields.

The great benefit of open-air preaching is that we get so many new-comers to hear the gospel who otherwise would never hear it. The gospel command is, "Go ye into all the world and preach the gospel to every creature," but it is so little obeyed that one would imagine that it ran thus, "Go into your own place of worship and preach the gospel to the few creatures who will come inside." "Go ye into the highways and hedges and compel them to come in,"—albeit it constitutes part of a parable, is worthy to be taken very literally, and in so doing its meaning will be best carried out. We ought actually to go into the streets and lanes and highways, for there are lurkers in the hedges, tramps on the highway, street-walkers, and lane-haunters, whom we shall never reach unless we pursue them into their own domains. Sportsmen must not stop at home and wait for the birds to come and be shot at, neither must fishermen throw their nets inside their boats and hope to take many fish. Traders *go* to the markets, they follow their customers and go out after business if it will not come to them; and so must we. Some of our brethren are prosing on and on, to empty pews and musty hassocks, while they might be conferring lasting benefit upon hundreds by quitting the old walls for a while, and seeking living stones for Jesus. Let them come out of Rehoboth and find room at the street corner, let them leave Salem and seek the peace of neglected souls, let them dream no longer at Bethel, but make an open space to be none other than the house of God, let them come down from Mount Zion, and up from Ænon, and even away from Trinity, and St. Agnes, and St. Michael-and-All-Angels, and St. Margaret-Pattens, and St. Vedast, and St. Ethelburga, and all the rest of them, and try to find new saints among the sinners who are perishing for lack of knowledge.

I have known street preaching in London remarkably blest to persons whose character and condition would quite preclude their having been found in a place of worship. I know, for instance, a Jewish friend who, on coming from Poland, understood nothing whatever of the English language. In going about the streets on the Sunday he noticed the numerous groups listening to earnest speakers. He had never seen such a thing in his own country, where the Russian police would be alarmed if groups were seen in conversation, and he was therefore all the more interested. As he acquired a little English he became more and more constant in his attendance upon street speakers; indeed, it was very much with the view of learning the language that he listened at the first. I am afraid that the English which he acquired was not of the very best, which judgment I form as much from what I have heard of open-air oratory as from having listened to our Jewish friend himself, whose theology is better than his English. However, that "Israelite indeed" has always reason to commend the street preachers. How many other strangers and foreigners may, by the same instrumentality, have become fellow-citizens with the saints and of the household of God we cannot tell. Romanists also are met with in this manner more frequently than some would suppose. It is seldom prudent to publish cases of conversion among Papists, but my own observation leads me to believe that they are far more common than they were ten years ago, and the gracious work is frequently commenced by what is heard of the gospel at our street corners.

Infidels, also, are constantly yielding to the word of the Lord thus brought home to them. The street evangelist, moreover, wins attention from those eccentric people whose religion can neither be described nor imagined. Such people hate the very sight of our churches and meeting houses, but will stand in a crowd to hear what is said, and are often most impressed when they affect the greatest contempt.

Besides, there are numbers of persons in great cities who have not fit clothes to worship in, according to the current idea of what clothes ought to be; and not a few whose persons as well as their garments are so filthy, so odorous, so unapproachable, that the greatest philanthropist and the most levelling democrat might desire to have a little space between himself and their lively individualities. There are others who, whatever raiment they wear, would not go into a chapel upon any consideration, for they consider it to be a sort of punishment to attend divine service. Possibly they remember the dull Sundays of their childhood and the dreary sermons they have heard when for a few times they have entered a church, but it is certain that they look upon persons who attend places of worship as getting off the punishment they ought to endure in the next world by suffering it in this world instead. The Sunday newspaper, the pipe, and the pot, have more charms for them than all the preachments of bishops and parsons, whether of church or dissent. The open-air evangelist frequently picks up these members of the "No church" party, and in so doing he often finds some of the richest gems that will at last adorn the Redeemer's crown: jewels, which, by reason of their roughness, are apt to be unnoticed by a more fastidious class of soul-winners. Jonah in the streets of Nineveh was heard by multitudes who would never have known of his existence if he had hired a hall; John the Baptist by the Jordan awakened an interest which would never have been aroused had he kept to the synagogue; and those who went from city to city proclaiming everywhere the word of the Lord Jesus would never have turned the world upside down if they had felt it needful to confine themselves to iron rooms adorned with the orthodox announcement, "The gospel of the grace of God will (D.V.) be preached here next Lord's day evening."

I am quite sure, too, that if we could persuade our friends in the country to come out a good many times in the year and hold a service in a meadow, or in a shady grove, or on the hill side, or in a garden, or on a common, *it would be all the better for the usual hearers.* The mere novelty of the place would freshen their interest, and wake them up. The slight change of scene would have a wonderful effect upon the more somnolent. See how mechanically they move into their usual place of worship, and how mechanically they go out again. They fall into their seats as if at last they had found a resting place; they rise to sing with an amazing effort, and they drop down before you have time for a doxology at the close of the hymn because they did not notice it was coming. What logs some regular hearers are! Many of them are asleep with their eyes open. After sitting a certain number of years in the same old spot, where the pews, pulpit, galleries, and all things else are always the same, except that they get a little dirtier and dingier every week, where everybody occupies the same position for ever and for evermore, and the minister's face, voice, tone are much the same from January to December,—you get to feel the holy quiet of the scene and listen to what is going on as though it were addressed to "the dull cold ear of death." As a miller hears his wheels as though he did not hear them, or a stoker scarcely notices the clatter of his engine after enduring it for a little time; or as a dweller in London never notices the ceaseless grind of the traffic; so do many members of our congregations become insensible to the most earnest addresses, and accept them as a matter of course. The preaching and the rest of it get to be so usual that they might as well not be at all. Hence a change of place might be useful, it might prevent monotony, shake up indifference, suggest thought, and in a thousand ways promote attention, and give new hope of doing good. A great fire which should burn some of our chapels to the ground might not be the greatest calamity which has ever occurred, if it only aroused some of those rivals of the seven sleepers of Ephesus who will never be moved so long as the old house and the old pews hold together. Besides, the fresh air and plenty of it is a grand thing for every mortal man, woman, and child. I preached in Scotland twice on a Sabbath day at Blairmore, on a little height by the side of the sea, and after discoursing with all my might to large congregations, to be counted by thousands, I did not feel one-half so much exhausted as I often am when addressing a few hundreds in some horrible black hole of Calcutta, called a chapel. I trace my freshness and freedom from lassitude at Blairmore to the fact that the windows could not be shut down by persons afraid of draughts, and that the roof was as high as the heavens are above the earth. My conviction is that a man could preach three or four times on a Sabbath out of doors with less fatigue than would be occasioned by one discourse delivered in an impure atmosphere, heated and poisoned by human breath, and carefully preserved from every refreshing infusion of natural air.

Tents are bad—unutterably bad: far worse than the worst buildings. I think a tent is the most objectionable covering for a preaching place that was ever invented. I am glad to see tents used in London, for the very worst place is better than none, and because they can easily be moved from place to place, and are not very expensive; but still, if I had my choice between having nothing at all and having a tent,

I should prefer the open air by far. Under canvas the voice is deadened and the labour of speaking greatly increased. The material acts as a wet blanket to the voice, kills its resonance, and prevents its travelling. With fearful exertion, in the sweltering air generated in a tent, you will be more likely to be killed than to be heard. You must have noticed even at our own College gatherings, when we number only some two hundred, how difficult it is to hear at the end of a tent, even when the sides are open, and the air is pure. Perhaps you may on that occasion attribute this fact in some degree to a want of attentiveness and quietness on the part of that somewhat jubilant congregation, but still even when prayer is offered, and all is hushed, I have observed a great want of travelling power in the best voice beneath a marquee.

If you are going to preach in the open air in the country, you will perhaps have *your choice of a spot wherein to preach*; if not, of course you must have what you can get, and you must in faith accept it as *the very best*. Hobson's choice of that or none makes the matter simple, and saves a deal of debate. Do not be very squeamish. If there should happen to be an available meadow hard by your chapel, select it because it will be very convenient to turn into the meeting-house should the weather prove unsuitable, or if you wish to hold a prayer-meeting or an after-meeting at the close of your address. It is well to preach before your regular services on a spot near your place of worship, so as to march the crowd right into the building before they know what they are about. Half-an-hour's out-of-door speaking and singing before your ordinary hour of assembly will often fill an empty house. At the same time, do not always adhere to near and handy spots, but choose a locality for the very opposite reason, because it is far away from any place of worship and altogether neglected. Hang up the lamps wherever there is a dark corner; the darker the more need of light. Paradise Row and Pleasant Place are generally the least paradisiacal and the most unpleasant: thither let your steps be turned. Let the dwellers in the valley of the shadow of death perceive that light has sprung up for them.

I have somewhere met with the recommendation always to preach with a wall behind you, but against that I respectfully enter my caveat. Have a care of what may be on the other side of the wall! One evangelist received a can of scalding water from over a wall with the kindly remark, "There's soup for Protestants!" and another was favoured with most unsavoury bespatterings from a vessel emptied from above. Gideon Ouseley began to preach in Roscommon with his back against the gable of a tobacco factory in which there was a window with a wooden door, through which goods were hoisted into the loft. Would you be surprised to learn that the window suddenly opened, and that from it descended a pailful of tobacco water, an acrid fluid most painful to the eyes? The preacher in after years knew better than to put himself in such a tempting position. Let his experience instruct you.

If I had my choice of a pitch for preaching, I should prefer to front a rising ground, or an open spot bounded at some little distance by a wall. Of course there must be sufficient space to allow of the congregation assembling between the pulpit and the bounding object in front, but I like to see an end, and not to shout into boundless space. I do not know a prettier site for a sermon than that which I occupied in my friend Mr. Duncan's grounds at Benmore. It was a level sweep of lawn, backed by rising terraces covered with fir-trees. The people could either occupy the seats below, or drop down upon the grassy banks, as best comported with their comfort, and thus I had part of my congregation in rising galleries above me, and the rest in the area around me. My voice readily ascended, and I conceive that if the people had been seated up the hill for half-a-mile they would have been able to hear me with ease. I should suppose that Wesley's favourite spot at Gwennap Pit must be somewhat after the same order. Amphitheatres and hillsides are always favourite spots with preachers in the fields, and their advantages will be at once evident to you.

My friend Mr. Abraham once produced for me a grand cathedral in Oxfordshire. The remains of it are still called "Spurgeon's Tabernacle," and may be seen near Minster Lovell, in the form of a quadrilateral of oaks. Originally it was the *beau ideal* of a preaching place, for it was a cleared spot in the thick forest of Witchwood, and was reached by roads cut through the dense underwood. I shall never forget those "alleys green," and the verdant walls which shut them in. When you reached the inner temple it consisted of a large square, out of which the underwood and smaller trees had been cut away, while a sufficient number of young oaks had been left to rise to a considerable height, and then overshadow us with their branches. Here was a truly magnificent cathedral, with pillars and arches: a temple not made with hands, of which we might truly say,

> "Father, thy hand
> Hath reared these venerable columns, thou
> Didst weave this verdant roof."

I have never, either at home or on the Continent, seen architecture which could rival my cathedral. "Lo, we heard of it at Ephratah: we found it in the fields of the wood." The blue sky was visible through our clerestory, and from the great window at the further end the sun smiled upon us toward evening. Oh, sirs, it was grand indeed, to worship thus beneath the vaulted firmament, beyond the sound of city hum, where all around ministered to quiet fellowship with God.

That spot is now cleared, and the place of our assembly has been selected at a little distance from it. It is of much the same character, only that my boundary walls of forest growth have disappeared to give place to an open expanse of ploughed fields. Only the pillars and the roof of my temple remain, but I am still glad, like the Druids, to worship among the oak trees. This year a dove had built her nest just above my head, and she continued flying to and fro to feed her young, while the sermon proceeded. Why not? Where should she be more at home than where the Lord of love and Prince of Peace was adored? It is true my arched cathedral is not waterproof, and other showers besides those of grace will descend upon the congregation, but this has its advantages, for it makes us the more grateful when the day is propitious, and the very precariousness of the weather excites a large amount of earnest prayer.

I once preached a sermon in the open air in haying time during a violent storm of rain. The text was, "He shall come down like rain upon the mown grass, as showers that water the earth," and surely we had the blessing as well as the inconvenience. I was sufficiently wet, and my congregation must have been drenched, but they stood it out, and I never heard that anybody was the worse in health, though, I thank God, I have heard of souls brought to Jesus under that discourse. Once in a while, and under strong excitement, such things do no one any harm, but we are not to expect miracles, nor wantonly venture upon a course of procedure which might kill the sickly and lay the foundations of disease in the strong.

I remember well preaching between Cheddar Cliffs. What a noble position! What beauty and sublimity! But there was great danger from falling pieces of stone, moved by the people who sat upon the higher portions of the cliff, and hence I would not choose the spot again. We must studiously avoid positions where serious accident might be possible. An injured head qualifies no one for enjoying the beauties of nature, or the consolations of grace. Concluding a discourse in that place, I called upon those mighty rocks to bear witness that I had preached the gospel to the people, and to be a testimony against them at the last great day, if they rejected the message. Only the other day I heard of a person to whom that appeal was made useful by the Holy Spirit.

Look well to the ground you select, that it is not swampy. I never like to see a man slip up to his knees in mire while I am preaching. Rushy places are often so smooth and green that we select them without noting that they are apt to be muddy, and to give our hearers wet feet. Always inconvenience yourself rather than your audience: your Master would have done so. Even in the streets of London a concern for the convenience of your hearers is one of the things which conciliates a crowd more than anything.

Avoid as your worst enemy the neighbourhood of the Normandy poplar. These trees cause a perpetual hissing and rustling sound, almost like the noise of the sea. Every leaf of certain kinds of poplar is in perpetual motion, like the tongue of Talkative. The noise may not seem very loud, but it will drown the best of voices. "The sound of a going in the tops of the mulberry trees" is all very well, but keep clear of the noise of poplars and some other trees, or you will suffer for it. I have had painful experience of this misery. The old serpent himself seemed to hiss at me out of those unquiet boughs.

Practised preachers do not care to have the sun directly in their faces if they can help it, neither do they wish their hearers to be distressed in like manner, and therefore they take this item into consideration when arranging for a service. In London we do not see that luminary often enough to be much concerned upon this point.

Do not try to preach against the wind, for it is an idle attempt. You may hurl your voice a short distance by an amazing effort, but you cannot be well heard even by the few. I do not often advise you to consider which way the wind blows, but on this occasion I urge you to do it, or you will labour in vain. Preach so that the wind carries your voice towards the people, and does not blow it down your throat, or you will have to eat your own words. There is no telling how far a man may be heard *with the wind*. In certain atmospheres and climates, as for instance in that of Palestine, persons might be heard for several miles; and single sentences of well-known speech may in England be recognised a long way off, but I should gravely doubt a man if he asserted that he understood a new sentence beyond the distance of a mile. Whitefield is reported to have been heard a mile, and I have been myself assured that I was heard for that distance, but I am somewhat sceptical.[1] Half-a-mile is surely enough, even with the wind, but you must make sure of that to be heard at all.

In the country it ought to be easy to find a fit place for preaching. One of the earliest things that a minister should do when he leaves College and settles in a country town or village is to begin open-air speaking. He will generally have no difficulty as to the position; the land is before him and he may choose according to his own

[1] From *Chambers' Book of Days* we borrow the following note: "Mrs. Oliphant, in her *Life of the Rev. Edward Irving,* states that he had been on some occasions clearly heard at the distance of half-a-mile. It has been alleged, however, that Black John Russell, of Kilmarnock, celebrated by Burns in no gracious terms, was heard, though not perhaps intelligibly, at the distance of a full mile. It would appear that even this is not the utmost stretch of the phenomenon. A correspondent of the *Jameson's Journal,* in 1828, states that, being at the west end of Dunfermline, he overheard part of a sermon then delivering at a tent at Cairneyhill by Dr. Black: he did not miss a word, 'though the distance must be something about two miles': the preacher has, perhaps, seldom been surpassed for distinct speaking and a clear voice: 'and the wind, which was steady and moderate, came in the direction of the sound.' "

sweet will. The market-cross will be a good beginning, then the head of a court crowded with the poor, and next the favourite corner of the idlers of the parish. Cheap-Jack's stand will make a capital pulpit on Sunday night during the village fair, and a wagon will serve well on the green, or in a field at a little distance, during the week-day evenings of the rustic festival. A capital place for an *al fresco* discourse is the green where the old elm trees, felled long ago, are still lying in reserve as if they were meant to be seats for your congregation; so also is the burial ground of the meeting-house where "the rude forefathers of the hamlet sleep." Consecrate it to the living and let the people enjoy "Meditations among the Tombs." Make no excuses, then, but get to work at once.

In London, or any other large town, it is a great thing to find a vacant spot where you can obtain a right to hold services at your pleasure. If you can discover a piece of ground which is not yet built over, and if you can obtain the use of it from the owner till he covers it, it will be a great acquisition, and worth a slight expense in fencing; for you are then king of the castle and disturbers will be trespassers. I suppose that such a spot is not often obtainable, especially by persons who have no money; but it is worth thinking about. It is a great gain when your place of worship has even a small outside space, like that at Surrey Chapel, or upon the Tabernacle steps; for here you are beyond the interference of the police or drunken men. If we have none of these, we must find street corners, triangles, quiet nooks, and wide spaces wherein to proclaim the gospel. Years ago I preached to enormous assemblies in King Edward's Road, Hackney, which was then open fields, but now not a spare yard remains. On those occasions the rush was perilous to life and limb, and there seemed no limit to the throngs. Half the number would have been safer. That open space has vanished, and it is the same with fields at Brixton, where in years gone by it was delightful to see the assembled crowds listening to the word. Burdened with the rare trouble of drawing too many together, I have been compelled to abstain from these exercises in London, but not from any lessened sense of their importance. With the Tabernacle always full I have as large a congregation as I desire at home, and therefore do not preach outside except in the country; but for those ministers whose area under cover is but small, and whose congregations are thin, the open air is the remedy whether in London or in the provinces.

In raising a new interest, and in mission operations, out of door services are a main agency. Get the people to *listen* outside that they may by-and-by *worship* inside. You want no pulpit, a chair will do, or the kerb of the road. The less formality the better, and if you begin by merely talking to the two or three around you and make no pretence of sermonizing you will do well. More good may be done by personal talk to one than by a rhetorical address to fifty. Do not purposely interfere with the thoroughfare, but if the crowd should accumulate do not hasten away in sheer fright: the policeman will let you know soon enough. You are most wanted, however, where you will be in no danger of impeding passers-by, but far more likely to be in danger yourself—I refer to those central courts and blind alleys in our great cities which lie out of the route of decency, and are known to nobody but the police, and to them principally through bruises and wounds. Talk of discovering the interior of Africa, we need explorers for Fryingpan Alley and Emerald-Island Court: the Arctic regions are well nigh as accessible as Dobinson's Rents and Jack Ketch's Warren. Heroes of the cross—here is a field for you more glorious than the Cid ever beheld when with his brave right arm he smote the Paynim hosts. "Who will bring me into the strong city? Who will lead me into Edom?" Who will enable us to win these slums and dens for Jesus? Who can do it but the Lord? Soldiers of Christ who venture into these regions must expect a revival of the practices of the good old times, so far as brickbats are concerned, and I have known a flower-pot fall accidentally from an upper window in a remarkably slanting direction. Still, if we are born to be drowned we shall not be killed by flower-pots. Under such treatment it may be refreshing to read what Christopher Hopper wrote under similar conditions more than a hundred years ago. "I did not much regard a little dirt, a few rotten eggs, the sound of a cow's horn, the noise of bells, or a few snowballs in their season; but sometimes I was saluted with blows, stones, brickbats, and bludgeons. These I did not well like: they were not pleasing to flesh and blood. I sometimes lost a little skin, and once a little blood, which was drawn from my forehead with a sharp stone. I wore a patch for a few days, and was not ashamed; I gloried in the cross. And when my small sufferings abounded for the sake of Christ, my comfort abounded much more. I never was more happy in my own soul, or blessed in my labours."

I am somewhat pleased when I occasionally hear of a brother's being locked up by the police, for it does him good, and it does the people good also. It is a fine sight to see the minister of the gospel marched off by the servant of the law! It excites sympathy for him, and the next step is sympathy for his message. Many who felt no interest in him before are eager to hear him when he is ordered to leave off, and still more so when he is taken to the station. The vilest of mankind respect a man who gets into trouble in order to do them good, and if they see unfair opposition excited they grow quite zealous in the man's defence.

I am persuaded that the more of open-air preaching there is in London the better. If it should become a nuisance to some it will be a blessing to others, if properly conducted. If it be the gospel which is spoken, and if the spirit of the preacher be one of love and truth, the results cannot be doubted: the bread cast upon the waters must be found again after many days. The gospel must, however, be preached in a manner worth the hearing, for mere noise-making is an evil rather than a benefit. I know a family almost driven out of their senses by the hideous shouting of monotonous exhortations, and the howling of "Safe in the arms of Jesus" near their door every Sabbath afternoon by the year together. They are zealous Christians, and would willingly help their tormentors if they saw the slightest probability of usefulness from the violent bawling: but as they seldom see a hearer, and do not think that what is spoken would do any good if it were heard, they complain that they are compelled to lose their few hours of quiet because two good men think it their duty to perform a noisy but perfectly useless service. I once saw a man preaching with no hearer but a dog, which sat upon its tail and looked up very reverently while its master orated. There were no people at the windows nor passing by, but the brother and his dog were at their post whether the people would hear or whether they would forbear. Once also I passed an earnest declaimer, whose hat was on the ground before him, filled with papers, and there was not even a dog for an audience, nor any one within hearing, yet did he "waste his sweetness on the desert air." I hope it relieved his own mind. Really it must be viewed as an essential part of a sermon that somebody should hear it: it cannot be a great benefit to the world to have sermons preached *in vacuo*.

As to *style in preaching out of doors*, it should certainly be very different from much of that which prevails within, and perhaps if a speaker were to acquire a style fully adapted to a street audience, he would be wise to bring it indoors with him. A great deal of sermonizing may be defined as saying nothing at extreme length; but out of doors verbosity is not admired, you must say something and have done with it and go on to say something more, or your hearers will let you know. "Now then," cries a street critic, "let us have it, old fellow." Or else the observation is made, "Now then, pitch it out! You'd better go home and learn your lesson." "Cut it short, old boy," is a very common admonition, and I wish the presenters of this advice gratis could let it be heard inside Ebenezer and Zoar and some other places sacred to long-winded orations. Where these outspoken criticisms are not employed, the hearers rebuke prosiness by quietly walking away. Very unpleasant this, to find your congregation dispersing, but a very plain intimation that your ideas are also much dispersed.

In the street, a man must keep himself alive, and use many illustrations and anecdotes, and sprinkle a quaint remark here and there.

To dwell long on a point will never do. Reasoning must be brief, clear, and soon done with. The discourse must not be laboured or involved, neither must the second head depend upon the first, for the audience is a changing one, and each point must be complete in itself. The chain of thought must be taken to pieces, and each link melted down and turned into bullets: you will need not so much Saladin's sabre to cut through a muslin handkerchief as Cœur de Lion's battle-axe to break a bar of iron. Come to the point at once, and come there with all your might.

Short sentences of words and short passages of thought are needed for out of doors. Long paragraphs and long arguments had better be reserved for other occasions. In quiet country crowds there is much force in an eloquent silence, now and then interjected; it gives people time to breathe, and also to reflect. Do not, however, attempt this in a London street; you must go ahead, or someone else may run off with your congregation. In a regular field sermon pauses are very effective, and are useful in several ways, both to speaker and listeners, but to a passing company who are not inclined for anything like worship, quick, short, sharp address is most adapted.

In the streets a man must from beginning to end be intense, and for that very reason he must be condensed and concentrated in his thought and utterance. It would never do to begin by saying, "My text, dear friends, is a passage from the inspired word, containing doctrines of the utmost importance, and bringing before us in the clearest manner the most valuable practical instruction. I invite your careful attention and the exercise of your most candid judgment while we consider it under various aspects and place it in different lights, in order that we may be able to perceive its position in the analogy of the faith. In its exegesis we shall find an arena for the cultured intellect, and the refined sensibilities. As the purling brook meanders among the meads and fertilizes the pastures, so a stream of sacred truth flows through the remarkable words which now lie before us. It will be well for us to divert the crystal current to the reservoir of our meditation, that we may quaff the cup of wisdom with the lips of satisfaction." There, gentleman, is not that rather above the average of word-spinning, and is not the art very generally in vogue in these days? If you go out to the obelisk in Blackfriars Road, and talk in that fashion, you will be saluted with "Go on, old buffer," or "*Ain't he fine?* MY EYE!" A very vulgar youth will cry, "What a mouth for a tater!" and another will shout in a tone of mock solemnity, "AMEN!" If you give them chaff they will cheerfully return it into your own bosom. Good measure, pressed down and running over will they mete out to you. Shams and shows will have no mercy from a street gathering. But have something to say, look them in the face, say what you mean, put it plainly, boldly, earnestly, courteously, and they will hear you. Never speak against time or for the sake of hearing your own voice, or you will obtain some information about your personal appearance or manner of oratory which will probably be more true than pleasing. "Crikey," says one, "wouldn't he do for an undertaker! He'd make 'em weep." This was a compliment paid to a melancholy brother whose tone is peculiarly funereal. "There, old fellow," said a critic on another occasion, "you go and wet your whistle. You must feel awfully dry after jawing away at that rate about nothing at all." This also was specially appropriate to a very heavy brother of whom we had aforetime remarked that he would make a good martyr, for there was no doubt of his burning well, he was so dry. It is sad, very sad, that such rude remarks should be made, but there is a wicked vein in some of us, which makes us take note that the vulgar observations are often very true, and "hold as 'twere the mirror up to nature." As caricature often gives you a more vivid idea of a man than a photograph would afford you, so do these rough mob critics hit off an orator to the life by their exaggerated censures. The very best speaker must be prepared to take his share of street wit, and to return it if need be; but primness, demureness, formality, sanctimonious long-windedness, and the affectation of superiority, actually invite offensive pleasantries, and to a considerable extent deserve them. Chadband or Stiggins in rusty black, with plastered hair and huge choker, is as natural an object of derision as Mr. Guido Fawkes himself. A very great man in his own esteem will provoke immediate opposition, and the affectation of supernatural saintliness will have the same effect. The less you are like a parson the more likely you are to be heard; and, if you are known to be a minister, the more you show yourself to be a man the better. "What do you get for that, governor?" is sure to be asked, if you appear to be a cleric, and it will be well to tell them at once that this is extra, that you are doing overtime, and that there is to be no collection. "You'd do more good if you gave us some bread or a drop of beer, instead of them tracts," is constantly remarked, but a manly manner, and the outspoken declaration that you seek no wages but their good, will silence that stale objection.

The *action* of the street preacher should be of the very best. It should be purely natural and unconstrained. No speaker should stand up in the street in a grotesque manner, or he will weaken himself and invite attack. The street preacher should not imitate his own minister, or the crowd will spy out the imitation very speedily, if the brother is anywhere near home. Neither should he strike an attitude as little boys do who say, "My name is Norval." The stiff straight posture with the regular up and down motion of arm and hand is too commonly adopted: and I would even more condemn the wild-raving-maniac action which some are so fond of, which seems to be a cross between Whitefield with both his arms in the air, and Saint George with both his feet violently engaged in trampling on the dragon. Some good men are grotesque by nature, and others take great pains to make themselves so. The wicked Londoners say, "What a cure!" I only wish I knew of a cure for the evil.

All mannerisms should be avoided. Just now I observe that nothing can be done without a very large Bagster's Bible with a limp cover. There seems to be some special charm about the large size, though it almost needs a little perambulator in which to push it about. With such a Bible full of ribbons, select a standing in Seven Dials, after the pattern of a divine so graphically described by Mr. McCree. Take off your hat, put your Bible in it, and place it on the ground. Let the kind friend who approaches you on the right hold your umbrella. See how eager the dear man is to do so! Is it not pleasing? He assures you he is never so happy as when he is helping good men to do good. Now close your eyes in prayer. When your devotions are over, *somebody will have profited by the occasion*. Where is your affectionate friend who held your umbrella and your hymn-book? Where is that well-brushed hat, and that orthodox Bagster? Where? oh, where? Echo answers, "Where?"

The catastrophe which I have thus described suggests that a brother had better accompany you in your earlier ministries, that one may watch while the other prays. If a number of friends will go with you and make a ring around you it will be a great acquisition, and if these can sing it will be still further helpful. The friendly company will attract others, will help to secure order, and will do good service by sounding forth sermons in song.

It will be very desirable to speak so as to be heard, but there is no use in incessant bawling. The best street preaching is not that which is done at the top of your voice, for it must be impossible to lay the proper emphasis upon telling passages when all along you are shouting with all your might. When there are no hearers near you, and yet people stand upon the other side of the road and listen, would it not be as well to cross over and so save a little of the strength which is now wasted? A quiet, penetrating, conversational style would seem to be the most telling. Men do not bawl and halloa when they are pleading in deepest earnestness; they have generally at such times less wind and a little more rain : less rant and a few more tears. On, on, on with one monotonous shout and you will weary everybody and wear out yourself. Be wise now, therefore, O ye who would succeed in declaring your Master's message among the multitude, and use your voices as common sense would dictate.

In a tract published by that excellent society "The Open Air Mission," I notice the following :

QUALIFICATIONS FOR OPEN-AIR PREACHERS

1. A good voice.
2. Naturalness of manner.
3. Self-possession.
4. A good knowledge of Scripture and of common things.
5. Ability to adapt himself to any congregation.
6. Good illustrative powers.
7. Zeal, prudence, and common sense.
8. A large, loving heart.
9. Sincere belief in all he says.
10. Entire dependence on the Holy Spirit for success.
11. A close walk with God by prayer.
12. A consistent walk before men by a holy life.

If any man has all these qualifications, the Queen had better make a bishop of him at once, yet there is no one of these qualities which could well be dispensed with.

Interruptions are pretty sure to occur in the streets of London. At certain places all will go well for months, but in other positions the fight begins as soon as the speaker opens his mouth. There are *seasons* of opposition: different schools of adversaries rise and fall, and accordingly there is disorder or quiet. The best tact will not always avail to prevent disturbance; when men are drunk there is no reasoning with them, and of furious Irish Papists we may say much the same. Little is to be done with such unless the crowd around will co-operate, as oftentimes they will, in removing the obstructor. Certain characters, if they find that preaching is going on, will interrupt by hook or by crook. They go on purpose, and if answered once and again they still persevere. One constant rule is to be always courteous and good tempered, for if you become cross or angry it is all over with you. Another rule is to keep to your subject, and never be drawn into side issues. Preach Christ or nothing: don't dispute or discuss except with your eye on the cross. If driven off for a moment always be on the watch to get back to your sole topic. Tell them the old, old story, and if they will not hear *that*, move on. Yet be adroit, and take them with guile. Seek the one object by many roads. A little mother-wit is often the best resource and will work wonders with a crowd. *Bonhomie* is the next best thing to grace on such occasions. A brother of my acquaintance silenced a violent Romanist by offering him his stand and requesting him to preach. The man's comrades for the very fun of the thing urged him on, but, as he declined, the dog in the manger fable was narrated and the disturber disappeared. If it be a real sceptic who is assailing you it is prudence to shun debate as much as possible, or ask him questions in return, for your business is not to argue but to proclaim the gospel. Mr. John McGregor says "Sceptics are of many kinds. Some of them ask questions to get answers, and others put difficulties to puzzle the people. An honest sceptic said to me in a crowd in Hyde-park, 'I have been trying to believe for these ten years, but there is a contradiction I *cannot* get over, and it is this: we are told that printing was invented not five hundred years ago, and yet that the Bible is five thousand years old, and I cannot for the life of me see how this can be.' Nay! the crowd did not laugh at this man. *Very few people in a crowd know much more than he did about the Bible.* But how deeply they drank in a half-hour's account of the Scripture manuscripts, their preservation, their translations and versions, their dispersion and collection, their collation and transmission, and the overwhelming evidence of their genuine truth!"

I remember an infidel on Kennington Common being most effectually stopped. He continued to cry up the beauties of *nature* and the works of *nature* until the preacher asked him if he would kindly tell them what nature was. He replied that "everybody knew what nature was." The preacher retorted, "Well, then, it will be all the easier for you to tell us." "Why, nature—nature," he said, "nature,—nature is nature." Of course, the crowd laughed and the wise man subsided.

Ignorance when it is allied with a coarse voluble tongue is to be met by letting it have rope enough. One fellow wanted to know "how Jacob *knew* that Esau hated him." He had hold of the wrong end of the stick that time, and the preacher did not enlighten him, or he would have set him up with ammunition for future encounters.

Our business is not to supply men with arguments by informing them of difficulties. In the process of answering them ministers have published the sentiments of infidels more widely than the infidels themselves could have done. Unbelievers only "glean their blunted shafts, and shoot them at the shield of truth again." Our object is not to conquer them in logical encounters, but to save their souls. Real difficulties we should endeavour to meet, and hence a competent knowledge of the evidences is most desirable; but honest objectors are best conversed with alone, when they are not ashamed to own themselves in the wrong, and this we could not expect of them in the crowd. Christ is to be preached whether men will believe in Him or no. Our own experience of His power to save will be our best reasoning, and earnestness our best rhetoric. The occasion will frequently suggest the fittest thing to say, and we may also fall back on the Holy Spirit who will teach us in the self-same hour what we shall speak.

The open-air speaker's calling is as honourable as it is arduous, as useful as it is laborious. God alone can sustain you in it, but with Him at your side you will have nothing to fear. If ten thousand rebels were before you and a legion of devils in every one of them you need not tremble. More is He that is for you than all they that be against you.

> "By all hell's host withstood,
>   We all hell's host o'erthrow;
> And conquering them through Jesus' blood,
>   We still to conquer go."

XIX

Posture, Action, Gesture, etc.

THE subjects of this lecture are to be *"Posture, Gesture, and Action in the Delivery of a Sermon."* I shall not attempt to draw any hard and fast line of division between the one and the other; for it would need a very highly discriminating mind to keep them separate; indeed, it could not be done at all, for they naturally merge into each other. As I have, after a fair trial, found it impossible to keep even "posture" and "gesture" in an absolutely unmingled state in my own mind, I have allowed them to run together; but I hope that no confusion will appear in the result.

The sermon itself is the main thing: its matter, its aim, and the spirit in which it is brought before the people, the sacred anointing upon the preacher, and the divine power applying the truth to the hearer: these are infinitely more important than any details of manner. Posture and action are comparatively small and inconsiderable matters; but still even the sandal in the statue of Minerva should be correctly carved, and in the service of God even the smallest things should be regarded with holy care. Life is made up of little incidents, and success in it often depends upon attention to minor details. Small flies make the apothecary's ointment to stink, and little foxes spoil the vines, and therefore small flies and little foxes should be kept out of our ministry. Doubtless, faults in even so secondary a matter as posture have prejudiced men's minds, and so injured the success of what would otherwise have been most acceptable ministries. A man of more than average abilities may, by ridiculous action, be thrown into the rear rank and kept there. This is a great pity, even if there were only one such case, but it is to be feared that many are injured by the same cause. Little oddities and absurdities of mode and gesture which wise men would endeavour not to notice are not overlooked by the general public; in fact, the majority of hearers fix their eyes mainly upon those very things, while those who come to scoff observe nothing else. Persons are either disgusted or diverted by the oddities of certain preachers, or else they want an excuse for inattention, and jump at this convenient one: there can be no reason why we should help men to resist our own endeavours for their good. No minister would willingly cultivate a habit which would blunt his arrows, or drift them aside from the mark; and, therefore, since these

272

minor matters of movement, posture, and gesture may have that effect, you will give them your immediate attention.

We very readily admit that action in preaching is an affair of minor consequence; for some who have succeeded in the highest sense have been exceedingly faulty from the rhetorician's point of view. At the present moment there is in Boston, U.S.A., a preacher of the very highest order of power, of whom a friendly critic writes: "In the opening sentences one or the other of his arms shakes at his side in a helpless fashion, as if it were made of caudal vertabræ loosely jointed. He soon exhibits a most engaging awkwardness, waddling about in a way to suggest that each leg is shorter than the other, and shaking his head and shoulder in ungainly emphasis. He raises one eyebrow in a quite impossible fashion. No one else can squint so." This is an instance of mind overcoming matter, and the excellence of the teaching condoning defects in utterance; but it would be better if no such drawbacks existed. Are not apples of gold all the more attractive for being placed in baskets of silver? Why should powerful teaching be associated with waddling and squinting? Still it is evident that proper action is, to say the least, not essential to success. Homer would appear to have considered the entire absence of gesture to be no detriment to eminent power in speech, for he pictures one of his greatest heroes as entirely abjuring it, though not without some sense of censure from his audience.

> "But when Ulysses rose, in thought profound,
> His modest eyes he fixed upon the ground;
> As one unskilled or dumb, he seemed to stand,
> Nor rais'd his head, nor stretched his sceptred hand.
> But when he speaks, what elocution flows!
> Soft as the fleeces of descending snows,
> The copious accents fall, with easy art;
> Melting they fall, and sink into the heart!
> Wondering we hear, and, fixed in deep surprise,
> Our ears refute the censures of our eyes."

Nor need we go back to the ancients for proof that an exceedingly quiet action may be connected with the highest power of eloquence, for several instances occur to us among the moderns. One may suffice: our own supremely gifted Robert Hall had no oratorical action, and scarcely any motion in the pulpit, except an occasional lifting or waving of the right hand, and in his most impassioned moments an alternate retreat and advance.

It is not so much incumbent upon you to acquire right pulpit action as it is to get rid of that which is wrong. If you could be reduced to motionless dummies, it would be better than being active and even vigorous incarnations of the grotesque, as some of our brethren have been. Some men by degrees fall into a suicidal style of preaching, and it is a very rare thing indeed to see a man escape when once he has entangled himself in the meshes of an evil mannerism. No one likes to tell them of their queer antics, and so they are unaware of them; but it is surprising that their wives do not mimic them in private and laugh them out of their awkwardness. I have heard of a brother who in his earlier days was most acceptable, but who afterwards dropped far behind in the race because he by degrees fell into bad habits: he spoke with a discordant whine, assumed most singular attitudes, and used such extraordinary mouthings that people could not hear him with pleasure. He developed into a man to be esteemed and honoured, but not to be listened to. Excellent Christian men have said that they did not know whether to laugh or to cry when they were hearing him preach: they felt as if they must laugh at the bidding of nature, and then they felt that they ought to cry from the impulse of grace when they saw so good a preacher utterly ruined by absurd affectations. If you do not care to cultivate proper action, at least be wise enough to steer clear of that which is grotesque or affected. There is a wide range between the fop, curling and perfuming his locks, and permitting one's hair to hang in matted masses like the mane of a wild beast. We should never advise you to practise postures before a glass, nor to imitate great divines, nor to ape the fine gentleman; but there is no need, on the other hand, to be vulgar or absurd. Postures and attitudes are merely a small part of the dress of a discourse, and it is not in dress that the substance of the matter lies: a man in fustian is "a man for a' that," and so a sermon which is oddly delivered may be a good sermon for all that; but still, as none of you would care to wear a pauper's suit if you could procure better raiment, so you should not be so slovenly as to clothe truth like a mendicant when you might array her as a prince's daughter.

Some men are naturally very awkward in their persons and movements. I suppose we must blame what the countryman called their "broughtens up." The rustic's gait is heavy, and his walk is slouching. You can see that his natural *habitat* is a ploughed field. On the pavement or the carpet he is suspicious of his footing, but down a muddy lane, with a mule's burden of earth on each boot, he progresses with ease, if not with elegance. There is a lumpishness and lubberliness innate in the elements of some men's constitutions. You could not make them elegant if you brayed them in a mortar among wheat with a pestle. The drill-sergeant is of the utmost use in our schools, and those parents who think that drill exercise is a waste of time are very much mistaken. There is a shape and handiness, a general propriety of form, which the human body acquires under proper drill which seldom comes in any other manner. Drill brings a man's shoulders down, keeps his arms from excessive swinging, expands the chest, shows him what to do with his hands, and, in a word, teaches a man how to walk uprightly, and to bring himself into something like ship-shape, without any conscious effort to do so, which effort would be a sure betrayal of his awkwardness. Very spiritual people will think me trifling, but indeed I am not. I hope the day will come when it will be looked upon as an essential part of education to teach a young man how to carry himself, and move without clumsiness.

It may happen that awkward gestures arise from feeble utterance, and a nervous consciousness of lack of power in that direction. Certain splendid men of our acquaintance are so modest as to be diffident, and hence they become hesitating in speech, and disarranged in manner. Perhaps no more notable instance of this can be mentioned than the late beloved Dr. James Hamilton. He was the most beautiful and chaste of speakers, with an action painful to the last degree. His biographer says: "In mental resources and acquirements he was possessed of great wealth; but in the capacity to utter his thoughts, with all the variation of tone and key which their nature required, yet so as to be thoroughly heard in a great edifice, he was far less gifted. In this department, accordingly, he was always pained by a conscious shortcoming from his own ideal. It is certain that lack of vocal force, and ready control over his intonations, largely detracted from the power and popularity of his preaching. In delicacy of conception, in the happy choice of idioms, in the command of striking and original imagery, and in the glow of evangelical fervour that pervaded all, he had few equals. These rare qualities, however, were shorn of half their strength, in as far as his public preaching was concerned, by the necessity under which he constantly lay of straining to make himself audible, by *standing on his tip-toes, and throwing out his words in handfuls, if so be they might reach the far-distant aisles.* If the muscles of his chest had been such as to enable him to stand solidly at ease, while his lips performed the task of articulation without the aid of auxiliary blasts from over-inflated lungs, James Hamilton would certainly have been followed by greater crowds, and obtained access for his message to a wider and more varied circle. But we do not know what counterbalancing evil might have come in along with such external success. Although with all his prayers and pains this thorn was still left in the flesh, the grand compensation remained: 'My grace is sufficient for thee; my strength is perfect in thy weakness.' What talents the Lord saw meet to bestow, he laid out with marvellous skill and diligence in the giver's service, and if some of the talents were withheld, the Withholder knows why. He hath done all things well." In this sentiment we heartily concur, but we should be sorry for any young man to submit at discretion to a similar defect, and ascribe it to the hand of the Lord. Dr. Hamilton did not so. He earnestly endeavoured to overcome his natural disadvantage, and to our knowledge took lessons of more than one professor of elocution. He did not take refuge in the sluggard's plea, but laboured hard to master the difficulty, and only failed because it was a physical defect beyond all remedy. Let us wherever we see awkwardness, which is evidently unavoidable, take little or no notice of it, and take care to commend the brother that he does so well under the circumstances; counting it no small achievement for a divine to cover by richness of thought and fitness of language the ungainliness of his outer man, thus making the soul triumph over the body. Yet should we ourselves be afflicted with any fault of manner, let us resolve to overcome it, for it is not an impossible task. Edward Irving was a striking instance of a man's power to improve himself in this respect. At first his manner was awkward, constrained, and unnatural; but by diligent culture his attitude and action were made to be striking aids to his eloquence.

Pulpits have much to answer for in having made men awkward. What horrible inventions they are! If we could once abolish them we might say concerning them as Joshua did concerning Jericho—"Cursed be he that buildeth this Jericho," for the old-fashioned pulpit has been a greater curse to the churches than is at first sight evident. No barrister would ever enter a pulpit to plead a case at the bar. How could he hope to succeed while buried alive almost up to his shoulders? The client would be ruined if the advocate were thus imprisoned. How manly, how commanding is the attitude in which Chrysostom is usually represented! Forgetting his robes for the moment one cannot but feel that such a natural posture is far more worthy of sublime truth than that of a person crouching over a sheet of paper, looking up very occasionally, and then revealing no more than his head and shoulders. Austin in his *Chironomia* very properly says, "Freedom is also necessary to gracefulness of action. No gestures can be graceful which are either confined by external circumstances, or restrained by the mind. If a man were obliged to address an assembly from a narrow window, through which he could not extend his arms and his head, it would be in vain for him to attempt graceful gesture. Confinement in every lesser degree must be proportionally injurious to grace; thus the crowded bar is injurious to the action of the advocate, and the enclosed and bolstered pulpit, which often cuts off more than half of his figure, is equally injurious to the graceful action of the preacher."

The late Thomas Binney was unable to endure a platform, and was known to fetch gowns and other materials to hang over the rails of an open rostrum, if he found himself placed in one: this must have arisen solely from the force of habit, for there can be no real advantage in being enclosed in a wooden pen. This feeling will no doubt retain the close pulpit in its place for awhile longer, but in ages to come men will find an argument for the divinity of our holy faith in the fact that it survived pulpits.

Ministers cannot be blamed for ungainly postures and attitudes when only a very small part of their bodies can be seen during a discourse. If it was the custom to preach as Paul did at Athens public speakers would become models of propriety. By the way, it is interesting to note that Raphael in his representation of Paul at Athens evidently had in his mind the apostle's utterance, "God dwelleth not in temples made with hands, neither is worshipped with man's hands": hence he delineates him as lifting his hands. I am indebted for this hint to G. W. Hervey, M.A., who has written a very able and comprehensive *"System of Rhetoric."*

Remarkable are the forms which pulpits have assumed according to the freaks of human fancy and folly. Twenty years ago they had probably reached their very worst. What could have been their design and intent it would be hard to conjecture. A deep wooden pulpit of the old sort might well remind a minister of his mortality, for it is nothing but a coffin set on end: but on what rational ground do we bury our pastors alive? Many of these erections resemble barrels, others are of the fashion of egg cups and wine glasses; a third class were evidently modelled after corn bins upon four legs; and yet a fourth variety can only be likened to swallows' nests stuck upon the wall. Some of them are so high as to turn the heads of the occupants when they dare to peer into the awful depths below them, and they give those who look up to the elevated preacher for any length of time a crick in the neck. I have felt like a man at the mast-head while perched aloft in these "towers of the flock." These abominations are in themselves evils, and create evils.

While I am upon pulpits I will make a digression, and remark for the benefit of deacons and churchwardens that I frequently notice in pulpits a most abominable savour of gas, which evidently arises from leakage in the gas-pipes, and is very apt to make a preacher feel half intoxicated, or to sicken him. We ought to be spared this infliction. Frequently, also, a large lamp is placed close to each side of the minister's head, thus cramping all his movements and placing him between two fires. If any complaints are made of the hot-headedness of our ministers, it is readily to be accounted for, since the apparatus for the purpose is arranged with great care. Only the other night I had the privilege, when I sat down in the pulpit, to feel as if some one had smitten me on the top of my head, and as I looked up there was an enormous Argand burner with a reflector placed immediately above me, in order to throw a light on my Bible: a very considerate contrivance no doubt, only the inventor had forgotten that his burners were pouring down a terrible heat upon a sensitive brain. One has no desire to experience an artificial *coup de soleil* while preaching; if we must suffer from such a calamity let it come upon us during our holidays, and let it befall us from the sun himself. No one in erecting a pulpit seems to think of the preacher as a man of like feelings and senses with other people; the seat upon which you are to rest at intervals is often a mere ledge, and the door handle runs into the small of your back, while when you stand up and would come to the front there is often a curious gutta-percha bag interposed between you and your pulpit. This gummy depositary is charitably intended for the assistance of certain deaf people, who are I hope benefited; they ought to be, for every evil should have a compensating influence. You cannot bend forward without forcing this contrivance to close up, and I for my own part usually deposit my pocket-handkerchief in it, which causes the deaf people to take the ends of the tubes out of their ears and to discover that they hear me well enough without them.

No one knows the discomfort of pulpits except the man who has been in very many, and found each one worse than the last. They are generally so deep that a short person like myself can scarcely see over the top of them, and when I ask for something to stand upon they bring me a hassock. Think of a minister of the gospel poising himself upon a hassock while he is preaching: a Boanerges and a Blondin in one person. It is too much to expect us to keep the balance of our minds and the equilibrium of our bodies at the same time. The tippings up, and overturnings of stools and hassocks which I have had to suffer while preaching rush on my memory now, and revive the most painful sensations. Surely we ought to be saved such petty annoyances, for their evil is by no means limited by our discomfort; if it were so, it would be of no consequence; but, alas! these little things often throw the mind out of gear, disconnect our thoughts, and trouble our spirit. We ought to rise superior to such trifles, but though the spirit truly is willing the flesh is weak. It is marvellous how the mind is affected by the most trifling matters: there can be no need to perpetuate needless causes of discomfort. Sydney Smith's story shows that we have not been alone in our tribulation. "I can't bear," said he, "to be imprisoned in the true orthodox way in my pulpit, with my head just peeping above the desk. I like to look down upon my congregation—to fire into them. The common people say I am a *bould preacher*, for I like to have my arms free, and to thump the pulpit. A singular *contretemps* happened to me once, when, to effect this, I had ordered the clerk to pile up some hassocks for me to stand on. My text was, 'We are perplexed, but not in despair; persecuted, but not forsaken; cast down, but not destroyed.' I had scarcely uttered these words, and was preparing to illustrate them, when I did so practically, and in a way I had not at all anticipated. My fabric of hassocks suddenly gave way; down I fell, and with difficulty prevented myself from being precipitated into the arms of my congregation, who, I must say, behaved very well, and recovered their gravity sooner than I could have expected."

But I must return to my subject, and I do so by repeating the belief that boxed-up pulpits are largely accountable for the ungainly postures which some of our preachers assume when they are out of their cages and are loose upon a platform. They do not know what to do with their legs and arms, and feel awkward and exposed, and hence drop into ridiculous attitudes. When a man has been accustomed to regard himself as an "animated bust" he feels as if he had become too long when he is made to appear at full length.

There can be no doubt *that many men are made awkward through fear.* It is not the man's nature, nor his pulpit, but his nervousness which makes a guy of him. To some it is a display of great courage even to stand before an audience, and to speak is an ordeal indeed: no wonder that their attitude is constrained, for they are twitching and trembling all over. Every nerve is in a state of excitement, and their whole body is tremulous with fear. Especially are they perplexed what to do with their hands, and they move them about in a restless, irregular, meaningless manner; if they could have them strapped down to their sides they might rejoice in the deliverance. One of the clergy of the Church of England, in pleading for the use of the manuscript, makes use of the remarkable argument that a nervous man by having to turn over the leaves of his discourse thus keeps his hands occupied; whereas, if he had no paper before him, he would not know what to do with them. It is an ill wind that blows no one any good, and it must be a very bad practice indeed which has not some remote and occasional advantages. For nervousness, however, there must be a more effectual treatment; the preacher should try to conquer the evil rather than look for a mode of concealing its outward manifestations. Practice is a great remedy, and faith in God is a still more potent cure. When the minister becomes accustomed to the people he stands at ease because he is at ease, he feels at home, and as to his hands or legs, or any other part of his person, he has no thought: he goes to work with all his heart, and drops into the positions most natural to an earnest man, and these are the most appropriate. Unstudied gestures, to which you never turned your thoughts for a moment, are the very best, and the highest result of art is to banish art, and leave the man as free to be graceful as the gazelle among the mountains.

Occasional oddities of posture and gesture may arise from the difficulty of finding the next word. An American observer some years ago said, "It is interesting, sometimes, to see the different ways in which different individuals get out of the same dilemma. Mr. Calhoun is not often at a loss for a word, but occasionally one sticks in his throat, in the pronunciation, like Macbeth's '*Amen.*' In such a case he gives a petulant twitch or two at his shirt collar, and runs his bony fingers through his long grey hair, till it fairly bristles again. Webster, when bothered for a word, or snarled up in a sentence, almost invariably scratches the inner corner of his left eye carefully with the third finger of his right hand. Failing in this, he rubs his nose quite fiercely with the bent knuckle of his thumb. As a *dernier ressort,* he springs his knees apart until his legs resemble an ellipsis, then plunging his hands deep into his pockets, he throws the upper section of his body smartly forward, and the word is '*bound* to come.'" A man ought to be forgiven for what he does when he is in an agony, but it would be a great gain if he never suffered such embarrassments, and so escaped from the consequent contortions.

Habit also frequently leads speakers into very singular movements, and to these they become so wedded that they cannot speak without them. Tugging at a button at the back of the coat, or twiddling the fingers, will be often seen, not as a part of the preacher's oratory, but as a sort of free accompaniment to it. Addison, in the *Spectator,* relates an amusing incident of this kind. "I remember, when I was a young man, and used to frequent Westminster Hall, there was a counsellor who never pleaded without a piece of packthread in his hand, which he used to twist about a thumb or a finger all the while he was speaking: the wags of those days used to call it the thread of his discourse, for he was not able to utter a word without it. One of his clients, who was more merry than wise, stole it from him one day in the midst of his pleading, but he had better have let it alone, for he lost his cause by his jest." Gentlemen who are as yet free from such little peculiarities should be upon their guard lest they should gradually yield to them; but, so long as they are mere trifles, observed only by the few, and not injurious to the preacher's efforts, no great stress needs to be laid upon them.

The posture of the minister should be natural, but his nature must not be of a coarse type; it should be graceful, educated nature. He should avoid especially those positions which are unnatural to a speaker, because they hamper the organs of utterance, or cramp his lungs. He should use his common sense, and not make it difficult for him to speak by leaning forward over the Bible or book-board. Bending over as if you were speaking confidentially to the persons immediately below may be tolerated occasionally, but as a customary position it is as injurious as it is ungraceful. Who thinks of stooping when he speaks in the parlour? What killing work it would be to conduct a long conversation while pressing the breathing apparatus against the edge of a table! Stand upright, get a firm position, and then speak like a man. A few orators even err in the other direction, and throw their heads far back as though they were addressing the angels, or saw a handwriting upon the ceiling. This also cometh of evil, and unless the occasional sublime apostrophe requires it, is by no means to be practised. John Wesley well says, "The head ought not to be held up too high, nor clownishly thrust too forward, neither to be cast down and hang, as it were, on the breast; nor to lean always on one or the other side; but to be kept modestly and decently upright, in its natural state and position. Further, it ought neither to be kept immovable, as a statue, nor to be continually moving and throwing itself about. To avoid both extremes, it should be turned gently, as occasion is, sometimes one way, sometimes the other; and at other times, remain, looking straight forward, to the middle of the auditory."

Too many men assume a slouching attitude, lolling and sprawling as if they were lounging on the parapet of a bridge and chatting with somebody down in a boat on the river. We do not go into the pulpit to slouch about, and to look free and easy, but we go there upon very solemn business, and our posture should be such as becomes our mission. A reverent and earnest spirit will not be indicated by a sluggish lounge or a careless slouch. It is said that among the Greeks even the ploughmen and herdsmen take up graceful attitudes without any idea that they are doing so. I think it is also true of the Italians, for wherever I have seen a Roman man or woman—no matter whether they are sleeping upon the Spagna steps, or sitting upon a fragment of the baths of Caracalla, or carrying a bundle on their heads, or riding a mule, they always look like studies for an artist; yet this is the last thing which ever crosses their minds. Those picturesque peasants have never taken lessons in calisthenics, nor do they trouble their heads as to how they appear to the foreigner; pure nature, delivered from mannerism, primness, and affectation, moulds their habits into gracefulness. We should be foolish to imitate Greeks or Italians, except in their freedom from all imitation, but it were well if we could copy their unconstrained and natural action. There is no reason why a Christian should be a clown, and there are a great many reasons why a minister should not be a boor. As Rowland Hill said that he could not see why Satan should have the best tunes, so neither can I see why he should have the most graceful speakers!

Now, leaving posture, let us more distinctly notice *action* in preaching; this also is a secondary and yet an important item. Our first observation shall be, *it should never be excessive*. In this matter bodily exercise profiteth little. We cannot readily judge when action is excessive, for what would be excessive in one man may be most fitting and proper in another. Different races employ different action in speaking. Two Englishmen will talk very quietly and soberly to one another compared with a couple of Frenchmen. Notice our Gallic neighbours: they talk all over, and shrug their shoulders, and move their fingers, and gesticulate most vehemently. Very well, then, we may allow a French preacher to be more demonstrative in preaching than an Englishman, because he is so in ordinary speech. I am not sure that a French divine is so as a matter of fact, but if he were so it could be accounted for by the national habit. If you and I were to converse in the Parisian fashion we should excite ridicule, and, in the same way, if we were to become violent and vehement in the pulpit we might run the same risk; for if Addison be an authority, English orators use less gestures than those of other countries. As it is with races so is it with men : some naturally gesticulate more than others, and if it be really natural, we have little fault to find. For instance, we cannot censure John Gough's marvellous gesticulation and perambulation, for he would not have been Gough without them. I wonder how many miles he walks in the course of one of his lectures! Did we not see him climb the sides of a volcano in pursuit of a bubble? How we pitied him as we saw him ankle deep in the hot ashes! Then he was away, away at the other end of the platform at Exeter Hall, apostrophising a glass of water; but he only stopped there a moment, and anon made another rush over the corns of the temperance brethren in the front row. Now, this was right enough for John Gough; but if you, John Smith or John Brown, commence these perambulations you will soon be likened to the wandering Jew, or to the polar bear, at the Zoological Gardens, which for ever goes backwards and forwards in its den. Martin Luther was wont to smite with his fist at such a rate that they show, at Eisenach, a board—I think a three-inch board—which he broke while hammering at a text. The truth of the legend has been doubted, for it has been asserted that those delicate hands, which could play so charmingly upon the guitar, could hardly have been treated so roughly; but if the hand be an index of its owner's character, we can well believe it, for strength and tenderness were marvellously combined in Luther. There was much delicacy and sensitiveness about Luther's mind, yet these never diminished, but rather increased, its tremendous energy. It is by no means difficult to believe that he could smash up a plank, from the style in which he struck out at the Pope; and yet we can well imagine that he would touch the strings of his guitar with a maiden's hand; even as David could play skilfully upon the harp, and yet a bow of steel was broken by his arms. John Knox is said at one time to have been so feeble that, before he entered the pulpit, you would expect to see him drop down in a fainting fit; but once before the audience he seemed as though he would "ding the pulpit in blads," which, being interpreted, means in English that he would knock it into shivers. That was evidently the style of the period when Protestants were fighting for their very existence, and the Pope and his priests and the devil and his angels were aroused to special fury: yet I do not suppose that Melancthon thought it needful to be quite so tremendous, nor did Calvin hammer and slash in a like manner. At any rate, you need not try to break three-inch boards, for there might be a nail in one of them; neither need you ding a pulpit into "blads," for you might find yourself without a pulpit if you did. Come upon consciences with a crash, and aim at breaking hard hearts by the power of the Spirit, but these require spiritual power; physical energy is not the power of God unto salvation.

It is very easy to overdo the thing so much as to make yourself appear ridiculous. Perhaps it was a keen perception of this danger which led Dr. Johnson to forbid action altogether, and to commend Dr. Watts very highly because "he did not endeavour to assist his eloquence by any gesticulations; for as no corporeal actions have any correspondence with theological truth, he did not see how they could enforce it." The great lexicographer's remark is nonsense, but if it should be thought weighty enough to reduce a preacher to absolute inaction, it will be better than overwrought posturing. When Nathan addressed David, I suppose that he delivered his parable very quietly, and that when the time came to say, "Thou art the man," he gave the king a deeply earnest look; but younger ministers imagine that the prophet strode into the middle of the room and, setting his right foot forward, pointed his finger like a pistol between the royal eyes, and giving a loud stamp of the foot, shouted, "THOU ART THE MAN." Had it been so done it is to be feared that the royal culprit would have had his thoughts turned from himself to the insane prophet, and would have called for his guard to clear the hall. Nathan was too solemnly in earnest to be indecently violent; and as a general rule we may here note that it is the tendency of deep feeling rather to subdue the manner than to render it too energetic. He who beats the air, and bawls, and raves, and stamps, means nothing; and the more a man really means what he says the less of vulgar vehemence will there be. John Wesley in his *Directions concerning Pronunciation and Gesture* cramps the preacher too much when he says, "He must never clap his hands, nor thump the pulpit. The hands should seldom be raised higher than the eyes:" but he probably had his eye upon some glaring case of extravagance. He is right, however, when he warns his preachers that "the hands should not be in perpetual motion, for this the ancients called the babbling of the hands."

Russell very wisely says: "True vehemence never degenerates into violence and vociferation. It is the force of inspiration,—not of frenzy. It is not manifested in the screaming and foaming, the stamping and the contortions, of vulgar excess. It is ever manly and noble, in its intensest excitement: it elevates,—it does not degrade. It never descends to the bawling voice, the guttural coarseness, the shrieking emphasis, the hysteric ecstacy of tone, the bullying attitude, and the clinched fist of extravagant passion."

When your sermon seems to demand of you a little imitative action, be peculiarly watchful lest you go too far, for this you may do before you are aware of it. I have heard of a young divine who in expostulation with the unconverted, exclaimed, "Alas, you shut your eyes to the light (here he closed both eyes); you stop your ears to the truth (here he put a finger into each ear); and you turn your backs upon salvation" (here he turned his back on the people). Do you wonder that when the people saw a man standing with his back to them and his fingers in his ears they all fell to laughing? The action might be appropriate, but it was overdone, and had better have been left undone. Violent gesture, even when commended by some, will be sure to strike others from its comic side. When Burke in the House of Commons flung down the dagger to show that Englishmen were making weapons to be used against their own countrymen, his action seems to me to have been striking and much to the purpose, and yet Sheridan said, "The gentleman has brought us the knife, where is the fork?" and Gilray wickedly caricatured him. The risks of too little action are by no means great, but you can plainly see that there are great perils in the other direction. Therefore, do not carry action too far, and if you feel that you are naturally very energetic in your delivery, repress your energies a little. Wave your hands a little less, smite the Bible somewhat more mercifully, and in general take matters rather more calmly.

Perhaps a man is nearest to the golden mean in action when his manner excites no remark either of praise or censure, because it is so completely of a piece with the discourse that it is not regarded as a separate item at all. That action which gains conspicuous notice is probably out of proportion, and excessive. Mr. Hall once spent an evening with Mrs. Hannah More, and his judgment upon her manners might well serve as a criticism upon the mannerisms of ministers. "Nothing striking, madam, certainly not. Her manners are too perfectly proper to be striking. Striking manners are bad manners, you know, madam. She is a perfect lady, and studiously avoids those eccentricities which constitute striking manners."

In the second place, *action should be expressive and appropriate.* We cannot express so much by action as by language, but one may express a few things with even greater force. Indignantly to open a door and point to it is quite as emphatic as the words, "Leave the room!" To refuse the hand when another offers his own is a very marked declaration of ill-will, and will probably create a more enduring bitterness than the severest words. A request to remain silent upon a certain subject could be well conveyed by laying the finger across the lips. A shake of the head indicates disapprobation in a very marked manner. The lifted eyebrows express surprise in a forcible style; and every part of the face has its own eloquence of pleasure and of grief. What volumes can be condensed into a shrug of the shoulders, and what mournful mischief that same shrug has wrought! Since, then, gesture and posture can speak powerfully, we must take care to let them speak correctly. It will never do to imitate the famous Grecian who cried, "O heaven!" with his finger pointing to the earth; nor to describe dying weakness by thumping upon the book-board. Nervous speakers appear to fire at random with their gestures, and you may see them wringing their hands while they are dilating upon the joys of faith, or grasping the side of the pulpit convulsively when they are bidding the believer hold all earthly things with a loose hand. Even when no longer timorous, brethren do not always manage their gestures so as to make them run parallel with their words. Men may be seen denouncing with descending fist the very persons whom they are endeavouring to comfort. No brother among you would, I hope, be so stupid as to clasp his hands while saying—"the gospel is not meant to be confined to a few. Its spirit is generous and expansive. It opens its arms to men of all ranks and nations." It would be an equal solecism if you were to spread forth your arms and cry, "Brethren, concentrate your energies! Gather them up, as a commander gathers his troops to the royal standard in the day of battle." Now, put the gestures into their proper places and see how diffusion may be expressed by the opened arms, and concentration by the united hands.

Action and tone together may absolutely contradict the meaning of the words. The Abbé Mullois tells us of a malicious wag who on hearing a preacher pronounce those terrible words, "Depart, ye cursed," in the blandest manner, turned to his companion and said, "Come here, my lad, and let me embrace you; that is what the parson has just expressed." This is a sad business, but by no means an uncommon one. What force may the language of Scripture lose through the preacher's ill-delivery! Those words which the French preacher pronounced in so ill a manner are very terrible, and I felt them to be so when a short while ago I heard them hissed forth in awful earnest, by an insane person who thought himself a prophet sent to curse myself and my congregation. "Depart, ye cursed" came forth from his lips like the mutterings of thunder, and the last word seemed to bite into the very soul, as with flaming eye and outstretched hand the fanatic flashed it upon the assembly.

Too many speakers appear to have taken lessons from Bendigo, or some other professor of the noble art of self-defence, for they hold their fists as if they were ready for a round. It is not pleasant to watch brethren preaching the gospel of peace in that pugnacious style; yet it is by no means rare to hear of an evangelist preaching a free Christ with a clinched fist. It is amusing to see them putting themselves into an attitude and saying, "Come unto me," and then, with a revolution of both fists, "and I will give you—rest." Better not suggest such ridiculous ideas, but they have been suggested more than once by men who earnestly desired above all things to make their hearers think of better things. Gentlemen, I am not at all surprised at your laughing, but it is infinitely better that you should have a hearty laugh at these absurdities *here* than that your people should laugh at you in the future. I am giving you no imaginary sketch, but one which I have seen myself and fear I may yet see again. Those awkward hands, if once brought into subjection, become our best allies. We can talk with them almost as well as with our tongues, and make a sort of silent music with them which will add to the charm of our words. If you have never read Sir Charles Bell on *The Hand,* be sure to do so, and note well the following passage: "We must not omit to speak of the hand as an instrument of expression. Formal dissertations have been written on this. But were we constrained to seek authorities, we might take the great painters in evidence, since by the position of the hands, in conformity with the figure, they have expressed every sentiment. Who, for example, can deny the eloquence of the hands in the Magdalens of Guido; their expression in the cartoons of Raphael, or in the "Last Supper," by Leonardo da Vinci? We see there expressed all that Quinctilian says the hand is capable of expressing. 'For other parts of the body,' says he, 'assist the speaker, but these, I may say, speak themselves. By them we ask, we promise, we invoke, we dismiss, we threaten, we intreat, we deprecate, we express fear, joy, grief, our doubts, our assent, our penitence: we show moderation, or profusion; we mark number and time.'"

The face, and especially the eyes, will play a very important part in all appropriate action. It is very unfortunate when ministers cannot look at their people. It is singular to hear them pleading with persons whom they do not see. They are entreating them to look to Jesus upon the cross! You wonder where the sinners are. The preacher's eyes are turned upon his book, or up to the ceiling, or into empty space. It seems to me that you *must* fix your eyes upon the people when you come to exhortation. There are parts of a sermon in which the sublimity of the doctrine may call for the uplifted gaze, and there are other portions which may allow the eyes to wander as you will; but when pleading time has come, it will be inappropriate to look anywhere but to the persons addressed. Brethren who never do this at all lose a great power. When Dr. Wayland was ill, he wrote, "Whether I am to recover my former health I know not. If, however, I should be permitted to preach again, I will certainly do what is in my power to learn to preach directly to men, *looking them in their faces,* and not looking at the paper on the desk."

The man who would be perfect in posture and gesture must regulate his whole frame, for in one case a man's most suitable action will be that of his head, and in another that of his hands, and in a third that of his trunk alone. Quinctilian says—"The sides should bear their part in the gesture. The motion, also, of the whole body contributes much to the effect in delivery: so much so that Cicero is of opinion that more can be done by its gesture than even by the hands themselves. Thus he says in his work *De Oratore*: 'There will be no affected motions of the fingers, no fall of the fingers to suit the measured cadence of the language; but he will produce gestures by the movements of his whole body and by the manly inflexion of his side.'"

I might multiply illustrations of what I mean by appropriate action, but these must suffice. Let the gesture tally with the words, and be a sort of running commentary and practical exegesis upon what you are saying. Here I must make a pause, hoping to continue the subject in my next lecture. But so conscious am I that many may think my subject so secondary as to be of no importance whatever, that I close by giving an instance of the careful manner in which great painters take heed to minute details, only drawing this inference, that if they are thus attentive to little things, much more ought we to be. Vigneul Marville says: "When I was at Rome I frequently saw Claude, who was then patronised by the most eminent persons in that city; I frequently met him on the banks of the Tiber, or wandering in the neighbourhood of Rome, amidst the venerable remains of antiquity. He was then an old man, yet I have seen him returning from his walk with his handkerchief filled with mosses, flowers, stones, etc., that he might consider them at home with that indefatigable attention which rendered him so exact a copier of nature. I asked him one day by what means he arrived at such an excellency of character among painters, even in Italy. 'I spare no pains whatever, even in the minutest trifles,' was the modest reply of this venerable genius."

XX

Posture, Action, Gesture, etc.

[SECOND LECTURE.]

THIS lecture begins at thirdly. If you remember, we have said that gesture should not be excessive, and secondly that it should be appropriate: now comes the third canon, *action and gesture should never be grotesque*. This is plain enough, and I shall not enforce it except by giving specimens of the grotesque, that you may not only avoid the identical instances, but all of a similar character. In all ages absurd gestures would appear to have been very numerous, for in an old author I find a long list of oddities, some of which it is to be hoped have taken their leave of this world, while others are described in language so forcible that it probably caricatures the actual facts. This writer says: "Some hold their heads immovable, and turned to one side, as if they were made of horn; others stare with their eyes as horribly as if they intended to frighten every one; some are continually twisting their mouths and working their chins while they are speaking, as if, all the time, they were cracking nuts; some like the apostate Julian, breathe insult, and express contempt and impudence in their countenances. Others, as if they personated the fictitious heroes in tragedy, gape enormously, and extend their jaws as widely as if they were going to swallow up everybody: above all, when they bellow with fury, they scatter their foam about, and threaten with contracted brow, and eyes like Saturn. *These*, as if they were playing some game, are continually making motions with their fingers, and, by the extraordinary working of their hands, endeavour to form in the air, I may almost say, all the figures of the mathematicians: *those*, on the contrary, have hands so ponderous, and so fastened down by terror, that they could more easily move beams of timber. Many labour so with their elbows, that it is evident, either that they had been formerly shoemakers themselves, or had lived in no other society than that of cobblers. Some are so unsteady in the motions of their bodies, that they seem to be speaking out of a cock-boat; others again are so unwieldy and uncouth in their motions, that you would think them to be sacks of tow painted to look like men. I have seen some who jumped on the platform and capered nearly in measure; men that exhibited the fuller's dance, and, as the old poet

288

says, expressed their wit with their feet. But who in a short compass is able to enumerate all the faults of gesture, and all the absurdities of bad delivery?" This catalogue might surely content the most voracious collector for the chamber of horrors, but it does not include the half of what may be seen in our own times by anyone who is able to ramble from one assembly to another. As children seem never to have exhausted their mischievous tricks, so speakers appear never to be at the end of their singular gestures. Even the best fall into them occasionally.

The first species of grotesque action may be named *the stiff*; and this is very common. Men who exhibit this horror appear to have no bend in their bodies and to be rigid about the joints. The arms and legs are moved as if they were upon iron hinges, and were made of exceedingly hard metal. A wooden anatomical doll, such as artists use, might well represent their limbs so straight and stiff, but it would fail to show the jerks with which those limbs are thrown up and down. There is nothing round in the action of these brethren; everything is angular, sharp, mechanical. If I were to set forth what I mean by putting myself into their rectangular attitudes I might be supposed to caricature more than one exceedingly able northern divine, and having the fear of this before my eyes, and, moreover, holding these brethren in supreme respect, I dare not go into very minute particulars. Yet it is supposable that these good men are themselves aware that their legs should not be set down as if they belonged to a linen-horse, or a huge pair of tongs, and that their arms should not be absolutely rigid like pokers. Oil for the joints has been suggested, but there appears to be a want of oil in the limbs themselves, which move up and down as if they belonged to a machine rather than to a living organism. Surely any sort of physical exercise might help to cure this mischief, which in some living preachers almost amounts to a deformity. On the platform of Exeter hall, gentlemen afflicted with unnatural stiffness not only furnish matter for the skilful caricaturist, but unfortunately call off the attention of their auditors from their admirable speeches by their execrable action. On a certain occasion we heard five or six remarks upon the awkwardness of the doctor's posturing, and only one or two encomiums upon his excellent speech. "People should not notice such trifles," remarks our friend Philo; but people do notice such trifles whether they ought to do so or not, and therefore it is well not to display them. It is probable that the whole of this lecture will be regarded by some very excellent people as beneath their notice, and savouring of questionable humour, but that I cannot help; for although I do not set so much value upon action as Demosthenes did when he made it the first, the second, and the third point in oratory, yet it is certain that much good speech is bereft of power through the awkward deportment of the speaker; and therefore if I may in any measure redress the evil I will cheerfully bear the criticism of my more sombre brethren. I am deeply in earnest, however playful my remarks may seem to be. These follies may be best shot at by the light arrows of ridicule, and therefore I employ them, not being of the same mind as those

"Who think all virtue lies in gravity,
And smiles are symptoms of depravity."

The second form of the grotesque is not unlike the first, and may be best distinguished as *the regular mechanical.* Men in this case move as if they were not living beings possessed of will and intellect, but as if they were automatons formed to go through prescribed movements at precise intervals. At the back of the Tabernacle a cottager has placed over his house a kind of vane, in the form of a little soldier, which lifts first one arm and then the other with rather an important air. It has made me smile many a time by irresistibly reminding me of ——, who alternately jerks each arm, or if he allows one arm to lie still, chops the other up and down as persistently as if he were moved by wind or by clockwork. Up and down, up and down the hand goes, turning neither to the right nor to the left, every other movement being utterly abjured, except this one monotonous ascent and descent. It matters little how unobjectionable a movement may be in itself, it will become intolerable if it be continued without variation. Ludovicus Cresollius, of Brittany, (1620) in his treatise upon the action and pronunciation of an orator, speaks somewhat strongly of a learned and polished Parisian preacher, who had aroused his ire by the wearisome monotony of his action. "When he turned himself to the left he spoke a few words accompanied by a moderate gesture of the hand, then bending to the right he acted the same part over again; then back again to the left, and presently to the right again: almost at an equal and measured interval of time he worked himself up to his usual gesture, and went through his one kind of movement. You could compare him only to the blind-folded Babylonian oxen going forward and turning back by the same path. I was so disgusted that I shut my eyes, but even so I could not get over the disagreeable impression of the speaker's manner."

The prevailing House of Commons' style, so far as I have seen it in public meetings, consists of an up and down movement of the back and hand; one seems to see the M.P. bowing to Mr. Speaker and the honourable house much as a waiter will do at an eating-house when he is receiving an order for an elaborate dinner. "Yes sir," "Yes sir," "Yes sir," with a jerk between each exclamation. The amusing rhyme with its short lines brings many a parliamentary speaker before my mind's eye:

"Mr. Tattat
You must not pat
Your arguments flat
On to the crown of another man's hat."

This is near akin to what has been accurately described as the pump-handle style. This is to be witnessed very frequently, and consists of a long series of jerkings of the arm, meant, perhaps, to increase emphasis, but really doing nothing whatever. Speakers of this sort remind us of Moore's conundrum, "Why is a pump like Lord Castlereagh?"

"Because it is a slender thing of wood,
   That up and down its awkward arm doth sway,
And coolly spout, and spout, and spout away
   In one weak, washy, everlasting flood."

Occasionally one meets with a saw-like action, in which the arm seems lengthened and contracted alternately. This motion is carried out to perfection when the orator leans over the rail, or over the front of the pulpit, and cuts downward at the people, like the top sawyer operating upon a piece of timber. One wonders how many planks a man would cut in the time if he were really working upon wood instead of sawing the air. We are all grateful for converted sawyers, but we trust they will feel at liberty to leave their saws behind them.

Much the same may be said for the numerous hammer-men who are at work among us, who pound and smite at a great rate, to the ruining of Bibles and the dusting of pulpit cushions. The predecessors of these gentlemen were celebrated by Hudibras in the oft-quoted lines,—

"And pulpit drum ecclesiastic,
   Was beat with fist instead of a stick."

Their one and only action is to hammer, hammer, hammer, without sense or reason, whether the theme be pleasing or pathetic. They preach with demonstration and power, but evermore the manifestation is the same. We dare not say that they smite with the fist of wickedness, but certainly they do smite, and that most vigorously. They set forth the sweet influences of the Pleiades and the gentle wooings of love with blows of the fist; and they endeavour to make you feel the beauty and the tenderness of their theme by strokes from their never-ceasing hammer.

Some of them are dull enough in all conscience, and do not even hammer with a hearty good will, and then the business becomes intolerable. One likes to hear a good noise, and see a man go in for hammering vehemently, if the thing must be done at all; but the gentleman we have in our mind seldom or never warms to his work, and merely smites because it is the way of him.

> "You can hear him swing his heavy sledge,
> With measured beat and slow."

If a man *must* strike, let him do it in earnest; but there is no need for perpetual pounding. There are better ways of becoming striking preachers than by imitating the divine of whom his precentor said that he had dashed the inwards out of one Bible and was far gone with another. In certain old Latin MSS. sermons, with notes in the margin, the preacher is recommended to shake the crucifix, and to hammer upon the pulpit *like Satan himself*! By this means he was to collect his thoughts; but one would not give much for thoughts thus collected. Have any of our friends seen these manuscripts and fallen in love with the directions? It would seem so.

Now, the jerking, sawing, pumping, and pounding might all be endurable and even appropriate if they were blended; but the perpetual iteration of any one becomes wearisome and unmeaning. The figures of Mandarins in a tea-shop, continually nodding their heads, and the ladies in wax which revolve with uniform motions in the hair-dresser's window, are not fit models for men who have before them the earnest work of winning men to grace and virtue. You ought to be so true, so real, so deeply in earnest, that mere mechanical movements will be impossible to you, and everything about you will betoken life, energy, concentrated faculty, and intense zeal.

Another method of the grotesque may be correctly called *the laborious*. Certain brethren will never fail in their ministry from want of physical exertion: when they mount the rostrum they mean hard work, and before long they puff and blow at it as if they were labourers working by the piece. They enter upon a sermon with the resolve to storm their way through it, and carry all before them: the kingdom of heaven suffereth violence with them in another sense besides that which is intended in Scripture. "How is your new minister getting on?" said an enquiring friend to a rustic hearer. "Oh," said the man, "he's sure to get on, for he drives at sin as if he were knocking down an ox." An excellent thing to do in spirit, but not to be performed literally. When I have occasionally heard of a wild brother taking off his collar and cravat, upon a very hot day, and even of his going so far as to divest himself of his coat, I have thought that he was only putting himself into a condition which the physical-force orator might desire, for he evidently regards a sermon as a battle or a wrestling match. An Irish thunderer of my acquaintance broke a chair during a declamation against Popery, and I trembled for the table also. A distinguished actor, who became a convert and a preacher late in life, would repeatedly strike the table or floor with his staff when he grew warm in a speech. He has made me wish to close my ears when the smart raps of his cane have succeeded each other with great rapidity and growing force. What was the peculiar use of the noise I could not tell, for we were all awake, and his voice was sufficiently powerful. One did not mind it, however, from the grand old man, for it suited the "fine frenzy" of his whole-hearted enthusiasm, but the noise was not so desirable as to be largely called for from any of us.

Laborious action is frequently a relic of the preacher's trade in former days: as an old hunter cannot quite forget the hounds, so the good man cannot shake off the habits of the shop. One brother who has been a wheelwright always preaches as if he were making wheels. If you understand the art of wheelwrighting, you can see most of the processes illustrated during one of his liveliest discourses. You can detect the engineer in another friend, the cooper in a third, and the grocer with his scales in a fourth. A brother who has been a butcher is pretty sure to show us how to knock down a bullock when he gets at all argumentative. As I have watched the discourse proceed from strength to strength, and the preacher has warmed to his work, I have thought to myself, "Here comes the pole-axe, there goes the fat ox, down falls the prize bullock." Now, these reminiscences of former occupations are never very blameworthy, and are at all times less obnoxious than the altogether inexcusable awkwardnesses of gentlemen who from their youth up have dwelt in the halls of learning. These will sometimes labour quite as much, but with far less likeness to useful occupations; they beat the air and work hard at doing nothing. Gentlemen from the universities are frequently more hideous in their action than commonplace people; perhaps their education may have deprived them of confidence, and made them all the more fidgety and awkward.

It has occurred to me that some speakers fancy that they are beating carpets, or chopping sticks, or mincing sausage-meat, or patting butter, or poking their fingers into people's eyes. Oh, could they see themselves as others see them, they might cease thus to perform before the public, and save their bodily exercise for other occasions. After all, I prefer the vigorous, laborious displays to the more easy and even stately airs of certain self-possessed talkers. One rubs his hands together with abounding self-satisfaction,

> "Washing his hands with invisible soap
> In imperceptible water,"

and meanwhile utters the veriest platitudes with the air of a man who is outdoing Robert Hall or Chalmers. Another pauses and looks round with a dignified air, as if he had communicated inestimable information to a highly favoured body of individuals who might reasonably be expected to rise in a state of intense excitement and express their overwhelming sense of obligation. Nothing has been said beyond the merest schoolboy talk; but the air of dignity, the attitude of authority, the very tone of the man, all show how thoroughly satisfied he is. This is not laborious preaching, but it occurs to me to mention it because it is the very reverse, and is so much more to be condemned. A few simpletons are, no doubt, imposed upon, and fancy that a man must be saying something great when he delivers himself in a pompous manner; but sensible persons are at first amused and afterwards disgusted with the big manner, "*à la grand seigneur.*" One of the great advantages of our College training is the certainty that an inflated mannerism is sure to be abated by the amiable eagerness with which all our students delight in rescuing a brother from this peril. Many wind-bags have collapsed in this room beneath your tender handling, never, I hope, to be puffed out to their former dimensions. There are some in the ministry of all the churches who would be marvellously benefited by a little of the very candid if not savage criticisms which have been endured by budding orators at your hands. I would that every minister who has missed such an instructive martyrdom could find a friend sufficiently honest to point out to him any oddities of manner into which he may insensibly have fallen.

But here we must not overlook another laborious orator who is in our mind's eye. We will name him the perpetual motion preacher, who is all action, and lifts his finger, or waves his hand, or strikes his palm at every word. He is never at rest for a moment. So eager is he to be emphatic that he effectually defeats his object, for where every word is emphasized by a gesture nothing whatever is emphatic. This brother takes off men's minds from his words to his movements: the eye actually carries the thoughts away from the ear, and so a second time the preacher's end is missed. This continual motion greatly agitates some hearers, and gives them the fidgets, and no wonder, for who can endure to see such incessant patting, and pointing, and waving? In action, as well as everything else, "let your moderation be known unto all men."

Thus I have mentioned three species of the grotesque—the stiff, the mechanical, and the laborious—and I have also glanced at the lazily dignified. I will close the list by mentioning two others. There is the *martial,* which also sufficiently borders on the grotesque to be placed in this category. Some preachers appear to be fighting the good fight of faith every time they stand before a congregation. They put themselves into a fencing attitude, and either stand on guard against an imaginary foe, or else assault the unseen adversary with stern determination. They could not look more fierce if they were

at the head of a regiment of cavalry, nor seem more satisfied at the
end of each division of discourse if they had fought a series of
Waterloos. They turn their heads on one side with a triumphant air,
as if about to say—"I have routed that enemy, and we shall hear no
more of *him*."

The last singularity of action which I shall place under this head
is the *ill-timed*. In this case the hands do not keep time with the lips.
The good brother is a little behindhand with his action, and therefore
the whole operation is out of order. You cannot at first make the
man out at all: he appears to chop and thump without rhyme or
reason, but at last you perceive that his present action is quite
appropriate to what he said a few seconds before. The effect is strange
to the last degree. It puzzles those who do not possess the key to it,
and when fully understood it loses none of its oddness.

Besides these oddities, there is a class of action which must, to
use the mildest term, be described as altogether *ugly*. For these a
platform is "generally necessary," for a man cannot make himself so
thoroughly ridiculous when concealed in a pulpit. To grasp a rail,
and to drop down lower and lower till you almost touch the ground
is supremely absurd. It may be a proper position as a prelude to an
agile gymnastic feat, but as an accompaniment to eloquence it is
monstrous; yet have I seen it more than once. I have found it difficult
to describe in words the extraordinary position, but a picture would
show how ridiculous it is and would render the attitude obsolete.
One or two brethren have disported themselves upon my platform
in this queer manner, and they are quite welcome to do the same
again, if upon seeing themselves thus roughly sketched they consider the posture to be commanding and impressive. It would be
far better for such remarkable performers if it were reported of them
as of that great Wesleyan, Richard Watson: "He stood perfectly erect,
and nearly all the action that he used was a slight motion of the right
hand, with occasionally a significant shake of the head."

The habit of shrugging the shoulders has been allowed to tyrannise
over some preachers. A number of men are round-shouldered by
nature, and many more seem determined to appear so, for when they
have anything weighty to deliver they back themselves up by elevating
their backs. An excellent preacher at Bristol, lately deceased, would
hunch first one shoulder and then another as his great thoughts
struggled forth, and when they obtained utterance he looked like a
hunchback till the effort was over. What a pity that such a habit had
become inveterate! How desirable to avoid its formation! Quinctilian
says: "Some people raise up their shoulders in speaking, but this is
a fault in gesture. Demosthenes, in order to cure himself of it, used
to stand in a narrow pulpit, and practise speaking with a spear hanging
over his shoulder, in such a manner that if in the heat of delivery he

failed to avoid this fault, he would be corrected by hurting himself against the point." This is a sharp remedy, but the gain would be worth an occasional wound if men who distort the human form could thus be cured of the fault.

At a public meeting upon one occasion a gentleman who appeared to be very much at home and to speak with a great deal of familiar superiority, placed his hands behind him under his coat tails, and thus produced a very singular figure, especially to those who took a side view from the platform. As the speaker became more animated, he moved his tails with greater frequency, reminding the observer of a water-wagtail. It must be seen to be appreciated, but one exhibition will be enough to convince any sensible man that however graceful a dress coat may be, it by no means ministers to the solemnity of the occasion to see the tails of that garment projecting from the orator's rear. You may also have seen at meetings the gentleman who places his hands on his hips, and either looks as if he defied all the world, or as if he endured considerable pain. This position savours of Billingsgate and its fish-women far more than of sacred eloquence. The arms *"akimbo,"* I think they call it, and the very sound of the word suggests the ridiculous rather than the sublime. We may drop into it for the moment rightly enough, but to deliver a speech in that posture is preposterous. It is even worse to stand with your hands in your trousers like the people one sees at French railway stations, who probably thrust their hands into their pockets because there is nothing else there, and nature abhors a vacuum. For a finger in the waistcoat pocket for a moment no one will be blamed, but to thrust the hands into the trousers is outrageous. An utter contempt for audience and subject must have been felt before a man could come to this. Gentlemen, because you are gentlemen, you will never need to be warned of this practice, for you will not descend to it. Once in a while before a superfinely genteel and affected audience a man may be tempted to shock their foolish gentility by a freedom and easiness which is meant to be the protest of a brusque manliness; but to see a man preach the gospel with his hands in his pockets does not remind you of either a prophet or an apostle. There are brethren who do this ever and anon who can afford to do it from their general force of character: these are the very men who should do nothing of the kind, because their example is powerful, and they are somewhat responsible for the weaklings who copy them.

Another unseemly style is nearly allied to the last, though it is not quite so objectionable. It may be seen at public dinners of the common order, where white waistcoats need a little extra display, and at gatherings of artisans where an employer has given his men a treat, and is responding to the toast of "the firm." Occasionally it is exhibited at religious meetings, where the speaker is a man of local importance, and feels that he is monarch of all he surveys. In this case the thumbs are inserted in the arm-holes of the waistcoat, and the speaker throws back his coat and reveals the lower part of the vest. I have called this the *penguin style*, and I am unable to find a better comparison. For a footman or a coachman at a *soirée*, or for a member of the United Order of Queer Fellows, this attitude may be suitable and dignified, and a venerable sire at a family gathering may talk to his boys and girls in that position; but for a public speaker, and much more for a minister, as a general habit, it is as much out of character as a posture can be.

First cousin to this fashion is that of holding on to the coat near the collar, as if the speaker considered it necessary to hold himself well in hand. Some grasp firmly, and then run the hands up and down as if they meant to double the coat in a new place, or to lengthen the collar. They appear to hang upon their coat-fronts like a man clutching at two ropes: one wonders the garment does not split at the back of the neck. This practice adds nothing to the force or perspicuity of a speaker's style, and its probable signification is, "I am quite at ease, and greatly enjoy hearing my own voice."

As it would be well to stamp out at many uglinesses as possible, I shall mention even those which are somewhat rare. I remember an able minister who was accustomed to look into the palm of his left hand while with his right he appeared to pick out his ideas therefrom. Divisions, illustrations, and telling points all seemed to be growing in his palm like so many flowers; and these he seemed carefully to take up by the roots one by one and exhibit to the people. It mattered little, for his thought was of a high order of excellence, but yet the action was by no means graceful.

A preacher of no mean order was wont to lift his fist to his brow and to tap his forehead gently, as if he must needs knock at the mind's door to wake up his thoughts: this also was more peculiar than forcible.

To point into the left hand with the first finger of the right as if boring small holes into it, or to use the aforesaid pointed finger as if you were stabbing the air, is another freak of action which has its amusing side.

Passing the hand over the brow when the thought is deep, and the exact word is not easy to find, is a very natural motion, but scratching the head is by no means equally advisable, though perhaps quite as natural. I have seen this last piece of action carried to considerable lengths, but I was never enamoured of it.

I cannot avoid mentioning an accidental grotesqueness which is exceedingly common. Some brethren always lay down the law with an outspread hand, which they continue to move up and down with the rhythm of every sentence. Now this action is excellent in its way if not carried on too monotonously, but unfortunately it is liable to accidents. If the earnest orator continues to lift his hand upward and downward he is in great danger of frequently presenting an aspect with regrettable implications. The action verges upon the symbolic, but unhappily the symbol has been somewhat vulgarized, and has been described as "putting the thumb of scorn to the nose of contempt." Some men unwittingly perpetrate this a score of times during a discourse.

You have laughed at these portraits which I have drawn for your edification—take care that no one has to laugh at you because you fall into these or similar absurdities of action.

I must confess, however, that I do not think so badly of any of these, or all of them put together, as I do of *the superfine* style, which is utterly despicable and abominable. It is worse than the commonly vulgar, for it is the very essence of vulgarity, flavoured with affectations and airs of gentility. Rowland Hill sketched the thing which I condemn in his portrait of Mr. Taplash; of course it was a more correct representation as to detail fifty years ago than it is now, but in the main features it is still sufficiently accurate: "The orator, when he first made his appearance, would be primmed and dressed up in the most finished style; not a hair would be found out of place on his empty pate, on which the barber had been exercising his occupation all the Sunday morning, and powdered till as white as the driven snow. Thus elegantly decorated, and smelling like a civet-cat, through an abundance of perfumery, he would scent the air as he passed. Then, with a most conceited skip, he would step into the pulpit, as though stepping out of a band-box; and here he had not only to display his elegant production, but his elegant self also: his delicate white hand exhibiting his diamond ring, while his richly-scented white handkerchief was unfurled, and managed with remarkable dexterity and art. His smelling-bottle was next occasionally presented to his nose, giving different opportunities to display his sparkling ring. Thus having adjusted the *important* business of the handkerchief and the smelling-bottle, he had next to take out his glass, that he might reconnoitre the fair part of his auditory, with whom he might have been gallanting and entertaining them with his cheap talk the day before: and these, as soon as he could catch their eye, he would favour with a simpering look, and a graceful nod."

This is a pungent version of Cowper's review of certain "messengers of grace" who "relapsed into themselves" when the sermon was ended: very little selves they must have been.

> "Forth comes the pocket mirror. First we stroke
> An eyebrow; next compose a straggling lock;
> Then with an air, most gracefully performed
> Fall back into our seat, extend an arm

And lay it at its ease with gentle care,
With handkerchief in hand depending low.
The better hand more busy gives the nose
Its bergamot, or aids the indebted eye.
With opera glass, to watch the moving scene,
And recognize the slow retiring fair.—
Now this is fulsome, and offends me more
Than in a churchman slovenly neglect
And rustic coarseness would."

"Rustic coarseness" is quite refreshing after one has been wearied with inane primness. Well did Cicero exhort orators to adopt their gestures rather from the camp or the wrestling ring than from the dancers with their effeminate niceties. Manliness must never be sacrificed to elegance. Our working classes will never be brought even to consider the truth of Christianity by teachers who are starched and fine. The British artisan admires manliness, and prefers to lend his ear to one who speaks in a hearty and natural style: indeed, working men of all nations are more likely to be struck by a brave negligence than by a foppish attention to personal appearances. The story told by the Abbé Mullois is, we suspect, only one of a numerous class. "A converted Parisian operative, a man of a wilful but frank disposition, full of energy and spirit, who had often spoken with great success at the clubs composed of men of his own class, was asked by the preacher who had led him to God, to inform him by what instrumentality he, who had once been so far estranged from religion, had eventually been restored to the faith. 'Your doing so,' said his interrogator, 'may be useful to me in my efforts to reclaim others.'

" 'I would rather not,' replied he, 'for I must candidly tell you that you do not figure very conspicuously in the case.'

" 'No matter,' said the other, 'it will not be the first time that I have heard the same remark.'

" 'Well, if you must hear it, I can tell you in a few words how it took place. A good woman had pestered me to read your little book —pardon the expression, I used to speak in that style in those days. On reading a few pages, I was so impressed that I felt a strong desire to see you.

" 'I was told that you preached in a certain church, and I went to hear you. Your sermon had some further effect upon me; but, to speak frankly, very little; comparatively, indeed, none at all. What did much more for me was your open, and simple, and good-natured manner, and, above all, your ill-combed hair; *for I have always detested those priests whose heads remind one of a hairdresser's assistant;* and I said to myself, "That man forgets himself on our behalf, we ought, therefore, to do something for his sake." Thereupon

I determined to pay you a visit, and you *bagged me*. Such was the beginning and end of the affair.' "

There are silly young ladies who are in raptures with a dear young man whose main thought is his precious person; these, it is to be hoped, are becoming fewer every day: but as for sensible men, and especially the sturdy workmen of our great cities, they utterly abhor foppery in a minister. Wherever you see affectation you find at once a barrier between that man and the commonsense multitude. Few ears are delighted with the voices of peacocks.

It is a pity that we cannot persuade all ministers to be *men*, for it is hard to see how otherwise they will be truly men of God. It is equally to be deplored that we cannot induce preachers to speak and gesticulate like other sensible persons, for it is impossible that they should grasp the masses till they do. All foreign matters of attitude, tone, or dress are barricades between us and the people: we must talk like men if we would win men. The late revival of millinery in the Anglican Church is for this reason, as well as for far graver ones, a step in the wrong direction. A hundred years ago the dressiness of the clergy was about as conspicuous as it is now, but it had no doctrinal meaning, and was mere foppery, if Lloyd is to be believed in his *Metrical Plea for Curates*.

He abuses rectors very heartily, and among the rest describes a canonical beau :

> "Behold Nugoso! wriggling, shuffling on,
> A mere church-puppet, an automaton
> In orders : note its tripping, mincing pace,
> Religion creams and mantles in its face!
> It's all religion from the top to toe!
> But milliners and barbers made it so.
> It wears religion in the modish way,
> It brushes, starches, combs it every day :
> Its orthodoxy lies in outward things,
> In beavers, cassocks, gowns, bands, gloves, and rings :
> It shows its learning by its doctor's hood,
> And proves its goodness,—'cause its clothes are good."

This fondness for comely array led to a stiff propriety in the pulpit: they called it "dignity," and prided themselves upon it. Propriety and decorum were their chief concern, and these were mingled with pomposity or foolish simpering according to the creature's peculiarities, until honest men grew weary of their hollow performances and turned away from such stilted ministrations. The preachers were too much concerned to be proper to have any concern to be useful. The gestures which would have made their words a little more intelligible they would not condescend to use, for what cared they for the vulgar?

if persons of taste were satisfied, they had all the reward they desired, and meanwhile the multitudes were perishing for lack of knowledge. God save us from fine deportment and genteel propriety if these are to keep the masses in alienation from the public worship of God.

In our own day this sickening affectation is, we hope, far more rare, but it still survives. We had the honour of knowing a minister who could not preach without his black kid gloves, and when he upon one occasion found himself in a certain pulpit without them, he came down into the vestry for them. Unfortunately one of the deacons had carried into his pew, not his own hat, as he intended, but the preacher's, and while this discovery was being made, the divine was in terrible trepidation, exclaiming, "I never do preach without gloves. I cannot do it. I cannot go into the pulpit till you find them." I wish he never had found them, for he was more fitted to stand behind a draper's counter than to occupy the sacred desk. Slovenliness of any sort is to be avoided in a minister, but manliness more often falls into this fault than into the other effeminate vice; therefore shun most heartily this worst error. Cowper says,

"In my soul I loathe all affectation,"

and so does every sensible man. All tricks and stage effects are unbearable when the message of the Lord is to be delivered. Better a ragged dress and rugged speech, with artless, honest manner, than clerical foppery. Better far to violate every canon of gracefulness than to be a mere performer, a consummate actor, a player upon a religious stage. The caricaturist of twenty years ago favoured me with the name of *Brimstone,* and placed side by side with me a simpering elocutionist whom he named *Treacle.* I was thoroughly satisfied with my lot, but I could not have said as much if I had been represented by the companion portrait. Molasses and other sugary matters are sickening to me. Jack-a-dandy in the pulpit makes me feel as Jehu did when he saw Jezebel's decorated head and painted face, and cried in indignation, "Fling her down."

It would greatly trouble me if any of my remarks upon grotesque action should lead even one of you to commence posturing and performing; this would be to fly from bad to worse. We mentioned that Dr. Hamilton took lessons from a master, in order to escape from his infirmity, but the result was manifestly not very encouraging, and I gravely fear that more faults are created than cured by professional teachers: perhaps the same result may follow from my own amateur attempt, but I would at least prevent that misfortune as far as possible by earnest warnings. Do not think of how you will gesticulate when you preach, but learn the art of doing the right thing without giving it any thought at all.

Our last rule is one which sums up all the others; *be natural in your action.* Shun the very appearance of studied gesture. Art is cold, only nature is warm; let grace keep you clear of all seeming, and in every action, and in every place, be truthful, even if you should be considered rough and uncultivated. Your mannerism must always be your own, it must never be a polished lie, and what is the aping of gentility, the simulation of passion, the feigning of emotion, or the mimicry of another man's mode of delivery but a practical lie.

> "Therefore, avaunt all attitude and stare,
> And start theatric, practised at the glass!"

Our object is to remove the excrescences of uncouth nature, not to produce artificiality and affectation; we would prune the tree and by no means clip it into a set form. We would have our students think of action while they are with us at college, that they may never have need to think of it in after days. The matter is too inconsiderable to be made a part of your weekly study when you get into the actual battle of ministerial life; you must attend to the subject now, and have done with it. You are not sent of God to court smiles but to win souls; your teacher is not the dancing-master, but the Holy Spirit, and your pulpit manner is only worth a moment's thought because it may hinder your success by causing people to make remarks about the preacher when you want all their thoughts for the subject. If the best action had this effect I would urge you to forswear it, and if the worst gestures would prevent such a result I would advise you to practise them. All that I aim at is to advocate quiet, graceful, natural movements, because they are the least likely to be observed. The whole business of delivery should be *one*; everything should harmonize; the thought, the spirit, the language, the tone, and the action should be all of a piece, and the whole should be, not for the winning of honour to ourselves, but for the glory of God and the good of men; if it be so there is no fear of your violating the rule as to being natural, for it will not occur to you to be otherwise. Yet have I one fear, and it is this: you may fall into a foolish imitation of some admired minister, and this will to some extent put you off from the right track. Each man's action should suit himself and grow out of his own personality. The style of Dr. Goliath, who is six feet high, will not fit the stature and person of our friend Short who is a Zaccheus among preachers; neither will the respectable mannerism of an aged and honoured divine at all befit the youthful Apollos who is barely out of his teens. I have heard that for a season quite a number of young Congregational ministers imitated the pastor of the Weigh House, and so there were little Binneys everywhere copying the great Thomas in everything except his thoughtful preaching. A rumour is current that there are one or two young Spurgeons about, but if so I hope that the reference is to my own sons, who have a right to the name by birth. If any of you become mere copyists of me I shall regard you as thorns in the flesh, and rank you among those whom Paul says "we suffer gladly." Yet it has been wisely said that every beginner must of necessity be for a time a copyist; the artist follows his master while as yet he has barely acquired the elements of the art, and perhaps for life he remains a painter of the school to which he at first attached himself; but as he becomes proficient he develops his own individuality, grows into a painter with a style of his own, and is all the better and none the worse for having been in his earliest days content to sit at a master's feet. It is of necessity the same in oratory, and therefore it may be too much to say never copy anyone, but it may be better to exhort you to imitate the best action you can find, in order that your own style during its formation may be rightly moulded. Correct the influence of any one man by what you see of excellence in others; but still create a manner of your own. Slavish imitation is the practice of an ape, but to follow another where he leads aright, *and there only,* is the wisdom of a prudent man. Still never let a natural originality be missed by your imitating the best models of antiquity, or the most esteemed among the moderns.

In conclusion, do not allow my criticisms upon various grotesque postures and movements to haunt you in the pulpit; better perpetrate them all than be in fear, for this would make you cramped and awkward. Dash at it whether you blunder or no. A few mistakes in this matter will not be half so bad as being nervous. It may be that what would be eccentric in another may be most proper in *you*; therefore take no man's dictum as applicable to every case, or to your own. See how John Knox is pictured in the well-known engraving. Is his posture graceful? Perhaps not. Yet is it not exactly what it should be? Can you find any fault with it? Is it not Knox-like, and full of power? It would not suit one man in fifty; in most preachers it would seem strained, but in the great Reformer it is characteristic, and accords with his life-work. You must remember the person, the times and his surroundings, and then the mannerism is seen to be well becoming a hero-preacher sent to do an Elijah's work, and to utter his rebukes in the presence of a Popish court which hated the reforms which he demanded. Be yourself as he was himself; even if you should be ungainly and awkward, be yourself. Your own clothes, though they be homespun, will fit you better than another man's, though made of the best broadcloth; you may follow your tutor's style of dress if you like, but do not borrow his coat, be content to wear one of your own. Above all, be so full of matter, so fervent, and so gracious that the people will little care how you hand out the word;

for if they perceive that it is fresh from heaven, and find it sweet and abundant, they will pay little regard to the basket in which you bring it to them. Let them, if they please, say that your bodily presence is weak, but pray that they may confess that your testimony is weighty and powerful. Commend yourself to every man's conscience in the sight of God, and then the mere mint and anise of posture will seldom be taken into account.

XXI

Earnestness: its Marring and Maintenance

IF *I* were asked—What in a Christian minister is the most essential quality for securing success in winning souls for Christ? I should reply, "earnestness": and if I were asked a second or a third time, I should not vary the answer, for personal observation drives me to the conclusion that, as a rule, real success is proportionate to the preacher's earnestness. Both great men and little men succeed if they are thoroughly alive unto God, and fail if they are not so. We know men of eminence who have gained a high reputation, who attract large audiences, and obtain much admiration, who nevertheless are very low in the scale as soul winners: for all they do in that direction they might as well have been lecturers on anatomy, or political orators. At the same time we have seen their compeers in ability so useful in the business of conversion that evidently their acquirements and gifts have been no hindrance to them, but the reverse; for by the intense and devout use of their powers, and by the anointing of the Holy Spirit, they have turned many to righteousness. We have seen brethren of very scanty abilities who have been terrible drags upon a church, and have proved as inefficient in their spheres as blind men in an observatory; but, on the other hand, men of equally small attainments are well known to us as mighty hunters before the Lord, by whose holy energy many hearts have been captured for the Saviour. I delight in M'Cheyne's remark, "It is not so much great talents that God blesses, as great likeness to Christ." In many instances ministerial success is traceable almost entirely to an intense zeal, a consuming passion for souls, and an eager enthusiasm in the cause of God, and we believe that in every case, other things being equal, men prosper in the divine service in proportion as their hearts are blazing with holy love. "The God that answereth by fire, let him be God"; and the man who has the tongue of fire, let him be God's minister.

Brethren, you and I must, as preachers, be always earnest in reference to our pulpit work. Here we must labour to attain the very highest degree of excellence. Often have I said to my brethren that the pulpit is the Thermopylæ of Christendom: there the fight will be lost or won. To us ministers the maintenance of our power in the pulpit should be our great concern; we must occupy that spiritual watch-tower with our hearts and minds awake and in full vigour. It will not avail us to be laborious pastors if we are not earnest preachers. We shall be forgiven a great many sins in the matter of pastoral visitation if the people's souls are really fed on the Sabbath-day; but fed they must be, and nothing else will make up for it. The failures of most ministers who drift down the stream may be traced to inefficiency in the pulpit. The chief business of a captain is to know how to handle his vessel; nothing can compensate for deficiency there, and so our pulpits must be our main care, or all will go awry. Dogs often fight because the supply of bones is scanty, and congregations frequently quarrel because they do not get sufficient spiritual meat to keep them happy and peaceful. The ostensible ground of dissatisfaction may be something else, but nine times out of ten deficiency in their rations is at the bottom of the mutinies which occur in our churches. Men, like all other animals, know when they are fed, and they usually feel good tempered after a meal; and so when our hearers come to the house of God, and obtain "food convenient for them," they forget a great many grievances in the joy of the festival, but if we send them away hungry they will be in as irritable a mood as a bear robbed of her whelps.

Now, in order that we may be acceptable, *we must be earnest when actually engaged in preaching.* Cecil has well said that the spirit and manner of a preacher often effect more than his matter. To go into the pulpit with the listless air of those gentlemen who loll about, and lean upon the cushion as if they had at last reached a quiet resting place, is, I think, most censurable. To rise before the people to deal out commonplaces which have cost you nothing, as if anything would do for a sermon, is not merely derogatory to the dignity of our office, but is offensive in the sight of God. We must be earnest in the pulpit for our own sakes, for we shall not long be able to maintain our position as leaders in the church of God if we are dull. Moreover, for the sake of our church members, and converted people, we must be energetic, for if we are not zealous, neither will they be. It is not in the order of nature that rivers should run uphill, and it does not often happen that zeal rises from the pew to the pulpit. It is natural that it should flow down from us to our hearers; the pulpit must therefore stand at a high level of ardour, if we are, under God, to make and to keep our people fervent. Those who attend our ministry have a great deal to do during the week. Many of them have family trials, and heavy personal burdens to carry, and they frequently come into the assembly cold and listless, with thoughts wandering hither and thither; it is ours to take those thoughts and thrust them into the furnace of our own earnestness, melt them by holy contemplation and by intense appeal, and pour them out into the mould of the truth. A blacksmith can do nothing when his fire is out, and in this respect he is the type of a minister. If all the lights in the outside world are quenched, the lamp which burns in the sanctuary ought still to remain undimmed; for that fire no curfew must ever be rung. We must regard the people as the wood and the sacrifice, well wetted a second and a third time by the cares of the week, upon which, like the prophet, we must pray down the fire from heaven. A dull minister creates a dull audience. You cannot expect the office-bearers and the members of the church to travel by steam if their own chosen pastor still drives the old broadwheeled waggon. We ought each one to be like that reformer who is described as *"Vividus vultus, vividi occuli, vividae manus, denique omnia vivida,"* which I would rather freely render— " countenance beaming with life, eyes and hands full of life, in fine, a vivid preacher, altogether alive."

> "Thy soul must overflow, if thou
> Another's soul would reach,
> It needs the overflow of heart
> To give the lips full speech."

The world also will suffer as well as the church if we are not fervent. We cannot expect a gospel devoid of earnestness to have any mighty effect upon the unconverted around us. One of the excuses most soporific to the conscience of an ungodly generation is that of half-heartedness in the preacher. If the sinner finds the preacher nodding while he talks of judgment to come, he concludes that the judgment is a thing which the preacher is dreaming about, and he resolves to regard it all as mere fiction. The whole outside world receives serious danger from the cold-hearted preacher, for it draws the same conclusion as the individual sinner : it perseveres in its own listlessness, it gives its strength to its own transient objects, and thinks itself wise for so doing. How can it be otherwise? If the prophet leaves his heart behind him when he professes to speak in the name of God, what can he expect but that the ungodly around him will persuade themselves that there is nothing in his message, and that his commission is a farce.

Hear how Whitefield preached, and never dare to be lethargic again. Winter says of him that "sometimes he exceedingly wept, and was frequently so overcome, that for a few seconds you would suspect he never would recover; and when he did, nature required some little time to compose herself. I hardly ever knew him go through a sermon without weeping more or less. His voice was often interrupted by his affections; and I have heard him say in the pulpit, 'You blame me for weeping; but how can I help it, when you will not weep for yourselves, although your own immortal souls are on the verge of destruction, and, for aught I know, you are hearing your last sermon, and may never more have an opportunity to have Christ offered to you?'"

Earnestness in the pulpit must be real. It is not to be mimicked. We have seen it counterfeited, but every person with a grain of sense could detect the imposition. To stamp the foot, to smite the desk, to perspire, to shout, to bawl, to quote the pathetic portions of other people's sermons, or to pour out voluntary tears from a watery eye will never make up for true agony of soul and real tenderness of spirit. The best piece of acting is but acting; those who only look at appearances may be pleased by it, but lovers of reality will be disgusted. What presumption!—what hypocrisy it is by skilful management of the voice to mimic the passion which is the genuine work of the Holy Ghost. Let mere actors beware, lest they be found sinning against the Holy Spirit by their theatrical performances. We must be earnest in the pulpit because we are earnest everywhere; we must blaze in our discourses because we are continually on fire. Zeal which is stored up to be let off only on grand occasions is a gas which will one day destroy its proprietor. Nothing but truth may appear in the house of the Lord; all affectation is strange fire, and excites the indignation of the God of truth. Be earnest, and you will *seem* to be earnest. A burning heart will soon find for itself a flaming tongue. To sham earnestness is one of the most contemptible of dodges for courting popularity; let us abhor the very thought. Go and be listless in the pulpit if you are so in your heart. Be slow in speech, drawling in tone, and monotonous in voice, if so you can best express your soul; even that would be infinitely better than to make your ministry a masquerade and yourself an actor.

But our zeal while in the act of preaching must be followed up by intense solicitude as to the after results; for if it be not so we shall have cause to question our sincerity. God will not send a harvest of souls to those who never watch or water the fields which they have sown. When the sermon is over we have only let down the net which afterwards we are to draw to shore by prayer and watchfulness. Here, I think, I cannot do better than allow a far abler advocate to plead with you, and quote the words of Dr. Watts: "Be very solicitous about the success of your labours in the pulpit. Water the seed sown, not only with public, but secret prayer. Plead with God importunately that he would not suffer you to labour in vain. Be not like that foolish bird the ostrich, which lays her eggs in the dust, and leaves them there regardless whether they come to life or not (Job xxxix. 14–17). God hath not given her understanding, but let not this folly be your character or practice; labour, and watch, and pray, that your sermons and the fruit of your studies may become words of Divine life to souls.

"It is an observation of pious Mr. Baxter (which I have read somewhere in his works), that he has never known any considerable success from the brightest and noblest talents, nor from the most excellent kind of preaching, nor even when the preachers themselves have been truly religious, if they have not had a solicitous concern for the success of their ministrations. Let the awful and important thought of souls being saved by our preaching, or left to perish and to be condemned to hell through our negligence,—I say, let this awful and tremendous thought dwell ever upon our spirits. We are made watchmen to the house of Israel, as Ezekiel was; and, if we give no warning of approaching danger, the souls of multitudes may perish through our neglect; but the blood of souls will be terribly required at our hands (Ezekiel iii. 17, etc.)."

Such considerations should make us instant in season and out of season, and cause us at all times to be clad with zeal as with a cloak. We ought to be all alive, and always alive. A pillar of light and fire should be the preacher's fit emblem. Our ministry must be emphatic, or it will never affect these thoughtless times; and to this end our hearts must be habitually fervent, and our whole nature must be fired with an all-consuming passion for the glory of God and the good of men.

Now, my brethren, it is sadly true that holy earnestness when we once obtain it may be easily damped; and as a matter of fact it is more frequently chilled in the loneliness of a village pastorate than amid the society of warm-hearted Christian brethren. Adam, the author of *Private Thoughts*, once observed that "a poor country parson, fighting against the devil in his parish, has nobler ideas than Alexander the Great ever had"; and I will add, that he needs more than Alexander's ardour to enable him to continue victorious in his holy warfare. Sleepy Hollow and Dormer's Land will be too much for us unless we pray for daily quickening.

Yet town life has its dangers too, and zeal is apt to burn low through numerous engagements, like a fire which is scattered abroad instead of being raked together into a heap. Those incessant knocks at our door, and perpetual visits from idle persons, are so many buckets of cold water thrown upon our devout zeal. We must by some means secure uninterrupted meditation, or we shall lose power. London is a peculiarly trying sphere on this account.

Zeal also is more quickly checked after long years of continuance in the same service than when novelty gives a charm to our work. Mr. Wesley says, in his fifteenth volume of *Journals and Letters*, "I know that, were I myself to preach one whole year in one place, I should preach both myself and most of my congregation asleep." What then must it be to abide in the same pulpit for many years! In such a case it is not the pace that kills, but the length of the race. Our God is evermore the same, enduring for ever, and he alone can enable us to endure even to the end. He, who at the end of twenty years' ministry among the same people is more alive than ever, is a great debtor to the quickening Spirit.

Earnestness may be, and too often is, diminished by neglect of study. If we have not exercised ourselves in the word of God, we shall not preach with the fervour and grace of the man who has fed upon the truth he delivers, and is therefore strong and ardent. An Englishman's earnestness in battle depends, according to some authorities, upon his being well fed: he has no stomach for the fight if he is starved. If we are well nourished by sound gospel food we shall be vigorous and fervent. An old blunt commander at Cadiz is described by Selden as thus addressing his soldiers: "What a shame will it be, you Englishmen, who feed upon good beef and beer, to let these rascally Spaniards beat you that eat nothing but oranges and lemons!" His philosophy and mine agree: he expected courage and valour from those who were well nourished. Brethren, never neglect your spiritual meals, or you will lack stamina and your spirits will sink. Live on the substantial doctrines of grace, and you will outlive and out-work those who delight in the pastry and syllabubs of "modern thought."

Zeal may, on the other hand, be damped by our studies. There is, no doubt, such a thing as feeding the brain at the expense of the heart, and many a man in his aspirations to be literary has rather qualified himself to write reviews than to preach sermons. A quaint evangelist was wont to say that Christ hung crucified beneath Greek, Latin, and Hebrew. It ought not to be so, but it has often happened that the student in college has gathered fuel, but lost the fire which is to kindle it. It will be to our everlasting disgrace if we bury our flame beneath the faggots which are intended to sustain it. If we degenerate into bookworms it will be to the old serpent's delight, and to our own misery.

True earnestness may be greatly lessened by levity in conversation, and especially by jesting with brother ministers, in whose company we often take greater liberties than we would like to do in the society of other Christians. There are excellent reasons for our feeling at home with our brethren, but if this freedom be carried too far we shall soon feel that we have suffered damage through vanity of speech. Cheerfulness is one thing, and frivolity is another; he is a wise man who by a serious happiness of conversation steers between the dark rocks of moroseness, and the quicksands of levity.

We shall often find ourselves in danger of being deteriorated in zeal by the cold Christian people with whom we come in contact. What terrible wet blankets some professors are! Their remarks after a sermon are enough to stagger you. You think that surely you have moved the very stones to feeling, but you painfully learn that these people are utterly unaffected. You have been burning and they are freezing; you have been pleading as for life or death and they have been calculating how many seconds the sermon occupied, and grudging you the odd five minutes beyond the usual hour, which your earnestness compelled you to occupy in pleading with men's souls.

If these frost-bitten men should happen to be the officers of the church, from whom you naturally expect the warmest sympathy, the result is chilling to the last degree, and all the more so if you are young and inexperienced: it is as though an angel were confined in an iceberg. "Thou shalt not yoke the ox and the ass together" was a merciful precept: but when a laborious, ox-like minister comes to be yoked to a deacon who is not another ox, it becomes hard work to plough. Some crabbed professors have a great deal to answer for in this matter. One of them not so very long ago went up to an earnest young evangelist who had been doing his best, and said, "Young man, do you call that preaching?" He thought himself faithful, but he was cruel and uncourteous, and though the good brother survived the blow it was none the less brutal. Such offences against the Lord's little ones are, I hope, very rare, but they are very grievous, and tend to turn aside our hopeful youth.

Frequently the audience itself, as a whole, will damp your zeal. You can see by their very look and manner that the people are not appreciating your warm-hearted endeavours, and you feel discouraged. Those empty benches also are a serious trial, and if the place be large, and the congregation small, the influence is seriously depressing: it is not every man who can bear to be "a voice crying in the wilderness." Disorder in the congregation also sadly afflicts sensitive speakers. The walking up the aisle of a woman with a pair of pattens, the squeak of a pair of new boots, the frequent fall of umbrellas and walking-sticks, the crying of infants, and especially the consistent lateness of half the assembly;—all these tend to irritate the mind, take it off from its object, and diminish its ardour. We hardly like to confess that our hearts are so readily affected by such trifles, but it is so, and not at all to be wondered at. As pots of the most precious ointment are more often spoilt by dead flies than by dead camels, so insignificant matters will destroy earnestness more readily than greater annoyances. Under a great discouragement a man pulls himself together, and then throws himself upon his God, and receives divine strength: but under lesser depressions he may possibly worry, and the trifle will irritate and fester till serious consequences follow.

Pardon my saying that the condition of your body must be attended to, especially in the matter of eating, for any measure of excess may injure your digestion and make you stupid when you should be fervent. From the memoir of Duncan Matheson I cull an anecdote which is much to the point: "In a certain place where evangelistic meetings were being held, the lay preachers, among whom was Mr. Matheson, were sumptuously entertained at the house of a Christian gentleman. After dinner they went to the meeting, not without some difference of opinion as to the best method of conducting the services of the evening. 'The Spirit is grieved; He is not here at all, I feel it,' said one of the younger, with a whine which somewhat contrasted with his previous unbounded enjoyment of the luxuries of the table. 'Nonsense,' replied Matheson, who hated all whining and morbid spirituality; 'Nothing of the sort. You have just eaten too much dinner, and you feel heavy.'" Duncan Matheson was right, and a little more of his common sense would be a great gain to some who are ultra spiritual, and attribute all their moods of feeling to some supernatural cause when the real reason lies far nearer to hand. Has it not often happened that dyspepsia has been mistaken for backsliding, and a bad digestion has been set down as a hard heart? I say no more: a word to the wise is enough.

Many physical and mental causes may operate to create apparent lethargy where there is at heart intense earnestness. Upon some of us a disturbed night, a change in the weather, or an unkind remark, will produce the most lamentable effect. But those who complain of want of zeal are often the most zealous persons in the world, and a confession of want of life is itself an argument that life exists, and is not without vigour. Do not spare yourselves and become self-satisfied; but, on the other hand, do not slander yourselves and sink into despondency. Your own opinion of your state is not worth much: ask the Lord to search you.

Long continued labour without visible success is another frequent damp upon zeal, though if rightly viewed it ought to be an incentive to sevenfold diligence. Quaint Thomas Fuller observes that "herein God hath humbled many painstaking pastors, in making them to be clouds to rain, not over Arabia the happy, but over Arabia the desert and stony." If non-success humbles us it is well, but if it discourages us, and especially if it leads us to think bitterly of more prosperous brethren, we ought to look about us with grave concern. It is possible that we have been faithful and have adopted wise methods, and are in our right place, and yet we have not struck the mark; we shall probably be heavily bowed down and feel scarcely able to continue the work; but if we pluck up courage and increase our earnestness we shall one day reap a rich harvest, which will more than repay us for all our waiting. "The husbandman *waiteth* for the precious fruits of the earth"; and with a holy patience begotten of zeal we must wait on, and never doubt that the time to favour Zion will yet come.

Nor must it ever be forgotten that the flesh is weak and naturally inclined to slumber. We need a constant renewal of the divine impulse which first started us in the way of service. We are not as arrows, which find their way to the target by the sole agency of the force with which they started from the bow; nor as birds, which bear within themselves their own motive power: we must be borne onward, like ships at sea, by the constant power of the heavenly wind, or we shall make no headway. Preachers sent from God are not musical boxes which, being once wound up, will play through their set tunes, but they are trumpets which are utterly mute until the living breath causes them to give forth a certain sound. We read of some who are dumb dogs, given to slumber, and such would be the character of us all if the grace of God did not prevent. We have need to watch against a careless, indifferent spirit, and if we do not so we shall soon be as lukewarm as Laodicea itself.

Remembering then, dear brethren, that we must be in earnest, and that we cannot counterfeit earnestness, or find a substitute for it, and that it is very easy for us to lose it, let us consider for a while the ways and means for retaining all our fervour and gaining more. If it is to continue, *our earnestness must be kindled at an immortal flame,* and I know of but one—the flame of the love of Christ, which many waters cannot quench. A spark from that celestial sun will be as undying as the source from whence it came. If we can get it, yea, if we have it, we shall still be full of enthusiasm, however long we may live, however greatly we may be tried, and however much for many reasons we may be discouraged. To continue fervent for life we must possess the fervour of heavenly life to begin with. Have we this fire? We must have the truth burnt into our souls, or it will not burn upon our lips. Do we understand this? The doctrines of grace must be part and parcel of ourselves, interwoven with the warp and woof of our being, and this can only be effected by the same hand which originally made the fabric. We shall never lose our love to Christ and our love to souls if the Lord has given them to us. The Holy Spirit makes zeal for God to be a permanent principle of life rather than a passion,—does the Holy Spirit rest upon us, or is our present fervour a mere human feeling? We ought upon this point to be seriously inquisitorial with our hearts, pressing home the question, Have we the holy fire which springs from a true call to the ministry? If not, why are we here? If a man *can* live without preaching, let him live without preaching. If a man can be content without being a soul-winner—I had almost said he had better not attempt the work, but I had rather say —let him seek to have the stone taken out of his heart, that he may feel for perishing men. Till then, as a minister, he may do positive mischief by occupying the place of one who might have succeeded in the blessed work in which *he* must be a failure.

The fire of our earnestness must burn upon the hearth of faith in the truths which we preach, and faith in their power to bless mankind when the Spirit applies them to the heart. He who declares what may or what may not be true, and what he considers upon the whole to be as good as any other form of teaching, will of necessity make a very feeble preacher. How can he be zealous about that which he is not sure of? If he knows nothing of the inward power of the truth within his own heart, if he has never tasted and handled of the good word of life, how can he be enthusiastic? But if the Holy Ghost has taught us in secret places, and made our soul to understand within itself the doctrine which we are to proclaim, then shall we speak evermore with the tongue of fire. Brother, do not begin to teach others till the Lord has taught *you*. It must be dreary work to parrot forth dogmas which have no interest for your heart, and carry no conviction to your understanding. I would prefer to pick oakum or turn a crank for my breakfast, like the paupers in the casual ward, rather than be the slave of a congregation and bring them spiritual meat of which I never taste myself. And then how dreadful the end of such a course must be! How fearful the account to be rendered at the last by one who publicly taught what he did not heartily believe, and perpetrated this detestable hypocrisy in the name of God!

Brethren, if the fire is brought *from* the right place *to* the right place, we have a good beginning; and the main elements of a glorious ending. Kindled by a live coal, borne to our lips from off the altar by the winged cherub, the fire has begun to feed upon our inmost spirit, and there it will burn though Satan himself should labour to stamp it out.

Yet the best flame in the word needs renewing. I know not whether immortal spirits, like the angels, drink on the wing, and feed on some superior manna prepared in heaven for them; but the probability is that no created being, though immortal, is quite free from the necessity to receive from without sustenance for its strength. Certainly the flame of zeal in the renewed heart, however divine, must be continually fed with fresh fuel. Even the lamps of the sanctuary needed oil. *Feed the flame, my brother, feed it frequently;* feed it with holy thought and contemplation, especially with thought about your work, your motives in pursuing it, the design of it, the helps that are waiting for you, and the grand results of it if the Lord be with you. Dwell much upon the love of God to sinners, and the death of Christ on their behalf, and the work of the Spirit upon men's hearts. Think of what must be wrought in men's hearts ere they can be saved. Remember, you are not sent to whiten tombs, but to open them, and this is a work which no man can perform unless, like the Lord Jesus at the grave of Lazarus, he groans in spirit; and even then he is powerless apart from the Holy Ghost. Meditate with deep solemnity upon the fate of the lost sinner, and, like Abraham, when you get up early to go to the place where you commune with God, cast an eye towards Sodom and see the smoke thereof going up like the smoke of a furnace. Shun all views of future punishment which would make it appear less terrible, and so take off the edge of your anxiety to save immortals from the quenchless flame. If men are indeed only a nobler kind of ape, and expire as the beasts, you may well enough let them die unpitied; but if their creation in the image of God ininvolves immortality, and there is any fear that through their unbelief they will bring upon themselves endless woe, arouse yourselves to the agonies of the occasion, and be ashamed at the bare suspicion of unconcern. Think much also of the bliss of the sinner saved, and like holy Baxter derive rich arguments for earnestness from "the saints' everlasting rest." Go to the heavenly hills and gather fuel there; pile on the glorious logs of the wood of Lebanon, and the fire will burn freely and yield a sweet perfume as each piece of choice cedar glows in the flame. There will be no fear of your being lethargic if you are continually familiar with eternal realities.

Above all, feed the flame with intimate fellowship with Christ. No man was ever cold in heart who lived with Jesus on such terms as John and Mary did of old, for *he* makes men's hearts burn within them. I never met with a half-hearted preacher who was much in communion with the Lord Jesus. The zeal of God's house ate up our Lord, and when we come into contact with him it begins to consume us also, and we feel that we cannot but speak the things which we have seen and heard in his company, nor can we help speaking of them with the fervour which comes out of actual acquaintance with them. Those of us who have been preaching for these five-and-twenty years sometimes feel that the same work, the same subject, the same people, and the same pulpit, are together apt to beget a feeling of monotony, and monotony may soon lead on to weariness. But then we call to mind another sameness, which becomes our complete deliverance; there is the same Saviour, and we may go to him in the same way as we did at the first, since he is "Jesus Christ the same yesterday, and to-day, and for ever." In his presence we drink in the new wine and renew our youth. He is the fountain, for ever flowing with the cool, refreshing water of life, and in fellowship with him we find our souls quickened into perpetual energy. Beneath his smile our long-accustomed work is always delightful, and wears a brighter charm than novelty could have conferred. We gather new manna for our people every morning, and as we go to distribute it we feel an anointing of fresh oil distilling upon us. "They that wait upon the Lord shall renew their strength; they shall mount up with wings as eagles; they shall run and not be weary; and they shall walk, and not faint." Newly come from the presence of him that walketh among the golden candlesticks we are ready to write or speak unto the churches in the power which he alone can give. Soldiers of Christ, you can only be worthy of your Captain by abiding in fellowship with him, and listening to his voice as Joshua did when he stood by Jordan, and enquired —"What saith my Lord unto his servant?"

Fan the flame as well as feed it. Fan it with much supplication. We cannot be too urgent with one another upon this point: no language can be too vehement with which to implore ministers to pray. There is for our brethren and ourselves an absolute necessity for prayer.

Necessity!—I hardly like to talk of that, let me rather speak of the deliciousness of prayer—the wondrous sweetness and divine felicity which come to the soul that lives in the atmosphere of prayer. John Fox said, "The time we spend with God in secret is the sweetest time, and the best improved. Therefore, if thou lovest thy life, be in love with prayer." The devout Mr. Hervey resolved on the bed of sickness —"If God shall spare my life, I will read less and pray more." John Cooke, of Maidenhead, wrote—"The business, the pleasure, the honour, and advantage of prayer press on my spirit with increasing force every day." A deceased pastor when drawing near his end, exclaimed, "I wish I had prayed more"; that wish many of us might utter. There should be special seasons for devotion, and it is well to maintain them with regularity; but the spirit of prayer is even better than the habit of prayer: to pray without ceasing is better than praying at intervals. It will be a happy circumstance if we can frequently bow the knee with devout brethren, and I think it ought to be a rule with us ministers never to separate without a word of prayer. Much more intercession would rise to heaven if we made a point of this, especially those of us who have been fellow-students. If it be possible, let prayer and praise sanctify each meeting of friend with friend. It is a refreshing practice to have a minute or two of supplication in the vestry before preaching if you can call in three or four warm-hearted deacons or other brethren. It always nerves me for the fight. But, for all that, to fan your earnestness to a vehement flame you should seek the spirit of continual prayer, so as to pray in the Holy Ghost, everywhere and always; in the study, in the vestry, and in the pulpit. It is well to be pleading evermore with God, when sitting down in the pulpit, when rising to give out the hymn, when reading the chapter, and while delivering the sermon; holding up one hand to God empty, in order to receive, and with the other hand dispensing to the people what the Lord bestows. Be in preaching like a conduit pipe between the everlasting and infinite supplies of heaven and the all but bound-less needs of men, and to do this you must reach heaven, and keep up the communication without a break. Pray *for* the people while you preach *to* them; speak with God for them while you are speaking with them for God. Only so can you expect to be continually in earnest. A man does not often rise from his knees unearnest; or, if he does, he had better return to prayer till the sacred flame descends upon his soul. Adam Clarke once said, "Study yourself to death, and then pray yourself alive again": it was a wise sentence. Do not attempt the first without the second; neither dream that the second can be honestly accomplished without the first. Work and pray, as well as watch and pray; but pray always.

Stir the fire also by frequent attempts at fresh service. Shake your-self out of routine by breaking away from the familiar fields of service and reclaiming virgin soil. I suggest to you, as a subordinate but very useful means of keeping the heart fresh, the frequent addition of new work to your usual engagements. I would say to brethren who are soon going away from the College, to settle in spheres where they will come into contact with but few superior minds, and perhaps will be almost alone in the higher walks of spirituality,—look well to yourselves that you do not become flat, stale, and unprofitable, and keep yourselves sweet by maintaining an enterprising spirit. You will have a good share of work to do, and few to help you in it, and the years will grind along heavily; watch against this, and use all means to prevent your becoming dull and sleepy, and among them use that which experience leads me to press upon you. I find it good for myself to have some new work always on hand. The old and usual enterprises must be kept up, but somewhat must be added to them. It should be with us as with the squatters upon our commons, the fence of our garden must roll outward a foot or two, and enclose a little more of the common every year. Never say "it is enough," nor accept the policy of "rest and be thankful." Do all you possibly can, and then do a little more. I do not know by what process the gentleman who advertises that he can make short people taller attempts the task, but I should imagine that if any result could be produced in the direction of adding a cubit to one's stature it would be by every morning reaching up as high as you possibly can on tiptoe, and, having done that, trying day by day to reach a little higher. This is certainly the way to grow mentally and spiritually,—"reaching forth to that which is before." If the old should become just a little stale, add fresh endeavours to it, and the whole mass will be leavened anew. Try it and you will soon discover the virtue of breaking up fresh ground, invading new provinces of the enemy, and scaling fresh heights to set the banner of the Lord thereon. This is, of course, a secondary expedient to those of which we have already spoken, but still it is a very useful one, and may greatly benefit you. In a country town, say of two thousand inhabitants, you will, after a time, feel, "Well, now, I have done about all I can in this place." What then? There is a hamlet some four miles off: set about opening a room there. If one hamlet is occupied, make an excursion to another, and spy out the land, and set the relief of its spiritual destitution before you as an ambition. When the first place is supplied, think of a second. It is your duty, it will also be your safeguard. Everybody knows what interest there is in fresh work. A gardener will become weary of his toil unless he is allowed to introduce new flowers into the hothouse, or to cut the beds upon the lawn in a novel shape; all monotonous work is unnatural and wearying to the mind, therefore it is wisdom to give variety to your labour.

Far more weighty is the advice, *keep close to God, and keep close to your fellow men whom you are seeking to bless.* Abide under the shadow of the Almighty, dwell where Jesus manifests himself, and live in the power of the Holy Ghost. Your very life lies in this. Whitefield mentions a lad who was so vividly conscious of the presence of God that he would generally walk the roads with his hat off. How I wish we were always in such a mood. It would be no trouble to maintain earnestness then.

Take care, also, to be on most familiar terms with those whose souls are committed to your care. Stand in the stream and fish. Many preachers are utterly ignorant as to how the bulk of the people are living; they are at home among books, but quite at sea among men. What would you think of a botanist who seldom saw real flowers, or an astronomer who never spent a night with the stars? Would they be worthy of the name of men of science? Neither can a minister of the gospel ʰe anything but a mere empiric unless he mingles with men, and studies character for himself. "Studies from the life,"—gentlemen, we must have plenty of these if we are to paint to the life in our sermons. Read men as well as books, and love *men* rather than opinions, or you will be inanimate preachers.

Get into close quarters with those who are in an anxious state. Watch their difficulties, their throes and pangs of conscience. It will help to make you earnest when you see their eagerness to find peace. On the other hand, when you see how little earnest the bulk of men remain, it may help to make you more zealous for their arousing. Rejoice with those who are finding the Saviour: this is a grand means of revival for your own soul. When you are enabled to bring a mourner to Jesus you will feel quite young again. It will be as oil to your bones to hear a weeping penitent exclaim, "I see it all now! I believe, and my burden is gone: I am saved." Sometimes the rapture of newborn souls will electrify you into apostolic intensity. Who could not preach after having seen souls converted? Be on the spot when grace at last captures the lost sheep, that by sharing in the Great Shepherd's rejoicings you may renew your youth. Be in at the death with sinners, and you will be repaid for the weary chase after them which it may be you have followed for months and years. Grasp them with firm hold of love, and say, "Yes, by the grace of God, I have really won these souls;" and your enthusiasm will flame forth.

If you have to labour in a large town I should recommend you to familiarize yourself, wherever your place of worship may be, with the poverty, ignorance, and drunkenness of the place. Go if you can with a City missionary into the poorest quarter, and you will see that which will astonish you, and the actual sight of the disease will make you eager to reveal the remedy. There is enough of evil to be seen even in the best streets of our great cities, but there is an unutterable depth of horror in the condition of the slums. As a doctor walks the hospitals, so ought you to traverse the lanes and courts to behold the mischief which sin has wrought. It is enough to make a man weep tears of blood to gaze upon the desolation which sin has made in the earth. One day with a devoted missionary would be a fine termination to your College course, and a fit preparation for work in your own sphere. See the masses living in their sins, defiled with drinking and Sabbath-breaking, rioting and blaspheming; and see them dying sodden and hardened, or terrified and despairing: surely this will rekindle expiring zeal if anything can do it. The world is full of grinding poverty, and crushing sorrow; shame and death are the portion of thousands, and it needs a great gospel to meet the dire necessities of men's souls. Verily it is so. Do you doubt it? Go and see for yourselves. Thus will you learn to preach a great salvation, and magnify the great Saviour, not with your mouth only, but with your heart; and thus will you be married to your work beyond all possibility of deserting it.

Death-beds are grand schools for us. They are intended to act as tonics to brace us to our work. I have come down from the bed-chambers of the dying, and thought that everybody was mad, and myself most of all. I have grudged the earnestness which men devoted to earthly things, and half said to myself,—Why was that man driving along so hastily? Why was that woman walking out in such finery? Since they were all to die so soon, I thought nothing worth their doing but preparing to meet their God. To be often where men die will help us to teach them both to die and to live. M'Cheyne was wont to visit his sick or dying hearers on the Saturday afternoon, for, as he told Dr. James Hamilton, "Before preaching he liked to look over the verge."

I pray you, moreover, measure your work in the light of God. Are you God's servant or not? If you are, how can your heart be cold? Are you sent by a dying Saviour to proclaim his love and win the reward of his wounds, or are you not? If you are, how can you flag? Is the Spirit of God upon you? Has the Lord anointed you to preach glad tidings to the poor? If he has not, do not pretend to it. If he has, go in this thy might, and the Lord shall be thy strength. Yours is not a trade, or a profession. Assuredly if you measure it by the tradesman's measure it is the poorest business on the face of the earth. Consider it as a profession: who would not prefer any other, so far as golden gains or worldly honours are concerned? But if it be a divine calling, and you a miracle-worker, dwelling in the supernatural, and working not for time but for eternity, then you belong to a nobler guild, and to a higher fraternity than any that spring of earth and deal with time. Look at it aright, and you will own that it is a grand thing to be as poor as your Lord, if, like him, you may make many rich; you will feel that it is a glorious thing to be as unknown and despised as were your Lord's first followers, because you are making him known, whom to know is life eternal. You will be satisfied to be anything or to be nothing, and the thought of self will not enter your mind, or only cross it to be scouted as a meanness not to be tolerated by a consecrated man. There is the point. Measure your work as it should be measured, and I am not afraid that your earnestness will be diminished. Gaze upon it by the light of the judgment day, and in view of the eternal rewards of faithfulness. Oh, brethren, the present joy of having saved a soul is overwhelmingly delightful; you have felt it, I trust, and know it now. To save a soul from going down to perdition brings to us a little heaven below, but what must it be at the day of judgment to meet spirits redeemed by Christ, who learned the news of their redemption from our lips! We look forward to a blissful heaven in communion with our Master, but we shall also know the added joy of meeting those loved ones whom we led to Jesus by our ministry. Let us endure every cross, and despise all shame, for the joy which Jesus sets before us of winning men for him.

One more thought may help to keep up our earnestness. Consider the great evil which will certainly come upon us and upon our hearers if we be negligent in our work. "They shall perish"—is not that a dreadful sentence? It is to me quite as awful as that which follows it,—"but their blood will I require at the watchman's hand." How shall we describe the doom of an unfaithful minister? And every unearnest minister is unfaithful. I would infinitely prefer to be consigned to Tophet as a murderer of men's bodies than as a destroyer of men's souls; neither do I know of any condition in which a man can perish so fatally, so infinitely, as in that of the man who preaches a gospel which he does not believe, and assumes the office of pastor over a people whose good he does not intensely desire. Let us pray to be found faithful always, and ever. God grant that the Holy Spirit may make and keep us so.

XXII

The Blind Eye and the Deaf Ear

HAVING often said in this room that a minister ought to have one blind eye and one deaf ear, I have excited the curiosity of several brethren, who have requested an explanation; for it appears to them, as it does also to me, that the keener eyes and ears we have the better. Well, gentlemen, since the text is somewhat mysterious, you shall have the exegesis of it.

A part of my meaning is expressed in plain language by Solomon, in the book of Ecclesiastes (vii. 21): "Also take no heed unto all words that are spoken; lest thou hear thy servant curse thee." The margin says, "Give not thy heart to all words that are spoken"—do not take them to heart or let them weigh with you, do not notice them, or act as if you heard them. You cannot stop people's tongues, and therefore the best thing is to stop your own ears and never mind what is spoken. There is a world of idle chit-chat abroad, and he who takes note of it will have enough to do. He will find that even those who live with him are not always singing his praises, and that when he has displeased his most faithful servants they have, in the heat of the moment, spoken fierce words which it would be better for him not to have heard. Who has not, under temporary irritation, said that of another which he has afterwards regretted? It is the part of the generous to treat passionate words as if they had never been uttered. When a man is in an angry mood it is wise to walk away from him, and leave off strife before it be meddled with; and if we are compelled to hear hasty language, we must endeavour to obliterate it from the memory, and say with David, "But I, as a deaf man, heard not. I was as a man that heareth not, and in whose mouth are no reproofs." Tacitus describes a wise man as saying to one that railed at him, "You are lord of your tongue, but I am also master of my ears"—you may say what you please, but I will only hear what I choose. We cannot shut our ears as we do our eyes, for we have no ear lids, and yet, as we read of him that "stoppeth his ears from hearing of blood," it is, no doubt, possible to seal the portal of the ear so that nothing contraband shall enter. We would say of the general gossip of the village, and of the unadvised words of angry friends— do not hear them, or if you must hear them, do not lay them to heart, for you also have talked idly and angrily in your day, and would even now be in an awkward position if you were called to account for every word that you have spoken, even about your dearest friend. Thus Solomon argued as he closed the passage which we have quoted, —"For oftentimes also thine own heart knoweth that thou thyself likewise hast cursed others."

In enlarging upon my text, let me say first,—when you commence your ministry make up your mind to begin with a clean sheet; *be deaf and blind to the longstanding differences which may survive in the church.* As soon as you enter upon your pastorate you may be waited upon by persons who are anxious to secure your adhesion to their side in a family quarrel or church dispute; be deaf and blind to these people, and assure them that bygones must be bygones with you, and that as you have not inherited your predecessor's cupboard you do not mean to eat his cold meat. If any flagrant injustice has been done, be diligent to set it right, but if it be a mere feud, bid the quarrelsome party cease from it, and tell him once for all that you will have nothing to do with it. The answer of Gallio will almost suit you: "If it were a matter of wrong or wicked lewdness, O ye Jews, reason would that I should bear with you: but if it be a question of words and names, and vain janglings, look ye to it; for I will be no judge of such matters." When I came to New Park-street Chapel as a young man from the country, and was chosen pastor, I was speedily interviewed by a good man who had left the church, having, as he said, been "treated shamefully." He mentioned the names of half-a-dozen persons, all prominent members of the church, who had behaved in a very unchristian manner to him, he, poor innocent sufferer, having been a model of patience and holiness. I learned his character at once from what he said about others (a mode of judging which has never misled me), and I made up my mind how to act. I told him that the church had been in a sadly unsettled state, and that the only way out of the snarl was for every one to forget the past and begin again. He said that the lapse of years did not alter facts, and I replied that it would alter a man's view of them if in that time he had become a wiser and a better man. However, I added, that all the past had gone away with my predecessors, that he must follow them to their new spheres, and settle matters with *them,* for I would not touch the affair with a pair of tongs. He waxed somewhat warm, but I allowed him to radiate until he was cool again, and we shook hands and parted. He was a good man, but constructed upon an uncomfortable principle, so that he came across the path of others in a very awkward manner at times, and if I had gone into his narrative and examined his case, there would have been no end to the strife. I am quite certain that, for my own success, and for the prosperity of the church, I took the wisest course by applying my blind eye to all disputes which dated previously to my advent. It is the extreme of unwisdom for a young man fresh from college, or from another charge, to suffer himself to be earwigged by a clique, and to be bribed by kindness and flattery to become a partisan, and so to ruin himself with one-half of his people. Know nothing of parties and cliques, but be the pastor of all the flock, and care for all alike. Blessed are the peacemakers, and one sure way of peacemaking is to let the fire of contention alone. Neither fan it, nor stir it, nor add fuel to it, but let it go out of itself. Begin your ministry with one blind eye and one deaf ear.

I should recommend the use of the same faculty, or want of faculty, with regard to finance in the matter of your own salary. There are some occasions, especially in raising a new church, when you may have no deacon who is qualified to manage that department, and, therefore, you may feel called upon to undertake it yourselves. In such a case you are not to be censured, you ought even to be commended. Many a time also the work would come to an end altogether if the preacher did not act as his own deacon, and find supplies both temporal and spiritual by his own exertions. To these exceptional cases I have nothing to say but that I admire the struggling worker and deeply sympathize with him, for he is overweighted, and is apt to be a less successful soldier for his Lord because he is entangled with the affairs of this life. In churches which are well established, and afford a decent maintenance, the minister will do well to supervise all things, but interfere with nothing. If deacons cannot be trusted they ought not to be deacons at all, but if they are worthy of their office they are worthy of our confidence. I know that instances occur in which they are sadly incompetent and yet must be borne with, and in such a state of things the pastor must open the eye which otherwise would have remained blind. Rather than the management of church funds should become a scandal we must resolutely interfere, but if there is no urgent call for us to do so we had better believe in the division of labour, and let deacons do their own work. We have the same right as other officers to deal with financial matters if we please, but it will be our wisdom as much as possible to let them alone, if others will manage them for us. When the purse is bare, the wife sickly, and the children numerous, the preacher *must* speak if the church does not properly provide for him; but to be constantly bringing before the people requests for an increase of income is not wise. When a minister is poorly remunerated, and he feels that he is worth more, and that the church could give him more, he ought kindly, boldly, and firmly to communicate with the deacons first, and if they do not take it up he should then mention it to the brethren in a sensible, business-like way, not as craving a charity, but as putting it to their sense of honour, that "the labourer is worthy of his hire." Let him say outright what he thinks, for there is nothing to be ashamed of, but there would be much more cause for shame if he dishonoured himself and the cause of God by plunging into debt: let him therefore speak to the point in a proper spirit to the proper persons, and there end the matter, and not resort to secret complaining. Faith in God should tone down our concern about temporalities, and enable us to practise what we preach, namely—"Take no thought, saying, What shall we eat? or, What shall we drink; or, Wherewithal shall we be clothed? for your heavenly Father knoweth that ye have need of all these things." Some who have pretended to live by faith have had a very shrewd way of drawing out donations by turns of the indirect corkscrew, but you will either ask plainly, like men, or you will leave it to the Christian feeling of your people, and turn to the items and modes of church finance a blind eye and a deaf ear.

The blind eye and the deaf ear will come in exceedingly well in connection with the gossips of the place. Every church, and, for the matter of that, every village and family, is plagued with certain Mrs. Grundys, who drink tea and talk vitriol. They are never quiet, but buzz around to the great annoyance of those who are devout and practical. No one needs to look far for perpetual motion, he has only to watch their tongues. At tea-meetings, Dorcas meetings, and other gatherings, they practise vivisection upon the characters of their neighbours, and of course they are eager to try their knives upon the minister, the minister's wife, the minister's children, the minister's wife's bonnet, the dress of the minister's daughter, and how many new ribbons she has worn for the last six months, and so on *ad infinitum*. There are also certain persons who are never so happy as when they are "grieved to the heart" to have to tell the minister that Mr. A. is a snake in the grass, that he is quite mistaken in thinking so well of Messrs. B. and C., and that they have heard quite "promiscuously" that Mr. D. and his wife are badly matched. Then follows a long string about Mrs. E., who says that she and Mrs. F. overheard Mrs. G. say to Mrs. H. that Mrs. J. should say that Mr. K. and Miss L. were going to move from the chapel and hear Mr. M., and all because of what old N. said to young O. about that Miss P. Never listen to such people. Do as Nelson did when he put his blind eye to the telescope and declared that he did not see the signal, and therefore would go on with the battle. Let the creatures buzz, and do not even hear them, unless indeed they buzz so much concerning one person that the matter threatens to be serious; then it will be well to bring them to book and talk in sober earnestness to them. Assure them that you are obliged to have facts definitely before you, that your memory is not very tenacious, that you have many things to think of, that you are always afraid of making any mistake in such matters, and that if they would be good enough to write down what they have to say the case would be more fully before you, and you could give more time to its consideration. Mrs. Grundy will not do that; she has a great objection to making clear and definite statements; she prefers talking at random.

I heartily wish that by any process we could put down gossip, but I suppose that it will never be done so long as the human race continues what it is, for James tells us that "every kind of beasts, and of birds, and of serpents, and of things in the sea, is tamed, and hath been tamed of mankind: but the tongue can no man tame; it is an unruly evil, full of deadly poison." What can't be cured must be endured, and the best way of enduring it is not to listen to it. Over one of our old castles a former owner has inscribed these lines—

> THEY SAY.
> WHAT DO THEY SAY?
> LET THEM SAY.

Thin-skinned persons should learn this motto by heart. The talk of the village is never worthy of notice, and you should never take any interest in it except to mourn over the malice and heartlessness of which it is too often the indicator.

Mayow in his *Plain Preaching* very forcibly says, "If you were to see a woman killing a farmer's ducks and geese, for the sake of having one of the feathers, you would see a person acting as we do when we speak evil of anyone, for the sake of the pleasure we feel in evil speaking. For the pleasure we feel is not worth a single feather, and the pain we give is often greater than a man feels at the loss of his property." Insert a remark of this kind now and then in a sermon, when there is no special gossip abroad, and it may be of some benefit to the more sensible: I quite despair of the rest.

Above all, never join in tale-bearing yourself, and beg your wife to abstain from it also. Some men are too talkative by half, and remind me of the young man who was sent to Socrates to learn oratory. On being introduced to the philosopher he talked so incessantly that Socrates asked for double fees. "Why charge me double?" said the young fellow. "Because," said the orator, "I must teach you two sciences: the one how to hold your tongue and the other how to speak." The first science is the more difficult, but aim at proficiency in it, or you will suffer greatly, and create trouble without end.

Avoid with your whole soul that spirit of suspicion which sours some men's lives, and *to all things from which you might harshly draw an unkind inference turn a blind eye and a deaf ear.* Suspicion makes a man a torment to himself and a spy towards others. Once begin to suspect, and causes for distrust will multiply around you, and your very suspiciousness will create the major part of them. Many a friend has been transformed into an enemy by being suspected. Do not, therefore, look about you with the eyes of mistrust, nor listen as an eavesdropper with the quick ear of fear. To go about the congregation ferreting out disaffection, like a gamekeeper after rabbits, is a mean employment, and is generally rewarded most sorrowfully. Lord Bacon wisely advises "the provident stay of enquiry of that which we would be loth to find." When nothing is to be discovered which will help us to love others we had better cease from the enquiry, for we may drag to light that which may be the commencement of years of contention. I am not, of course, referring to cases requiring discipline which must be thoroughly investigated and boldly dealt with, but I have upon my mind mere personal matters where the main sufferer is yourself; here it is always best not to know, nor to wish to know, what is being said about you, either by friends or foes. Those who praise us are probably as much mistaken as those who abuse us, and the one may be regarded as a set off to the other, if indeed it be worth while taking any account at all of man's judgment. If we have the approbation of our God, certified by a placid conscience, we can afford to be indifferent to the opinions of our fellow men, whether they commend or condemn. If we cannot reach this point we are babes and not men.

Some are childishly anxious to know their friend's opinion of them, and if it contain the smallest element of dissent or censure, they regard him as an enemy forthwith. Surely we are not popes, and do not wish our hearers to regard us as infallible! We have known men become quite enraged at a perfectly fair and reasonable remark, and regard an honest friend as an opponent who delighted to find fault; this misrepresentation on the one side has soon produced heat on the other, and strife has ensued. How much better is gentle forbearance! You must be able to bear criticism, or you are not fit to be at the head of a congregation; and you must let the critic go without reckoning him among your deadly foes, or you will prove yourself a mere weakling. It is wisest always to show double kindness where you have been severely handled by one who thought it his duty to do so, for he is probably an honest man and worth winning. He who in your early days hardly thinks you fit for the pastorate may yet become your firmest defender if he sees that you grow in grace, and advance in qualification for the work; do not, therefore, regard him as a foe for truthfully expressing his doubts; does not your own heart confess that his fears were not altogether groundless? Turn your deaf ear to what you judge to be his harsh criticism, and endeavour to preach better.

Persons from love of change, from pique, from advance in their tastes, and other causes, may become uneasy under our ministry, and it is well for us to know nothing about it. Perceiving the danger, we must not betray our discovery, but bestir ourselves to improve our sermons, hoping that the good people will be better fed and forget their dissatisfaction. If they are truly gracious persons, the incipient evil will pass away, and no real discontent will arise, or if it does you must not provoke it by suspecting it.

Where I have known that there existed a measure of disaffection to myself, I have not recognised it, unless it has been forced upon me, but have, on the contrary, acted towards the opposing person with all the more courtesy and friendliness, and I have never heard any more of the matter. If I had treated the good man as an opponent, he would have done his best to take the part assigned him, and carry it out to his own credit; but I felt that he was a Christian man, and had a right to dislike me if he thought fit, and that if he did so I ought not to think unkindly of him; and therefore I treated him as one who was a friend to my Lord, if not to me, gave him some work to do which implied confidence in him, made him feel at home, and by degrees won him to be an attached friend as well as a fellow-worker. The best of people are sometimes out at elbows and say unkind things; we should be glad if our friends could quite forget what we said when we were peevish and irritable, and it will be Christlike to act towards others in this matter as we would wish them to do towards us. Never make a brother remember that he once uttered a hard speech in reference to yourself. If you see him in a happier mood, do not mention the former painful occasion: if he be a man of right spirit he will in future be unwilling to vex a pastor who has treated him so generously, and if he be a mere boor it is a pity to hold any argument with him, and therefore the past had better go by default.

It would be better to be deceived a hundred times than to live a life of suspicion. It is intolerable. The miser who traverses his chamber at midnight and hears a burglar in every falling leaf is not more wretched than the minister who believes that plots are hatching against him, and that reports to his disadvantage are being spread. I remember a brother who believed that he was being poisoned, and was persuaded that even the seat he sat upon and the clothes he wore had by some subtle chemistry become saturated with death; his life was a perpetual scare, and such is the existence of a minister when he mistrusts all around him. Nor is suspicion merely a source of disquietude, it is a moral evil, and injures the character of the man who harbours it. Suspicion in kings creates tyranny, in husbands jealousy, and in ministers bitterness; such bitterness as in spirit dissolves all the ties of the pastoral relation, eating like a corrosive acid into the very soul of the office and making it a curse rather than a blessing. When once this terrible evil has curdled all the milk of human kindness in a man's bosom, he becomes more fit for the detective police force than for the ministry; like a spider, he begins to cast out his lines, and fashions a web of tremulous threads, all of which lead up to himself and warn him of the least touch of even the tiniest midge.

There he sits in the centre, a mass of sensation, all nerves and raw wounds, excitable and excited, a self-immolated martyr drawing the blazing faggots about him, and apparently anxious to be burned. The most faithful friend is unsafe under such conditions. The most careful avoidance of offence will not secure immunity from mistrust, but will probably be construed into cunning and cowardice. Society is almost as much in danger from a suspecting man as from a mad dog, for he snaps on all sides without reason, and scatters right and left the foam of his madness. It is vain to reason with the victim of this folly, for with perverse ingenuity he turns every argument the wrong way, and makes your plea for confidence another reason for mistrust. It is sad that he cannot see the iniquity of his groundless censure of others, especially of those who have been his best friends and the firmest upholders of the cause of Christ.

> "I would not wrong
> Virtue so tried by the least shade of doubt.
> Undue suspicion is more abject baseness
> Even than the guilt suspected."

No one ought to be made an offender for a word; but, when suspicion rules, even silence becomes a crime. Brethren, shun this vice by renouncing the love of self. Judge it to be a small matter what men think or say of you, and care only for their treatment of your Lord. If you are naturally sensitive do not indulge the weakness, nor allow others to play upon it. Would it not be a great degradation of your office if you were to keep an army of spies in your pay to collect information as to all that your people said of you? And yet it amounts to this if you allow certain busybodies to bring you all the gossip of the place. Drive the creatures away. Abhor those mischief-making, tattling handmaidens to strife. Those who will fetch will carry, and no doubt the gossips go from your house and report every observation which falls from your lips, with plenty of garnishing of their own. Remember that, as the receiver is as bad as the thief, so the hearer of scandal is a sharer in the guilt of it. If there were no listening ears there would be no talebearing tongues. While you are a buyer of ill wares the demand will create the supply, and the factories of falsehood will be working full time. No one wishes to become a creator of lies, and yet he who hears slanders with pleasure and believes them with readiness will hatch many a brood into active life.

Solomon says "a whisper separateth chief friends" (Prov. xvi. 28). Insinuations are thrown out, and jealousies aroused, till "mutual coolness ensues, and neither can understand why; each wonders what can possibly be the cause. Thus the firmest, the longest, the warmest, and most confiding attachments, the sources of life's sweetest joys, are broken up perhaps for ever."[1] This is work worthy of the arch-fiend himself, but it could never be done if men lived out of the atmosphere of suspicion. As it is, the world is full of sorrow through this cause, a sorrow as sharp as it is superfluous. This is grievous indeed! Campbell eloquently remarks, "The ruins of old friendships are a more melancholy spectacle to me than those of desolated palaces. They exhibit the heart which was once lighted up with joy all damp and deserted, and haunted by those birds of ill omen that nestle in ruins." O suspicion, what desolations thou hast made in the earth!

Learn to disbelieve those who have no faith in their brethren. Suspect those who would lead you to suspect others. A resolute unbelief in all the scandalmongers will do much to repress their mischievous energies. Matthew Pool in his Cripplegate Lecture says, "Common fame hath lost its reputation long since, and I do not know anything which it hath done in our day to regain it; therefore it ought not to be credited. How few reports there are of any kind which, when they come to be examined, we do not find to be false! For my part, I reckon, if I believe one report in twenty, I make a very liberal allowance. Especially distrust reproaches and evil reports, because these spread fastest, as being grateful to most persons, who suppose their own reputation to be never so well grounded as when it is built upon the ruins of other men's." Because the persons who would render you mistrustful of your friends are a sorry set, and because suspicion is in itself a wretched and tormenting vice, resolve to turn towards the whole business your blind eye and your deaf ear.

Need I say a word or two about the wisdom of *never hearing what was not meant for you*. The eavesdropper is a mean person, very little if anything better than the common informer; and he who says he *overheard* may be considered to have heard over and above what he should have done.

Jeremy Taylor wisely and justly observes, "Never listen at the door or window, for besides that it contains in it a danger and a snare, it is also invading my neighbour's privacy, and a-laying that open, which he therefore encloses that it might not be open." It is a well worn proverb that listeners seldom hear any good of themselves. Listening is a sort of larceny, but the goods stolen are never a pleasure to the thief. Information obtained by clandestine means must, in all but extreme cases, be more injury than benefit to a cause. The magistrate may judge it expedient to obtain evidence by such means, but I cannot imagine a case in which a minister should do so. Ours is a mission of grace and peace; we are not prosecutors who search out condemnatory evidence, but friends whose love would cover a multitude of offences. The peeping eyes of Canaan, the son of Ham, shall

[1] Dr. Wardlaw on Proverbs.

never be in our employ; we prefer the pious delicacy of Shem and Japhet, who went backward and covered the shame which the child of evil had published with glee.

To opinions and remarks about yourself turn also as a general rule the blind eye and the deaf ear. Public men must expect public criticism, and as the public cannot be regarded as infallible, public men may expect to be criticized in a way which is neither fair nor pleasant. To all honest and just remarks we are bound to give due measure of heed, but to the bitter verdict of prejudice, the frivolous faultfinding of men of fashion, the stupid utterances of the ignorant, and the fierce denunciations of opponents, we may very safely turn a deaf ear. We cannot expect those to approve of us whom we condemn by our testimony against their favourite sins; their commendation would show that we had missed our mark. We naturally look to be approved by our own people, the members of our churches, and the adherents of our congregations, and when they make observations which show that they are not very great admirers, we may be tempted to discouragement if not to anger: herein lies a snare. When I was about to leave my village charge for London, one of the old men prayed that I might be "delivered from the bleating of the sheep." For the life of me I could not imagine what he meant, but the riddle is plain now, and I have learned to offer the prayer myself. Too much consideration of what is said by our people, whether it be in praise or in depreciation, is not good for us. If we dwell on high with "that great Shepherd of the sheep" we shall care little for all the confused bleatings around us, but if we become "carnal, and walk as men," we shall have little rest if we listen to this, that, and the other which every poor sheep may bleat about us. Perhaps it is quite true that you were uncommonly dull last Sabbath morning, but there was no need that Mrs. Clack should come and tell you that Deacon Jones thought so. It is more than probable that having been out in the country all the previous week, your preaching was very like milk and water, but there can be no necessity for your going round among the people to discover whether they noticed it or not. Is it not enough that your conscience is uneasy upon the point? Endeavour to improve for the future, but do not want to hear all that every Jack, Tom, and Mary may have to say about it. On the other hand, you were on the high horse in your last sermon, and finished with quite a flourish of trumpets, and you feel considerable anxiety to know what impression you produced. Repress your curiosity: it will do you no good to enquire. If the people should happen to agree with your verdict, it will only feed your pitiful vanity, and if they think otherwise your fishing for their praise will injure you in their esteem. In any case it is all about yourself, and this is a poor theme to be anxious about; play the man, and do not demean yourself by seeking compliments like little children when dressed in new clothes, who say, "See my pretty frock." Have you not by this time discovered that flattery is as injurious as it is pleasant? It softens the mind and makes you more sensitive to slander. In proportion as praise pleases you censure will pain you. Besides, it is a crime to be taken off from your great object of glorifying the Lord Jesus by petty considerations as to your little self, and, if there were no other reason, this ought to weigh much with you. Pride is a deadly sin, and will grow without your borrowing the parish water-cart to quicken it. Forget expressions which feed your vanity, and if you find yourself relishing the unwholesome morsels confess the sin with deep humiliation. Payson showed that he was strong in the Lord when he wrote to his mother, "You must not, certainly, my dear mother, say one word which even looks like an intimation that you think me advancing in grace. I cannot bear it. All the people here, whether friends or enemies, conspire to ruin me. Satan and my own heart, of course, will lend a hand; and if you join too, I fear all the cold water which Christ can throw upon my pride will not prevent its breaking out into a destructive flame. As certainly as anybody flatters and caresses me my heavenly Father has to whip me: and an unspeakable mercy it is that he condescends to do it. I can, it is true, easily muster a hundred reasons why I should not be proud, but pride will not mind reason, nor anything else but a good drubbing. Even at this moment I feel it tingling in my fingers' ends, and seeking to guide my pen." Knowing something myself of those secret whippings which our good Father administers to his servants when he sees them unduly exalted, I heartily add my own solemn warnings against your pampering the flesh by listening to the praises of the kindest friends you have. They are injudicious, and you must beware of them.

A sensible friend who will unsparingly criticize you from week to week will be a far greater blessing to you than a thousand undiscriminating admirers if you have sense enough to bear his treatment, and grace enough to be thankful for it. When I was preaching at the Surrey Gardens, an unknown censor of great ability used to send me a weekly list of my mispronunciations and other slips of speech. He never signed his name, and that was my only cause of complaint against him, for he left me in a debt which I could not acknowledge. I take this opportunity of confessing my obligations to him, for with genial temper, and an evident desire to benefit me, he marked down most relentlessly everything which he supposed me to have said incorrectly. Concerning some of these corrections he was in error himself, but for the most part he was right, and his remarks enabled me to perceive and avoid many mistakes. I looked for his weekly memoranda with much interest, and I trust I am all the better for them. If I had repeated a sentence two or three Sundays before, he would say, "See same expression in such a sermon," mentioning number and page. He remarked on one occasion that I too often quoted the line

"Nothing in my hands I bring,"

and, he added, "we are sufficiently informed of the vacuity of your hands." He demanded my authority for calling a man *covechus*; and so on. Possibly some young men might have been discouraged, if not irritated, by such severe criticisms, but they would have been very foolish, for in resenting such correction they would have been throwing away a valuable aid to progress. No money can purchase ouspoken honest judgment, and when we can get it for nothing let us utilize it to the fullest extent. The worst of it is that of those who offer their judgments few are qualified to form them, and we shall be pestered with foolish, impertinent remarks, unless we turn to them all the blind eye and the deaf ear.

In the case of false reports against yourself, for the most part use the deaf ear. Unfortunately liars are not yet extinct, and, like Richard Baxter and John Bunyan, you may be accused of crimes which your soul abhors. Be not staggered thereby, for this trial has befallen the very best of men, and even your Lord did not escape the envenomed tongue of falsehood. In almost all cases it is the wisest course to let such things die a natural death. A great lie, if unnoticed, is like a big fish out of water, it dashes and plunges and beats itself to death in a short time. To answer it is to supply it with its element, and help it to a longer life. Falsehoods usually carry their own refutation somewhere about them, and sting themselves to death. Some lies especially have a peculiar smell, which betrays their rottenness to every honest nose. If you are disturbed by them the object of their invention is partly answered, but your silent endurance disappoints malice and gives you a partial victory, which God in his care of you will soon turn into a complete deliverance. Your blameless life will be your best defence, and those who have seen it will not allow you to be condemned so readily as your slanderers expect. Only abstain from fighting your own battles, and in nine cases out of ten your accusers will gain nothing by their malevolence but chagrin for themselves and contempt from others. To prosecute the slanderer is very seldom wise. I remember a beloved servant of Christ who in his youth was very sensitive, and, being falsely accused, proceeded against the person at law. An apology was offered, it withdrew every iota of the charge, and was most ample, but the good man insisted upon its being printed in the newspapers, and the result convinced him of his own unwisdom. Multitudes, who would otherwise have never heard of the libel, asked what it meant, and made comments thereon, generally concluding with the sage remark that he must have done something imprudent to provoke such an accusation. He was heard to say that so long as he lived he would never resort to such a method again, for he felt that the public apology had done him more harm than the slander itself. Standing as we do in a position which makes us choice targets for the devil and his allies, our best course is to defend our innocence by our silence and leave our reputation with God. Yet there are exceptions to this general rule. When distinct, definite, public charges are made against a man he is bound to answer them, and answer them in the clearest and most open manner. To decline all investigation is in such a case practically to plead guilty, and whatever may be the mode of putting it, the general public ordinarily regard a refusal to reply as a proof of guilt. Under mere worry and annoyance it is by far the best to be altogether passive, but when the matter assumes more serious proportions, and our accuser defies us to a defence, we are bound to meet his charges with honest statements of fact. In every instance counsel should be sought of the Lord as to how to deal with slanderous tongues, and in the issue innocence will be vindicated and falsehood convicted.

Some ministers have been broken in spirit, driven from their position, and even injured in character by taking notice of village scandal. I know a fine young man, for whom I predicted a career of usefulness, who fell into great trouble because he at first allowed it to be a trouble and then worked hard to make it so. He came to me and complained that he had a great grievance; and so it was a grievance, but from beginning to end it was all about what some half-dozen women had said about his procedure after the death of his wife. It was originally too small a thing to deal with,—a Mrs. Q. had said that she should not wonder if the minister married the servant then living in his house; another represented her as saying that he ought to marry her, and then a third, with a malicious ingenuity, found a deeper meaning in the words, and construed them into a charge. Worst of all, the dear sensitive preacher must needs trace the matter out and accuse a score or two of people of spreading libels against him, and even threaten some of them with legal proceedings. If he could have prayed over it in secret, or even have whistled over it, no harm would have come of the tittle-tattle; but this dear brother could not treat the slander wisely, for he had not what I earnestly recommend to you, namely, a blind eye and a deaf ear.

Once more, my brethren, the blind eye and the deaf ear will be useful to you *in relation to other churches and their pastors*. I am always delighted when a brother in meddling with other people's business burns his fingers. Why did he not attend to his own concerns and not episcopize in another's diocese? I am frequently requested by members of churches to meddle in their home disputes; but unless they come to me with authority, officially appointing me to be umpire, I decline. Alexander Cruden gave himself the name of "the Corrector," and I have never envied him the title. It would need a peculiar inspiration to enable a man to settle all the controversies of our churches, and as a rule those who are least qualified are the most eager to attempt it. For the most part interference, however well intentioned, is a failure. Internal dissensions in our churches are very like quarrels between man and wife: when the case comes to such a pass that they must fight it out, the interposing party will be the victim of their common fury. No one but Mr. Verdant Green will interfere in a domestic battle, for the man of course resents it, and the lady, though suffering from many a blow, will say, "You leave my husband alone; he has a right to beat me if he likes." However great the mutual animosity of conjugal combatants, it seems to be forgotten in resentment against intruders; and so, amongst the very independent denomination of Baptists, the person outside the church who interferes in any manner is sure to get the worst of it. Do not consider yourself to be the bishop of all the neighbouring churches, but be satisfied with looking after Lystra, or Derbe, or Thessalonica, or whichever church may have been allotted to your care, and leave Philippi and Ephesus in the hands of their own pastors. Do not encourage disaffected persons in finding fault with their minister, or in bringing you news of evils in other congregations. When you meet your brother ministers do not be in a hurry to advise them; they know their duty quite as well as you know yours, and your judgment upon their course of action is probably founded upon partial information supplied from prejudiced sources. Do not grieve your neighbours by your meddlesomeness. We have all enough to do at home, and it is prudent to keep out of all disputes which do not belong to us. We are recommended by one of the world's proverbs to wash our dirty linen at home, and I will add another line to it, and advise that we do not call on our neighbours while their linen is in the suds. This is due to our friends, and will best promote peace. "He that passeth by and meddleth with strife belonging not to him, is like one that taketh a dog by the ears"—he is very apt to be bitten, and few will pity him. Bridges wisely observes that "Our blessed Master has read us a lesson of godly wisdom. He healed the contentions in his own family, but when called to meddle with strife belonging not to him, he gave answer—'Who made me a judge or a divider over you?'" Self-constituted judges win but little respect; if they were more fit to censure they would be less inclined to do so. Many a trifling difference within a church has been fanned into a great flame by ministers outside who had no idea of the mischief they were causing: they gave verdicts upon *ex parte* statements, and so egged on opposing persons who felt safe when they could say that the neighbouring ministers quite agreed with them. My counsel is that we join the "Know-nothings," and never say a word upon a matter till we have heard both sides; and, moreover, that we do our best to avoid hearing either one side or the other if the matter does not concern us.

Is not this a sufficient explanation of my declaration that I have one blind eye and one deaf ear, and that they are the best eye and ear I have?

XXIII

On Conversion as Our Aim

THE grand object of the Christian ministry is the glory of God. Whether souls are converted or not, if Jesus Christ be faithfully preached, the minister has not laboured in vain, for he is a sweet savour unto God as well in them that perish as in them that are saved. Yet, as a rule, God has sent us to preach in order that through the gospel of Jesus Christ the sons of men may be reconciled to Him. Here and there a preacher of righteousness, like Noah, may labour on and bring none beyond his own family circle into the ark of salvation; and another, like Jeremiah, may weep in vain over an impenitent nation; but, for the most part, the work of preaching is intended to save the hearers. It is ours to sow even in stony places, where no fruit rewards our toil; but still we are bound to look for a harvest, and mourn if it does not appear in due time.

The glory of God being our chief object, we aim at it by seeking the edification of saints and the salvation of sinners. It is a noble work to instruct the people of God, and to build them up in their most holy faith: we may by no means neglect this duty. To this end we must give clear statements of gospel doctrine, of vital experience, and of Christian duty, and never shrink from declaring the whole counsel of God. In too many cases sublime truths are held in abeyance under the pretence that they are not practical; whereas the very fact that they are revealed proves that the Lord thinks them to be of value, and woe unto us if we pretend to be wiser than He. We may say of any and every doctrine of Scripture—

"To give it then a tongue is wise in man."

If any one note is dropped from the divine harmony of truth the music may be sadly marred. Your people may fall into grave spiritual diseases through the lack of a certain form of spiritual nutriment, which can only be supplied by the doctrines which you withhold. In the food which we eat there are ingredients which do not at first appear to be necessary to life; but experience shows that they are requisite to health and strength. Phosphorus will not make flesh, but it is wanted for bone; many earths and salts come under the same description—they are necessary in due proportion to the human economy. Even thus certain truths which appear to be little adapted for spiritual nutriment are, nevertheless, very beneficial in furnishing believers with backbone and muscle, and in repairing the varied organs of Christian manhood. We must preach "the whole truth," that the man of God may be thoroughly furnished unto all good works.

Our great object of glorifying God is, however, to be mainly achieved by the winning of souls. We *must* see souls born unto God. If we do not, our cry should be that of Rachel "Give me children, or I die." If we do not win souls, we should mourn as the husbandman who sees no harvest, as the fisherman who returns to his cottage with an empty net, or as the huntsman who has in vain roamed over hill and dale. Ours should be Isaiah's language uttered with many a sigh and groan —"Who hath believed our report? and to whom is the arm of the Lord revealed?" The ambassadors of peace should not cease to weep bitterly until sinners weep for their sins.

If we intensely desire to see our hearers believe on the Lord Jesus, how shall we act in order to be used of God for producing such a result? This is the theme of the present lecture.

Since conversion is a divine work, we must take care that we *depend entirely upon the Spirit of God,* and look to Him for power over men's minds. Often as this remark is repeated, I fear we too little feel its force; for if we were more truly sensible of our need of the Spirit of God, should we not study more in dependence upon His teaching? Should we not pray more importunately to be anointed with His sacred unction? Should we not in preaching give more scope for His operation? Do we not fail in many of our efforts, because we practically, though not doctrinally, ignore the Holy Ghost? His place as God is on the throne, and in all our enterprises He must be first, midst, and end: we are instruments in His hand, and nothing more.

This being fully admitted, what else should be done if we hope to see conversions? *Assuredly we should be careful to preach most prominently those truths which are likely to lead to this end.* What truths are those? I answer, we should first and foremost preach *Christ, and Him crucified.* Where Jesus is exalted souls are attracted —"I, if I be lifted up, will draw all men unto me." The preaching of the cross is to them that are saved the wisdom of God and the power of God. The Christian minister should preach all the truths which cluster around the person and work of the Lord Jesus, and hence he must declare very earnestly and pointedly *the evil of sin,* which created the need of a Saviour. Let him show that sin is a breach of the law, that it necessitates punishment, and that the wrath of God is revealed against it. Let him never treat sin as though it were a trifle, or a misfortune, but let him set it forth as exceeding sinful. Let him go into particulars, not superficially glancing at evil in the gross, but mentioning various sins in detail, especially those most current at the time: such as that all-devouring hydra of drunkenness, which devastates our land; lying, which in the form of slander abounds on all sides; and licentiousness, which must be mentioned with holy delicacy, and yet needs to be denounced unsparingly. We must especially reprove those evils into which our hearers have fallen, or are likely to fall. Explain the ten commandments and obey the divine injunction: "show my people their transgressions, and the house of Jacob their sins." Open up the spirituality of the law as our Lord did, and show how it is broken by evil thoughts, intents, and imaginations. By this means many sinners will be pricked in their hearts. Old Robbie Flockhart used to say, "It is of no use trying to sew with the silken thread of the gospel unless we pierce a way for it with the sharp needle of the law." The law goes first, like the needle, and draws the gospel thread after it: therefore preach concerning sin, righteousness, and judgment to come. Let such language as that of the fifty-first Psalm be often explained: show that God requireth truth in the inward parts, and that purging with sacrificial blood is absolutely needful. Aim at the heart. Probe the wound and touch the very quick of the soul. Spare not the sterner themes, for men must be wounded before they can be healed, and slain before they can be made alive. No man will ever put on the robe of Christ's righteousness till he is stripped of his fig leaves, nor will he wash in the fount of mercy till he perceives his filthiness. Therefore, my brethren, we must not cease to declare the law, its demands, its threatenings, and the sinner's multiplied breaches of it.

Teach the depravity of human nature. Show men that sin is not an accident, but the genuine outcome of their corrupt hearts. Preach the doctrine of the natural depravity of man. It is an unfashionable truth; for nowadays ministers are to be found who are very fine upon "the dignity of human nature." The "lapsed state of man"—that is the phrase—is sometimes alluded to, but the corruption of our nature, and kindred themes are carefully avoided: Ethiopians are informed that they may whiten their skins, and it is hoped that leopards will remove their spots. Brethren, you will not fall into this delusion, or, if you do, you may expect few conversions. To prophesy smooth things, and to extenuate the evil of our lost estate, is not the way to lead men to Jesus.

Brethren, *the necessity for the Holy Ghost's divine operations* will follow as a matter of course upon the former teaching, for dire necessity demands divine interposition. Men must be told that they are dead, and that only the Holy Spirit can quicken them; that the Spirit works according to His own good pleasure, and that no man can claim his visitations or deserve his aid. This is thought to be very discouraging teaching, and so it is, but men need to be discouraged when they are seeking salvation in a wrong manner. To put them out of conceit of their own abilities is a great help toward bringing them to look out of self to another, even the Lord Jesus. The doctrine of election and other great truths which declare salvation to be all of grace, and to be, not the right of the creature, but the gift of the Sovereign Lord, are all calculated to hide pride from man, and so to prepare him to receive the mercy of God.

We must also set before our hearers the justice of God and *the certainty that every transgression will be punished*. Often must we

> "Before them place in dread array,
> The pomp of that tremendous day
> When Christ with clouds shall come."

Sound in their ears the doctrine of the second advent, not as a curiosity of prophecy, but as a solemn practical fact. It is idle to set forth our Lord in all the tinkling bravery of an earthly kingdom, after the manner of brethren who believe in a revived Judaism; we need to preach the Lord as coming to judge the world in righteousness, to summon the nations to His bar, and to separate them as a shepherd divideth the sheep from the goats. Paul preached of righteousness, temperance, and judgment to come, and made Felix tremble: these themes are equally powerful now. We rob the gospel of its power if we leave out its threatenings of punishment. It is to be feared that the novel opinions upon annihilation and restoration which have afflicted the Church in these last days have caused many ministers to be slow to speak concerning the last judgment and its issues, and consequently the terrors of the Lord have had small influence upon either preachers or hearers. If this be so it cannot be too much regretted, for one great means of conversion is thus left unused.

Beloved brethren, we must be most of all clear upon the great soul-saving doctrine of the *atonement*; we must preach a real bona fide substitutionary sacrifice, and proclaim pardon as its result. Cloudy views as to atoning blood are mischievous to the last degree; souls are held in unnecessary bondage, and saints are robbed of the calm confidence of faith, because they are not definitely told that "God hath made Him to be sin for us, who knew no sin, that we might be made the righteousness of God in Him." We must preach substitution straightforwardly and unmistakeably, for if any doctrine be plainly taught in Scripture it is this,—"The chastisement of our peace was upon Him, and with His stripes we are healed." "He, His own self, bare our sins in His own body on the tree." This truth gives rest to the conscience by showing how God can be just, and the justifier of him that believeth. This is the great net of gospel fishermen: the fish are drawn or driven in the right direction by other truths, but this is the net itself.

If men are to be saved, we must in plainest terms preach *justification by faith,* as the method by which the atonement becomes effectual in the soul's experience. If we are saved by the substitutionary work of Christ, no merit of ours is wanted, and all men have to do is by a simple faith to accept what Christ has already done. It is delightful to dwell on the grand truth that "This man, after He had offered one sacrifice for sins for ever, sat down on the right hand of God." O glorious sight—the Christ sitting down in the place of honour because His work is done. Well may the soul rest in a work so evidently complete.

Justification by faith must never be obscured, and yet all are not clear upon it. I once heard a sermon upon "They that sow in tears shall reap in joy," of which the English was, "Be good, very good, and though you will have to suffer in consequence, God will reward you in the end." The preacher, no doubt, believed in justification by faith, but he very distinctly preached the opposite doctrine. Many do this when addressing children, and I notice that they generally speak to the little ones about *loving* Jesus, and not upon believing in Him. This must leave a mischievous impression upon youthful minds and take them off from the true way of peace.

Preach earnestly *the love of God in Christ Jesus,* and magnify the abounding mercy of the Lord; but always preach it in connection with His justice. Do not extol the single attribute of love in the method too generally followed, but regard love in the high theological sense, in which, like a golden circle, it holds within itself all the divine attributes: for God were not love if He were not just, and did not hate every unholy thing. Never exalt one attribute at the expense of another. Let boundless mercy be seen in calm consistency with stern justice and unlimited sovereignty. The true character of God is fitted to awe, impress, and humble the sinner: be careful not to misrepresent your Lord.

All these truths and others which complete the evangelical system are calculated to lead men to faith; therefore make them the staple of your teaching.

Secondly, if we are intensely anxious to have souls saved we must not only preach the truths which are likely to lead up to this end, but we must *use modes of handling those truths which are likely to conduce thereto.* Do you enquire, what are they? First, you must do a great deal by way of *instruction.* Sinners are not saved *in* darkness but *from* it; "that the soul be without knowledge, it is not good." Men must be taught concerning themselves, their sin, and their fall; their Saviour, redemption, regeneration, and so on. Many awakened souls would gladly accept God's way of salvation if they did but know it; they are akin to those of whom the apostle said, "And now, brethren, I wot that through ignorance ye did it." If you will instruct them God will save them: is it not written, "the entrance of thy word giveth light"? If the Holy Spirit blesses your teaching, they will see how wrong they have been, and they will be led to repentance and faith. I do not believe in that preaching which lies mainly in shouting, "Believe! believe! believe!" In common justice you are bound to tell the poor people what they are to believe. There must be instruction, otherwise the exhortation to believe is manifestly ridiculous, and must in practice be abortive. I fear that some of our orthodox brethren have been prejudiced against the free invitations of the gospel by hearing the raw, undigested harangues of revivalist speakers whose heads are loosely put together. The best way to preach sinners to Christ is to preach Christ to sinners. Exhortations, entreaties, and beseechings, if not accompanied with sound instruction, are like firing off powder without shot. You may shout, and weep, and plead, but you cannot lead men to believe what they have not heard, nor to receive a truth which has never been set before them. "Because the preacher was wise, he still taught the people knowledge."

While giving instructions it is wise to *appeal to the understanding*. True religion is as logical as if it were not emotional. I am not an admirer of the peculiar views of Mr. Finney, but I have no doubt that he was useful to many; and his power lay in his use of clear arguments. Many who knew his fame were greatly disappointed at first hearing him, because he used few beauties of speech and was as calm and dry as a book of Euclid; but he was exactly adapted to a certain order of minds, and they were convinced and convicted by his forcible reasoning. Should not persons of an argumentative cast of mind be provided for? We are to be all things to all men, and to these men we must become argumentative and push them into a corner with plain deductions and necessary inferences. Of carnal reasoning we would have none, but of fair, honest pondering, considering, judging, and arguing the more the better.

The class requiring logical argument is small compared with the number of those who need to be pleaded with, by way of *emotional persuasion*. They require not so much reasoning as heart-argument —which is logic set on fire. You must argue with them as a mother pleads with her boy that he will not grieve her, or as a fond sister entreats a brother to return to their father's home and seek reconciliation: argument must be quickened into persuasion by the living warmth of love. Cold logic has its force, but when made red hot with affection the power of tender argument is inconceivable. The power which one mind can gain over others is enormous, but it is often best developed when the leading mind has ceased to have power over itself. When passionate zeal has carried the man himself away his speech becomes an irresistible torrent, sweeping all before it. A man known to be godly and devout, and felt to be large-hearted and self-sacrificing, has a power in his very person, and his advice and recommendation carry weight because of his character; but when he comes to plead and to persuade, even to tears, his influence is wonderful, and God the Holy Spirit yokes it into His service. Brethren, we must *plead.* Entreaties and beseechings must blend with our instructions. Any and every appeal which will reach the conscience and move men to fly to Jesus we must perpetually employ, if by any means we may save some. I have sometimes heard ministers blamed for speaking of themselves when they are pleading, but the censure need not be much regarded while we have such a precedent as the example of Paul. To a congregation who love you it is quite allowable to mention your grief that many of them are unsaved, and your vehement desire, and incessant prayer for their conversion. You are doing right when you mention your own experience of the goodness of God in Christ Jesus, and plead with men to come and taste the same. We must not be abstractions or mere officials to our people; but we must plead with them as real flesh and blood, if we would see them converted. When you can quote yourself as a living instance of what grace has done, the plea is too powerful to be withheld through fear of being charged with egotism.

Sometimes, too, we must change our tone. Instead of instructing, reasoning and persuading, we must come to *threatening,* and declare the wrath of God upon impenitent souls. We must lift the curtain and let them see the future. Show them their danger, and warn them to escape from the wrath to come. This done, we must return to *invitation,* and set before the awakened mind the rich provisions of infinite grace which are freely presented to the sons of men. In our Master's name we must give the invitation, crying, "Whosoever will, let him take the water of life freely." Do not be deterred from this, my brethren, by those ultra-Calvinistic theologians who say, "You may instruct and warn the ungodly, but you must not invite or entreat them." And why not? "Because they are dead sinners, and it is therefore absurd to invite them, since they cannot come." Wherefore then may we warn or instruct them? The argument is so strong, if it be strong at all, that it sweeps away all modes of appeal to sinners, and they alone are logical who, after they have preached to the saints, sit down and say, "The election hath obtained it, and the rest were blinded." On what ground are we to address the ungodly at all? If we are only to bid them do such things as they are capable of doing without the Spirit of God, we are reduced to mere moralists. If it be absurd to bid the dead sinner believe and live, it is equally vain to bid him consider his state, and reflect upon his future doom. Indeed, it would be idle altogether were it not that true preaching is an act of faith, and is owned by the Holy Spirit as the means of working spiritual miracles. If we were by ourselves, and did not expect divine interpositions, we should be wise to keep within the bounds of reason, and persuade men to do only what we see in them the ability to do. We should then bid the living live, urge the seeing to see, and persuade the willing to will. The task would be so easy that it might even seem to be superfluous; certainly no special call of the Holy Ghost would be needed for so very simple an undertaking. But, brethren, where is the mighty power and the victory of faith if our ministry is this and nothing more? Who among the sons of men would think it a great vocation to be sent into a synagogue to say to a perfectly vigorous man, "Rise up and walk," or to the possessor of sound limbs, "Stretch out thine hand." He is a poor Ezekiel whose greatest achievement is to cry, "Ye living souls, live."

Let the two methods be set side by side as to practical result, and it will be seen that those who never exhort sinners are seldom winners of souls to any great extent, but they maintain their churches by converts from other systems. I have even heard them say, "Oh, yes, the Methodists and Revivalists are beating the hedges, but we shall catch many of the birds." If I harboured such a mean thought I should be ashamed to express it. A system which cannot touch the outside world, but must leave arousing and converting work to others, whom it judges to be unsound, writes its own condemnation.

Again, brethren, if we wish to see souls saved, we must be wise as to *the times* when we address the unconverted. Very little common sense is spent over this matter. Under certain ministries there is a set time for speaking to sinners, and this comes as regularly as the hour of noon. A few crumbs of the feast are thrown to the dogs under the table at the close of the discourse, and they treat your crumbs as you treat them, namely, with courteous indifference. Why should the warning word be always at the hinder end of the discourse when hearers are most likely to be weary? Why give men notice to buckle on their harness so as to be prepared to repel our attack? When their interest is excited, and they are least upon the defensive, then let fly a shaft at the careless, and it will frequently be more effectual than a whole flight of arrows shot against them at a time when they are thoroughly encased in armour of proof. Surprise is a great element in gaining attention and fixing a remark upon the memory, and times for addressing the careless should be chosen with an eye to that fact. It may be very well as a rule to seek the edification of the saints in the morning discourse, but it would be wise to vary it, and let the unconverted sometimes have the chief labour of your preparation and the best service of the day.

Do not close a single sermon without addressing the ungodly, but at the same time set yourself seasons for a determined and continuous assault upon them, and proceed with all your soul to the conflict. On such occasions aim distinctly at immediate conversions; labour to remove prejudices, to resolve doubts, to conquer objections, and to drive the sinner out of his hiding-places at once. Summon the church-members to special prayer, beseech them to speak personally both with the concerned and the unconcerned, and be yourself doubly upon the watch to address individuals. We have found that our February meetings at the Tabernacle have yielded remarkable results: the whole month being dedicated to special effort. Winter is usually the preacher's harvest, because the people can come together better in the long evenings, and are debarred from out-of-door exercises and amusements. Be well prepared for the appropriate season when "kings go forth to battle."

Among the important elements in the promotion of conversion are your own tone, temper, and spirit in preaching. If you preach the truth in a dull, monotonous style, God *may* bless it, but in all probability he will not; at any rate the tendency of such a style is not to promote attention, but to hinder it. It is not often that sinners are awakened by ministers who are themselves asleep. A hard, un-feeling mode of speech is also to be avoided; want of tenderness is a sad lack, and repels rather than attracts. The spirit of Elijah may startle, and where it is exceedingly intense it may go far to prepare for the reception of the gospel; but for actual conversion more of John is needed,—love is the winning force. We must love men to Jesus. Great hearts are the main qualifications for great preachers, and we must cultivate our affections to that end. At the same time our manner must not degenerate into the soft and saccharine cant which some men affect who are for ever *dearing* everybody, and fawning upon people as if they hoped to soft-sawder them into godli-ness. Manly persons are disgusted, and suspect hypocrisy when they hear a preacher talking molasses. Let us be bold and outspoken, and never address our hearers as if we were asking a favour of them, or as if they would oblige the Redeemer by allowing Him to save them. We are bound to be lowly, but our office as ambassadors should prevent our being servile.

Happy shall we be if we preach believingly, always expecting the Lord to bless his own word. This will give us a quiet confidence which will forbid petulance, rashness, and weariness. If we ourselves doubt the power of the gospel, how can we preach it with authority? Feel that you are a favoured man in being allowed to proclaim the good news, and rejoice that your mission is fraught with eternal benefit to those before you. Let the people see how glad and confident the gospel has made you, and it will go far to make them long to partake in its blessed influences.

Preach very solemnly, for it is a weighty business, but let your matter be lively and pleasing, for this will prevent solemnity from souring into dreariness. Be so thoroughly solemn that all your faculties are aroused and consecrated, and then a dash of humour will only add intenser gravity to the discourse, even as a flash of lightning makes midnight darkness all the more impressive. Preach to one point, concentrating all your energies upon the object aimed at. There must be no riding of hobbies, no introduction of elegancies of speech, no suspicion of personal display, or you will fail. Sinners are quick-witted people, and soon detect even the smallest effort to glorify self. Forgo everything for the sake of those you long to save. Be a fool for Christ's sake if this will win them, or be a scholar, if that will be more likely to impress them. Spare neither labour in the study, prayer in the closet, nor zeal in the pulpit. If men do not judge their souls to be worth a thought, compel them to see that their minister is of a very different opinion.

Mean conversions, expect them, and prepare for them. Resolve that your hearers shall either yield to your Lord or be without excuse, and that this shall be the immediate result of the sermon now in hand. Do not let the Christians around you wonder when souls are saved, but urge them to believe in the undiminished power of the glad tidings, and teach them to marvel if no saving result follows the delivery of the testimony of Jesus. Do not permit sinners to hear sermons as a matter of course, or allow them to play with the edged tools of Scripture as if they were mere toys; but again and again remind them that every true gospel sermon leaves them worse if it does not make them better. Their unbelief is a daily, hourly sin; never let them infer from your teaching that they are to be pitied for continuing to make God a liar by rejecting His Son.

Impressed with a sense of their danger, give the ungodly no rest in their sins; knock again and again at the door of their hearts, and knock as for life and death. Your solicitude, your earnestness, your anxiety, your travailing in birth for them God will bless to their arousing. God works mightily by this instrumentality. But our agony for souls must be real and not feigned, and therefore our hearts must be wrought into true sympathy with God. Low piety means little spiritual power. Extremely pointed addresses may be delivered by men whose hearts are out of order with the Lord, but their result must be small. There is a something in the very tone of the man who has been with Jesus which has more power to touch the heart than the most perfect oratory: remember this and maintain an unbroken walk with God. You will need much night-work in secret if you are to gather many of your Lord's lost sheep. Only by prayer and fasting can you gain power to cast out the worst of devils. Let men say what they will about sovereignty, God connects special success with special states of heart, and if these are lacking he will not do many mighty works.

In addition to earnest preaching it will be wise to use other means.
If you wish to see results from your sermons you must be accessible
to enquirers. A meeting after every service may not be desirable, but
frequent opportunities for coming into direct contact with your people
should be sought after, and by some means created. It is shocking to
think that there are ministers who have no method whatever for
meeting the anxious, and if they do see here and there one, it is because
of the courage of the seeker, and not because of the earnestness of the
pastor. From the very first you should appoint frequent and regular
seasons for seeing all who are seeking after Christ, and you should
continually invite such to come and speak with you. In addition to
this, hold numerous enquirers' meetings, at which the addresses shall
be all intended to assist the troubled and guide the perplexed, and
with these intermingle fervent prayers for the individuals present, and
short testimonials from recent converts and others. As an open confession of Christ is continually mentioned in connection with saving
faith, it is your wisdom to make it easy for believers who are as yet
following Jesus by night to come forward and avow their allegiance
to him. There must be no persuading to make a profession, but there
should be every opportunity for so doing, and no stumbling-block
placed in the way of hopeful minds. As for those who are not so far
advanced as to warrant any thought of baptism, you may be of the
utmost benefit to them by personal intercourse, and therefore you
should seek it. Doubts may be cleared away, errors rectified, and
terrors dispelled by a few moments' conversation; I have known
instances in which a life-long misery has been ended by a simple
explanation which might have been given years before. Seek out the
wandering sheep one by one, and when you find all your thoughts
needed for a single individual, do not grudge your labour, for your
Lord in His parable represents the good shepherd as bringing home
His lost sheep, not in a flock, but one at a time upon His shoulders,
and rejoicing so to do.

With all that you can do your desires will not be fulfilled, for soul-
winning is a pursuit which grows upon a man; the more he is rewarded
with conversions the more eager he becomes to see greater numbers
born unto God. Hence you will soon discover that *you need help if
many are to be brought in.* The net soon becomes too heavy for one
pair of hands to drag ashore when it is filled with fishes; and your
fellow-helpers must be beckoned to your assistance. Great things are
done by the Holy Spirit when a whole church is aroused to sacred
energy: then there are hundreds of testimonies instead of one, and
these strengthen each other; then advocates for Christ succeed each
other and work into each other's hands, while supplication ascends
to heaven with the force of united importunity; thus sinners are en-
compassed with a cordon of earnest entreaties, and heaven itself is

called into the field. It would seem hard in some congregations for a sinner to be saved, for whatever good he may receive from the pulpit is frozen out of him by the arctic atmosphere with which he is surrounded: and on the other hand some churches make it hard for men to remain unconverted, for with holy zeal they persecute the careless into anxiety. It should be our ambition, in the power of the Holy Ghost, to work the entire church into a fine missionary condition, to make it like a Leyden jar charged to the full with divine electricity, so that whatever comes into contact with it shall feel its power. What can one man do alone? What can he not do with an army of enthusiasts around him? Contemplate at the outset the possibility of having a church of soul-winners. Do not succumb to the usual idea that we can only gather a few useful workers, and that the rest of the community must inevitably be a dead weight: it may possibly so happen, but do not set out with that notion or it will be verified. The usual need not be the universal; better things are possible than anything yet attained; set your aim high and spare no effort to reach it. Labour to gather a church alive for Jesus, every member energetic to the full, and the whole in incessant activity for the salvation of men. To this end there must be the best of preaching to feed the host into strength, continual prayer to bring down the power from on high, and the most heroic example on your own part to fire their zeal: then under the divine blessing a common-sense management of the entire force cannot fail to produce the most desirable issues. Who among you can grasp this idea and embody it in actual fact?

To call in another brother every now and then to take the lead in evangelistic services will be found very wise and useful; for there are some fish that never will be taken in your net, but will surely fall to the lot of another fisherman. Fresh voices penetrate where the accustomed sound has lost effect, and they tend also to beget a deeper interest in those already attentive. Sound and prudent evangelists may lend help even to the most efficient pastor, and gather in fruit which he has failed to reach; at any rate it makes a break in the continuity of ordinary services, and renders them less likely to become monotonous. Never suffer jealousy to hinder you in this. Suppose another lamp should outshine yours, what will it matter so long as it brings light to those whose welfare you are seeking? Say with Moses, "Would God all the Lord's servants were prophets." He who is free from selfish jealousy will find that no occasion will suggest it; his people may be well aware that their pastor is excelled by others in talent, but they will be ready to assert that he is surpassed by none in love to their souls. It is not needful for a loving son to believe that his father is the most learned man in the parish; he loves him for his own sake, and not because he is superior to others. Call in every now and then a warm-hearted neighbour, utilize the talent in the church itself, and procure the services of some eminent soul-winner, and this may, in God's hands, break up the hard soil for you, and bring you brighter days.

In fine, beloved brethren, by any means, by all means, labour to glorify God by conversions, and rest not till your heart's desire is fulfilled.

XXIV

Illustrations in Preaching

THE TOPIC now before us is the use of illustrations in our sermons. Perhaps we shall best subserve our purpose by working out an illustration in the present address; for there is no better way of teaching the art of pottery than by making a pot. Quaint Thomas Fuller says, "reasons are the pillars of the fabric of a sermon; but similitudes are the windows which give the best lights." The comparison is happy and suggestive, and we will build up our discourse under its direction.

The chief reason for the construction of windows in a house is, as Fuller says, *to let in light*. Parables, similes, and metaphors have that effect; and hence we use them to *illustrate* our subject, or, in other words, to *"brighten it with light,"* for that is Dr. Johnson's literal rendering of the word *illustrate*. Often when didactic speech fails to enlighten our hearers we may make them see our meaning by opening a window and letting in the pleasant light of analogy. Our Saviour, who is the light of the world, took care to fill his speech with similitudes, so that the common people heard him gladly: his example stamps with high authority the practice of illuminating heavenly instruction with comparisons and similes. To every preacher of righteousness as well as to Noah, wisdom gives the command, "A window shalt thou make in the ark." You may build up laborious definitions and explanations and yet leave your hearers in the dark as to your meaning; but a thoroughly suitable metaphor will wonderfully clear the sense. The pictures in *The Illustrated London News* give us a far better idea of the scenery which they represent than could be conveyed to us by the best descriptive letter-press; and it is much the same with Scriptural teaching: abstract truth comes before us so much more vividly when a concrete example is given, or the doctrine itself is clothed in figurative language. There should, if possible, be at least one good metaphor in the shortest address; as Ezekiel, in his vision of the temple, saw that even to the little chambers there were windows suitable to their size. If we are faithful to the spirit of the gospel we labour to make things plain: it is our study to be simple and to be understood by the most illiterate of our hearers; let us, then, set forth many a metaphor and parable before the people. He wrote wisely who said, "The world below me is a glass in which I may see the world above. The works of God are the shepherd's calendar and the ploughman's alphabet." Having nothing to conceal, we have no ambition to be obscure. Lycophron declared that he would hang himself upon a tree if he found a person who could understand his poem entitled "The Prophecy of Cassandra." Happily no one arose to drive him to such a misuse of timber. We think we could find brethren in the ministry who might safely run the same risk in connection with their sermons. Still have we among us those who are like Heraclitus, who was called "the Dark Doctor" because his language was beyond all comprehension. Certain mystical discourses are so dense that if light were admitted into them it would be extinguished like a torch in the Grotta del Cane: they are made up of the palpably obscure and the inexplicably involved, and all hope of understanding them may be abandoned. This style of oratory we do not cultivate. We are of the same mind as Joshua Shute, who said: "That sermon has most learning in it that has most plainness. Hence it is that a great scholar was wont to say, 'Lord, give me learning enough, that I may preach plain enough.'"

Windows greatly add to the pleasure and agreeableness of a habitation, and so do *illustrations make a sermon pleasurable and interesting.* A building without windows would be a prison rather than a house, for it would be quite dark, and no one would care to take it upon lease; and, in the same way, a discourse without a parable is prosy and dull, and involves a grievous weariness of the flesh. The preacher in Solomon's Ecclesiastes "sought to find out acceptable words," or, as the Hebrew has it, "words of delight": surely, figures and comparisons are delectable to our hearers. Let us not deny them the salt of parable with the meat of doctrine. Our congregations hear us with pleasure when we give them a fair measure of imagery: when an anecdote is being told they rest, take breath, and give play to their imaginations, and thus prepare themselves for the sterner work which lies before them in listening to our profounder expositions. Riding in a third-class carriage some years ago in the eastern counties, we had been for a long time without a lamp; and when a traveller lighted a candle, it was pleasant to see how all eyes turned that way, and rejoiced in the light: such is frequently the effect of an apt simile in the midst of a sermon, it lights up the whole matter, and gladdens every heart. Even the little children open their eyes and ears, and a smile brightens up their faces as we tell a story; for they, too, rejoice in the light which streams in through our windows. We dare say they often wish that the sermon were all illustrations, even as the boy desired to have a cake made all of plums; but that must not be: there is a happy medium, and we must keep to it by making our discourse pleasant hearing, but not a mere pastime. No reason exists why the preaching of the gospel should be a miserable operation either to the speaker or to the hearer. Pleasantly profitable let all our sermons be.

A house must not have thick walls without openings, neither must a discourse be all made up of solid slabs of doctrine without a window of comparison or a lattice of poetry; if so, our hearers will gradually forsake us, and prefer to stay at home and read their favourite authors whose lively tropes and vivid images afford more pleasure to their minds.

Every architect will tell you that he looks upon his windows as *an opportunity for introducing ornament into his design.* A pile may be massive, but it cannot be pleasing if it is not broken up with windows and other details. The palace of the popes at Avignon is an immense structure; but the external windows are so few that it has all the aspect of a colossal prison, and suggests nothing of what a palace should be. Sermons need to be broken up, varied, decorated, and enlivened; and nothing can do this so well as the introduction of types, emblems, and instances. Of course, ornament is not the main point to be considered; but still, many little excellences go to make up perfection, and this is one of the many, and therefore it should not be overlooked. When wisdom built her house she hewed out her seven pillars, for glory and for beauty, as well as for the support of the structure; and shall we think that any rough hovel is good enough for the beauty of holiness to dwell in? Certainly a gracious discourse is none the better for being bereft of every grace of language. Meretricious ornament we deprecate, but an appropriate beauty of speech we cultivate. Truth is a king's daughter, and her raiment should be of wrought gold; her house is a palace, and it should be adorned with "windows of agate and gates of carbuncle."

Illustrations tend to enliven an audience and quicken attention. Windows, when they will open, which, alas, is not often the case in our places of worship, are a great blessing by refreshing and reviving the audience with a little pure air, and arousing the poor mortals who are rendered sleepy by the stagnant atmosphere. A window should, according to its name, be a wind-door, through which a breath of air may visit the audience; even so, an original figure, a noble image, a quaint comparison, a rich allegory, should open upon our hearers a breeze of happy thought, which will pass over them like life-giving breath, arousing them from their apathy, and quickening their faculties to receive the truth. Those who are accustomed to the soporific sermonizings of certain dignified divines would marvel greatly if they could see the enthusiasm and lively delight with which congregations listen to speech through which there flows a quiet current of happy, natural illustration. Arid as a desert are many volumes of discourses which are to be met with upon the booksellers' dust-covered shelves; but if in the course of a thousand paragraphs they contain a single simile, it is as an oasis in the Sahara, and serves to keep the reader's soul alive. In fashioning a discourse think little of the bookworm, which will be sure of its portion of meat however dry your doctrine, but have pity upon those hungering ones immediately around you who must find life through your sermon or they will never find it at all. If some of your hearers sleep on they will of necessity wake up in eternal perdition, for they hear no other helpful voice.

While we thus commend illustrations for necessary uses, it must be remembered that they are not the strength of a sermon any more than a window is the strength of a house; and for this reason, among others, *they should not be too numerous*. Too many openings for light may seriously detract from the stability of a building. We have known sermons so full of metaphors that they became weak, and we had almost said *crazy*, structures. Sermons must not be nosegays of flowers, but sheaves of wheat. Very beautiful sermons are generally very useless ones. To aim at elegance is to court failure. It is possible to have too much of a good thing: a glass house is not the most comfortable of abodes, and besides other objectionable qualities it has the great fault of being sadly tempting to stone-throwers. When a critical adversary attacks our metaphors he generally makes short work of them. To friendly minds images are arguments, but to opponents they are opportunities for attack; the enemy climbs up by the window. Comparisons are swords with two edges which cut both ways; and frequently what seems a sharp and telling illustration may be wittily turned against you, so as to cause a laugh at your expense: therefore do not rely upon your metaphors and parables. Even a second-rate man may defend himself from a superior mind if he can dexterously turn his assailant's gun upon himself. Here is an instance which concerns myself, and I give it for that reason, since these lectures have all along been autobiographical. I give a cutting from one of our religious papers. "Mr. Beecher has been neatly tripped up in *The Sword and the Trowel*. In his *Lectures on Preaching* he asserts that Mr. Spurgeon has succeeded 'in spite of his Calvinism'; adding the remark that 'the camel does not travel any better, nor is it any more useful, because of the hump on its back.' The illustration is not a felicitous one, for Mr. Spurgeon thus retorts: 'Naturalists assure us the camel's hump is of great importance in the eyes of the Arabs, who judge of the condition of their beasts by the size, shape, and firmness of their humps. The camel feeds upon his hump when he traverses the wilderness, so that in proportion as the animal travels over the sandy wastes, and suffers from privation and fatigue, the mass diminishes; and he is not fit for a long journey till the hump has regained its proportions. Calvinism, then, is the spiritual meat which enables a man to labour on in the ways of Christian service; and, though ridiculed as a hump by those who are only lookers-on, those who traverse the weary paths of a wilderness experience know too well its value to be willing to part with it, even if Beecher's splendid talents could be given in exchange.'"

Illustrate, by all means, but do not let the sermon be all illustrations, or it will be only suitable for an assembly of simpletons. A volume is all the better for engravings, but a scrap-book which is all woodcuts is usually intended for the use of little children. Our house should be built up with the substantial masonry of doctrine, upon the deep foundation of inspiration; its pillars should be of solid Scriptural argument, and every stone of truth should be carefully laid in its place; and then the windows should be ranged in due order, "three rows" if we will: "light against light," like the house of the forest of Lebanon. But a house is not erected for the sake of the windows, nor may a sermon be arranged with the view of fitting in a favourite apologue. A window is merely a convenience subordinate to the entire design, and so is the best illustration. We shall be foolish indeed if we compose a discourse to display a metaphor; as foolish as if an architect should build a cathedral with the view of exhibiting a stained glass window. We are not sent into the world to build a Crystal Palace in which to set out works of art and elegancies of fashion; but as wise master-builders we are to edify, spiritual house for the divine inhabiting. Our building is intended to last, and is meant for everyday use, and hence it must not be all crystal and colour. We miss our way altogether, as gospel ministers, if we aim at flash and finery.

It is impossible to lay down a rule as to how much adornment shall be found in each discourse: every man must judge for himself in that matter. True taste in dress could not be readily defined, yet everyone knows what it is; and there is a literary and spiritual taste which should be displayed in the measuring out of tropes and figures in every public speech. "Ne quid nimis" is a good caution: do not be too eager to garnish and adorn. Some men seem never to have enough of metaphors: each one of their sentences must be a flower. They compass sea and land to find a fresh piece of coloured glass for their windows, and they break down the walls of their discourses to let in superfluous ornaments, till their productions rather resemble a fantastic grotto than a house to dwell in. They are grievously in error if they think that thus they manifest their own wisdom, or benefit their hearers. I could almost wish for a return of the window-tax if it would check these poetical brethren. The law, I believe, allowed eight windows free from duty, and we might also exempt "a few, that is eight" metaphors from criticism; but more than that ought to pay heavily. Flowers upon the table at a banquet are well enough; but as nobody can live upon bouquets, they will become objects of contempt if they are set before us in lieu of substantial viands. The difference between a little salt with your meat and being compelled to empty the salt-cellar is clear to all; and we could wish that those who pour out so many symbols, emblems, figures, and devices would remember that nausea in oratory is not more agreeable than in food. Enough is as good as a feast; and too many pretty things may be a greater evil than none at all.

It is a suggestive fact that the tendency to abound in metaphor and illustration becomes weaker as men grow older and wiser. Perhaps this may, in a measure, be ascribed to the decay of their imagination; but it also occurs at the same time as the ripening of their understanding. Some may have to use fewer figures of necessity, because they do not come to them as aforetime; but this is not always the case. I know that men who still possess great facility in imagery find it less needful to employ that faculty now than in their earlier days, for they have the ear of the people, and they are solemnly resolved to fill that ear with instruction as condensed as they can make it. When you begin with a people who have not heard the gospel, and whose attention you have to win, you can hardly go too far in the use of figure and metaphor. Our Lord Jesus Christ used very much of it; indeed, "without a parable spake he not unto them"; because they were not educated up to the point at which they could profitably hear pure didactic truth. It is noticeable that after the Holy Ghost had been given, fewer parables were used, and the saints were more plainly taught of God. When Paul spoke or wrote to the churches in his epistles he employed few parables, because he addressed those who were advanced in grace and willing to learn. As Christian minds made progress the style of their teachers became less figurative, and more plainly doctrinal. We seldom see engravings in the classics of the college; these are reserved for the spelling-books of the dame-school. This should teach us wisdom, and suggest that we are to be bound by no hard and fast rules, but should use more or less of any mode of teaching according to our own condition and that of our people.

Illustrations should really cast light upon the subject in hand, otherwise they are sham windows, and all shams are an abomination. When the window-tax was still in force many people in country houses closed half their lights by plastering them up, and then they had the plaster painted to look like panes; so that there was still the appearance of a window, though no sunlight could enter. Well do I remember the dark rooms in my grandfather's parsonage, and my wonder that men should have to pay for the light of the sun. Blind windows are fit emblems of illustrations which illustrate nothing, and need themselves to be explained. Grandiloquence is never more characteristic than in its figures; there it disports itself in a very carnival of bombast. We could quote several fine specimens of sublime spread-eagleism and magnificent nonsense, but one alone may suffice as a favourable sample of a form of display which is rather more common across the water than in these old-fashioned regions. The author's name we will not mention, but the extract is given verbatim, and is taken from a sermon upon "To die is gain." Let the young preacher ponder and wonder, but let him not imitate. We give the whole passage for the sake of *the frigate bird,* and the *granite-porphyry-jasper staircase.*

"There is a bird that mariners call the 'frigate bird,' of strange habits and of strange power. Men see him in all climes, but never yet has human eye seen him near the earth. With wings of mighty stretch, high borne, he sails along. Men of the far north see him at midnight moving on amid auroral fires, sailing along with set wings amid those awful flames, taking the colour of the waves of light which swell and heave around him. Men in the tropics see him at hottest noon, his plumage all incarnadined by the fierce rays that smite innocuous upon him. Amid their ardent fervour, he bears along, majestic, tireless. Never was he known to stoop from his lofty line of flight, never to swerve. To many he is a myth, to all a mystery. Where is his perch? [*This is fine indeed. Let us add, "Who shall lay salt on his tail?"*] Where does he rest? Where was he brooded? None know. They only know that above cloud, above the reach of tempest, above the tumult of transverse currents, this bird of heaven (so let us call him) on self-supporting vans that disdain to beat the air on which they rest, moves grandly on. [*Grand idea! The critter flies without moving his wings, disdaining to beat the air, as well he may, for he beats all creation.*] So shall my hope be. At either pole of life, above the clouds of sorrow, superior to the tempests that beat upon me, on lofty and tireless wing, scorning the earth, it shall move along. Never shall it stoop, never swerve from its sublime line of flight. They shall see it in the morning of my life; they shall see it in its hot noon-day; and when the shadows fall, my sun having set, using your style of speech; but, using mine, when the shadows disappear, my sun having risen, the last they see of me shall be this hope of gain dying, as it sails out on steady wing, and disappears amid the everlasting light.

"I feel, friends, that no exhortation of mine will lift you to this pedestal of hewn granite, on which it is given to monumental piety to stand. [*Quite right: an exhortation cannot very well lift a body on to a pedestal; it needs a leg or an arm to do that. But what is monumental piety?*] Only by analysis, by meditation, by thought that ponders in the night time the majestic utterances of Scripture, and by the open lattice—or, better yet, beneath the grand dome—bows in prayer, and holds communion with the possibilities that stand beyond this life, like unfilled thrones waiting for occupants. Only in this way, and in others suggested by the Spirit to minds fit to receive them, will you or any ever rise to the level of the emotion which dictated the text. Where is Paul to-day? Where does he stand, who, from his prison at Rome, sent out this immortal saying? Is there one of us that has verified the statement that to die is gain? Not one. [*Pretty safe question! Who among us has been dead?*] We know he walks in glory. He moves amid the majestic spaces where even Deity is not cramped. [*Eloquent or blasphemous, which?*] After all his struggles, he has entered into rest. Yet what has he received that is not in reserve for us? What has he that has not come to him in the way of gift? And is not his God mine and yours? Will the eternal Father feed with a partial hand? Will He discriminate, and become a respecter of persons, even at His own table? Piety can never receive into its mind the awful suspicion. Our Father feeds his children alike; and the garments that they wear are cut from a royal fabric, even His righteousness. They shine like suns brought by the action of a sublime movement into conjunction. Rise, then, my friends, ye people of His love; rise and climb with me the mighty stairway whose steps are changed from granite to porphyry, and from porphyry to jasper, as we ascend, until our feet, pure as itself, stand on the sea of crystal which stretches in seamless purity before the throne." [*Upstairs to the sea! And up three pair of stairs too! Sublime idea, or, at least, within a step of it.*]

This piece of high-flown oratory sheds light upon nothing, and does not in the faintest degree enable us to understand the reason why "to die is gain." The object of language of this kind is not to instruct the hearer, but to dazzle him, and if possible to impress him with the idea that his minister is a wonderful orator. He who condescends to use clap-trap of any kind deserves to be debarred the pulpit for the term of his natural life. Let your figures of speech really represent and explain your meaning, or else they are dumb idols, which ought not to be set up in the house of the Lord.

It may be well to note that *illustrations should not be too prominent*, or, to pursue our figure, they should not be painted windows, attracting attention to themselves rather than letting in the clear light of day. I am not pronouncing any judgment upon windows adorned with "glass of various colours which shine like meadows decked in the flowers of spring"; I am looking only to my illustration. Our figures are meant not so much to be seen as to be seen through. If you take the hearer's mind away from the subject by exciting his admiration of your own skill in imagery, you are doing evil rather than good. I saw in one of our exhibitions a portrait of a king; but the artist had surrounded his majesty with a bower of flowers so exquisitely painted that everyone's eye was taken away from the royal figure. All the resources of the painter's art had been lavished upon the accessories, and the result was that the portrait, which should have been all in all, had fallen into a secondary place. This was surely an error in portrait-painting, even though it might be a success in art. We have to set forth Christ before the people, "evidently crucified among them," and the loveliest emblem or the most charming image which calls the mind away from our divine subject is to be conscientiously foresworn. Jesus must be all in all: His gospel must be the beginning and end of all our discoursing; parable and poesy must be under His feet, and eloquence must wait upon Him as His servant. Never by any possibility must the minister's speech become a rival to his subject; that were to dishonour Christ, and not to glorify Him. Hence the caution that the illustrations be not too conspicuous.

Out of this last observation comes the further remark that *illustrations are best when they are natural, and grow out of the subject.* They should be like those well-arranged windows which are evidently part of the plan of a structure, and not inserted as an afterthought, or for mere adornment. The cathedral of Milan inspires my mind with extreme admiration; it always appears to me as if it must have grown out of the earth like a colossal tree or rather like a forest of marble. From its base to its loftiest pinnacle every detail is a natural outgrowth, a portion of a well developed whole, essential to the main idea; indeed, part and parcel of it. Such should a sermon be; its exordium, divisions, arguments, appeals, and metaphors should all spring out of itself; nothing should be out of living relation to the rest; it should seem as if nothing could be added without being an excrescence, and nothing taken away without inflicting damage. There should be flowers in a sermon, but the bulk of them should be the flowers of the soil; not dainty exotics, evidently imported with much care from a distant land, but the natural upspringing of a life natural to the holy ground on which the preacher stands. Figures of speech should be congruous with the matter of the discourse; a rose upon an oak would be out of place, a lily springing from a poplar would be unnatural: everything should be of a piece and have a manifest relationship to the rest. Occasionally a little barbaric splendour may be allowed after the manner of Thomas Adams and Jeremy Taylor and other masters in Israel, who adorn truth with rare gems, and gold of Ophir, fetched from far. Yet I would have you note what Dr. Hamilton says of Taylor, for it is a warning to those who aim at winning the ear of the multitude. "Thoughts, epithets, incidents, images came trooping round with irrepressible profusion, and they were all so apt and beautiful, that it was hard to send any of them away. And so he tried to find a place and use for all,—for 'flowers and wings of butterflies,' as well as 'wheat;'—and if he could not fabricate links of his logical chain out of 'the little rings of the vine,' and 'the locks of a new-weaned boy,' he could at least decorate his subject with exquisite adornments. The passages from his loved Austin and Chrysostom, and not less beloved Seneca and Plutarch, the scholar knows how to pardon. The squirrel is not more tempted to carry nuts to his hoard than the bookish author is tempted to transfer to his own pages fine passages from his favourite authors. Alas! he little knows how flat and meaningless they are to those who have not traversed the same walks, and shared the delight with which he found great spoil. To him each polished shell recalls its autumnal tale of woods, and groves, and sunshine showering through the yellow leaves; but to the quaint collection 'the general public' very much prefer a pint of filberts from a huckster's barrow." No illustrations are half so telling as those which are taken from familiar objects. Many fair flowers grow in foreign lands; but those are dearest to the heart which bloom at our own cottage door.

Elaboration into minute points is not commendable when we are using figures. The best light comes in through the clearest glass: too much paint keeps out the sun. God's altar of old was to be made of earth, or of unhewn stone, "for," said the word, "if thou lift up thy tool upon it, thou hast polluted it" (Ex. xx. 25). A laboured, artificial style, upon which the graver's tool has left abundant marks, is more consistent with human pleadings in courts of law, or in the forum, or in the senate, than with prophetic utterances delivered in the name of God and for the promotion of His glory. Our Lord's parables were as simple as tales for children, and as naturally beautiful as the lilies which sprang up in the valleys where he taught the people. He borrowed no legend from the Talmud, nor fairy tale from Persia, neither fetched he his emblems from beyond the sea; but he dwelt among his own people, and talked of common things in homely style, as never man spake before, and yet as any observant man should speak. His parables were like himself and his surroundings; and were never strained, fantastic, pedantic, or artificial. Let us imitate Him, for we shall never find a model more complete, or more suitable for the present age. Opening our eyes, we shall discover abundant imagery all around. As it is written, "The word is nigh thee," so also is the analogy of that word near at hand:

> "All things around me whate'er they be
> That I meet as the chance may come,
> Have a voice and a speech in them all—
> Birds that hover, and bees that hum,
> The beast of the field or the stall;
> The trees, leaves, rushes, and grasses;
> The rivulet running away;
> The bird of the air as it passes;
> Or the mountains that motionless stay,
> And yet those immovable masses
> Keep changing, as dreams do, all day." [1]

[1] Slightly altered from *Fables in Song.* By Robert Lord Lytton. William Blackwood and Sons. 1874. 2 vols.

There will be little need to borrow from the recondite mysteries of human art, nor to go deep into the theories of science; for in nature golden illustrations lie upon the surface, and the purest is that which is uppermost and most readily discerned. Of natural history in all its branches we may well say, "the gold of that land is good": the illustrations furnished by everyday phenomena seen by the plough-man and the waggoner are the very best which earth can yield. An illustration is not like a prophet, for it has most honour in its own country; and those who have oftenest seen the object are those who are most gratified by the figure drawn from it.

I trust that it is scarcely necessary to add that *illustrations must never be low or mean.* They may not be high-flown, but they should always be in good taste. They may be homely, and yet chastely beautiful; but rough and coarse they should never be. A house is dishonoured by having dirty windows, cobwebbed and begrimed, patched with brown paper, or stuffed up with rags: such windows are the insignia of a hovel rather than a house. About our illustrations there must never be even the slightest trace of anything that would shock the most delicate modesty. We like not that window out of which Jezebel is looking. Like the bells upon the horses, our lightest expressions must be holiness unto the Lord. Of that which suggests the grovelling and the base we may say with the apostle, "Let it not be once named among you, as becometh saints." All our windows should open towards Jerusalem, and none towards Sodom. We will gather our flowers always and only from Emmanuel's land; and Jesus Himself shall be their savour and sweetness, so that when He lingers at the lattice to hear us speak of Himself He may say "Thy lips, O my spouse, drop as the honeycomb: honey and milk are under thy tongue." That which grows beyond the border of purity and good repute must never be bound up in our garlands, nor placed among the decorations of our discourses. That which would be exceedingly clever and telling in a stump orator's speech, or in a cheap-jack's harangue, would be disgusting from a minister of the gospel. Time was when we could have found far too many specimens of censurable coarseness, but it would be ungenerous to mention them now that such things are on all hands condemned.

Gentlemen, take care that your windows are not broken, or even cracked: in other words, *guard against confused metaphors and limping illustrations.* Sir Boyle Roche is generally credited with some of the finest specimens of metaphorical conglomerate. We should imagine that the passage is mythical in which he is represented as saying, "I smell a rat; I see it floating in the air; I'll nip it in the bud." Minor blunderings are frequent enough in the speech of our own countrymen. An excellent temperance advocate exclaimed, "Comrades, let us be up and doing! Let us take our axes on our shoulders, and plough the

waste places till the good ship Temperance sails gaily over the land."
We well remember, years ago, hearing a fervent Irish clergyman
exclaim, "Garibaldi, sir, he is far too great a man to play second fiddle
to such a wretched luminary as Victor Emanuel." It was at a public
meeting, and therefore we were bound to be proper; but it would have
been a great relief to our soul if we might have indulged in a hearty
laugh at the spectacle of Garibaldi with a fiddle, playing to a luminary;
for a certain nursery rhyme jingled in our ears, and sorely tried our
gravity. A poetic friend thus encouragingly addresses us,—

> "March on, however rough the road,
>   Though foes obstruct thy way,
> Deaf to *the barking curs that would*
>   *Ensnare thy feet astray*."

The other evening a brother expressed his desire that we might "all
be winners of souls, and bring the Lord's blood-bought jewels to cast
their crowns at His feet." The words had such a pious ring about
them that the audience did not observe the fractured state of the
expression. One of your own number hoped "that every student might
be enabled to sound the gospel trumpet with such a clear and certain
sound *that the blind might see*." Perhaps he meant that they should
open their eyes with astonishment at the terrific blast; but the figure
would have been more congruous if he had said "that the deaf should
hear." A Scotch writer, in referring to a proposal to use an organ in
divine service, says : "Nothing will *stem this avalanche* of will-worship
and gross sin but the *falling back on the Word of God*."

The Daily News in reviewing a book written by an eminent Nonconformist minister, complained that his metaphors were apt to be a
little unmanageable, as when he spoke of something which had
remained a secret until a strangely potent key was inserted among
the hidden wards of the parental heart, and a rude wrench flung wide
the floodgates and set free the imprisoned stream. However, there is
no wonder that ordinary mortals commit blunders in figurative speech
when even his late Infallible Holiness Pius IX said of Mr. Gladstone
that he "had suddenly come forward like a viper assailing the barque
of St. Peter." A viper assailing a barque is rather too much for the
most accommodating imagination, although some minds are ready for
any marvels.

One of those reviews which reckon themselves to be the cream of
the cream took pains to inform us that the Dean of Chichester, being
the select preacher at St. Mary's, Oxford, "seized the opportunity to
smite the Ritualists hip and thigh, *with great volubility and vivacity*."
Samson smote his foes with a great slaughter; but language is flexible.

These blunders are to be quoted by the page : I have given enough
to let you see how readily the pitchers of metaphor may be cracked,

and rendered unfit to carry our meaning. The ablest speaker may occasionally err in this direction; it is not a very serious matter, and yet like a dead fly it may spoil sweet ointment. A few brethren of my acquaintance are always off the lines; they muddle up every figure they touch, and as soon as they approach a metaphor we look for an accident. It might be wisdom on their part to shun all figures of speech till they know how to use them; for it is a great pity when illustrations are so confused as both to darken the sense and create diversion. Muddled metaphors are muddles indeed; let us give the people good illustrations or none at all.

At this point I will close my lecture, which is only meant to be an introduction to my subject, and not a full treatment of it.

XXV

Anecdotes from the Pulpit

It is pretty generally admitted that sermons may wisely be adorned with a fair share of illustrations; but anecdotes used to that end are still regarded by the prudes of the pulpit with a measure of suspicion. They will come down low enough to quote an emblem, they will deign to use poetic imagery; but they cannot stoop to tell a simple, homely story. They would probably say in confidence to their younger brethren, "Beware how you lower yourselves and your sacred office by repeating anecdotes, which are best appreciated by the vulgar and uneducated." We would not retort by exhorting all men to abound in stories, for there ought to be discrimination. It is freely admitted that there are useful and admirable styles of oratory which would be disfigured by a rustic tale; and there are honoured brethren whose genius would never allow them to relate a story, for it would not appear suitable to their mode of thought. Upon these we would not even by implication hint at a censure; but when we are dealing with others who seem to be somewhat, and are not what they seem, we feel no tenderness; nay, we are even moved to assail their stilted greatness. If they sneer at anecdotes, we *smile* at them and their sneers, and wish them more sense and less starch. Affectation of intellectual superiority and love of rhetorical splendour have prevented many from setting forth gospel truth in the easiest imaginable manner, namely, by analogies drawn from common events. Because they could not condescend to men of low estate they have refrained from repeating incidents which would have accurately explained their meaning. Fearing to be thought vulgar, they have lost golden opportunities. As well might David have refused to sling one of the smooth stones at Goliath's brow because he found it in a common brook.

From individuals so lofty in their ideas nothing is likely to flow down to the masses of the people but a glacial eloquence,—a river of ice. Dignity is a most poor and despicable consideration unless it be the dignity of turning many to righteousness; and yet divines who have had scarcely enough of real dignity to save themselves from contempt, have swollen "huge as high Olympus" through the affectation of it. A young gentleman, after delivering an elaborate discourse, was told that not more than five or six in the congregation had been able to understand him. This he accepted as a tribute to his genius; but I take leave to place him in the same class with another person who was accustomed to shake his head in the most profound manner that he might make his prelections the more impressive, and this had some effect with the groundlings, until a shrewd Christian woman made the remark that he did shake his head certainly, but that *there was nothing in it.* Those who are too refined to be simple need to be refined again. Luther has well put it in his Table-Talk: "Cursed are all preachers that in the church aim at high and hard things; and neglecting the saving health of the poor unlearned people, seek their own honour and praise, and therefore try to please one or two great persons. *When I preach I sink myself deep down.*" It may be superfluous to remind you of the oft-quoted passage from George Herbert's *Country Parson,* and yet I cannot omit it, because it is so much to my mind: "The Parson also serves himself of the judgments of God, as of those of ancient times, so especially of the late ones; and those most which are nearest to his parish; for people are very attentive at such discourses, and think it behoves them to be so when God is so near them, and even over their heads. Sometimes he tells them stories and sayings of others, according as his text invites him; for them also men heed, and remember better than exhortations; which, though earnest, yet often die with the sermon, especially with country people, which are thick, and heavy, and hard to raise to a point of zeal and fervency, and need a mountain of fire to kindle them, but stories and sayings they will well remember."

It ought never to be forgotten that the great God Himself, when He would instruct men, employs histories and biographies. Our Bible contains doctrines, promises, and precepts; but these are not left alone, the whole book is vivified and illustrated by marvellous records of things said and done by God and by men. He who is taught of God values the sacred histories, and knows that in them there is a special fulness and forcibleness of instruction. Teachers of Scripture cannot do better than instruct their fellows after the manner of the Scriptures.

Our Lord Jesus Christ, the great teacher of teachers, did not disdain the use of anecdotes. To my mind it seems clear that certain of His parables were facts and, consequently, anecdotes. May not the story of the Prodigal Son have been a literal truth? Were there not actual instances of an enemy sowing tares among the wheat? May not the rich fool who said—"Take thine ease," have been a photograph taken from the life? Did not Dives and Lazarus actually figure on the stage of history? Certainly the story of those who were crushed by the fall of the tower of Siloam, and the sad tragedy of the Galilaeans, "whose blood Pilate had mingled with their sacrifices," were matters of current Jewish gossip, and our Lord turned both of them to good account. What HE did we need not be ashamed to do. That we may do it with all wisdom and prudence let us seek the guidance of the Divine Spirit which rested upon Him so continually.

I shall make up this present address by quoting the examples of great preachers, beginning with the era of the Reformation, and following on without any very rigid chronological order down to our own day. Examples are more powerful than precepts; hence I quote them.

First, let me mention that grand old preacher, *Hugh Latimer*, the most English of all our divines; and one whose influence over our land was undoubtedly most powerful. Southey says, "Latimer more than any other man promoted the Reformation by his preaching"; and in this he echoes the more important utterance of Ridley, who wrote from his prison, "I do think that the Lord hath placed old father Latimer to be his standard-bearer in our age and country against his mortal foe, Antichrist." If you have read any of his sermons, you must have been struck with the number of his quaint stories, seasoned with a homely humour which smacks of that Leicestershire farmhouse wherein he was brought up by a father who did yeoman's service, and a mother who milked thirty kine. No doubt we may attribute to these stories the breaking down of pews by the overwhelming rush of the people to hear him; and the general interest which his sermons excited. More of such preaching, and we should have less fear of the return of Popery. The common people heard him gladly, and his lively anecdotes accounted for much of their eager attention. A few of these narratives one could hardly repeat, for the taste of our age has happily improved in delicacy; but others are most admirable and instructive. Here are three of them:

THE FRIAR'S MAN AND THE TEN COMMANDMENTS

"I will tell you now a pretty story of a friar, to refresh you withal. A limiter of the grey friars in the time of his limitation preached many times, and had but one sermon at all times; which sermon was of the ten commandments. And because this friar had preached this sermon so often, one that heard it before told the friar's servant that his master was called 'Friar John Ten Commandments': wherefore the servant showed the friar his master thereof, and advised him to preach of some other matters; for it grieved the servant to hear his master derided. Now, the friar made answer saying, 'Belike, then, thou canst say the ten commandments well, seeing thou hast heard them so many a time.' 'Yea,' said the servant 'I warrant you.' 'Let me hear them,' saith the master; then he began,— 'Pride, covetousness, lechery,' and so numbered the deadly sins for the ten commandments. And so there be many at this time, which be weary of the old gospel; they would fain hear some new things: they think themselves so perfect in the old, when they be no more skilful than this servant was in his ten commandments."

ST. ANTHONY AND THE COBBLER

"We read a pretty story of St. Anthony, which, being in the wilderness, led there a very hard and straight life, insomuch as none at that time did the like. To whom came a voice from heaven, saying, 'Anthony, thou art not so perfect as is a cobbler that dwelleth at Alexandria.' Anthony, hearing this, rose up forthwith, and took his staff and went till he came to Alexandria, where he found the cobbler. The cobbler was astonished to see so reverend a father to come into his house. Then Anthony said unto him, 'Come and tell me thy whole conversation, and how thou spendest thy time.' 'Sir,' said the cobbler, 'as for me, good works I have none, for my life is but simple and slender; I am but a poor cobbler. In the morning, when I arise, I pray for the whole city wherein I dwell, specially for all such neighbours and poor friends as I have. After, I set me at my labour, where I spend the whole day in getting of my living, and keep me from all falsehood; for I hate nothing so much as I do deceitfulness: wherefore, when I make to any man a promise, I keep it and do it truly: and so spend my time poorly with my wife and children, whom I teach and instruct as far as my wit will serve me, to fear and dread God. This is the sum of my simple life.'

"In this story you see how God loveth those that follow their vocation, and live uprightly without any falsehood in their dealing. This Anthony was a great and holy man, yet this cobbler was as much esteemed before God as he."

THE DANGER OF PROSPERITY

"I read once a story of a good bishop, which rode by the way and was weary, being yet far off from any town; therefore seeing a fair house, he went thither, and was very well and honourably received: there were great preparations made for him, and a great banquet; all things were in plenty. Then the man of the house set out his prosperity, and told the bishop what riches he had, in what honours and dignities he was, how many fair children he had, what a virtuous wife God had provided for him, so that he had no lack of any manner of thing, he had no trouble nor vexations, neither outward nor inward. Now this holy man, hearing the good estate of that man, called one of his servants, and commanded him to make ready the horses: for the bishop thought that God was not in that house because there was no temptation there: he took his leave and went his ways. Now when he came a two or three mile off, he remembered his book which he had left behind him; he sent his man back again to fetch that book, and when the servant came again the house was sunken and all that was in it. Here it appeareth that it is a good thing to have temptation. This man thought himself a jolly fellow, because all things went well with him. But he knew not St. James's lesson: *Beatus qui suffert tentationem*, 'Blessed is he that endureth temptation.' Let us therefore learn here, not to be irksome when God layeth his cross upon us."

Let us take a long leap of about a century, and we come to *Jeremy Taylor*, another bishop, whom I mention immediately after *Latimer* because he is apparently such a contrast to that homely divine, while yet in very truth he has a measure of likeness to him as to the point now in hand. They both rejoiced in figure and metaphor, and equally delighted in incident and narrative. True, the one would talk of John and William, and the other of Anexagoras and Scipio; but actual scenes were the delight of each. In this respect Jeremy Taylor may be said to be Latimer turned into Latin. Jeremy Taylor is as full of classical allusions as a king's palace is full of rare treasures, and his language is of the lofty order which more becomes a patrician audience than a popular assembly; but when you come to the essence of things, you see that if Latimer is homely, so also Taylor narrates incidents which are *homely to him*; but his home is among philosophers of Greece and senators of Rome. This being understood, we venture to say that no one used more anecdotes than this splendid poet-preacher. His biographer truly says,—"It would be hard to point out a branch of learning or of scientific pursuit to which he does not occasionally allude; or any author of eminence, either ancient or modern, with whom he does not evince himself acquainted. He more than once refers to obscure stories in ancient writers, as if they were of necessity as familiar to all his readers as to himself; as for instance, he talks of 'poor Attillius Aviola,' and again of 'the Libyan lion that brake loose into his wilderness and killed two Roman boys.'" In all this he is eminently select and classical, and therefore I the more freely introduce him here; for there can be no reason why our anecdotes should all be rustic; we, too, may rifle the treasures of antiquity, and make the heathen contribute to the gospel, even as Hiram of Tyre served under Solomon's direction for the building of the temple of the Lord.

I am no admirer of Taylor's style in other respects, and his teaching seems to be at times semi-popish; but in this place I have only to deal with him upon one particular, and of that matter he is an admirable example. He lavishes classic stories even as an Asiatic queen bedecks herself with countless pearls. Out of a single sermon I extract the following, which may suffice for our purpose:

STUDENTS PROGRESSING BACKWARDS

"Menedemus was wont to say, 'that the young boys that went to Athens, the first year were wise men, the second year philosophers, the third orators, and the fourth were but plebeians, and understood nothing but their own ignorance.' And just so it happens to some in the progresses of religion; at first they are violent and active, and then they satiate all the appetites of religion; and that which is left is, that they were soon weary, and sat down in displeasure, and return to the world, and dwell in the business of pride or money; and, by this time, they understand that their religion is declined, and passed from the heats and follies of youth to the coldness and infirmities of old age."

THE PROUD MAN WHO BOASTED OF HIS HUMILITY

"He was noted for a vain person, who, being overjoyed for the cure (as he thought) of his pride, cried out to his wife, *'Cerne, Dionysia, deposui fastum;'* 'Behold, I have laid aside all my pride.'"

DIOGENES AND THE YOUNG MAN

"Diogenes once spied a young man coming out of a tavern or place of entertainment, who, perceiving himself observed by the philosopher, with some confusion stepped back again, that he might, if possible, preserve his fame with that severe person. But Diogenes told him, *Quanto magis intraveris, tanto magis eris in caupona:* 'The more you go back, the longer you are in the place where you are ashamed to be seen.' He that conceals his sin still retains that which he counts his shame and burden."

No examples will have greater weight with you than those taken from among the Puritans, in whose steps it is our desire to walk, though, alas! we follow with feeble feet. Certain of them abounded in anecdotes and stories: *Thomas Brooks* is a signal instance of the wise and wealthy use of holy fancy. I put him first, because I reckon him to be the first in the special art which is now under consideration. He hath dust of gold; for even in the margins of his books there are sentences of exceeding preciousness, and hints at classic stories. His style is clear and full; he never so exceeds in illustration as to lose sight of his doctrine. His floods of metaphor never drown his meaning, but float it upon their surface. If you have never read his works I almost envy you the joy of entering for the first time upon his *Unsearchable Riches*, trying his *Precious Remedies*, tasting his *Apples of Gold*, communing with his *Mute Christian*, and enjoying his other masterly writings. Let me give you a taste of his quality in the way of anecdotes. Here are a few brief ones which lie almost upon the same page; but he so abounds with them that you may readily cull scores of better ones for yourselves.

MR. WELCH WEEPING

"A soul under special manifestations of love weeps that it can love Christ no more. Mr. Welch, a Suffolk minister, weeping at table, and being asked the reason of it, answered, it was because he could love Christ no more. The true lovers of Christ can never rise high enough in their love to Christ; they count a little love to be no love; great love to be but little; strong love to be but weak; and the highest love to be infinitely below the worth of Christ, the beauty and glory of Christ, the fulness, sweetness, and goodness of Christ. The top of their misery in this life is, that they love so little, though they are so much beloved."

SUBMISSIVE SILENCE

"Such was the silence of Philip the Second, king of Spain, that when his invincible Armada, that had been three years a-fitting, was lost, he gave command that all over Spain they should give thanks to God and the saints that it was no more grievous."

FAVOURITES SUBMITTING TO THEIR LORDS

"When Tiribazus, a noble Persian, was arrested, at first he drew his sword and defended himself; but when they charged him in the king's name, and informed him that they came from the king, and were commanded to bring him to the king, he yielded willingly. Seneca persuaded his friend to bear his affliction quietly, because he was the emperor's favourite, telling him that it was not lawful for him to complain whilst Cæsar was his friend. So saith the holy Christian, Oh, my soul! be quiet, be still; all is in love, all is a fruit of Divine favour."

SIR PHILIP SIDNEY

"A religious commander being shot in battle, when the wound was searched and the bullet cut out, some standing by, pitying his pain, he replied, 'Though I groan, yet I bless God I do not grumble. God allows His people to groan, though not to grumble.'"

Thomas Adams, the Conforming Puritan, whose sermons are full of rugged force and profound meaning, never hesitated to insert a story when he felt that it would enforce his teaching. His starting-point is ever some Biblical sentence, or scriptural history; and this he works out with much elaboration, bringing to it all the treasures of his mind. As Stowell says, "Fables, anecdotes, classical poetry, gems from the fathers and other old writers, are scattered over almost every page." His anecdotes are usually rough-and-ready ones, and might be compared to those of Latimer, only they are not so genial; their humour is generally grim and caustic. The following may serve as fair specimens:

THE HUSBAND AND HIS WITTY WIFE

"The husband told his wife, that he had one ill quality, he was given to be angry without cause; she wittily replied, that she would keep him from that fault, for she would give him cause enough. It is the folly of some that they will be offended without cause, to whom the world promises that they shall have causes enough. 'In the world ye shall have tribulation.'"

THE SERVANT AT THE SERMON

"It is ordinary with many to commend the lecture to others' ears, but few commend it to their own hearts. It is morally true what the Christian Tell-truth relates: A servant coming from church, praiseth the sermon to his master. He asks him what was the text. Nay, quoth the servant, it was begun before I came in. What then was his conclusion? He answered, I came out before it was done. But what said he in the midst? Indeed I was asleep in the midst. Many crowd to get into the church, but make no room for the sermon to get into them."

THE PICTURE OF A HORSE

"One charged a painter to draw him *equum volitantem*, a trotting or prancing horse; and he (mistaking the word) drew him *equum volutantem*, a wallowing or tumbling horse, with his heels upward. Being brought home, and the bespeaker blaming his error; I would have him prancing, and you have made him tumbling. If that be all, quoth the painter, it is but turning the picture wrong side uppermost, and you have your desire. Thus in their quodlibetical discourses they can but turn the lineaments, and the matter is as they would have it. I speak not this to disgrace all their learning, but their fruitless, needless disputes and arguments, who find themselves a tongue, where the Scripture allows them none."

THE PIRATE

"As when the desperate pirate, ransacking and rifling a bottom, was told by the master, that though no law could touch him for the present, he should answer it at the day of judgment; replied, Nay, if I may stay so long ere I come to it, I will take thee and thy vessel too. A conceit wherewith too many land-thieves, oppressors, flatter themselves in their hearts, though they dare not utter it with their lips."

William Gurnall, the author of *The Christian in Complete Armour*, must surely have been a relater of pertinent stories in his sermons, since even in his set and solid writings they occur. Perhaps I need not have made the distinction between his writings and his preaching, for it appears from the preface that his *Christian in Complete Armour* was preached before it was printed. In vivid imagery every page of his famous book abounds, and whenever this is the case we are sure to light upon short narratives and striking incidents. He is as profuse in illustration as either Brooks, Watson, or Swinnock. Happy Lavenham to have been served by such a pastor! By the way, this *Complete Armour* is beyond all others a preacher's book: I should think that more discourses have been suggested by it than by any other uninspired volume. I have often resorted to it when my own fire has been burning low, and I have seldom failed to find a glowing coal upon Gurnall's hearth. John Newton said that if he might read only one book beside the Bible, he would choose *The Christian in Complete Armour,* and Cecil was of much the same opinion. J. C. Ryle has said of it, "You will often find in a line and a half some great truth, put so concisely, and yet so fully, that you really marvel how so much thought could be got into so few words." One or two stories from the early part of his great work must suffice for our purpose.

BIRD SAFE IN A MAN'S BOSOM

"A heathen could say, when a bird (feared by a hawk) flew into his bosom, 'I will not betray thee unto thine enemy, seeing thou comest for sanctuary unto me.' How much less will God yield up a soul unto its enemy, when it takes sanctuary in His Name, saying, 'Lord, I am hunted with such temptation, dogged with such a lust; either thou must pardon it, or I am damned; mortify it, or I shall be a slave to it; take me into the bosom of thy love for Christ's sake; castle me in the arms of thy ever-lasting strength; it is in thy power to save me from, or give me up into, the hands of my enemy: I have no confidence in myself or any other; into thy hands I commit my cause, my life, and rely on thee.' This dependence of a soul undoubtedly will awaken the almighty power of God for such a one's defence: He hath sworn the greatest oath that can come out of His blessed lips, even by Himself, that such as 'flee for refuge' to hope in Him shall have 'strong consolation': Hebrews vi. 17, 18."

THE PRINCE WITH HIS FAMILY IN DANGER

"Suppose a king's son should get out of a beseiged city, where he hath left his wife and children (whom he loves as his own soul), and these all ready to die by sword or famine, if supply come not the sooner; could this prince, when arrived at his father's house, please himself with the delights of the court, and forget the distress of his family? or rather would he not come post to his father (having their cries and groans always in his ears), and, before he ate or drank, do his errand to his father, and entreat him, if ever he loved him, that he would send all the force of his kingdom to raise the siege, rather than any of his dear relations should perish? Surely, sirs, though Christ be in the top of His preferment, and out of the storm in regard of His own person, yet His children, left behind in the midst of sin's, Satan's, and the world's batteries, are in His heart, and shall not be forgotten a moment by Him. The care He takes in our business appeared in the speedy despatch He made of His Spirit to His apostles' supply, which, as soon as He was warm in His seat at His Father's right hand, He sent, to the incomparable comfort of His apostles and us that to this day, yea, to the end of the world, do or shall believe on Him."

JOHN CARELESS

"When God honours a person to suffer for His truth, this is a great privilege: 'Unto you it is given not only to believe, but to suffer for His sake.' God doth not use to give worthless gifts to His saints, there is some preciousness in it which a carnal eye cannot see. Faith, you will say, is a great gift; but perseverance greater, without which faith would be little worth, and perseverance in suffering is above both honourable. This made *John Careless,* an English martyr (who though he died not at the stake, yet in prison for Christ), say, 'Such an honour 'tis as angels are not permitted to have; therefore, God forgive me mine unthankfulness.'"

MR. BENBRIDGE

"Oh, how many die at the gallows as martyrs in the devil's cause for felonies, rapes, and murders! He might withdraw His grace, and leave thee to thy own cowardice and unbelief, and then thou wouldst soon show thyself in thy colours. The stoutest champions for Christ have been taught how weak they are if Christ steps aside. Some that have given great testimony of their faith and resolution in Christ's cause, even to come so near dying for His name as to give themselves to be bound to the stake, and fire to be kindled upon them, yet their hearts have failed; as that holy man, Mr. Benbridge, who in our English martyrology, who thrust the faggots from him, and cried out, *'I recant, I recant!'* Yet this man, when reinforced in his faith, and indued with power from above, was able within the space of a week after that sad foil, to die at the stake cheerfully. He that once overcame death for us, 'tis He that always overcame death in us."

John Flavel is a name which I shall have to quote in another lecture, for he is greatest in metaphor and allegory; but in the matter of anecdote his preaching is a fine example. It was said of his ministry that he who was unaffected by it must either have had a very soft head or a very hard heart. He had a fund of striking incidents, and a faculty of happy illustration, and as he was a man in whose manner cheerfulness was blended with solemnity, he was popular in the highest degree both at home and abroad. He sought out words which might suit the sailors of Dartmouth and farmers of Devon, and therefore he has left behind him his *Navigation Spiritualized,* and his *Husbandry Spiritualized,* a legacy for each of the two orders of men who plough the sea and the land. He was a man worth making a pilgrimage to hear. What a crime it was to silence his heaven-touched lips by the abominable Act of Uniformity! Instead of quoting several passages from his sermons, each one containing an anecdote, I have thought it as well to give a mass of stories as we find them in his prelections upon :

PROVIDENCE IN CONVERSION

"A scrap of paper accidentally coming to view hath been used as an occasion of conversion. This was the case of a minister of Wales, who had two livings, but took little care of either. He being at a fair, bought something at a pedlar's standing, and rent off a leaf of Mr. Perkin's catechism to wrap it in; and reading a line or two of it, God sent it home so as it did the work."

"The marriage of a godly man into a carnal family hath been ordered by Providence for the conversion and salvation of many therein. Thus we read, in the life of that renowned English worthy, Mr. John Bruen, that, in his second match, it was agreed that he should have one year's diet in his mother-in-law's house. During his abode there that year (saith Mr. Clark) the Lord was pleased by his means graciously to work upon her soul, as also upon his wife's sister, and half-sister, their brothers, Mr. William and Mr. Thomas Fox, with one or two of the servants in that family."

"Not only the reading of a book, or hearing of a minister, but (which is most remarkable) the very mistake of forgetfulness of a minister hath been improved by Providence for this end and purpose. Augustine, once preaching to his congregation, forgot the argument which he first proposed, and fell upon the errors of the Manichees, beside his first intention; by which discourse he converted one Firmus, his auditor, who fell down at his feet weeping, and confessing he had lived a Manichee many years. Another I knew, who, going to preach, took up another Bible than that he had designed, in which, not only missing his notes, but the chapter also in which his text lay, was put to some loss thereby; but after a short pause he resolved to speak to any other Scripture that might be presented to him, and accordingly read the text, 'The Lord is not slack concerning his promise' (2 Pet. iii. 9); and though he had nothing prepared, yet the Lord helped him to speak both methodically and pertinently from it; by which discourse a gracious change was wrought upon one in the congregation, who hath since given good evidence of a sound conversion, and acknowledged this sermon to be the first and only means thereof."

"Going to hear a sermon in *jest* hath proved some men's conversion in *earnest*. Mr. Firmin, in his *Real Christian*, tells us of a notorious drunkard, whom the drunkards called 'Father,' that one day would needs go to hear what Wilson said, out of no other design, it seems, but to scoff at the holy man; but in the prayer before sermon, his heart began to thaw, and when he read his text, which was, 'Sin no more, lest a worse thing come unto thee' (John v. 14), he could not contain; and in that sermon the Lord changed his heart, though formerly so bitter an enemy that the minister on lecture-days was afraid to go to church before his shop door. 'Lo, these are parts of his ways; but how little a portion is heard of him?'"

George Swinnock, for some years chaplain to Hampden, had the gift of illustration largely developed, as his works prove. Some of his similes are far-fetched, and the growth of knowledge has rendered certain of them obsolete; but they served his purpose, and made his teaching attractive. After deducting all his fancies, which in the present age would be judged to be strained, there remains "a rare amount of sanctified wit and wisdom"; and sparkling here and there we spy out a few telling stories, mostly of classic origin:

THE PRAYER OF PAULINUS

"It was the speech of Paulinus, when his city was taken by the barbarians, *Domine, ne excrucier ob aurem et argentum:* 'Lord, let me not be troubled for my silver and gold which I have lost, for thou art all things.' As Noah, when the whole world was overwhelmed with water, had a fair epitome of it in the ark, having all sorts of beasts and fowls there; so he that in a deluge hath God to be his God, hath the original of all mercies. He who enjoyeth the ocean may rejoice, though some drops are taken from him."

QUEEN ELIZABETH AND THE MILKMAID

"Queen Elizabeth envied the milkmaid when she was in prison; but had she known the glorious reign which she was to have for forty-four years, she would not have repined at the poor happiness of so mean a person. Christians are too prone to envy the husks which wandering sinners fill themselves with here below; but would they set before them their glorious hopes of a heaven, how they must reign with Christ for ever and ever, they would see little reason for their repining."

THE BELIEVING CHILD

"I have read a story of a little child about eight or nine years old, that being extremely pinched with hunger, looked one day pitifully necessitous on her mother, and said, 'Mother, do you think that God will starve us?' The mother answered, 'No, child, He will not.' The child replied, 'But if He do, yet we must love Him and serve Him.' Here was language that spake a well-grown Christian. For indeed God brings us to want and misery, to try us whether we love Him for His own sake, or for our own sakes; for those excellencies that are in Him, or for those mercies we have from Him; to see whether we will say with the cynic to Antisthenes, *Nullus tam darus erit baculus,* etc. 'There should be no cudgel so crabbed as to beat me from thee.'"

FASHIONABLE RELIGION

"I have read of a popish lady in Paris, that when she saw a glorious procession to one of their saints, cried out, 'Oh, how fine is our religion beyond that of the Hugenots!—they have a mean and beggarly religion, but ours is full of bravery and solemnity.' But as heralds say of a coat of arms, if it be full of gays and devices, it speaks a mean descent; so truly that manner of worship which is mingled with men's inventions speaks its descent to be mean—namely, from man."

THE BUSY DUKE

"The French Duc d'Alva could say, when he was asked by Henry the Fourth whether he had seen the eclipse of the sun, that he had so much

business to do upon earth, that he had no time to look up to heaven.
Sure I am, the Christian may say with more truth and conscience, that
he hath so much business to do for heaven, that he hath no time to mind
vain or earthly things."

Thomas Watson was one of the many Puritan preachers who won
the popular ear by their frequent illustrations. In the clear flowing
stream of his teaching we find pearls of anecdote very frequently.
No one ever grew weary under such pleasant yet weighty discourse
as that which we find in his *Beatitudes.* Let two quotations serve to
show his skill.

THE VESTAL AND THE BRACELETS

"Most men think because God hath blessed them with an estate, therefore they are blessed. Alas! God often gives these things in anger. He
loads His enemies with gold and silver; as Plutarch reports of Tarpeia,
a Vestal nun, who bargained with the enemy to betray the Capitol of
Rome to them, in case she might have the golden bracelets on their left
hands, which they promised; and being entered into the Capitol, they
threw not only their bracelets, but their bucklers, too, upon her, through
the weight thereof she was pressed to death. God often lets men have
the golden bracelets of worldly substance, the weight whereof sinks them
into hell. Oh, let us *superna anhelare,* get our eyes 'fixed' and our hearts
'united' to God the supreme good; this is to pursue blessedness as in a
chase."

HEDGEHOG AND CONIES

"The Fabulist tells a story of the hedgehog that came to the cony-
burrows in stormy weather, and desired harbour, promising that he would
be a quiet guest; but when once he had gotten entertainment, he did set
up his prickles, and did never leave till he had thrust the poor conies out
of their burrows: so covetousness, though it hath many fair pleas to
insinuate and wind itself into the heart, yet as soon as you have let it in,
this thorn will never cease pricking till it hath choked all good beginnings,
and thrust all religion out of your hearts."

I think this must suffice to represent the men of the Puritanic period,
who added to their profound theology and varied learning a zeal to
be understood, and a skill in setting forth truth by the help of every-
day occurrences. The age which followed them was barren of spiritual
life, and was afflicted by a race of rhetorical divines, whose words had
little connection with *the Word* of life. The scanty thought of the
Queen Anne dignitaries needed no aid of metaphor or parable: there
was nothing to explain to the people; the utmost endeavour of these
divines was to hide the nakedness of their discourses with the fig-
leaves of Latinized verbiage. Living preaching was gone, spiritual
life was gone, and consequently a pulpit was set up which had no
voice for the common people; no voice, indeed, for anybody except

the mere formalist, who is content if decorum be observed and respectability maintained. Of course, our notion of making truth clear by stories did not suit the dignified death of the period, and it was only when the dry bones began to be stirred that the popular method was again brought to the front.

The illustrious *George Whitefield* stands, with Wesley, at the head of that noble army who led the Revival of the last century. It is not at this present any part of my plan to speak of his matchless eloquence, unquenchable earnestness, and incessant labour; but it is quite according to the run of my lecture to remind you of his own saying,—"I use market language." He employed pure, good, flowing English; but he was as simple as if he spoke to children. Although by no means abounding in illustration, yet he always employed it when needed, and he narrated incidents with great power of action and emphasis. His stories were so told that they thrilled the people : they saw as well as heard, for each word had its proper gesture. One reason why he could be understood at so great a distance was the fact that the eye helped the ear. As specimens of his anecdotes I have selected these which follow :

THE TWO CHAPLAINS

"You cannot do without the grace of God when you come to die. There was a nobleman that kept a deistical chaplain, and his lady a Christian one; when he was dying, he says to his chaplain,—'I liked you very well when I was in health; but it is my lady's chaplain I must have when I am sick.'"

NEVER SATISFIED

"My dear hearers, there is not a single soul of you all that are satisfied in your stations : is not the language of your hearts when apprentices, We think we shall do very well when journeymen; when journeymen, that we should do very well when masters; when single, that we shall do well when married; and to be sure you think you shall do well when you keep a carriage. I have heard of one who began low : he first wanted a house; then, says he, 'I want two, then four, then six'; and when he had them, he said, 'I think I want nothing else.' 'Yes,' says his friend, 'you will soon want another thing, that is, a hearse-and-six to carry you to your grave'; and that made him tremble."

DR. MANTON'S HEART

"A good woman, who was charmed with Dr. Manton, said, 'Oh, sir, you have made an excellent sermon to-day; I wish I had your heart.' 'Do you so?' said he, 'good woman; you had better not wish for it; for if you had it, you would wish for your own again.' The best of men see themselves in the worst light."

Fearing that the quotation of any more examples might prove tedious, I would only remind you that such men as Berridge, Rowland

Hill, Matthew Wilks, Christmas Evans, William Jay, and others who have but lately departed from us, owed much of their attractiveness to the way in which they aroused their audiences, and flashed truth into their faces by well-chosen anecdotes. Time calls upon me to have done, and how can I come to a better close than by mentioning one living man, who, above all others, has in two continents stirred the masses of the people?—I refer to D. L. Moody. This admirable brother has a great aversion to the printing of his sermons; and well he may have, for he is incessantly preaching, and has no time allowed him for preparation of fresh discourses; and therefore it would be great unwisdom on his part to print at once those addresses with which he is working through a campaign. We hope, however, that when he has done with a sermon he will never suffer it to die out, but give it to the church and to the world through the press. Our esteemed brother has a lively, telling style, and he thinks it wise frequently to fasten a nail with the hammer of anecdote. Here are four or five extracts from the little book entitled *Arrows and Anecdotes by D. L. Moody,* by John Lobb:

THE IDIOT'S MOTHER

"I know a mother who has an idiot child. For it she gave up all society, almost everything, and devoted her whole life to it. 'And now,' said she, 'for fourteen years I have tended it and loved it, and it does not even know me. Oh! it is breaking my heart!' Oh! how the Lord must say this of hundreds here! Jesus comes here, and goes from seat to seat, asking if there is a place for Him. Oh! will not some of you take Him into your hearts?"

SURGEON AND PATIENT

"When I was in Belfast I knew a doctor who had a friend, a leading surgeon there, and he told me that the surgeon's custom was, before performing any operation, to say to the patient: 'Take a good look at the wound, and then fix your eyes on me, and don't take them off till I get through the operation.' I thought at the time that was a good illustration. Sinner, take a good look at the wound to-night, and then fix your eyes on Christ, and don't take them off. It is better to look at the remedy than at the wound."

THE ORPHAN'S PRAYER

"A little child, whose father and mother had died, was taken into another family. The first night she asked if she could pray as she used to do. They said, 'Oh, yes.' So she knelt down, and prayed as her mother had taught her; and, when that was ended, she added a little prayer of her own: 'Oh, God, make these people as kind to me as father and mother were.' Then she paused, and looked up, as if expecting the answer, and added: 'Of course He will.' How sweetly simple was that little one's faith! She expected God to 'do,' and, of course, she got her request."

THE ROLL-CALL

"A soldier lay on his dying couch during our last war, and they heard him say, 'Here!' They asked him what he wanted, and he put up his hand and said: 'Hush! they are calling the roll of heaven, and I am answering to my name'; and presently he whispered: 'Here!' and he was gone."

NO HOME BEYOND THE GRAVE

"I have been told of a wealthy man who died recently. Death came unexpectedly to him, as it almost always does; and he sent out for his lawyer to draw his will. And he went on willing away his property; and when he came to his wife and child, he said he wanted them to have the home. But the little child didn't understand what death was. She was standing near, and she said, 'Papa, have you got a home in that land you are going to?' The arrow reached that heart; but it was too late. He saw his mistake. He had got no home beyond the grave."

I will weary you no longer. You may safely do what the most useful of men have done before you. Copy them not only in their use of illustration, but in their wisely keeping it in subservience to their design. They were not story-tellers, but preachers of the gospel; they did not aim at the entertainment of the people, but at their conversion. Never did they go out of their way to drag in a telling bit which they had been saving up for display, and never could anyone say of their illustrations that they were

> "Windows that exclude the light,
> And passages that lead to nothing."

Keep you the due proportion of things lest I do worse than lose my labour, by becoming the cause of your presenting to the people strings of anecdotes instead of sound doctrines, for that would be as evil a thing as if you offered to hungry men flowers instead of bread, and gave to the naked gauze of gossamer instead of woollen cloth.

XXVI

The Uses of Anecdotes and Illustrations

THE USES of anecdotes and illustrations are manifold; but we may reduce them to seven, so far as our present purposes are concerned, not for a moment imagining that this will be a complete list.

We use them, first, *to interest the mind and secure the attention of our hearers.* We cannot endure a sleepy audience. To us, a slumbering man is no man. Sydney Smith observed that, although Eve was taken out of the side of Adam while he was asleep, it was not possible to remove sin from men's hearts in that manner. We do not agree with Hodge, the hedger and ditcher, who remarked to a Christian man with whom he was talking, "I loikes Sunday, I does; I loikes Sunday." "And what makes you like Sunday?" "'Cause, you see, it's a day of rest; I goes down to the old church, I gets into a pew, and puts my legs up, and I thinks o' nothin'." It is to be feared that in town as well as in country this thinking of nothing is a very usual thing. But your regard for the sacred day, and the ministry to which you are called, and the worshipping assembly, will not allow you to give your people the chance of thinking of nothing. You want to arouse every faculty in them to receive the Word of God, that it may be a blessing to them.

We want to win attention at the commencement of the service, and to hold it till the close. With this aim, many methods may be tried; but possibly none will succeed better than the introduction of an interesting story. This sets Hodge listening, and although he will miss the fresh air of the fields, and begin to feel drowsy in your stuffy chapel, another tale will stir him to renewed attention. If he hears some narrative in connection with his village or county, you will have him "all there," and you may then hope to do him good.

The anecdote in the sermon answers the purpose of an engraving in a book. Everybody knows that people are attracted by volumes with pictures in them; and that, when a child gets a book, although it may pass over the letterpress without observation, it is quite sure to pause over the woodcuts. Let us not be too great to use a method which many have found successful. We must have attention. In some audiences, we cannot get it if we begin with solid instruction; they are not desirous of being taught, and consequently they are not in a condition to receive the truth if we set it before them nakedly.

Now for a bunch of flowers to attract these people to our table, for afterwards we can feed them with the food they so much need. Just as the Salvation Army goes trumpeting and drumming through the streets to draw the people into the barracks, so may an earnest man spend the first few minutes with an unprepared congregation in waking the folks up, and enticing them to enter the inner chamber of the truth. Even this awakening prelude must have in it that which is worthy of the occasion; but if it is not up to your usual average in weight of doctrine, it may not only be excused, but commended, if it prepares the audience to receive that which is to follow. Ground-bait may catch no fish; but it answers its purpose if it brings them near the bait and the hook.

A congregation which has been well instructed, and is mainly made up of established believers, will not need to be addressed in the same style as an audience gathered fresh from the world, or a meeting of dull, formal churchgoers. Your common-sense will teach you to suit your manner to your audience. It is possible to maintain profound and long-continued attention without the use of an illustration; I have frequently done so in the Tabernacle when it has been mainly filled with church-members; but when my own people are away, and strangers fill their places, I bring out all my store of stories, similes, and parables.

I have sometimes told anecdotes in the pulpit, and very delicate and particular people have expressed their regret and horror that I should say such things; but when I have found that God has blessed some of the illustrations I have used, I have often thought of the story of the man with a halbert, who was attacked by a nobleman's dog, and, of course, in defending himself, he killed the animal. The nobleman was very angry, and asked the man how he dared to kill the dog; and the man replied that, if he had not killed it, the dog would have bitten him, and torn him in pieces. "Well," said the nobleman, "but you should not have struck it on the head with the halbert; why did you not hit it with the handle?" "My lord," answered the man, "so I would if it had tried to bite me with its tail." So, when I have to deal with sin, some people say, "Why don't you address it delicately? Why don't you speak to it in courtly language?" And I answer, "So I would if it would bite me with its tail; but as long as ever I find that it deals roughly with me, I will deal roughly with it; and any kind of weapon that will help to slay the monster, I shall not find unfitted to my hand."

We cannot afford, in these days, to lose any opportunity of getting hold of the public ear. We must use every occasion that comes in our way, and every tool that is likely to help us in our work; and we must rouse up all our faculties, and put forth all our energies, if that by any means we may get the people to heed that which they are so slow to regard, the great story of righteousness, temperance, and judgment to come. We shall need to read much, and to study hard, or else we shall not be able to influence our day and generation for good. I believe that the greatest industry is necessary to make a thoroughly efficient preacher, and the best natural ability, too; and it is my firm conviction that, when you have the best natural ability, you must supplement it with the greatest imaginable industry if you are really to do much service for God among this crooked and perverse generation.

The fool in Scotland, who got into the pulpit before the preacher arrived, was requested by the minister to come down. "Nay, nay," answered the man, "you come up, too, for it will take both of us to move this stiff-necked generation." It will certainly take all the wisdom that we can obtain to move the people among whom our lot is cast; and if we do not use every lawful means of interesting the minds of our hearers, we shall find that they will be like a certain other congregation, in which the people were all asleep except one poor idiot. The minister, woke them up, and tried to reprove them by saying, "There, you were all asleep except poor Jock the idiot"; but his rebuke was cut short by Jock, who exclaimed, "And if I had not been an idiot, I should have been asleep, too."

I will leave the moral of that well-known story to speak for itself, and will pass on to my second point, which is, that the use of anecdotes and illustrations *renders our preaching life-like and vivid*. This is a most important matter. Of all things that we have to avoid, one of the most essential is that of giving our people the idea, when we are preaching, that we are acting a part. Everything theatrical in the pulpit, either in tone, manner, or anything else, I loathe from my very soul. Just go into the pulpit, and talk to the people as you would in the kitchen, or the drawing-room, and say what you have to tell them in your ordinary tone of voice. Let me conjure you, by everything that is good, to throw away all stilted styles of speech, and anything approaching affectation. Nothing can succeed with the masses except naturalness and simplicity. Why, some ministers cannot even give out a hymn in a natural manner! "Let us sing to the praise and glory of God," [spoken in the tone that is sometimes heard in churches or chapels]—who would ever think of speaking like that at the tea-table? "I shall be greatly obliged if you will kindly give me another cup of tea," [spoken in the same unnatural way]—you would never think of giving any tea to a man who talked like that; and if we preach in that stupid style, the people will not believe what we say; they will think it is our business, our occupation, and that we are doing the whole thing in a professional manner. We must shake off professionalism of every kind, as Paul shook off the viper into the fire;

and we must speak as God has ordained that we should speak, and not by any strange, out-of-the-way, new-fangled method of pulpit oratory.

Our Lord's teaching was amazingly life-like and vivid; it was the setting out of truth before the eye, not as a flat picture, but as in a stereoscope, making it stand up, with all its lines and angles of beauty in life-like reality. That was a fine living sermon when he took a little child, and set him in the midst of the disciples; and that was another powerful discourse when he preached about abstaining from carking cares, and stooped down, and plucked a lily (as I suppose he did) and said, "Consider the lilies of the field, how they grow; they toil not, neither do they spin." I can readily suppose that some ravens were flying just over his head, and that he pointed to them, and said, "Consider the ravens; for they neither sow nor reap; which neither have storehouse nor barn; and God feedeth them." There was a life-likeness, you see, a vividness, about the whole thing. We cannot always literally imitate our Lord, as we have mostly to preach in places of worship. It is a blessing that we have so many houses of prayer, and I thank God that there are so many of them springing up all around us; yet I should praise the Lord still more if half the ministers, who preach in our various buildings, were made to turn out of them, and to speak for their Master in the highways, and byways, and anywhere that the people would go to listen to them. We are to go out into all the world, and preach the gospel to every creature, not to stop in our chapels waiting for every creature to come in to hear what we have to say. A sportsman, who should sit at his parlour window, with his gun loaded all ready for shooting partridges, would probably not make up a very heavy bag of game. No, he must put on his buskins, and tramp off over the fields, and then he will get a shot at the birds he is seeking. So must we do, brethren, we must always have our buskins ready for field work, and be ever on the watch for opportunities of going out among the souls of men, that we may bring them back as trophies of the power of the gospel we have to proclaim.

It might not be wise for us to try to make our sermons life-like and vivid in the style in which quaint old Matthew Wilks sometimes did; as when, one Sabbath morning, he took into the pulpit a little box, and after a while opened it, and displayed to the congregation a small pair of scales, and then, turning over the leaves of the Bible with great deliberation, held up the balances, and announced as his text, "Thou art weighed in the balances, and art found wanting." I think, however, that was puerile rather than powerful. I like Matthew Wilks better when, on another occasion, his text being, "See that ye walk circumspectly," he commenced by saying, "Did you ever see a tom cat walking on the top of a high wall that was covered with bits of broken glass bottles? If so, you had just then an accurate illustration

of what is meant by the injunction, 'See that ye walk circumspectly.'"
There is the case, too, of good "Father Taylor", who, preaching in
the streets in one of the towns of California, stood on the top of a
whisky-barrel. By way of illustration, he stamped his foot on the
cask, and said, "This barrel is like man's heart, full of evil stuff; and
there are some people who say that, if sin is within you, it may just
as well come out." "No," said the speaker, "it is not so; now here is
this whisky that is in the barrel under my foot; it is a bad thing, it is
a damnable thing, it is a devilish thing, but as long as it is kept tightly
bunged up in the barrel, it certainly will not do the hurt that it will
if it is taken over to the liquor-bar, and sold out to the drunkards of
the neighbourhood, sending them home to beat their wives, or kill
their children. So, if you keep your sins in your own heart, they will
be evil and devilish, and God will damn you for them; but they will
not do so much hurt to other people, at any rate, as if they are seen
in public." Stamping his foot again on the barrel, the preacher said,
"Suppose you try to pass this cask over the boundaries of the country,
and the custom-house officer comes, and demands the duty upon its
contents. You say that you will not let any of the whisky get out;
but the officer tells you that he cannot allow it to pass. So, if it were
possible for us to abstain from outward sin, yet, since the heart is
full of all manner of evil, it would be impossible for us to pass the
frontiers of heaven, and to be found in that holy and happy place."
That I thought to be somewhat of a life-like illustration, and a
capital way of teaching truth, although I should not like always to
have a whisky-barrel for a pulpit, for fear the head might fall in, and
I might fall in, too.

I should not recommend any of you to be so life-like in your
ministry as that notable French priest, who, addressing his congregation, said, "As to the Magdalenes, and those who commit the sins of
the flesh, such persons are very common; they abound even in this
church; and I am going to throw this mass-book at a woman who is
a Magdalene," whereupon all the women in the place bent down their
heads. So the priest said, "No, surely, you are not all Magdalenes; I
hardly thought that was the case; but you see how your sin finds you
out!" Nor should I even recommend you to follow the example of
the clergyman, who, when a collection was to be made for lighting
and warming the church, after he had preached some time, blew out
the candles on both sides of the pulpit, saying that the collection was
for the lights and the fires, and he did not require any light, for he
did not read his sermon, "but," he added, "when Roger gives out
the Psalm presently, you will want a light to see your books; so the
candles are for yourselves. And as for the stove, I do not need its
heat, for my exercise in preaching is sufficient to keep me warm;
therefore you see that the collection is wholly for yourselves on this

occasion. Nobody can say that the clergy are collecting for themselves this time, for on this Sunday it is wholly for your own selves." I thought the man was a fool for making such remarks, though I find that his conduct has been referred to as being a very excellent instance of boldness in preaching.

There is a story told about myself, which, like very many of the tales told about me, is a *story* in two senses. It is said that, in order to show the way in which men backslide, I once slid down the banisters of the pulpit. I only mention this, in passing, because it is a remarkable fact that, at the time the story was told, my pulpit was fixed in the wall, and there was no banister, so that the reverend fool (which he would have been if he had done what people said) could not have performed the antic if he had been inclined to attempt it. But the anecdote, although it is not true, serves all the purposes of the life-likeness I have tried to describe.

You probably recollect the instance of Whitefield depicting the blind man, with his dog, walking on the brink of a precipice, and his foot almost slipping over the edge. The preacher's description was so graphic, and the illustration so vivid and life-like, that Lord Chesterfield sprang up, and exclaimed, "Good God! he's gone!" but Whitefield answered, "No, my lord, he is not quite gone; let us hope that he may yet be saved." Then he went on to speak of the blind man as being led by his reason, which is only like a dog, showing that a man led only by reason is ready to fall into hell. How vividly one would see the love of money set forth in the story told by our venerable friend, Mr. Rogers, of a man who, when he lay a-dying, would put his money in his mouth because he loved it so, and wanted to take some of it with him! How strikingly is the non-utility of worldly wealth, as a comfort to us in our last days, brought before us by the narrative in which good Jeremiah Burroughes speaks of a miser who had his money bags laid near his hand on his dying bed! He kept taking them up, and saying, "Must I leave you? Must I leave you? Have I lived all these years for you, and now must I leave you?" And so he died. There is a tale told of another, who had many pains in his death, and especially the great pain of a disturbed conscience. He also had his money bags brought, one by one, with his mortgages, and bonds, and deeds, and putting them near his heart, he sighed, and said, "These won't do; these won't do; these won't do; take them away! What poor things they all are when I most need comfort in my dying moments!"

How distinctly love to Christ is brought out in the story of John Lambert, fastened to the stake, and burning to death, yet clapping his hands as he was burning, and crying out, "None but Christ! None but Christ!" until his nether extremities were burned, and he fell from the chains into the fire, still exclaiming in the midst of the flames. "None but Christ! None but Christ!" How clearly the truth stands out before you when you hear such stories as these! You can realize it almost as well as if the incident happened before your eyes. How well you can see the folly of misunderstanding between Christians in Mr. Jay's story of two men who were walking from opposite directions on a foggy night! Each saw what he thought was a terrible monster moving towards him, and making his heart beat with terror; as they came nearer to each other, they found that the dreadful monsters were brothers. So, men of different denominations are often afraid of one another; but when they get close to each other, and know each other's hearts, they find out that they are brethren after all. The story of the negro and his master well illustrates the need of beginning at the beginning in heavenly things, and not meddling with the deeper points of our holy religion till we have learned its elements thoroughly. A poor negro was labouring hard to bring his master to a knowledge of the truth, and was urging him to exercise faith in Christ, when he excused himself because he could not understand the doctrine of election. "Ah! Massa," said the negro, "don't you know what comes before de Epistle to de Romans? You must read de Book de right way; de doctrine ob election is in Romans, and dere is Matthew, Mark, Luke, and John, first. You are only in Matthew yet; dat is about repentance; and when you get to John, you will read where de Lord Jesus Christ said dat God so loved de world, dat he gave his only begotten Son, dat whosoever believeth in him should not perish, but hab everlasting life." So, brethren, you can say to your hearers, "You will do better by reading the four Gospels first than by beginning to read in Romans; first study Matthew, Mark, Luke, and John, and then you can go on to the Epistles."

But I must not keep on giving you illustrations, because so many will suggest themselves. I have given you sufficient to show that they do make our preaching vivid and life-like; therefore, the more you have of them, the better. At the same time, gentlemen, I must warn you against the danger of having too many anecdotes in any one sermon. You ought, perhaps, to have a dish of salad on the table; but if you ask your friends to dinner, and give them nothing but salad, they will not fare very well, and will not care to come to your house again.

Thirdly, anecdotes and illustrations may be used *to explain either doctrines or duties to dull understandings*. They may, in fact, be the very best form of exposition. A preacher should instance, and illustrate, and exemplify his subject, so that his hearers may have real acquaintance with the matter he is bringing before them. If a man attempted to give me a description of a piece of machinery, he would possibly fail to make me comprehend what it was like; but if he will have the goodness to let me see a drawing of the various sections, and then of the whole machine, I will, somehow or other, by hook or by crook, make out how it works. The pictorial representation of a thing is always a much more powerful means of instruction than any mere verbal description ever could be. It is just in this way that anecdotes and illustrations are so helpful to our hearers. For instance, take this anecdote as illustrating the text, "Thou, when thou prayest, enter into thy closet, and when thou hast shut thy door, pray to thy Father which is in secret." A little boy used to go up into a hay-loft to pray; but he found that, sometimes, persons came up, and disturbed him; therefore, the next time he climbed into the loft, he pulled the ladder up after him. Telling this story, you might explain how the boy thus entered into his closet, and shut the door. The meaning is not so much the literal entrance into a closet, or the shutting of the door, as the getting away from earthly sources of distraction, pulling up the ladder after us, and keeping out anything that might come in to hinder our secret devotions. I wish we could always pull the ladder up after us when we retire for private prayer; but many things try to climb that ladder. The devil himself will come up to disturb us if he can; and he can get into the hay-loft without any ladder.

What a capital exposition of the fifth commandment was that which was given by Corporal Trim, when he was asked, "What dost thou mean by honouring thy father and thy mother?" and he answered, "Please, your honour, it is allowing them a shilling a week out of my pay when they grow old." That was an admirable explanation of the meaning of the text. Then, if you are trying to show how we are to be doers of the Word, and not hearers only, there is a story of a woman who, when asked by the minister what he had said on Sunday, replied that she did not remember the sermon; but it had touched her conscience, for when she got home she burned her bushel, which was short measure. There is another story which also goes to show that the gospel may be useful even to hearers who forget what they have heard. A woman is called upon by her minister on the Monday, and he finds her washing wool in a sieve, holding it under the pump. He asks her, "How did you enjoy last Sabbath's discourses?" and she says that they did her much good. "Well, what was the text?" She does not recollect. "What was the subject?" "Ah! sir, it is quite gone from me," says the poor woman. Does she remember any of the remarks that were made? No, they are all gone. "Well then, Mary," says the minister, "it could not have done you much good." Oh! but it had done her a great deal of good; and she explained it to him by saying, "I will tell you, sir, how it is; I put this wool in the sieve under the pump, I pump on it, and all the water runs through the sieve, but then it washes the wool. So it is with your sermon; it comes into my heart, and then it runs right through my poor memory, which is like a sieve, but it washes me clean, sir."

You might talk for a long while about the cleansing and sanctifying power of the Word, and it would not make such an impression upon your hearers as that simple story would.

What finer exposition of the text "Weep with them that weep," can you have than this pretty anecdote? "Mother," said little Annie, "I cannot make out why poor Widow Brown likes me to go in to see her; she says I do comfort her so; but, mother, I cannot say anything to comfort her, and as soon as she begins crying, I put my arms round her neck, and I cry, too, and she says that that comforts her." And so it does; that is the very essence of the comfort, the sympathy, the fellow-feeling that moved the little girl to weep with the weeping widow. Mr. Hervey thus illustrates the great truth of the different appearance of sin to the eye of God and the eye of man. He says that you may take a small insect, and with the tiniest needle make a puncture in it so minute that you can scarcely see it with the naked eye; but when you look at it through a microscope, you see an enormous rent, out of which there flows a purple stream, making the creature seem to you as though it had been smitten with the axe that killeth an ox. It is but a defect of our vision that we cannot see things correctly; but the microscope reveals them as they really are. Thus you may explain to your hearers how God's microscopic eye sees sin in its true aspects. Suppose that you wanted to set forth the character of Caleb, who followed the Lord fully; it would greatly help many of your people if you said that the name Caleb signifies a dog, and then showed how a dog follows his master. There is his owner on horseback, riding along the miry roads; but the dog keeps as close to him as he can, no matter how much mud and dirt are splashed upon him, and not heeding the kicks he might get from the horse's heels. Even so should we follow the Lord. If you wish to exemplify the shortness of time, you might bring in the poor sempstress, with her little piece of candle, stitching away to get her work done before the light went out.

Many preachers find the greatest difficulty in getting suitable metaphors to set forth simple faith in the Lord Jesus Christ. There is a capital anecdote of an idiot, who was asked by the minister, who was trying to instruct him, whether he had a soul. To the utter consternation of his kind teacher, he replied, "No, I have no soul." The preacher said he was greatly surprised, after he had been taught for years, that he did not know better than that; but the poor fellow thus explained himself, "I had a soul once, but I lost it; and Jesus Christ came and found it, and now I let Him keep it, for it is His, it does not belong to me any longer." That is a fine picture of the way of salvation by simple faith in the substitution of the Lord Jesus Christ; and the smallest child in the congregation might be able to understand it through the story of the poor idiot.

Fourthly, *there is a kind of reasoning in anecdotes and illustrations*, which is very clear to illogical minds; and many of our hearers, unfortunately, have such minds, yet they can understand illustrative instances and stubborn facts. Truthful anecdotes are facts, and facts are stubborn things. Instances, when sufficiently multiplied, as we know by the inductive philosophy, prove a point. Two instances may not prove it; but twenty may prove it to a demonstration. Take the very important matter of answers to prayer. You can prove that God answers prayer by quoting anecdote after anecdote, that you know to be authentic, of instances in which God has really heard and answered prayer. Take that capital little book by Mr. Prime on the Power of Prayer; there, I believe you have the truth upon this subject demonstrated as clearly as you could have it in any proposition in Euclid. I think that, if such a number of facts could be instanced in connection with any question relating to geology or astronomy, the point would be regarded as settled. The writer brings such abundant proofs of God's having heard prayer, that even men who reject inspiration ought, at least, to acknowledge that this is a marvellous phenomenon for which they cannot account by any other explanation than the one which proclaims that there is a God who sitteth in heaven, and who hath respect unto the cry of his people upon the earth.

I have heard of some persons who have had objections to labour for the conversion of their children on the ground that God would save his own without any effort on our part. I remember making one man wince who held this view, by telling him of a father who would never teach his child to pray, or have him instructed even as to the meaning of prayer. He thought it was wrong, and that such work ought to be left to God's Holy Spirit. The boy fell down, and broke his leg, and had to have it taken off; and all the while the surgeon was amputating it, the boy was cursing and swearing in the most frightful manner. The good surgeon said to the father, "You see, you would not each your boy to pray, but the devil evidently had no objection to teach him to swear." That is the mischief of it; if we do not try our best to bring our children to Christ, there is another who will do his worst to drag them down to hell. A mother once said to her sick son, who was about to die, and was in a dreadful state of mind, "My boy, I am sorry you are in such trouble; I am sure I never taught you any hurt." "No, mother," he answered, "but you never taught me any good; and therefore there was room for all sorts of evil to get into me." All these stories will be to many people the very best kind of argument that you could possibly use with them. You bring to them facts, and these facts reach their conscience, even though it is imbedded in several inches of callousness.

I do not know of any reasoning that would explain the need of submission to the will of God better than the telling of the story, which Mr. Gilpin gives us in his Life, of his being called in to pray with a woman whose boy was very ill. The good man asked that God would, if it were his will, restore the dear child to life and health, when the mother interrupted him, and said, "No, I cannot agree to such a prayer as that; I cannot put it in that shape, it must be God's will to restore him. I cannot bear that my child should die; pray that he may live whether it is God's will or not." He answered, "Woman, I cannot pray that prayer, but it is answered; your child will recover, but you will live to rue the day that you made such a request." Twenty years after, there was a woman carried away in a fainting fit from under a drop at Tyburn, for her son had lived long enough to bring himself to the gallows by his crimes. The mother's wicked prayer had been heard, and God had answered it. So, if you want to prove the power of the gospel, do not go on expending words to no purpose, but tell the stories of cases you have met with that illustrate the truth you are enforcing, for such anecdotes will convince your hearers as no other kind of reasoning can. I think that is clear enough to every one of you.

Anecdotes are useful, also, because they often appeal very forcibly to human nature. In order to rebuke those who profane the Sabbath, tell the story of the gentleman who had seven sovereigns, and who met with a poor fellow, to whom he gave six out of the seven, and then the wicked wretch turned round and robbed him of the seventh. How clearly that sets forth the ingratitude of our sinful race in depriving God of that one day out of the seven which he has set apart for his own service! This story appeals to nature, too. Two or three boys come round one of their companions, and they say to him, "Let us go and get some cherries out of your father's garden." "No," he replies, "I cannot steal, and my father does not wish those cherries to be picked." "Oh! but then your father is so kind, and he never beats you." "Ah! I know that is true," answers the boy, "and that is the very reason why I would not steal his cherries." This would show that the grace and goodness of God do not lead his children to licentiousness; but, on the contrary, they restrain them from sin. This story, also, appeals to human nature, and shows that the fathers of the Church are not always to be depended upon as fountains of authority. A nobleman had heard of a certain very old man, who lived in a village, and he sought out and found him, and ascertained that he was seventy years of age. He was talking with him, supposing him to be the oldest inhabitant, when the man said, "Oh! no, sir, I am not the oldest; I am not the father of the village; there is an older one, my father, who is still alive." So, I have heard of some who have said that they turned away from "the fathers" of the Church to the very old fathers, that is, away from what are commonly called "the patristic fathers", back to the apostles, who are the true fathers and grandfathers of the Christian Church.

Sometimes, anecdotes have force in them on account of their appealing to the sense of the ludicrous. Of course, I must be very careful here, for it is a sort of tradition of the fathers that it is wrong to laugh on Sundays. The eleventh commandment is, that we are to love one another, and then, according to some people, the twelfth is, "Thou shalt pull a long face on Sunday." I must confess that I would rather hear people laugh than I would see them asleep in the house of God; and I would rather get the truth into them through the medium of ridicule than I would have the truth neglected, or leave the people to perish through lack of reception of the truth. I do believe in my heart that there may be as much holiness in a laugh as in a cry; and that, sometimes, to laugh is the better thing of the two, for I may weep, and be murmuring, and repining, and thinking all sorts of bitter thoughts against God; while, at another time, I may laugh the laugh of sarcasm against sin, and so evince a holy earnestness in the defence of the truth. I do not know why ridicule is to be given up to Satan as a weapon to be used against us, and not to be employed by us as a weapon against him. I will venture to affirm that the Reformation owed almost as much to the sense of the ridiculous in human nature as to anything else, and that those humorous squibs and caricatures, that were issued by the friends of Luther, did more to open the eyes of Germany to the abominations of the priesthood than the more solid and ponderous arguments against Romanism. I know no reason why we should not, on suitable occasions, try the same style of reasoning. "It is a dangerous weapon," it will be said, "and many men will cut their fingers with it." Well, that is their own look-out; but I do not know why we should be so particular about their cutting their fingers if they can, at the same time, cut the throat of sin, and do serious damage to the great adversary of souls.

Here is a story that I should not mind telling on a Sunday for the benefit of certain people, who are good at hearing sermons and attending prayer-meetings, but who are very bad hands at business. They never work on Sundays because they never work on any day of the week; they forget that part of the commandment which says, "Six days shalt thou labour," which is just as binding as the other part, "The seventh day is the sabbath of the Lord thy God : in it thou shalt not do any work." To these people who never labour because they are so heavenly-minded, I would tell the story of a certain monk, who entered a monastery, but who would not work in the fields, or the garden, or at making clothes, or anything else, because, as he told the superior, he was a spiritually-minded monk. He wondered, when the dinner-hour approached, that there came to him no summons from the refectory. So he went down to the prior, and said, "Don't

the brethren eat here? Are you not going to have any dinner?"
The prior said, "We do, because we are carnal; but you are so spiritual
that you do not work, and therefore you do not require to eat; that
is why we did not call you. The law of this monastery is that, if any
man will not work, neither shall he eat."

That is a good story of the boy in Italy who had his Testament
seized, and who said to the *gendarme*, "Why do you seize this book?
Is it a bad book?" "Yes," was the answer. "Are you sure the book
is bad?" he enquired; and again the reply was, "Yes." "Then, why
do you not seize the Author of it if it is a bad book?" That was a
fine piece of sarcasm at those who had a hatred of the Scriptures, and
yet professed to have love to Christ. That is another good story of our
friend the Irishman, who, when he was asked by the priest what
warrant an ignorant man such as he was had for reading the Bible,
said, "Truth, but I have a search-warrant; for it says, 'Search the
Scriptures; for in them ye think ye have eternal life: and they are
they which testify of me.'"

This story would not be amiss, I think, as a sort of ridiculous argument showing what power the gospel ought to have over the human
mind. Dr. Moffat tells us of a certain Kaffir, who came to him, one
day, saying that the New Testament, which the missionary had given
him a week before, had spoiled his dog. The man said that his dog
had been a very good hunting dog, but that he had torn the Testament
to pieces, and eaten it up, and now he was quite spoiled. "Never
mind," said Dr. Moffat, "I will give you another Testament." "Oh!"
said the man, "it is not that that troubles me, I do not mind the dog
spoiling the book, for I could buy another; but the book has spoiled
the dog." "How is that?" enquired the missionary; and the Kaffir
replied, "The dog will be of no use to me now, because he has eaten
the Word of God, and that will make him love his enemies, so that
he will be of no good for hunting." The man supposed that not even
a dog could receive the New Testament without being sweetened in
temper thereby; that is, in truth, what ought to be the case with all
who feed upon the gospel of Christ. I should not hesitate to tell that
story after Dr. Moffat, and I should, of course, use it to show that,
when a man has received the truth as it is in Jesus, there ought to be
a great change in him, and he ought never to be of any use to his old
master again.

When the priests were trying to pervert the natives of Tahiti to
Romanism, they had a fine picture which they hoped would convince
the people of the excellence of the Church of Rome. There were
certain dead logs of wood: whom were they to represent? They were
the heretics, who were to go into the fire. And who were these small
branches of the tree? They were the faithful. Who were the larger
ones? They were the priests. And who were the next? They were

the cardinals. And who was the trunk of the tree? Oh, that was the pope! And the root, whom did that set forth? Oh, the root was Jesus Christ! So the poor natives said, "Well, we do not know anything about the trunk, or the branches; but we have got the root, and we mean to stick to that, and not give it up." If we have the root, if we have Christ, we may laugh to scorn all the pretensions and delusions of men.

These stories may make us laugh, but they may also smite error right through the heart, and lay it dead; and they may, therefore, lawfully be used as weapons with which we may go forth to fight the Lord's battles.

Fifthly, another use of anecdotes and illustrations lies in the fact that *they help the memory to grasp the truth*. There is a story told— though I will not vouch for the truth of it—of a certain countryman, who had been persuaded by some one that all Londoners were thieves; and, therefore, on coming to London for the first time, he tried to secure his watch by putting it into his waistcoat pocket, and then covering it all over with fish-hooks. "Now," he thought, "if any gentleman tries to get my watch, he will remember it." The story says that, as he was walking along, he desired to know the time himself, and put his own hand into his pocket, forgetting all about the fish-hooks. The effect produced upon him can better be imagined than described. Now, it seems to me that a sermon should always be like that countryman's pocket, full of fish-hooks, so that, if anybody comes in to listen to it, he will get some forget-me-not, some remembrancer, fastened in his ear, and it may be, in his heart and conscience. Let him drop in just at the end of the discourse, there should be something at the close that will strike and stick. As when we walk in our farmer friends' fields, there are certain burrs that are sure to cling to our clothes; and brush as we may, some of the relics of the fields remain upon our garments, so there ought to be some burr in every sermon that will stick to those who hear it.

What do you remember best in the discourses you heard years ago? I will venture to say that it is some anecdote that the preacher related. It may possibly be some pithy sentence; but it is more probable that it is some striking story which was told in the course of the sermon. Rowland Hill, a little while before he died, was visiting an old friend, who said to him, "Mr. Hill, it is now sixty-five years since I first heard you preach; but I remember your text, and a part of your sermon." "Well," asked the preacher, "what part of the sermon do you recollect?" His friend answered, "You said that some people, when they went to hear a sermon, were very squeamish about the delivery of the preacher. Then you said, 'Supposing you went to hear the will of one of your relatives read, and you were expecting a legacy from him; you would hardly think of criticizing the manner in which the lawyer read the will; but you would be all attention to hear whether anything was left to you, and if so, how much; and that is the way to hear the gospel.' " Now, the man would not have recollected that for sixty-five years if Mr. Hill had not put the matter in that illustrative form. If he had said, "Dear friends, you must listen to the gospel for its own sake, and not merely for the charms of the preacher's oratory, or those delightful soaring periods which gratify your ears," if he had put it in the very pretty manner in which some people can do the thing, I will be bound to say that the man would have remembered it as long as a duck recollects the last time it went into the water, and no longer; for it would have been so common to have spoken in that way; but putting the truth in the striking manner that he did, it was remembered for sixty-five years.

An American gentleman related the following anecdote, which just answers the purpose I have in view, so I will pass it on to you. He said, "When I was a boy, I used to hear the story of a tailor who lived to a great age, and became very wealthy, so that he was an object of envy to all who knew him. His life, as all lives will, drew to a close; but before he passed away, feeling some desire to benefit the members of his craft, he gave out word that, on a certain day, he would be happy to communicate to all the tailors of the neighbourhood the secret by which they might become wealthy. A great number of knights of the thimble came, and while they waited in anxious silence to hear the important revelation, he was raised up in his bed, and with his expiring breath uttered this short sentence, *"Always put a knot in your thread."* That is why I recommend you, brethren, to use anecdotes and illustrations, because they put knots in the thread of your discourse. What is the use of pulling the end of your thread through the material on which you are working? Yet, has it not been the case with very many of the sermons to which we have listened, or the discourses we have ourselves delivered? The bulk of what we have heard has just gone through our minds without leaving any lasting impression, and all we recollect is some anecdote that was told by the preacher.

There is an authenticated case of a man being converted by a sermon eighty-five years after he had heard it preached. Mr. Flavel, at the close of a discourse, instead of pronouncing the usual benediction, stood up, and said, "How can I dismiss you with a blessing, for many of you are 'Anathema Maranatha', because you love not the Lord Jesus Christ?" A lad of fifteen heard that remarkable utterance; and eighty-five years afterwards, sitting under a hedge, I think in Virginia, the whole scene came vividly before him as if it had been but the day before; and it pleased God to bless Mr. Flavel's words to his conversion, and he lived three years longer to bear good testimony that he had felt the power of the truth in his heart.

Sixthly, anecdotes and illustrations are useful because *they frequently arouse the feelings*. They will not do this, however, if you tell the same stories over and over again ever so many times. I recollect, when I first heard that wonderful story about "There is another man," I cried a good deal over it. Poor soul, just rescued, half-dead, with only a few rags on him, and yet he said, "There is another man," needing to be saved. The second time I heard the story, I liked it, but I did not think it was quite so new as at first; and the third time I heard it, I thought that I never wanted to hear it again. I do not know how many times I have heard it since; but I can always tell when it is coming out. The brother draws himself up, and looks wonderfully solemn, and in a sepulchral tone says, "There is another man," and I think to myself, "Yes, and I wish there had not been," for I have heard that story till I am sick and tired of it. Even a good anecdote may get so hackneyed that there is no force in it, and no use in retailing it any longer.

Still, a live illustration is better for appealing to the feelings of an audience than any amount of description could possibly be. When Mr. Beecher brought a beautiful slave girl, with her manacles on, into his pulpit, he did more for the anti-slavery cause than he might have done by the most eloquent harangue. What we want in these times is not to listen to long prelections upon some dry subject, but to hear something practical, something matter-of-fact, that comes home to our every-day reasoning; and when we get this, then our hearts are soon stirred.

I have no doubt that the sight of a death-bed would move men much more than that admirable work called *Drelincourt on Death*, a book which, I should think, nobody has ever been able to read through. There may have been instances of persons who have attempted it; but I believe that, long before they have reached the latter end, they have been in a state of asphyxia or coma, and have been obliged to be rubbed with hot flannels; and the book has had to be removed to a distance before they could recover. If you have not read *Drelincourt on Death*, I believe I know what you have read, that is, the ghost story that is stitched in at the end of the book. The work would not sell, the whole impression was upon the shelves of the bookseller, when Defoe wrote the fiction entitled, "A True Relation of the Apparition of Mrs. Veal after her death to Mrs. Bargrave," in which *Drelincourt on Death* is recommended by the apparition as the best book on the subject. This story had not a vestige or shadow of truth in it, it was all a piece of imagination; but it was put in at the end of the book, and then the whole edition was speedily cleared out, and more were wanted. It may be something like that very often with your sermons; only you must tell the people of what has actually occurred, and so you will retain their attention, and reach their hearts.

Many have been moved to self-sacrifice by the story of the Moravians, in South Africa, who saw a large enclosed space of ground, in which there were persons rotting away with leprosy, some without arms and some without legs; and these Moravians could not preach to the poor lepers without going in there themselves for life to rot with them, and they did so. Two more of the same noble band of brethren sold themselves into slavery in the West Indies, in order that they might be allowed to preach to the slaves. When you can give such instances as these of missionary disinterestedness and devotedness, it will do more to arouse a spirit of enthusiasm for foreign missions than all your closely-reasoned arguments could possibly do.

Who has not heard and felt the force of the story of the two miners, when the fuse was burning, and only one could escape, and the Christian man cried out to his unconverted companion, "Escape for your life, because, if you die, you are lost; but if I die, it is all right with me; so you go."

The fool's plan, too, I have sometimes used as a striking illustration. There was a little boat which got wrecked, and the man in it was trying to swim to shore, but the current was too strong for him. After he had been drowned an hour, a man said, "I could have saved him," and when they asked him how he could have saved him, he described a plan that seemed to be most excellent and feasible, by which the man might, no doubt, have been saved; but then, unfortunately, by that time he was drowned! So, there are some who are always wise just too late, some who may have to say to themselves, when such and such a one is gone the way of all living, "What might I not have done for him if I had but taken him in time!" Brethren, let that anecdote be a reminder to us all that we should seek to be wise in winning souls before it is too late to rescue them from everlasting destruction.

Seventhly, and lastly, anecdotes and illustrations are exceedingly useful because *they catch the ear of the utterly careless.* Something is wanted in every sermon for this class of people; and an anecdote is well calculated to catch the ear of the thoughtless and the ungodly. We really desire their salvation, and we would bait our trap in any way possible by which we might catch them for Christ. We cannot expect our young people to come and listen to learned doctrinal disquisitions that are not at all embellished with anything that interests their immature minds. Nay, even grown-up people, after the toils of the week, some of them busy till early on the Sunday morning, cannot be expected to attend to long prosaic discourses which are not broken by a single anecdote.

Oh, dear, dear, dear! How I do pity those unpractical brethren who do not seem to know to whom they are preaching! "Ah!" said a brother once, "whenever I preach, I do not know where to look, and so I look up at the ventilator." Now, there is not anybody up in the ventilator; there cannot be supposed to be anybody there, unless the angels of heaven are listening there to hear the words of truth. A minister should not preach *before* the people, but he should preach right *at* them; let him look straight at them; if he can, let him search them through and through, and take stock of them, as it were, and see what they are like, and then suit his message to them.

I have often seen some poor fellow standing in the aisle at the Tabernacle. Why, he looks just like a sparrow that has got into a church, and cannot get out again! He cannot make out what sort of service it is; he begins to count how many people sit in the front row in the gallery, and all kinds of ideas pass through his mind. Now I want to attract his attention; how shall I do it? If I quote a text of Scripture, he may not know what it means, and may not be interested in it. Shall I put a bit of Latin into the sermon, or quote the original Hebrew or Greek of my text? That will not do for such a man. What shall I do? Ah! I know a story that will, I believe, just fit him. Out it comes, and the man does not look up at the gallery any more; but he is wondering whatever the preacher is at. Something is said that so exactly suits his case that he begins to ask himself who has been telling the minister about him, and he thinks, "Why, I know; my wife comes to hear this man sometimes, so she has been telling him all about me!" Then he feels curious to hear more, and while he is looking up at the preacher, and listening to the truth that is being proclaimed, the first gleam of light on divine things dawns upon him; but if we had kept on with our regular discourse, and had not gone out of our way, what might have become of that man, I cannot tell. "They say I ramble," said Rowland Hill, in a sermon I have been reading this afternoon; "they say I ramble, but it is because you ramble, and I am obliged to ramble after you. They say I do not stick to my subject; but, thank God, I always stick to my object, which is, the winning of your souls, and bringing you to the cross of Jesus Christ!"

Mr. Bertram aptly illustrates the way in which men are engrossed in worldly cares by telling the story of the captain of a whaling ship, whom he tried to interest in the things of God, and who said, "It is no use, sir; your conversation will not have any effect upon me. I cannot hear what you are saying, or understand the subject you are talking about. I left my home to try to catch whales, I have been a year and nine months looking for whales, sir, and I have not caught a whale yet. I have been ploughing the deep in search of whales; when I go to bed, I dream of whales; and when I get up in the morning, I wonder if there will be any whales caught that day; there is a whale in my heart, sir, a whale in my brain, and it is of no use for you to talk to me about anything else but whales." So, your people have their business in their heads, and in their hearts, they want to make a fortune, and retire; or else they have a family of children to bring up, and Susan must be married, and John must be got into a situation, and it is no use for you to talk to them about the things of God unless you can drive away the whales that keep floundering and splashing about.

There is a merchant, perhaps, who has just thought of some bad bill; or another has looked across the building, and noticed a piece of ribbon of a particular colour, and he thinks, "Yes, I ought to have had a larger stock of that kind of thing, I see that it is getting fashionable!" or it may be that one of the hearers has caught sight of his neighbour, and he thinks he must pay him a visit on the morrow; and so people's thoughts are occupied with all sorts of subjects beside that of which the preacher is speaking. You ask me how I know that this is the case. Well, I know because I have been guilty of the same offence myself; I find this occurs when I am listening to another brother preaching. I do not think, when I am preaching, that I get on very well; but sometimes, when I go into the country, and take the morning and evening services, and then hear some one else in the afternoon, I think, "Well, really, when I was up there, I thought I was a stick: but *now!* I only wish I had my turn again!" Now, this is very wrong, to let such thoughts come into our minds; but as we are all very apt to wander, the preacher should carry anecdotes and illustrations into the pulpit, and use them as nails to fasten the people's attention to the subject of his sermon.

Mr. Paxton Hood once said, in a lecture that I heard him deliver, "Some preachers expect too much of their hearers; they take a number of truths into the pulpit as a man might carry up a box of nails; and then, supposing the congregation to be posts, they take out a nail, and expect it to get into the post by itself. Now that is not the way to do it. You must take your nail, hold it up against the post, hammer it in, and then clinch it on the other side; and then it is that you may expect the great Master of assemblies to fasten the nails so that they will not fall out." We must try thus to get the truth into the people, for it will never get in of itself; and we must remember that the hearts of our hearers are not open, like a church door, so that the truth may go in, and take its place, and sit upon its throne to be worshipped there. No, we have often to break open the doors with great effort, and to thrust the truth into places where it will not at first be a welcome guest, but where, afterwards, the better it is known, the more it will be loved.

Illustrations and anecdotes will greatly help to make a way for the truth to enter; and they will do it by catching the ear of the careless and the inattentive. We must try to be like Mr. Whitefield, of whom a shipbuilder said, "When I have been to hear anybody else preach, I have always been able to lay down a ship from stem to stern; but when I listen to Mr. Whitefield, I cannot even lay the keel." And another, a weaver, said, "I have often, when I have been in church, calculated how many looms the place would hold; but when I listen to that man, I forget my weaving altogether." You must endeavour, brethren, to make your people forget matters relating to this world by interweaving the whole of divine truth with the passing things of every day, and this you will do by a judicious use of anecdotes and illustrations.

Now, gentlemen, these seven reasons—that they interest the mind and secure the attention of our hearers, that they render the teaching vivid and life-like, that they explain some difficult passages to dull understandings, that they help the reasoning faculties of certain minds, that they aid the memory, that they arouse the feelings, and that they catch the ear of the careless—have reconciled me for many a day to the use of anecdotes and illustrations, and I think it is very likely that they will reconcile you to the use of them, too.

At the same time, I must repeat what I before said, we must take care that we do not let our anecdotes and illustrations be like empty casks that carry nothing. We must not have it truthfully said of our sermons, as was said by a certain lady, who, after having heard a clergyman preach, was asked what she thought of the sermon, and whether there was not much spirit in it. "Oh, yes!" she replied, "it was all spirit; there was no body to it at all." There must be some "body" in every discourse, some really sound doctrine, some suitable instruction for our hearers to carry home; not merely stories to amuse them, but solid truth to be received in the heart, and wrought out in the life. If this be so with your sermons, my dear brethren, I shall not have spoken to you this afternoon in vain upon the uses of anecdotes and illustrations.

XXVII

Where Can We find Anecdotes and Illustrations?

DEAR BRETHREN, after my last lecture to you, upon the uses of anecdotes and illustrations, you are probably quite ready to employ them in your discourses; but some of you may ask, "Where can we get them?" At the very beginning of this afternoon's talk, let me say that *nobody need make anecdotes* in order to interest a congregation. I have heard of one, who called to see a minister on a Friday, and he was told by the servant that her master could not be seen, for he was up in his study "making anecdotes." That kind of work will not do for a Christian minister. I would also bid you beware of the many common anecdotes, which are often repeated, but which I half suspect could not be proved to be matters of fact. Whenever I have the slightest suspicion about the truth of a story, I drop it at once; and I think that everyone else should do the same. So long as the anecdotes are current, and are generally believed, and provided they can be used for a profitable purpose, I believe they may be told, without any affirmation as to their truthfulness being made in a court of justice; but the moment any doubt comes across the mind of the preacher as to whether the tale is at least founded on fact, I think he had better look for something else, for he has the whole world to go to as a storehouse of illustration.

If you want to interest your congregation, and keep up their attention, you can find anecdotes and illustrations in many channels, like golden grains glistening amongst the mountain streams. For instance, there is *current history*. You may take up the daily newspaper, and find illustrations there. In my little shilling book, *The Bible and the Newspaper,* I have given specimens of how this may be done; and when I was preparing the present lecture, I took up a newspaper to see if I could find an illustration in it, and I soon found one. There was an account of a man at Wandsworth, who was discovered, with a gun and a dog, trespassing on some gentleman's preserves, and he said that he was only looking for mushrooms! Can you imagine what the gun and the dog had to do with mushrooms? However, the keeper felt in the man's pocket, and, laying hold of something soft, asked, "What is this?" "Oh!" said the poacher, "it is only a rabbit."

When it was suggested to him that the creature's ears were too long for a rabbit, he said that it was only a leveret, whereas it proved to be a very fine and plump hare. The man then said that he had found the hare lying near some mushrooms, but his intention was to get the mushrooms only! Now, that is a capital illustration. As soon as ever you lay hold of a man, and begin to accuse him of sin, he says, "Sin, sir! Oh, dear no! I was only doing a very proper thing, just what I have a perfect right to do; I was looking for mushrooms, I was not poaching!" You press him a little more closely, and try to bring him to conviction of sin; and then he says, "Well, perhaps it was hardly the thing, it may have been a little amiss; but it was only a rabbit!" When the man cannot any longer deny that he is guilty of sin, he says that it was only a very little one; and it is long before you can get him to admit that sin is exceeding sinful; indeed, no human power can ever produce genuine conviction in the heart of a single sinner; it must be the work of the Holy Spirit.

I also read, in the same newspaper, of a calamitous shipwreck, caused through the lack of lights. You could easily turn that incident to account by using it to illustrate the destruction of souls through the want of a knowledge of Christ. I have no doubt, if you were to take up any of this morning's daily papers, you would very readily find an abundance of illustrations. Mr. Newman Hall, in addressing us once, said that every Christian minister ought to read regularly his Bible and *The Times* newspaper. I should imagine, from the usual mode of his address, that he does so himself. Whether you read that particular paper, or any other, you should somehow keep yourselves well stored with illustrations taken from the ordinary transactions going on round about you. I pity even a Sunday-school teacher, much more a minister of the gospel, who could not make use of such incidents as the terrible burning of the church at Santiago, the great fire at London Bridge, the entrance into London of the Princess Alexandra, the taking of the census; and, indeed, anything that attracts public attention. There is in all these events an illustration, a simile, an allegory, which may point a moral, and adorn a tale.

You may sometimes adapt *local history* to the illustration of your subject. When a minister is preaching in any particular district, he will often find it best to catch the ears of the people, and engross their attention, by relating some anecdote that relates to the place where they live. Whenever I can, I get the histories of various counties; for, having to go into all sorts of country towns and villages to preach, I find that there is a great deal of useful material to be dug out of even dull, dry, topographical books. They begin, perhaps, with the name of John Smith, labourer, the man who keeps the parish register, and winds up the parish clock, and makes mouse-traps, and catches rats, and does fifty other useful things; but if you have the patience

to read on, you will find much information that you could get nowhere else, and you will probably meet with many incidents and
anecdotes that you can use as illustrations of the truth you are seeking
to set forth.

Preaching at Winslow, in Buckinghamshire, it would not be at all
amiss to introduce the incident of good Benjamin Keach, the pastor
of the Baptist church in that town, standing in the pillory in the
market-place in the year 1664, "for writing, printing, and publishing
a schismatical book, entitled, *The Child's Instructor; or, a New and
Easy Primmer.*" I do not think, however, that, if I were preaching at
Wapping, I should call the people "*Wapping* sinners", as Rowland
Hill is said to have done, when he told them that "Christ could save
old sinners, great sinners, yea, even Wapping sinners!" At Craven
Chapel, it would be most appropriate to tell the story of Lord Craven,
who was packing up his goods to go into the country at the time of
the Great Plague of London, when his servant said to him, "My lord,
does your God live only in the country?" "No," replied Lord Craven,
"He is here as well as there." "Well, then," said the servant, "if I were
your lordship, I think I would stop here; you will be as safe in the
city as in the country"; and Lord Craven did stop there, relying upon
the good providence of God.

Beside this, brethren, you have the marvellous storehouse of *ancient
and modern history*—Roman, Greek, and English—with which, of
course, you are seeking to become well acquainted. Who can possibly
read the old classic tales without feeling his soul on fire? As you
rise from their perusal, you will not merely be familiar with the events
which happened in "the brave days of old," but you will have learnt
many lessons that may be of service in your preaching to-day. For
instance, there is the story of Phidias and the statue of the god which
he had carved. After he had finished it, he had chiselled in the corner,
in small letters, the word "Phidias", and it was objected that the statue
could not be worshipped as a god, nor considered sacred, while it
bore the sculptor's name. It was even seriously questioned whether
Phidias should not be stoned to death because he had so desecrated
the statue. How could he dare, they asked, to put his own name on
the image of a god? So, some of us are very apt to want to put our
little names down at the bottom of any work which we have done
for God, that we may be remembered, whereas we ought rather to
upbraid ourselves for wishing to have any of the credit of that which
God the Holy Ghost enables us to do.

Then there is that other story of an ancient sculptor, who was about
to put the image of a god into a heathen temple, although he had
not finished that portion of the statue which was to be imbedded in
the wall. The priest demurred, and declared that the statue was not

completed. The sculptor said, "That part of the god will never be seen, for it will be built into the wall." "The gods can see in the wall," answered the priest. In like manner, the most private parts of our life, those secret matters than can never reach the human eye, are still under the ken of the Almighty, and ought to be attended to with the greatest care. It is not sufficient for us to maintain our public reputation among our fellow-creatures, for our God can see in the wall, He notices our coldness in the closest of communion, and He perceives our faults and failures in the family.

Trying once to set forth how the Lord Jesus Christ delights in His people because they are His own handiwork, I found a classic story of Cyrus extremely useful. When showing a foreign ambassador round his garden, Cyrus said to him, "You cannot possibly take such an interest in these flowers and trees as I do, for I laid out the whole garden myself, and every plant here I planted with my own hand. I have watered them, and I have seen them grow, I have been a husbandman to them, and therefore I love them far better than you can." So, the Lord Jesus Christ loves the fair garden of His Church, because He laid it all out, and planted it with His own gracious hand, and He has watched over every plant, and nourished and cherished it.

The days of the Crusaders are a peculiarly rich period for noble stories that will make good illustrations. We read that the soldiers of Godfrey de Bouillon, when they came within sight of the city of Jerusalem, were so charmed with the view that they fell on their faces, and then rose to their feet, and clapped their hands, and made the mountains ring with their shouts of joy. Thus, when we get within sight of the New Jerusalem, our happy home on high, whose name is ever dear to us, we will make our dying chamber ring with hallelujahs, and even the angels shall hear our songs of praise and thanksgiving. It is also recorded, concerning this same Godfrey, that, when he had entered Jerusalem at the head of his victorious army, he refused to wear the crown with which his soldiers wanted to deck his brow, "For," said he, "why should I wear a crown of gold in the city where my Lord wore a crown of thorns?" This is a good lesson for us to learn for ourselves, and to teach to our people. In the world where Christ was despised and rejected of men, it would be unseemly for a Christian to be seeking to win earthly honours, or ambitiously hunting after fame. The disciple must not think of being above his Master, nor the servant above his Lord.

Then you might easily make an illustration out of that romantic story, which may or may not be true, of Queen Eleanor sucking the poison out of her husband's wounded arm. Many of us, I trust, would be willing, as it were, to suck out all the slander and venom from the arm of Christ's Church, and to bear any amount of suffering ourselves, so long as the Church itself might escape and live. Would not any one of you, my brethren, gladly put his lips to the unvenomed wounds of the Church to-day, and suffer even unto death, sooner than let the doctrines of Christ be impugned, and the cause of God be dishonoured?

What a fine field of illustration lies open to you in *religious history!* It is difficult to tell where to begin digging in this mine of precious treasure. The story of Luther and the Jew might be used to set forth the evil of sin, and how to avoid it. A Jew was seeking an opportunity of stabbing the Reformer; but Luther received a portrait of the would-be murderer, so that, wherever he went, he was on his guard against the assassin. Using this fact himself as an illustration, Luther said, "God knows that there are sins that would destroy us, and He has therefore given us portraits of them in His Word, so that, wherever we see them, we may say, 'That is a sin that would stab me; I must beware of that evil thing, and keep out of its way.'"

Stout Hugh Latimer, in that famous story of an incident in his trial before several bishops, brings out very clearly the omnipresence and omniscience of God, and the care that we ought to exercise in the presence of One who can read our most secret thoughts and imaginations. He says, "I was once in examination before five or six bishops, where I had much trouble; thrice every week I came to examinations, and many traps and snares were laid to get something. . . . At last, I was brought forth to be examined in a chamber hung with arras, where I was wont to be examined; but now at this time the chamber was somewhat altered. For whereas, before, there was wont always to be a fire in the chimney, now the fire was taken away, and an arras hung over the chimney, and the table stood near the fire-place. There was, amongst the bishops who examined me, one with whom I had been very familiar, and took him for my great friend, an aged man, and he sat next to the table's end. Then, amongst all other questions, he put forth a very subtle and crafty one, and such a one, indeed, as I could not think so great danger in. And when I should make answer, 'I pray you, Mr. Latimer,' said one, 'speak out; I am very thick of hearing, and there may be many that sit far off.' I marvelled at this, that I was bid to speak out, and began to suspect, and give an ear to the chimney; and there I heard a pen writing in the chimney behind the cloth. They had appointed one there to write all mine answers, for they made sure that I should not start from them; and there was no starting from them. God was my good Lord, and gave me answer, else I could never have escaped." Preaching, some years afterwards, Latimer himself told the story, and applied the illustration. "My hearer," said he, "there is a recording pen always at work behind the arras, taking down all thou sayest, and noting all thou doest, therefore be thou careful that thy words and acts are worthy of record in God's Book of Remembrance."

You might aptly illustrate the doctrine of God's special providential care of His servants by relating the story of John Knox, who, one evening, refused to sit in his usual seat, though he did not know any particular reason for so acting. No one was allowed to occupy that chair, and during the evening, a shot came in through the window, and struck a candlestick that stood immediately opposite where John Knox would have been sitting if he had taken his accustomed place. There is also the case of the godly minister, who, in escaping from his persecutors, went into a hay-loft, and hid himself in the hay. The soldiers went into the place, pricking and thrusting with their swords and bayonets, and the good man even felt the cold steel touch the sole of his foot, and the scratch which was made remained for years: yet his enemies did not discover him. Afterwards, a hen came and laid an egg every day hard by the place where he was hidden, and so he was sustained as well as preserved until it was safe for him to leave his hiding-place. It was either the same minister, or one of his persecuted brethren, who was providentially protected by such a humble agent as a spider. This is the story as I have read it: "Receiving friendly warning of an intended attempt to apprehend him, and finding men were on his track, he took refuge in a malt-house, and crept into the empty kiln, where he lay down. Immediately after, he saw a spider lower itself across the narrow entrance by which he had got in, thus fixing the first line of what was soon wrought into a large and beautiful web. The weaver and the web, placed directly between him and the light, were very conspicuous. He was so much struck with the skill and diligence of the spider, and so much absorbed in watching her work, that he forgot his own danger. By the time the network was completed, crossing and re-crossing the mouth of the kiln in every direction, his pursuers came into the malt-house to search for him. He noted their steps, and listened to their cruel words while they looked about. Then they came close to the kiln, and he overheard one say to another, 'It's no use to look in *there*; the old villain can never be there: *look at that spider's web; he could never have got in there without breaking it.*' Without further search they went to seek elsewhere, and he escaped safely out of their hands."

There is another story, I have somewhere met with, of a prisoner, during the American war, who was put into a cell in which there was a little slit through which a soldier's eye always watched him day and night. Whatever the prisoner did, whether he ate, or drank, or slept, the sentinel's eye was perpetually gazing at him; and the thought of it, he said, was perfectly dreadful to him, it almost drove him mad; he could not bear the idea of having that man's eye always scrutinizing him. He could scarcely sleep; his very breathing became a misery, because, turn which way he would, he could never escape from the gaze of that soldier's eye. That story might be used as an illustration of the fact that God's omniscient eye is always looking at every one of us.

I remember making two or three of my congregation speak out pretty loudly by telling them this story, which I read in an American tract. I suppose it may be true; I receive it as reliable, and I wish I could tell it as it is printed. A Christian minister, residing near the backwoods, took a walk one evening for silent meditation. He went much farther than he intended, and, missing the track, wandered away into the woods. He kept on endeavouring to find the road to his home; but failed to do so. He was afraid that he would have to spend the night in some tree; but suddenly, as he was going forward, he saw the glimmer of lights in the distance, and therefore pressed on, hoping to find shelter in a friendly cottage. A strange sight met his gaze; a meeting was being held in a clearing in the middle of the woods, the place being lit up with blazing pine-torches. He thought, "Well, here are some Christian people met to worship God; I am glad that what I thought was an awkward mistake in losing my way has brought me here; I may, perhaps, both do good and get good."

To his horror, however, he found that it was an atheistical gathering, and that the speakers were venting their blasphemous thoughts against God with very great boldness and determination. The minister sat down, full of grief. A young man declared that he did not believe in the existence of God, and dared Jehovah to destroy him then and there if there was such a God. The good man's heart was meditating how he ought to reply, but his tongue seemed to cleave to the roof of his mouth; and the infidel orator sat down amidst loud acclamations of admiration and approval. Our friend did not wish to be a craven, or to hold back in the day of battle, and therefore he was almost inclined to rise and speak, when a hale, burly man, who had passed the meridian of life, but who was still exceedingly vigorous, and seemed a strong, muscular clearer of the backwoods, rose and said, "I should like to speak if you will give me a hearing. I am not going to say anything about the topic which has been discussed by the orator who has just sat down; I am only going to tell you a fact: will you hear me?" "Yes, yes," they shouted; it was a free discussion, so they would hear him, especially as he was not going to controvert. "A week ago," he began, "I was working up yonder, on the river's bank, felling trees. You know the rapids down below. Well, while I was at my employment, at some little distance from them, I heard cries and shrieks, mingled with prayers to God for help. I ran down to the water's edge, for I guessed what was the matter. There I saw a young man, who could not manage his boat; the current was getting the mastery of him, and he was drifting down the stream, and ere long, unless someone had interposed, he would most certainly have been swept over the falls, and carried down to a dreadful death. I saw that young man kneel down in the boat, and pray to the Most High God, by the love of Christ, and by His precious blood, to save him. He confessed that he had been an infidel; but said that, if he might but be delivered this once, he would declare his belief in God. I at once sprang into the river. My arms are not very weak, I think, though they are not so strong as they used to be. I managed to get into the boat, turned her round, brought her to the shore, and so I saved that young man's life; and that young man is the one who has just sat down, and who has been denying the existence of God, and daring the Most High to destroy him!" Of course, I used that story to show that it was an easy thing to brag and boast about holding infidel sentiments in a place of safety; but that, when men come into peril of their lives, then they talk in a very different fashion.

There is a capital story, which exemplifies the need of going up to the house of God, not merely to listen to the preacher, but to seek the Lord. A certain lady had gone to the communion in a Scotch church, and had greatly enjoyed the service. When she reached her home, she enquired who the preacher was, and she was informed that it was Mr. Ebenezer Erskine. The lady said that she would go again, the next Sabbath, to hear him. She went, but she was not profited in the least; the sermon did not seem to have any unction or power about it. She went to Mr. Erskine, and told him of her experience at the two services. "Ah! madam," said he, "the first Sabbath you came to meet the Lord Jesus Christ, and you had a blessing; but the second Sabbath you came to hear Ebenezer Erskine, and you had no blessing, and you had no right to expect any." You see, brethren, a preacher might talk to the people, in general terms, about coming to worship God, and not merely to hear the minister, yet no effect might be produced by his words, for there might not be anything sufficiently striking to remain in the memory; but after such an anecdote as this one about Mr. Erskine and the lady, who could forget the lesson that was intended to be taught?

Well now, supposing that you have exhausted all the illustrations to be found in current history, in local history, in ancient and modern history, and in religious history,—which I do not think you will do unless you are yourselves exhausted,—you may then turn to *natural history*, where you will find illustrations and anecdotes in great abundance; and you need never feel any qualms of conscience about using the facts of nature to illustrate the truths of Scripture, because there is a sound philosophy to support the use of such illustrations. It is a fact that can easily be accounted for, that people will more readily receive the truth of revelation if you link it with some kindred truth in natural history, or anything that is visible to the eye, than if you give them a bare statement of the doctrine itself. Besides, there is this important fact that must not be forgotten, the God who is the Author of revelation, is also the Author of creation, and providence, and history, and everything else from which you ought to draw your illustrations. When you use natural history to illustrate the Scriptures, you are only explaining one of God's books by another volume that He has written.

It is just as if you had before you two works by one author, who had, in the first place, written a book for children; and then, in the second place, had prepared a volume of more profound instruction for persons of riper years, and higher culture. At times, when you found obscure and difficult passages in the work meant for the more advanced scholars, you would refer to the little book which was intended for the younger folk, and you would say, "We know that this means so-and-so, because that is how the matter is explained in the book for beginners." So creation, providence, and history, are all books which God has written for those to read who have eyes, written for those who have ears to hear his voice in them, written even for carnal men to read, that they may see something of God therein. But the other glorious Book is written for you who are taught of God, and made spiritual and holy. Oftentimes, by turning to the primer, you will get something out of that simple narrative which will elucidate and illustrate the more difficult classic, for that is what the Word of God is to you.

There is a certain type of thought which God has followed in all things. What He made with His Word has a similarity to the Word itself by which He made it; and the visible is the symbol of the invisible, because the same thought of God runs through it all. There is a touch of the divine finger in all that God has made; so that the things which are apparent to our senses have certain resemblances to the things which do not appear. That which can be seen, and tasted, and touched, and handled, is meant to be to us the outward and visible sign of a something which we find in the Word of God, and in our spiritual experience, which is the inward and the spiritual grace; so that there is nothing forced and unnatural in bringing nature to illustrate grace; it was ordained of God for that very purpose. Range over the whole of creation for your similes; do not confine yourself to any particular branch of natural history. The congregation of one very learned doctor complained that he gave them spiders continuously by way of illustration. It would be better to give the people a spider or two occasionally, and then to vary the instruction by stories, and anecdotes, and similes, and metaphors drawn from geology, astronomy, botany, or any of the other sciences which will help to shed a side light upon the Scriptures.

If you keep your eyes open, you will not see even a dog following his master, nor a mouse peeping up from his hole, nor will you hear even a gentle scratching behind the wainscot without getting something to weave into your sermons if your faculties are all on the alert. When you go home to-night, and sit by your fireside, you ought not to be able to take up your domestic cat without finding that which will furnish you with an illustration. How soft are pussy's pads, and yet, in a moment, if she is angered, how sharp will be her claws! How like to temptation, soft and gentle when first it cometh to us, but how deadly, how damnable the wounds it causeth ere long!

I recollect using, with very considerable effect in a sermon in the Tabernacle, an incident that occurred in my own garden. There was a dog which was in the habit of coming through the fence, and scratching in my flower-beds, to the manifest spoiling of the gardener's toil and temper. Walking in the garden, one Saturday afternoon, and preparing my sermon for the following day, I saw the four-footed creature,—rather a scurvy specimen, by-the-by,—and having a walking-stick in my hand, I threw it at him with all my might, at the same time giving him some good advice about going home. Now, what should my canine friend do but turn round, pick up the stick in his mouth, and bring it, and lay it down at my feet, wagging his tail all the while in expectation of my thanks and kind words? Of course, you do not suppose that I kicked him, or threw the stick at him any more. I felt quite ashamed of myself, and I told him that he was welcome to stay as long as he liked, and to come as often as he pleased. There was an instance of the power of non-resistance, submission, patience, and trust, in overcoming even righteous anger. I used that illustration in preaching the next day, and I did not feel that I had at all degraded myself by telling the story.

Most of us have read Alphonse Karr's book, *A Tour round my Garden*. Why does not somebody write *A Tour round my Dining-table*, or, *A Tour round my Kitchen*? I believe a most interesting volume of the kind might be written by any man who had his eyes open to see the analogies of nature. I remember that, one day, when I lived in Cambridge, I wanted a sermon very badly; and I could not fix upon a subject, when, all at once, I noticed a number of birds on the slates of the opposite house. As I looked closely at them, I saw that there was a canary, which had escaped from somebody's house, and a lot of sparrows had surrounded it, and kept pecking at it. There was my text at once: "Mine heritage is unto me as a speckled bird, the birds round about are against her."

Once more, brethren, if you cannot find illustrations in natural history, or any of the other histories I have mentioned, *find them anywhere*. Anything that occurs around you, if you have but brains in your head, will be of service to you; but if you are really to interest and profit your congregations, you will need to keep your eyes open, and to use all the powers with which the Lord has endowed you. If you do so, you will find that, in simply walking through the streets, something or other will suggest a passage of Scripture, or will help you, when you have chosen your text, to open it up to the people so as really to arrest their attention, and convey the truth to their minds and hearts.

For instance, the snow to-day covered all the ground, and the black soil looked fair and white. It is thus with some men under transient reformations; they look as holy, and as heavenly, and as pure as though they were saints; but when the sun of trial arises, and a little heat of temptation cometh upon them, how soon do they reveal their true blackness, and all their surface goodliness melteth away!

The whole world is hung round by God with pictures; and the preacher has only to take them down, one by one, and hold them up before his congregation, and he will be sure to enlist their interest in the subject he is seeking to illustrate. But he must have his own eyes open, or he will not see these pictures. Solomon said, "The wise man's eyes are in his head," and addressing such a man, he wrote, "Let thine eyes look right on, and let thine eyelids look straight before thee." Why does he speak of seeing with the eyelids? I think he means that the eyelids are to shut in what the eyes have perceived. You know that there is all the difference in the world between a man with eyes and one with no eyes. One sits down by a stream, and sees much to interest and instruct him; but another, at the same place, is like the gentleman of whom Wordsworth wrote:

> "A primrose by a river's brim
> A yellow primrose was to him,
> And it was nothing more."

If you find any difficulty in illustrating your subject, I should strongly recommend you to *try to teach children* whenever you can get an opportunity of doing so. I do not know a better way of schooling your own mind to the use of illustrations than frequently to take a class in the Sunday-school, or to give addresses to the scholars as often as you can; because, if you do not illustrate *there,* you will have your lesson or your address illustrated for you very strikingly. You will find that the children will do it by their general worry and inattention, or by their talk and play. I used to have a class of boys when I was a Sunday-school teacher, and if I was ever a little dull, they began to make wheels of themselves, twisting round on the forms on which they sat. That was a very plain intimation to me that I must give them an illustration or an anecdote; and I learned to tell stories partly by being obliged to tell them. One boy, whom I had in the class, used to say to me, "This is very dull, teacher; can't you pitch us a yarn?" Of course he was a naughty boy, and you may suppose that he went to the bad when he grew up, though I am not at all sure that he did; but I used to try and pitch him the yarn that he wanted in order to get his attention again. And I dare say that some of our hearers, if they were allowed to speak out during the sermon, would ask us to pitch them a yarn, that is, to give them something to interest them. I believe that one of the best things you can do to teach either the old or the young is to give them plenty of anecdotes and illustrations.

I think it would be very useful to some of you who are not yet adept at the art of illustration if you were to *read books in which there is an abundance of metaphor, simile, and emblem.* I am not going fully into that subject on this occasion, because this lecture is only preliminary to the next two that I hope to deliver, in which I will try to give you a list of cyclopædias of anecdotes and illustrations, and books of fables, emblems, and parables; but I advise you to study such works as Gurnall's *Christian in Complete Armour,* or Matthew Henry's *Commentary,* with the distinct view of noticing all the illustrations, emblems, metaphors, and similes that you can find. I should even select *non*-comparisons; I like Keach's *Metaphors* where he points out the disparity between the type and the Anti-type. Sometimes, the contrasts between different persons or objects will be as instructive as their resemblances.

When you have read the book once, and tried to mark all the figures, go through it again, and note all the illustrations you missed in your first reading. You will probably have missed many; and you will be suprised to find that there are *illustrations even in the words themselves.* How frequently a word is itself a picture! Some of the most expressive words that are found in human language are like rich gems, which have passed before your eye very often, but you have not had time to handle or to value them. In your second examination of the book, you will notice, perhaps, what eluded you the first time, and you will find many illustrations which are merely hinted at, instead of being given at length. Do as I have recommended with a great many books. Get copies that you can afford to mark with a coloured pencil, so that you will be sure to see the illustrations readily; or put them down in one of your note-books.

I am sure that those brethren who begin early to keep a record of such things act wisely. The commonplace-books of the old Puritans were invaluable to them. They would never have been able to have compiled such marvellous works as they did if they had not been careful in collecting and arranging their matter under different heads; and thus, all that they had ever read upon any subject was embalmed and preserved, and they could readily refer to any point that they might require, and refresh their memories, and verify their quotations. Some of us, who are very busy, may be excused from that task; we must do the best we can, but some of you, who go to smaller charges, in the country especially, ought to keep a commonplace-book, or else I am afraid you will get to be very commonplace yourselves.

Your selection of similes, metaphors, parables, and emblems will not be complete unless you also *search the Scriptures to find the illustrations that are recorded there.* Biblical allusions are the most effective methods of illustrating and enforcing the truths of the gospel; and the preacher who is familiar with his Bible will never be at a loss for an instance of that which "is profitable for doctrine, for reproof, for correction, for instruction in righteousness." The Lord must have meant us thus to use His Word, otherwise He would not have given us, in the Old Testament, such a number of types and symbols of truths to be afterwards more fully revealed under the gospel dispensation.

Such a collection of illustrations as I have suggested will come very handy to you in future days, and you will be reminded, by the comparisons and figures used by others, to make comparisons and figures for yourself. Familiarity with anything makes us *au fait* at it; we can learn to do almost anything by practice. I suppose that I could, by degrees, learn to make a tub if I spent my time with a man engaged in that business. I should know how to put the staves and the hoops if I stayed long enough in the cooper's yard; and I have no doubt that any of you could learn anything you desired provided you had sufficient time and opportunity. So, if you search for illustrations, you will learn to make them for yourselves.

That brings me to my last point. I began this lecture by warning you against the practice of making anecdotes; I close it by advising you often to *set yourself the task of making illustrations.* Try to make comparisons from the things round about you. I think it would be well, sometimes, to shut the door of your study, and say to yourself, "I will not go out of this room until I have made at least half-a-dozen good illustrations." The Chinese say that the intellect lies in the stomach, and that the affections are there, too. I think they are right on the latter point, because, you know, if you are ever very fond of anybody,—your wife, for instance,—you say that you could eat her; and you also say that such and such a person is very sweet. So, too, the intellect may lie in the stomach; and consequently, when you have been shut in for two or three hours, and begin to want your dinner or tea, you may be quickened into the making of the six illustrations I have mentioned as a minimum. Your study would be a veritable prison if you could not make as many useful comparisons as that from the different objects in the room. I should say that a prison itself would furnish suggestions for making many metaphors. I do not wish you to go to prison for that purpose; but if you ever do get there, you ought to be able to learn how to preach in an interesting manner upon such a passage as this,—"Bring my soul out of prison;" or this, "He was there in the prison. But the Lord was with Joseph."

If you cannot get your brains to work in the house, you might take a walk, and say to yourself, "I will wander over the fields, or I will get into the garden, or I will stroll in the wood, and see if I cannot find some illustration or other. You might even go and look in at a shop-window, and see if there are not some illustrations to be discovered there. Or you might stand still a little while, and hear what people say as they go by; or stop where there is a little knot of idlers, and try to hear what they are talking about, and see what symbol you can make out of it. You should also spend as much time as you can visiting the sick; that will be a most profitable thing to do, for in that sacred service you will have many opportunities of getting illustrations from the tried children of God as you hear their varied experiences. It is wonderful what pages of a new cyclopædia of illustrative teaching you might find written out with indelible ink if you went visiting the sick, or even in talking with children. Many of them will say things that you will be able to quote with good effect in your sermons. At any rate, do make up your mind that you will attract and interest the people by the way in which you set the gospel before them. Half the battle lies in making the attempt, in coming to this determined resolution, "God helping me, I will teach the people by parables, by similes, by illustrations, by anything that will be helpful to them; and I will seek to be a thoroughly interesting preacher of the Word."

I earnestly hope you will practise the art of making illustrations. I will try to prepare a little set of exercises for you to do week by week. I shall give you some subject, and some object, between which there is a likeness; and I shall get you to try to see the resemblance, and to find out what comparisons can be instituted between them. I shall also, if I can, give you some subject without an object, and then say to you, "Illustrate that; tell us, for instance, what virtue is like." Or, sometimes, I may give you the object without the subject, thus,—"A diamond; how will you use that as an illustration?" Then, sometimes, I may give you neither the subject nor the object, but just say, "Bring me an illustration." I think we might, in this way, make a set of exercises which would be very useful to you all.

The way to get a mind worth having is to get one well stored with things worth keeping. Of course, the man who has the most illustrations in his head, will be the one who will use the most illustrations in his discourses. There are some preachers who have the bump of illustration fully developed; they are sure to illustrate their subject, they cannot help it. There are some men who always see "likes"; they catch a comparison long before others see it. If any of you say that you are not good at illustrating, I reply, "My brother, you must try to grow horns if you have not any on your head." You may never be able to develop any vast amount of imagination or fancy if you do not possess it at the first,—just as it is hard to make a cheese out of a millstone,—but by diligent attention to this matter, you may improve upon what you now are. I do believe that some fellows have a depression in their craniums where there ought to be a bump. I knew a young man, who tried hard to get into this College; but he never saw how to join things together unless he tied them by their tails. He brought out a book; and when I read it, I found at once that it was full of my stories and illustrations; that is to say, every illustration or story in the book was one that I had used, but there was not one of them that was related as it ought to have been. This man had so told the story that it was not there at all; the very point which I had brought out he had carefully omitted, and every bit of it was told correctly except the one thing that was the essence of the whole. Of course, I was glad that I did not have that brother in the College; he might have been an ornament to us by his deficiencies, but we can do without such ornaments; indeed, we have had enough of them already.

Finally, dear brethren, do try with all your might to get the power to see a parable, a simile, an illustration, wherever it is to be seen; for to a great extent this is one of the most important qualifications of the man who is to be a public speaker, and especially of the man who is to be an efficient preacher of the gospel of Christ. If the Lord Jesus made such frequent use of parables, it must be right for us to do the same.

XXVIII

The Sciences as Sources of Illustration

ASTRONOMY

I PROPOSE, brethren, if I am able to do it,—and I am somewhat dubious upon that point,—to give you a set of lectures at intervals upon THE VARIOUS SCIENCES AS SOURCES OF ILLUSTRATION. It seems to me that every student for the Christian ministry ought to know at least something of every science; he should intermeddle with every form of knowledge that may be useful in his life's work. God has made all things that are in the world to be our teachers, and there is something to be learned from every one of them; and as he would never be a thorough student who did not attend all classes at which he was expected to be present, so he who does not learn from all things that God has made will never gather all the food that his soul needs, nor will he be likely to attain to that perfection of mental manhood which will enable him to be a fully-equipped teacher of others.

I shall commence with the science of ASTRONOMY; and you will, at the beginning, understand that I am not going to deliver an astronomical lecture, nor to mention all the grand facts and details of that fascinating science; but I intend simply to use *astronomy as one of the many fields of illustration that the Lord has provided for us.* Let me say, however, that the science itself is one which ought to receive much attention from all of us. It relates to many of the greatest wonders in nature, and its effect upon the mind is truly marvellous. The themes on which astronomy discourses are so grand, the wonders disclosed by the telescope are so sublime that, very often, minds that have been unable to receive knowledge through other channels have become remarkably receptive while they have been studying this science. There is an instance of a brother, who was one of the students in this College, and who seemed to be a dreadful dolt; we really thought he never would learn anything, and that we should have to give him up in despair. But I introduced to him a little book called *The Young Astronomer*; and he afterwards said that, as he read it, he felt just as if something had cracked inside his head, or as if some string had been snapped. He had laid hold of such enlarged thoughts

413

that I believe his cranium did actually experience an expansion which it ought to have undergone in his childhood, and which it did undergo by the marvellous force of the thoughts suggested by the study of even the elements of astronomical science.

This science ought to be the special delight of ministers of the gospel, for surely it brings us into closer connection with God than almost any other science does. It has been said that an undevout astronomer is mad. I should say that an undevout man of any sort is mad,—with the worst form of madness; but, certainly, he who has become acquainted with the stars in the heavens, and who yet has not found out the great Father of lights, the Lord who made them all, must be stricken with a dire madness. Notwithstanding all his learning, he must be afflicted with a mental incapacity which places him almost below the level of the beasts that perish.

Kepler, the great mathematical astronomer, who has so well explained many of the laws which govern the universe, closes one of his books, his *Harmonics,* with this reverent and devout expression of his feelings: "I give thee thanks, Lord and Creator, that thou hast given me joy through thy creation; for I have been ravished with the work of thy hands. I have revealed unto mankind the glory of thy works, as far as my limited spirit could conceive their infinitude. Should I have brought forward anything that is unworthy of thee, or should I have sought my own fame, be graciously pleased to forgive me." And you know how the mighty Newton, a very prince among the sons of men, was continually driven to his knees as he looked upwards to the skies, and discovered fresh wonders in the starry heavens. Therefore, the science which tends to bring men to bow in humility before the Lord should always be a favourite study with us whose business it is to inculcate reverence for God in all who come under our influence.

The science of astronomy would never have become available to us in many of its remarkable details if it had not been for the discovery or invention of the *telescope.* Truth is great, but it does not savingly affect us till we become personally acquainted with it. The knowledge of the gospel, as it is revealed to us in the Word of God, makes it true to us; and oftentimes the Bible is to us what the telescope is to the astronomer. The Scriptures do not make the truth; but they reveal it in a way in which our poor, feeble intellect, when enlightened by the Holy Spirit, is able to behold and comprehend it.

From a book[1] to which I am indebted for many quotations in this lecture, I learn that the telescope was discovered in this singular manner: "A maker of spectacles at Middleburg stumbled upon the

[1] *The Heavens and the Earth.* A popular Handbook of Astronomy. By Thomas Milner, M.A., F.R.G.S. Religious Tract Society. (Now out of print.)

discovery owing to his children directing his attention to the enlarged appearance of the weathercock of a church, as accidentally seen through two spectacle-glasses, held between the fingers some distance apart. This was one of childhood's inadvertent acts; and seldom has there been a parallel example of mighty results springing out of such a trivial circumstance. It is strange to reflect upon the playful pranks of boyhood being connected in their issue, and at no distant date, with enlarging the known bounds of the planetary system, resolving the nebula of Orion, and revealing the richness of the firmament." In a similar way, a simple incident has often been the means of revealing to men the wonders of divine grace. What a certain individual only meant to be trifling with divine things, God has overruled for his soul's salvation. He stepped in to hear a sermon as he might have gone to the theatre to see a play; but God's Spirit carried the truth to his heart, and revealed to him the deep things of the kingdom, and his own personal interest in them.

I think that incident of the discovery of the telescope might be usefully employed as an illustration of the connection between little causes and great results, showing how the providence of God is continually making small things to be the means of bringing about wonderful and important revolutions. It may often happen that what seems to us to be a matter of pure accident, with nothing at all notable about it, may really have the effect of changing the entire current of our life, and it may be influential also in turning the lives of many others in quite a new direction.

When once the telescope had been discovered, then the numbers and position and movements of the stars became increasingly visible, until at the present time we are able to study the wonders of the stellar sky, and continually to learn more and more of the marvels that are there displayed by the hand of God. The telescope has revealed to us much more of the sun, and the moon, and the stars, than we could ever have discovered without its aid. Dr. Livingstone, on account of his frequently using the sextant when he was travelling in Africa, was spoken of by the natives as the white man who could bring down the sun, and carry it under his arm. That is what the telescope has done for us, and that is what faith in the gospel has done for us in the spiritual heavens; it has brought down to us the Father, the Son, and the Holy Spirit, and given us the high eternal things to be our present possession, and our perpetual joy.

Thus, you see, the telescope itself may be made to furnish us with many valuable illustrations. We may also turn to good account the lessons to be learned by the study of the stars for the purpose of navigation. The mariner, crossing the trackless sea, by taking astronomical observations, can steer himself with accuracy to his desired haven. Captain Basil Hall tells us, in the book I have previously mentioned, that "he once sailed from San Blas, on the West Coast of Mexico; and, after a voyage of eight thousand miles, occupying eighty-nine days, he arrived off Rio de Janeiro, having in this interval passed through the Pacific Ocean, rounded Cape Horn, and crossed the South Atlantic, without making land, or seeing a single sail except an American whaler. When within a week's sail of Rio, he set seriously about determining, by lunar observations, the position of his ship, and then steered his course by those common principles of navigation which may be safely employed for short distances between one known station and another. Having arrived within what he considered, from his computations, fifteen or twenty miles of the coast, he hove to, at four o'clock in the morning, to await the break of day, and then bore up, proceeding cautiously on account of a thick fog. As this cleared away, the crew had the satisfaction of seeing the great Sugar-Loaf Rock, which stands on one side of the harbour's mouth, so nearly right ahead that they had not to alter their course above a point in order to hit the entrance of the port. This was the first land they had seen for nearly three months, after crossing so many seas, and being set backwards and forwards by innumerable currents and foul winds. The effect upon all on board was electric; and, giving way to their admiration, the sailors greeted the commander with a hearty cheer."

In a similar manner, we also sail by guidance from the heavenly bodies, and we have for a long season no sight of land, and sometimes do not even see a passing sail; and yet, if we take our observations correctly, and follow the track which they point out, we shall have the great blessing, when we are about to finish our voyage, of seeing, not the great Sugar-Loaf Rock, but the Fair Haven of Glory right straight before us. We shall not have to alter our course even a single point; and, as we sail into the heavenly harbour, what songs of joy will we raise, not in glorification of our own skill, but in praise of the wondrous Captain and Pilot who has guided us over life's stormy sea, and enabled us to sail in safety even where we could not see our way!

Kepler makes a wise remark, when speaking about the mathematical system by which the course of a star could be predicted. After describing the result of his observations, and declaring his firm belief that the will of the Lord is the supreme power in the laws of nature, he says, "But if there be any man who is too dull to receive this science, I advise that, leaving the school of astronomy, he follow his own path, and desist from this wandering through the universe; and, lifting up his natural eyes, with which he alone can see, pour himself out in his own heart, in praise of God the Creator; being certain that he gives no less worship to God than the astronomer, to whom God has given to see more clearly with his inward eye, and who, for what he has himself discovered, both can and will glorify God."

That is, I think, a very beautiful illustration of what you may say to any poor illiterate man in your congregation, "Well, my friend, if you cannot comprehend this system of theology which I have explained to you, if these doctrines seem to you to be utterly incomprehensible, if you cannot follow me in my criticism upon the Greek text, if you cannot quite catch the poetical idea that I tried to give you just now, which is so charming to my own mind, nevertheless, if you know no more than that your Bible is true, that you yourself are a sinner, and that Jesus Christ is your Saviour, go on your way, and worship and adoré, and think of God as you are able to do. Never mind about the astronomers, and the telescopes, and the stars, and the sun, and the moon; worship the Lord in your own fashion. Altogether apart from my theological knowledge, and my explanation of the doctrines revealed in the Scriptures, the Bible itself, and the precious truth you have received into your own soul, through the teaching of the Holy Spirit, will be quite enough to make you an acceptable worshipper of the Most High God."

I suppose you are all aware that among the old systems of astronomy was one which placed the earth in the centre, and made the sun, and the moon, and the stars revolve around it. "Its three fundamental principles were the immobility of the earth, its central position, and the daily revolution of all the heavenly bodies around it in circular orbits."

Now, in a similar fashion, there is a way of making a system of theology of which man is the centre, by which it is implied that Christ and His atoning sacrifice are only made for man's sake, and that the Holy Spirit is merely a great Worker on man's behalf, and that even the great and glorious Father is to be viewed simply as existing for the sake of making man happy. Well, that may be the system of theology adopted by some; but, brethren, we must not fall into that error, for, just as the earth is not the centre of the universe, so man is not the grandest of all beings. God has been pleased highly to exalt man; but we must remember how the psalmist speaks of him: "When I consider thy heavens, the work of thy fingers, the moon and the stars, which thou hast ordained; what is man, that thou art mindful of him; and the son of man, that thou visitest him?" In another place, David says, "Lord, what is man, that thou takest knowledge of him! or the son of man, that thou makest account of him! Man is like to vanity: his days are as a shadow that passeth away." Man cannot be the centre of the theological universe, he is altogether too insignificant a being to occupy such a position, and the scheme of redemption must exist for some other end than that of merely making man happy, or even of making him holy. The salvation of man must surely be first of all for the glory of God; and you have discovered the right form of Christian doctrine when you have found the system that has

God in the centre, ruling and controlling according to the good pleasure of His will. Do not dwarf man so as to make it appear that God has no care for him; for if you do that, you slander God. Give to man the position that God has assigned to him; by doing so, you will have a system of theology in which all the truths of revelation and experience will move in glorious order and harmony around the great central orb, the Divine Sovereign Ruler of the universe, God over all, blessed for ever.

You may, however, any one of you, make another mistake by imagining yourself to be the centre of a system. That foolish notion is a good illustration, I think. There are some men whose fundamental principles are, first of all, their own immobility: what they are, they always are to be, and they are right, and no one can stir them; secondly, their position is central, for them suns rise and set, and moons do wax and wane. For them, their wives exist; for them, their children are born; for them, everything is placed where it appears in God's universe; and they judge all things according to this one rule, "How will it benefit *me*?" That is the beginning and the end of their grand system, and they expect the daily revolution, if not of all the heavenly bodies, certainly of all the earthly bodies around them. The sun, the moon, and the eleven stars are to make obeisance to them. Well, brethren, that is an exploded theory so far as the earth is concerned, and there is no truth in such a notion with reference to ourselves. We may cherish the erroneous idea; but the general public will not, and the sooner the grace of God expels it from us, the better, so that we may take our proper position in a far higher system than any of which we can ever be the centre.

THE SUN, then, not the earth, is the centre of the solar system; which system, mark you, is propably only one little insignificant corner of the universe, although it includes such a vast space that if I could give you the actual figures you would not be able to form the slightest idea of what they really represented. Yet that tremendous system, compared with the whole of God's universe, may be only like a single grain of dust on the sea-shore, and there may be myriads upon myriads of systems, some of which are made up of innumerable systems as large as ours, and the great sun himself may only be a planet revolving round a greater sun, and this world only a little satellite to the sun, never yet observed by the astronomers who, it may be, live in that remoter sun still farther off. It is a marvellous universe that God has made; and however much of it we may have seen, we must never imagine that we have discovered more than a very small portion of the worlds upon worlds that God has created.

The earth, and all the planets, and all the solid matter of the universe, are controlled, as you know, by the force of attraction. We are kept in our place in the world, in going round the sun, by two forces, the one called centripetal, which draws us towards the sun, and the other called centrifugal, which is generally illustrated by the tendency of drops of water on a trundled mop to fly off at a tangent from the circle they are describing.

Now, I believe that, in like manner, there are two forces which are ever at work upon all of us, the one which draws us towards God, and the other which drives us away from Him, and we are thus kept in the circle of life; but, for my part, I shall be very glad when I can pass out of that circle, and get away from the influence of the centrifugal force. I believe that, the moment I do so,—as soon as ever the attraction which draws me away from God is gone,—I shall be with Him in heaven; that I do not doubt. Directly one or other of the two forces which influence human life shall be exhausted, we shall have either to drift away into the far-off space, through the centrifugal force,—which God forbid!—or else we shall fly at once into the central orb, by the centripetal force, and the sooner that glorious end of life comes, the better will it be for us. With Augustine, I would say, "All things are drawn to their own centre. Be thou the Centre of my heart, O God, my Light, my only Love!"

The sun himself is an enormous body; he has been measured, but I think I will not burden you with the figures, since they will convey to you no adequate idea of his actual size. Suffice it to say that, if the earth and the moon were put inside the sun, there would be abundance of room for them to go on revolving in their orbits just as they are now doing; and there would be no fear of their knocking against that external crust of the sun which would represent to them the heavens.

It takes about eight minutes for light to reach us from the sun. We may judge of the pace at which that light comes when we reflect that a cannon-ball, rushing with the swiftest possible velocity, would take seven years to get there, and that a train, travelling at the rate of thirty miles an hour, and never stopping for refreshments, would require more than three hundred and fifty years before it would reach the terminus. You may thus form some slight idea of the distance that we are from the sun; and this, I think, furnishes us with a good illustration of faith. There is no man who can know, except by faith, that the sun exists. That he did exist eight minutes ago, I know, for here is a ray of light that has just come from him, and told me that; but I cannot be sure that he is existing at this moment. There are some of the fixed stars, that are at such a vast distance from the earth, that a ray of light from them takes hundreds of years to reach us; and, for aught we know, they may have been extinct long ago. Yet we still put them down in our chart of the heavens, and we can only keep them there by faith, for as, "through faith we understand that the worlds were framed by the word of God," so it is only by faith that we can know that any of them now exist. When we come to examine the matter closely, we find that our eyesight, and all our faculties and senses, are not sufficient to give us positive conviction with regard to these heavenly bodies; and therefore we still have to exercise faith; so is it to a high degree in spiritual affairs, we walk by faith, not by sight.

That the sun has spots upon his face, is a fact which everybody notices. Just so; and if you are suns, and are never so bright, yet if you have any spots upon you, you will find that people will be very quick to notice them, and to call attention to them. There is often much more talk about the sun's spots than there is about his luminous surface; and, after the same fashion, more will be said about any spots and imperfections that men may discover in our character than about any excellencies that they may see in us. It was for some time asserted that there were no spots or specks whatever on the sun. Many astronomers, with the aid of the telescope, as well as without it, discovered these blemishes and patches on the face of the sun; but they were assured by men who ought to have known, namely, by the reverend fathers of the church, that it was impossible that there could be anything of the kind. The book I have previously quoted says: "Upon Scheiner, a German Jesuit, reporting the evidence of his senses to his provincial superior, the latter positively refused to believe him. 'I have read,' said he 'Aristotle's writings from end to end many times, and I can assure you that I have nowhere found in them anything similar to what you mention. Go, my son, and tranquillize yourself: be assured that what you take for spots in the sun are the faults of your glasses, or of your eyes.'" So, brethren, we know the force of bigotry, and how men will not see what is perfectly plain to us, and how, even when facts are brought before them, they cannot be made to believe in them, but will attribute them to anything but that which is the real truth. I am afraid that the Word of God itself has often been treated just in that way. Truths that are positively and plainly revealed there are stoutly denied, because they do not happen to fit in with the preconceived theories of unbelievers.

There have been a great many attempts to explain what the spots upon the sun really are. One theory is, that the solar orb is surrounded by a luminous atmosphere, and that the spots are open spaces in that atmosphere through which we see the solid surface of the sun. I cannot see any reason why that theory should not be the truth; and, if it be so, it seems to me to explain the first chapter of Genesis, where we are told that God created the light on the first day, though he did not make the sun until the fourth day. Did he not make the light first, and then take the sun, which otherwise might have been a dark world, and put the light on it as a luminous atmosphere? The two things certainly might very well fit in with one another; and if these spots are really openings in the luminous atmosphere through which we see the dark surface of the sun, they are admirable illustrations of the spots that men see in us. We are clothed with holiness as with a garment of light; but every now and then there is a rift through which observers can see down into the dark body of natural depravity that still is in the very best of us.

It is a dangerous thing to look at the sun with unprotected eyes. Some have ventured to look at it with glasses that have no colouring in them, and they have been struck blind. There have been several instances of persons who have inadvertently neglected to use a proper kind of glass before turning the telescope to the sun, and so have been blinded. This is an illustration of our need of a Mediator, and of how necessary it is to see God through the medium of Christ Jesus our Lord; else might the excessive glory of the Deity utterly destroy the faculty of seeing God at all.

The effect of the sun upon the earth, I shall not dwell upon now, as that may rather concern another branch of science than astronomy. It will suffice to say that living plants will sometimes grow without the sun, as you may have seen them in a dark cellar; but how blanched they are when existing under such circumstances! What must have been the pleasure with which Humboldt entered into the great subterranean cave called the Cueva del Guacharo, in the district of Caraccas! It is a cavern inhabited by nocturnal, fruit-eating birds, and this was what the great naturalist saw: "Seeds, carried in by the birds to their young, and dropped, had sprung up, producing tall, blanched, spectral stalks, covered with half-formed leaves; but it was impossible to recognize the species from the change in form, colour, and aspect, which the absence of light had occasioned. The native Indians gazed upon these traces of imperfect organization with mingled curiosity and fear, as if they were pale and disfigured phantoms banished from the face of the earth."

So, brethren, think what you and I would be without the light of God's countenance. Picture a church growing, as some churches do grow, without any light from heaven, a cavern full of strange birds and blanched vegetation. What a terrible place for anyone to visit! There is a cave of that sort at Rome, and there are others in various parts of the earth; but woe unto those who go to live in such dismal dens!

What a wonderful effect the light of God's countenance has upon men who have the divine life in them, but who have been living in the dark! Travellers tell us that, in the vast forests of the Amazon and the Orinoco, you may sometimes see, on a grand scale, the influence of light in the colouring of the plants when the leaf-buds are developing. One says: "Clouds and rain sometimes obscure the atmosphere for several days together, and during this time the buds expand themselves into leaves. But these leaves have a pallid hue till the sun appears, when, in a few hours of clear sky and splendid sunshine, their colour is changed to a vivid green. It has been related that, during twenty days of dark, dull weather, the sun not once making his appearance, the leaves were expanded to their full size, but were almost white. One forenoon, the sun began to shine in full brightness, when the colour of the forest changed so rapidly that its progress might be marked. By the middle of the afternoon, the whole, for many miles, presented the usual summer dress."

That is a beautiful illustration, it seems to me, that does not want any opening up; you can all make the application of it to the Lord Jesus for yourselves. As Dr. Watts sings:

> "In darkest shades if He appear,
>   My dawning is begun;
> He is my soul's sweet morning star,
>   And He my rising sun."

Then we begin to put on all sorts of beauty, as the leaves are painted by the rays of the sun. We owe every atom of colour that there is in any of our virtues, and every trace of flavour that there is in any of our fruits, to those bright sunbeams that come streaming down to us from the Sun of righteousness, who carries many other blessings besides healing beneath His wings.

The effect of the sun upon vegetation can be observed among the flowers in your own garden. Notice how they turn to him whenever they can; the sunflower, for instance, follows the sun's course as if he were himself the sun's son, and lovingly looked up to his father's face. He is very much like a sun in appearance, and I think that is because he is so fond of turning to the sun. The innumerable leaves of a clover field bend towards the sun; and all plants, more or less, pay deference to the sunlight to which they are so deeply indebted. Even the plants in the hothouse, you can observe, do not grow in that direction you would expect them to do if they wanted warmth, that is, towards the stove-pipe, whence the heat comes, nor even to the spot where most air is admitted; but they will always, if they possibly can, send out their branches and their flowers towards the sun. That is how we ought to grow towards the Sun of righteousness; it is for our soul's health that we should turn our faces towards the Sun, as Daniel prayed with his windows open towards Jerusalem. Where Jesus is, there is our Sun; towards him let us constantly incline our whole being.

Not very long ago I met with the following remarkable instance of the power of rays of light transmitted from the sun. Some divers were working at Plymouth Breakwater; they were down in the diving-bell, thirty feet below the surface of the water; but a convex glass, in the upper part of the bell, concentrated the sun's rays full upon them, and burnt their caps. As I read this story, I thought it was a capital illustration of the power there is in the gospel of our Lord Jesus Christ. Some of our hearers are fully thirty feet under the waters of sin, if they are not even deeper down than that; but, by the grace of God, we will yet make them feel the blessed burning power of the truths we preach, even if we do not succeed in setting them all on fire with this powerful glass. Perhaps, when you were a boy, you had a burning-glass, and when you were out with a friend who did not know what you had in your pocket, while he was sitting very quietly by your side, you took out your glass, and held it for a few seconds over the back of his hand until he felt something rather hot just there. I like the man who, in preaching, concentrates the rays of the gospel on a sinner till he burns him. Do not scatter the beams of light; you can turn the glass so as to diffuse the rays instead of concentrating them; but the best way of preaching is to focus Jesus Christ, the Sun of righteousness, right on a sinner's heart. It is the best way in the world to get at him; and if he is thirty feet under the water, this burning-glass will enable you to reach him; only mind that you do not use your own candle instead of the Sun, for that will not answer the same purpose.

Sometimes the sun suffers eclipse, as you know. The moon intrudes between us and the sun, and then we cannot see the great orb of day. I suppose we have all seen one total eclipse, and we may see another. It is a very interesting sight; but it appears to me that people take a great deal more notice of the sun when he is eclipsed than they do when he is shining clearly. They do not stand looking at him, day after day, when he is pouring forth his bright beams in unclouded glory; but as soon as ever he is eclipsed, then they are out in their thousands, with their glasses, and every little boy in the street has a fragment of smoked glass through which he watches the eclipse of the sun.

Thus, brethren, I do not believe that our Lord Jesus Christ ever receives so much attention from men as when he is set forth as the suffering Saviour, evidently crucified among them. When the great eclipse passed over the Sun of Righteousness, then all eyes were fixed upon Him, and well they might be. Do not fail to tell your hearers continually about that awful eclipse on Calvary; but mind that you also tell them all the effects of that eclipse, and that there will be no repetition of that stupendous event.

> "Lo! the sun's eclipse is o'er;
> Lo! he sets in blood no more."

Speaking of eclipses reminds me that there is, in the book I have mentioned, a striking description of one given by a correspondent who wrote to the astronomer Halley. He took his stand at Haradow Hill, close to the east end of the avenue of Stonehenge, a very capital place for observation, and there he watched the eclipse. He says of it: "We were now enveloped in a total and palpable darkness, if I may be allowed the expression. It came on rapidly, but I watched so attentively that I could perceive its progress. It came upon us like a great black cloak thrown over us, or like a curtain drawn from that side. The horses we held by the bridle seemed deeply struck by it, and pressed closely to us with marks of extreme surprise. As well as I could perceive, the countenances of my friends wore a horrible aspect. It was not without an involuntary exclamation of wonder that I looked around me at this moment. It was the most awful sight I had ever beheld in my life."

So, I suppose, it must be in the spiritual realm. When the Sun of this great world suffered eclipse, then were all men in darkness; and when any dishonour comes upon the cross of Christ, or upon Christ Himself, then is each Christian himself in darkness of a horrible kind. He cannot be in the light if his Lord and Master is in the shade.

One observer describes what he saw in Austria, where, it appears, all the people made the eclipse a time for keeping holiday, and turned out together on the plain with various modes of observing the wonderful sight. This writer says: "The phenomenon, in its magnificence, had triumphed over the petulance of youth, over the levity which some persons assume as a sign of superiority, over the noisy indifference of which soldiers usually make profession. A profound stillness also reigned in the air: the birds had ceased to sing." The more curious thing is that, in London, after an eclipse, when the cocks found that the sun shone out again, they all began crowing as though they joyfully thought that the daylight had broken through the gloom of night.

Yet this wonderful phenomenon does not appear to have always attracted the attention of all persons who might have witnessed it. History says that, at one time, there was a battle being fought, I think, in Greece, and, during its progress, there came on a total eclipse of the sun; but the warriors went on fighting all the same, indeed, they never noticed the extraordinary occurrence. That shows us how strong passions may make us forget surrounding circumstances, and it also teaches us how a man's engagements on earth may make him oblivious of all that is transpiring in the heavens. We read, just now, of how those horses, that were standing idly on Salisbury Plain, trembled during the eclipse; but another writer tells us that the horses in Italy, that were busily occupied in drawing the carriages, do not appear to have taken the slightest notice of the phenomenon, but to have gone on their way the same as usual. Thus, the engagements of a worldly man are often so engrossing in their character that they prevent him from feeling those emotions which are felt by other men, whose minds are more at liberty to meditate upon them.

I met with a very pretty story, concerning an eclipse, which you will probably like to hear. A poor little girl, belonging to the commune of Sièyes, in the Lower Alps, was tending her flock on the mountain-side at six o'clock on a bright summer morning. The sun had risen, and was dissipating the vapours of the night, and everyone thought that there would be a glorious, unclouded day; but gradually the light darkened until the sun had wholly disappeared, and a black orb took the place of the glowing disc, while the air became chill, and a mysterious gloom pervaded the whole region. The little child was so terrified by the circumstance, which was certainly unusual, that she began to weep, and cried out loudly for help. Her parents, and other friends, who came at her call, did not know anything about an eclipse, so they were also astounded and alarmed; but they tried to comfort her as best they could. After a short time, the darkness passed away from the face of the sun, and it shone out as before, and then the little girl cried aloud, in the *patois* of the district, "O beautiful sun!" and well she might. When I read the story, I thought that, when my heart had suffered eclipse, and the presence of Christ had gone for a while, and then had come back again, how beautiful the Sun seemed to me, even more bright and fair than before the temporary darkness. Jesus seemed to shine on me with a brighter light than ever before, and my soul cried out in an ecstasy of delight, "O beautiful Sun of righteousness!"

That story must, I think, close our illustrations derived from the sun; for we want also to learn all we can from his planets, and if we intend to pay a visit to them all, we shall have to travel far, and to travel fast, too.

The nearest planet that revolves around the sun is MERCURY, which is about 37,000,000 miles from the great luminary. Mercury, therefore, receives a far greater allowance of light and heat from the sun than comes to us upon the earth. It is believed that, even at the poles of Mercury, water would always boil; that is to say, if the planet is constituted at all as this world is. None of us could possibly live there; but that is no reason why other people should not, for God could make some of his creatures to live in the fire just as well as He could make others to live out of it. I have no doubt that, if there are inhabitants there, they enjoy the heat. In a spiritual sense, at any rate, we know that men who live near to Jesus dwell in the divine flame of love.

Mercury is a comparatively small planet; its diameter is about 2,960 miles, while that of the earth is 7,975. Mercury rushes round the sun in eighty-eight days, travelling at the rate of nearly 110,000 miles in an hour, while the earth traverses only 65,000 miles in the same time. Fancy crossing the Atlantic in about two or three minutes! It is an instance of the wisdom of God that Mercury appears to be the densest of the planets. You see, that part of a machine in which there is the most rapid whirl, and the greatest wear and tear, ought to be made of the strongest material; and Mercury is made very strong in order to bear the enormous strain of its swift motion, and the great heat to which it is subjected.

This is an illustration of how God fits every man for his place; if He means me to be Mercury,—the messenger of the gods, as the ancients called him,—and to travel swiftly, He will give me a strength proportioned to my day. In the formation of every planet, adapting it to its peculiar position, there is a wonderful proof of the power and forethought of God; and in a similar manner does He fit human beings for the sphere they are each called to occupy.

I like to see in Mercury a picture of the child of God who is full of grace. Mercury is always near the sun; indeed, so near that it is itself very seldom seen. I think Copernicus said that he never did see it, although he had long watched for it with great care, and he deeply regretted that he had to die without having ever seen this planet. Others have observed it, and it has been quite a treat for them to be able to watch its revolutions. Mercury is usually lost in the rays of the sun; and that is where you and I ought to be, so close to Christ, the Sun of righteousness, in our life and in our preaching, that the people who are trying to observe our movements can scarcely see us at all. Paul's motto must be ours: "Not I, but Christ."

Mercury, also, in consequence of being so near the sun, is apparently the least understood of any of the planets. It has, perhaps, given more trouble to the astronomers than any other member of the heavenly family; they have paid great attention to it, and tried to find out all about it; but they have had a very difficult task, for it is generally lost in the solar glory, and never seen in a dark portion of the heavens. So, I believe, brethren, that the nearer we live to Christ, the greater mystery shall we be to all mankind. The more we are lost in His brightness, the less will they be able to understand us. If we were always what we should be, men would see in us an illustration of the text, "Ye are dead, and your life is hid with Christ in God." Like Mercury, we ought also to be so active in our appointed orbit that we should not give observers time to watch us in any one position; and next, we should be so absorbed in the glory of Christ's presence, that they would not be able to perceive us.

When Mercury is seen from the earth, it is never visible in its brightness, for its face is always turned towards the sun. I am afraid that, whenever any of us are seen very much, we usually appear only as black spots; when the preacher is very prominent in a sermon, there is always a darkness. I like gospel preaching to be all Christ, the Sun of righteousness, and no black spot at all; nothing of ourselves, but all of the Lord Jesus. If there are any inhabitants of Mercury, the sun must appear to them four or five times as large as he does to us; the brightness would be insufferable to our eyes. It would be a very splendid sight if one could gaze upon it; and thus, the nearer you get to Christ, the more you see of Him, and the more He grows in your esteem.

The next planet to Mercury is VENUS; it is about 66,000,000 miles from the sun, and is a little smaller than the earth, its diameter being 7,510 miles, compared with our 7,975. Venus goes round the sun in 225 days, travelling at the rate of 80,000 miles an hour. When the Copernican system of astronomy was fairly launched upon the world, one of the objections to it was stated thus: "It is clear that Venus does not go round the sun, because, if it does, it must present the same aspect as the moon, namely, it must sometimes be a crescent, at other times a half-moon, or it must assume the form known as *gibbous*, and sometimes it must appear as a complete circle. But," said the objector, pointing to Venus, "she is always the same size; look at her, she is not at all like the moon." This was a difficulty that some of the earlier astronomers could not explain; but when Galileo was able to turn his newly made telescope to the planet, what did he discover? Why, that Venus does pass through similar phases to those of the moon! We cannot always see the whole of it enlightened, yet I suppose it is true that the light of Venus always appears about the same to us. You will perceive in a moment why that is; when the planet's face is turned toward us, it is at the greatest distance from the earth; consequently, the light that reaches us is no more than when it is closer, but has its face at last partly turned away from us. To my mind, the two facts are perfectly reconcilable; and so is it, I believe, with some of the doctrines of grace that perplex certain people. They say, "How do you make these two things agree?" I reply, "I do not know that I am bound to prove how they agree. If God had told me, I would tell you; but as He has not done so, I must leave the matter where the Bible leaves it." I may not have discovered the explanation of any apparent difference between the two truths, and yet, for all that, the two things may be perfectly consistent with one another.

Venus is both the morning star and "the star of the evening, beautiful star." It has been called Lucifer, and Phosphorus, the light-bringer, and also Hesperus, the vesper star. You perhaps remember how Milton, in *Paradise Lost*, refers to this double character and office of Venus:

"Fairest of stars! last in the train of night,
   If better thou belong not to the dawn;
   Sure pledge of day, that crown'st the smiling morn
   With thy bright circlet: praise him in thy sphere,
   While day arises, that sweet hour of prime."

Our Lord Jesus Christ calls Himself, "the bright and morning star." Whenever He comes into the soul, He is the sure harbinger of that everlasting light which shall go no more down for ever. Now that Jesus, the Sun of righteousness, has gone from the gaze of man, you and I must be like evening stars, keeping as close as we can to the great central Sun, and letting the world know what Jesus was like by our resemblance to Him. Did He not say to His disciples, "Ye are the light of the world"?

The next little planet that goes round the sun is THE EARTH. Its distance from the sun varies from about ninety-two to ninety-five millions of miles. Do not be discouraged, gentlemen, in your hopes of reaching the sun, because you are nothing like so far away as the inhabitants of Saturn; if there are any residents there, they are about ten times as far from the sun as we are. Still, I do not suppose you will ever take a seat in Sol's fiery chariot; at least, not in your present embodied state; it is far too warm a place for you to be at home there. The earth is somewhat larger than Venus, and it takes much longer to go round the sun, it is twelve months on its journey, or, speaking exactly, 365 days, 6 hours, 9 minutes, and 10 seconds. This world is a slow-going concern; and I am afraid it is less to the glory of God than any other world that he has made. I have not seen it from a distance; but I should suspect that it never shines anything like so brightly as Venus; for, through sin, a cloud of darkness has enveloped it. I suppose that, in the millennial days, the curtain will be drawn back, and a light will be thrown upon the earth, and that it will then shine to the glory of God like its sister stars that have never lost their pristine brightness. I think there have been some curtains drawn up already; every sermon, full of Christ, that we preach, rolls away some of the mists and fogs from the surface of the planet; at any rate, morally and spiritually, if not naturally.

Still, brethren, though the earth travels slowly, when compared with Mercury and Venus, yet, as Galileo said, it does move, and at a pretty good rate, too. I dare say, if you were to walk for twenty minutes, and you knew nothing about the speed at which the earth is travelling, you would be surprised if I assured you that you had in that short space of time gone more than 20,000 miles; but it would be a fact. This book, which has already given us much useful information, says: "It is a truly astonishing thought that, 'awake, asleep, at home, abroad,' we are constantly carried round with the terrestrial mass, at the rate of eleven miles a minute, and are, at the same time, travelling with it in space with a velocity of sixty-six thousand miles an hour. Thus, during the twenty minutes consumed in walking a mile from our thresholds, we are silently conveyed more than twenty thousand miles from one portion of space to another; and, during a night of eight hours' rest, or tossing to and fro, we are unconsciously translated through an extent equal to twice the distance of the lunar world."

We do not take any notice of this movement, and so it is that little things, which are near and tangible, often seem more notable than great things which are more remote. This world impresses many men with far greater force than the world to come has ever done, because they look only upon the things that are seen and temporal. "But," perhaps you say, "we do not feel ourselves moving." No, but you are moving, although you are not conscious of it. So, I think that, sometimes, when a believer in Christ does not feel himself advancing in divine things, he need not fret on that account; I am not certain that those who imagine themselves to be growing spiritually are really doing so. Perhaps they are only growing a cancer somewhere; and its deadly fibres make them fancy there is a growth within them. Alas! so there is; but it is a growth unto destruction.

When a man thinks that he is a full-grown Christian, he reminds me of a poor boy whom I used to see. He had such a splendid head for his body that he had often to lay it on a pillow, for it was too weighty for his shoulders to carry, and his mother told me that, when he tried to stand up, he often tumbled down, overbalanced by his heavy head. There are some people who appear to grow very fast, but they have water on the brain, and are out of due proportion; but he who truly grows in grace does not say, "Dear me! I can feel that I am growing; bless the Lord! Let's sing a hymn, 'I'm a growing! I'm a growing!'" I have sometimes felt that I was growing smaller, brethren; I think that is very possible, and a good thing, too. If we are very great in our own estimation, it is because we have a number of cancers, or foul gatherings, that need to be lanced, so as to let out the bad matter that causes us to boast of our bigness.

It is a good thing that we do not feel ourselves moving, for, as I before reminded you, we walk by faith, not by sight. Yet I know that we are moving, and I am persuaded that I shall return, as nearly as the earth's revolution permits, to this exact spot this day twelvemonth. If they are looking down at me from Saturn, they will spy me out somewhere near this same place, unless the Lord should come in the meantime, or he should call me up to be with Him.

If we did feel the world move, it would probably be because there was some obstruction in the heavenly road; but we go on so softly, and gently, and quietly, that we do not perceive it. I believe that growth in grace is very much after the same fashion. A babe grows, and yet does not know that he grows; the seed unconsciously grows in the earth, and so we are developing in the divine life until we come to the fulness of the stature of men in Christ Jesus.

Waiting upon the earth is THE MOON. In addition to her duty as one of the planets revolving round the sun, she has the task of attending upon the earth, doing much useful service for it, and at night lighting it with her great reflector-lamp, according to the allowance of oil she has available for shedding her beams upon us. The moon also operates upon the earth by her powers of attraction; and as the water is the more mobile part of our planet, the moon draws it towards herself, so making the tides; and those tides help to keep the whole world in healthful motion; they are a sort of life-blood to it.

The moon undergoes eclipse, sometimes very frequently, and a great deal more often than the sun; and this phenomenon has occasioned much terror. Among some tribes, an eclipse of the moon is an occasion for the greatest possible grief. Sir R. Schomberg thus describes a total lunar eclipse in San Domingo: "I stood alone upon the flat roof of the house which I inhabited, watching the progress of the eclipse. I pictured in imagination the lively and extraordinary scene which I once witnessed in the interior of Guiana, among the untutored and superstitious Indians, how they rushed out of their huts when the first news of the eclipse came, gibbered in their tongue, and, with violent gesticulations, threw up their clenched fists towards the moon. When, as on this occasion, the disc was perfectly eclipsed, they broke out in moanings, and sullenly squatted upon the ground, hiding their faces between their hands. The females remained, during this strange scene, within their huts. When, shining like a sparkling diamond, the first portion of the moon, that had disencumbered itself from the shadow, became visible, all eyes were turned towards it. They spoke to each other with subdued voices; but their observations became louder and louder, and they quitted their stooping position as the light increased. When the bright disc announced that the monster which wanted to stifle the Queen of Night had been overcome, the great joy of the Indians was expressed in that peculiar whoop, which, in the stillness of the night, may be heard for a great distance."

Want of faith causes the most extraordinary fear, and produces the most ridiculous action. A man who believes that the moon, though temporarily hidden, will shine forth again, looks upon an eclipse as a curious phenomenon worthy of his attention, and full of interest; but the man who really fears that God is blowing out the light of the moon, and that he shall never see its bright rays any more, feels in a state of terrible distress. Perhaps he will act as the Hindoos and some of the Africans do during an eclipse; they beat old drums, and blow bullocks' horns, and make all manner of frightful noises, to cause the dragon who is supposed to have swallowed the moon to vomit it up again. That is their theory of an eclipse, and they act accordingly; but once know the truth, and know especially the glorious truth that "All things work together for good to them that love God, to them that are the called according to his purpose," and we shall not be afraid of any dragon swallowing the moon, nor of anything else that the fears of men have made them imagine. If we are ignorant of the truth, every event that occurs, which may be readily enough accounted for from God's point of view, may cause the utmost terror, and drive us, perhaps, into the wildest follies.

The next planet to the earth is MARS; fiery Mars, generally shining with a ruddy light. It used to be thought that the colour of Mars' "blood-red shield" was caused by the absorption of the solar rays; but this idea has been refuted, and it is now believed to be due to the colour of its soil. According to the former idea, an angry man, who is like Mars, the god of war, must be one who has absorbed all other colours for his own use, and only shows the red rays to others; while the more modern notion, that the soil of the planet gives it its distinctive colour, teaches us that, where there is a fiery nature, there will be a warlike exhibition of it unless it is restrained by grace. Mars is about 140,000,000 miles from the sun; it is much smaller than our earth, its equatorial diameter being 4,363 miles. Travelling at the rate of 53,600 miles an hour, it takes 687 days to complete its revolution round the sun.

Between the orbits of Mars and Jupiter, there is a wide zone, in which, for many centuries, no planets were visible; but the astronomers said within themselves, "There must surely be something or other between Mars and Jupiter." They could not find any great planets; but as telescopes became larger, and more powerful, they observed that there was a great number of ASTEROIDS or PLANETOIDS, as some term them. I do not know how many there are, for they are like some of our brethren's families, they are daily increasing. Some hundreds of them have already been discovered; and by the aid of telescopic photography, we may expect to hear of the finding of many more. The first asteroid was identified on the first day of the present century, and was named Ceres. Many of them have been called by female mythological names, I suppose because they are the smaller planets, and it is considered gallant to give them ladies' names. They appear to vary from about 20 to 200 miles in diameter; and many have thought that they are the fragments of some planet that once revolved between Mars and Jupiter, but that has been blown up, and gone to pieces in a general wreck.

Those meteoric stones, which sometimes fall to the earth, but which much more frequently, at certain seasons of the year, are seen shooting across the midnight sky, may also be fragments of the aforesaid world which has perished. At all events, since the fathers fell asleep, all things have not continued as they were; there have been changes in the starry world to let men know that other changes will yet come. These blocks of meteoric matter are flying through space, and when they get within the range of our atmosphere there is an opposing medium; they have to drive through it at an enormous rapidity, and so they become burning hot, and thus they become visible. And, in like manner, I believe that there are plenty of good men in the world who are invisible till they get to be opposed, and being opposed, and having the love of God driving them on with tremendous momentum, they become red-hot with holy fervour, they overcome all opposition, and then they become visible to the eye of mankind. For my part, I rather like to pass through an opposing medium. I think that we all want to travel in that kind of atmosphere just to give us the sacred friction that will fully develop the powers with which we have been entrusted. If God has given us force, it is not at all a bad thing for us to be put where there is opposition, because we shall not be stopped by it, but shall by that very process be made to shine all the brighter as lights in the world.

Beyond the space which is occupied by the asteroids, is the magnificent planet, JUPITER, the brightest star which we see, except Venus; and yet he is very, very far away. His mean distance from the sun is about 475,000,000 miles; that is, more than five times as far off as we are. Even here, we are so far away that we do not often see the sun; but Jupiter is five times as far from the sun, and it takes him 4,333 days, or nearly twelve of our years, to go round the great luminary, travelling at a speed of 27,180 miles an hour. The reason why Jupiter is so bright is, partly, because of his great size, for he is nearly 90,000 miles in diameter, while the earth is less than 8,000, and it may be partly because he is better constituted for reflecting, or else, at that distance, his magnitude would not avail him. And brethren, if you and I are put in difficult positions, where we seem to be unable to shine to the glory of God, we must ask the Lord specially to constitute us so that we can better reflect his brightness, and so produce as good an effect as our brethren who are placed in more favourable positions.

Jupiter is attended by four moons.[1] These satellites were discovered soon after the invention of the telscope; yet there were several persons

[1] "In September, 1892, a fifth satellite was discovered through the great telescope at the Lick Observatory on Mount Hamilton, California."—*The Voices of the Stars.* By J. E. Walker, M.A. Elliot Stock.

who would not believe in their existence, and one of our excellent friends, the Jesuits, of course, was strongest in his determination that he never would, by any process, be convinced of that which others knew to be a fact. He was asked to look through a telescope in order to see that it was really so; but he declined because he said that, perhaps, if he did so, he would be obliged to believe it; and as he had no desire to do so, he refused to look. Are there not some who act thus toward the truths of revelation? Some time after, the Jesuit fell under the anger of good Kepler, and being convinced that he was in the wrong, he went to the astronomer, and begged his pardon. Kepler told him that he would forgive him, but he would have to inflict a penance upon him. "What will it be?" he enquired. "Why," said Kepler, "you must look through that telescope." That was the direst punishment the Jesuit could possibly receive; for, when he looked through the instrument, he was obliged to say that he did see what he had formerly denied, and he was obliged to express his conviction of the truth of the astronomer's teaching. So, sometimes, to make a man see the truth is a very severe penalty to him. If he does not want to see it, it is a good thing to compel him to look at it. There are a great many brethren, who are not Jesuits, and who yet are not anxious to know the whole truth; but I hope that you and I, Brethren, will always desire to learn all that the Lord has revealed in His Word.

This was the argument of Sizzi, an astronomer of some note, who tried to prove that Jupiter's moons could not exist. I wonder whether you can see the flaw in it: "There are seven windows given to animals in the domicile of the head, through which the air is admitted to the tabernacle of the body, to enlighten, to warm, and to nourish it; which windows are the principal parts of the microcosm, or little world, two nostrils, two eyes, two ears, and one mouth. So, in the heavens, as in a microcosm, or great world, there are two favourable stars, Jupiter and Venus; two unpropitious, Mars and Saturn; two luminaries, the sun and the moon; and Mercury alone undecided and indifferent, from which, and from many other phenomena of nature, such as the seven metals, etc., which it were tedious to enumerate, we gather that the number of planets is necessarily seven. Moreover, the satellites are invisible to the naked eye, and therefore can exercise no influence over the earth, and therefore would be useless, and therefore do not exist. Besides, as well the Jews and other ancient nations, as modern Europeans, have adopted the division of the week into seven days, and have named them from the seven planets. Now, if we increase the number of the planets, this whole system falls to the ground."

I think, brethren, that I have heard the same kind of argument advanced many times with reference to spiritual matters; that is, an argument from theory against fact; but facts will always overturn theories all the world over, only that, sometimes, it takes a good while before the facts can be absolutely proved.

It is a singular thing, and another instance of the power and wisdom of God, that though the satellites of Jupiter are constantly being eclipsed, as is natural enough from their rapid revolutions around him, yet they are never all eclipsed at one time. One moon may be eclipsed, and perhaps another, or even three out of the four; but there is always one left shining; and, in like manner, God never takes away all the comfort of His people at once, there is always some ray of light to cheer them.

There is a great deal more to be learned from Jupiter; but having introduced you to him, I will leave you to examine him for yourselves, and to get all you can out of him.

Far, far beyond Jupiter is SATURN. That respectable planet has been very much slandered, but I am happy to inform you that he does not deserve such treatment. He is nearly 900,000,000 miles from the sun. I wonder whether any brother here, with a large mind, has any idea of what a million is; I do not suppose that he has, and I am sure that I have not. It takes a vast deal of thinking to comprehend what a million means; but to realize what is meant by a million miles, is altogether beyond one's mental grasp. A million pins would be something enormous; but a million miles! And here we are talking of nine hundred millions of miles; well, I give up all thought of understanding what that is so long as I am in this finite state. Why, when you speak of nine hundred millions, you might as well say nine hundred billions at once; for the one term is almost as incomprehensible as the other; and yet, please to recollect that this vast space is to our great God only a mere hand's-breadth compared with the immeasurable universe that he has created.

I said that Saturn had been greatly slandered, and so he has. You know that we have, in our English language, the word "saturnine", as a very uncomplimentary description of certain individuals. When a man is praised for being very hearty and genial, he is said to be jovial, in allusion to Jove, or Jupiter, the brightly-shining planet; but a person of an opposite temperament is called saturnine, because it is supposed that Saturn is a dull planet, dreadfully dreary, and that his influences are malignant and baneful. If you have read some of the astrological books which I have had the pleasure of studying, you have there been told that, if you had been born under the influence of Saturn, you might almost as well have been born under the influence of Satan, for it will come to about the same thing in the end. He is supposed to be a very slow sort of individual, his symbol is the hieroglyphic of lead; but he is really a very light and buoyant personage. His diameter is about nine times as great as that of the earth, and while in volume he is equal to 746 worlds as large as ours, his weight is only equal to 92 such globes. The densities of the planets appear to diminish according to their distance from the sun, not in regular proportion, but still very largely so; and there seems to be no reason why those which are most remote, and travel slowly, should be made so dense as those which are nearer the central orb, and revolve more quickly around him.

This useful volume, from which I have already given you several extracts, says: "Instead, therefore, of sinking like lead in the mighty waters, he would float upon the liquid, if an ocean could be found sufficiently capacious to receive him. John Goad, the well-known astro-meteorologist, declared the planet not to be such a 'plumbeous blue-nosed fellow' as all antiquity had believed, and the world still supposed. But it was the work of others to prove it. For six thousand years or so, Saturn concealed his personal features, interesting family, and strange appurtenances,—the magnificent out-buildings of his house,—from the knowledge of mankind. But he was caught at last by a little tube, pointed at him from a slope of the Apennines, the holder of which, in invading his privacy, cared not to ask leave, and deemed it no intrusion." When that "little tube" was turned upon him, he was found to be a most beautiful planet, one of the most varied and most marvellous of all the planetary worlds.

Take that as an illustration of the falseness of slander, and of how some persons are very much bemired and bespattered because people do not know them. This planet, which was so despised, turned out to be a very beautiful object indeed; and, instead of being very dull, and what the word saturnine usually means, he is bright and glorious. Saturn also has no less than eight satellites to attend him; and, in addition, he has three magnificent rings, of which Tennyson has sung:

> "Still as, while Saturn whirls, his steadfast shade
> Sleeps on his luminous rings."

Saturn has only about a hundredth part of the light from the sun as compared with what we receive; and yet, I suppose, the atmosphere might be so arranged that he might have as much solar light as we have; but even if the atmosphere is of the same kind as ours, Saturn would still have as much light as we have in an ordinary London fog. I am speaking, of course, of the light from the sun; but then we cannot tell what illuminating power the Lord may have put in the planet himself; and beside that, he has his eight moons, and his three shining rings, which have a brilliance that we cannot either imagine or describe. What must it be to see a marvellous arch of light rising to a height of 37,570 miles above the planet, and having the enormous span of 170,000 miles! If you were at the equator of Saturn, you would only see the rings as a narrow band of light; but if you could journey towards the poles, you would see above you a tremendous arch, blazing with light, like some of the vast reflectors that you see hung up in large buildings where they cannot get sufficient sunlight. The reflector helps to gather up the rays of light, and throw them where they are needed; and I have no doubt that these rings act like reflectors to Saturn. It must be a wonderful world to live in if there are inhabitants there; they get compensations which fully make up for their disadvantages in being so far away from the sun. So is it in the spiritual world, what the Lord withholds in one direction he makes up in another; and those who are far removed from the means of grace, and Christian privileges, have an inward light and joy, which others, with greater apparent advantages, might almost envy.

Journeying again in the heavens, far, far beyond Saturn, we come to URANUS, or HERSCHEL, as it is sometimes called, after the astronomer who discovered it in 1781. The mean distance of Uranus from the sun is believed to be about 1,754,000,000 miles; I give you the figures, but neither you nor I can have the slightest conception of the distance they represent. To be an observer standing on Uranus, the sun would probably appear only as a far-away speck of light; yet the planet revolves around the sun at about 15,000 miles an hour, and occupies about eighty-four of our years in completing one journey. Uranus is said to be equal in volume to seventy-three or seventy-four earths, and to be attended by four moons. I do not know much about Uranus, therefore I do not intend to say much about him.

That may serve as an illustration of the lesson that a man had better say as little as possible concerning anything of which he knows only a little; and that is a lesson which many people need to learn. For instance, there are probably more works on the Book of Revelation than upon any other part of the Scriptures, and, with the exception of just a few, they are not worth the paper on which they are printed. Then, next to the Book of Revelation, in this respect, is the Book of Daniel; and because it is so difficult to explain, many men have written upon it, but as a rule the result of their writing has been that they have only confuted and contradicted one another. Let us, brethren, preach what we know; and say nothing of that of which we are ignorant.

We have gone a long way, in imagination, in travelling to the planet Uranus; but we have not yet completed our afternoon's journey. It was observed by certain astronomers that the orbit of Uranus sometimes deviated from the course they had marked in their chart of the heavens; and this convinced them that there was another planetary body, not then discovered, which was exerting an unseen but powerful influence upon Uranus.

This fact, that these huge worlds, with so many millions of miles of space between them, do retard or accelerate each other's movements, is to me a beautiful illustration of the influence that you and I have upon our fellow-men. Whether consciously or unconsciously, we either impede a man's progress in the path that leads to God, or else we quicken his march along the heavenward way. "None of us liveth to himself."

The astronomers came to the conclusion that there must be another planet, previously unknown to them, that was disturbing the motion of Uranus. Unknown to one another, an Englishman, Mr. Adams, of Cambridge, and a Frenchman, M. Leverrier, set to work to find out the position in which they expected the heavenly body to be discovered, and their calculations brought them to almost identical results. When the telescopes were pointed to that part of the heavens where the mathematical astronomers believed the planet would be found, it was at once discovered, shining with a pale and yellow light, and we now know it by the name of NEPTUNE.

The volume before me thus speaks of the two methods of finding a planet, the one worker using the most powerful telescope, and the other making mathematical calculations: "To detect a planet by the eye, or to track it to its place by the mind, are acts as incommensurable as those of muscular and intellectual power. Recumbent on his easy chair, the practical astronomer has but to look through the cleft in his revolving cupola, in order to trace the pilgrim star in its course; or, by the application of magnifying power, to expand its tiny disc, and thus transfer it from among its sidereal companions to the planetary domains. The physical astronomer, on the contrary, has no such auxiliaries: he calculates at noon, when the stars disappear under a meridian sun; he computes at midnight, when clouds and darkness shroud the heavens; and from within that cerebral dome which has no opening heavenwards, and no instrument but the eye of reason, he sees in the disturbing agencies of an unseen planet, upon a planet by him equally unseen, the existence of the disturbing agent, and from the nature and amount of its action he computes its magnitude, and indicates its place."

What a grand thing is reason! Far above the mere senses, and then faith is high above reason; only, in the case of the mathematical astronomer of whom we are thinking, reason was a kind of faith. He argued, "God's laws are so-and-so and so-and-so. This planet Uranus is being disturbed, some other planet must have disturbed it, so I will search and find out where he is;" and when his intricate calculations were completed, he put his finger on Neptune as readily as a detective lays his hand on a burglar, and a great deal sooner;

indeed, it seems to me that it is often easier to find a star than to catch a thief.

Neptune had long been shining before he was discovered and named; and you and I, brethren, may remain unknown for years, and possibly the world may never discover us; but I trust that our influence, like that of Neptune, will be felt and recognized, whether we are seen of men, or only shine in solitary splendour to the glory of God.

Well, we have travelled in thought as far as Neptune, which is about 2,748,000,000 miles from the sun; and, standing there, we look over into space, and there are myriads, and myriads, and myriads of miles in which there appear to be no more planets belonging to the solar system. There may be others that have not been discovered yet; but, as far as we know, beyond Neptune there is a great gulf fixed.

There are, however, what I may call "leapers" in the system, which, without the use of a pole, are able to cross this gulf; they are THE COMETS. These comets are, as a rule, so thin,—a mere filmy mass of vapour,—that when they come flashing into our system, and rushing out again, as they do, they never disturb the motion of a planet. And there are some terrestrial comets about, that I know, that go to various towns, and blaze away for a time; but they have no power to disturb the planets revolving there in their regular course. The power of a man does not consist in rushing to and fro, like a comet, but in steadily shining year after year like a fixed star. The astronomer Halley says, "If you were to condense a comet down to the thickness of the ordinary atmosphere, it would not fill a square inch of space." So thin is a comet, that you might look through five thousand miles of it, and see just as easily as if it were not there. It is well to be transparent, brethren; but I hope you will be more substantial than most of the comets of which we have heard.

Comets come with great regularity, though they seem to be very irregular. Halley prophesied that the comet of 1682, of which little had been previously known, would return at regular intervals of about seventy-five years. He knew that he would not live to see its reappearance; but he expressed the hope that when it did return, his prophecy might be remembered. Various astronomers were looking out for it, and they hoped it might arrive at the time foretold, because, otherwise, ignorant people would not believe in astronomy. But the comet came back all right; so their minds were set at rest, and Halley's prediction was verified.

Among the stories concerning comet-watching, there is one that contains an illustration and a lesson also. "Messier, who had acquired the name of 'the comet-hunter', from the number he discovered, was particularly anxious upon the occasion. Of great simplicity of character, his zeal after comets was often displayed in the oddest manner.

While attending the death-bed of his wife, and necessarily absent from his observatory, the discovery of one was snatched from him by Montaigne de Limoges. This was a grievous blow. A visitor began to offer him consolation on account of his recent bereavement, when Messier, thinking only of the comet, answered, 'I had discovered twelve; alas, to be robbed of the thirteenth by that Montaigne!' But instantly recollecting himself, he exclaimed, 'Ah! cette pauvre femme!' and went on deploring wife and comet together." He evidently lived so much in the heavens that he forgot his wife; and if science can sometimes carry a man away from all the trials of this mortal life, surely our heavenly life ought to lift us up above all the distractions and cares that afflict us.

The return of a comet is frequently announced with great certainty. This paragraph appeared in a newspaper: "On the whole, it may be considered as tolerably certain that the comet will become visible in every part of Europe about the latter end of August, or the beginning of September next. It will most probably be distinguishable by the naked eye, like a star of the first magnitude, but with a duller light than that of a planet, and surrounded with a pale nebulosity, which will slightly impair its splendour. On the night of the 7th of October, the comet will approach the well-known constellation of the Great Bear; and between that and the 11th, it will pass directly through the seven conspicuous stars of that constellation. Towards the close of November, the comet will plunge among the rays of the sun, and disappear, and not issue from them, on the other side, until the end of December. This prospectus of the movements of a body, invisible at the time, millions of miles away, is nearly as definite as the early advertisements of coaching between London and Edinburgh. Let us now place the observations of the eye alongside the anticipations of science, and we shall find that science has proved almost absolutely correct."

Just think of the calculations, gentlemen, that were necessary, for, though a comet does not interfere with the course of a planet, a planet interferes very considerably with the course of a comet; so that, in their calculations, the astronomers had to recollect the track in which the comet would have to travel. Thinking of him as a way-worn traveller, we remember that he will have to go by Neptune's bright abode, and Neptune will be sure to give him a cup of tea; then he will journey on as far as Uranus, and put up for the night there; in the morning, he will pay an early visit to Saturn, and he will stay there for breakfast; he will dine with Jupiter; by and by he will reach Mars, and there will be sure to be a row there; and he will be glad when he gets to Venus, and, of course, he will be detained by her charms. You will, therefore, very readily see, gentlemen, that the calculations as to the return of a comet are extremely difficult, and yet the astronomers do estimate the time to a nicety. This science is a very marvellous one, not only for what it reveals, but for the talent which it brings out, and the lessons it continually teaches us about the wonderful works of our great Father.

We have done with the solar system, and even with those interlopers which come to us every now and then from far remote systems, for a comet, I suppose, is only seen for a month, or a week, and then sometimes does not reappear for hundreds of years. Where have they gone all that while? Well, they have gone somewhere, and they are serving the purpose of the God who made them, I dare say; but, for my own part, I would not like to be a comet in God's system. I would like to have my fixed place, and keep on shining for the Lord there. I have lived in London for a good many years, and I have seen many comets come and go during that time. Oh, the great lights I have seen rush by! They have gone off into some unknown sphere, as comets usually do. I have generally noticed that, when men are going to do so much more than everybody else, and they are so amazingly pompous over it, their history is usually pretty accurately described by that simple simile of going up like a rocket, and coming down like a stick.

I do not know whether you can, in imagination, lean over the battlements of this little solar system, and see what there is beyond it. Do not narrow your minds, gentlemen, to a few hundred millions of miles! If you look out for a long way indeed, you will begin to see a star. I should only be uttering meaningless words if I told you its distance from us; yet there are others, of those that we are able to see, that are almost immeasurably farther away. They have taken a deal of trouble to send us a ray of light such a vast distance, to inform us that they are getting on very well, and that, though they are at such a distance from us, they still enjoy themselves as best they can in our absence.

These stars, as the common people look at them, seem to be scattered about in the heavens, as we say, "anyhow." I always admire that charming variety; and I am thankful to God that he has not set the stars in straight lines, like rows of street-lamps. Only think, brethren, how it would be if we looked up at night, and saw the stars all arranged in rows, like pins on a paper! Bless the Lord, it is not so! He just took a handful of bright worlds, and scattered them about the sky, and they dropped into most beautiful positions, so that people say, "There is the Great Bear;" and, "That is Charles's Wain," and every countryman knows the Reaping-hook. Have you not seen it, brethren? Others say, "That is the Virgin, and that is the Ram, and that is the Bull," and so on.

I think that naming of the various constellations is very like a good deal of mystical preaching that there is nowadays. The preachers say, "That is so-and-so, and that is so-and-so." Well, perhaps it is so; but I do not see it. You may imagine anything you like in the constellations of the heavens. I have pictured a fortress in the fire, and watched it being built up, and seen little soldiers come and pull it all down. You can see anything in the fire, and in the sky, and in the Bible, if you like to look for it in that way; you do not see it in reality, it is only a freak of your imagination. There are no bulls and bears in the heavens. There may be a virgin, but she is not to be worshipped as the Romanists teach. I hope you all know the pole-star; you ought also to know the pointers; they point to the pole-star, and that is just what we ought to do, to direct the poor slaves of sin and Satan to the true Star of liberty, our Lord and Saviour, Jesus Christ.

Then there are the Pleiades; almost anybody can tell you where they are. They are a cluster of apparently little stars, but they are intensely bright. They teach me that, if I am a very little man, I must try to be very bright; if I cannot be like Aldebaran, or some of the brightest gems of the sky, I must be as bright as I can in my own particular sphere, and be as useful there as if I were a star of the first magnitude. Then, on the other side of the globe, they look up to the Southern Cross. I dare say one of our brethren from Australia will give you a private lecture upon that constellation. It is very beautiful to think of the Cross being the guide of the mariner; it is the best guide anyone can have, either this side of the tropics, or the other.

Beside the stars, there are vast luminous bodies which are called NEBULÆ. In some parts of the heavens, there are enormous masses of light-matter; they were supposed by some to be the material out of which worlds were made. These were the lumps of mortar, out of which, according to the old atheistic theory, worlds grew by some singular process of evolution; but when Herschel turned his telescope upon them, he very soon put the nose of that theory out of joint, for he discovered that these nebulæ were simply enormous masses of stars, such myriads upon myriads of miles away, that, to our sight, they looked just like a little dust of light.

There are many wonderful things to be learned about the stars, to which I hope you will give your earnest attention as you have the opportunity. Among the rest is this fact, that some stars have ceased to be visible to us. Tycho Brahé said that, on one occasion he found a number of villagers looking up at the sky; and, on asking them why they were gazing at the heavens, they told him that a new star had suddenly appeared. It shone brightly for a few months, and then vanished. Many times, a starry world has seemed to turn red, as if it were on fire; it has apparently burned, and blazed away, and then disappeared. Kepler, writing concerning such a phenomenon, says: "What it may portend is hard to determine; and thus much only is certain, that it comes to tell mankind either nothing at all, or high and weighty news, quite beyond human sense and understanding." In allusion to the opinions of some, who explained the novel object by the Epicurean doctrine of a fortuitous combination of atoms, he remarks, with characteristic oddity, yet good sense, "I will tell these disputants,—my opponents,—not my opinion, but my wife's. Yesterday, when weary with writing, and my mind quite dusty with considering these atoms, I was called to supper, and a salad that I had asked for was set before me. 'It seems, then,' said I, aloud, 'that if pewter dishes, leaves of lettuce, grains of salt, drops of water, vinegar, and oil, and slices of egg, had been flying about in the air from all eternity, it might at last happen, by chance, that there would come a salad.' 'Yes,' says my wife, 'but not one so nice or well dressed as this which I have made for you.'"

So I should think; and if the fortuitous combination of atoms could not make a salad, it is not very likely that they could make a world. I once asked a man, who said that the world was a fortuitous concourse of atoms, "Have you ever chanced to have no money, and to be away where you knew nobody who would give you a dinner?" He replied, "Yes, I have." "Well, then," said I, "did it ever happen to you that a fortuitous concourse of atoms made a leg of mutton for you, with some nice boiled turnips, and caper sauce, for your dinner?" "No," he said, "it has not." "Well," I answered, "a leg of mutton, at any rate, even with turnips and caper sauce included, is an easier thing to make than one of these worlds, like Jupiter or Venus."

We are told, in the Word of God, that one star differeth from another star in glory; yet one that is small may give more light to us than a larger star which is farther away. Some stars are what is called variable, they appear larger at one time than another. Algol, in the head of Medusa, is of this kind. We are told that "The star, at the brightest, appears of the second magnitude, and remains so for about two days, fourteen hours. Its light then diminishes, and so rapidly, that in three and a half hours it is reduced to the fourth magnitude. It wears this aspect rather more than fifteen minutes, then increases, and in three and a half hours more resumes its former appearance." I am afraid that many of us are variable stars; if we do sometimes wax dim, it will be well if we regain our brightness as quickly as Algol does. Then there are thousands of double stars. I hope that you will each get a wife who will always shine with you, and never eclipse you, for a double star may be very bright at one time, and sometimes be eclipsed altogether. There are also triple stars, or systems, and quadruple systems, and there are, in some cases, hundreds or thousands all spinning round one another, and around their central luminaries.

Wonderful combinations of glory and beauty may be seen in the stellar sky; and some of these stars are red, some blue, some yellow, all the colours of the rainbow are represented in them. It would be very wonderful to live in one of them, and to look across the sky, and see all the glories of the heavens that God has made. On the whole, however, for the present, I am quite content to abide upon this little planet, especially as I am not able to change it for another home, until God so wills it.

We want to hear from you. Please send your comments about this book to us in care of zreview@zondervan.com. Thank you.